THE KINGFISHER

VISUAL
FACTFINDER

Stars and Planets • Planet Earth • The Living World
Science and Technology • World History • Countries of the World

THE KINGFISHER
VISUAL
FACTFINDER

Stars and Planets • Planet Earth • The Living World
Science and Technology • World History • Countries of the World

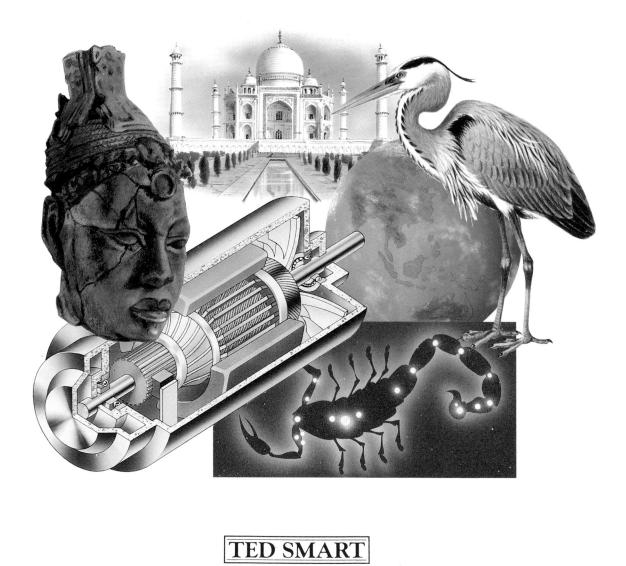

TED SMART

Authors

STARS AND PLANETS
James Muirden

PLANET EARTH
Michael Allaby, Neil Curtis

THE LIVING WORLD
Brian Williams

SCIENCE AND TECHNOLOGY
Brian Williams

WORLD HISTORY
Ken Hills

COUNTRIES OF THE WORLD
Brian Williams

Series Editor
Michèle Byam

Series Designer and Art Editor
Ralph Pitchford

Editors
Andrea Moran, Cynthia O'Neill

Designers and Art Editors
Shaun Barlow, Sandra Begnor, Nigel Bradley, John Kelly,
Cathy Tincknell, Steve Woosnam-Savage

Picture Research
Elaine Willis, Su Alexander

Production Manager
Julia Mather

Additional editorial help from
Joan Angelbeck, Stuart Atkinson, Nicky Barber, Hilary Bird,
Catherine Bradley, Catherine Headlam

Additional art preparation by
Matthew Gore, Andy Archer, Julian Ewart, Mustafa Sidki,
Martin Wilson, Janet Woronkowicz

KINGFISHER
Kingfisher Publications Plc
New Penderel House
283-288 High Holborn
London WC1V 7HZ

First published in 1993 by Kingfisher Publications Plc
The material in this edition was previously published in six individual volumes in 1993

This edition produced for
The Book People Ltd,
Hall Wood Avenue,
Haydock,
St Helens WA11 9UL

Copyright © Kingfisher Publications Plc 1993

British Library Cataloguing in Publication Data
A catalogue record for this book is available
from the British Library

ISBN 1 85697 074 4

BILLIONS
For many years there have been two meanings for the word 'billion'. In Britain
and Continental Europe the word indicates one million million; in the United States one thousand
million. Today international usage is following the US meaning, so all references to 'billion' in
the statistics in this book are to be taken as one thousand million.

Typeset by Southern Positives and Negatives (SPAN), Lingfield, Surrey
Colour Reproduction by Scantrans, Singapore
Printed in China

CONTENTS

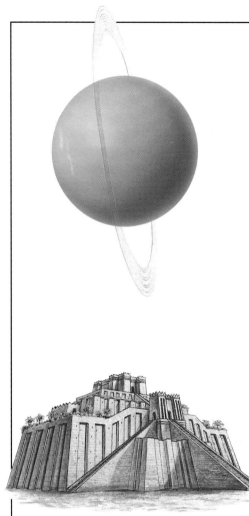

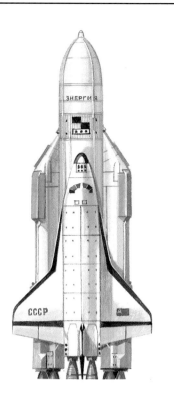

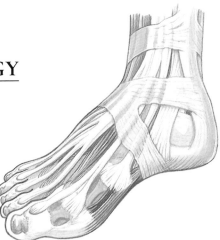

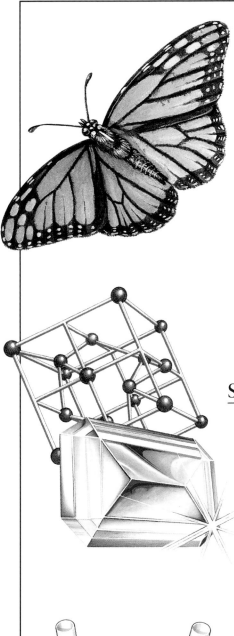

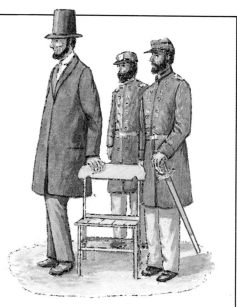

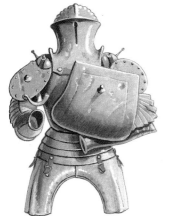

An image of the Earth taken by the Meteosat weather satellite. The 'realistic' colouring was added by computer.

STARS
— AND —
PLANETS

Centuries ago, early civilizations looked to the skies and thought that the Earth must be the centre of the Universe, with the Sun and stars in orbit around it. As our understanding of the Universe grew, human beings began to realize how small and unimportant the Earth is. It is just one small planet whirling around an ordinary star, in a galaxy of at least 100 billion stars. But we are right to believe that the Earth is special, too. Despite thousands of years of observing the stars and, very recently, space exploration, we have yet to discover signs of other intelligent life in the Universe.

Stars and Planets provides an illustrated guide to our knowledge of space. Topics covered range from the Sun and the planets, to theories on the beginning of the Universe. The life and death of stars is explained, and astronomical achievements through history are listed. There is still a great deal we do not know about the Universe. The final section highlights the space technology that has made distant planets familiar to us, and that may help us to learn more about space in the future.

James Muirden

COSMIC TIME

A Timescale of the Universe

The Universe is everything that exists. All the planets, stars and the 'star cities', or galaxies, are part of the Universe, and so is all of space. The Universe has no centre, or edge – it seems to go on for ever. Most astronomers believe that the Universe began about 15 billion years ago, in a huge explosion they call the Big Bang. They think that during the Big Bang the raw material of everything found in the Universe was created in an instant of time, far shorter than anything we can measure or imagine. There is evidence to support this idea, because the galaxies in the Universe seem to be flying apart, as if from an explosion. Scientists have also detected the faint heat-waves left over from a vast explosion. Since time began with the Big Bang, we cannot ask what caused the explosion, as nothing can exist without time. The Big Bang is the ultimate mystery.

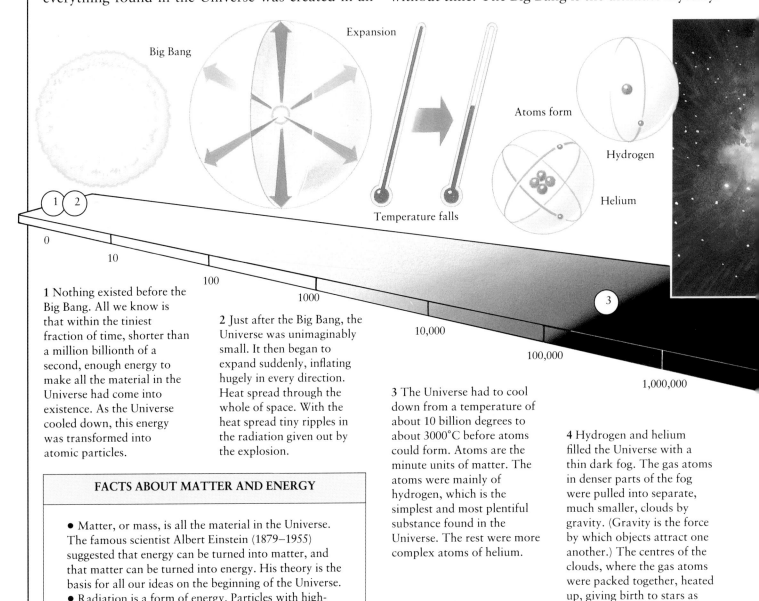

Big Bang

Expansion

Temperature falls

Atoms form

Hydrogen

Helium

0

10

100

1000

10,000

100,000

1,000,000

1 Nothing existed before the Big Bang. All we know is that within the tiniest fraction of time, shorter than a million billionth of a second, enough energy to make all the material in the Universe had come into existence. As the Universe cooled down, this energy was transformed into atomic particles.

2 Just after the Big Bang, the Universe was unimaginably small. It then began to expand suddenly, inflating hugely in every direction. Heat spread through the whole of space. With the heat spread tiny ripples in the radiation given out by the explosion.

3 The Universe had to cool down from a temperature of about 10 billion degrees to about 3000°C before atoms could form. Atoms are the minute units of matter. The atoms were mainly of hydrogen, which is the simplest and most plentiful substance found in the Universe. The rest were more complex atoms of helium.

4 Hydrogen and helium filled the Universe with a thin dark fog. The gas atoms in denser parts of the fog were pulled into separate, much smaller, clouds by gravity. (Gravity is the force by which objects attract one another.) The centres of the clouds, where the gas atoms were packed together, heated up, giving birth to stars as the galaxies formed.

FACTS ABOUT MATTER AND ENERGY

- Matter, or mass, is all the material in the Universe. The famous scientist Albert Einstein (1879–1955) suggested that energy can be turned into matter, and that matter can be turned into energy. His theory is the basis for all our ideas on the beginning of the Universe.
- Radiation is a form of energy. Particles with high-energy are a form of radiation. Some radiation, like that from a fire, can be felt as heat.

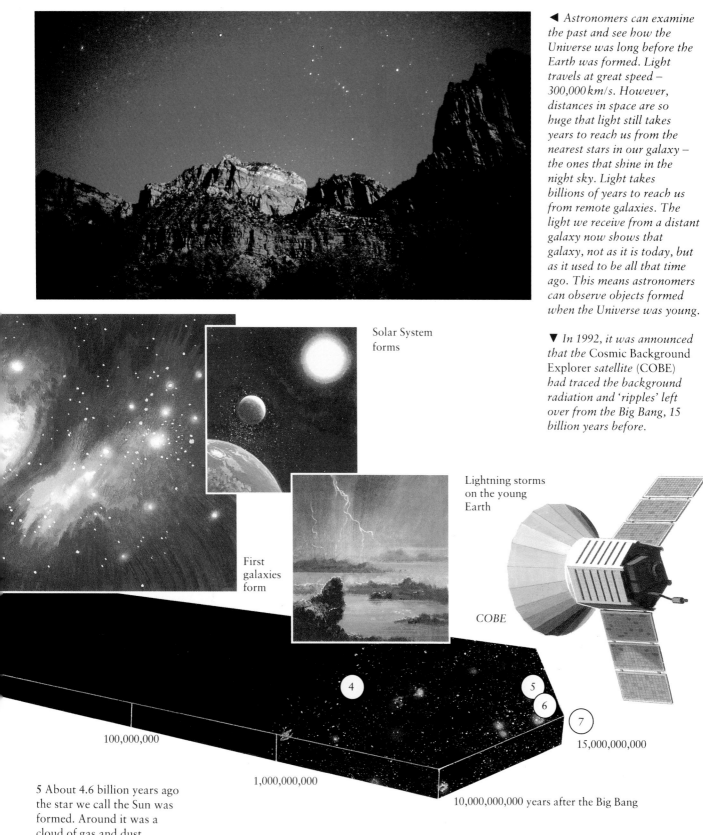

◀ *Astronomers can examine the past and see how the Universe was long before the Earth was formed. Light travels at great speed – 300,000 km/s. However, distances in space are so huge that light still takes years to reach us from the nearest stars in our galaxy – the ones that shine in the night sky. Light takes billions of years to reach us from remote galaxies. The light we receive from a distant galaxy now shows that galaxy, not as it is today, but as it used to be all that time ago. This means astronomers can observe objects formed when the Universe was young.*

▼ *In 1992, it was announced that the Cosmic Background Explorer satellite (COBE) had traced the background radiation and 'ripples' left over from the Big Bang, 15 billion years before.*

Solar System forms

Lightning storms on the young Earth

First galaxies form

COBE

100,000,000

1,000,000,000

10,000,000,000 years after the Big Bang

15,000,000,000

5 About 4.6 billion years ago the star we call the Sun was formed. Around it was a cloud of gas and dust containing substances such as carbon and oxygen. These had been formed in older stars and blasted out into space when the stars died. These substances came together to form the planets.

6 The first living cells appeared on Earth 3.5 billion years ago. How life began is uncertain. Maybe lightning storms provided the energy to start chemical reactions in the 'soup' of elements on the young planet.

7 It has taken one ten-thousandth of the time since the Big Bang for recognizable humans to develop from apes. Today, scientists try to work out the story of the Universe by sending into space satellites which look back across time.

THE SOLAR SYSTEM

Beginnings

We live on a small rocky planet we call the Earth, which travels through space on a path, or orbit, around a star we call the Sun. The Earth is part of the Solar System – the name we give to the Sun and the family of planets, asteroids and comets that orbit it. This family reaches far into space – the Solar System is about a million times wider than Earth. 'Solar' means 'of the Sun', and the Sun is by far the most important member of the family. It is about 740 times more massive than all the planets put together. Because of its great size, it has a powerful gravitational pull, and this pull keeps the Solar System together and controls the movements of the planets. The Solar System began about 4.6 billion years ago, when a cloud of hydrogen, helium and a tiny percentage of other elements, started to condense into a cluster of stars. One of these stars was the Sun.

THE BIRTH OF THE SOLAR SYSTEM

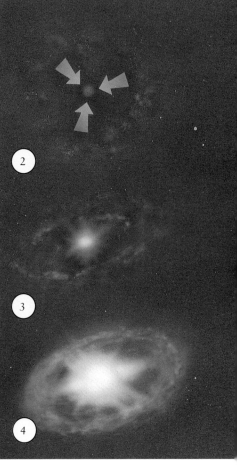

The 'empty' space between stars in fact contains hydrogen atoms and tiny grains of solid material. The grains lie very far apart from each other. However, in some regions of a galaxy the grains are found much closer together, forming dark clouds of gas and dust. These regions are called nebulae.

Stars are formed from a nebula when the material in the nebula is given a shake, making it break up into much smaller nebulae (1). For example, a star might explode nearby and send out powerful energy waves. In some colliding galaxies, stars are formed where nebulae meet and pass through each other.

The gravity of a small dark nebula, or globule, begins to pull itself inwards (2). Pressure causes the centre to heat up. The dark cloud may take less than 100,000 years to change into a shining star (3). The baby star spins on its axis, throwing off two spiral arms that form a ring around it (4).

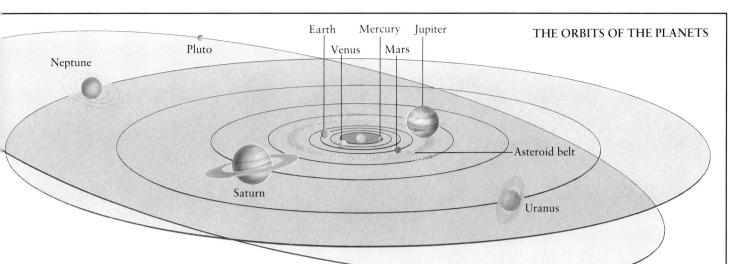

THE ORBITS OF THE PLANETS

▲ *The planets go round the Sun in elliptical orbits, which means they follow a path shaped like a flattened circle. Pluto's orbit is also tilted.*

PLANET	SPEED IN ORBIT (kilometres/second)
Mercury	47.9
Venus	35.0
Earth	29.8
Mars	24.1
Jupiter	13.1
Saturn	9.6
Uranus	6.8
Neptune	5.4
Pluto	4.7

The Sun's gravity pulls the planets inwards. At the same time, the planets' own energy of motion is trying to fling them off into space. These two forces balance exactly. The closer a planet is to the Sun, the faster it has to move to maintain this balance.

As a star like the Sun forms, the force of its inwards collapse heats its centre. When the temperature inside the star reaches millions of degrees, nuclear reactions are able to start. These send a new wave of energy outwards (5) which stops the star shrinking further, and also blasts the remains of the nebula out into space.

The ring of gas and dust thrown out by our young Sun began to collect into fragments and solid grains of matter. Once these 'planetesimals' reached a certain size, their gravity began to pull in other, smaller fragments, and they grew rapidly (6). Gradually they turned into the planets we know today (7).

The inner planets have hard surfaces. The giant outer planets grew into rocky globes too, but they then attracted the hydrogen and helium gases and icy particles that collected in the cold regions of the Solar System. Some smaller planetesimals became asteroids (*see pages 42–43*); others became moons of the planets.

The Sun

The Sun lies at the centre of our Solar System, a fiercely-hot ball of gas nearly 1.4 million kilometres wide. Its appearance changes all the time: prominences leap from the Sun into space, and dark spots appear on its surface. Since its birth, some 4.6 billion years ago, the Sun has been the power station for the Earth and the other planets, providing them with their light and heat. The source of the Sun's energy lies deep inside its centre, where the nuclear reactions that keep it shining take place.

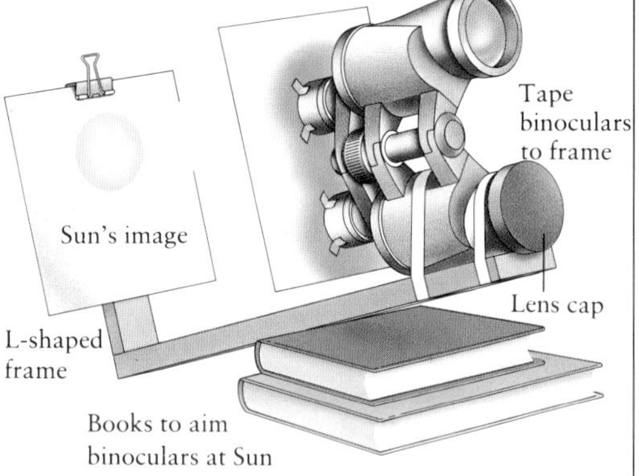

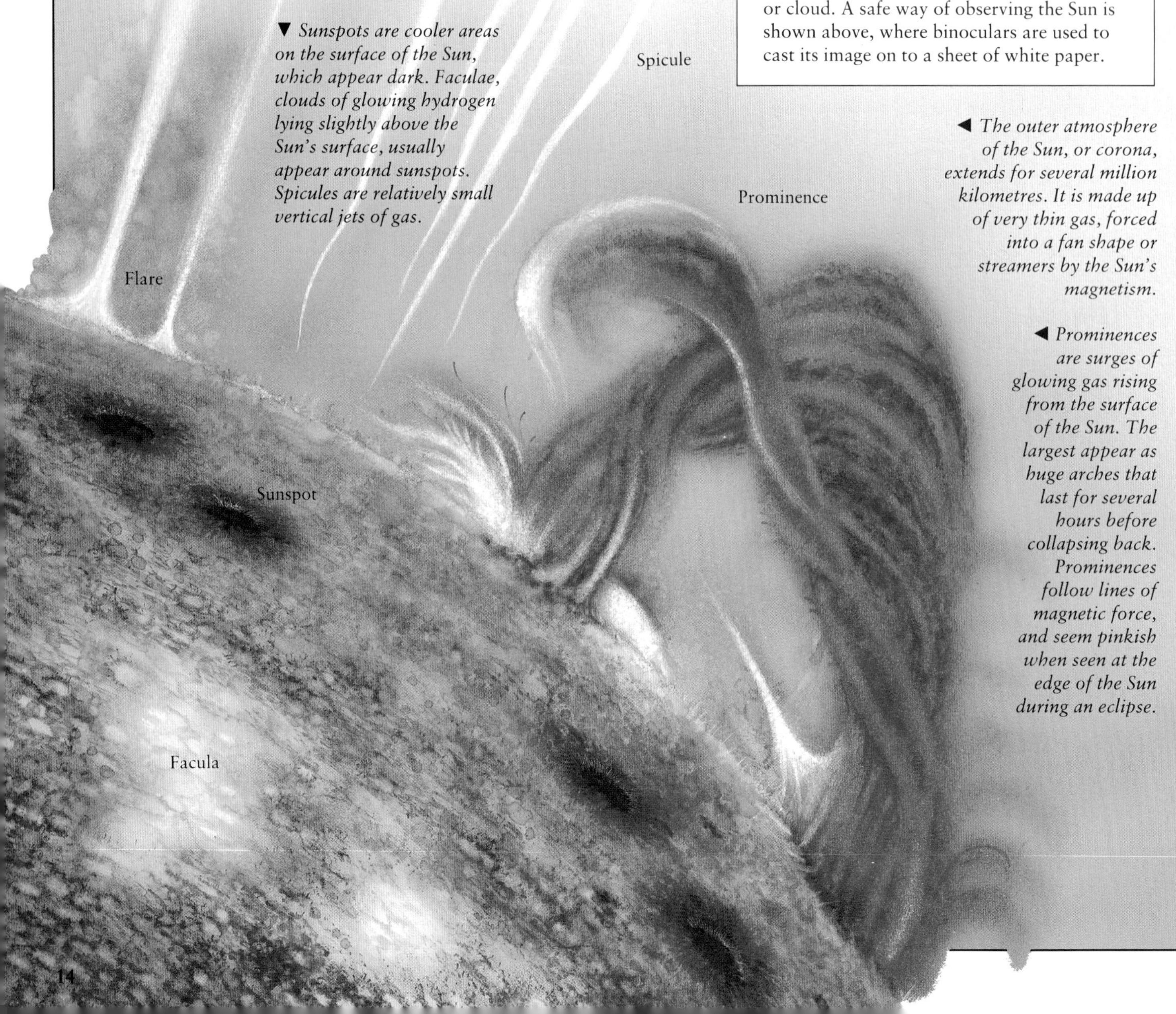

◀ *Flares are violent explosions that usually occur over sunspots. They last only a few minutes but can upset the Earth's magnetic field and put fierce gusts of energy into the solar wind (see page 16).*

▼ *Sunspots are cooler areas on the surface of the Sun, which appear dark. Faculae, clouds of glowing hydrogen lying slightly above the Sun's surface, usually appear around sunspots. Spicules are relatively small vertical jets of gas.*

Spicule

Prominence

◀ *The outer atmosphere of the Sun, or corona, extends for several million kilometres. It is made up of very thin gas, forced into a fan shape or streamers by the Sun's magnetism.*

◀ *Prominences are surges of glowing gas rising from the surface of the Sun. The largest appear as huge arches that last for several hours before collapsing back. Prominences follow lines of magnetic force, and seem pinkish when seen at the edge of the Sun during an eclipse.*

Flare

Sunspot

Facula

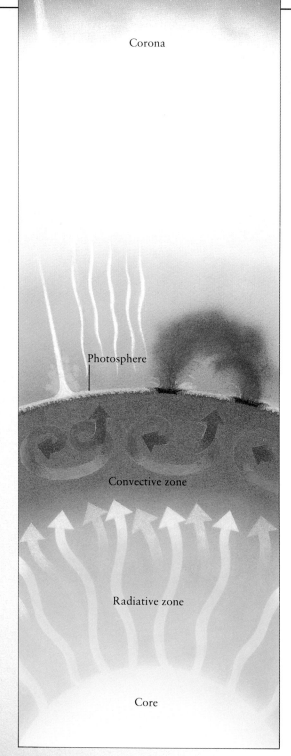

Corona

Photosphere

Convective zone

Radiative zone

Core

THE STRUCTURE OF THE SUN
Light and heat are produced in the core of the Sun. This energy then flows in waves through the radiative zone, with sufficient force to stop the vast bulk of the Sun collapsing inwards under gravity. The energy waves are weakened by this journey so that when they reach the convective zone they can radiate no further. Instead, the energy waves reach the visible surface of the Sun (the photosphere) by a violent churning motion called convection.

HOW THE SUN SHINES
The temperature at the centre of the Sun is about 15 million °C. Here, the atoms that make up its main gas, hydrogen, have so much energy that they break apart, coming together again as helium gas. During this reaction, a burst of energy is given out. This energy drives the Sun. It is thought the Sun contains enough hydrogen to keep giving out energy for billions of years. As it uses up its fuel, our star will change *(below)*.

▶ *The Sun will continue to shine almost unchanged for several billion years. Meanwhile, the Earth will continue to pass through Ice Ages and warm periods as its orbit goes through a regular cycle of slight change.*

◀ *In about 5 billion years' time, energy from the Sun's huge core will make its outer layers expand. As our star swells and grows hotter, the water on Earth will start to boil away. Life forms will suffocate in the great heat.*

▶ *As the Sun turns into a red giant star, Earth will be scorched to a cinder and its atmosphere will be stripped away. A few million years later the thin outer layers of the Sun will have consumed the Earth; Mars will probably escape.*

◀ *After the red giant stage, lasting about 100 million years, the Sun will run out of nuclear fuel. If will shrink and become a white dwarf star. From the surface of Mars (left) it will be a dim pinpoint. The Earth will no longer exist.*

The Sun

Every second, the Sun loses 7 million tonnes of material, but all the material lost so far only amounts to less than 0.01 percent of its mass since it started shining. Of this amount, 4 million tonnes are turned into energy when protons and neutrons fuse together, giving out radiation and falling into the core. The Sun's lifetime is not limited by the amount of its fuel, but by the growth of its core. When the core reaches a certain size, the Sun will expand and it will start to destroy the Earth *(see page 15)*.

▶ *The Sun is blasting material into space at the rate of about 3 million tonnes per second. This material is ejected at such speed that it escapes from the Sun's gravity and passes out of the Solar System altogether. This stream of particles is called the solar wind. It consists of atomic particles; these are magnetic, and force the planets' magnetic fields into a distorted pear shape.*

(see page 15)

AN ECLIPSE OF THE SUN

Sun

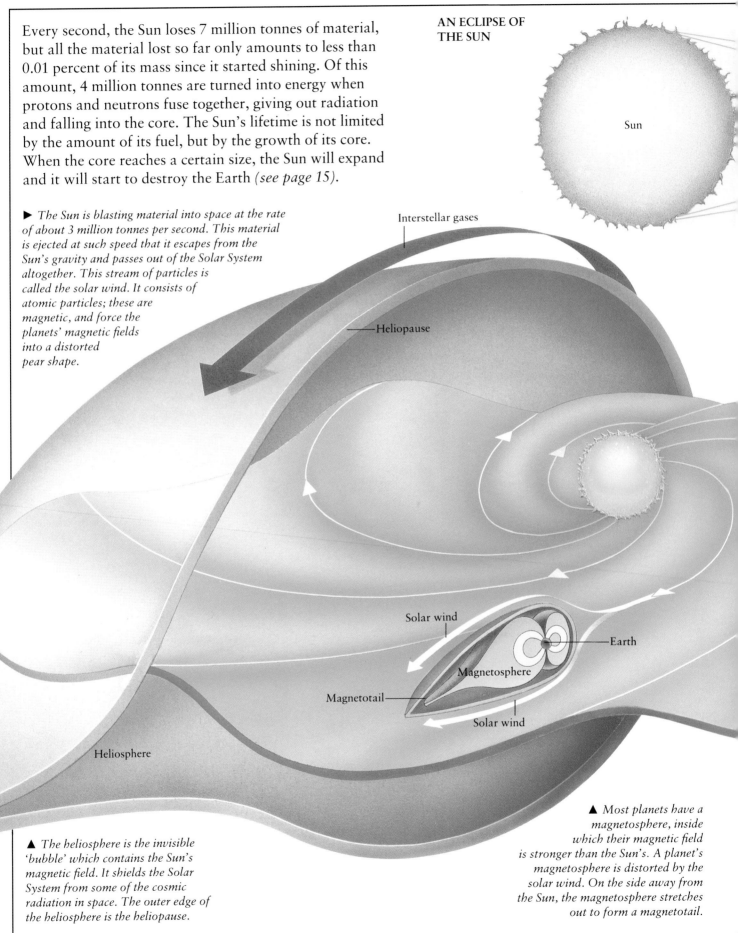

Interstellar gases

Heliopause

Solar wind

Earth

Magnetosphere

Magnetotail

Solar wind

Heliosphere

▲ *The heliosphere is the invisible 'bubble' which contains the Sun's magnetic field. It shields the Solar System from some of the cosmic radiation in space. The outer edge of the heliosphere is the heliopause.*

▲ *Most planets have a magnetosphere, inside which their magnetic field is stronger than the Sun's. A planet's magnetosphere is distorted by the solar wind. On the side away from the Sun, the magnetosphere stretches out to form a magnetotail.*

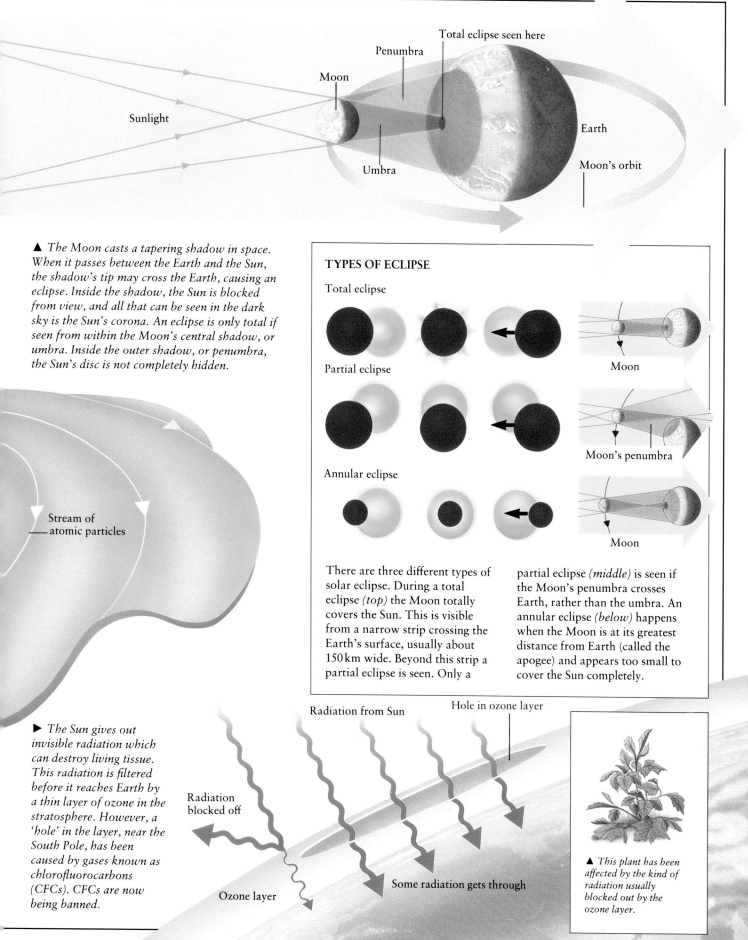

Total eclipse seen here

Penumbra

Moon

Sunlight

Umbra

Earth

Moon's orbit

▲ *The Moon casts a tapering shadow in space. When it passes between the Earth and the Sun, the shadow's tip may cross the Earth, causing an eclipse. Inside the shadow, the Sun is blocked from view, and all that can be seen in the dark sky is the Sun's corona. An eclipse is only total if seen from within the Moon's central shadow, or umbra. Inside the outer shadow, or penumbra, the Sun's disc is not completely hidden.*

Stream of atomic particles

TYPES OF ECLIPSE

Total eclipse

Partial eclipse

Moon

Moon's penumbra

Annular eclipse

Moon

There are three different types of solar eclipse. During a total eclipse *(top)* the Moon totally covers the Sun. This is visible from a narrow strip crossing the Earth's surface, usually about 150 km wide. Beyond this strip a partial eclipse is seen. Only a partial eclipse *(middle)* is seen if the Moon's penumbra crosses Earth, rather than the umbra. An annular eclipse *(below)* happens when the Moon is at its greatest distance from Earth (called the apogee) and appears too small to cover the Sun completely.

▶ *The Sun gives out invisible radiation which can destroy living tissue. This radiation is filtered before it reaches Earth by a thin layer of ozone in the stratosphere. However, a 'hole' in the layer, near the South Pole, has been caused by gases known as chlorofluorocarbons (CFCs). CFCs are now being banned.*

Radiation from Sun

Hole in ozone layer

Radiation blocked off

Ozone layer

Some radiation gets through

▲ *This plant has been affected by the kind of radiation usually blocked out by the ozone layer.*

The Planets

A planet is a large body, made of gas, metal or rock, that orbits a star. We know of nine planets that orbit our Sun. All of them were formed at the same time, from the same cloud of gas and dust around the Sun, but there are great differences between them. The four inner terrestrial planets (Mercury, Venus, Earth and Mars) are rock and metal. Jupiter, Saturn, Uranus and Neptune are mainly liquid and ice; these giant outer bodies are the gaseous planets. Distant Pluto does not fit in either group.

THE DENSITY OF THE PLANETS

Compared with the gaseous planets, the inner rocky planets have no more than a thin skin of atmosphere. They contain much more material per unit of volume than the gaseous planets do; and this means that they are much denser. Water has a density of one gram per cubic centimetre. The Earth is five and a half times denser than water. Saturn, however, is *less* dense than water. It could float on a huge ocean.

▼ *Although Mercury is the innermost planet, it is not the hottest. It does have the shortest year, going round the Sun once every 88 days. It has a cratered surface, and no moons, or satellites.*

▼ *Venus is the brightest object in the sky, but the planet is not shining by its own light. Venus is bright because the clouds that cover its surface reflect the Sun's light very well. All the planets shine by reflection.*

Mercury

Sun

Venus

Earth

Mars

Jupiter

▲ *The Earth is the only planet with liquid water on its surface. It is also the densest planet – almost eight times as dense as Saturn.*

▲ *The highest mountain and the deepest valleys in the Solar System are found on Mars, so it may once have been the most volcanically active planet.*

▲ *The largest planet, Jupiter, also spins fastest on its axis – its day lasts less than 10 hours. This very rapid spin produces a force which makes the planet's liquid body bulge outwards at the equator.*

MEASURING DISTANCES IN SPACE

Astronomers use special units to represent the huge distances in space. The distance between stars is measured in light-years: one light-year is equal to the distance travelled by a beam of light in one year, or 9.46 million million kilometres. The basic unit of distance within the Solar System is the astronomical unit, or AU. One AU is the average distance from the Earth to the Sun – about 149,600,000 km.

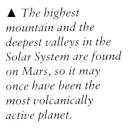

Mercury 0.39 AU
Venus 0.72 AU
Earth 1 AU
Mars 1.52 AU
Jupiter 5.20 AU
Saturn 9.54 AU
Uranus 19.19 AU

0　1　2　3　4　5　6　7　8　9　10　11　12　13　14　15　16　17　18　19　20　21　22　23

FACTS ABOUT THE PLANETS

● We owe much of our knowledge about the Solar System to space probes. These unmanned spacecraft have investigated nearly every planet, sending back pictures to Earth. The *Voyager* probes were especially important. Between 1979 and 1989 the probes sent back close-up pictures of the four giant planets and their moons, and discovered rings around Jupiter, Uranus and Neptune.

● Only Mercury and Venus have no moons, or natural satellites, at all. Saturn has the greatest number of moons: 18.
● The planets are named after ancient Greek and Roman gods; for example, Jupiter is named after the chief of the Roman gods.

● After the formation of the Solar System, leftover rocky debris in the cloud of particles around the Sun kept striking the planets as they formed. Mercury and our Moon still show the scars of impacts, but the Earth's craters have been smoothed out by weather and movements of the planet's surface. This main bombardment ended 3.9 billion years ago; some major impacts have happened since.

▼ *Saturn used to be known as 'the planet with the rings'. Ring systems have now been discovered around all the giant planets, but Saturn's system is by far the largest and most complicated. Only Saturn's rings can be seen through a telescope from Earth.*

Uranus

◄ *Almost nothing was known about Uranus until the space probe* Voyager 2 *flew past it in 1986. Uranus' axis is tipped over so that it spins almost sideways.*

Pluto

Neptune

Saturn

▲ *Until 1999, Neptune will be the outermost planet in the Solar System, since Pluto's orbit has brought it briefly closer to the Sun. Neptune has a cold, windswept, cloudy surface.*

▲ *We know very little about distant Pluto, which was only discovered in 1930. It is the smallest planet, and is probably made of ice. No space probe has ever visited this mysterious world.*

Pluto 29.6 AU (at its closest)   Neptune 30.1 AU   Pluto 49.5 AU (at its furthest)

26 27 28 29 30 31 32 33 34 35 36 37 38 39 40 41 42 43 44 45 46 47 48 49 50

Mercury

Mercury is the innermost planet. It is a dead, airless world, which whirls through space in the merciless glare of the Sun. The one spacecraft to have visited it was *Mariner 10* in 1974, which photographed half the planet. During its daytime, which lasts for about three Earth months, it is so hot that lead would run like water over the rocks. But at night its surface is colder than icy Jupiter. Mercury holds two records for the major planets of the Solar System: the longest day and the shortest year.

▲ *Mercury is the second smallest of the planets, after Pluto. It is also smaller than two satellites, Jupiter's Ganymede and Saturn's Titan. Because it is so close to the Sun, it is bombarded by the solar wind. (Distances not to scale.)*

Earth

◀ *Mercury's surface is heavily scarred with craters. They are the result of collisions during the first few hundred million years of the Solar System's history. There are also lava flows, which must have occurred early in Mercury's history as they are also cratered.*

▼ *Mercury's distance from the Sun changes as it completes its orbit. From the planet's surface, the Sun would appear 1.5 times bigger when Mercury is closest than when it is farthest away.*

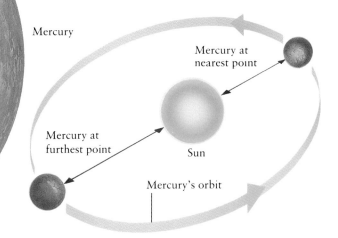

Mercury

Mercury at nearest point

Mercury at furthest point

Sun

Mercury's orbit

MERCURY DATAFILE

Diameter: 4880 km
Mass: 0.06 × Earth
Density: 5.4 (water = 1)
Minimum distance from Sun: 45.9 million km
Maximum distance from Sun: 69.7 million km
Minimum distance from Earth: 45 million km
Day/night: 176 Earth days
Length of year: 88 Earth days
Tilt of axis: 0° 0′
Surface gravity: 0.38 × Earth
Temperature: −185°C to 430°C
Satellites: 0

STRUCTURE

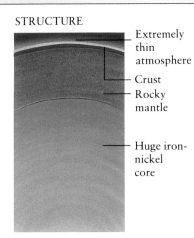

- Extremely thin atmosphere
- Crust
- Rocky mantle
- Huge iron-nickel core

FACTS ABOUT MERCURY

- The length of Mercury's year is shorter than its day. The planet has the shortest year in the Solar System – only 88 Earth days – but sunrise to sunrise on Mercury takes 176 Earth days.
- It is possible that some of Mercury's rocky mantle was knocked off by an impact with another body. This would explain the size of its huge iron core.

▲ *The smooth plains between the craters on Mercury suggest the planet might once have been a volcanic world. Following the formation of the Solar System, lava flows would have filled in the heavily cratered areas remaining after the bombardment of the planets.*

▼ *There is practically no atmosphere on Mercury to reflect the light of the Sun, and so the sky is always black. The Sun takes about three of our months to pass across the sky, but some of the deepest craters have been in darkness for billions of years. The surface is crossed with huge wrinkle ridges, such as Discovery Rupes, 3 km high and about 500 km long.*

Impact with
huge object

Shock waves travel
through the planet

Caloris Basin,
1300 km across

Ridges form on
the opposite side
of Mercury

THE FORMATION OF THE CALORIS BASIN

The dominant feature on Mercury is the Caloris Basin. It is an ancient, lava-filled crater about 1300 km across – a quarter of the planet's diameter. It is thought the basin was formed when a huge body, about 100 km across, crashed into Mercury. Shock waves from the collision travelled right around the planet, meeting on the opposite point and throwing up a confusion of ridges. Half the Caloris Basin was in darkness when visited by *Mariner 10*, so that it has never been seen properly.

THE FORMATION OF RIDGES

Mercury is the second densest of all the planets, so it must have a large metallic core, presumably of iron. When heated or cooled, iron changes its size much more than rock. So as the hot core cooled over the hundreds of millions of years after the planet formed, it began to shrink, making the hard crust go loose and wrinkled like the skin on a dried apple. These wrinkle ridges are known as rupes, and are found all over Mercury. They are up to 3 km high.

Crater

Core shrinks

Mantle and crust
are squeezed as
core shrinks

Core shrinks
as it cools

Venus

Through a telescope Venus appears as a gleaming silvery gem. But appearances deceive, because the planet is in fact a rocky waste, hotter than Mercury and spread out under a choking carbon dioxide atmosphere that is denser than water. Sulphuric acid droplets fall on the surface from clouds that permanently cast an orange gloom. The surface features shown on these pages (mountains, craters and volcanoes) were detected by spacecraft radar – the only way of probing the thick clouds.

▲ *Although the surface conditions are totally different, Venus is almost a twin of the Earth in size. Venus is very hot because its thick atmosphere is very efficient at holding in the Sun's heat. (Distances not to scale.)*

◀ *The orbit of Venus lies between the Earth and the Sun. This means it can only be seen in the twilight after sunset or before sunrise. Venus is sometimes called the morning star or the evening star.*

Earth

Venus

▼ *Venus' atmosphere is almost entirely made up of carbon dioxide, produced in vast amounts from erupting volcanoes when the planet was young. Sunlight penetrates the atmosphere and warms the surface of the planet. The ground radiates heat waves but they cannot escape back into space because of the thick cloud layer. The heat is trapped, warming the planet still more.*

▲ *The surface of Venus is completely hidden by dense clouds.*

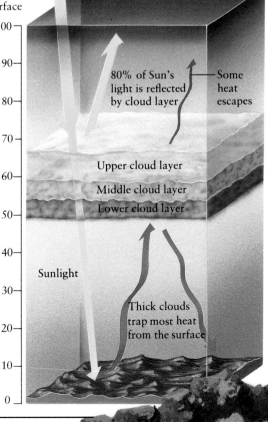

km above the surface

80% of Sun's light is reflected by cloud layer

Some heat escapes

Upper cloud layer

Middle cloud layer

Lower cloud layer

Sunlight

Thick clouds trap most heat from the surface

VENUS DATAFILE

Diameter: 12,104 km
Mass: 0.82 × Earth
Density: 5.2 (water = 1)
Minimum distance from Sun:
   108 million km
Maximum distance from Sun:
   109 million km
Minimum distance from Earth:
   42 million km
Day/night: 117 Earth days
Length of year: 225 Earth days
Tilt of axis: 12° 42′
Surface gravity: 0.90 × Earth
Temperature: 480°C average
Satellites: 0

STRUCTURE

Atmosphere

Crust

Mantle

Partly-molten metallic core

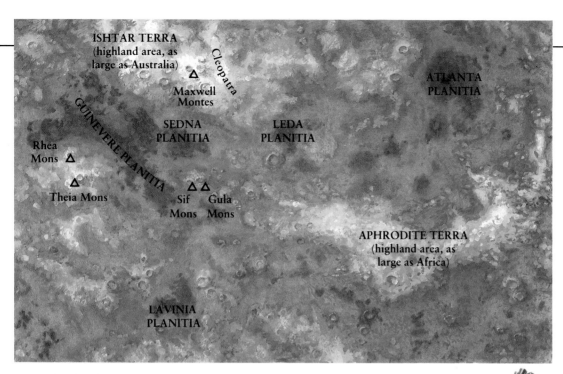

ISHTAR TERRA
(highland area, as
large as Australia)

Cleopatra

Maxwell
Montes

ATLANTA
PLANITIA

GUINEVERE PLANITIA

SEDNA
PLANITIA

LEDA
PLANITIA

Rhea
Mons △

Theia Mons △

Sif
Mons △

Gula
Mons △

APHRODITE TERRA
(highland area, as
large as Africa)

LAVINIA
PLANITIA

◀ *An artist's impression of Venus' surface, based on radar information. The highland areas, or continents, are coloured yellow. The mountain Maxwell Montes is 12 km high. Its peaks are the second highest in the Solar System. About 80 percent of the surface of Venus is covered with dusty, rocky lava plains, which have smothered most of the early craters. A well-known crater, Cleopatra, is 160 km across.*

▶ *The Magellan spacecraft mapped 99 percent of the surface of Venus in 1990– 1992. It recorded features as small in size as a football pitch.*

◀ *Maat Mons is a volcanic feature on Venus, 8 km high. Radar information from Magellan was processed by computer technology to produce this image.*

▶ *Sulphur dioxide from early volcanic activity has helped to form dense sulphuric acid clouds. These spread in a corrosive mist over the surface of Venus.*

The Earth

As far as we know, the Earth is unique in the Solar System for two reasons: it has liquid water on its surface, and it supports life. Both are probably dependent on each other. Without water, the type of plant life we know could not have flourished; without plant life, oxygen would not have been released into the early carbon dioxide atmosphere to make air for animals to breathe. A permanent carbon dioxide covering might have created a similar atmosphere to that on Venus, turning Earth's surface into a desert.

▲ The blue-white Earth is the largest of the four inner terrestrial planets. Its colour contrasts strongly with that of its neighbouring planets – jewel-bright Venus and reddish Mars. (Distances not to scale.)

▼ The Earth's atmosphere is about 78 percent nitrogen, 21 percent oxygen and one percent other gases. Half of the Earth's atmospheric material is found in the troposphere, 10 km high. The stratosphere contains the ozone layer which absorbs dangerous ultraviolet rays from the Sun. The mesosphere is where small space bodies, meteoroids, burn up because of air resistance.

Earth

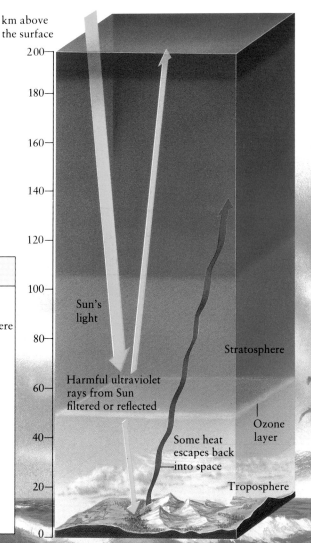

km above the surface

Sun's light

Harmful ultraviolet rays from Sun filtered or reflected

Some heat escapes back into space

Stratosphere

Ozone layer

Troposphere

EARTH DATAFILE

Diameter: 12,756 km
Mass: 5.9 thousand billion billion tonnes
Density: 5.5 (water = 1)
Minimum distance from Sun: 147 million km
Maximum distance from Sun: 152 million km
Day/night: 24 h
Length of year: 365 days 5 h
Tilt of axis: 23° 27'
True rotation period: 23 h 56 min
Maximum temperature: 58°C
Minimum temperature: −89°C
Satellites: 1

STRUCTURE

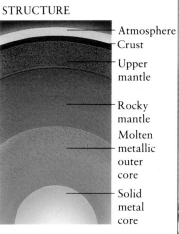

Atmosphere
Crust
Upper mantle
Rocky mantle
Molten metallic outer core
Solid metal core

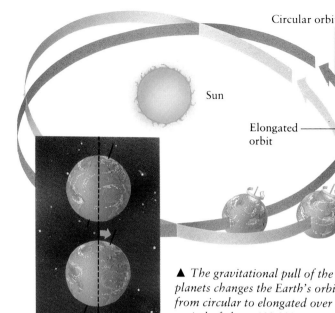

Circular orbit

Sun

Elongated orbit

▲ *The gravitational pull of the planets changes the Earth's orbit from circular to elongated over a period of about 100,000 years.*

▶ *The Earth has had a number of Ice Ages, the last one thousands of years ago. These may have been caused by changes in the shape of the Earth's orbit and the tilt of its axis. Today, summers are warm and winters cool. But changes to Earth's orbit and tilt could mean that the temperature hardly changes and winter snow does not melt in the summer. Instead, ice reflects the Sun's radiation back into space, the temperature falls further, and an Ice Age begins.*

Earth's axis tilts over thousands of years

Snow evaporates, causing cloud cover

Cloud reflects Sun's heat away from Earth, causing temperature to fall further

▲ *The tilt of Earth's axis varies by 3° over a 40,000 year period. The greater the tilt, the greater the difference in the seasons.*

▼ *The Earth's surface water is in a delicate balance. Vapour rises from the sea, condenses as clouds, and falls back as rain or snow.*

THE CHANGING SURFACE

The crust of the Earth is not an unbroken shell, but is made up of several giant plates of solid rock. The plates are floating on the moving molten rock of the Earth's mantle beneath. The Earth's surface is constantly changing because of the great forces created by these plates as they drift. If two plates move against each other the crust may be forced up in mountain chains. An example is the Andes chain, which runs down South America. In the middle of the oceans, ridges form where the sea floor is spreading, as rock from the mantle wells up and forms new crust. The ridge marks the edge of a plate.

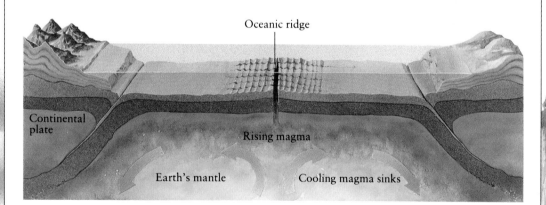

Oceanic ridge

Continental plate

Rising magma

Earth's mantle

Cooling magma sinks

The Moon

The Moon is the Earth's satellite, a pitted rocky body orbiting our planet. It has no light of its own, but seems bright in the sky as it reflects the light of the Sun. The Moon is a fossilized world, where little has happened during the last 3 billion years – but it had a violent past. After the Moon formed, its surface was cratered by bodies that crashed into it between 3 and 4 billion years ago, exploding on the surface. The craters have not worn away, but display the Moon's history for all to see.

▲ *The crater Eratosthenes measures 61 km across. It must have been formed after the lava plains that surround it, otherwise it would have been melted down by the flood of hot rock.*

▼ *The diameter of the Moon is roughly equal to the distance across Australia.*

BAY OF RAINBOWS

SEA OF SHOWERS

SEA OF SERENITY

Eratosthenes

SEA OF CRISES

OCEAN OF STORMS

SEA OF TRANQUILITY

Copernicus

SEA OF FERTILITY

SEA OF CLOUDS

SEA OF NECTAR

SEA OF MOISTURE

HUMBOLDT'S SEA

SOUTHERN SEA

◄ *The side of the Moon turned towards Earth has huge lava plains, called maria. The pull of Earth's gravity strained and weakened this side, pulling it out of shape. As a result, lava flowed out through cracks in the crust, flooding the older craters to form lava plains.*

◄ *The far side of the Moon is covered with craters and mountain ranges. The lunar mountains were not caused by crustal movements but are the surviving walls of huge, ancient craters. With no Earth shining in the sky, the nights must be very dark indeed.*

MOON DATAFILE

STRUCTURE

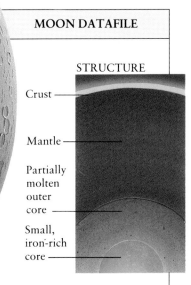

Crust

Mantle

Partially molten outer core

Small, iron-rich core

Diameter: 3476 km
Mass: 0.01 x Earth
Density: 3.3 (water = 1)
Minimum distance from Earth: 356,000 km
Maximum distance from Earth: 407,000 km
Day/night: 29.5 Earth days
True time to orbit Earth: 27.3 Earth days
Lunar month (cycle of phases): 29.5 Earth days
True rotation period: 27.3 days
Maximum temperature: 110°C
Minimum temperature: −170°C

HOW THE CRATERS WERE FORMED

Most of the craters on the Moon were formed when smaller bodies, a few kilometres across, crashed into its surface. A body striking the surface of the Moon at a speed greater than 10 km/s would explode, blasting out a crater about 10 times its own width. Silica, a glassy substance found in rock, might be squirted out for hundreds of kilometres. The silica would form bright rays, extending out of the crater. The violent impact on the floor of the crater would create a shock wave, making the floor spring back up as a central mountain.

1 Meteorite

2 Rocky material thrown out

3 Mountain formed in centre of crater

Settled rays of silicate rock

4 Dust settles in crater over time

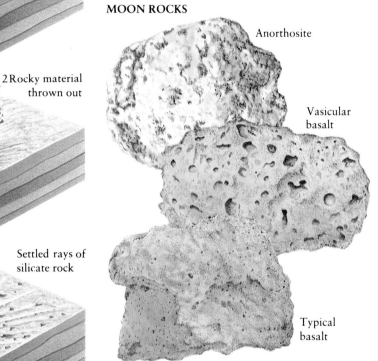

MOON ROCKS

Anorthosite

Vasicular basalt

Typical basalt

▲ The US Apollo project answered a number of questions about the Moon, confirming that its surface is firm and the core is still hot.

◄ Compared with Earth rocks, the samples brought back from the Moon by the Apollo project contain more of some elements such as titanium, and less of others such as gold. The ages of the Moon rock samples range from about 4.5 billion years (not long after the birth of the Moon) to 3.1 billion years – the time when the lava plains formed.

FACTS ABOUT THE MOON

- The Moon has no atmosphere, and so there is no wind or weather either. As a result, the astronauts' footprints will last for centuries.
- Today, laser beams can measure the distance to the Moon with an accuracy of about 10 cm.

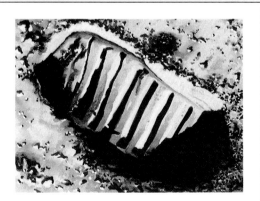

The Earth and the Moon

It would be hard to imagine two rocky worlds more different than the Earth and the Moon – yet they orbit each other almost as a double planet. Most satellites are much smaller than the planet controlling them, but the diameter of the Moon is a quarter of the Earth's diameter. The Moon is a very useful body for us, lightening half the nights every month as it reflects the Sun's light. Yet it may also block the light sent from the Sun during a solar eclipse, casting a black shadow on part of the Earth.

THE FORMATION OF THE MOON

Despite the closeness of the Moon to the Earth, we are still unable to say for certain how our satellite formed. A century ago it was believed that the molten Earth, spinning very fast, became unstable and threw a large blob of material into orbit. This theory has now been abandoned because, for this to happen, the Earth would have to spin once in only two and a half hours, which seems impossible. Three other theories have been put forward; they are illustrated here.

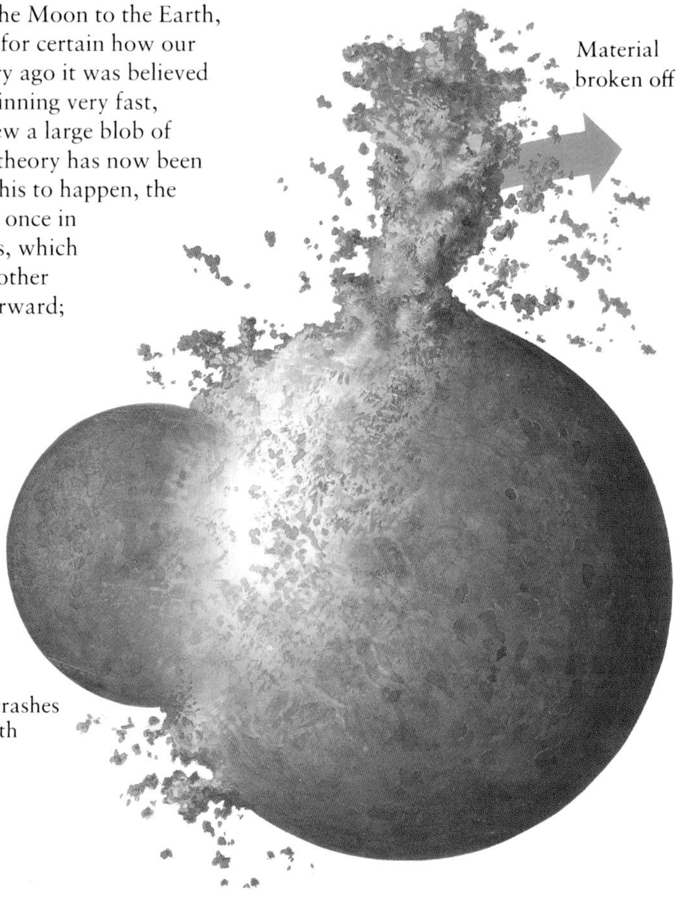

Material broken off

1 Body crashes into Earth

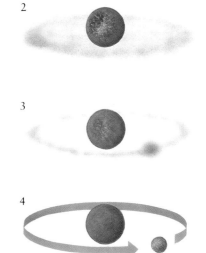

2

3

4

◄ *Samples from the surface of the Moon show that its rocks have a very different composition from those on the Earth. If the Moon ever did form part of our planet, it could have been broken off by a collision with a planet-sized body (1). This body added different material to the debris thrown off into space (2). The debris formed an orbiting cloud (3) which finally condensed into the Moon (4).*

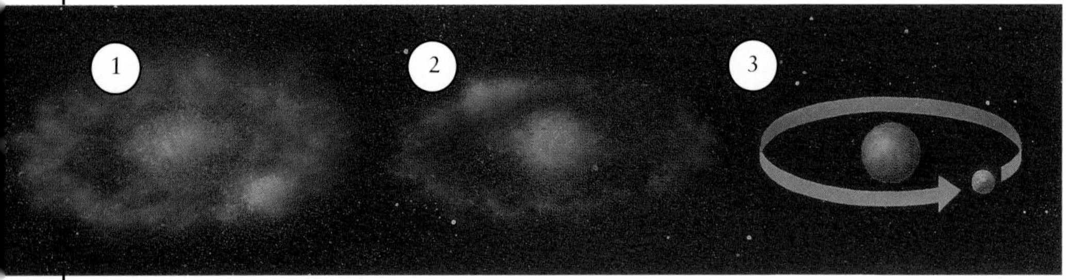

◄ *The Earth and the Moon may have formed together as a double planet from the cloud of debris left over after the formation of the Sun. This idea is attractive because it does not assume an unlikely event, such as a collision. But if the two bodies formed so closely together, then why are their surface rocks so different? And why does the Moon have such a small iron core compared with the Earth?*

1 2 3

▶ *The capture theory assumes that the Moon was a passing body caught by the Earth's gravity. This explains its different composition. However, calculations show that a capture is far less likely than a collision with another body.*

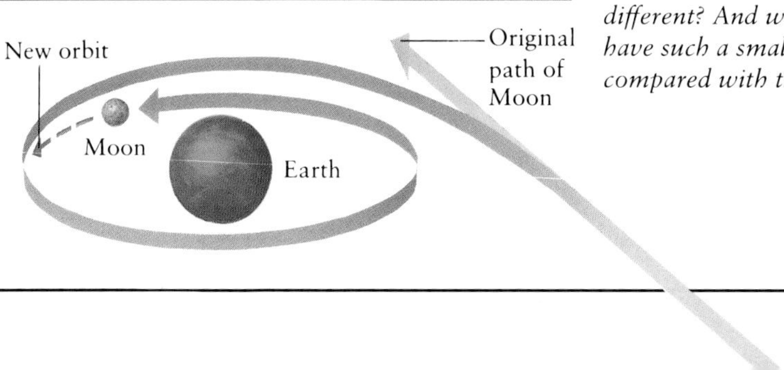

New orbit

Moon   Earth

Original path of Moon

◄ In this photograph, taken by Apollo 11, the blue and white Earth contrasts with the bare lunar surface. The Moon's weak gravity could not hold on to any atmosphere, and so it became just a huge ball of stone, exposed to fierce temperature extremes of day and night. The photo is often called 'Earthrise'. However, this is not accurate. The Earth never rises or sets in the Moon's sky, since the same hemisphere of the Moon is always turned towards the Earth.

THE PHASES OF THE MOON

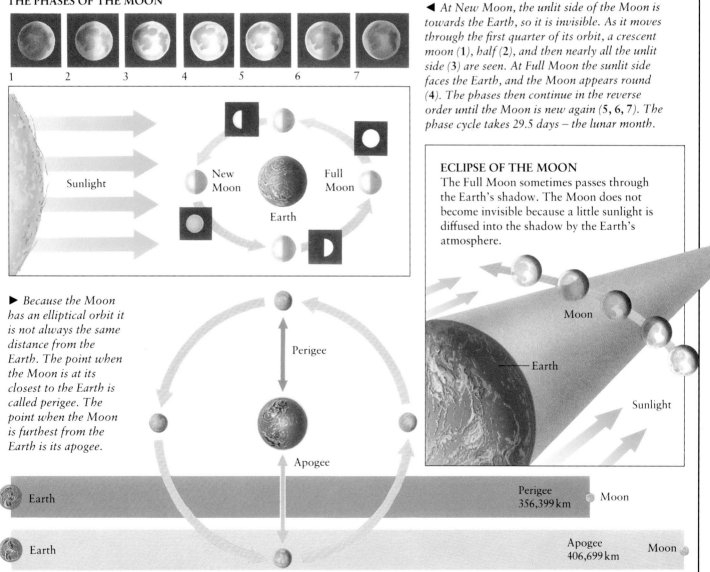

◄ At New Moon, the unlit side of the Moon is towards the Earth, so it is invisible. As it moves through the first quarter of its orbit, a crescent moon (1), half (2), and then nearly all the unlit side (3) are seen. At Full Moon the sunlit side faces the Earth, and the Moon appears round (4). The phases then continue in the reverse order until the Moon is new again (5, 6, 7). The phase cycle takes 29.5 days – the lunar month.

ECLIPSE OF THE MOON

The Full Moon sometimes passes through the Earth's shadow. The Moon does not become invisible because a little sunlight is diffused into the shadow by the Earth's atmosphere.

► Because the Moon has an elliptical orbit it is not always the same distance from the Earth. The point when the Moon is at its closest to the Earth is called perigee. The point when the Moon is furthest from the Earth is its apogee.

Perigee

Apogee

Earth

Perigee
356,399 km

Moon

Earth

Apogee
406,699 km

Moon

Mars

This mysterious planet has intrigued skywatchers for centuries. It shines very brightly when closest to the Earth, moving quickly in front of the stars, and it has a strong, reddish colour. Less than a century ago, many people believed in Martians, and the possibility of finding some kind of life form inspired the *Viking* missions in 1976. Although apparently dead and inhospitable, Mars is the only planet selected for possible human exploration, and further visits by unmanned spacecraft are planned.

▲ *Mars is the outermost of the rocky planets. A vast gap, twice the diameter of its own orbit, separates Mars from Jupiter. Most of the asteroids, or minor planets, are found in this gap. (Distances not to scale.)*

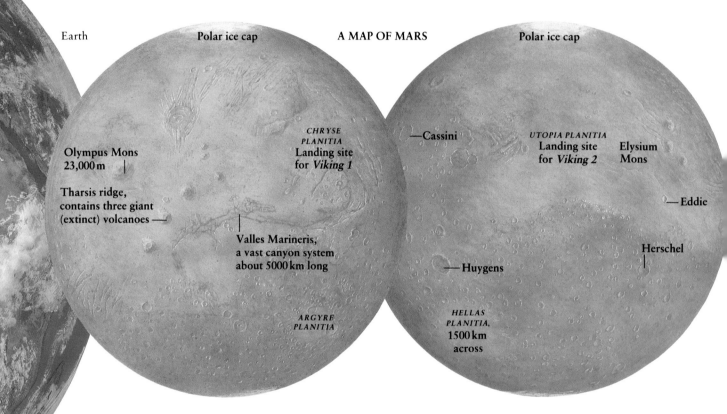

A MAP OF MARS

Earth

Polar ice cap

Polar ice cap

Olympus Mons 23,000 m

Tharsis ridge, contains three giant (extinct) volcanoes —

CHRYSE PLANITIA
Landing site for *Viking 1*

Valles Marineris, a vast canyon system about 5000 km long

ARGYRE PLANITIA

—Cassini

UTOPIA PLANITIA
Landing site for *Viking 2*

Elysium Mons

—Eddie

Herschel

—Huygens

HELLAS PLANITIA, 1500 km across

MARS DATAFILE

Diameter: 6787 km
Mass: 0.11 × Earth
Density: 3.9 (water = 1)
Minimum distance from Sun: 206 million km
Maximum distance from Sun: 249 million km
Minimum distance from Earth: 56 million km
Day/night: 24 h 37 min
Length of year: 687 Earth days
Tilt of axis: 25° 12′
Surface gravity: 0.38 × Earth
Temperature: − 110°C to 0°C
Satellites: 2

STRUCTURE

— Atmosphere
— Crust

— Mantle

— Iron core

MARTIAN ATMOSPHERE

The atmosphere on Mars is mainly carbon dioxide with nitrogen, argon and other gases. At a height of about 30 km, winds can raise huge dust-clouds. At night, carbon dioxide freezes on parts of the surface as hoar frost. Traces of water can form thin hazes at dusk and dawn.

Thick cloud layer

Carbon dioxide gas

Dust-clouds

SATELLITES OF MARS

Deimos is about 15 km long, and covered with small craters. From Mars, Deimos would appear as an almost star-like object, remaining above the horizon for two nights at a time.

Deimos

Phobos

Phobos is larger and closer to Mars than Deimos. It is about 27 km long. It orbits Mars in only seven and a half hours, so that it rises in the west and sets in the east about four hours later.

Viking Lander

▲ *This view of the surface of Mars was taken by the* Viking 2 *lander* (left). *It shows a desert of rocks, each up to about 30 cm across, under an orange sky.*

▼ *The colour of Mars' sky comes from wind-borne dust blown from the reddish surface. Early in the planet's history, when it was warmer and damp, the iron-rich surface rusted, turning Mars into a red planet.*

FACTS ABOUT MARS

● About 4 billion years ago, Mars may have been warm enough for water to run in rivers over its surface.
● Phobos, the inner moon, goes around the planet three times while Mars spins on its axis once. This means that Phobos' 'month' is shorter than Mars' day.
● The Valles Marineris is an enormous canyon system running for some 4000 km along the surface of Mars. In some places it is 6 km deep.
● Did a *Viking* orbiter record a landslide on Mars in 1978? Two close-up pictures of part of the Valles Marineris, taken two and a half minutes apart, appear to show a sudden cloud of dust about 600 m high.

▶ *Roughly half of the Martian surface shows signs of past volcanic activity. The volcanic mountain Olympus Mons rises 23 km above the plain. It is the highest peak in the Solar System, and shows how violent the volcanic activity must have been. Elsewhere on Mars, there are winding valleys that look just like dried-up river beds.*

Dust cloud storm

Giant volcano

Crater

◀ *Some craters on Mars seem almost as unchanged as those found on the Moon.*

Jupiter

Jupiter is by far the largest planet in the Solar System – it is so huge that all the other planets could be squeezed inside it. It spins faster than any of the other planets too, so that its day lasts less than 10 hours. Jupiter is made up of about 90 percent hydrogen and 10 percent helium, with traces of other elements. Its core must be hotter than the surface of the Sun, but the clouds exposed to space are bitterly cold. Its vivid stripes are cloud markings, drawn out into dark belts and light zones by Jupiter's rapid spin.

▲ *Although Jupiter is the largest planet, it has only a thousandth of the Sun's mass. Even the smallest and dimmest known stars contain about a hundred times as much material as Jupiter. (Distances not to scale.)*

▶ *The details of Jupiter's appearance are always changing. The cloud belts are caused by clouds of frozen ammonia, ammonium hydrosulphide, water ice and other compounds being swept through the outer layers of the planet at speeds of up to 400 km/h. Some markings have lasted for decades.*

Earth

Jupiter

▶ *The Great Red Spot is a vast whirlpool on the surface of Jupiter. About twice the Earth's diameter, it draws material up from below as it rotates every six days. This cloud feature has been observed for a century, and possibly longer. The colour, which sometimes fades away for several years, may be caused by sunlight reacting with chemicals in the clouds to release red phosphorus.*

▲ *The ring around Jupiter is about 6500 km wide and 30 km thick. It is surrounded by a much fainter 20,000 km-wide halo. The ring is made up of particles which measure about 0.01 mm across. Another ring of sulphur particles lies in Io's orbit.*

JUPITER'S ATMOSPHERE

The clouds of Jupiter lie in the upper 200 km of the atmosphere – less than one percent of the distance to the centre. The planet is made up of almost pure hydrogen and helium, compressed to a fiercely-hot liquid. This churning liquid generates a powerful magnetic field and electric currents, which produce radio waves.

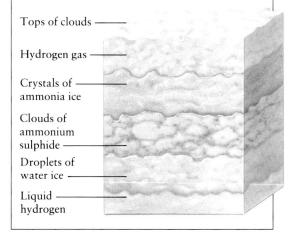

Tops of clouds

Hydrogen gas

Crystals of ammonia ice

Clouds of ammonium sulphide

Droplets of water ice

Liquid hydrogen

JUPITER DATAFILE

Diameter: 142,800 km (equator)
Mass: 318 × Earth
Density: 1.3 (water = 1)
Minimum distance from Sun: 741 million km
Maximum distance from Sun: 816 million km
Minimum distance from Earth: 590 million km
Day/night: 9 h 50 min (equator)
Length of year: 11.9 Earth years
Tilt of axis: 3°
Surface gravity: 2.7 × Earth
Temperature: −150°C
Satellites: 16 known

STRUCTURE

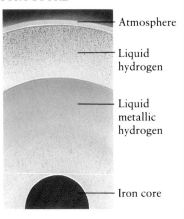

Atmosphere

Liquid hydrogen

Liquid metallic hydrogen

Iron core

EXPLORING JUPITER

The *Galileo* probe should reach Jupiter in 1995. The main craft will study the planet itself and its satellites. A probe will also be released into Jupiter's atmosphere to record the conditions and chemical make-up of the outer layers, before it is destroyed by the fierce pressure. *Galileo* was launched in 1989. It used the gravity of Venus and the Earth to speed it on its way to Jupiter.

Flyby Earth (1), 1990

Flyby Earth (2), 1992

Flyby Venus, 1990

Galileo launch, 1989

Arrives at Jupiter, 1995

Galileo probe

THE GALILEAN SATELLITES

Jupiter's four large satellites were discovered by Galileo Galilei (1564–1642) with his primitive telescope in 1610. They include Ganymede, the largest satellite in the Solar System. Although the satellites can be seen using binoculars, the *Voyager* spacecraft produced our first detailed view of their surfaces in 1979. (*Their sizes are shown to scale here.*)

◄ *Callisto, the outermost Galilean satellite, is covered with ancient craters. However, unlike our Moon, there is no sign of any later lava flows. All the satellites keep the same face turned inwards towards Jupiter.*

▲ *Ganymede is the largest satellite in the Solar System, 5262 km across. Parts of its crust may once have drifted over the hot rock beneath, as happened on Earth.*

A volcano explodes on Io

► *Europa is covered in ice many kilometres thick, making it the smoothest known body anywhere. The dark streaks may be fractures in the surface, filled with ice.*

► *Io is a sulphur-covered volcanic world. Constant eruptions shoot material 200 km into space before it falls back on to the orange-yellow surface.*

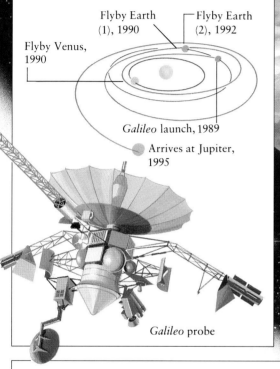

Saturn

Saturn has been known for centuries as the ringed planet. In fact, due to the *Voyager* space probes we now know that all four giant planets have rings, although Saturn's rings are by far the most impressive. There is less cloud detail visible on Saturn than on Jupiter. This may be because a layer of haze makes it hard to see what cloud belts lie lower down. However, about three times every century violent storms disturb the calm surface and cause brilliant white 'spots' to break out on the planet.

▲ *Like the other giant planets, Saturn spins so quickly that its equator now bulges outward noticeably. This gives the planet a slightly squashed look. The bulge is due to centrifugal force.* (Distances not to scale.)

▶ *The cloud features on Saturn are difficult to make out, but* Voyager 2 *recorded details including a 'Great Brown Spot' near the north pole.*

▶ *Under this calm-looking surface, material is being swept round at speeds of up to 1800 km/h. In 1990 a huge white eruption was easily visible from the Earth through telescopes.*

Earth

Saturn

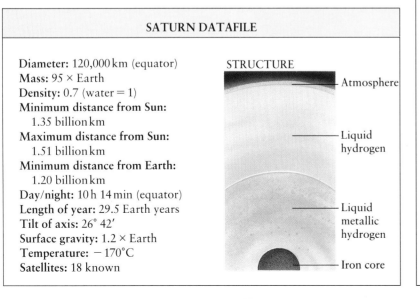

▲ *Saturn's rings extend for over 74,000 km, but are only a few kilometres deep. Although they seem to be divided into several wide zones, they are really thousands of separate narrow ringlets. The rings could be the remains of a small satellite, 100 km across.*

Cassini division

▲ *The Cassini Division is a wide zone in the rings where the particles are scattered. They have been pulled into different orbits by Saturn's moons.*

SATURN'S ATMOSPHERE
The cloud layers form a skin as thin as apple peel over the hydrogen and helium body of Saturn. *Voyager 2* had a much clearer view of the cloud forms than *Voyager 1* did, when it passed nine months earlier. This suggests that the upper ammonia haze varies in transparency.

SATURN DATAFILE

Diameter: 120,000 km (equator)
Mass: 95 × Earth
Density: 0.7 (water = 1)
Minimum distance from Sun:
　1.35 billion km
Maximum distance from Sun:
　1.51 billion km
Minimum distance from Earth:
　1.20 billion km
Day/night: 10 h 14 min (equator)
Length of year: 29.5 Earth years
Tilt of axis: 26° 42′
Surface gravity: 1.2 × Earth
Temperature: −170°C
Satellites: 18 known

STRUCTURE
— Atmosphere
— Liquid hydrogen
— Liquid metallic hydrogen
— Iron core

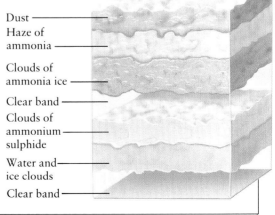

Dust
Haze of ammonia
Clouds of ammonia ice
Clear band
Clouds of ammonium sulphide
Water and ice clouds
Clear band

▲ *The* Cassini *spacecraft will be launched in 1997 and is planned to reach Saturn in 2002. It will orbit Saturn and study Titan, the largest moon. A probe will be dropped into Titan's atmosphere.*

SATURN'S SATELLITES

Saturn has more known moons than any other planet. There are 18 satellites confirmed so far, of which 12 were discovered by the *Voyager* probes. The existence of other satellites is suspected. The moons range from the second largest in the Solar System (Titan, 5150 km across) to the second smallest (Pan, at 20 km across only slightly larger than Mars' Deimos). Titan is the only moon in the Solar System to have its own thick atmosphere, which makes it a prime target for the planned *Cassini* mission. Phoebe is the furthest moon from the planet, orbiting at 13 million km distance.

Titan

▲ *The main gases found in Titan's thick orange atmosphere are nitrogen and methane, with traces of organic compounds including ethane and ethyne. These compounds form the crude beginnings of molecules found in living cells. Titan's hidden surface could be a deep-frozen record of how more advanced organic molecules formed naturally out of simple gases.*

▲ Voyager 1 *visited Saturn in 1980. It sent back this image of the unique oval red cloud feature in Saturn's southern hemisphere.*

▶ *Saturn's rings are made up of billions of particles in orbit around the planet, ranging in size from grains to large rocks.*

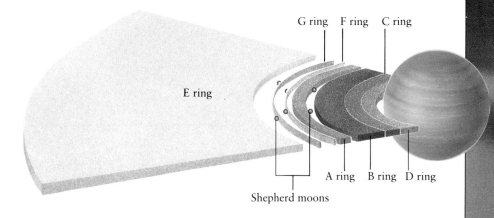

RINGS AND SHEPHERD MOONS

Only rings A, B and C are visible from the Earth. The particles in the brightest ring, B, seem to be icy. Calculations suggest that ice would eventually be dulled by fine space dust. Since this has not yet happened, the rings are probably less than a billion years old. The gravity of tiny satellites, known as shepherd moons, appears to control the position of some of the orbiting particles. For example, Prometheus and Pandora, each less than 150 km across, orbit on either side of the narrow F ring.

G ring F ring C ring

E ring

Shepherd moons

A ring B ring D ring

Uranus

Before the last decade, chance played a large part in our understanding of Uranus. Barely visible with the naked eye, the planet was discovered by accident in 1781. Two centuries later its faint ring system was also discovered by accident. Apart from the fact that it orbits the Sun on its side and has a family of satellites, little else was known. In the course of a few days in January 1986, pictures taken by the space probe *Voyager 2* transformed our knowledge of this remote giant.

▲ *Uranus has the volume of more than 60 Earths. The tilt of its axis means that its 'north' pole is pointing slightly south. Uranus has a backward, or retrograde, spin – as do Venus and Pluto. (Distances not to scale.)*

DISCOVERING URANUS

Uranus was discovered by William Herschel (1738–1822), a musician from Germany who settled in Bath, England and became fascinated by astronomy. In 1781 he was looking at the sky with his home-made telescope when he noticed a 'star' that showed as a small disc. The discovery earned Herschel royal recognition.

Earth

Voyager 2

Uranus

► *Uranus has many rings – nine major ones and many more faint ones. They are made up of roughly metre-sized pieces of rock, with little ice or dust. Some of Uranus' rings have been created or controlled by shepherd moons orbiting beside them* (see page 35).

URANUS DATAFILE

Diameter: 51,000 km (equator)
Mass: 14.5 × Earth's mass
Density: 1.3 (water = 1)
Minimum distance from Sun:
  2.74 billion km
Maximum distance from Sun:
  3.01 billion km
Minimum distance from Earth:
  2.59 billion km
Day/night: 17 h 14 min
Length of year: 84 Earth years
Tilt of axis: 82°
Surface gravity: 0.93 × Earth
Temperature: − 200°C
Satellites: 15

STRUCTURE

— Atmosphere of hydrogen, helium and methane

— Mantle of ammonia, water and methane ice

— Iron silicate core

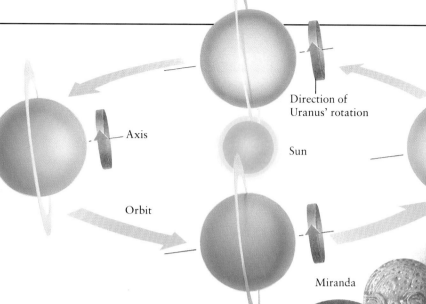

▶ *The strange tilt of Uranus may be the result of a collision with another large body, soon after it had formed. The effect is that each pole spends about 40 years in constant summer sunlight, and then another 40 in continual winter darkness. At the present time, one of the poles is almost facing the Sun. However, Voyager 2 took measurements that showed that the winter side was not as cold as expected, because of heat flowing back from the sunlit face.*

Direction of
Uranus' rotation

Axis

Sun

Orbit

Miranda

Ariel

Titania

THE SATELLITES OF URANUS

Five satellites were already known from Earth-based observation, but *Voyager* discovered ten more, each less than 100 km across. Unlike the mythological names for most Solar System satellites, the moons of Uranus are named after Shakespearean characters: for example, Desdemona, Portia and Oberon.

▼ *Very few craters can be seen on Miranda, which suggests that the body formed after the main bombardment of craters (see page 19). It is possible that the original moon broke up and the pieces came together again.*

▶ *Miranda is 480 km across, a curious, patchwork moon. There may be ice-cliffs on its surface towering 20 km high.*

▶ *The surface of Ariel has few craters. It is possible that old, large craters have been melted down by volcanic activity in the past.*

▲ *Uranus' largest satellite, Titania, is an ice-covered world. Long valleys cross a landscape of craters, which measure up to 400 km across.*

▼ *From Miranda's strange surface, Uranus looms vast in the black sky. Only when its equator is edge-on to the Sun will the planet appear completely sunlit.*

Neptune

Neptune was discovered in 1846 as a result of the effect of its gravitational pull on Uranus. Its brilliant blue methane atmosphere looks calm and cold (it has a temperature of −210°C). But *Voyager 2* discovered winds ripping through Neptune's atmosphere at 2200 km/h, the fiercest winds in the Solar System. The winds travel in a different direction to the planet's spin. Neptune's large satellite, Triton, was also surprising – despite being the coldest land surface in the Solar System, it has plumes of gas erupting into space.

▲ *Neptune is a little smaller than Uranus. It is the outermost giant planet, and for 20 years in every 250 years, when Pluto comes closest to the Sun (as in 1979–1999), it is also the outermost planet. (Distances not to scale.)*

Earth

▶ *Methane gas, which reflects blue light well, gives Neptune its intense colour.*

Neptune

▶ *Voyager 2 found four faint rings around Neptune. The three brighter rings have been called Galle, Adams and Leverrier, after the three people involved in the discovery of Neptune.*

◀ *Some cloud features appear and vanish in just a few minutes, rising up from the warmer layers and sinking again as they cool down. Long-lasting features, such as the Great Dark Spot and some of the white clouds, are being forced along by the fierce currents.*

▲ *Neptune's rings are all very narrow. Galle is only 15 km wide, and Adams, the widest, is less than 50 km across.*

NEPTUNE DATAFILE

Diameter: 49,500 km (equator)
Mass: 17.2 × Earth
Density: 1.8 (water = 1)
Minimum distance from Sun:
4.46 billion km
Maximum distance from Sun:
4.54 billion km
Minimum distance from Earth:
4.31 billion km
Day/night: 17 h 6 min
Length of year: 165 Earth years
Tilt of axis: 29° 36′
Surface gravity: 1.2 × Earth
Temperature: −210°C
Satellites: 8

STRUCTURE

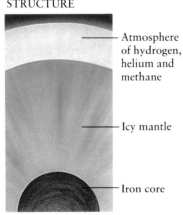

— Atmosphere of hydrogen, helium and methane

— Icy mantle

— Iron core

Leverrier

▲ *The Sun's gravity rules the planets, but their own much weaker gravity also pulls at each other. The independent calculations of John Couch Adams in England and Urbain Leverrier in France in 1845 showed that an unknown planet was pulling Uranus from its true path. These calculations led to the discovery of Neptune by Johann Galle in Germany.*

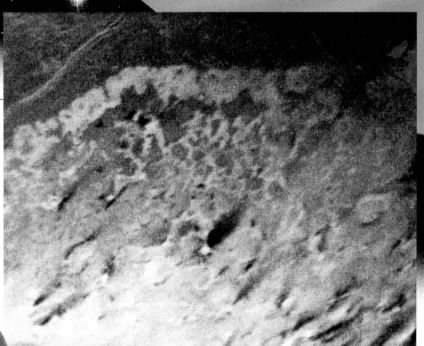

▶ *The Great Dark
Spot was discovered by*
Voyager 2. *Large enough
to contain the Earth, the
spot changes in size and shape as
the material inside it is slowly
churned round once every 16 days. A
much smaller dark spot, known as D2, was
also seen in Neptune's southern hemisphere;
both spots were observed for several weeks.*

SATELLITES OF NEPTUNE

Neptune has eight satellites, six of them
discovered by *Voyager 2*. The five tiny
inner satellites orbit Neptune faster than
it spins. The next, Proteus, is 415 km
across. Nereid, the small outermost
satellite discovered from Earth, takes a
year to make one orbit, sweeping close
to Neptune and then far out into space,
like a comet.

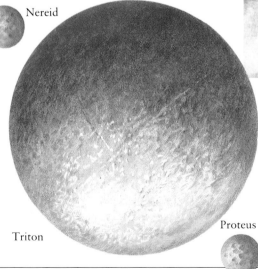

Nereid

Triton

Proteus

TRITON

The largest of Neptune's satellites, Triton,
is 2705 km across, with a crust of rock-
hard ice at a temperature of −235°C.
Although its gravity is too weak to hold on
to a proper atmosphere, a very thin layer of
nitrogen is fed by plumes of gas from the
surface. Triton orbits Neptune backwards;
this suggests that the satellite was captured
by the planet's gravity, or suffered a space
accident that altered its path.

▲ *This close-up of
Triton's south pole
was taken by* Voyager
2. *The space probe
was only 190,000 km
from Triton's surface.
The white material
may be frost, and the
long dark streaks may
be dust, blown by
surface winds.*

Pluto and Beyond

Uranus and Neptune have slightly erratic orbits. The cause of this was suspected to be the pull of gravity from a ninth planet. This led to the discovery of Pluto in 1930 during a thorough search of the sky for 'Planet X' by the American astronomer Clyde Tombaugh. We still know very little about Pluto. It is the only planet we have not observed in close-up from a spacecraft and is too far away to see in detail with a telescope.

▲ *Tiny Pluto, on the frontier of the Solar System, is smaller than our Moon and only twice the diameter of the largest asteroid. Its eccentric orbit carries it closer than Neptune to the Sun at perihelion. (Distances not to scale.)*

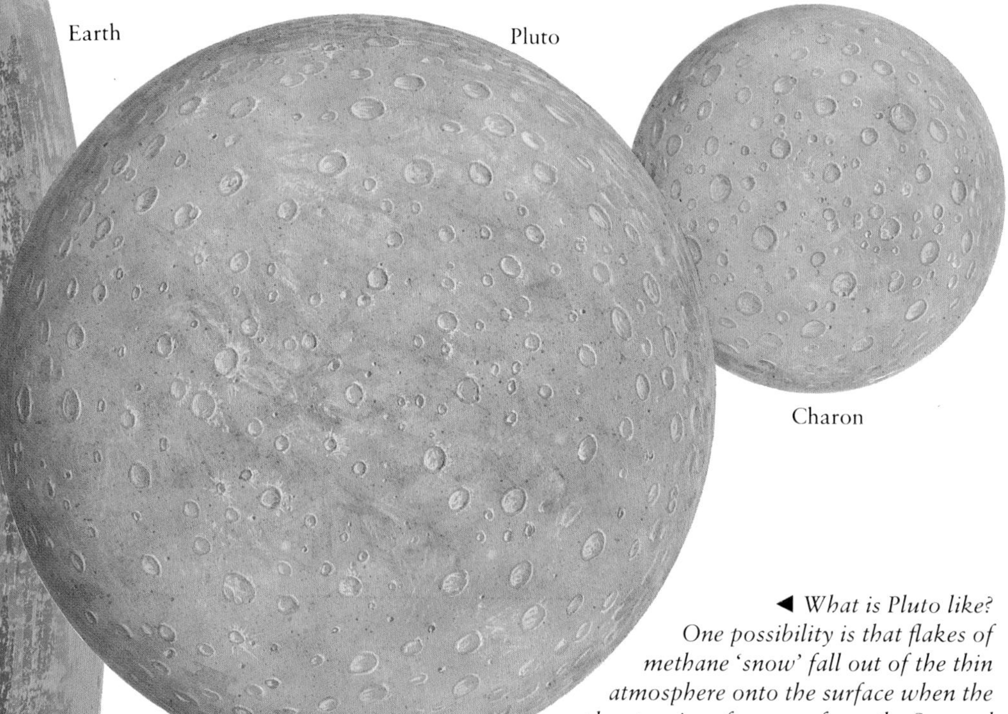

Earth

Pluto

Charon

◀ *No telescope has seen Pluto, or its moon Charon, in detail. We can only guess at their appearance. Charon was detected from Earth in 1978. It is about half the size of Pluto, with a diameter of 1200 km. Pluto and Charon orbit each other like a double planet. Each one keeps the same hemisphere facing towards the other, and at certain periods during Pluto's year Charon is eclipsed at each revolution.*

◀ *What is Pluto like? One possibility is that flakes of methane 'snow' fall out of the thin atmosphere onto the surface when the planet swings far away from the Sun and the surface temperature falls. When it approaches perihelion again, the increasing warmth turns the methane snow back into gas, and the atmosphere is restored.*

▼ *The clearest image we have of Pluto and Charon comes from the HST (see pages 70–71). The photo shows their relative sizes, but they are farther apart than it appears here.*

PLUTO DATAFILE

Diameter: 2250 km
Mass: 0.002 × Earth
Density: Approx 2 (water = 1)
Minimum distance from Sun:
    4.44 billion km
Maximum distance from Sun:
    7.39 billion km
Minimum distance from Earth:
    4.3 billion km
Day/night: 6 Earth d 9 h
Length of year: 248 Earth years
Tilt of axis: 62° 24′
Surface gravity: 0.03 × Earth
Temperature: −230°C
Satellites: 1

STRUCTURE

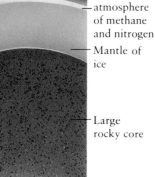

Thin atmosphere of methane and nitrogen

Mantle of ice

Large rocky core

PLUTO'S ORBIT

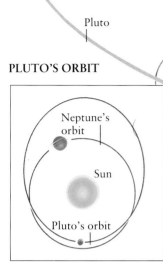

Pluto has an eccentric orbit. Between 1979 and 1999 the planet's orbit brings it closer to the Sun than Neptune, so that at the moment Neptune is the 'last' planet. Pluto's orbit may be a clue to other puzzles of the outer Solar System. Why do Pluto and Charon spin backwards? Why does Neptune's moon Triton orbit backwards? Was Pluto once a moon of Neptune? If *Voyager* had flown past Pluto on its journey across the Solar System, perhaps it would have answered some of these questions.

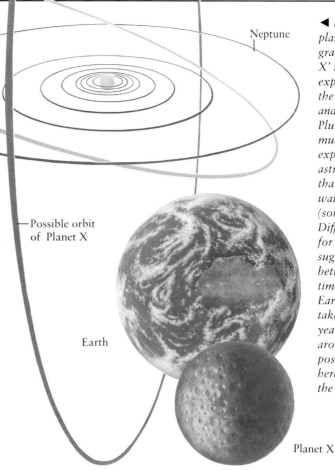

◄ Is there a tenth planet? The pull of gravity from 'Planet X' was needed to explain wanderings in the orbits of Uranus and Neptune. When Pluto turned out to be much smaller than expected, some astronomers thought that Planet X was still waiting to be found (some still do). Different calculations for Planet X have suggested masses between 0.35 and five times that of the Earth. Planet X may take from 200 to 1000 years to travel once around the Sun. One possible orbit is shown here, looping above the Solar System.

▼ From the icy surface of Pluto, Charon would appear seven times the diameter of our own Moon. Charon does not rise or set, because the same side of Pluto always faces it.

CHARON'S EFFECT ON PLUTO'S SPIN

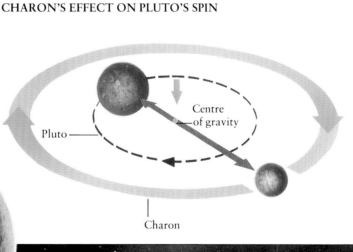

Two orbiting objects revolve around their centre of gravity, or barycentre. In the case of the Earth and the smaller Moon, the barycentre is inside the Earth. However, Charon has a quarter of Pluto's mass. This pulls the barycentre to a point in space between them, so that Pluto, as well as Charon, moves in a circle.

Minor Planets and Meteoroids

In the early days of the Solar System there was debris everywhere, as grains of solid matter grew together into larger objects. The planets and the larger satellites were the most successful, but countless other smaller bodies formed as well. Some passed too near a planet, especially Jupiter, whose gravity stopped them growing into a major planet. Other bodies, moving in the wide space between the orbits of Mars and Jupiter, collided and broke up. The remains of these are known as asteroids, or minor planets.

FACTS ABOUT THE MINOR PLANETS

- Ceres was the first minor planet, or asteroid, to be discovered, in 1801.
- Some asteroids have orbits that take them very close to Earth. One, called Hermes, has come within 777,000 km of us. However, the threat of an asteroid colliding with Earth is very small – the likelihood is perhaps one direct hit every 250,000 years.

► *The asteroid belt is found between the orbits of Mars and Jupiter. It probably contains about 100,000 bodies larger than one kilometre across. Over 3000 of the largest have been given names. The largest, Ceres, has a diameter of 1000 km. The orbits of some unusual asteroids are shown* right. *As well as these, asteroid 1991 DA travels well past Jupiter. The asteroids known as the Trojans share Jupiter's orbit. At its closest point to the Sun the asteroid Phaethon glows red-hot, as it passes twice as close to the Sun as the planet Mercury.*

THE ASTEROID BELT

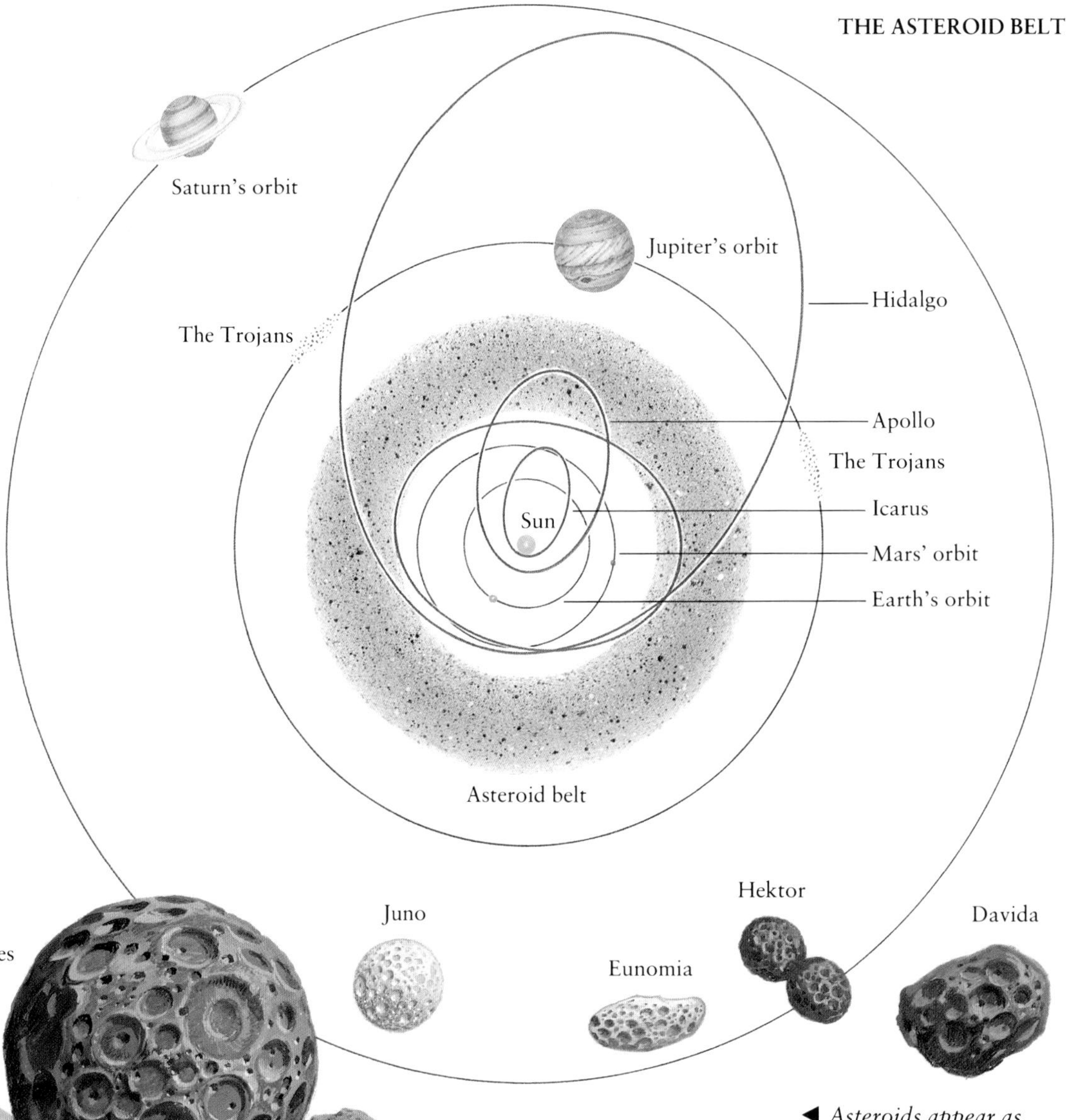

Saturn's orbit
Jupiter's orbit
Hidalgo
The Trojans
Apollo
The Trojans
Sun
Icarus
Mars' orbit
Earth's orbit
Asteroid belt
Juno
Hektor
Davida
Eunomia

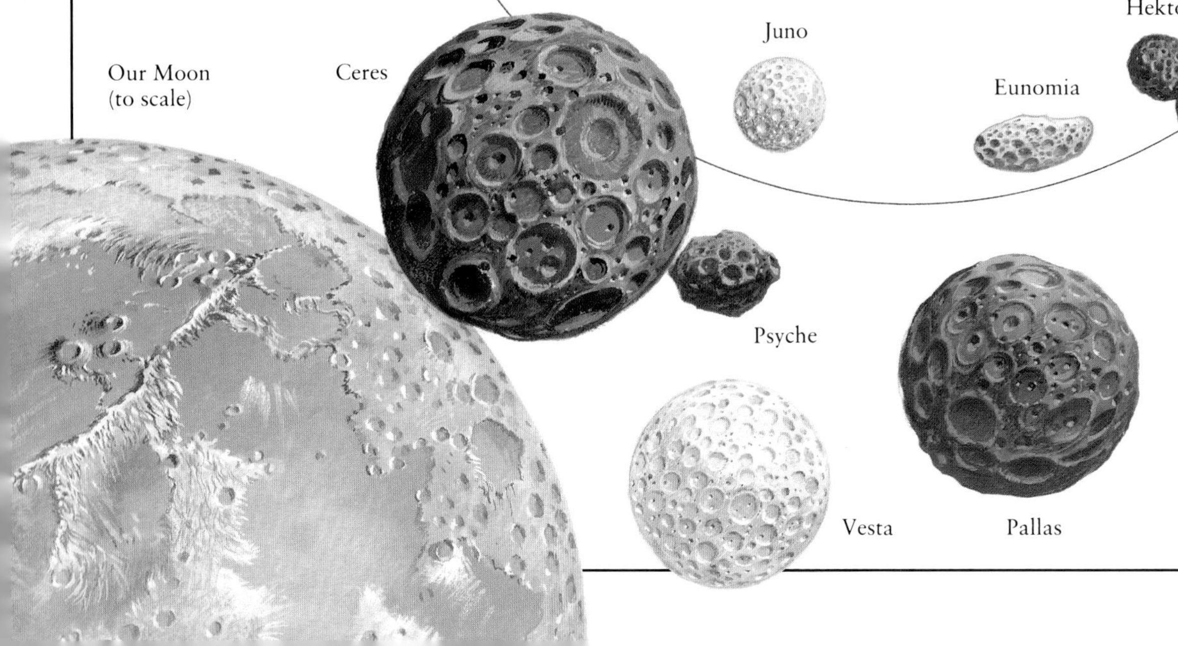

Our Moon
(to scale)
Ceres
Psyche
Vesta
Pallas

◄ *Asteroids appear as pinpoints of light in the sky. One asteroid, Gaspra, has been photographed by the* Galileo *spacecraft. The pictures reveal a long, impact-marked body. Some asteroids must be irregular in shape because their brightness changes as they rotate.*

◄ *An especially bright meteor is called a fireball. Any meteor large enough to travel through the Earth's atmosphere and hit the ground is called a meteorite. These are thought to be pieces of minor planets or comets. Some meteorites are stony, others are metallic – presumably from the crust or core of a broken mini-planet. A few meteorites are made of very crumbly rock.*

METEOROIDS

Many meteoroids are particles thrown out from the crumbly nucleus of a comet *(see pages 44–45)*. They exist by the million, travelling along the comet's orbit in huge swarms, although the grains may be kilometres apart. Meteoroids themselves are invisible, but if they collide with the Earth's atmosphere (at speeds ranging from 10 to 40 km/s) they evaporate in a streak of light – forming meteors or 'shooting stars'.

▼ *If the Earth passes through a large swarm of meteoroids, many meteors may be seen every hour. This is a meteor shower. The meteor shower below is connected with the comet Tempel-Tuttle.*

► *Ordinary meteors usually burn up at a height of about 50 km above Earth. Anything larger than a small stone will light up the sky as a fireball. It may explode, or hit the ground as a meteorite.*

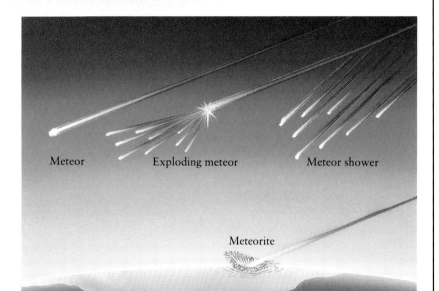

Meteor   Exploding meteor   Meteor shower

Meteorite

▼ *The Old Woman meteorite was discovered in California in 1976. It weighs 2758 kg, making it the second largest meteorite ever found in the United States. It is made of iron and nickel, and may once have formed part of the molten core of a small planet that broke up about 4 billion years ago.*

Comets

It is easy to understand how the unexpected sight of a comet's long, bright tail in the sky must have terrified ancient civilizations. Today we know that comets are just lumps of ice and rock, travelling from the far outer Solar System to orbit our Sun. As a comet nears the Sun the ice melts, giving off jets of gas and releasing clouds of dusty rock particles. From Earth this gas and dust is seen as a dramatic tail, shining by reflected sunlight, and stretching for millions of kilometres.

Crumbling particles of rock and ice

Nucleus

Jets of gas given off

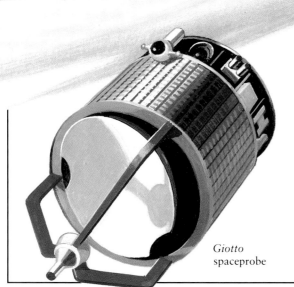

Giotto
spaceprobe

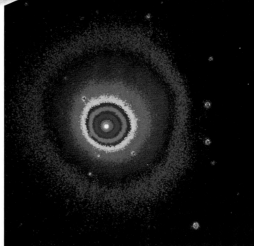

▲ *Comets are named after the person who discovers them. Comet West, discovered by Richard West in 1976, was one of the brightest of recent times.*

◀ *The solid part of a comet, called its nucleus, may be only a few kilometres across, but it may produce a cloud, or coma, of dust and gas 10 times the Earth's diameter. (Illustration not to scale.)*

◀ *Probably the most famous comet of all is Halley, which returns every 76 years. On its appearance in 1985–1986, it was visited by the* Giotto *probe (far left). As Halley neared our planet this false colour image was taken from Earth. The different colours show different levels of brightness (white is brightest). The nucleus gives out gas and dust in circular rings.*

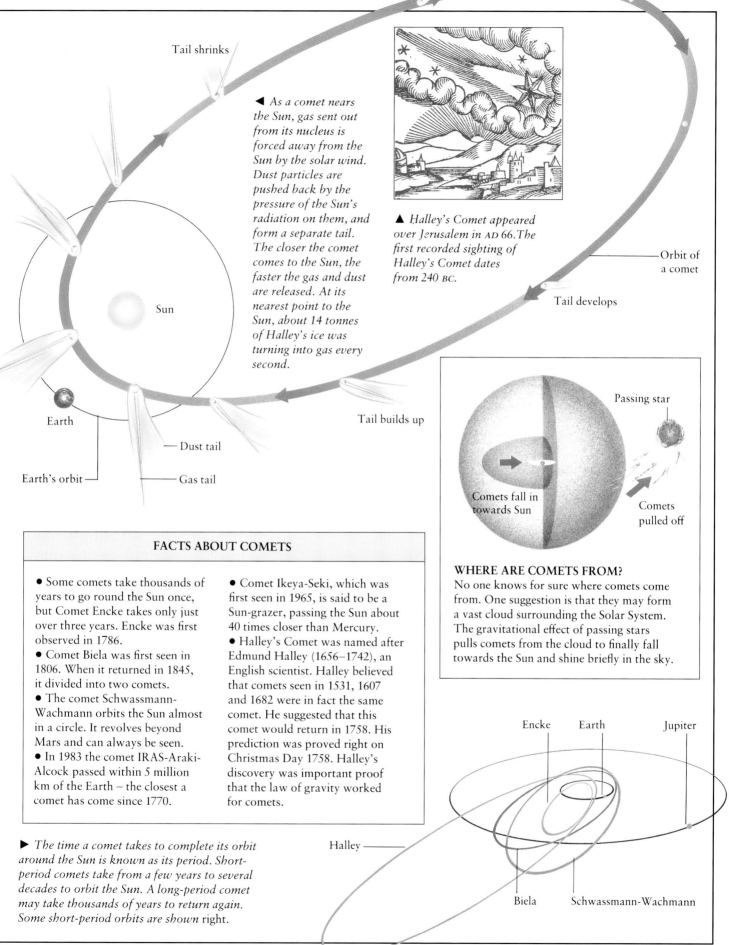

Tail shrinks

◀ As a comet nears the Sun, gas sent out from its nucleus is forced away from the Sun by the solar wind. Dust particles are pushed back by the pressure of the Sun's radiation on them, and form a separate tail. The closer the comet comes to the Sun, the faster the gas and dust are released. At its nearest point to the Sun, about 14 tonnes of Halley's ice was turning into gas every second.

▲ Halley's Comet appeared over Jerusalem in AD 66. The first recorded sighting of Halley's Comet dates from 240 BC.

Sun

Orbit of a comet

Tail develops

Earth

Tail builds up

Earth's orbit

Dust tail

Gas tail

Passing star

Comets fall in towards Sun

Comets pulled off

FACTS ABOUT COMETS

● Some comets take thousands of years to go round the Sun once, but Comet Encke takes only just over three years. Encke was first observed in 1786.
● Comet Biela was first seen in 1806. When it returned in 1845, it divided into two comets.
● The comet Schwassmann-Wachmann orbits the Sun almost in a circle. It revolves beyond Mars and can always be seen.
● In 1983 the comet IRAS-Araki-Alcock passed within 5 million km of the Earth – the closest a comet has come since 1770.

● Comet Ikeya-Seki, which was first seen in 1965, is said to be a Sun-grazer, passing the Sun about 40 times closer than Mercury.
● Halley's Comet was named after Edmund Halley (1656–1742), an English scientist. Halley believed that comets seen in 1531, 1607 and 1682 were in fact the same comet. He suggested that this comet would return in 1758. His prediction was proved right on Christmas Day 1758. Halley's discovery was important proof that the law of gravity worked for comets.

WHERE ARE COMETS FROM?
No one knows for sure where comets come from. One suggestion is that they may form a vast cloud surrounding the Solar System. The gravitational effect of passing stars pulls comets from the cloud to finally fall towards the Sun and shine briefly in the sky.

Encke   Earth   Jupiter

▶ The time a comet takes to complete its orbit around the Sun is known as its period. Short-period comets take from a few years to several decades to orbit the Sun. A long-period comet may take thousands of years to return again. Some short-period orbits are shown right.

Halley

Biela   Schwassmann-Wachmann

BEYOND THE SOLAR SYSTEM

The Milky Way

The Sun is just one of a hundred billion stars, existing in space in a vast 'star-city'. This city is our galaxy, which we call the Milky Way. The softly-shining band of light in our night sky is also called the Milky Way, and is the edge-on view of our own galaxy. The Milky Way is spiral in shape, and the Sun is found out towards its 'edge'. The galaxy is so huge that it would take a beam of light about 130,000 years to cross from one edge to the other, even though light travels at almost 300,000 kilometres a second. Huge areas of the Milky Way are unexplored because our view of them is so poor – it is like trying to see people at the other side of a crowd. Dark clouds block the light from the centre of the galaxy, increasing the astronomers' problems. However, observing other galaxies has helped to build up a picture of what our own is like.

THE MILKY WAY
The Milky Way is a barred spiral galaxy, with two arms that rotate slowly. The area in which our Sun is found takes about 225 million years to go around once. At the centre is a bright halo of old stars that formed with the galaxy, 14 billion years ago. The arms contain vast nebulae of gas and dust where new stars are being born.

HOW A GALAXY BEGINS
Galaxies begin as huge masses of dark gas. As they shrink under the pressure of gravity (**1**), the gas at the centre becomes dense enough to start forming stars. Some galaxies start spinning (**2**), and if the spin is fast enough it forces the outer areas into a flat disc, forming a spiral (**3**) or barred spiral galaxy. Galaxies that spin slowly or not at all become spherical or elliptical in shape.

1

2

3

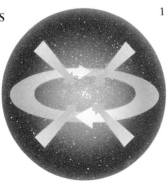

▲ *A slowly-spinning mass of gas starts to collapse, and the first stars are formed at the centre. As the cloud shrinks, its turning speed increases.*

▲ *Gas clouds meet in the swirling disc, and attract more clouds because of their extra gravity. Stars start to form here too.*

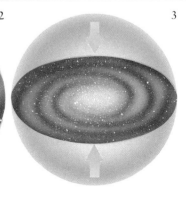

▲ *There is no gas left at the centre to make new stars, but the arms are rich in raw star material. The galaxy is now in its prime of life.*

◄ This panorama of our galaxy was obtained by combining several photographs taken of the Milky Way from different parts of the world. If you imagine the right and left ends joined together, with your head inside the ring, this is how the Milky Way would appear to someone floating in space.

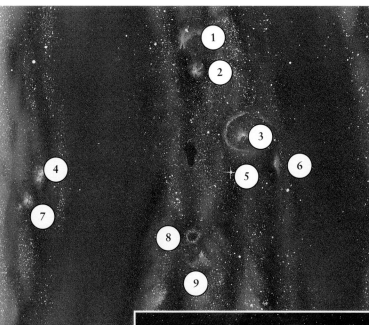

▼ The Orion Nebula is about 30 light-years across and 1600 light-years away. It was once dark, but millions of years ago stars began forming inside it, and their radiation makes the nebula glow.

▲ The Milky Way is rich in dark nebulae. However, the galaxy is foggy with tiny particles that act as a colour filter. The effect causes objects like this nebula to appear red to us on Earth.

▲ Within the main arms of the Milky Way are smaller arms where stars and nebulae are more closely connected. This illustration shows some of the Sun's neighbours in the galaxy.

1 Cone Nebula
2 Rosette Nebula
3 Orion Nebula
4 Lagoon Nebula
5 Solar System
6 California Nebula
7 Trifid Nebula
8 Vela Supernova Remnant
9 N American Nebula

MILKY WAY DATAFILE

Diameter:
  130,000 light-years
Thickness of spiral arms:
  3000 light-years (approx.)
Thickness of central bulge:
  10,000 light-years
Diameter of central bulge:
  20,000 light-years
Total mass: 110 billion × Sun
Average density (estimate):
  0.00000000000000000007
  (water = 1)
Age: 14 billion years
Time to rotate once:
  (Position of Sun)
  225 million years
Distance of Sun from centre:
  30,000 light-years
Satellite galaxies: 2

Clusters and Superclusters

Just as stars are born in groups or clusters, so do galaxies often exist in groups. Our galaxy belongs to a cluster of some 32 galaxies, called the Local Group. Most of the galaxies in the Local Group are small and faint, and would be invisible to us if they were much further away. Beyond the edge of the Local Group, astronomers have discovered thousands of other groups of galaxies in the Universe. These groups in turn seem to form looser groups in space, known as superclusters.

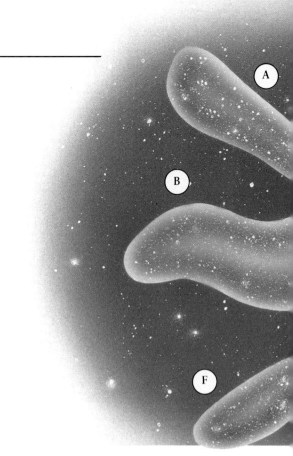

TYPES OF GALAXY

◀ *Galaxies are put into classes according to their shape. Irregular galaxies (class Irr) are usually smaller than the Milky Way. The gravity of much larger galaxies nearby may have pulled them out of shape – for example, the Magellanic Clouds, in the grip of the Milky Way.*

▶ *Elliptical galaxies seem to have no nebulae, which means they cannot form any more stars. They are scaled from E0 (almost spherical) to E7 (very elongated). The largest known galaxies are giant ellipticals, but dwarf ellipticals are also very common.*

◀ *Ordinary spiral galaxies are classed from Sa (very tight arms) to Sc (very loose arms). Another type, S0, has a very large centre, or nucleus, which is more like an elliptical galaxy's. Until very recently the Milky Way galaxy was thought to be an Sb or Sc type.*

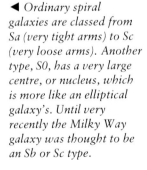

▶ *Barred spiral galaxies, classed from SBa (tight arms) to SBc (loose arms), have centres with a short bar of stars across them. The spiral arms begin at the ends of this bar. Astronomers have recently found evidence that there is such a bar in our own Milky Way galaxy.*

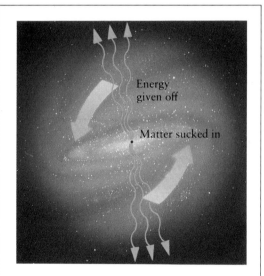

Energy given off

Matter sucked in

QUASARS

The strangest galaxies known are the far-off objects called quasars. Although they cannot be seen in any detail, they seem to be galaxies that are sending out huge amounts of energy from a small area of space near their centre. Some quasars are as bright as thousands of galaxies like the Milky Way. The source of this energy could be the presence of a black hole at the galaxy's centre, which is sucking gas and whole stars into it *(see pages 56–57)*. As it is sucked in, this material spins around the black hole almost at the speed of light, sending huge amounts of energy into space.

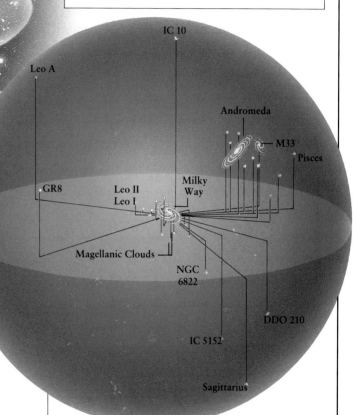

◄ *The Local Supercluster contains several thousand galaxies, scattered across 100 million light-years of space. The Milky Way galaxy is near the outer edge of the Canes Venatici cloud.*

KEY
A Virgo III cloud
B Virgo II cloud
C Virgo I cloud
D Canes Venatici cloud
E Canes Venatici spur
F Crater cloud
G Leo II cloud

SUPERCLUSTERS

The Local Group is a fairly small cluster of galaxies, belonging to a collection of other small clusters called the Canes Venatici cloud. A much larger group of galaxies, the Virgo cluster, is about 60 million light-years away. It lies at the centre of our Local Supercluster – a collection of major clouds of galaxies. The entire supercluster measures over 100 million light-years across. In the diagram *(above)*, the galaxy clusters are shown with sharp boundaries to help make their shapes more clear. In reality, the clusters are much more scattered throughout space. Notice how the central Virgo I cloud is round, while the others are elongated, pointing inwards towards it as if stretched by the pull of its gravity. This has occurred because Virgo I, although not particularly large, contains about 20 percent of all the galaxies in the supercluster.

▲ *The 32 galaxies detected in our Local Group range from the Andromeda galaxy, the largest, to tiny irregular galaxies. The Milky Way is second in order of size, one of only three spiral galaxies in the Group. The galaxies can be pictured scattered in space, inside an imaginary sphere about 5 million light-years across.*

FACTS ABOUT THE LOCAL GROUP

● The Andromeda galaxy is the largest in the Local Group. It may contain 400 billion stars.
● The Milky Way's nearest neighbours in space are the two Magellanic Clouds, 200,000 light-years away. They are satellites of the Milky Way.
● A belt of fast moving gas, called the Magellanic Stream, connects our galaxy to the two Magellanic Clouds.

● M33 in Triangulum is the third largest member of the Local Group.
● The most distant galaxy in our Local Group is Leo A, 5 million light-years away.
● Dwarf elliptical galaxies are probably the commonest type of galaxy in the Universe, but they are so dim that we can only make out the 15 or so near to us in the Local Group.

▶ *An exploding star, or supernova, plays an important part in a galaxy's development. Such stars scatter extra elements into space, besides the original hydrogen and helium, to build up new stars. The last nearby supernova was seen in the Large Magellanic Cloud in 1987.*

Cosmology

Cosmology is the study of how the Universe began and how it will be in the future. The Universe may go on getting bigger for ever. Alternatively, the galaxies may come together, until finally they collide and explode in the violence of a 'Big Crunch'. Cosmologists try to work out the likely fate of the Universe. They believe they have traced the development of the Universe right back to a fraction of a second after the Big Bang, but they do not know what caused the Big Bang itself.

THE FATE OF THE UNIVERSE

What is the future of the Universe? It may keep on expanding; it may collapse and end; or it may even be one of a series of universes. It all depends upon how much material the Universe contains. As the galaxies fly apart after the Big Bang, their gravitational attraction is slowing them down. But the gravity between bodies in space becomes weaker as they move farther apart, so the slowing-down effect becomes less as the Universe expands. There is a thin dividing line between there not being enough matter in the Universe, so that gravity is too weak ever to stop the expansion; and there being too much matter, so that everything rushes together in a 'Big Crunch'.

AN EVER-EXPANDING UNIVERSE

Big Bang

Galaxies fly apart after the Big Bang

A FINITE UNIVERSE

Big Bang

FACTS ABOUT THE UNIVERSE

- There are clues to show that the Big Bang happened. For one thing, the galaxies are still flying apart from the explosion. In 1965 astronomers found a very feeble warmth in space, which is a trace of the fantastic heat created by the Big Bang.
- Some astronomers believe the Universe must contain 'missing mass'. This is invisible material, which astronomers believe exists because of the effect of its gravity. If the Universe does not contain this material, then after the Big Bang it should have expanded so fast that galaxies could not have formed at all. The missing mass has not been detected yet, but it may add up to roughly ten times the mass of the stars and nebulae that are visible.

RED SHIFT

Light travels in waves, and the colour of light depends upon wavelength. Waves of blue light are much closer together than waves of red light. If a very fast-moving object is sending out light, then the light waves will be squashed ahead of it, and stretched out behind. This means that the light from the approaching object seems bluish. Light from an object travelling fast away from someone appears reddish. This is called a red shift.

Reddish light detected on Earth

Galaxy moving away from Earth

◀ *Distant galaxies show a colour shift towards red. These galaxies are moving away at speeds of thousands of kilometres a second, and their light waves are stretched by this speed, making them look redder in colour than they really are. This change of colour is not seen by the eye, but is detected with an instrument called a spectrograph. Astronomers can use the red shift to measure the speed at which a galaxy travels.*

▼ *Galaxies and clusters of galaxies twist and loop themselves through space like strings of frogspawn. Is there almost as much invisible matter in the supposedly empty space between the strings?*

Gravity cannot stop the expansion of the Universe

Gravity stops expansion of the the Universe

▼ *If the Big Crunch happened, the sky would grow as hot as the Sun. Finally, everything would vanish into a black hole.*

A SERIES OF UNIVERSES
A completely new Universe begins

▼ *Time and space would end if the Universe ended. A new Universe would have to start everything again. It would not be the old one recycled.*

Big Crunch   Big Bang

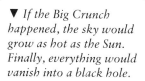

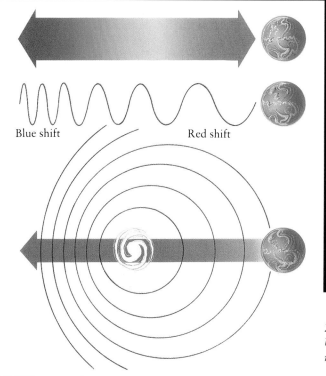

Blue shift   Red shift

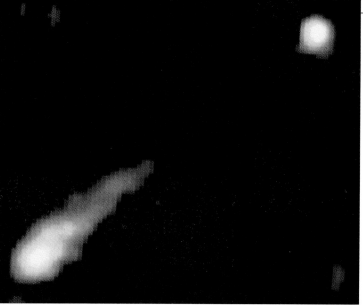

▲ *Red shift measurements of the quasar 3C 273 show that it is 2.1 billion light-years away, and travelling at 50,000 km/s. As the Universe expands, distant galaxies move away faster than galaxies nearby. Their distance can be calculated from their red shift.*

THE STARS

The Life of a Star

A star is born inside a huge nebula of gas and dust (called 'gust'). A nebula starts to shrink into much smaller nebulae when it receives a 'shake', perhaps after colliding with another nebula, or being hit by the shock waves of an exploding star. Eventually the nebula will break up into a cluster of baby stars, containing a mixture of bright, medium and dim stars. Although all these stars are born at the same time, their lifetimes and endings will be very different, according to the amount of material they contain. Generally, a massive star has a shorter life than a less massive star. Stars are sources of light and heat. They also process and recycle material, turning some of the hydrogen and helium that were created at the beginning of the Universe into other elements. These include carbon and oxygen, which are the building blocks of life.

▶ A medium hot star, like the Sun, gives out much less energy than the brightest stars. This means it will shine steadily for billions of years before it begins to expand. The dimmer the star, the longer its life.

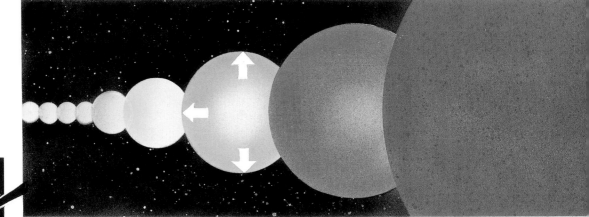

▲ The main sequence period for both a medium hot star and a very hot, bright star (below) is the time when the star is shining steadily by turning hydrogen into helium. The star grows slightly hotter and brighter during this time. When the star's core of used helium reaches a certain size it is a crisis point in its life. The core of the star collapses under the force of its gravity and becomes still hotter. Now even helium starts nuclear reactions.

▲ This new energy source is so powerful that part of the star is blown outwards. The outer layers cool to a reddish colour. At this stage in its life the star is known as a 'red giant'. At its greatest size, the diameter of a red giant may be a hundred times that of the original star, which forms the core of the red giant.

▶ A very bright, very hot star may shine at full power for only a few million years before it uses up all its fuel. Although it has more fuel than a medium star, it uses it up much faster, and has only a brief life.

Blue
giant

Red
dwarf

Main sequence star
(such as the Sun)

Red giant

White
dwarf

Neutron
star

Black hole

▲ Although our Sun shines
with a yellow light, not all stars are yellow.
Stars vary in size, brightness and temperature.
The hottest stars shine with a white-blue light;
they have a diameter up to 20 times greater than
our Sun, and so are known as blue giants. The
dim, cool stars known as red dwarfs are about a
quarter of the Sun's diameter. Huge red giant
stars have outer layers that have blown away
from the core of energy, becoming cooler and so
redder. They can be 500 times the Sun's width.
A dim white dwarf will give out little light and
may be only a few percent of the Sun's width.

◀ In a white dwarf,
the star's atoms are
crushed together
hundreds of times more
tightly than normal. A
neutron star is a dead
star, made from the
solid nuclei of atoms,
the densest material in
the Universe. If it is
massive enough, a
neutron star will
become a black hole.

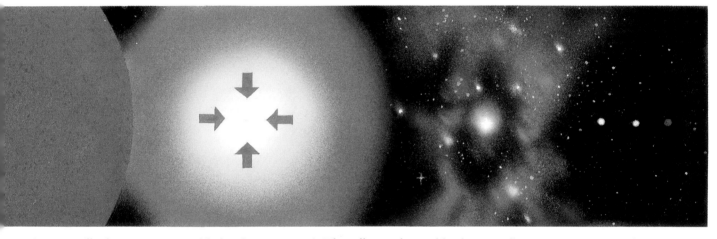

▲ Eventually the core runs out of fuel and
collapses completely, because it is no longer
producing enough energy to balance the
shrinking force of gravity. This is the end of
nuclear reactions in the star's core. If the star is
much more massive than our Sun, its collapse
gives out so much energy that the star is blown
to pieces in a supernova explosion (below).

▲ The collapse of a star like the Sun will not
result in a dramatic supernova explosion.
Instead, the star will shrink to a hot body the
size of a small planet. The star is now called a
white dwarf. The gravity of a massive star,
however, will be so strong it will crush the nuclei
of the star's atoms together, making a tiny, very
dense, neutron star (below).

▲ An ordinary star,
after becoming a white
dwarf, cools into a
dead black dwarf.

▼ If a neutron star has
a mass greater than
five Suns it will form a
black hole.

Extraordinary Stars

If you think of a star as a body similar to our Sun, then the different stars shown here may surprise you. Not all stars shine at constant levels. Some change greatly in brightness during years or even days; these are known as variable stars. Other stars, called pulsars, spin faster than a washing machine. Twenty percent of all known stars have a partner, around which they orbit in a binary system. Occasionally the transfer of gas in a binary system can lead to the drama of an exploding star, or supernova.

VARIABLE STARS
A variable star may be an unstable star that goes through a stage when it starts to swell and shrink, changing its brightness. Other variable stars may occur in binary systems where gas passes from one star to another, causing a sudden flare. A few variable stars do not actually give out less light at all, but seem to do so because they orbit each other in a binary system, and the light from one star is blocked for a time by its 'partner'.

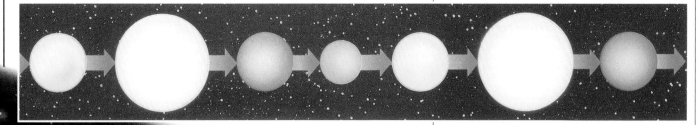

▲ *One kind of variable star will change in brightness as it changes size, perhaps over the course of a few days. This type of star is known as a pulsating variable.*

The brightest known type of exploding star is a Type I supernova. It starts as a binary system (**1**) with two ordinary stars in close orbit. The more massive star, A, develops more quickly, turning into a red giant while star B still shines normally.

B's gravity attracts gas from the outer layers of the red giant A on to its own surface (**2**). Finally only the white dwarf core of the red giant is left.

Star B now has so much extra mass that it too grows into a red giant (**3**). The remains of star A continue to shine as a white dwarf, about the size of the planet Uranus and much fainter than B.

◄ *Wolf-Rayet stars are the hottest stars known. The one at the centre of this nebula has a surface temperature of about 50,000°C.*

Gas from B begins flowing back on to A (**4**). A's mass increases again: disaster. The energy produced inside a star stops it from collapsing under its own weight. However, a white dwarf has used up most of its nuclear fuel. If too much mass is added, A won't be able to hold its shape.

When the mass of a white dwarf becomes 1.4 times that of our Sun, its outer layers fall in with such force that the temperature rises to several billion degrees. The blast of energy blows the star apart (**5**).

PULSAR

In 1967, radio astronomers at Cambridge, England, were trying out a new telescope. It began to record bursts of radiation that repeated every couple of seconds. At first the Cambridge astronomers thought that this might be an intelligent message from space, but soon they realised that they had discovered a new kind of star – a pulsar. From that chance discovery, more than 400 radio pulsars were discovered in the next 20 years.

▶ *A pulsar is a rapidly spinning neutron star. Its fierce magnetic field squirts light and radio waves into beams of energy that sweep round as the star turns. If the beam crosses Earth the star is detected by the pulse of its radiation.*

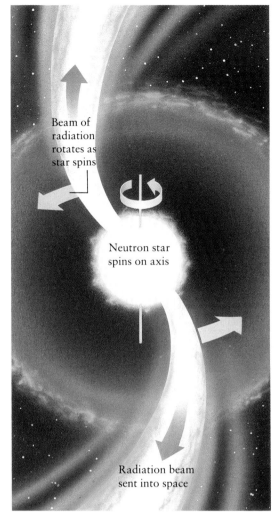

Beam of radiation rotates as star spins

Neutron star spins on axis

Radiation beam sent into space

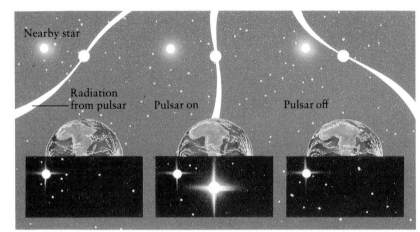

Nearby star

Radiation from pulsar

Pulsar on

Pulsar off

▲ *Pulsars flash on and off when their radiation beam passes across the Earth. Even the slowest pulsar sends out one pulse every four seconds. The most rapid spins 622 times a second. Why do neutron stars spin so much faster than the original star? Find the answer by watching an ice skater spin on the ice. As the skater shrinks by folding her arms up close to her body, she speeds up. A star collapsing into a tiny neutron star has the same effect.*

5

The cloud of debris is hurled through space at up to 40,000 km/s, forming a nebula rich in carbon and oxygen (6).

6

BINARY STARS

In some binary systems the two stars (1) may be very close, orbiting each other in a few hours; in others, the stars are millions of kilometres apart. Often, one star is more massive than the other and has evolved, perhaps into a red giant (2). Although the stars in a binary system appear to revolve around each other, they are really moving around their common centre of gravity (3).

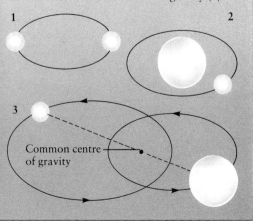

1

2

3

Common centre of gravity

Black Holes and Neutron Stars

When a massive star dies, it may leave behind a heavy core which becomes a neutron star – the smallest, densest kind of star. If the force of gravity around the neutron star is strong enough, a black hole could be the result. These fascinating objects occur when gravity is so strong that space acts like a one-way funnel. Anything – light rays or moving solid matter – that passes into this funnel is compressed to nothing and disappears from our Universe. A black hole is the end of space and time.

▼ *A binary system containing a black hole will be ablaze with radiation, because material from the other star is energized as it spirals into the black hole.*

WHAT IS A BLACK HOLE LIKE?

A black hole is caused by a very dense object, such as a massive neutron star, which creates a powerful gravitational field, a kind of space funnel, in a small space. An object passing close enough will be pulled into the space funnel; once something has been pulled into a black hole it can never escape.

A BLACK HOLE IN THE MILKY WAY?

A faint object in the Milky Way galaxy, normally about a million times too faint to be seen with the naked eye, sometimes gives out bursts of X-rays. Known as V404 Cygni, it is the most likely black hole in our galaxy. V404 Cygni is a binary system. The two stars orbit each other in 6.5 days. One star may be similar to the Sun, the other is a very dense object about six times as massive as the Sun – safely over the 'black hole' limit.

▲ *A black hole on its own in space would be difficult to detect. But if it is near another star, the pull of the black hole's gravity may draw material from the star into a whirling ring that gives off bursts of X-rays. If astronomers detect a star-like object that is giving out high-energy radiation they have probably found a black hole.*

NEUTRON STARS

All objects in the Universe are made of atoms, and atoms consist of atomic particles in rapid motion. The forces holding an atom in shape are very powerful. But even they can be broken. When a star runs out of nuclear fuel and collapses, the pressure at the centre can be so enormous that the atoms themselves are compressed into a tiny ball of solid neutrons (consisting of protons and electrons forced together), millions of times smaller and denser than the original star.

▼ In order to collapse into a neutron star, a star must have a mass about 1.4 times the Sun's mass. This is called the mass limit. Such a star would be over a hundred times the Earth's diameter, but it would shrink into a neutron star about 20 km across – the size of a large city.

▲ If the Earth was compressed into solid neutrons, it would be a ball the diameter of a large sports field. A marble made of solid neutrons would weigh about as much as a million fully-laden juggernauts.

20 km across

Star Distance, Star Brightness

To measure the distance of a star from Earth, astronomers use parallax (*see opposite*). The first star distance was measured in 1838, marking a milestone in astronomy. As more star distances were catalogued, astronomers realized that some nearby stars appeared fainter than more distant ones, instead of the other way round as expected. It was proof that stars had different brightnesses, or luminosities. This formed the basis for the classification of stars into the families that are recognized today.

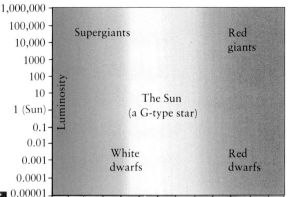

◄ *A group of stars close together in the sky is known as a star cluster. Clusters such as the Pleiades (left) are very useful for astronomers, because the stars are all the same distance away from Earth. So if one star looks brighter than another, it must be more luminous by that amount. The Pleiades are very young, maybe a hundred million years old, and the brightest members are very hot, main sequence stars.*

▲ *The Hertzsprung-Russell Diagram plots the temperature and luminosity of stars. Generally, the more material a star has, the hotter it is. A blue giant star is found in the upper left of the Diagram. The Sun, a yellow star of average size, lies in the middle, or main sequence. Few stars do not belong to the main sequence. Red giant stars lie in the upper right of the Diagram. Lower left stars are white dwarfs – very hot, but dim.*

STAR DISTANCE AND MAGNITUDE

From our Solar System certain groups of stars all seem to be the same distance away from Earth, forming star patterns called constellations. In fact the stars that make up these constellations are different distances from Earth, as the diagram of the stars in Orion (the hunter) shows. Elsewhere in the galaxy, these stars would not appear to be grouped together at all.

▶ *Star brightness is rated in magnitude: the smaller the number, the brighter the star. In Orion, the bright star Rigel is magnitude 0, while Mintaka and Alnitak are both magnitude 2.*

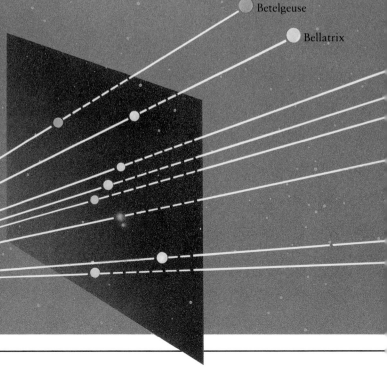

PARALLAX

When you move your head from side to side, nearby objects that you can see seem to you to move more than distant ones. This is called parallax. Astronomers use parallax to find out how far away stars are from Earth. They take two measurements of the direction of a star about six months apart, when the Earth is on opposite sides of its orbit and has moved 300 million km through space. From the slight change in the star's position, its distance can be calculated. The further the star, the smaller the change.

Star A

Star B

Sun

Earth in July

Earth in January

◀ *A very hot star will look bluish-white, and a cooler one, yellow. Stars may be classified according to temperature (far left). Letters stand for different temperature bands. Our yellow Sun is a G star. The table (left) shows the luminosity of average stars in these classes.*

	W
	O B
	A
	F
	G
	K
	M
	R
	N S

	−1
	0
	1
	2
	3
	4
	5
	6
	7

FACTS ABOUT STARS

- The nearest star to our Sun is Proxima Centauri, 4.2 light-years away. It is a dim, red dwarf star.
- Sirius is the brightest star in our sky.
- The dimmest stars we are able to detect from Earth are about a thousand million million million times fainter than the dimmest star visible with the naked eye.
- The oldest known star is thought to be CS 22876 − 32. It may be 15 billion years old.
- There are many newborn stars visible. An example is L1551, which is being born now in a nebula 500 light-years away.
- Pulsar PSR 1957 + 20 is the fastest spinning star. It revolves 622 times a second.
- The supernova seen in AD 1006 appeared about forty times brighter than Venus.

Mintaka

Alnilam

Alnitak

Orion Nebula

◀ *From Earth, star A looks brighter than star B because it is closer, although yellow A is less luminous than blue-white B. The absolute magnitude of a star is how bright it would appear seen from 32.6 light-years away.*

Rigel

Saiph

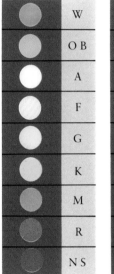
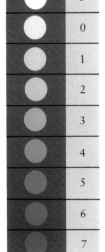

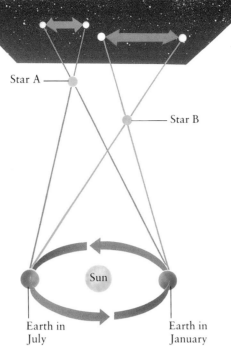

▲ *From Earth, all the stars of Orion seem to be the same distance away, forming a particular pattern in our night sky. But Betelgeuse is 330 light-years away, while Mintaka is 2300 light-years from Earth.*

The Moving Sky

To an observer on Earth, the stars appear to be attached to the inside of a vast hollow globe which spins round the Earth from east to west once a day. This view is not true. It is the Earth, and not the sky, that is spinning. All the same, it is often useful for astronomers to pretend that this globe, or celestial sphere, in the sky really does exist. The Earth's poles, and lines of latitude and longitude, can then all be marked on the celestial sphere. This helps astronomers to map the position of stars in the sky.

▶ *The celestial sphere appears to spin around the north and south celestial poles, which line up with the Earth's axis. It is divided up into 24 segments, running from the north to the south pole. In an hour it turns through one of these segments, carrying the stars steadily around the sky. The stars form easily recognizable patterns in the night sky. These patterns are called constellations. They are always in the same place on the celestial sphere, so their position can be noted. Astronomers can use the constellations to know where to find a particular star.*

▶ *The celestial equator is a projected circle, in line with the Earth's Equator. To an observer standing on the Equator, stars lying near the celestial equator pass overhead.*

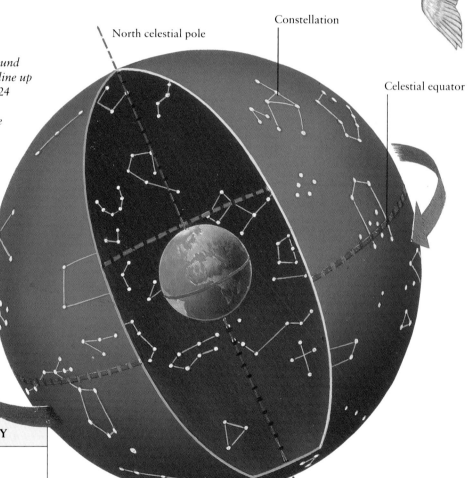

North celestial pole

Constellation

Celestial equator

South celestial pole

FACTS ABOUT THE MOVING SKY

• An observer always has part of the celestial sphere blocked out by the Earth. For example, the famous constellation Crux (the Cross), which lies near the south celestial pole, cannot be seen from European countries or from much of North America.
• Different constellations are seen from Earth in summer and winter. Orion, for example, is high in the midnight sky in January but cannot be seen in July at all. This is because the Earth's movement has positioned the Sun between it and Orion. The best time to look for a particular star is during the time of year when it is on the opposite side of the Earth to the Sun.

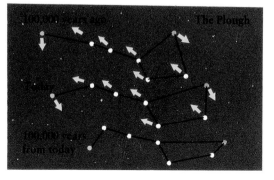

100,000 years ago

The Plough

100,000 years from today

◀ *The stars are moving through space at great speed, which means the star patterns are changing very slowly. The Plough in Ursa Major is an example. Five stars in this group are moving one way, and two the opposite way.*

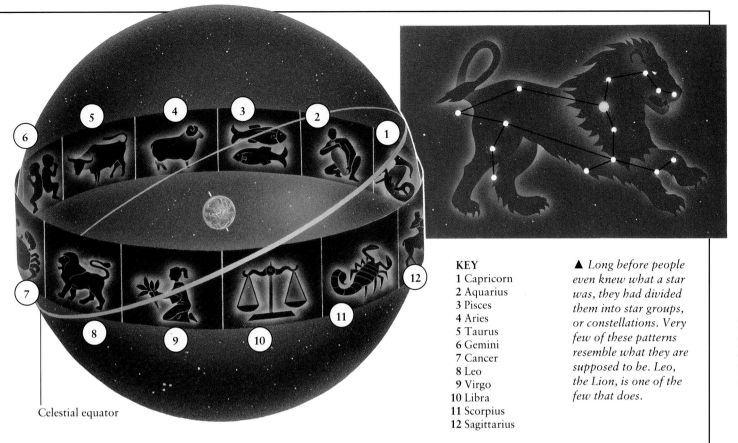

Celestial equator

KEY
1 Capricorn
2 Aquarius
3 Pisces
4 Aries
5 Taurus
6 Gemini
7 Cancer
8 Leo
9 Virgo
10 Libra
11 Scorpius
12 Sagittarius

▲ Long before people even knew what a star was, they had divided them into star groups, or constellations. Very few of these patterns resemble what they are supposed to be. Leo, the Lion, is one of the few that does.

▲ During a year, the Sun appears to take a particular path through the celestial sphere. This path marks the centre of the band of sky known as the Zodiac. There are twelve divisions of the Zodiac, each one represented by a constellation. The Sun seems to spend about one month in each constellation.

▶ This old star map shows the southern part of the celestial sphere. The dashed circle marks the path of the Sun, and the south pole is shown a little way above the centre. Unlike the north celestial pole, the south pole does not have a bright star near it. At the foot of the map the celestial equator is marked, in line with Earth's Equator.

The Constellations

Most people think of a constellation as a group of stars. In fact a constellation is a definite area of the celestial sphere, with internationally-agreed boundaries. The areas fit together to make up the sky. The maps show major constellations of the sky. The faintest stars are those with the smallest dots; these should just be visible with the naked eye from built-up areas. The outline of the Milky Way is shown, but this can only be seen properly under dark country skies.

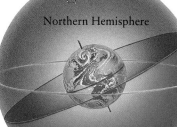

Northern Hemisphere

Southern Hemisphere

◀ *Each map shows one complete celestial hemisphere, as seen by someone standing at the North or South Pole. The celestial equator is the dividing line between the two maps, and the Earth's axis points to the celestial poles, at the centre of each.*

CONSTELLATION FACTS

● In total, the sky contains 88 constellations. Most of these were named in ancient times. In AD 150 the Greek astronomer, Ptolemy, described 48 star patterns, including well-known ones such as Ursa Major (the Great Bear). Many of these were recorded by Babylonian astronomers before 2000 BC. Between the 16th and 18th centuries AD, when explorers began venturing into the Southern Hemisphere, new parts of the celestial sphere came into view, and more constellations were added to the ancient ones.
● The largest constellation is Hydra (the Water Snake); the smallest constellation is Crux (the Cross).
● The faintest space object visible with the naked eye appears dimly in the Andromeda constellation. It is the Andromeda galaxy, 2.2 million light-years away.

NORTHERN HEMISPHERE

▲ *Ursa Minor (the Little Bear) is a constellation of the Northern Hemisphere. The bright star at the very tip of the bear's tail is the Pole Star, Polaris. Ursa Minor is visible from northern Europe and North America all year round.*

NORTHERN HEMISPHERE

1 *Equuleus* Little Horse
2 *Delphinus* Dolphin
3 *Pegasus* Pegasus
4 *Pisces* Fishes
5 *Cetus* Whale
6 *Aries* Ram
7 *Triangulum* Triangle
8 *Andromeda* Andromeda
9 *Lacerta* Lizard
10 *Cygnus* Swan
11 *Sagitta* Arrow
12 *Aquila* Eagle
13 *Lyra* Lyre
14 *Cepheus* Cepheus
15 *Cassiopeia* Cassiopeia
16 *Perseus* Perseus
17 *Camelopardus* Giraffe
18 *Auriga* Charioteer
19 *Taurus* Bull
20 *Orion* Orion (hunter)
21 *Lynx* Lynx
22 *Polaris* Pole Star
23 *Ursa Minor* Little Bear
24 *Draco* Dragon
25 *Hercules* Hercules
26 *Ophiuchus* Serpent Bearer
27 *Serpens* Serpent
28 *Corona Borealis* Northern Crown
29 *Boötes* Herdsman
30 *Ursa Major* Great Bear

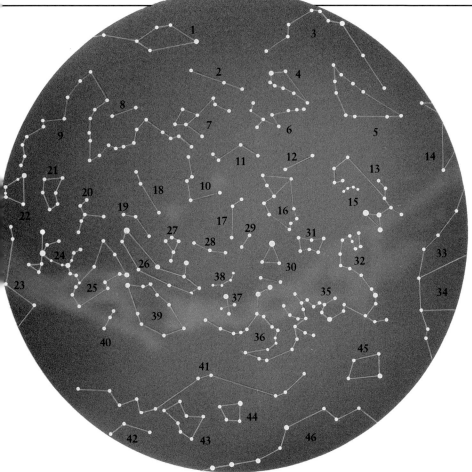

SOUTHERN HEMISPHERE

Australia

New Zealand

The constellation known as Crux, or the (Southern) Cross, appears on the flags of both Australia and New Zealand. The constellation contains five stars of different brightness. On Australia's flag the smallest star is shown with only five points, two less than the other stars. Only four stars appear on New Zealand's flag, all with the same number of points.

31 *Gemini* Twins
32 *Cancer* Crab
33 *Canis Minor* Little Dog
34 *Hydra* Water Snake
35 *Leo* Lion
36 *Leo Minor* Little Lion
37 *Canes Venatici* Hunting Dogs
38 *Coma Berenices* Berenice's Hair
39 *Virgo* Virgin

SOUTHERN HEMISPHERE
1 *Cetus* Whale
2 *Sculptor* Sculptor
3 *Aquarius* Water Bearer
4 *Piscis Austrinus* Southern Fish
5 *Capricornus* Sea-Goat
6 *Grus* Crane
7 *Phoenix* Phoenix
8 *Fornax* Furnace
9 *Eridanus* River Eridanus
10 *Hydrus* Lesser Water Snake
11 *Tucana* Toucan
12 *Indus* Indian
13 *Sagittarius* Archer
14 *Aquila* Eagle
15 *Corona Australis* Southern Crown
16 *Pavo* Peacock
17 *Octans* Octant

18 *Dorado* Swordfish
19 *Pictor* Painter
20 *Columba* Dove
21 *Lepus* Hare
22 *Orion* Orion (hunter)
23 *Monoceros* Unicorn
24 *Canis Major* Great Dog
25 *Puppis* Poop (of Argo)
26 *Carina* Keel (of Argo)
27 *Volans* Flying Fish
28 *Chamaeleon* Chameleon
29 *Apus* Bird of Paradise
30 *Triangulum Australe* Southern Triangle
31 *Ara* Altar
32 *Scorpius* Scorpion

33 *Serpens* Serpent
34 *Ophiuchus* Serpent Bearer
35 *Lupus* Wolf
36 *Centaurus* Centaur
37 *Crux* (Southern) Cross
38 *Musca* Fly
39 *Vela* Sails (of Argo)
40 *Pyxis* Mariner's Compass
41 *Hydra* Water Snake
42 *Sextans* Sextant
43 *Crater* Cup
44 *Corvus* Crow
45 *Libra* Scales
46 *Virgo* Virgin

◄ *The constellation Scorpius (the Scorpion) can be seen in the Southern Hemisphere. The most prominent star is Antares in its body, a giant star about 500 light-years away. Antares is 10,000 times more luminous than our Sun.*

OBSERVING THE SKIES

The Birth of Astronomy

The people of early civilizations must have been aware of the fixed patterns of the stars in the sky, their repeated appearance and disappearance with the seasons, and the strange 'wanderings' of the objects that we now call the planets. However, with no way of understanding their true nature, their astrological significance seemed the most important thing about them. The night sky was divided up into constellations, and they and the planets were given names. But right up until the beginning of the 17th century most people thought that the Earth was at the centre of the Universe.

Astronomical knowledge took a major leap forward in the early 17th century. The newly-invented telescope was first turned to the sky, and Johannes Kepler proved that the planets move around the Sun, not the Earth. Modern astronomy was born.

ANCIENT ASTRONOMY
In ancient civilizations astronomy was closely linked to astrology, the belief that events in the sky can affect the lives of people on Earth. The positions of the planets were observed for astrological predictions. The duties of priests and astronomers overlapped. For example, the Babylonian ziggurat below was half-temple and half-observatory.

A ziggurat

▲ *Astronomers in China were charting the positions of the stars as early as the 1300s BC. The Plough constellation appears on this old star map.*

▶ *This Egyptian mummy case shows Nut, the sky goddess, surrounded by the signs of the Zodiac. Many of the signs are still in use today.*

◀ *Stonehenge in England dates from about 5000 years ago. The Hele Stone (in the distance) seems to have been accurately placed to mark the position of midsummer sunrise. This event was important. In an age without calendars, the Sun's position as it rose and set was the simplest guide to the year's seasons.*

VIEWS OF THE UNIVERSE

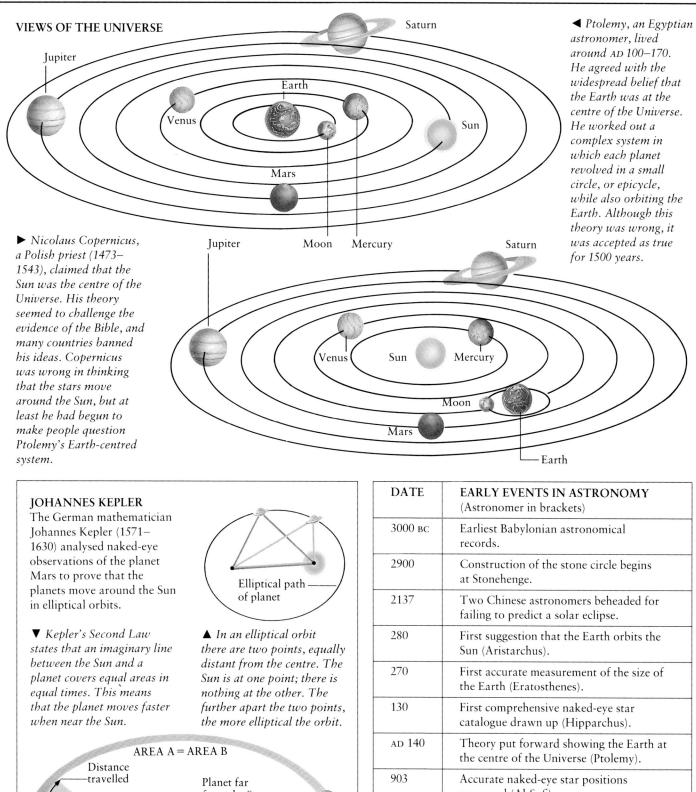

Jupiter

Saturn

Earth

Venus

Sun

Mars

Jupiter   Moon   Mercury

Saturn

Jupiter

Venus   Sun   Mercury

Moon

Mars

Earth

◄ *Ptolemy, an Egyptian astronomer, lived around* AD *100–170. He agreed with the widespread belief that the Earth was at the centre of the Universe. He worked out a complex system in which each planet revolved in a small circle, or epicycle, while also orbiting the Earth. Although this theory was wrong, it was accepted as true for 1500 years.*

► *Nicolaus Copernicus, a Polish priest (1473–1543), claimed that the Sun was the centre of the Universe. His theory seemed to challenge the evidence of the Bible, and many countries banned his ideas. Copernicus was wrong in thinking that the stars move around the Sun, but at least he had begun to make people question Ptolemy's Earth-centred system.*

JOHANNES KEPLER

The German mathematician Johannes Kepler (1571–1630) analysed naked-eye observations of the planet Mars to prove that the planets move around the Sun in elliptical orbits.

Elliptical path of planet

▼ *Kepler's Second Law states that an imaginary line between the Sun and a planet covers equal areas in equal times. This means that the planet moves faster when near the Sun.*

▲ *In an elliptical orbit there are two points, equally distant from the centre. The Sun is at one point; there is nothing at the other. The further apart the two points, the more elliptical the orbit.*

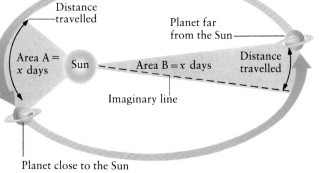

AREA A = AREA B

Distance travelled

Planet far from the Sun

Area A = *x* days

Sun

Area B = *x* days

Distance travelled

Imaginary line

Planet close to the Sun

DATE	EARLY EVENTS IN ASTRONOMY (Astronomer in brackets)
3000 BC	Earliest Babylonian astronomical records.
2900	Construction of the stone circle begins at Stonehenge.
2137	Two Chinese astronomers beheaded for failing to predict a solar eclipse.
280	First suggestion that the Earth orbits the Sun (Aristarchus).
270	First accurate measurement of the size of the Earth (Eratosthenes).
130	First comprehensive naked-eye star catalogue drawn up (Hipparchus).
AD 140	Theory put forward showing the Earth at the centre of the Universe (Ptolemy).
903	Accurate naked-eye star positions measured (Al-Sufi).
1054	Supernova seen in the constellation Taurus (Chinese observers).
1433	The most complete star catalogue yet published (Ulugh Beigh).
1543	Theory published suggesting the Sun is the centre of the Universe (Nicolaus Copernicus).
1572	Supernova visible in daylight in Cassiopeia (Studied by Tycho Brahe).

Optical Astronomy

In dim light, the pupil of the human eye opens up to about 7 mm across. Even this tiny 'light collector' is able to see the Andromeda galaxy, 2 million light-years away. A telescope is an artificial eye with a larger opening, or aperture, which collects more light than the human eye. Therefore it makes stars look brighter, and can reveal fainter and more distant objects. In 1608 a new age of astronomy began when the first telescope was made by a Dutchman, Hans Lippershey.

▼ *William Herschel (1738–1822) built large reflecting telescopes in order to study very faint objects. His largest telescope, with an aperture of 120 cm, was set up in his garden in England. The observer stood on the platform below the mouth of the tube.*

GALILEO'S DISCOVERIES

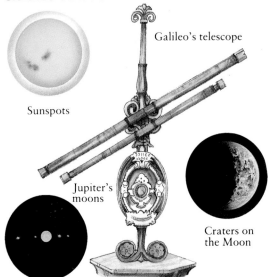

Sunspots

Galileo's telescope

Jupiter's moons

Craters on the Moon

▼ *Early refracting telescopes had to be very long in order to give a clear image. The telescope and observer had no protection from the weather. These fragile structures were called aerial telescopes.*

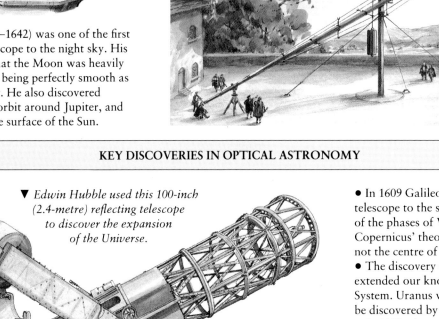

Galileo Galilei (1564–1642) was one of the first people to turn a telescope to the night sky. His first discovery was that the Moon was heavily cratered, rather than being perfectly smooth as Ptolemy had thought. He also discovered four large moons in orbit around Jupiter, and observed spots on the surface of the Sun.

KEY DISCOVERIES IN OPTICAL ASTRONOMY

▼ *Edwin Hubble used this 100-inch (2.4-metre) reflecting telescope to discover the expansion of the Universe.*

- In 1609 Galileo first turned a telescope to the sky; his observations of the phases of Venus confirmed Copernicus' theory that the Earth is not the centre of the Universe.
- The discovery of Uranus in 1781 extended our knowledge of the Solar System. Uranus was the first planet to be discovered by telescope.
- In 1838 telescopic observation meant the distance to a star could be measured for the first time – by F W Bessel in Germany.
- In the 1920s Edwin Hubble used his observations at Mt Wilson to show that the Universe is expanding.

▼ *Large astronomical telescopes are always reflectors, because mirrors are easier to make than lenses. This telescope at Mt Palomar, California, USA, has a reflector 5 metres across.*

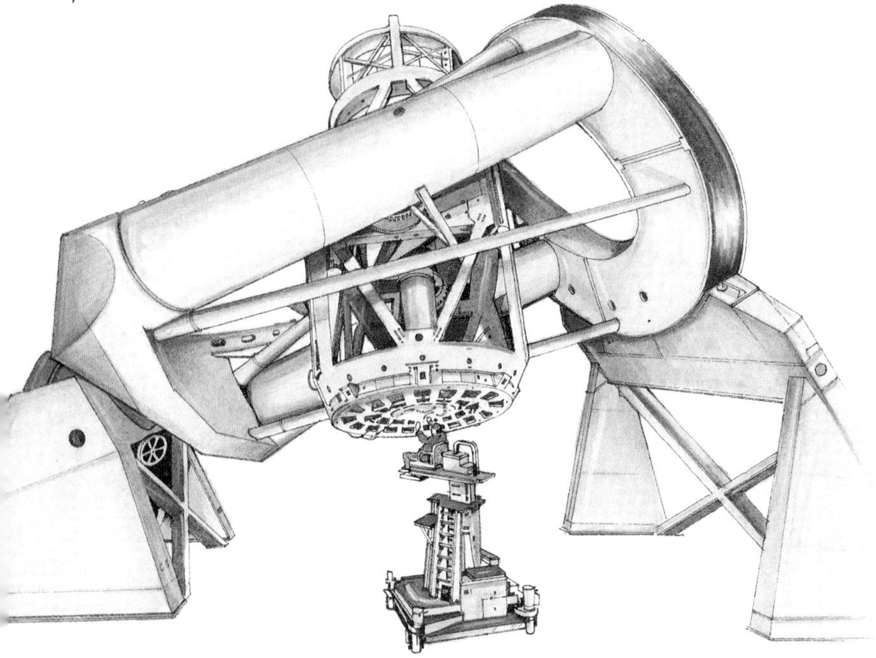

◄ *To see distant objects in more detail, astronomers need larger telescopes. A single large mirror is difficult and costly to build. The Multiple Mirror Telescope at Mt Hopkins, Arizona, USA uses six 1.8-metre mirrors mounted in one frame. Their combined collecting area is equal to that of a single 4.5-metre telescope, but is cheaper to build.*

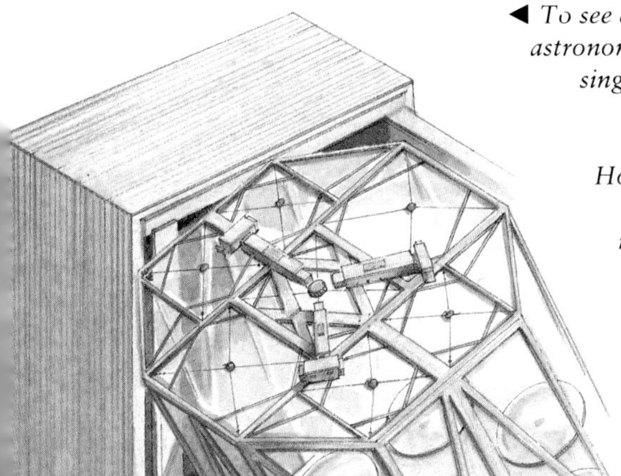

TYPES OF TELESCOPE

The two basic types of telescope used in optical astronomy are refractors and reflectors. A refracting telescope uses a lens to form a large, upside down image. The first telescopes were refractors. The first reflecting telescope was built by Isaac Newton in 1668. A reflector uses a large curved mirror instead of a lens. The mirror gathers light, which is reflected off a second mirror into the eyepiece. The Cassegrain is another type of reflecting telescope.

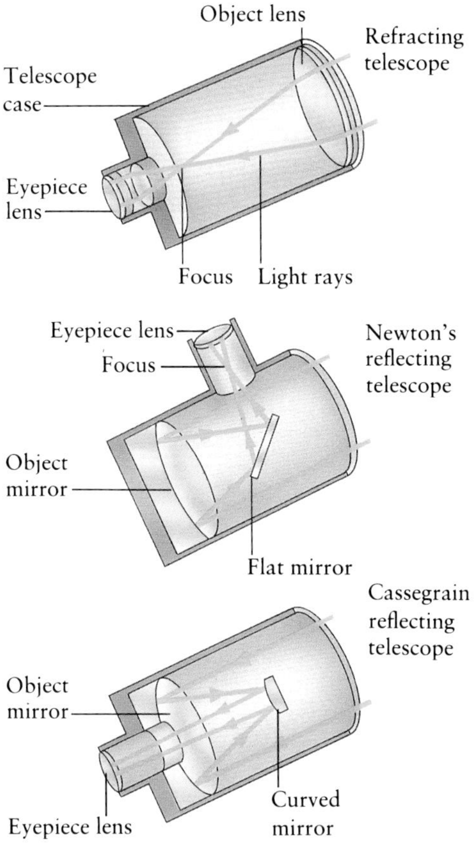

Object lens

Refracting telescope

Telescope case

Eyepiece lens

Focus   Light rays

Eyepiece lens

Focus

Newton's reflecting telescope

Object mirror

Flat mirror

Cassegrain reflecting telescope

Object mirror

Eyepiece lens

Curved mirror

▼ *Astronomers study the sky from observatories. Modern observatories are built on mountains, far from city lights which would interfere with the view. This observatory at La Palma in the Canary Islands is 2400 m above sea-level.*

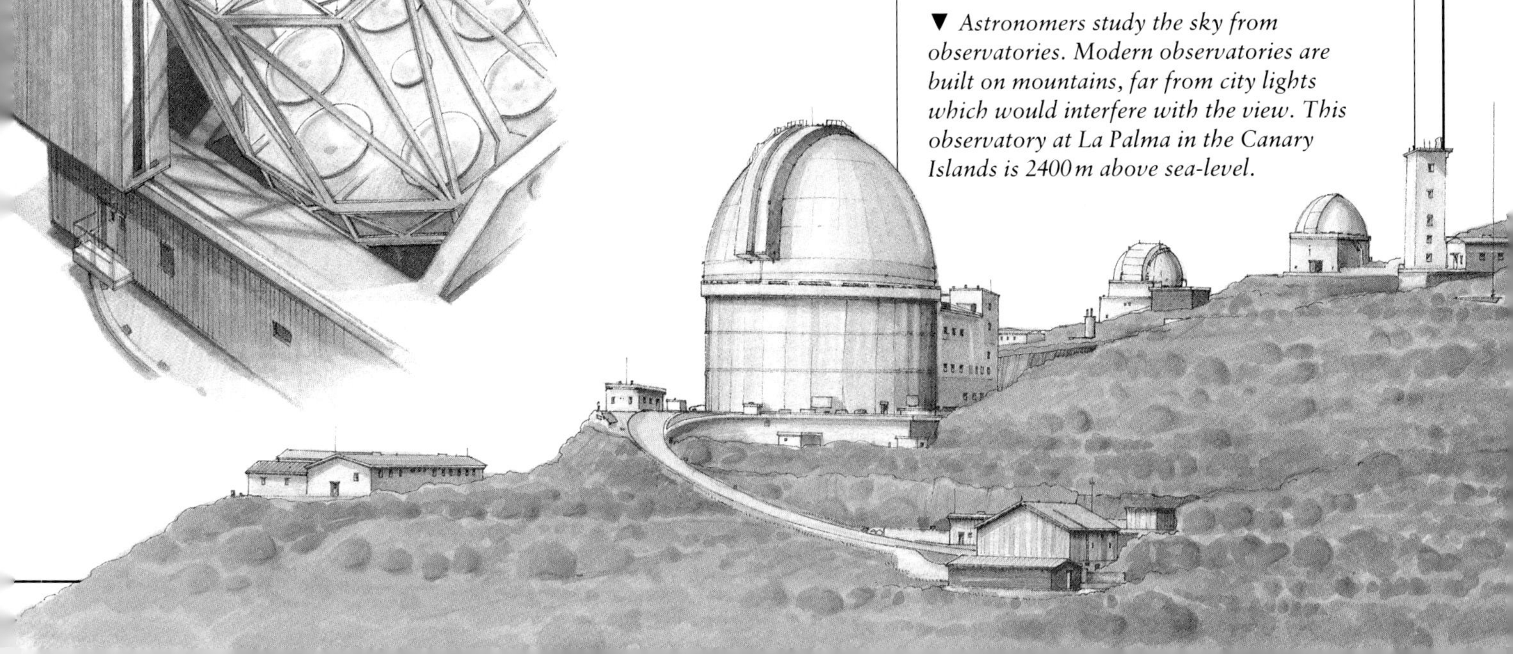

Radio Telescopes

As well as sending out visible light, many astronomical objects also send out radio waves, which are invisible. The Earth's atmosphere is completely clear to radio waves, which can pass through even the thickest clouds. For this reason, radio telescopes are very important in astronomy. Radio telescopes are a special kind of telescope that can collect radio waves and so 'see' objects that are too dim or distant to be seen with ordinary telescopes. Quasars and pulsars were discovered by radio telescopes.

HOW A RADIO TELESCOPE WORKS

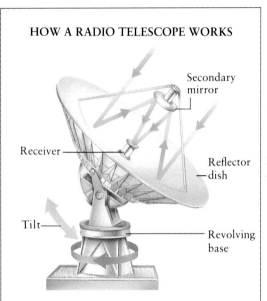

Secondary mirror

Receiver

Tilt

Reflector dish

Revolving base

Most radio telescopes use a concave dish to collect radio waves from space. The radio waves are reflected onto an antenna, which sends the signal to an amplifier to be strengthened. The signal will be processsed by a computer which can turn it into images. Radio waves have less energy than light waves, so radio telescopes must have a large dish to detect faint objects.

▲ This unusual radio telescope at Nançay, France, has a fixed curved reflector. A second, movable reflector directs the radio waves from space on to its surface.

▶ The main radio telescope at the Parkes Observatory, Australia has a 64-metre dish. The largest 'steerable' radio telescope in the world is at Effelsberg, Germany and has a 100-metre dish.

▶ Only a little of the energy sent out by space objects passes completely through the Earth's atmosphere. This energy includes the visible light waves detectable by optical telescopes, as well as the short-wave radio waves picked up by radio telescopes. Some infrared radiation reaches the Earth's surface, but our atmosphere blocks most other forms of radiation from space.

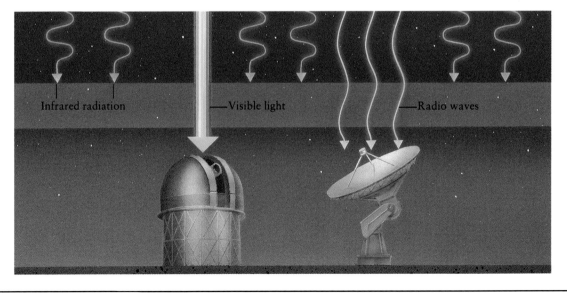

Infrared radiation — Visible light — Radio waves

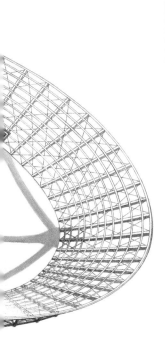

MAJOR RADIO OBSERVATORIES
● National Radio Astronomy Observatory, Socorro, New Mexico, USA, includes the Very Large Array (VLA) *(below)*.
● Arecibo, Puerto Rico (305-metre dish, pointing directly upwards).
● Green Bank, West Virginia, USA (new 100-metre dish being installed by 1995).
● Australia Telescope, Culgoora, New South Wales (six 22-metre dishes, linked by computer to act like a much larger telescope).
● Effelsberg, Germany (100-metre dish).
● Jodrell Bank, England (76-metre dish).

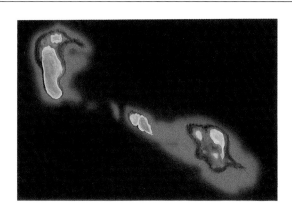

▲ *The clouds emitted by galaxy Centaurus A were recorded by the Very Large Array and turned into images by computer. They do not send out visible light.*

◀ *The VLA consists of 27 dish aerials, each 25 m across.*

▶ *Before 1900 no one had any idea how the Sun or other stars shone, and many people believed that the Milky Way was the most important galaxy in the Universe, since no other galaxies had been identified. Some of the important astronomical advances made this century appear here.*

FURTHER FACTS

A radio telescope need not be a metal dish. The radio telescope that led to the discovery of the first pulsar was a collection of wires and poles, built in a field in Cambridge, England, in 1967. A simple metal bar may act as an antenna for radio waves.

DATE	KEY EVENT
1908	Ejnar Hertzsprung (Denmark) and Henry Russell (USA) discover that most stars belong to an orderly family, the 'main sequence'.
1912	Cepheid variable stars discovered by Henrietta Leavitt (USA). They are important as their distance can be measured very accurately.
1915	Albert Einstein (Switzerland) publishes the General Theory of Relativity.
1923	Edwin Hubble (USA) observes Cepheids in the Andromeda Galaxy and measures the first distance between galaxies.
1929	Hubble proves that the galaxies are moving away from each other, and that the Universe is expanding.
1930	Clyde Tombaugh (USA) discovers Pluto while searching for 'Planet X'.
1932	Karl Jansky first detects radio waves from space at Holmdel, New Jersey, USA.
1937	First radio telescope dish built, measuring 9.4 metres across.
1958	The Earth's radiation belts discovered by James Van Allen's equipment on the American satellite *Explorer 1*.
1961	Quasar 3C 273 is the first to be discovered, by radio astronomers at Cambridge, England.
1965	Big Bang background radiation discovered by Arno Penzias and Robert Wilson at Holmdel, New Jersey, USA.
1967	Pulsars discovered by Jocelyn Bell and Anthony Hewish at Cambridge, England.
1990	Light recorded from furthest ever point to date.
1990	Hubble Space Telescope launched.

Space Telescopes

Putting a telescope into space, above the blocking, blurring effect of Earth's atmosphere, sounds like an astronomer's dream. The Hubble Space Telescope (HST) is the latest and largest satellite designed to observe space objects. However, there are problems too. Carrying a telescope into space is an expensive and difficult business. If anything goes wrong while the telescope is in orbit there is no one to mend it, and its power supplies will eventually wear out.

TELESCOPES IN SPACE

Some space observations are impossible from the Earth's surface because our atmosphere blocks out some types of radiation. X-rays and gamma rays from the Sun, red dwarfs and exploding galaxies such as Centaurus A are blocked, as well as infrared rays from cool objects such as comets and nebulae. The atmospheric currents around Earth even affect visible light, making the stars twinkle. Images obtained in space are perfectly steady and so more detail can be seen. An orbiting telescope can also observe the whole sky, which cannot be done from anywhere on the Earth's surface.

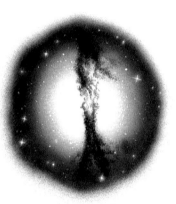

Centaurus A galaxy

Red dwarf

Comet

▲ *The Earth's atmosphere blocks much radiation sent out by space objects. Radio waves are reflected back into space at a height of about 300 km. Gamma rays and X-rays are absorbed at about 50 km; few infrared rays descend below 20 km. Only visible light and short-wavelength radio waves can reach the telescopes on the Earth's surface.*

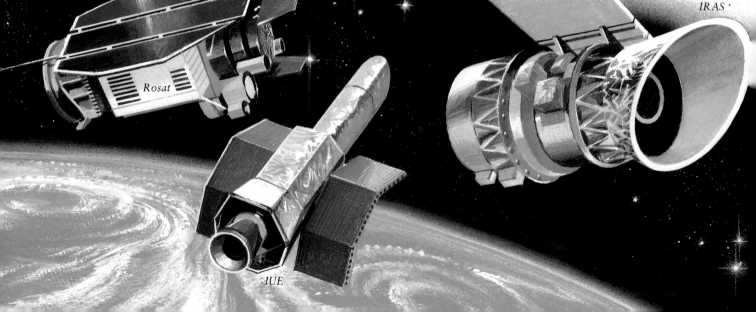

IRAS

Rosat

IUE

▶ *The Hubble Space Telescope, launched in 1990, orbits above Earth's surface and uses a mirror 2.4m across. It is the largest telescope ever to be put into orbit, and should be able to see objects 100 times fainter than telescopes on Earth can detect. HST's observations are sent down to radio telescopes around the Earth.*

◀ *The HST is really a giant video camera. In its 'wide-field' setting it can produce images of complete star clusters and nebulae. In 'faint-object' mode it can probe the space around a single star. It can also study the spectrum of a star or galaxy. Altogether there are five completely different ways in which the HST can be used.*

Communication antenna

Door

Secondary mirror

Solar panel

Primary mirror

Communication antenna

▼ *Apart from the HST, other satellites orbit the Earth, sending back valuable information on space objects. Rosat, launched in 1990, is expected to record about 100,000 X-ray sources. These include dim stars, such as red dwarfs, which also give out some X-rays. The* International Ultraviolet Explorer, *(IUE), was launched in 1978. The IUE studies ultraviolet light coming from stars. It is in a special orbit over the Atlantic Ocean so that its signals are received* directly by stations in Spain and America. *The* Infra-Red Astronomy Satellite *(IRAS) was put into orbit in 1983. It discovered many young, invisible, cool stars, as well as several comets, including the comet IRAS-Araki-Alcock in 1983. The planned launch of the* Advanced X-ray Astrophysics Facility *satellite (AXAF) is in the late 1990s.*

▼ *The HST has recorded an expanding cloud 50 times the diameter of the Solar System, surrounding a binary star, R Aquarii. Here, gas from a red giant is regularly detonated by its hot white dwarf companion. Material in the cloud is twisted by magnetic fields in space.*

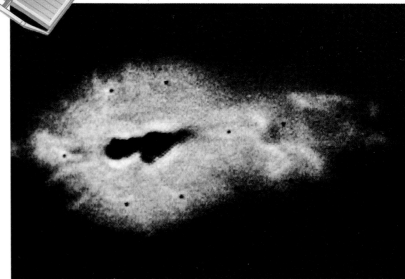

AXAF

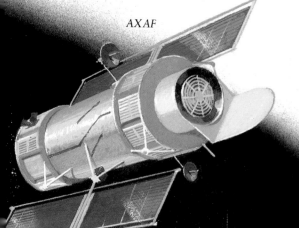

FACTS ABOUT SPACE TELESCOPES

● After launch, the HST would not focus properly. Investigation showed that the mirror was accidentally polished to the wrong curve. It cannot be changed, but small mirrors can be installed during a Shuttle maintenance mission to correct the fault.

● By computer-processing the originals to remove most of the blurred focus, some spectacular images have been obtained by the HST. However, this can only be done if the object is bright. Even then, the telescope is not showing as much detail as it should.

SPACE EXPLORATION

A Rocket to the Moon

Space travel was a fantastic dream for centuries. But to leave the Earth behind, it was necessary to build an engine powerful enough to travel at 11 km/s, the speed needed to beat the pull of Earth's gravity. During this century, the invention of liquid fuelled rockets has made space exploration possible. Rockets are the only vehicles powerful enough to carry spacecraft away from the surface of the Earth. Since 1957, rockets have carried hundreds of satellites into orbit, where they may gather information about our Universe. Rockets have launched space probes to other planets. Early Soviet rockets were powerful enough to launch cosmonauts (Soviet astronauts) into orbit, where they started building experimental space stations. And to fly astronauts to the Moon, US space scientists constructed the three-stage *Saturn V*, the largest rocket ever built.

TO THE MOON AND BACK
(**1**) Rocket stages 1 and 2 launch craft into orbit and fall away. (**2**) Rocket orbits Earth then carries on to Moon. (**3**) Command and Service Module (CSM) turns round; locks with Lunar Module (LM). (**4**) Astronauts enter LM; LM separates from CSM. (**5**) LM lands; CSM orbits Moon. (**6**) Astronauts carry out tasks; LM blasts off and re-connects with CSM. (**7**) LM ditched. (**8**) Re-entry.

Earth

◄ *As the* Apollo *spacecraft approached Earth on its return from the Moon, small rockets were used to alter its course slightly. This ensured that the Command Module (CM) containing the three astronauts was on target for its fall towards Earth.*

LAUNCH TO SPLASHDOWN
The 110-metre rocket *Saturn V* launched *Apollo 11* to the Moon on 16 July 1969. On 20 July, Buzz Aldrin and Neil Armstrong stood on the Moon's surface while the third crew member, Michael Collins, orbited in the Command Module (CM).

The CM was the only part of the spacecraft to return to Earth. Once it re-entered Earth's atmosphere its parachutes opened, slowing the CM down. Early US missions would splashdown into the ocean, where the crew would be rescued by helicopters.

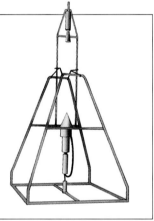

◄ *The Lunar Module (LM) blasted off from the Moon with the two astronauts travelling in the upper cabin. The lower half was left behind on the Moon.*

Moon

6
4
5
7
3

▲ *Once the final stage of the launch vehicle* Saturn V *had been jettisoned, the* Apollo *crew were carried to the Moon in the combined Command and Service Module (CSM). The Command*

Module (CM) carried the crew, the flight equipment and the communications instruments, while the Service Module (SM) contained fuel supplies and the spacecraft's rocket engines.

ROCKET INVENTORS

Rocket-propelled spacecraft were first seriously studied by the Russian scientist Konstantin Tsiolkovsky (1857–1935). Herman Oberth (1894–1989) experimented in Germany with small solid-fuel rockets. The first rocket to use liquid fuel *(right)* was built in 1926 by the American physicist Robert H. Goddard (1882–1945).

▼ *Some of the most significant rockets are shown here. Of these, the V2 rocket was first used during World War II. The* Long March *rocket was China's first successful launcher. The Russian* Energiya *launcher boosts the* Buran *shuttle into orbit.* Titan 3 *launches satellites, as does* Ariane, *the European Space Agency's rocket.*

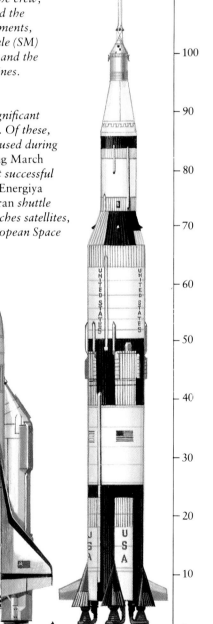

Height in metres

Saturn V

V2
Atlas
Titan 3
Long March III
Ariane
Vostok
Energiya launcher and *Buran* shuttle

Astronaut to scale

Artificial Earth Satellites

An artificial satellite is a spacecraft placed in orbit around a planet. About two thousand satellites have now been launched, for a number of purposes. Military satellites can spy, guide missiles, and even be weapons themselves. Communications satellites relay television, radio and telephone transmissions. Weather satellites help with weather forecasting and also give immediate warning of cyclones. Scientific satellites may carry out studies of the Earth and its environment, or observe space objects.

▶ *Satellites are put into orbit aboard rockets or the Space Shuttle. The speed at which a satellite is launched has to be exactly right, or the satellite will fly off into space (1) or return to the ground (2). An orbiting satellite launched at the right speed will keep 'falling' at the same rate as the Earth's surface curves beneath it (3), and so will never land.*

1 Too fast

2 Too slow

3 Right speed

TYPES OF ORBIT

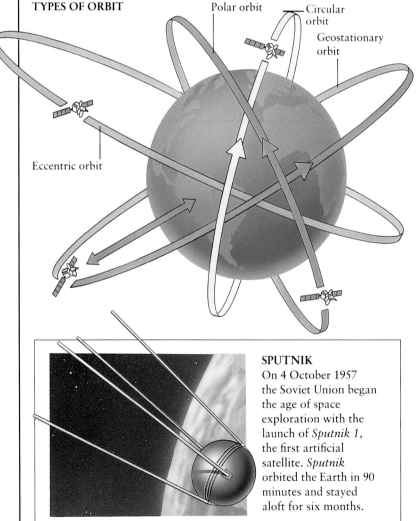

Polar orbit

Circular orbit

Geostationary orbit

Eccentric orbit

◀ *Satellite orbits can pass right over both the poles so that all the Earth's surface can be surveyed. In a geostationary orbit, the satellite always faces the same part of the Earth. A circular orbit means that the satellite is always the same height above the surface of Earth, but if the satellite's orbit is eccentric this distance will keep changing.*

SPUTNIK
On 4 October 1957 the Soviet Union began the age of space exploration with the launch of *Sputnik 1*, the first artificial satellite. *Sputnik* orbited the Earth in 90 minutes and stayed aloft for six months.

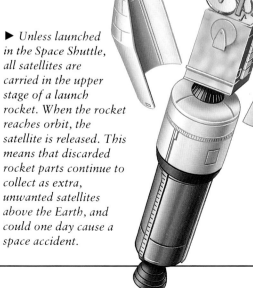

▶ *Unless launched in the Space Shuttle, all satellites are carried in the upper stage of a launch rocket. When the rocket reaches orbit, the satellite is released. This means that discarded rocket parts continue to collect as extra, unwanted satellites above the Earth, and could one day cause a space accident.*

▼ *The advantage of launching a satellite from the Space Shuttle, such as the SBS-4 satellite, is that astronauts can make last-minute adjustments before the satellite is released. Rocket motors on the satellite itself can be used to send it into an eccentric or geostationary orbit if required.*

SATELLITE FIRSTS

● *Sputnik 2* (USSR, 1957) launched the first living creature into space – a dog called Laika, who spent a week in orbit.

● *Explorer 1* (USA, 1958) was the US' first successful satellite. It detected belts of radiation around the Earth.

● *Solar Max* (USA 1980), a satellite designed to study the Sun by taking X-ray pictures of solar flares, failed nine months after launch. It became the first satellite to be repaired in space, by an historic Space Shuttle mission in 1984.

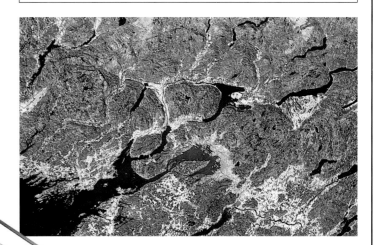

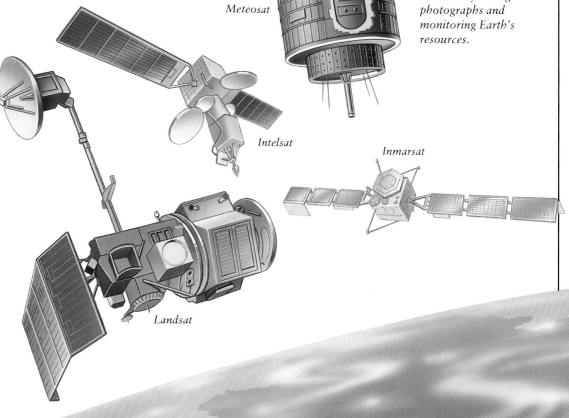

Meteosat

▲ *The* Landsat *satellites orbit Earth at a height of 1000 km, continually taking photographs and monitoring Earth's resources.*

Intelsat

Inmarsat

Landsat

► *Of the various types of satellite launched,* Intelsat 5 *was a communications satellite. It has now been replaced by* Intelsat 6, *which can carry up to 33,000 telephone channels.* Inmarsat *is also a communications satellite. It allows ship-to-shore telephone calls. The weather satellite* Meteosat, *launched in 1977, was the first in a continuing series of weather satellites. The* Landsat *satellites are designed to map the Earth's surface and collect information on the environment.*

Space Probes

The first successful space probe was *Luna 2* (USSR), which hit the Moon in 1959. Since then, probes have visited every planet in the Solar System apart from Pluto. These robot explorers have provided close-up pictures of worlds billions of kilometres away. The images are so clear that it is hard to appreciate the technical problems faced and overcome. For example, the *Voyager 2* pictures from the edge of the Solar System were transmitted using the same voltage as two car batteries!

SPACE PROBE DATAFILE

The first successful visits by spacecraft (date in brackets refers to encounter with planet):

Moon: *Luna 2* (USSR 1959); Lander *Luna 9* (USSR 1966); Orbiter *Luna 10* (USSR 1966)

Mercury: *Mariner 10* (USA 1974)

Venus: *Mariner 2* (USA 1962); Lander *Venera 7* (USSR 1970); Orbiter *Venera 9* (USSR 1975)

Mars: *Mariner 4* (USA 1965); Orbiter *Mariner 9* (USA 1971); Lander *Viking 1* (USA 1976)

Jupiter: *Pioneer 10* (USA 1973)

Saturn: *Pioneer 11* (USA 1979)

Uranus: *Voyager 2* (USA 1986)

Neptune: *Voyager 2* (USA 1989)

Asteroid: *Galileo* (USA 1991) examined Gaspra during its flight to Jupiter

Comet: *Giotto* (Europe 1986) examined Halley

▼ *The first artificial object to reach another world was the Soviet probe* Luna 2, *which crashed into the Moon on 13 September 1959.* Luna 1 *had missed.*

▼ Luna 9 *was the first spacecraft to make a soft landing on the Moon, on 3 February 1966. It returned the first pictures of the Moon's surface.*

Luna 2

Luna 9

Mariner 10

◄ Mariner 10 *was the first probe to visit two planets. It flew past Venus and then Mercury in 1974.*

◄ Pioneer-Venus 2 *sent four probes into the atmosphere of Venus on 9 December 1978, while Pioneer-Venus 1 went into orbit.*

Mariner 2

THE FIRST VEHICLE ON THE MOON
The Lunokhods were unmanned Moon cars launched by the USSR in 1970 and 1973. They were controlled from Earth by radio, and travelled the surface collecting information.

Pioneer-Venus 2

▶ Mariner 2 *was the first successful probe to visit a planet. It flew past Venus on 14 December 1962 and made temperature measurements.*

SLINGSHOT LAUNCH

To the Sun via Jupiter! Space probes can be speeded on their way, or have their course changed, by using the pull of another planet's gravity as a free energy source. The *Ulysses* probe, launched in 1990, used Jupiter's gravity to swing it into a vertical path that will pass above the Sun's poles.

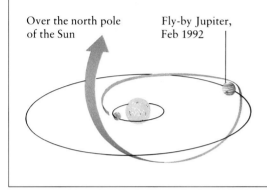

Over the north pole of the Sun

Fly-by Jupiter, Feb 1992

Ulysses

◀ *The* Ulysses *space probe will reach the Sun in 1995. It will record the solar wind and the Sun's magnetism, as well as travelling above both the Sun's poles.* Ulysses *should increase our knowledge about our star greatly.*

DEEP SPACE NETWORK

There is no second chance to receive data transmitted by a space probe, so there must always be a receiving station on the Earth able to make contact. The Deep Space Network (DSN) has three main stations around the world so that all directions in the Solar System are covered.

Red

Blue

Green

▲ *Colour pictures were made from separate red, blue and green images taken by* Voyager.

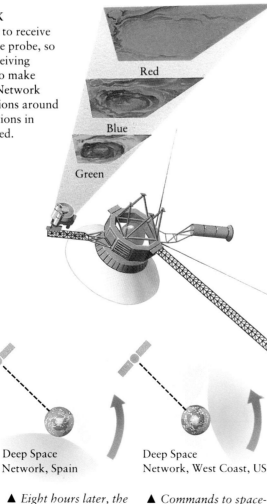

Deep Space Network, Australia

Deep Space Network, Spain

Deep Space Network, West Coast, US

▲ *A telescope in Australia uses a 64-metre diameter radio telescope to receive signals.*

▲ *Eight hours later, the Spanish station near Madrid is facing the same direction in space.*

▲ *Commands to spacecraft are usually sent from the Goldstone station in California, USA.*

PIONEER-VENUS 2

Pioneer-Venus 2 acted as a carrier to four smaller probes on the way to Venus in 1978. As it approached Venus, *Pioneer* launched its four probes towards different parts of the planet. The main probe was launched first, the smaller probes four days later.

Probes released 13 million km from Venus

Large probe reaches atmosphere first

Parachute opens and aeroshell abandoned

Probe reaches surface 56 minutes after entering atmosphere

Life in Space

When an astronaut travels into space, the familiar background to life – day and night, gravity, natural air, sunshine and exercise – is suddenly cut off. Astronauts undergo vigorous training to cope with the artificial space environment. Just to endure lift-off, which makes the body feel like it is being squashed, astronauts have to be extremely fit. As everything in the cabin is weightless, astronauts have to learn how to eat, sleep, move and keep healthy in a world without gravity.

FACTS ABOUT PEOPLE IN SPACE

April 12, 1961: First man in space (Yuri Gagarin, USSR).
June 16, 1963: First woman in space (Valentina Tereshkova, USSR).
March 18, 1965: First spacewalk (Alexei Leonov, USSR).

Valentina Tereshkova

US/USSR link-up

Yuri Gagarin

Challenger explosion

December 1968: First manned flight around the Moon (*Apollo 8*, USA).
July 20, 1969: First Moon landing (*Apollo 11*, USA).
May 1973: First fully successful space station (*Skylab*, USA).
July 1975: First docking of US and Soviet spacecraft (*Apollo 18* and *Soyuz 19*).
April 12, 1981: First Space Shuttle launched (*Columbia*, US).
January 28, 1986: *Challenger* shuttle explodes, killing all seven people on board. Crew includes teacher Christa McAuliffe.

▼ *A spacesuit must provide a supply of oxygen, remove carbon dioxide and other waste products, maintain atmospheric pressure and keep the astronaut comfortably warm. The latest suits worn on Shuttle flights allow the astronauts to spend many hours outside the spacecraft. These are known as Extra Vehicular Activity (EVA) suits.*

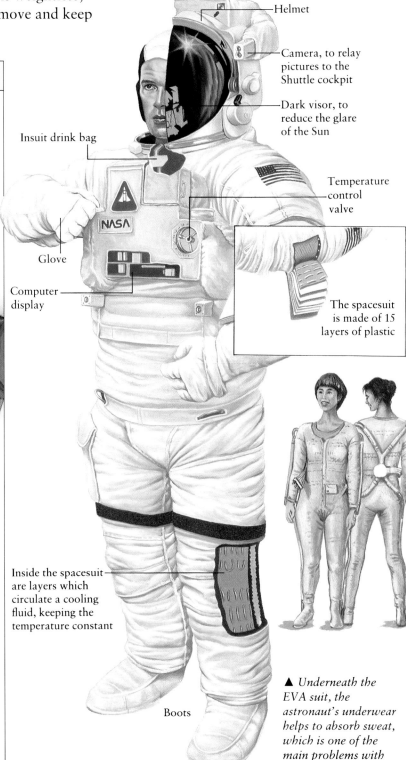

Helmet

Camera, to relay pictures to the Shuttle cockpit

Dark visor, to reduce the glare of the Sun

Insuit drink bag

Temperature control valve

NASA

Glove

Computer display

The spacesuit is made of 15 layers of plastic

Inside the spacesuit are layers which circulate a cooling fluid, keeping the temperature constant

Boots

▲ *Underneath the EVA suit, the astronaut's underwear helps to absorb sweat, which is one of the main problems with an airtight garment.*

▼ *There is no gravity in space, so liquid and food particles from an astronaut's dinner would float around the cabin. To prevent this, astronauts' food and drink is specially packaged.*

SPACE WALKING
When floating free in space, an astronaut has nothing to push against to start themselves moving and no way of stopping either. The Manned Manoeuvring Unit (MMU) used by US astronauts contains several small rocket thrusters pointing in different directions. When fired, the astronaut moves in the opposite direction. Lines tethering the astronaut to the spacecraft are no longer used with MMUs, as they could become dangerously tangled.

▼ *When sleeping, an astronaut is tied to the bunk or uses a secured sleeping suit. Sleep is timetabled, because there is no day or night in space.*

Shuttle lavatory

◄ *Astronauts who are spending a long time in a spacesuit wear a nappy. The Shuttle lavatory (left) is designed to contain solid and liquid waste.*

Growing crystals

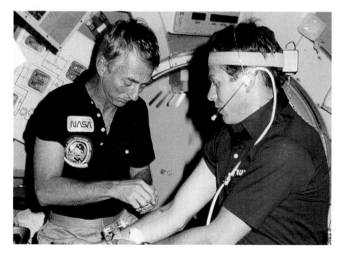

▲ *The health of astronauts is very important. The blood's circulation is affected by weightlessness, and this can cause sickness. Muscles may also start to deteriorate.*

Gravity and plants

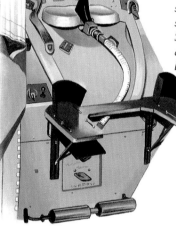

► *Some Space Shuttle flights have carried a laboratory called Spacelab into orbit. Spacelab is used for experiments on the effects of weightlessness. Some of these experiments have been carried out on living things to discover how zero gravity affects them. Spacelab scientists have studied the growth of pine seedlings and the way a spider spins a web. Other experiments are related to industrial processes, such as the growth of crystals.*

Space Shuttles and Space Stations

The flight of the first Space Shuttle, *Columbia*, in 1981 heralded a new era in space exploration – the launch of reusable spacecraft. Before then, all spacecraft were used only once, making a space mission an expensive business. The Shuttle can take off like a rocket but land like a glider, and may be used many times. Soon Shuttle spacecraft will be involved with the ambitious *Freedom* project. This is planned to be the biggest ever permanently occupied space station; it may be completed by AD 2000.

Eight minutes after lift-off – fuel tank falls away

▼ *The* Freedom *space station will consist of a number of cylindrical modules launched into Earth orbit by the Space Shuttle. Some of these modules will be laboratories, researching space biology and human survival in space.*

Two minutes after lift-off – booster rockets fall away from orbiter

▼ *Although launched by the Shuttle, a number of nations are constructing different parts of the* Freedom *space station. For example, the European Space Agency is providing one of the laboratory modules, to be called* Columbus.

An early design for the *Freedom* space station

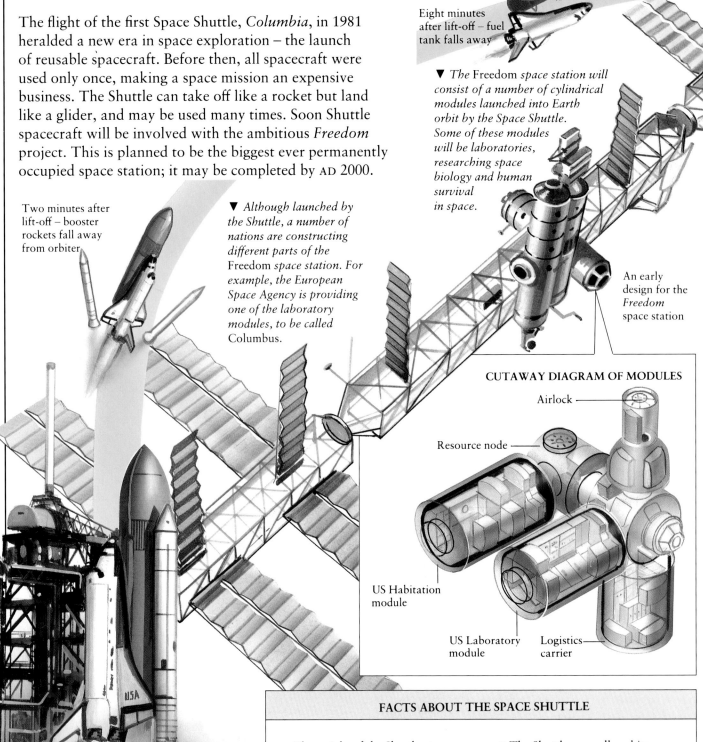

CUTAWAY DIAGRAM OF MODULES

Airlock

Resource node

US Habitation module

US Laboratory module

Logistics carrier

LAUNCHING THE SHUTTLE
The Shuttle is launched on the back of a huge fuel tank. The two side rocket boosters use solid fuel and are recovered. The main tank contains liquid fuel and burns up as it falls back to Earth over the Indian Ocean. The Shuttle's own rockets take it into final orbit.

FACTS ABOUT THE SPACE SHUTTLE

- The weight of the Shuttle at launch is 2000 tonnes – as much as 50 fully-laden juggernauts.
- Each of the four Shuttles is designed to make up to a hundred launches in a 20-year lifetime.
- On re-entry into the atmosphere, parts of the Shuttle's surface reach a temperature of 1600°C.
- Seventy percent of the Shuttle is covered with heat-resistant tiles.

- The Shuttle normally orbits 220 km above the Earth, but to launch the Hubble Space Telescope in 1990 the *Discovery* Shuttle reached the record height of 614 km.
- An extra piece of cargo on this flight was an eyepiece that Edwin Hubble used when taking the photographs that showed the expansion of the Universe!

Boosted
into orbit

Satellite
released
into orbit

THE SHUTTLE'S FUTURE

There are currently
four Shuttles in use
(*Columbia, Discovery,
Atlantis* and
Endeavour). The first,
Columbia, is now 12
years old, but they are
all expected to carry
on flying until the
end of the century.

▼ *In 1992 the Shuttle
was used to perform
repairs on the* Intelsat
communications satellite.

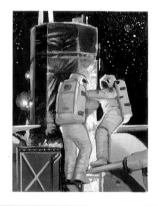

► Skylab *(USA,
1973–1974) was a
laboratory orbiting
Earth. It was visited
by three crews, the last
remaining in space for
84 days.*

Skylab

► Salyut 1 *(USSR,
1971) was the first
operational space
station. It was
visited by one
cosmonaut, who
spent 23 days aboard.*

▼ *After launching six
more Salyut space
stations, the USSR
launched Mir in 1986.
New compartments
have been added since,
and some cosmonauts
have stayed in Mir
for up to a year.*

Re-entry into
atmosphere

Salyut

RE-ENTRY
The Shuttle fires its engines
for just 150 seconds to start
its descent to Earth. It then
uses air resistance to slow it
down until it lands like an
ordinary glider.

Landing on a runway

Mir

The Future in Space

The biggest problem facing the future of space exploration is not technology but cost. Because the Shuttle is still a very expensive craft to operate, several nations are working on a Space Plane which could take off and land using an ordinary airfield. Highly-advanced jet engines would lift the Space Plane through the atmosphere, and a rocket would then carry it into orbit. Another cost-cutting project is the Solar Sail, which would use energy sent out by the Sun to 'blow' spacecraft between the planets.

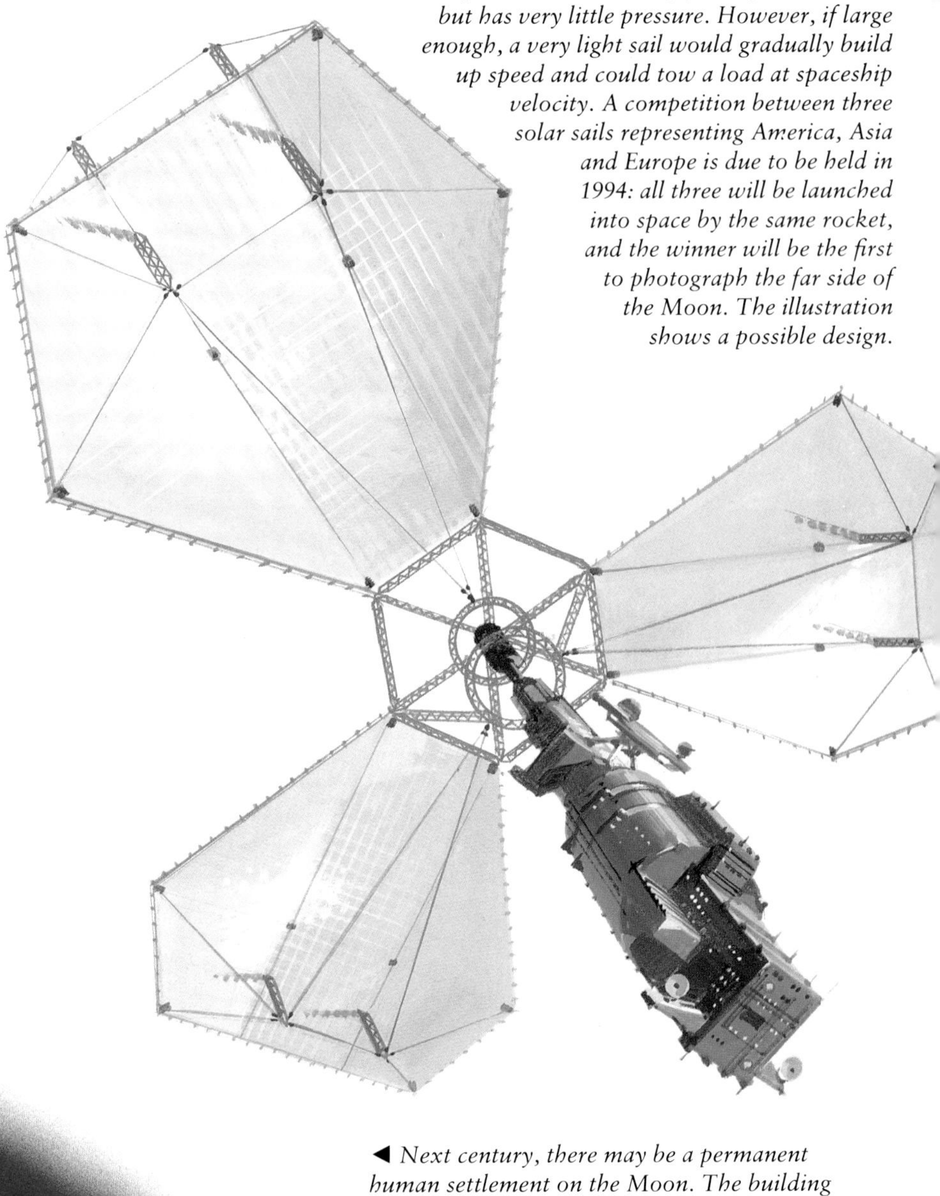

CODED MESSAGES
This message to possible other life forms was transmitted in radio code in 1974 towards a star cluster in the constellation Hercules. It will arrive in about the year 26,000.

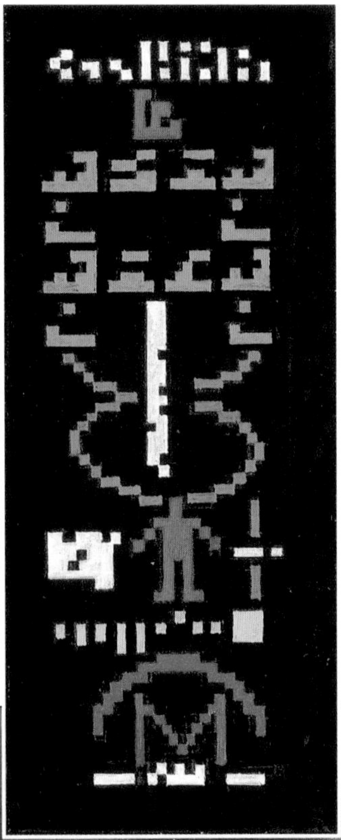

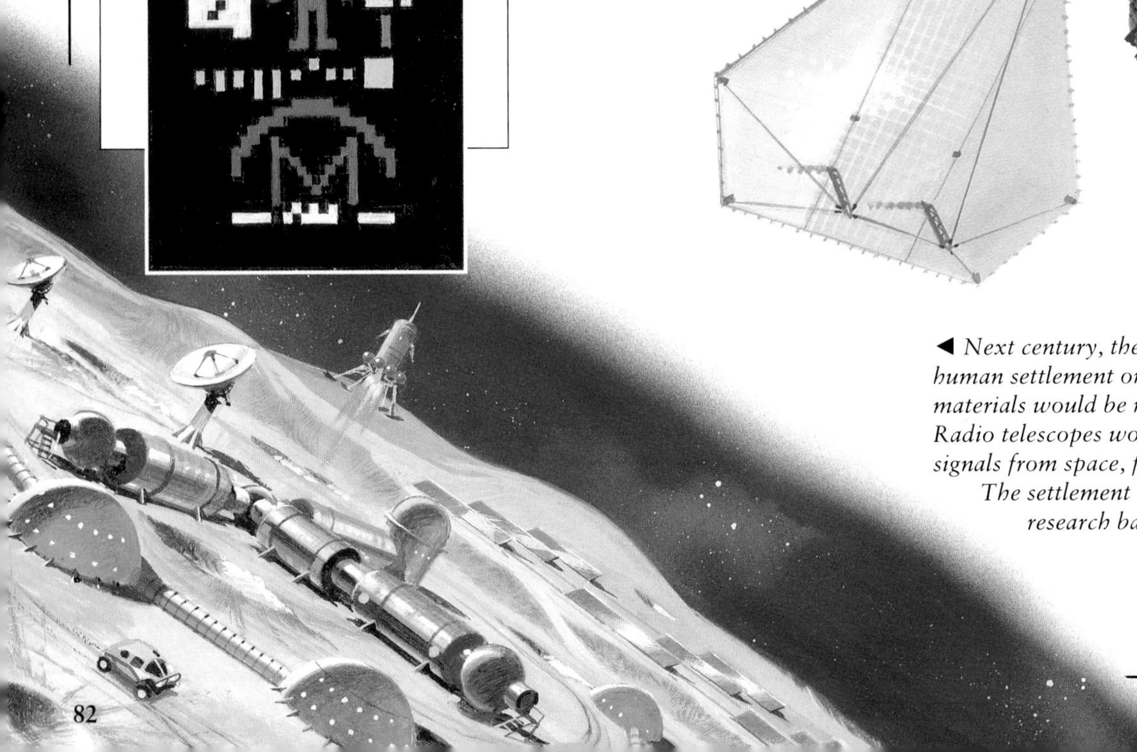

▼ *The solar wind of protons and electrons sent out by the Sun travels very fast (up to 900 km/s) but has very little pressure. However, if large enough, a very light sail would gradually build up speed and could tow a load at spaceship velocity. A competition between three solar sails representing America, Asia and Europe is due to be held in 1994: all three will be launched into space by the same rocket, and the winner will be the first to photograph the far side of the Moon. The illustration shows a possible design.*

◄ *Next century, there may be a permanent human settlement on the Moon. The building materials would be mined from the Moon itself. Radio telescopes would search the sky for signals from space, free from Earth's radio noise. The settlement would be an important research base for scientists.*

▲ *A few asteroids
are known to be
made of almost pure
metal rather than rock,
probably from the cores of
much larger bodies broken
up in ancient collisions. As
well as iron and nickel the
asteroids must contain
platinum and other rare
metals. One day it may be
possible to catch a passing
asteroid and propel it into
Earth orbit for mining.*

▼ *Space cities might one day
be built mainly from materials
mined on the Moon and
placed elsewhere in the Earth's
orbit around the Sun.*

ORBITING POWER STATIONS
Launching solar energy collectors into
orbit around the Earth has several
advantages over power stations on the
Earth's surface. The solar collectors
(above) can be placed in orbits where
they receive continuous sunlight, and the
Sun's radiation is much stronger without
the atmosphere to absorb so much of its
energy. The collected energy would be
beamed back, using lasers, to receiving
stations on the Earth, where it would
power electric generators.

GAZETTEER

Words in **bold** indicate an entry elsewhere in the Gazetteer or the Glossary.

Aldebaran: Red **giant star** that forms the eye of the **constellation** Taurus, the Bull. A hundred times as **luminous** as the Sun; 68 **light-years** away.

Andromeda galaxy: Nearest spiral **galaxy**, 2.2 million **light-years** away. May contain 400 billion stars. The Andromeda galaxy is the most distant object visible with the naked eye.

Antares: Red **supergiant star** that shines in the **constellation** of Scorpius. Wider than the Earth's **orbit** around the **Sun**; 500 **light-years** away and 10,000 times as **luminous** as the Sun.

Arcturus: Red giant and the brightest star found in the **constellation** of Boötes, the Herdsman. About 100 times as **luminous** as the **Sun**; 34 **light-years** away. Arcturus is the fourth-brightest star in the sky.

Ariel: Moon of **Uranus**, 1158 km across; orbits the planet in 2.52 days. Some of the craters on its surface are surrounded by white deposits, like those on our **Moon**. Ariel is crossed by many smooth valleys.

Barnard's Star: Fourth closest star to the **Sun**, a **red dwarf** six **light-years** away. Less than 0.001 percent as **luminous** as our Sun.

Betelgeuse: Red **supergiant star** that shines in Orion. Larger than the orbit of **Mars**, and about 40,000 times as **luminous** as our **Sun**; 330 **light-years** away. Betelgeuse may eventually turn into a **supernova.**

Callisto: Satellite of **Jupiter**, 4800 km across; orbits the planet in 16.7 days. Surface is very densely cratered.

Canopus: Giant **star** that shines in the **constellation** Carina, the Keel. Much hotter than the **Sun** and about 400 times as **luminous**; 74 **light-years** away. Second brightest star in the sky after **Sirius**.

Capella: Yellow giant star that shines in the **constellation** Auriga, the Charioteer. About the same temperature as the **Sun** but 100 times as **luminous**; 41 **light-years** away.

Centaurus A: Giant elliptical **galaxy**, 16 million **light-years** away. Seems to be erupting, sending out strong radio signals as well as X-rays. The nearest radio galaxy to our Solar System.

Ceres: The largest **asteroid** and the first to be discovered. About 1000 km across; it orbits the **Sun** every 4.6 Earth years.

Charon: Pluto's only known **satellite**, 1200 km across. The two bodies **orbit** each other at a distance of 19,130 km in 6.38 days.

Chiron: Once thought to be an unusual **asteroid**, orbiting the **Sun** between Saturn and Uranus; now classed as a **comet**. A faint hazy **coma** is sometimes seen around it.

Crab Nebula: Expanding cloud from an exploding star (**supernova**) observed by Chinese astronomers in 1054. About 3600 **light-years** away. Material from the supernova is flying outwards at more than 1000 km/s. At the centre of the Crab Nebula is the **pulsar** CM Tauri, which pulses 30 times a second.

Cygnus A: Galaxy, and the strongest source of radio waves in the entire sky. However, it is so far away that it appears as a dim speck even with the strongest telescopes.

Cygnus X-1: Powerful X-ray source. This radiation is believed to come from gas heated to 10 million °C as it is dragged down on to a neutron star – or possibly into a black hole – from the other star in a binary system.

Deimos: Satellite of **Mars**, measuring about 11 km by 15 km. Orbits Mars in 1.26 days.

Dione: Heavily cratered **satellite** of **Saturn**, 1120 km across; orbits Saturn in 2.7 days. The tiny satellite Helene shares its orbit.

Earth: Third planet from the **Sun**, 12,756 km across. Two-thirds of the surface is covered with liquid water. Only planet known to support life.

Enceladus: Satellite of **Saturn**, about 500 km across; orbits the planet in 1.4 days. Has a smooth icy surface with few craters.

Europa: Satellite of **Jupiter**, 3138 km across; takes 3.6 days to orbit the planet. A smooth world, made of ice.

Ganymede: Satellite of **Jupiter**, 5262 km across; orbits Jupiter in 7.2 days. Largest satellite in the **Solar System**. Ganymede is cratered, but unlike our **Moon** also shows signs that its crust has moved and folded, creating mountains and valleys.

Halley's Comet: Most famous of all **comets**, orbiting the Sun in 76 years on average. Last passed close to the Sun in 1985–1986 and will do so again in 2061.

Hyperion: Satellite of **Saturn**, irregular body about 300 km across; orbits the planet in 21.3 days.

Iapetus: Satellite of **Saturn**, 1500 km across; takes 79 days to complete an orbit. One of Iapetus' hemispheres is coal-black, the other, much paler.

Io: Satellite of **Jupiter**, 3630 km across and orbiting in 1.8 days. Most active body in the **Solar System** – its surface is a waste of sulphur deposits and spouting volcanoes.

Jupiter: Largest planet in the **Solar System**. Its diameter at the equator is 142,800 km; its day lasts less than 10 hours. Has no solid surface and is principally made of hydrogen. Most famous surface feature is the cyclone known as the Great Red Spot.

Local Group: Cluster of more than 30 **galaxies**, including the **Milky Way** and the **Andromeda galaxy**. Extends over 5 million **light-years** of space.

Local Supercluster: 'Cluster of clusters' of **galaxies**; includes the **Local Group**, also a much larger group known as the **Virgo Cluster**, and many other clusters and galaxies. About 100 million **light-years** across.

Magellanic Clouds: Two satellite galaxies of the **Milky Way**, dwarf irregulars less than 200,000 **light-years** away.

Mars: Fourth planet from the **Sun**; 6787 km across. Has little **atmosphere** and appears dead, but parts of its surface wrinkled and split open when it was young and hot. Features that look like dried-up river beds suggest water once ran on Mars.

Mercury: Innermost planet, only 4880 km across. Crater-covered, its rocks are oven-hot where they are exposed to the **Sun**.

Milky Way: Spiral **galaxy** containing at least 100 billion stars, including the **Sun**. Larger than many galaxies, but much smaller than some. Probably formed about 14 billion years ago.

Mimas: Satellite of **Saturn**, 392 km across; orbits the planet in only 23 hours. One of the craters on Mimas' surface is a quarter of the satellite's own diameter.

Miranda: Satellite of Uranus, 480 km across; orbits the planet in 1.4 days. Perhaps the most puzzling satellite in the Solar System, it looks as if it has been roughly put together using separate lumps of material.

Missing mass: Invisible matter believed to be present in the Universe because of its gravitational effect. Amounts to approximately 10 times the mass of the stars and nebulae that are visible.

Moon: Earth's satellite, 3476 km in diameter; orbits Earth in 27.3 days. Like most satellites in the Solar System, has a crater-covered surface. The smoother plains caused by lava flooding through the crust are not as common as on other satellites.

Neptune: Usually, the eighth planet from the Sun; 49,500 km across. It has a surface of methane gas, disturbed by winds at speeds of over 2000 km/h.

Nereid: Satellite of Neptune, about 300 km across; takes 360 days to orbit the planet once, in a very eccentric orbit. Nereid was almost certainly a passing body captured by Neptune's gravity.

Oberon: Satellite of Uranus, 1524 km across; orbits in 13.5 days. Has an icy, cratered surface, but is also crossed by valleys several hundred kilometres long where the crust has split open.

Omega Centauri: One of over a hundred globular star clusters that surround the centre of the Milky Way galaxy. Probably formed at the same time as the galaxy. Omega Centauri contains at least a million stars and lies about 17,000 light-years away.

Phobos: Satellite of Mars, only 27 km long; orbits Mars in under 8 hours.

Phoebe: Satellite of Saturn, 220 km across; takes 550 days to orbit once, travelling round the planet in the opposite direction to most other bodies in the Solar System.

Planet X: Original name given to Pluto before it was discovered. Some astronomers believe that there may be another planet-sized body in the outer Solar System, beyond Pluto's orbit.

Pleiades: Cluster of stars about 250 light-years away, often called the Seven Sisters. The stars were formed less than a hundred million years ago, making the cluster one of the youngest in the sky.

Pluto: Ninth planet, 2200 km across. Pluto takes 248 years to orbit the Sun. In 2113, at its furthest point from the Sun, it will be 7.4 billion km away – 50 times further than Earth.

Polaris, the Pole Star: Yellow giant star, about 300 light-years away; 1500 times as luminous as the Sun. To someone standing at the North Pole, Polaris would be overhead.

Proxima Centauri: Closest star to the Sun, 4.2 light-years away. A red dwarf about 10,000 times dimmer than the Sun. Belongs to a triple-star system which includes the bright binary Alpha Centauri, known as Rigel or Rigel Kent.

Quasar 3C 273: The first quasar to be discovered – a galaxy sending out as much energy as hundreds of ordinary galaxies. One of the nearest quasars to our Solar System.

Rhea: Crater-covered satellite of Saturn, 1530 km across; takes 4.5 days to orbit the planet.

Rigel: Brilliant supergiant star, 850 light-years away. About 40,000 times as luminous as the Sun; the seventh brightest star in the sky. Shines in the constellation Orion.

Saturn: Sixth planet from the Sun, with a diameter of 120,000 km, making it second to Jupiter in size. Saturn's bright rings are visible from Earth with a telescope.

Sirius: The brightest star in the sky, only 9 light-years away and about 25 times more luminous than the Sun. Has a dim white dwarf companion that was once much brighter than Sirius, but has already passed through the red giant stage.

SN 1987A: Bright supernova that erupted in the large Magellanic Cloud on 24 February 1987. Reached a peak brightness of about 50 million Suns.

Solar System: The Sun, its family of planets and their satellites, the asteroids and comets.

Sun: Yellow main sequence star at the centre of the Solar System, 1,392,000 km across and about 4.6 billion years old. It is 8 'light-minutes' away from Earth.

Tethys: Satellite of Saturn, 1060 km across. Orbits the planet in 1.9 days. Shares its orbit with two other tiny moons, Telesto and Calypso. Its craters include one 400 km across.

Titan: Satellite of Saturn, 5150 km across; orbits Saturn in 15.9 days. Second largest satellite in the Solar System. Has a methane atmosphere about 200 km deep.

Titania: Largest satellite of Uranus, 1172 km across; orbits the planet in 4.1 days. Titania is heavily cratered and has wide valleys, as though the hard surface split open in its youth.

Triton: Satellite of Neptune, 2705 km across; orbits the planet in 5.9 days, travelling backwards like Phoebe in Saturn's family. Spouts of nitrogen gas rising from its frigid, partly-cratered surface were observed by the *Voyager* space probe.

Umbriel: Satellite of Uranus, 1172 km across. Orbits the planet in 4.1 days. Has a very dark surface, covered with craters.

Uranus: The seventh planet, with a diameter of 51,000 km. Discovered with a telescope in 1781. The planet rotates tipped over on its side, instead of almost upright like all the other planets except Pluto.

Van Allen Belts: Two rings of atomic particles – protons and electrons – trapped by the Earth's magnetism around the Equator. The small inner belt is about 300 km above the Earth's surface, the large outer belt about 22,000 km away.

Vega: Main sequence star, 26 light-years away. Shines in the constellation of Lyra. Vega is slightly more luminous than Sirius, but because it is further away Sirius seems brighter in the night sky.

Venus: The second planet, Venus is 41 million kilometres closer to the Sun than Earth. Heat has been trapped under the dense clouds that cover its surface, making it the hottest world in the Solar System.

Virgo Cluster: Large cluster of several hundred galaxies, about 50 million light-years away. Near its centre is a giant elliptical galaxy, M87, which sends out strong X-rays.

1992 QB1: Recently-discovered, this body marks a new frontier of the Solar System. Orbit size is not accurately known, but its diameter is probably not more than 200 km. It will eventually be given a permanent name. Probably other bodies in this twilight zone are awaiting discovery.

GLOSSARY

Words in **bold** indicate an entry elsewhere in the Gazetteer or the Glossary.

Aerolite: Type of **meteorite**, made up of stony material; probably from the rocky crust of an ancient planetary body that broke up.

Airglow: Very dim glow that makes the night sky, even when seen from the darkest places on **Earth**, slightly brighter than the true blackness of space; caused by weak **aurorae**.

Albedo: The amount of sunlight a planet or **satellite** reflects back into space. The **Moon**'s albedo is only 7 percent because the rocks absorb the light. **Venus**' albedo is 80 percent because its atmosphere reflects light well.

Aphelion: Point on a planet's orbit at which it is furthest from the **Sun**; **Earth** is at aphelion around July 4th.

Apogee: Point on a **satellite**'s orbit at which it is furthest from the planet.

Artificial satellite: Spacecraft put into orbit around a heavenly body.

Asteroid: One of countless thousands of small bodies orbiting the Sun; over 90 percent are found between the orbits of **Mars** and **Jupiter**. Most are less than a kilometre across, although the largest, **Ceres**, is about 1000 km across. Also known as minor planets.

Astronomical Unit (AU): Average distance of the **Earth** from the **Sun**; equal to 149,597,870 km.

Atmosphere: Layer of gas around a planet or star, held down by gravity. Small bodies with weak gravity, such as the **Moon**, have no atmosphere.

Atom: Smallest part or unit of an **element**, containing **protons**, **neutrons** and **electrons**. Hydrogen is the simplest atom, with just one proton and one electron.

Aurora: Night-time display of coloured lights which occurs when atomic particles pouring from the **Sun** strike gas **atoms** in the upper atmosphere and cause them to give out light.

Axis: Imaginary line through the centre of a star or planet, around which it spins. The **Earth**'s axis passes through the North and South **Poles**.

Big Bang: In theory, a huge explosion which saw the start of the **Universe** about 15 billion years ago.

Binary star: Two stars in orbit around each other.

Black dwarf: The cold dark corpse of an ordinary star, such as the **Sun**, after it has run out of fuel. Since they do not shine, no black dwarfs have yet been observed.

Black hole: Body with such strong **gravity** that nothing can escape, not even **light waves**; thought to be formed by the collapse of stars heavier than the **Sun**.

Brown dwarf: 'Failed star', which did not get hot enough at the core for **nuclear reactions** to start, but is too large to be a planet.

Captured rotation: Movement of a **satellite** which keeps one half always facing inwards as it orbits the parent planet; for example, our **Moon**. Such bodies used to spin quickly, but tides have raised a slight bulge on one side of the satellite, which has been slowed down and finally captured by the planet's **gravity**.

Celestial sphere: An imaginary hollow sphere with the **Earth** at its centre, on which the stars and planets seem to lie. As the Earth spins on its **axis**, the bodies seem to drift across the sky.

Cepheids: Important family of **variable stars**. These are **giant stars**, much more **luminous** than the Sun, which brighten and fade every few days as they swell and shrink.

Chromosphere: Lower part of the **Sun**'s atmosphere, about 2000 km thick. Can be seen to shine deep pink during a total **eclipse**.

Coma: Hazy head of a **comet**, where gas and solid particles are escaping from the solid nucleus.

Comet: Body made of crumbling rock and ice, usually just a few kilometres across, which regularly passes near the **Sun** before swinging off into distant space. The Sun's heat may cause solid particles and gas to pour off in a long tail.

Conjunction: Moment which occurs when two astronomical bodies, one of them a planet or the **Moon**, pass close by each other in the sky. The Star of Bethlehem may have been a conjunction of two bright planets.

Constellation: A group of stars found together in a definite area of the sky; 88 are recognized officially.

Corona: Outer atmosphere of the **Sun**, above the **chromosphere**; it extends several million kilometres into space.

Cosmology: The study of the Universe, how it began, and how it has evolved.

Crater: One of many scars on the surface of the rocky planets and almost all the **satellites**, produced by collisions with smaller bodies. Most formed at least 3 billion years ago. The **Earth**'s craters have been smoothed out by weather and surface movements.

Dust: In astronomy, the miniscule grains of carbon which gather in vast clouds, or **nebulae**, many **light-years** across.

Dwarf star: Name given to most ordinary, or **main sequence**, stars. The Sun is a yellow dwarf. There are also **red**, **white** and **black dwarfs**.

Eclipse: Occurs when the **Moon** passes into **Earth**'s shadow (eclipse of the **Moon**), or when it passes in front of the **Sun** (eclipse of the Sun). Other bodies in the **Solar System**, and even **binary stars**, can eclipse each other.

Ecliptic: The path that the **Sun** seems to follow around the **celestial sphere** each year; in fact, it is the **Earth** that is moving around its orbit.

Electron: Subatomic particle with a negative electric charge.

Element: Substance containing just one kind of **atom**; common examples on **Earth** are oxygen and nitrogen.

Ellipse: The oval shape of the path followed by a planet, **satellite** or **comet**. Ellipses may be almost perfect circles, like the **Earth**'s orbit round the **Sun**, or very long and narrow, like the orbits of many comets.

Equation of Time: Difference between the correct local time and the time shown by the **Sun**'s shadow on a sundial. In early November the **Sun** is 16 minutes 'fast', while in the middle of February it is 14 minutes 'slow'.

Escape velocity: Speed at which a body needs to move if it is to escape completely from the gravity of a planet or **satellite**: 2.4 km/s for the **Moon**, 11.2 km/s for the **Earth** and 60.2 km/s for **Jupiter**.

Fireball: A very bright **meteor**. Some land on **Earth** as **meteorites**.

Galaxy: Vast collection of stars, **star clusters** and **nebulae**; generally either spiral, elliptical or irregular in shape. Dwarf galaxies may number just a few million stars – giant galaxies can contain a million, million stars.

Giant planets: In order from the **Sun**: **Jupiter**, **Saturn**, **Uranus** and **Neptune**.

Giant stars: Old stars that have begun to expand and cool as they use up their hydrogen fuel. Red giants are the oldest, and have swollen up into a red mist. The **Sun** will eventually become a red giant. Blue giant stars have surface temperatures of 12,000°C – much hotter than the Sun or a red giant star.

Globules: Protostars – dark clouds of **dust** and gas about one **light-year** across. Each globule is shrinking and heating up at the centre, and in a few thousand years will start to shine as a baby star.

Granulation: The mottled **photosphere** of the **Sun**, caused by hot gas breaking the surface and sinking back again.

Gravity: Force which attracts the bodies in the Universe towards each other.

Infrared radiation: Sent out by cool stars and **nebulae**. Difficult to study from **Earth** and so satellites such as *IRAS* have been used instead. Infrared **wavelength** is longer than visible light but shorter than radio waves.

Ionosphere: Layer of **electrons** and **atoms** about 70 km above the **Earth**'s surface. Reflects certain radio waves, which can pass from one station on Earth to another by bouncing off the ionosphere.

Light wave: A beam of light consists of energy waves – about 2000 in every millimetre. Red light has a longer wavelength than blue light. The waves contain packets of energy, called photons, and travel through empty space at a speed of 299,792.5 km/s.

Light-year: Distance a wave of light will travel through empty space in a year – 9,460,700,000,000 km. Used as a measure of distances in space.

Luminosity: Measure of how much light and heat a **star** gives out. Depends on its size and temperature. **Supergiant** stars are a million times more luminous than the Sun, but **red dwarfs** only a ten-thousandth of the Sun's luminosity are known to exist.

Lunation: The lunar month – the period from one New Moon to the next, lasting 29.5 days.

Magnetosphere: Stars and planets have their own magnetism. The magnetosphere is the surrounding space where atomic particles are trapped by this magnetism.

Magnitude: Apparent magnitude measures the brightness of a star as it appears in the sky. Absolute magnitude is the real brightness or luminosity of a star.

Main sequence: The family of normal stars, ranging from very bright and hot white stars, through cooler yellow stars like the **Sun**, down to the coolest dim **red dwarfs**.

Mass: Amount of material in a body. Different from weight (the force of **Earth**'s gravity pulling on a body).

Mesosphere: Belt of **atmosphere** lying between 50 km and 80 km above the Earth's surface.

Meteor: Streak of light left by a **meteoroid** as it burns up in the atmosphere.

Meteorite: Fallen **meteoroid**. Some are mainly stony (**aerolites**), others mainly nickel and iron (**siderites**).

Meteoroid: Body orbiting the **Sun**. They range in size from a grain of sand to extremely rare ones several metres across. They are only seen when they burn up in the atmosphere as a **meteor** or **fireball**. Large ones may land as a **meteorite**.

Midnight Sun: In summer, the part of the **Earth**'s surface near the Pole is bathed in constant light and the **Sun** never sets, even shining at midnight.

Nebula: Cloud of **dust** and gas, usually many **light-years** across, in a **galaxy**. Stars are formed inside nebulae. Smaller nebulae can be thrown out into space when a **supernova** explodes.

Neutron: Atomic particle with no electric charge. Neutrons are found in the nucleus of every **element** except hydrogen.

Neutron star: Solid atomic matter remaining after the centre of a **supergiant** star collapses in a **supernova** explosion.

Nova: Faint star which increases greatly in brightness almost overnight. Occurs in a **binary** system when gas passes from one star to another, causing an explosion.

Nucleus: Central part of an **atom**, containing **neutrons** and **protons** (apart from hydrogen, which has no neutrons).

Occultation: Occurs when the **Moon** or a planet passes in front of a star, blocking it from view.

Opposition: A planet is at opposition when it lies opposite to the **Sun** in the sky. This means that it rises above the horizon at sunset, and sets at sunrise.

Orbit: Path traced out by a planet or **comet** around the Sun, or a **satellite** around a planet. Every orbit is an **ellipse**.

Ozone layer: Form of oxygen, high up in the atmosphere, which blocks out dangerous radiation from the **Sun**.

Parallax: If you move your head or body from side to side, a nearby object seems to move in front of more distant ones. This is parallax. The distance of nearby stars can be worked out by seeing how much they move in front of remote stars as the **Earth** follows its orbit around the **Sun**.

Penumbra: Partly-shaded ring around the dark centre of a shadow, such as the shadow cast by the **Earth** on the **Moon** during a lunar **eclipse**. The lighter outer part of a **sunspot** is also called the penumbra.

Periastron: The smallest distance apart of two **stars** in a **binary** star system, as we see them orbiting each other.

Perigee: Point on a **satellite's** orbit where it is closest to the planet. In the case of the **Moon**, it is about 51,000 km closer at perigee than at **apogee**.

Perihelion: Point on the elliptical orbit of a planet where it is closest to the **Sun**. The **Earth** is at perihelion around January 2nd.

Period: The length of time taken by a body to go once round its orbit.

Phase: The shape in which the sunlit part of the **Moon** or a planet appears in the sky. The **Moon, Mercury** and **Venus** all change from a thin crescent to a complete circle.

Photosphere: Shining surface of the **Sun**. Its temperature is about 5800°C.

Planet: Body orbiting a star and giving out no light of its own. May be mainly rock, like the **Earth,** or mainly frozen or liquid gas, like **Jupiter**.

Planetary nebula: Shell of gas thrown out by a star after a **nova** or **supernova** explosion.

Poles: The two points on a spinning body, such as a planet or star, where the **axis** passes through the surface.

Prominence: Eruption of hydrogen gas from the **Sun**'s surface. Some prominences last for weeks, others may shoot off into space at 400 km/s.

Proper motion: The very slow change of position of the stars in the sky as thousands of years pass.

Proton: Atomic particle with a positive electric charge. Protons and **neutrons** form the nucleus of an **atom**, and the number of protons always equals the number of **electrons**.

Pulsar: Neutron star sending out a beam of light and radio waves as it spins. Each time this beam sweeps across the **Earth** we receive a pulse of **radiation**.

Quasar: Object producing as much energy as a hundred ordinary **galaxies**. Quasars are too far away from **Earth** to observe clearly, but seem to be galaxies with a special powerhouse at the centre.

Radiation: Energy, and the way it passes through space, in pulses radiating outwards like ripples across a pond. X-rays, light waves and radio waves are different forms of radiation, with different wavelengths.

Red dwarf: Main sequence star with less **mass** than the **Sun**. Its surface temperature is only about 3000°C and it is less than a thousandth as **luminous** as the Sun.

Red shift: Because the Universe is expanding, the **galaxies** are flying away from us. This spreads the light waves from the galaxies further apart, making them seem redder.

Retrograde motion: The planets appear to move slowly in front of the stars, from west to east. However, when they are near **opposition** the Earth's speed makes them seem to move backwards, or 'retrograde'.

Rings: Belts of solid particles – small rocky bodies, ice and dust – orbiting the four **giant planets**. The particles may have come from a **satellite** that broke up in orbit.

Saros: Period of 18 years, 10 days and 8 hours. Ancient astronomers found that **eclipses** of the **Sun** and **Moon** repeat after this interval.

Satellite: Body orbiting a planet. So far, 60 natural satellites have been found in the Solar System. Also known as a moon. *See also* **artificial satellite**.

Scintillation: *see* **twinkling**.

Seasons: Change from summer to winter; occurs because each of the Earth's poles turns towards and then away from the **Sun** during the course of the year.

Sidereal day: Time the **Earth** takes to rotate on its **axis** – 23 hours, 56 minutes and 4 seconds; measured by the stars rather than the **Sun**.

Siderite: Meteorite, consisting mainly of metal. Probably came from the iron-nickel core of an ancient planetary body that broke up.

Solar day: Time the **Earth** takes to rotate on its axis, measured by the **Sun**; exactly 24 hours long.

Solar wind: Steady outward blast of atomic particles from the **Sun**, reaching to the furthest part of the **Solar System**.

Spectral type: A way of classifying stars into groups according to the nature of their **spectrum**.

Spectrum: Colour range produced when light passes through a prism. Different **elements** produce their own pattern of bright or dark lines in a spectrum.

Star: Ball of hot gas which gives out heat and light as a result of atomic reactions deep inside it.

Star cluster: Group of stars which formed from the same **nebula**. Open clusters are usually young and contain a few hundred stars of many different kinds. Globular clusters contain many thousands of old **red giant** stars, packed much more closely together.

Steady state: Theory put forward about 50 years ago, stating that the **Universe** has always existed. It has been given up because the **Big Bang** theory is far better at explaining the discoveries of astronomers.

Stratosphere: Belt of **atmosphere** lying between 10 km and 50 km above the **Earth's** surface.

Sunspot: Region of the **photosphere** 500°C cooler than its surroundings.

Sunspot cycle: Period of time, about every 11 years, when **sunspots**, flares and **aurorae** become more common. The next period of maximum activity will occur around the year 2001.

Supergiant: Rare type of star, several times as massive as the Sun and up to a million times as **luminous**. A supergiant will probably end its life as a **supernova**.

Supernova: Complete destruction of a **supergiant** star in an explosion as bright as a whole **galaxy**. A **neutron star**, or even a **black hole**, may be all that is left.

Terrestrial planets: The inner planets: **Mercury, Venus, Earth** and **Mars**.

Tides: The gravity of two nearby space bodies makes them pull at each other's surface, producing tides.

Transit: Occurs when a **satellite** passes in front of a planet. **Mercury** and **Venus** sometimes transit the **Sun**, appearing as round black spots against the **photosphere**.

Troposphere: Lower layer of the Earth's atmosphere; is about 10 km high at the poles, and 16 km at the Equator.

Twinkling: Caused by heat currents in the **atmosphere** passing in front of the stars. The telescopic image dances, and fine detail is blurred. Large telescopes are usually built at a high altitude, where twinkling is less severe. Also known as scintillation.

Ultraviolet light: Invisible **radiation** sent out by the **Sun** and other stars. Most of it is blocked by the **Earth's atmosphere**, especially the **ozone layer**. Its wavelength is shorter than visible light, but longer than X-rays.

Umbra: Dark central part of a shadow, surrounded by the **penumbra**. The darkest part of a **sunspot** is also called the umbra.

Universe: All of space and everything that exists in it. The Universe is infinite – it has no end. *See also* **Big Bang, Steady state**.

Variable stars: Stars which change in brightness. Eclipsing variables are **binary stars** where one star regularly blocks the light from the other one. Intrinsic variables are single stars whose **luminosity** changes.

Wavelength: The distance between waves of **radiation**. Examples are: long wave radio with waves of up to several thousand metres; heat radiation, waves of about 1 mm; visible light, about 2000 waves/mm; X-rays, about 10,000,000 waves/mm.

White dwarf: Remains of a star, after it has become a **red giant**. Its surface is very hot, but because it has shrunk so small it is less than a hundredth as bright as the Sun.

Zodiac: A band of sky 20° wide with the **ecliptic** passing along the centre. The **Moon** and all the **planets** (except **Pluto**) always lie within it. The Zodiac passes through the 12 Zodiacal **constellations**.

PLANET EARTH

I t has been only in the last decade or two that we have been able to appreciate our world in all its splendour – since satellites have sent back photographs of our watery globe. Without such pictures it is hard to imagine that Earth is a ball-shaped planet travelling around the Sun through the vastness of space.

But scientists and thinkers have been unravelling the mysteries of Earth for centuries – observing volcanoes, wondering what causes earthquakes, unearthing fossils and prospecting for minerals. From their observations we have come to a better understanding of how our world works – from the hot, dense bowels of the planet to the surrounding envelope of air.

Planet Earth offers an up-to-date and easy-to-understand account of our physical world. In it you will read about the origins and structure of the Earth, how volcanoes erupt, and why continents drift. The major landscapes of the world are described, as are the oceans, the atmosphere and weather, and the Earth's resources. Essential facts and figures complete this comprehensive study of our extraordinary planet.

Neil Curtis

OUR PLANET

The Earth in Space

Viewed from space, the Earth appears as a round ball that shines bright and blue. People have not always seen the Earth in this way. Aristotle (384–322 BC), a philosopher in ancient Greece, and other scholars believed that any problem could be solved by thinking carefully about it. He believed that the Earth was at the centre of the Universe, and that the Moon, Sun, planets and stars orbited around it. You might come to the same conclusion, if you lived on a desert island, with no radio, television, computers, or newspapers, and had no telescope to study the night sky. Indeed, you might not even guess you were on a spherical planet floating in space. At best, if you watched a ship disappearing beneath the horizon, you might work out that the world's surface was curved. Today, we know that the Earth is one of a system of planets orbiting the Sun.

▶ *The Earth is not completely round. It is flattened at the poles and bulges slightly at the Equator. Clouds swirl continuously above the surface. Over two-thirds of the Earth is covered by water. Most of this water is contained in the oceans.*

EARTH DATAFILE

Diameter at the poles: 12,713 km
Diameter at the Equator: 12,756 km
Circumference (distance around the Earth at the Equator): 40,091 km
Volume: about one thousand billion cu km
Mass: 5.9 thousand billion billion tonnes
Average density: 5.5 (water = 1)
Surface area: 510 million sq km
Percentage of surface area covered by water: 71 percent
Age: 4.6 billion years
Age of the oldest-known rocks: 3.7 billion years
Distance to the Moon: *maximum* 406,697 km, *minimum* 356,400 km
Average distance to the Sun: 152 million km
Average thickness of the crust: 20 km
Average thickness of the mantle: 2800 km
Average diameter of the core: 6964 km
Temperature at the centre: 4500°C

▶ *Before modern mapping techniques, the peoples of the Earth had very different ideas of it. These ideas included the belief that the Earth (and the Sun) were gods and that the Earth was flat.*

Egyptian Sun Disc

15th century
World Map

Pluto · Neptune · Uranus · Saturn · Jupiter · Mars · Earth · Venus · Mercury · Sun

THE EARTH'S POSITION

Our Sun has a solar system of nine planets around it. The planets' characteristics are related to their distance from the Sun. Earth is one of the small inner planets, along with Mercury, Venus and Mars. Closest to the Sun, Mercury and Venus are extremely hot. Each day on Mercury lasts over two Earth-months, during which its surface heats up to 450°C, and then cools to −170°C during the long night. Venus is even hotter, because of the greenhouse effect of its carbon dioxide atmosphere (see page 159). Next is Earth – the only planet with liquid water, and conditions suitable for life. Beyond Earth, Mars resembles a cold, red stony desert. Colder still are the giant outer planets Jupiter, Saturn, Uranus and Neptune. They are partly made of gases such as hydrogen and helium. Pluto is the smallest planet and is thought to be ice.

THE BIRTH OF THE EARTH

The Earth was formed at the same time as the Sun and the other planets in the Solar System. About 4.6 billion years ago, a rotating cloud of dust and gas, called a nebula, contracted under the pull of gravity. The pressure and temperature at the centre of the nebula became so great it triggered a nuclear reaction. Some of the hydrogen in the cloud fused into helium, releasing great amounts of energy. This was the birth of the Sun. Farther from the centre, material surrounding the Sun cooled and collided, building up into larger bodies, which eventually became the planets.

Sun being formed

Earth

LINES ON EARTH

The Earth spins on an axis. The imaginary points on the Earth's surface where this axis projects are called the geographical poles.

The Equator is an imaginary circle drawn around the Earth at an equal distance from the North and South Poles. Imaginary circles drawn parallel to the Equator are called lines of latitude. The latitude of the Equator is 0°, while the poles are 90° North and 90° South. Great circles drawn through the poles give lines of longitude. Zero longitude runs through Greenwich, London.

Greenwich Meridian · Line of latitude · Tropic of Cancer · Equator · Tropic of Capricorn · Line of longitude

▲ Imaginary lines of latitude and longitude form a grid upon the Earth's surface for navigation and map-making. The tropics are two lines of latitude which mark the farthest limits where the Sun appears overhead.

Viking's view of the edge of a flat Earth

Aztec view of the Universe

North · West · Earth · East · South

Modern world map

Satellite image of the Earth

Gravity and the Earth

Gravity is the force of attraction that every object in the Universe exerts on every other object. It is the weakest force known in physics, but its effects extend across the huge distances of space. The greater the mass of an object, the larger its gravitational attraction, but the further away it is, the smaller the force. Gravitational forces are largely responsible for the orbits of bodies around the Sun and the orbit of our satellite, the Moon, around the Earth. These forces also give rise to the seasons and the tides.

THE EARTH'S DAY

The Earth's day is the time it takes to spin once on its axis (a little under 24 hours). If the Earth's axis was at right angles to its orbit, the length of a day would be the same all over the Earth. In fact, the Earth's axis is tilted by 23° 27′. This means that people in the hemisphere tilted towards the Sun see the Sun passing higher across the sky, and daylength is longer. The hemisphere tilted away from the Sun has a shorter day.

► *Twice a year, on 21 March and 23 September, day and night are of equal length all over the Earth.*

THE EARTH'S YEAR

The Earth's year is the time taken for it to complete one orbit of the Sun (365 days, 5 hours, 48 minutes and 46 seconds). The year is divided into 365 days, but every fourth year, a leap year, has 366 days to make up the extra time. In a leap year there are 29 days in February.

THE SEASONS

Since the Earth's axis is tilted, the hemispheres are at different angles to the Sun. This gives rise to the seasons. In winter the days are cold and short and in summer they are long and warm. At the Equator, daylength varies little throughout the year, and the seasons are linked to rainfall.

Sun

21 December
Winter begins in
Northern Hemisphere,
summer begins in
Southern Hemisphere

21 March
Spring begins in
Northern Hemisphere,
autumn in Southern
Hemisphere

21 June
Summer begins in
Northern Hemisphere,
winter begins in
Southern Hemisphere

Sun

Earth

Moon

▲ *In the Northern Hemisphere, summer begins officially on 21 June, the longest day of the year. In the Southern Hemisphere this is the shortest day.*

THE PULL OF GRAVITY

The sea rises and falls every 12 hours and 26 minutes. These tides are caused by the gravity of the Moon, and also the Sun. The Moon's gravity pulls the oceans on the side of the Earth nearest to it more than it pulls the Earth itself, causing a bulge of water, or tide. On the opposite side, the Earth is pulled more than the oceans, and this leaves behind a slightly smaller bulge.

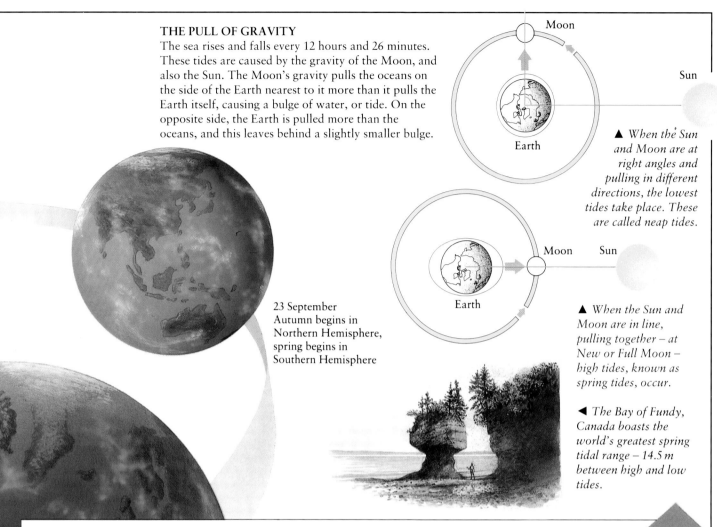

Moon

Sun

Earth

▲ *When the Sun and Moon are at right angles and pulling in different directions, the lowest tides take place. These are called neap tides.*

Moon Sun

Earth

23 September Autumn begins in Northern Hemisphere, spring begins in Southern Hemisphere

▲ *When the Sun and Moon are in line, pulling together – at New or Full Moon – high tides, known as spring tides, occur.*

◀ *The Bay of Fundy, Canada boasts the world's greatest spring tidal range – 14.5 m between high and low tides.*

THE EARTH'S ENERGY BALANCE

The Sun gives out radiation and can be thought of as the Earth's power plant. It supplies the energy that drives the Earth's climate and weather. It is the energy source for all plant life and, therefore, for all animal life as well. At a temperature of some 15 million °C, the Sun's fuel source, hydrogen, fuses into helium (the hydrogen atoms combine to form helium atoms) and releases energy. Our planet receives just one two-thousand millionth of the energy that the Sun generates.

▶ *Thirty percent of the available radiation is reflected directly back into space by clouds, or by the surface of the planet.*

▼ *Radiation reflected by the Earth is absorbed by gases in the atmosphere such as carbon dioxide. The energy is then radiated again, some of it returning to Earth.*

Radiation reflected back to space

Radiation from Sun

Radiation reflected to Earth's surface

▶ *About 70 percent of the Sun's radiation that reaches the Earth is absorbed and then radiated back again. Of this 70 percent, 25 percent is absorbed by the atmosphere and the rest by the planet itself.*

Absorption by atmosphere

The Structure of the Earth

Although earthquakes can have catastrophic effects, they can also reveal a great deal about the Earth's structure. The shock waves pass through the Earth in different ways and can be recorded by scientists using sensitive instruments called seismometers. Scientists have been able to identify three main zones according to density: the thin outer crust, the mantle below and the core in the centre. The upper layers of the Earth are also categorized as the hydrosphere, lithosphere and asthenosphere.

▼ *The Earth's crust is divided into oceanic crust and continental crust, both of which originate in the mantle. The thicker continental crust can vary from about 35 km thick to as much as 50 km beneath mountain ranges. It is made mainly from pale, granite-like rocks.*

▼ *The lithosphere is the upper, rocky layer of the Earth. It includes the crust and the top, brittle part of the mantle, and can be up to 300 km thick.*

▼ *The hydrosphere is the water (mainly the oceans and seas) on the Earth's surface. After the Earth was formed, water vapour in the atmosphere condensed to form the hydrosphere.*

▶ *The thinner rocky crust beneath the oceans is only about 5 km thick. It is made up mainly of dark rocks called basalt and gabbro and has been formed in the last 200 million years.*

▶ *The asthenosphere is the layer of the mantle beneath the lithosphere which is in an almost fluid or 'plastic' state, so that it behaves like an extremely thick liquid.*

THE MOHOLE PROJECT

Rocks on the surface of the Earth can easily be examined. But the inside of the planet is hidden from scientists, except when volcanic eruptions spew out material. The boundary between the crust and the mantle is called the Mohorovičić discontinuity, after a Croatian scientist. In the 1960s, an attempt was made to drill through the ocean crust to take samples of the mantle. The 'Mohole' project was abandoned because of increasing costs.

Oceanic crust

Continental crust

Enlarged section of lithosphere

Lithosphere

Asthenosphere

Outer core

Mantle

Inner core

Crust

Mantle

Crust

MAGNETIC ATTRACTION

The Earth's magnetic field extends far into space. The Sun showers the Earth with charged atomic particles – the solar wind – which are affected by the Earth's magnetic field (magnetosphere). In places where the magnetosphere is dense, the atomic particles are trapped in two layers around the Earth. These layers are called the Van Allen belts.

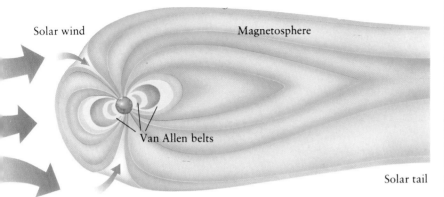

Solar wind

Magnetosphere

Van Allen belts

Solar tail

Solar wind

Earth's magnetic field

Lines of force

◄ The Earth is magnetic and behaves rather like a bar magnet with a magnetic field. The Earth's magnetic poles and the geographic poles do not exactly coincide.

THE EARTH'S MAGNETISM

Homing pigeon

Magnetism is a property of materials such as iron, and of electric currents, in which moving charged particles develop a force of attraction. The Earth is magnetic and has magnetic poles and a magnetic field. If a magnetized needle is floated in a bowl of water it will align itself with the Earth's magnetic poles. This is a simple compass and can be used for navigation, although the difference between the geographic poles and the magnetic poles (magnetic variation) must be taken into account. Magnetic variation changes over time. It appears that the magnetic poles are 'wandering', but it is actually the continents that are moving over them.

Some animals, such as pigeons, have been shown to use the Earth's magnetic field to navigate. If they are released in areas where there is some kind of magnetic disturbance, homing pigeons seem to lose their way.

Magnetic compass

◄ The aurora australis or the southern lights, is a 'curtain' of spectacular lights in the sky. They are caused by the collision of the solar wind with the Earth's atmosphere. The aurora borealis occurs at the North Pole.

THE CORE AND MANTLE

Lying beneath the Earth's crust, the mantle is about 2800 km thick. It is made up of dark rock. The central zone of the Earth is called the core. It is divided into inner and outer zones. The inner core is solid, but the outer core is liquid. Both are dense and hot, and consist mainly of nickel and iron.

THE CRUST

These are the main elements that make up the crust:

Oxygen	Calcium
Silicon	Sodium
Aluminium	Potassium
Iron	Magnesium

Land, Water and Air

The elements that make up the land, water and air of Earth are constantly being recycled as they combine, break up and recombine. For example, the air around Earth is unstable. It is too rich in the reactive gases oxygen, nitrogen and methane, and too poor in carbon dioxide to be in balance chemically. But Earth's air is ideal for life. The British scientist, James Lovelock, has developed the Gaia hypothesis, in which he suggests that it is life itself which maintains the conditions that it needs.

THE WATER CYCLE

Almost 80 percent of the rain that falls goes into the oceans, the rest falls on to land. When the Sun's rays heat the Earth's surface, water evaporates back into the atmosphere. Over 80 percent of it evaporates from the oceans. Some of the rest is returned to the atmosphere by transpiration from plants. As the water in the atmosphere cools, it condenses to form clouds. Some of this water falls to Earth again as rain.

Water vapour condenses and forms clouds

Rain and sn

Transpiration from plants

Water vapour in atmosphere

Evaporation from seas and lakes

Rivers flow back to oceans

Water vapour cools and forms rain

Groundwater runs off

Water vapour 0.05%

Moisture in soil 0.2%

Rivers and lakes 0.35%

Salt water lakes and inland seas 0.4%

▲ *The world's water is constantly being recycled. If the process of evaporation from the oceans and the ground, and transpiration from the Earth's plants suddenly stopped, there would be enough rain held in the atmosphere to last for 10 days.*

▶ *Most of the world's water is found in the oceans. Of the 3 percent of water that is not in the sea, over 75 percent is locked up in the ice caps and glaciers of the Arctic and Antarctic.*

Fresh water 3%

Groundwater 22%

Ice sheets and glaciers 77%

Seawater 97%

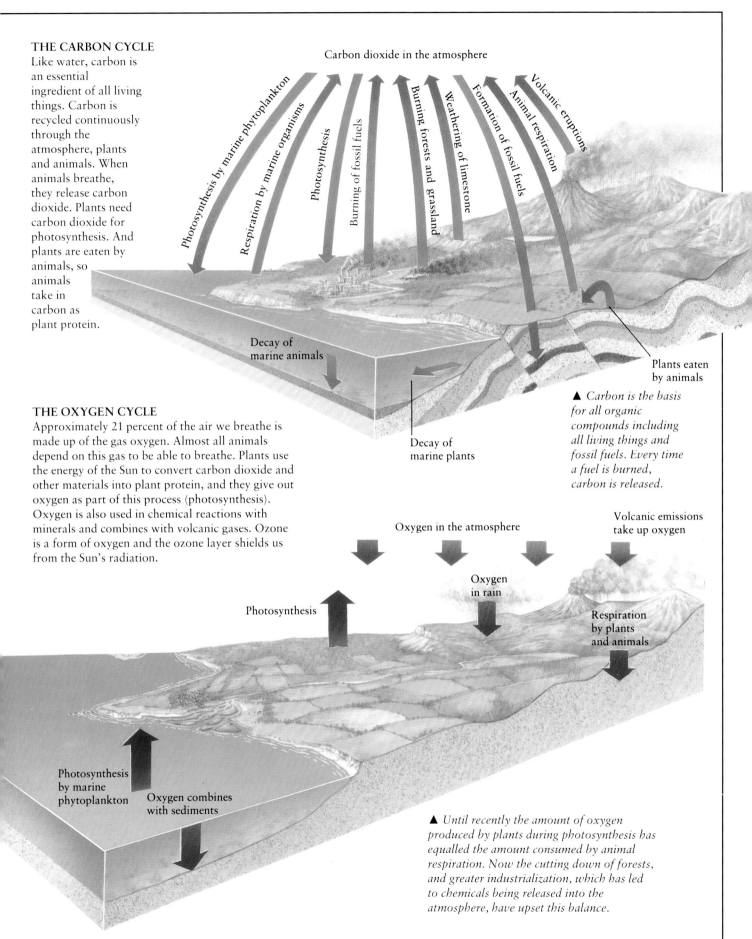

THE CARBON CYCLE

Like water, carbon is an essential ingredient of all living things. Carbon is recycled continuously through the atmosphere, plants and animals. When animals breathe, they release carbon dioxide. Plants need carbon dioxide for photosynthesis. And plants are eaten by animals, so animals take in carbon as plant protein.

Carbon dioxide in the atmosphere

Photosynthesis by marine phytoplankton

Respiration by marine organisms

Photosynthesis

Burning of fossil fuels

Burning forests and grassland

Weathering of limestone

Formation of fossil fuels

Animal respiration

Volcanic eruptions

Decay of marine animals

Decay of marine plants

Plants eaten by animals

▲ *Carbon is the basis for all organic compounds including all living things and fossil fuels. Every time a fuel is burned, carbon is released.*

THE OXYGEN CYCLE

Approximately 21 percent of the air we breathe is made up of the gas oxygen. Almost all animals depend on this gas to be able to breathe. Plants use the energy of the Sun to convert carbon dioxide and other materials into plant protein, and they give out oxygen as part of this process (photosynthesis). Oxygen is also used in chemical reactions with minerals and combines with volcanic gases. Ozone is a form of oxygen and the ozone layer shields us from the Sun's radiation.

Oxygen in the atmosphere

Volcanic emissions take up oxygen

Oxygen in rain

Photosynthesis

Respiration by plants and animals

Photosynthesis by marine phytoplankton

Oxygen combines with sediments

▲ *Until recently the amount of oxygen produced by plants during photosynthesis has equalled the amount consumed by animal respiration. Now the cutting down of forests, and greater industrialization, which has led to chemicals being released into the atmosphere, have upset this balance.*

THE LAND

Earthquakes

Earthquakes are among the most serious natural disasters: the ground shakes, and may crack; poorly constructed buildings collapse; dams are destroyed; huge ocean waves flood the land; gas mains rupture; and fires break out. Many hundreds or even thousands of people may be killed or left homeless as a result.

Earthquakes occur because within the Earth's asthenosphere, stress causes the semi-plastic rocks to move very slowly. This builds up strain within the more brittle rocks of the lithosphere above. Eventually, the brittle rocks break and the stress is released as shock waves. Earthquakes can take place at depths of up to 720km. But those that have effects at the surface usually occur no deeper than 70km. Every year there are about 1000 earthquakes around the world that are strong enough to cause some damage.

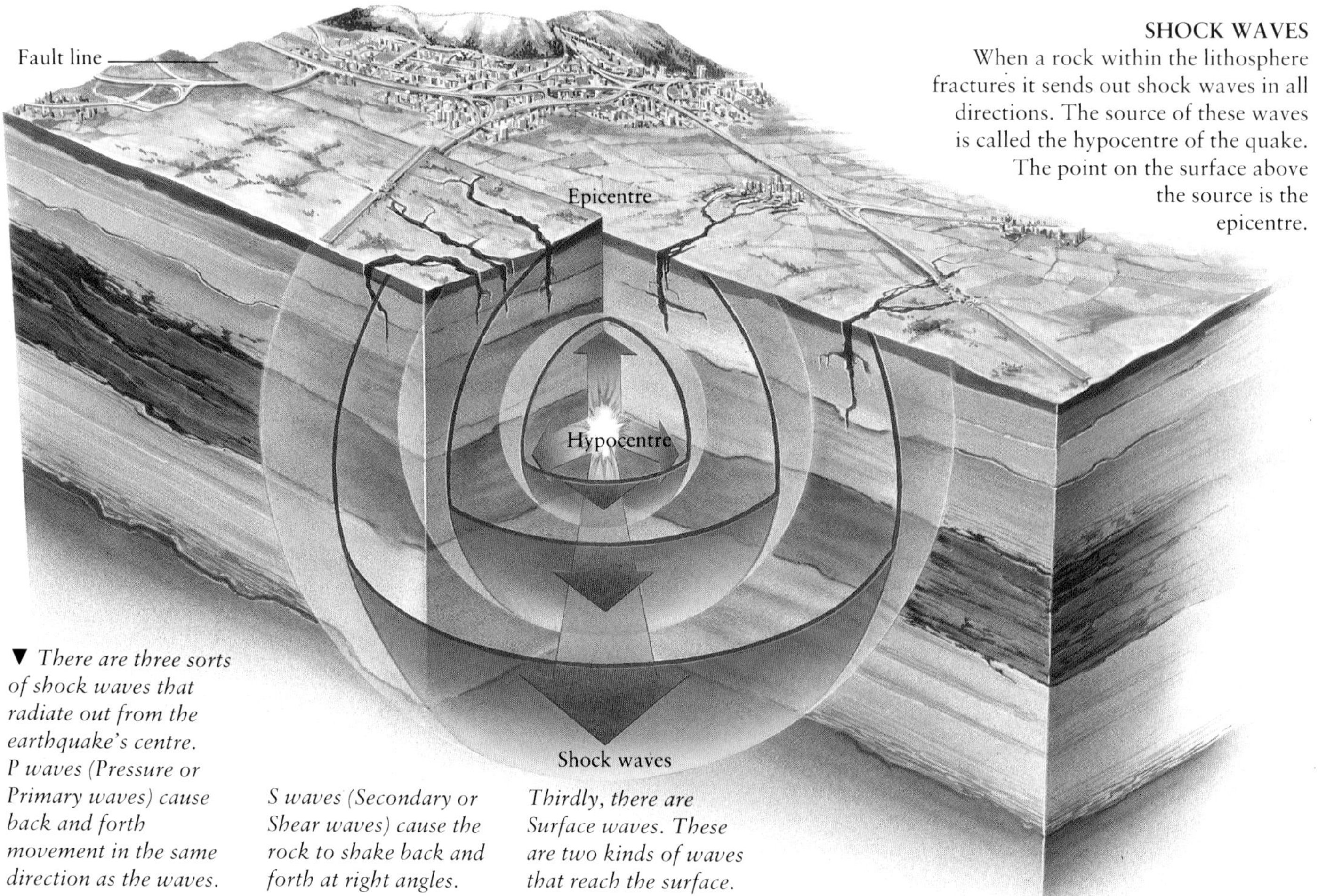

SHOCK WAVES

When a rock within the lithosphere fractures it sends out shock waves in all directions. The source of these waves is called the hypocentre of the quake. The point on the surface above the source is the epicentre.

Fault line

Epicentre

Hypocentre

Shock waves

▼ There are three sorts of shock waves that radiate out from the earthquake's centre. P waves (Pressure or Primary waves) cause back and forth movement in the same direction as the waves.

S waves (Secondary or Shear waves) cause the rock to shake back and forth at right angles.

Thirdly, there are Surface waves. These are two kinds of waves that reach the surface.

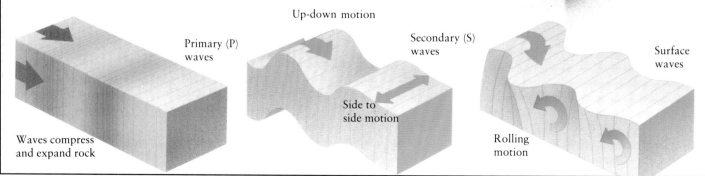

Up-down motion

Primary (P) waves

Secondary (S) waves

Surface waves

Side to side motion

Waves compress and expand rock

Rolling motion

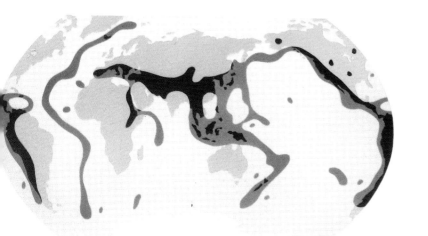

EARTHQUAKE ZONES

Scientists continuously monitor earthquakes, and plot the sites of major quakes on a map. A distinct pattern has emerged showing that, with a few exceptions, earthquakes take place in a number of definite zones. Earthquakes happen where there are deep trenches in the ocean bed with groups of islands nearby, such as around the Pacific.

In earthquake areas, seismologists try to work out whether stress is building up in the rocks. If the area is quiet for a long time, it may be that stress is building up and may eventually cause a major earthquake. Seismologists can also use one or more seismometers to detect the tiny shock waves that occur before an earthquake.

 Earthquake zones

FACTS ABOUT EARTHQUAKES

- The strongest earthquake ever recorded took place at Lebu on the west coast of Chile in South America, on 22 May 1960. It measured 8.3 on the Richter scale.
- Historical records indicate that in July of the year 1201, more than a million people were killed during an earthquake which affected the eastern Mediterranean area.
- The highest tsunami ever recorded hit the island of Ishigaki to the west of Taiwan in April 1771. It is thought to have reached a height of 85 m.
- In 1750 an earthquake caused widespread panic and confusion in London, a city where earthquakes are virtually unknown.
- The costliest earthquake in terms of property damage destroyed 570,000 buildings on the Kwanto plain, Japan, 1923.

Trans-America Pyramid, San Francisco, USA

▲ When an earthquake takes place under the sea bed, it may produce a wave in the sea. In the open ocean the wave may hardly be noticed. But if it reaches shallow water near a coast, the wave may rise to heights of 30 m or more. These giant waves are called tsunamis.

EARTHQUAKE SCALES

The intensity of earthquakes is measured on two scales. The Mercalli scale, based on observable effects, ranges from 'not felt' at 1 to 'total devastation' at scale 12. The Richter scale is based on the size of the shock waves produced.

Mercalli and Richter Scales

1	<3	Very slight: detected by instruments only
2	3–3.4	Feeble: felt by people resting
3	3.5–4	Slight: like heavy lorries passing
4	4.1–4.4	Moderate: windows rattle
5	4.5–4.8	Rather strong: wakes sleeping people
6	4.9–5.4	Strong: trees sway, walls crack
7	5.5–6	Very strong: people fall over, buildings crack
8	6.1–6.5	Destructive: chimneys fall, buildings move
9	6.6–7	Ruinous: heavy damage to buildings, ground cracks
10	7.1–7.3	Disastrous: most buildings destroyed, landslides
11	7.4–8.1	Very disastrous: railways and pipelines break
12	>8.1	Catastrophic: total devastation

EARTHQUAKE DAMAGE

If a large earthquake occurs where people live then there may be casualties as buildings collapse. Fire has always been a hazard, originally as buildings fell on domestic fires and burned, and now as gas mains break and catch fire.

▲ In 1906, the San Andreas fault moved 6.5 m, causing an earthquake that destroyed San Francisco, USA. Much of the city burned down as the gas mains broke and caught fire.

PREVENTING COLLAPSE

When an earthquake strikes, badly built houses collapse. It is, however, possible to construct buildings, even skyscrapers, that will resist collapse. Earthquake-proof buildings must have their foundations built into the solid rock, and they must be able to bend without shattering.

Volcanoes

A volcano is any kind of natural opening, or fissure, in the Earth's crust through which hot molten rock (called lava), ash, steam, gas and other material is spewed. The heat comes from within the Earth's mantle. The word 'volcano' (after Vulcan, the Roman god of fire and metalworking) is also used to describe the cone of lava and ash that builds up around the opening. The shape depends on the type of eruption. Volcanic activity may take place under the sea as well as on land, and sometimes creates new land.

▶ *Sometimes, a volcano may explode very violently, emptying the lava chamber that feeds it. The roof and walls may then collapse, leaving a hole called a caldera.*

Ash and smoke

TYPES OF VOLCANOES

Peléan eruption

Hawaiian eruption

▲ *Mount Pelé is a volcano on Martinique, West Indies. In an explosive Peléan eruption the lava is thick and the volcano gives out glowing, gas-charged clouds.*

▲ *The cones created by a Hawaiian eruption are big at the bottom and slope gently because the lava, which pours out in fountains, is quite runny.*

Strombolian eruption

Plinian eruption

▲ *Stromboli is an active volcano on an island north of Sicily. A Strombolian eruption occurs regularly, but with small explosions.*

Vulcanian eruption

▲ *Pliny the Elder died in AD 79 when Vesuvius erupted and the Roman city of Pompeii was destroyed. A Plinian eruption is explosive with great clouds of ash and volcanic rock, or pumice. A vulcanian eruption (left), after Vulcano, near Stromboli, is characterized by rare explosions of almost solid magma thrown long distances.*

INSIDE A VOLCANO

A typical volcano, with a crater and a cone of solidified lava and ash, is called a central type. The activity takes place in a chimney-like 'pipe' or vent through which the material erupts. Far below the vent is a chamber of molten rock (magma) containing dissolved gases. Gas bubbling out of the magma keeps the vent open. Sometimes, lava and other material may break through further down the sides of the volcano and a secondary or parasite core is formed.

Caldera

Lava flow

FAMOUS ERUPTIONS

Eruptions occur when the pressure in the chamber and vent has built up and the material breaks through.

Mt Etna, Sicily, 1669

Mt St Helens, USA, 1980

Taupa, New Zealand AD 130

Vesuvius, Italy AD 79

Cotopaxi, Ecuador, 1877

Mauna Loa, Hawaii, 1872

► *The zone of volcanoes that surround the Pacific Ocean is known as the circum-Pacific 'ring of fire'. Earthquakes also occur in this region.*

▼ *A geyser is an opening in the Earth which, from time to time, shoots a fountain of boiling water high into the air. The water at the bottom of the geyser boils before that at the top.*

Geyser

▼ *When a volcanic opening gives out only gas and steam, it is known as a fumarole.*

Volcanic cone

Fumarole

Layers of ash and lava

Central vent

Side vent

Magma chamber

◄ *The Hawaiian islands formed over a hot spot. Forty million years ago the plate turned, bending the island chain.*

Movement of plate

Island chain

Hot spot

HOT SPOTS

These are areas of volcanic activity on the Earth's crust which are not always on the edge of a crustal plate (*see pages 108–109*). As the plate drifts over the hot spot, semi-liquid rock (magma) in the mantle rises as it is heated from below and volcanic activity takes place. The volcano may form an island. Volcanic activity on the island decreases as it moves away from the hot spot.

BEST DOCUMENTED EXPLOSION

Mount St Helens is a volcanic cone in Washington State, in northwestern United States. In May 1980 the volcano exploded, hurling hot ash, rocks, gas and steam high into the air, and leaving the mountain 400 m lower. Following the main eruption, there were more blasts of steam and hot gas which destroyed millions of trees up to 30 km away. Many animals choked to death but only a few people died because scientists had predicted the eruption and the area had been evacuated. Later, ash from the volcano was found as far south as Colorado.

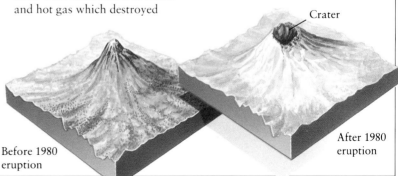

Crater

Before 1980 eruption

After 1980 eruption

Krakatau, Indonesia, 1883

Santorini, Aegean Sea, 1628 BC

Tamboro, Indonesia, 1815

Drifting Continents

The coastlines of eastern South America and West Africa could fit together like pieces in a jigsaw. This match was noticed in the 17th century. However, it was not until 1912 that Alfred Wegener proposed that all the land masses of the world had originally formed one super-continent, which he called Pangaea. This could not be explained until the early 1960s, when scientists discovered that the rocky plates of the Earth's lithosphere were moving, floating on the more mobile rock below.

▶ *As well as the matching coastlines, there is other evidence that there was once a single continent. There are remains of an ancient mountain belt, between 470 and 350 million years old, which are now separated by the Atlantic ocean. These mountains were created by what was a continuous belt of geological activity.*

Africa

South America

India

Antarctica

Australia

Fold mountains

EVOLVING EARTH

The supercontinent, Pangaea is thought to have evolved some 280 million years ago, at the end of the Carboniferous Period. By mid-Jurassic times, 150 million years ago, Pangaea had split into a northern continent, Laurasia, and a southern continent, Gondwanaland. By the end of the Cretaceous, about 65 million years ago, Gondwanaland was breaking up, although North America had not yet split from Eurasia.

300 million years ago

▶ *Two hundred million years ago Pangaea may have looked like this.*

200 million years ago

Tethys Ocean

Pangaea

65 million years ago

Laurasia

Tethys Ocean

Gondwanaland

PLANT AND ANIMAL DISTRIBUTION

Some fossils also tell us that the continents were once joined. For example, fossils of the plant *Glossopteris* and the animals *Mesosaurus* and *Lystrosaurus* have all been found in the southern continents which are now widely separated.

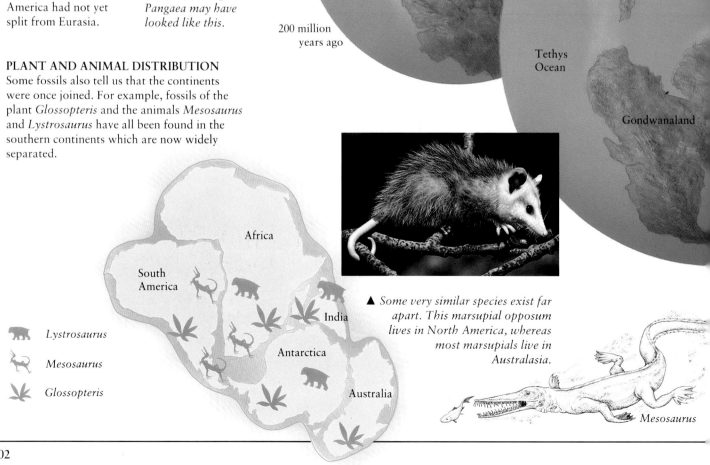

Africa

South America

India

Antarctica

Australia

🐾 *Lystrosaurus*

🦌 *Mesosaurus*

🌿 *Glossopteris*

▲ *Some very similar species exist far apart. This marsupial opposum lives in North America, whereas most marsupials live in Australasia.*

Mesosaurus

TODAY

The present distribution of the continents has taken place in the last 65 million years. Today, the drift still continues. The Atlantic Ocean is getting wider by several centimetres a year, the Pacific Ocean is getting smaller, and the Red Sea is part of a crack in the crust that will widen to produce a new ocean millions of years in the future.

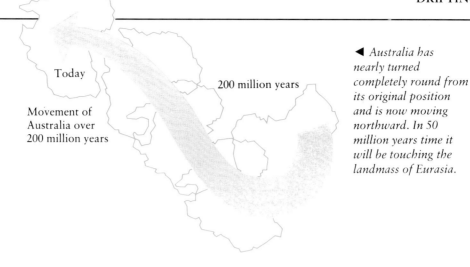

Today

Movement of Australia over 200 million years

200 million years

◀ *Australia has nearly turned completely round from its original position and is now moving northward. In 50 million years time it will be touching the landmass of Eurasia.*

Today

▼ *The world begins to look more familiar 65 million years ago. The widening South Atlantic Ocean has separated Africa and South America, and Madagascar has split from Africa, but Australia and Antarctica are still joined.*

25 million years ago

North America

Eurasia

Africa

South America

ALFRED WEGENER (1880–1930)

Alfred Wegener was born in Berlin, in Germany. He studied meteorology at the Universities of Heidelberg, Innsbruck in Austria, and in Berlin. In 1924 he returned to Graz, in Austria, to become professor of meteorology and geophysics.

In 1910 the American scientist F. B. Taylor put forward the idea that whole continents could have drifted across the surface of the planet. This theory was taken up in 1911 by H. B. Baker and then by Wegener in 1912 who developed his theory of continental drift, known as the Wegener hypothesis. He published *Origins of Continents and Oceans* in which he explained his ideas. Wegener also suggested that with the shifting land masses, the magnetic poles moved about. He died in Greenland on his fourth expedition there.

Plate Tectonics

The word 'tectonics' comes from the Greek *tekton*, meaning 'builder'. The theory suggests that the surface of the Earth is made up of rigid plates of lithosphere which 'float' on the more mobile asthenosphere. Owing to movements in the asthenosphere, the plates are in constant motion. It explains many of the major processes of the Earth, such as the drifting of continents, mountain building, and earthquake and volcanic activity. Much of this activity occurs at the edges, or margins, of the plates.

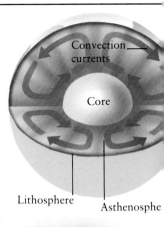

▶ *Movements of the plates of lithosphere may be driven by convection currents in the asthenosphere. Hot currents rise, then cool as they reach the surface. At the same time, cooler currents sink down. This movement carries the crustal plates.*

SEA-FLOOR SPREADING

Down the middle of the Atlantic Ocean floor is a ridge where volcanic activity takes place. This ridge marks a plate margin. Along the ridge are cracks where molten rocks push up to form new crust. The crust spreads away from the ridge, and the ocean basin widens.

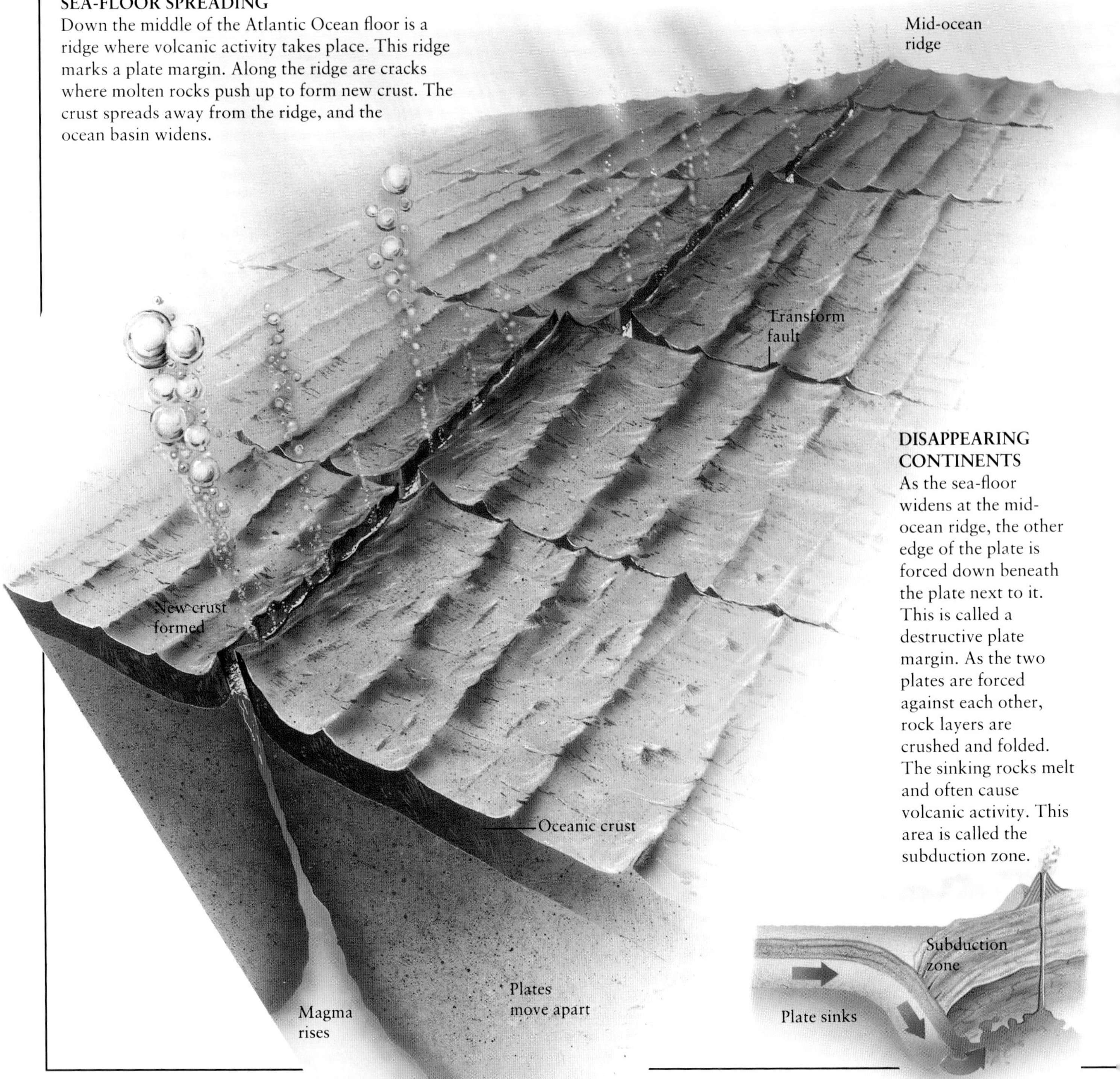

Mid-ocean ridge

Transform fault

New crust formed

Oceanic crust

DISAPPEARING CONTINENTS

As the sea-floor widens at the mid-ocean ridge, the other edge of the plate is forced down beneath the plate next to it. This is called a destructive plate margin. As the two plates are forced against each other, rock layers are crushed and folded. The sinking rocks melt and often cause volcanic activity. This area is called the subduction zone.

Magma rises

Plates move apart

Subduction zone

Plate sinks

ICELAND

Iceland is situated on the mid-Atlantic ridge between Greenland and Scandinavia. It was formed from eruptions from the ridge and is still getting wider by 2.5 cm a year. This activity means that it is a volcanic island, with geysers and hot springs.

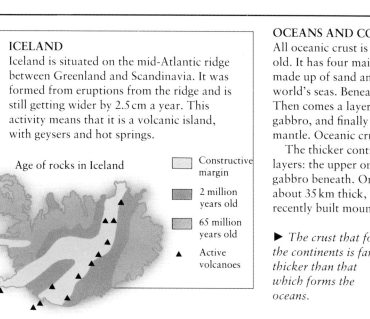

Age of rocks in Iceland

- Constructive margin
- 2 million years old
- 65 million years old
- ▲ Active volcanoes

OCEANS AND CONTINENTS

All oceanic crust is less than 200 million years old. It has four main layers. The top layer is made up of sand and mud laid down in the world's seas. Beneath it is a layer of basalt. Then comes a layer of another dark rock called gabbro, and finally a thin layer above the mantle. Oceanic crust is about 11 km thick.

The thicker continental crust has only two layers: the upper one is mainly granite, with gabbro beneath. On average, continental crust is about 35 km thick, but may be 50 km thick under recently built mountains.

▶ *The crust that forms the continents is far thicker than that which forms the oceans.*

Andes Mountains

Montana, USA

Continental crust

Oceanic crust

NORTH AMERICAN PLATE

EURASIAN PLATE

Japan Trench

Mid-Atlantic Ridge

COCOS PLATE

CARIBBEAN PLATE

AFRICAN PLATE

PACIFIC PLATE

SOUTH AMERICAN PLATE

Java Trench

NAZCA PLATE

East Pacific Rise

Mid Indian Ridge

INDO-AUSTRALIAN PLATE

ANTARCTIC PLATE

- – – Plate margin
- —— Transform faults

◀ *The Earth's crust is made up of eight main plates and several smaller ones. The edges of these plates are marked by ridges and trenches. New crust is formed at the ridges and destroyed at the trenches. Large faults, known as transform faults, occur at right-angles to the mid-oceanic ridges. As new crust is created in the mid-Atlantic, the North American and South American plates are moving westwards. India continues to move northwards, and the Himalayas get higher as it collides with the Eurasian plate, which is travelling eastwards. The African plate continues its drift to the northwest as the Red Sea opens up.*

▶ *Running from the northeast of Scotland to the southwest, a series of lochs follows the line of the Great Glen. This valley is a good example of a tear fault (see page 108).*
Some 400 million years ago, the land north of the fault slid southwest by 100 km.

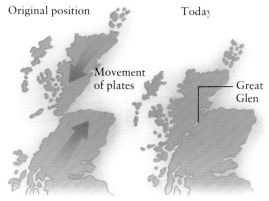

Original position

Today

Movement of plates

Great Glen

FACTS ABOUT PLATE TECTONICS

- When lavas cool and harden into rock, some minerals are magnetized in the direction of the Earth's magnetic poles at that time. About every 400,000–500,000 years, the Earth's magnetic poles reverse.
- By measuring the ages and magnetism of rocks on either side of the mid-Atlantic ridge, geologists have proved that the Atlantic is widening.
- The Atlantic widens by 1–5 cm a year.
- It has taken about 200 million years to separate South America from Africa and create the Atlantic Ocean, and about 40 million years for Australia and the Antarctic to move apart to their present positions.

Mountains

A mountain is an area of high ground which is higher (over 300 m) than a hill. A group of mountains is called a range. The greatest mountain ranges are the European Alps, the Andes of South America, the Rockies of North America, and – the highest of all – the Himalayas of Asia. It takes millions of years for mountains to be formed. The process is going on continuously as sections of the Earth's crust are thrust, folded and broken, pushing up rocks to make new mountains.

HOW MOUNTAINS ARE FORMED

The surface of the Earth is made up of giant slow-moving plates of crust and mantle. Where two continental plates collide, a mountain belt is thrust slowly upwards. The sediments of the ocean floor are squeezed into folds, which may be thousands of metres high. The folds may then be overturned, one on top of the other. Beneath the chain of mountains is a thick layer of continental crust.

THE HIMALAYAS

The high mountains of the Himalayas mark a region of the Earth's crust where two continental plates are colliding. The Indo-Australian plate is pushing north into the Eurasian plate. Eventually the two continents will become locked together.

Eurasian Plate

Tethys Ocean

Indo-Australian Plate

Ocean floor

Oceanic crust

Movement of plate

Continental crust

India

Himalayas

Today

65 million years ago

135 million years ago

▼ *About 45 million years ago, India and Eurasia crashed. Continental crust is light so it was thrust up into complex folds to form mountains. All the sediments that were laid down in the ocean also buckled and folded.*

Himalayas

Folded and uplifted ocean floor

Ocean closes over

Ocean floor is compressed

◀ *Running across the Tethys Ocean was a deep trench. As India and the Eurasian plate drifted closer, the crust under the ocean was dragged downwards along the trench and the ocean sediments built up at the edge of the plate. The Tethys Ocean gradually closed up.*

◀ *Debris worn from the land was deposited in the Tethys Ocean as thick layers of sediment. The northward movement of the plate pushed forward the ocean floor, up and over the scrunched edge of the Eurasian plate.*

◀ *After Pangaea broke up about 200 million years ago, the Indo-Australian plate began to move north. Around 45 million years ago it smashed into the larger, heavier Eusasian plate pushing up the Himalaya Mountains.*

MOUNTAIN ROOTS

The Earth's crust is thought to 'float' on denser material beneath. It has been shown that mountains have roots that support them. Like an iceberg, much of it is hidden below the surface.

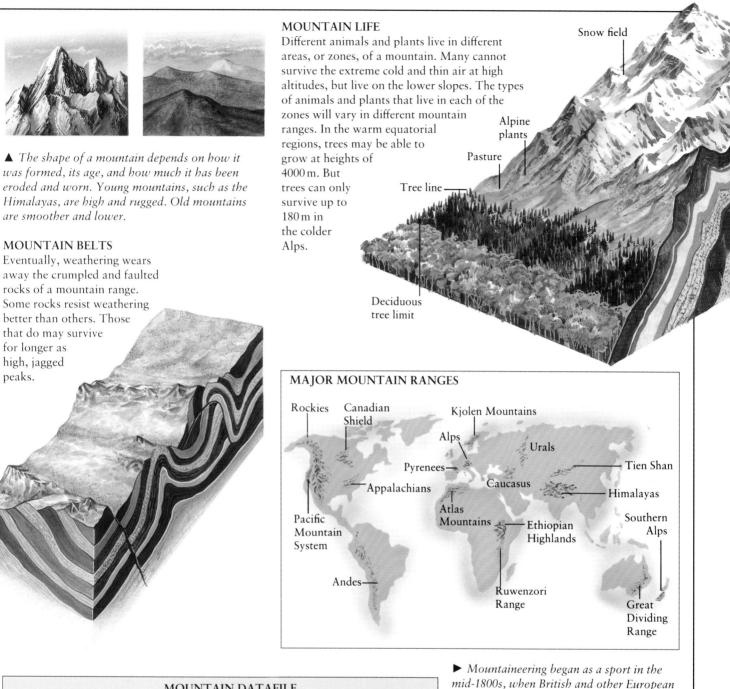

▲ *The shape of a mountain depends on how it was formed, its age, and how much it has been eroded and worn. Young mountains, such as the Himalayas, are high and rugged. Old mountains are smoother and lower.*

MOUNTAIN BELTS

Eventually, weathering wears away the crumpled and faulted rocks of a mountain range. Some rocks resist weathering better than others. Those that do may survive for longer as high, jagged peaks.

MOUNTAIN LIFE

Different animals and plants live in different areas, or zones, of a mountain. Many cannot survive the extreme cold and thin air at high altitudes, but live on the lower slopes. The types of animals and plants that live in each of the zones will vary in different mountain ranges. In the warm equatorial regions, trees may be able to grow at heights of 4000 m. But trees can only survive up to 180 m in the colder Alps.

Snow field

Alpine plants

Pasture

Tree line

Deciduous tree limit

MAJOR MOUNTAIN RANGES

Rockies

Canadian Shield

Kjolen Mountains

Alps

Urals

Pyrenees

Tien Shan

Appalachians

Caucasus

Himalayas

Pacific Mountain System

Atlas Mountains

Ethiopian Highlands

Southern Alps

Andes

Ruwenzori Range

Great Dividing Range

MOUNTAIN DATAFILE

The world's highest peaks (14 over 8000 metres) are in the Himalaya-Karakoram ranges.

Top 5 in Asia
1 Mount Everest 8848 m
2 Godwin-Austin (K2) 8610 m
3 Kanchenjunga 8598 m
4 Makalu 8480 m
5 Dhaulagiri 8169 m

Highest in other continents
6 Aconcagua (South America) 6960 m
7 McKinley (North America) 6194 m
8 Kilimanjaro (Africa) 5895 m
9 Elbrus (Europe) 5633 m
10 Vinson Massif 5140 m (Antarctica)
11 Mt Wilhelm (Oceania) 4509 m

▶ *Mountaineering began as a sport in the mid-1800s, when British and other European climbers tried to scale the peaks of the Alps. On 29 May 1953, mountaineering history was made when the New Zealander, Edmund Hillary (1919–), and his Sherpa guide, Tenzing Norgay (1914–86), reached the summit of Mount Everest, the world's highest peak. In 1975, the Japanese climber Junko Tabei (1939–) became the first woman to climb Everest.*

Bending and Breaking

If you hit a rock hard enough with a hammer, it will break. It is harder to imagine rocks bending. But when movements in the Earth cause stress to build up over a long period of time, the layers of rock may break or bend. A break in the rocks is known as a fault. When rock layers bend into waves, or sometimes overturn until they are upside-down, they are said to have folded. There are different kinds of folds and faults, depending on the type of rock, and the force that has pushed or pulled it.

FOLDS BEFORE FAULTS

If you take several layers of paper, hold them by the edges and then push, they will bend into a dome. If you try the same experiment with some cardboard, it will probably not bend as easily, and may break. Rocks can behave more like the paper than the cardboard. When they are pushed or pulled, they may recover if the stress is removed. But if the rock is brittle and it is deformed too much it will break. It will bend if it is more elastic.

THE PARTS OF A FAULT

The angle made by the fault and the horizontal is called the dip. If the angle is measured from the vertical it is called the hade. The relative movements of the blocks of rock on either side of the fault are known as its slip; the vertical movement when the blocks have slipped up or down the dip, as the throw.

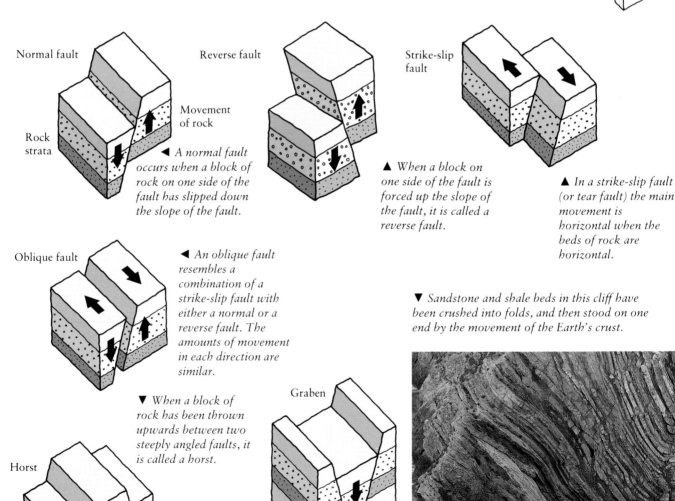

Normal fault

Reverse fault

Strike-slip fault

Rock strata

Movement of rock

◀ *A normal fault occurs when a block of rock on one side of the fault has slipped down the slope of the fault.*

▲ *When a block on one side of the fault is forced up the slope of the fault, it is called a reverse fault.*

▲ *In a strike-slip fault (or tear fault) the main movement is horizontal when the beds of rock are horizontal.*

Oblique fault

◀ *An oblique fault resembles a combination of a strike-slip fault with either a normal or a reverse fault. The amounts of movement in each direction are similar.*

▼ *When a block of rock has been thrown upwards between two steeply angled faults, it is called a horst.*

Graben

Horst

▼ *Sandstone and shale beds in this cliff have been crushed into folds, and then stood on one end by the movement of the Earth's crust.*

▲ *A graben is a down-thrown block of rock between two steeply angled normal faults.*

THE GREAT RIFT VALLEY

When a graben occurs on a very large scale, it is called a rift valley. Such valleys are usually quite straight and may be hundreds of kilometres long. The Great Rift Valley stretches from Turkey to Mozambique. In East Africa it divides in two, with the north-eastern rift running from Ethiopia to Zambia. The south-western rift curves through Uganda and Tanzania and contains some of the great East African lakes.

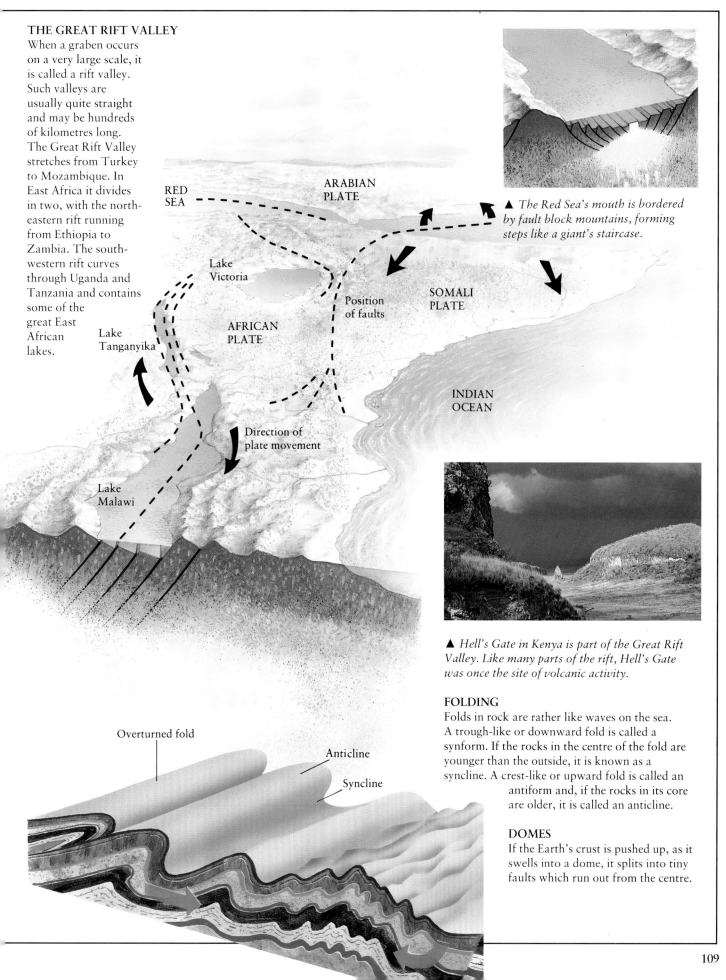

ARABIAN PLATE

RED SEA

Lake Victoria

Position of faults

SOMALI PLATE

AFRICAN PLATE

Lake Tanganyika

INDIAN OCEAN

Lake Malawi

Direction of plate movement

▲ *The Red Sea's mouth is bordered by fault block mountains, forming steps like a giant's staircase.*

▲ *Hell's Gate in Kenya is part of the Great Rift Valley. Like many parts of the rift, Hell's Gate was once the site of volcanic activity.*

FOLDING

Folds in rock are rather like waves on the sea. A trough-like or downward fold is called a synform. If the rocks in the centre of the fold are younger than the outside, it is known as a syncline. A crest-like or upward fold is called an antiform and, if the rocks in its core are older, it is called an anticline.

DOMES

If the Earth's crust is pushed up, as it swells into a dome, it splits into tiny faults which run out from the centre.

Overturned fold

Anticline

Syncline

Rocks

Granite, sandstone, chalk, marble and slate are all different types of rock. The pebbles you find on the beach are rocks that have been worn down and smoothed by the action of the sea. The stones that are used to build structures from small cottages to magnificent cathedrals are rocks. Not all rocks are hard; clay is a type of rock, but is quite soft. Petrologists (scientists who study rocks) might define a rock as any natural mass of mineral matter that makes up the Earth's crust.

IGNEOUS ROCKS

Granite is coarse-grained because it has cooled slowly. Syenite is similar to granite but less common. Basalt is fine-grained, almost black and has cooled quickly.

Granite

Basalt

Syenite

HOW ROCKS ARE FORMED

There are three main groups of rocks. Igneous rocks are formed from lava hurled out of a volcano, or from hot magma forced up through the ground. Sedimentary rocks are made from sediments formed by the erosion and weathering of other rocks. The sediments are carried by wind or water to the sea, where they are deposited and harden to rock. Metamorphic rocks are rocks that have been changed by heat and/or pressure.

Sedimentary rocks

Limestone

SEDIMENTARY ROCKS

Sandstone is made from grains of sand which have been naturally cemented together. The red rock of Devon, England is a typical sandstone. Chalk is made up of millions of tiny calcium carbonate (lime) skeletons.

Chalk

Sandstone

GEOLOGICAL TIMESCALE

For the last 150 years, scientists have been working out the ages of rocks. Unless they have been overturned, the oldest rocks are deeper than younger ones. Rocks can be related to a scale of different ages.

Millions of years ago

	4600	570	505	440	410	360
Period		Precambrian	Cambrian	Ordovician	Silurian	Devonian
Era						PALAEOZOIC

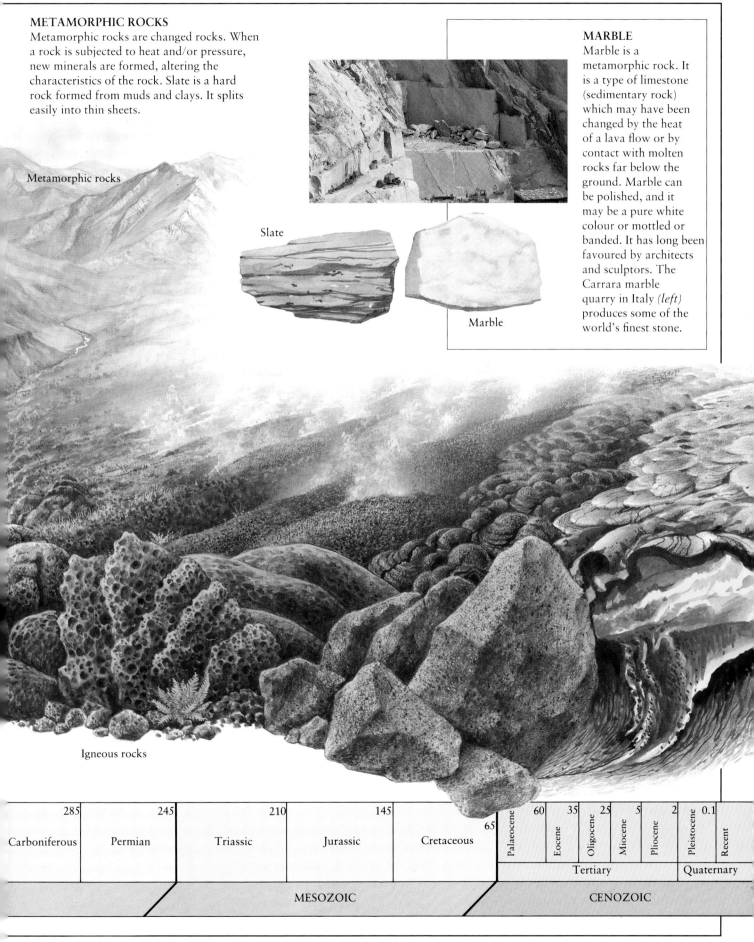

METAMORPHIC ROCKS
Metamorphic rocks are changed rocks. When a rock is subjected to heat and/or pressure, new minerals are formed, altering the characteristics of the rock. Slate is a hard rock formed from muds and clays. It splits easily into thin sheets.

Metamorphic rocks

Slate

Marble

MARBLE
Marble is a metamorphic rock. It is a type of limestone (sedimentary rock) which may have been changed by the heat of a lava flow or by contact with molten rocks far below the ground. Marble can be polished, and it may be a pure white colour or mottled or banded. It has long been favoured by architects and sculptors. The Carrara marble quarry in Italy *(left)* produces some of the world's finest stone.

Igneous rocks

285	245	210	145		60	35	25	5	2	0.1	
Carboniferous	Permian	Triassic	Jurassic	Cretaceous	65	Palaeocene	Eocene	Oligocene	Miocene	Pliocene	Pleistocene	Recent
						Tertiary					Quaternary
		MESOZOIC				CENOZOIC					

Minerals and Gems

Minerals are the building blocks of rocks. All rocks, igneous, sedimentary or metamorphic, are composed of minerals. A mineral is a chemical compound that occurs naturally. Each different mineral is made up of crystals of a particular chemical. Minerals can be identified by their hardness, colour, the way they reflect light, the way they break, and their density. Sometimes, using a hand lens, you can even identify the shape of the individual crystals of a mineral within a rock.

▲ *One of the commonest minerals is salt. Common salt is sodium chloride and occurs naturally in the sea. When an inland lake in a hot region evaporates, the salts are left behind as crystals, forming a salt-pan, or growing to form pillars such as these, in the Dead Sea.*

ROCK-FORMING MINERALS

Rocks are made up of mineral grains. The most common minerals making up igneous rocks include quartz, plagioclase and olivine. Augite is found in metamorphic rocks. Dolomite makes up limestone sedimentary rocks.

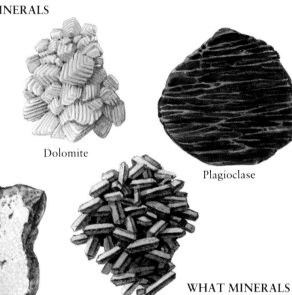

Dolomite

Plagioclase

Olivine

Augite

HOW MINERALS ARE FORMED

All minerals are originally formed from hot magma. When the magma cools, crystals of minerals appear. These first crystals may sink in the magma so that the composition of the magma changes with depth. Thus, a sequence of minerals is formed in the rocks as the magma cools.

WHAT MINERALS ARE MADE OF

About 90 different chemical elements are found naturally in the Earth's crust. But almost 99 percent of all minerals are made of just eight elements: oxygen, silicon, aluminium, iron, calcium, sodium, potassium and magnesium. Some minerals, such as gold and diamond, consist of a single element. These minerals are called native elements.

▶ *In areas of volcanic activity, hot water under pressure may force its way into cracks in the rocks. The water contains dissolved minerals. The minerals may crystallize on the sides of the crack forming a*

Opencast mine

Layers of rock

Lighter minerals form near the top

Igneous intrusion (magma)

vein. Important ore minerals (containing metals) are formed in this way.

FACTS ABOUT MINERALS AND GEMS

- There are at least 2000 minerals that have been named and identified. However, most rocks are made up of no more than 12 different classes of minerals – the rock-forming minerals.
- The most common element in the Earth's crust is oxygen, forming over 46 percent by weight. The second most common element is silicon at just over 27 percent by weight. Quartz is silicon dioxide. Quartz is a very common mineral.
- The largest diamond ever found was the Cullinan diamond, discovered in a mine in South Africa in 1905. It was 3106 carats, which means it weighed more than 600 g.
- The highest price ever paid for a diamond was more than £6 million.
- The largest cut emerald was 86,136 carats (well over 17 kg). It was found in Brazil and was valued in 1982 at £718,000.

CRYSTAL SYSTEMS

Cubic
(diamond)

Monoclinic (augite)

Hexagonal
(emerald)

Triclinic
(plagioclase)

Tetragonal
(zircon)

Orthorhombic
(olivine)

▲ *Many minerals form crystals. The shape of a crystal is determined by the arrangement of its atoms. A crystal has many flat faces. The angles between each face are characteristic of a given type of crystal. The whole crystal is symmetrical. On the basis of its symmetry, any crystal can be included within one of just six (sometimes seven) crystal systems.*

▼ *Most minerals are formed underground when heat and pressure transforms one form of rock into another. The minerals in molten rock or dissolved in very hot water crystallize out of solution as the temperature falls. Lighter minerals occur above denser minerals. If the crystals form slowly then gemstones may form.*

GEMSTONES

A gemstone is a mineral which is especially beautiful, and rare. Gems are formed under particular conditions of temperature and pressure, when the right minerals are present and crystals can form. These conditions are found deep in the Earth's crust. A gem may have a beautiful colour: deep green emeralds, or brilliant red rubies. Or its surface may show a rainbow of colours when it is moved, as in the case of opal.

Silver

Gold

▲ *Gold and silver are elements. Diamond and graphite are both forms of carbon but their atoms are arranged differently. Diamond is the hardest known naturally occurring substance. It may occur as gem-quality stones. Graphite is soft, black, and feels greasy.*

Diamond

Graphite

▼ *Under the sea, minerals dissolved in water crystallize around the vents of faults or fissures in the Earth's crust. They also precipitate (become solid) in the sea water above the sea floor.*

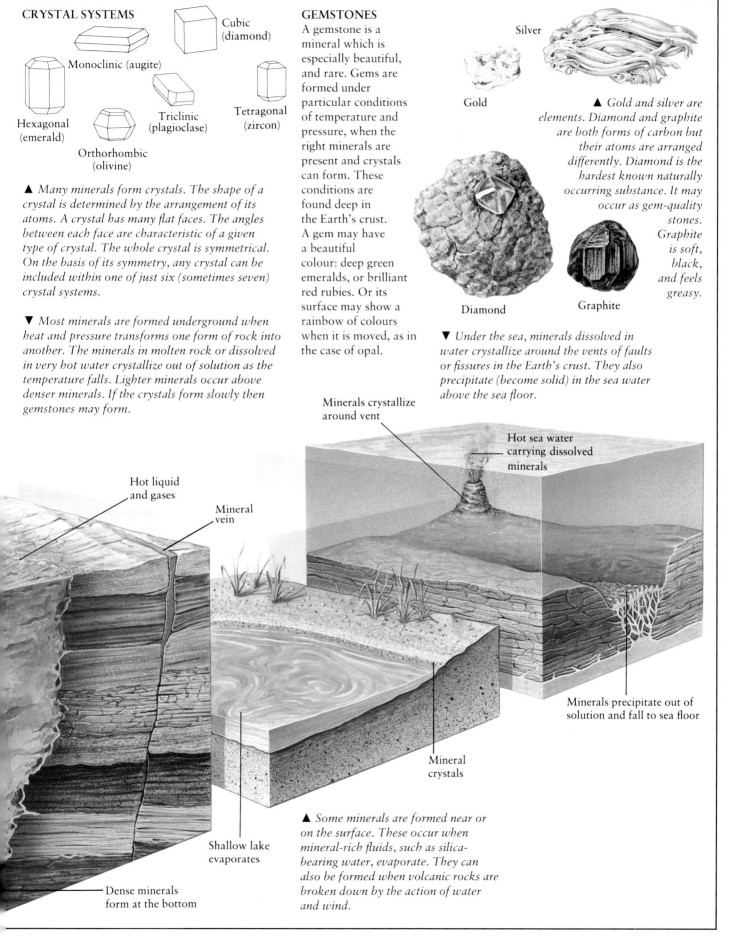

Minerals crystallize
around vent

Hot sea water
carrying dissolved
minerals

Hot liquid
and gases

Mineral
vein

Minerals precipitate out of
solution and fall to sea floor

Mineral
crystals

Shallow lake
evaporates

▲ *Some minerals are formed near or on the surface. These occur when mineral-rich fluids, such as silica-bearing water, evaporate. They can also be formed when volcanic rocks are broken down by the action of water and wind.*

Dense minerals
form at the bottom

Frozen in Time

The word fossil comes from the Latin, *fossilis*, meaning 'dug up'. Until the beginning of the 18th century, fossil meant anything that was dug out of the ground. Now we use the word to describe any remains of animals or plants that lived before about 10,000 years ago. The term is also used to describe the 'fossil fuels' – coal, oil and gas – because these fuels have been formed from the remains of ancient plants and animals. Fossils include skeletons, teeth, tracks, leaves and even plant pollen.

HOW FOSSILS ARE FORMED

Most fossils are found in sedimentary rocks, such as limestone or shale, which have been formed in the sea. Fossils of sea creatures are therefore much more common than those of land creatures. Those land animals and plants that have been preserved are usually found in sediments in a lake, river or estuary.

The soft parts of an animal or plant – the flesh, or a delicate shoot – will decay more quickly after the creature dies than its hard parts. So shells, teeth and bones are much more likely to be preserved as fossils than skin or organs. But sometimes, even an animal's last meal may be preserved as a fossil.

▼ *When sap runs down a tree trunk, it may trap an insect climbing up. The sap hardens into a golden-brown resin called amber, with the insect preserved inside it.*

Oil may seep up through the ground to form tar pits. An animal may fall into a pit and its remains be preserved. Parts of ancient plants are often preserved in coal.

Fossil insect in amber

Fossil leaf in coal

Tar pit

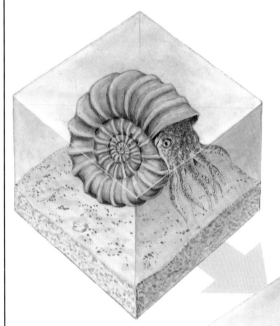

◀ *When a sea animal, such as an ammonite, dies, its body will sink to the sea bed. If there are swift currents the shell may be swept around. The shell will quickly break up and itself become part of the sediment on the sea bed.*

▶ *If the current is not very strong, the animal will settle and sediment will fall rapidly to the sea bed, burying it. This protects the animal from being eaten and destroyed by scavengers. The animal's soft parts rot away leaving the shell.*

▲ *As the shell is buried under more and more sediment, the material around it hardens into rock as the individual grains become squeezed together. The shell may remain in its original form or it may be replaced with minerals such as quartz or lime.*

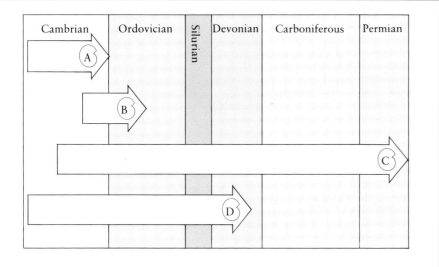

Cambrian	Ordovician	Silurian	Devonian	Carboniferous	Permian
A	B			C	D

DATING ROCKS FROM FOSSILS

Many types of animal and plant survived on Earth for only a limited period of time. Ammonites, the pterosaurs and dinosaurs all died out, or became extinct. The fossils of extinct animals can be used to date the surrounding rock. This is because these fossils cannot be found in rocks that are younger than the time at which the animal disappeared. Rocks of a known age can also be used to date fossils.

MOULDS AND CASTS

Sometimes a shell may be dissolved away by acid waters seeping through the rock. The shape of the shell might be preserved in the surrounding rock – a mould. If the mould is then filled with new mineral material, the resulting fossil is called a cast.

▼ *Eventually, the effects of weathering and erosion may wear away the sedimentary rocks and expose the fossil. Or the fossil may be found in a quarry face, or because of road cutting. It is as though the sea animal has been frozen in time.*

▲ *Over many millions of years, the sea may retreat. The rocks in which the fossil lies may become faulted and folded because of movements within the Earth's crust. What was once the sea bed may be thrown up into a newly formed mountain range.*

▲ *Even though it is not the original animal that has been preserved, scientists can still learn a lot from the fossil.*

Shaping the Earth

The world's highest mountain is Mount Everest in the Himalaya range, soaring to 8848 m. Britain's highest mountain, Ben Nevis, is 1343 m. Both mountains were created by similar processes of mountain building, so why should one be nearly seven times the height of the other? Part of the answer lies in the effects of weathering and erosion. Ben Nevis is a very old mountain and has been worn down over hundreds of millions of years by the action of wind, rain, ice and snow.

WEATHERING AND EROSION

Rocks are often formed inside the Earth, at high pressures and temperatures. At the Earth's surface, when rocks are exposed, the conditions are quite different. It is this change that causes rocks and minerals to break up. Physical weathering breaks down the rocks into smaller particles, such as sands or grits. In chemical weathering, the minerals that form the rocks are dissolved by the action of water together with oxygen and carbon dioxide in the air. Once the rocks have been broken down by weathering, the bits are transported elsewhere by ice, wind, running water or gravity. This is called erosion. Sometimes the actions of people can increase erosion by removing plants that hold the soil together.

▲ *Plant roots can also break down rock. They work their way into tiny cracks in a rock. As the roots grow, they widen the cracks. Eventually, the force of the roots can shatter the rock. Worms eat large amounts of soil, passing out the waste as casts which can then be washed away by rain.*

▼ *These desert rocks have been scoured by sand-carrying wind into strange pillars appearing from the dunes.*

▼ *Rain containing dissolved carbon dioxide from the air is a weak acid and will dissolve calcite, the main mineral found in limestones.*

Scree formed by frost erosion

Erosion of river valley

▼ *Rivers carry weathered rock debris to the coast. The finest particles may be carried out to sea.*

Erosion and weathering of folded rocks at surface

Rock tower weathered by wind and rain

▶ *When water freezes, it expands. If water finds its way into cracks in rocks and then freezes, it pushes out against the rock. This may cause the rock to shatter.*

◀ *Rocks may be subjected to high temperatures during the day, and very low ones at night. They expand and contract and this causes them to split.*

SLUMPS AND SLIDES

Gravity often causes erosion. Soil may slide slowly down a slope as a result of disturbance caused by wetting and drying. And gravity can cause loose material to slump. If the material is dry, some kind of shock, such as an earthquake, may cause soil and rock to slump.

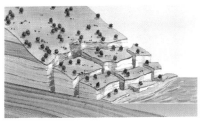

▲ *Soil may creep slowly downhill, pulled by gravity.*

▲ *A shock may cause clay to liquefy to form a mud flow.*

▲ *In a landslide, material falls quite quickly, but the material may*

fall from a break along a plane or curved surface.

FACTS ABOUT CAVES AND CAVERNS

- The world's deepest cave is at Rousseau Jean Bernard, in France. It is 1535 m deep.
- The longest cave system in the world is at least 530 km long. It is under the Mammoth Cave National Park, Kentucky, USA. This limestone plateau also boasts more than 60,000 swallow or sink holes.
- The world's biggest cavern is the Sarawak Chamber in Sarawak, Indonesia. It is 700 m long, 300 m wide and 70 m high, and is supported only by its sides.
- Gaping Gyll, a sink hole in North Yorkshire, descends vertically for more than 110 m.
- The longest stalactite in the world is in a cavern in County Clare in Ireland. It is over 7 m long.
- Near Lozère in southern France, there is a stalagmite that has now reached 29 m in height.

CAVES AND CAVERNS

Limestone may be weathered into a pavement of blocks. As acid water works its way down through cracks in limestone, it widens the cracks into passageways. When the water meets a layer it cannot drain through, it runs down until it finds an exit. In this way underground streams and rivers are formed. They dissolve away the limestone to form potholes, caves and caverns.

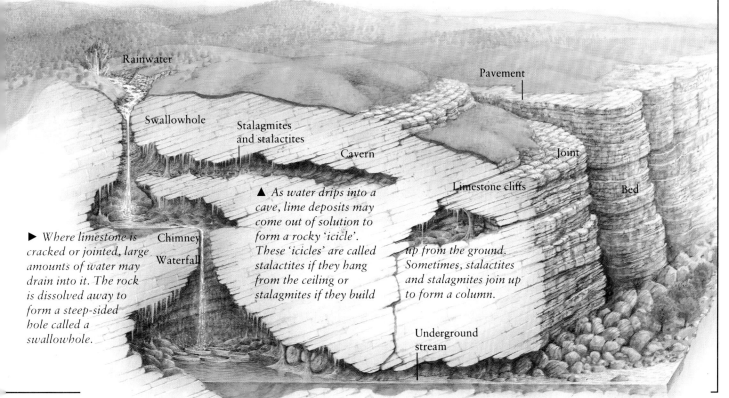

Rainwater

Swallowhole

Stalagmites and stalactites

Cavern

Pavement

Joint

Limestone cliffs

Bed

Chimney

Waterfall

▶ *Where limestone is cracked or jointed, large amounts of water may drain into it. The rock is dissolved away to form a steep-sided hole called a swallowhole.*

▲ *As water drips into a cave, lime deposits may come out of solution to form a rocky 'icicle'. These 'icicles' are called stalactites if they hang from the ceiling or stalagmites if they build*

up from the ground. Sometimes, stalactites and stalagmites join up to form a column.

Underground stream

The Work of Ice

Water freezes into solid ice at 0°C. As the density of water is greatest at 4°C, ice floats on top of cold water. This is important because it allows animals and plants to survive below the ice on a river, lake or even the ocean, provided the water does not freeze solid. A large block of ice that floats in the sea is called an iceberg. A large mass of ice on the surface of the land is called a glacier. Glaciers, originally made of snow, are very powerful and their action carves distinctive landscapes.

GLACIERS

Glaciers will form in places where so much snow falls during the winter that not all of it melts or evaporates in the summer. Glaciers are often found high up in mountains at the heads of valleys. Above the snow line, snow accumulates as a permanent snow field.

Depth (m)

Fresh snow

0

Né vé

1

Compacted snow

10

Ice

25

Compressed glacier ice

100

Impermeable ice

200

ICE AGES

A period when part of the Earth is permanently covered by ice is called an Ice Age. We are living in an Ice Age at the moment. There are permanent ice sheets at the North and South Poles. The extent of the ice varies with the seasons. However, there have been times in the past when larger areas of continents have been covered with ice. This was because the Earth's climate was cooler then.

Present extent of ice sheet
Farthest extent of ice sheet

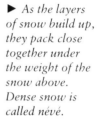

▶ As the layers of snow build up, they pack close together under the weight of the snow above. Dense snow is called névé.

▶ Air is squeezed out of the névé while water runs into it and freezes. The névé becomes denser.

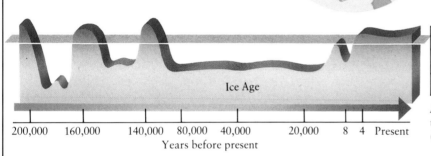

Ice Age

15°
10°
5°
0°

Average July temperatures (°C)

| 200,000 | 160,000 | 140,000 | 80,000 | 40,000 | 20,000 | 8 | 4 | Present |

Years before present

▲ Eventually the white snow is turned into clear, bluish ice, forming a glacier.

GLACIATION

About 2 million years ago, the Earth's climate cooled and polar ice spread southwards, covering Europe as far south as the Severn Estuary, Britain. In places, the European ice sheet was as thick as the Greenland ice sheet is today. The results of glaciation can be seen today. Valleys contained huge glaciers, creeping slowly downhill. As a glacier moved its scouring action wore away the sides and floor of its valley, deepening it. Glaciated valleys can be recognized by their smooth U-shape. And because ice does not meander as the river did, the valley is straightened out and old spurs truncated.

▼ A glacier carries with it rock debris from its valley. As the snout of the glacier melts, some debris is dropped, forming a ridge called a terminal moraine.

Snout

Meltwater

Terminal moraine

FACTS ABOUT ICE

- Today, permanent ice covers more than 10 percent of the Earth's surface.
- During the last Ice Age, over 28 percent of the planet was engulfed in ice. The Scandinavian ice sheet was 3000 m thick.
- During the Ice Ages, the average temperature of the Earth was only about 3°C lower than it is today.
- The world's longest glacier is the Antarctic Lambert Glacier which is over 400 km in length.
- The fastest moving glacier, in Greenland, flows at up to 24 m a day.
- The greatest thickness of ice is in the Antarctic and measures almost 5000 m.
- The biggest iceberg ever sighted was more than 31,000 sq km in size.
- The highest iceberg ever seen was 167 m.

▶ *A typical river valley is a V shape. A moving glacier carries a great deal of rock with it. It works rather like sandpaper, wearing away at the valley until its shape is like a U.*

▼ *The head of a glaciated valley is weathered and eroded into an armchair-shape known as a cirque (or a cwm in Wales, or a corrie in Scotland). Where more than one cirque is linked, a knife-like ridge or a pyramid-shaped peak may result.*

Pyramidal peak

Cirque

Crevasses

Movement of glacier

Lateral moraine

▶ *Sometimes a glacier picks up large blocks of rock and dumps them a long distance away. These are called glacial erratics.*

◀ *Lakes may form in the armchair-shaped cirques made by glaciers.*

GLACIAL LAKES

Lakes are a common feature of a landscape that has been glaciated. Indeed, there are more glacial lakes than all other kinds put together. A lake may form in a hollow that the ice has worn in softer rocks, or in holes in the uneven surface where a glacier has deposited a lot of debris.

WATER

Oceans and Seas

Over 70 percent of the Earth's surface is covered by water – the rivers, lakes, oceans and seas. This watery layer is sometimes referred to as the hydrosphere. There is also water locked up as ice – mainly at the poles – and still more exists as vapour in the atmosphere and as moisture in the soil. But about 97 percent of the planet's water is in the seas, and it is salty. The oceans are not evenly distributed around the globe, and most of the world's land areas are to be found in the Northern Hemisphere. The world's biggest ocean is the Pacific. It occupies almost twice the area of the next biggest ocean, the Atlantic, and is also far deeper. Much of the Pacific coast is bounded by mountain ranges, such as the Andes. This means that there are few major rivers flowing into the Pacific Ocean. Many large rivers flow into the Atlantic, carrying sediment from the land.

BEYOND THE LAND

The ocean floor can be separated into two main zones: the deep ocean basin, and the shallower area at the edge of the land, called the continental margin. The gentle slope from the edge of the land down to about 500 m is the continental shelf. Further out to sea, the ocean bed falls away more steeply down the continental slope, between 1500 and 3500 m to the abyssal plain. Deep submarine canyons form in the continental slope, where currents of muddy water from the mouths of rivers rush down the slope. These currents deposit their sediments in a fan shape.

Atlantic Ocean
106,000,000 sq km

Pacific Ocean
166,242,500 sq km

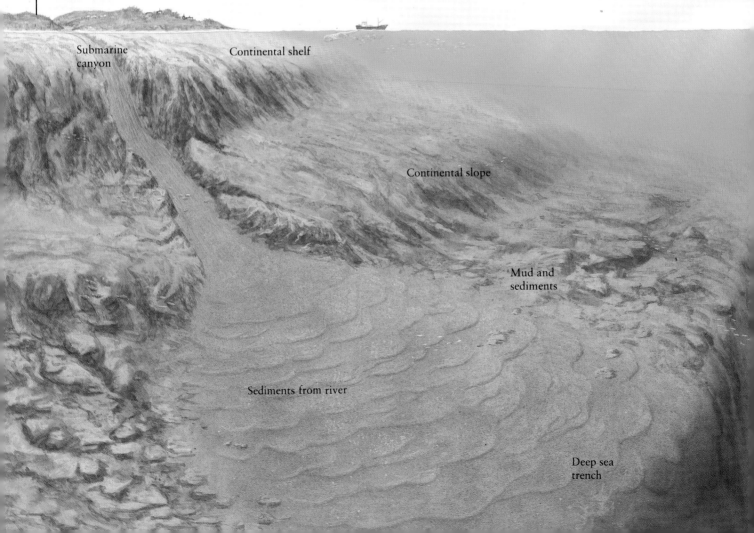

Submarine canyon

Continental shelf

Continental slope

Mud and sediments

Sediments from river

Deep sea trench

THE OCEANS

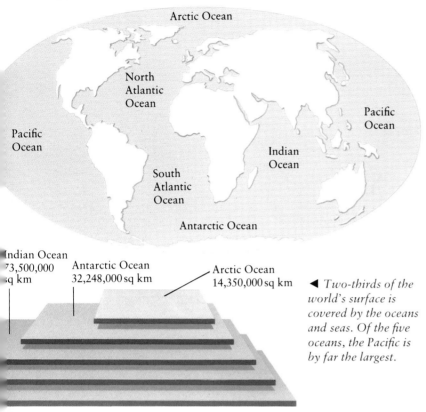

Arctic Ocean

North Atlantic Ocean

Pacific Ocean

Pacific Ocean

Indian Ocean

South Atlantic Ocean

Antarctic Ocean

Indian Ocean
73,500,000 sq km

Antarctic Ocean
32,248,000 sq km

Arctic Ocean
14,350,000 sq km

◀ *Two-thirds of the world's surface is covered by the oceans and seas. Of the five oceans, the Pacific is by far the largest.*

CORAL REEFS AND ATOLLS

Corals are sea animals related to jellyfishes. An individual, known as a polyp, has a cylinder-like trunk which is fixed at one end and has a mouth at the other. Some corals live in vast colonies and build massive, limey skeletons which accumulate into reefs.

MOUNTAINS AND CANYONS

The mountains of the oceans are very tall indeed. Mauna Kea, Hawaii, is really the peak of a mountain which starts on the sea bottom. Measured from there it is taller than Everest. Similarly, the Grand Canyon is dwarfed by the Marianas Trench in the Pacific Ocean. A volcanic mountain under the sea is called a seamount. If it breaks the surface, it becomes an island. Its top may be eroded and flattened so it no longer breaks the sea surface. Now it is known as a guyot.

Grand Canyon 1600 m

Mount Everest 8848 m

Mauna Kea 10,205 m

Marianas Trench 11,000 km

◀ *Close to mid-ocean ridges, there are holes in the sea floor where hot liquids and gases leak into the water from the hot rocks beneath. These liquids include metal oxides and sulphides which give a smoke-like effect as they mix with the cold sea water. Some animals live near the 'smokers', feeding on the sulphides.*

◀ *Coral reefs form when a new volcanic island rises from the sea over a hot spot. A fringing coral reef grows up round the island.*

◀ *The coral grows as fast as the sea floor sinks, or the sea level rises, to give a barrier reef with a lagoon between it and the island.*

◀ *Eventually the island disappears, leaving an atoll enclosing an empty lagoon, or a ring-shaped reef. Finally the coral is also covered by the rising waters, or sinks with the subsiding sea bed.*

The Life of the Ocean

The world of the oceans and seas has sometimes been called 'inner space.' Humans have made use of the sea for thousands of years – for food, transport or as a waste dump, for example. However, it has been only in comparatively recent times that people have been able to use machines to explore the fascinating world beneath the surface. The sea also has a considerable effect upon the land and the life that lives there. Water heats and cools quite slowly, and the oceans moderate the world's climate.

▶ *The sea tastes salty because it contains common salt and other minerals. On average the salinity of the sea is 35 parts per thousand. Some inland lakes and seas are saltier than the oceans – the Dead Sea is 250 parts per thousand.*

Chlorine 55%
Sodium 30%
Sulphates 8%
Magnesium 4
Calcium 1%
Potassium 1%

OCEAN CURRENTS

Warm water is less dense than, and rises through, colder water. In the deep waters of the oceans, these differences in temperature and density create currents. In the top 500 m of water, it is the winds that drive the currents. The ocean's currents follow the prevailing wind directions. Therefore in each ocean basin, there is a roughly circular movement of water called a gyre.

➡ Warm water
➡ Cold water

▼ *Near the Equator, the ocean's main currents are blown towards the west. Near the poles, they are blown eastwards.*

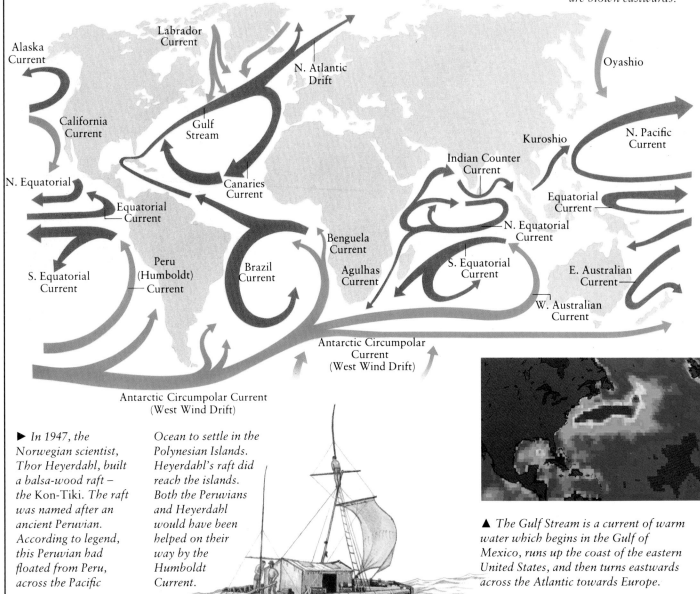

Alaska Current
Labrador Current
N. Atlantic Drift
Oyashio
California Current
Gulf Stream
Kuroshio
N. Pacific Current
N. Equatorial
Canaries Current
Indian Counter Current
Equatorial Current
Equatorial Current
N. Equatorial Current
Benguela Current
N. Equatorial Current
S. Equatorial Current
Peru (Humboldt) Current
Brazil Current
Agulhas Current
S. Equatorial Current
E. Australian Current
S. Equatorial Current
W. Australian Current
Antarctic Circumpolar Current (West Wind Drift)
Antarctic Circumpolar Current (West Wind Drift)

▶ *In 1947, the Norwegian scientist, Thor Heyerdahl, built a balsa-wood raft – the Kon-Tiki. The raft was named after an ancient Peruvian. According to legend, this Peruvian had floated from Peru, across the Pacific Ocean to settle in the Polynesian Islands. Heyerdahl's raft did reach the islands. Both the Peruvians and Heyerdahl would have been helped on their way by the Humboldt Current.*

▲ *The Gulf Stream is a current of warm water which begins in the Gulf of Mexico, runs up the coast of the eastern United States, and then turns eastwards across the Atlantic towards Europe.*

THE THERMOCLINE

The waters of the top 100 m of the seas are mixed by the wind. Beneath this, the water temperature falls rapidly. The boundary between the two levels is the thermocline. It prevents nutrients in the water from moving upwards.

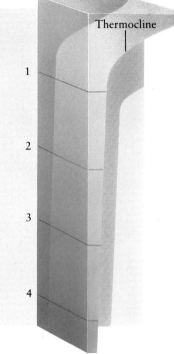

Depth (km)

Thermocline

1

2

3

4

BROTHER AND SISTER

El Niño (the Spanish word for a boy) is the name given to an occasional change in the world's weather pattern. This change, in turn, affects the circulation of the world's oceans.

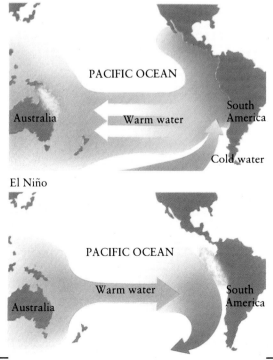

Normal Conditions

PACIFIC OCEAN

Australia   Warm water   South America

Cold water

El Niño

PACIFIC OCEAN

Australia   Warm water   South America

▶ *Sunlight penetrates water to about 900 m. But only in the top 100 m is there enough light for plants to photosynthesize. Seaweeds that live in upper waters are green and those below are reddish.*

LIFE IN THE SEA

The sea provides support and food for countless animals and plants. Although some kinds of sea creatures may exist in vast numbers, less than 15 percent of the world's species of animals live in the oceans. And 98 percent of these dwell on the sea floor.

◀ *Usually, food-rich waters well up along the coast of Peru, but during El Niño the winds change and the upwelling of cold, rich water is stopped. Instead, warm water arrives at the coast killing much of the wildlife and bringing famine to the people. La Niña (the Spanish for a girl) is the name given to a second occasional weather pattern which has the opposite effect to El Niño. When it occurs, it brings drought to some parts of the world while others are subjected to freak rains and floods.*

Plankton

Small fish

Sharks

Squid

Angler fish

Deep sea shrimp

◀ *Below 900 m the oceans are pitch black. At depths greater than 2000 m, strange creatures survive. Some of them give out their own light signals. Beardworms and fishes called rat-tails live here but there may be other even weirder animals that scientists have yet to discover.*

THE SARGASSO SEA

As ocean currents circulate, they sometimes trap areas of relatively calm water. The Sargasso in the western North Atlantic is surrounded by the Florida Current. It is often windless and is choked with seaweed. It is the birthplace of common eels.

The Seashore

Many scientists are worried that, if the greenhouse effect (*see page 159*) is allowed to continue, there will be a warming of the Earth's climate. If they are correct, then some of the polar ice would melt and sea levels across the world would rise. This could be disastrous for low-lying coastal regions. But this has already happened, about 10 to 15,000 years ago, towards the end of the last Ice Age. The effect continued until only a few thousand years ago. So most of the world's coasts are quite young features.

THE POWER OF THE SEA

Even the everyday action of a relatively calm sea may erode a coastline. Waves, armed with rocks, will hammer their load against the shore. And the sea will pick up and carry off any loose debris. The to-ing and fro-ing of rocks can smooth and round them into pebbles. Where the sea comes into contact with limestones, it may actually dissolve away the rock.

THE CHANGING COASTS

There are different types of coastline: narrow, pebbly or sandy beaches with a steep cliff at the back; broad beaches which slope down to the sea; the shore might be rocky. The coast may be cut by bays or deep inlets called fjords. Where parts of the coast are being eroded by the sea, you will see bays and high cliffs. This high coast is said to be retreating before the advance of the sea. At a retreating coastline the beach helps to resist the power of the sea. The sea also builds up parts of the coast. Waves carry sand and shingle, which is deposited in some places, building up a marsh, a beach or a spit. This creates a low, sloping coastline.

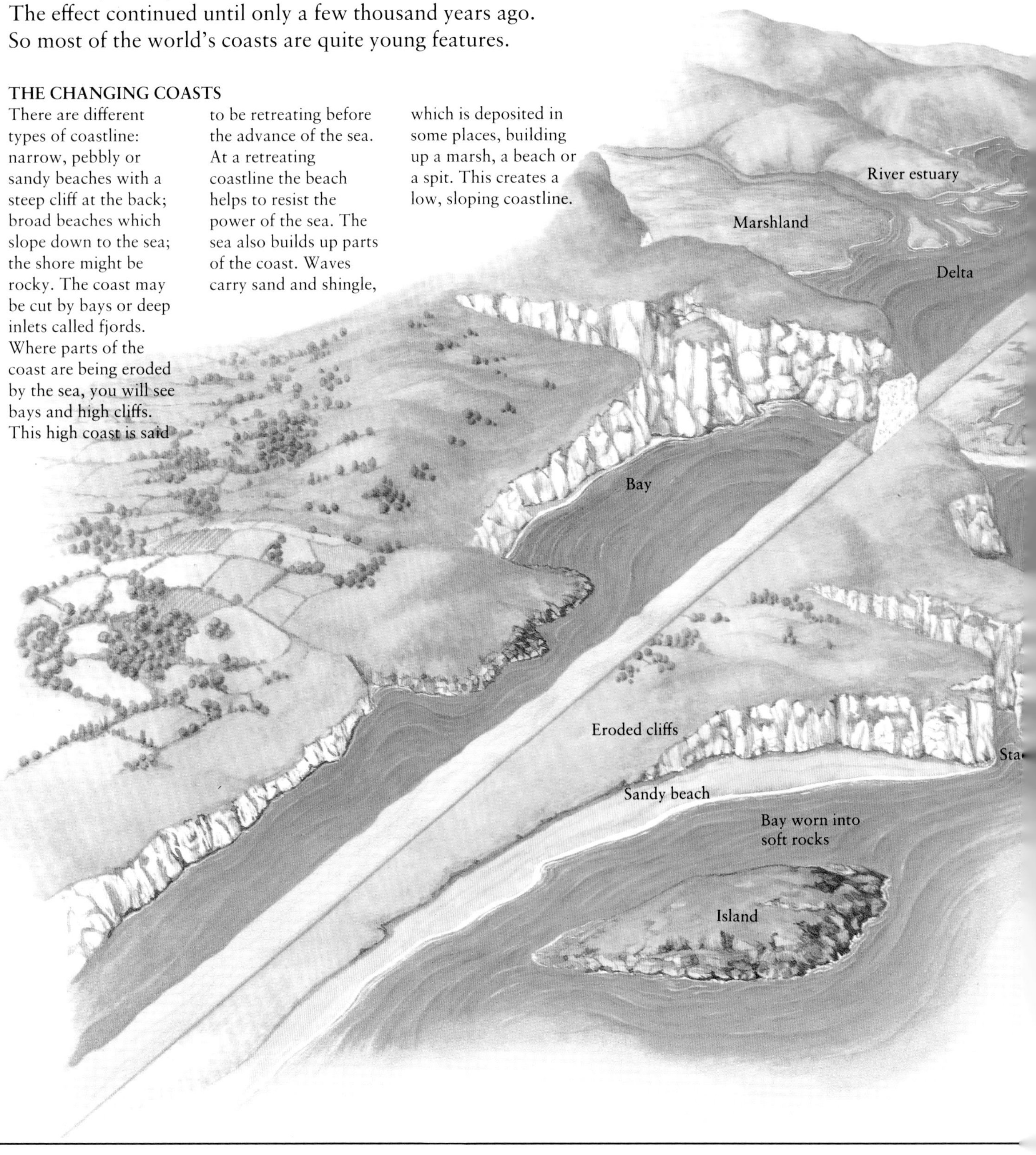

River estuary

Marshland

Delta

Bay

Eroded cliffs

Sandy beach

Sta•

Bay worn into soft rocks

Island

▼ *The seashore is constantly changing. Where coastal rocks are soft the features will change quickly, but where the rocks are hard, they will only be eroded slowly. A shore may feature cliffs, wide bays, rocky headlands, river deltas and estuaries.*

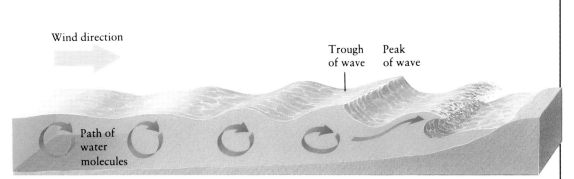

Wind direction

Trough of wave   Peak of wave

Path of water molecules

▲ *Waves are caused mainly by the wind. A wave's height depends on the strength of the wind and the area of sea it is blowing over. The motion of a water particle is almost circular until the wave meets the slope of the beach.*

SHIFTING SANDS

When a wave breaks on a beach the uprush of water (swash) carries sand and shingle towards the land. The returning backwash takes some material back down the beach.

Longshore current

Path of sand

Spit

◄ *The steep-sided inlets along the coast of countries such as Norway, Scotland and New Zealand are called fjords. They are the remains of glaciated river valleys which have been flooded at a retreating coastline.*

SPITS AND BARS

Sometimes, fence-like barriers are used to prevent longshore currents carrying beach material along the shore. But where longshore drift occurs, the sand and shingle can be dropped into deeper water. This builds up to form a new area of land called a spit, which will continue to grow (*left*). Sand dunes and marshes often build up behind the spit. Sometimes a spit will grow right across a bay to form a bar.

▲ *Waves may hit the beach at an angle, and a longshore current carries sand along the shore.*

Bar

goon

Arch

▲ *After years of battering, the seashore may feature wide, sandy beaches where the rock was soft; an island where a headland has been cut off from the shore; stacks and arches where weaknesses in the cliffs have been worn away; and a spit at the mouth of a bay.*

FACTS ABOUT THE SEASHORE

● During a big storm, a wave can crash against the shore with a pressure of almost 30,000 kilograms per square metre!
● After an Ice Age, when the ice sheets melt and their weight is removed from the land, the land may rise slowly, like a bobbing cork on water. At the coastline, the original beach will be raised high and dry and a new beach is formed at sea level.

▲ *The sea may sweep away more than the beach. Villages on a clay cliff in Yorkshire, England, have been undercut, and the erosion is still continuing.*

Rivers

Although rivers make up only a tiny percentage of all the surface water on Earth, they are very important. They wear away and form the landscape around us. River valleys have been barriers to the movement of people. Rivers themselves have provided vital transport links from the sea to inland areas. Where bridges have been built to cross rivers, villages, towns and cities have grown up. And of course, rivers have supplied food, and water for drinking, washing and irrigation.

BIRTH AND DEATH OF A RIVER

Some rivers start life as springs. Others are fed by melting glaciers. Most rivers come from the rain and snow that fall on uplands. Water runs along the surface in small rivulets. These rivulets may join to form a small stream. This will then begin to erode a valley. The valley sides themselves provide slopes for other tributary streams to flow down. As the amount of water increases, the river grows bigger. At the end of its journey, the river flows to the sea.

▼ *When a landscape has been newly uplifted, the land surface is steep and irregular and the river naturally follows the pattern of the land. This is known as a consequent river.*

Glacier

Meltwater

Waterfall

Rapids

Stream

Spring

FACTS ABOUT RIVERS

- The longest river in the world is the River Nile in Africa. Running from its source in Burundi to the Mediterranean, the Nile is 6670 km long.
- The second longest river, the Amazon in South America, is 6448 km. It runs from its source in the Andes Mountains of Peru to the southern Atlantic.
- The Amazon has more than 1100 tributaries, and it carries much more water than the Nile.
- Rivers can carry amazing amounts of sediment. The Huang He (Yellow River) in China has deposited rich silt over 141,645 sq km in its flood plain and delta.

▼ *Where a river flows across hard rocks towards softer rocks, the softer rocks will be eroded. This creates an abrupt increase in the slope of the river valley. As a result, the river flows more quickly and fiercely, as rapids. If the rock is eroded enough for its face to be vertical, the river will cascade over a waterfall.*

WATERFALLS
The world's longest unbroken falls of water:

Angel Falls, Venezuela 978 m

Yosemite Falls, USA 739 m

Mardalsfossen, Norway 655 m

Tugela, Africa 614 m

RIVER SHAPES

If a river flows quickly down a steep slope, over hard rocks, it will tend to cut a deep cleft, or gorge, in the land.

Where the river flows more slowly, over softer rocks, the valley will be worn back and widened out into an open V-shape.

MEANDERS AND OXBOW LAKES

When the channel of a river flows in a snake-like pattern across the broad floor of its valley, it is said to meander. On the inner side of each curve, the river deposits sand and silt. On the outer bend, the bank is eroded away and the channel deepens. Gradually new land is built up on the inner side of the bend, and more land is eroded away on the outer side. This makes the course of the river move, or migrate, into an increasingly wide meander. As the bends migrate, the valley gradually widens and flattens. If a flood occurs, the river may cross the neck of the loop, cutting off the old channel and forming an oxbow lake.

Meander

▲ *Some meanders will swell out into much broader loops than others.*

Loop widens

▲ *The neck of the loop may become very narrow as the loop develops.*

Oxbow lake

▲ *The old channel may be cut off to form an area of water called an ox bow lake.*

Tributary stream

River

Oxbow lake

Meander

Flood plain

Estuary

River mouth

▲ *As the river moves farther away from its source, its valley becomes shallower and smoother. The slope of the valley floor decreases, until it is almost flat. The river valley is broader.*

▶ *As the river reaches its mouth it slows right down, dropping the sediments it has been carrying. Its valley is wide, sloping gently to the sea. The river may meander, breaking up into a number of channels.*

Lakes and Swamps

A lake is an area of water completely surrounded by land. Lakes may contain fresh or salt water. Some, such as the Caspian, the salt lake between south-eastern Europe and Asia, are big enough to be thought of as inland seas. The water in a lake may seep from its basin and it may also evaporate. So, for a lake to continue to exist, it must be fed with water at the same rate or faster than the water is being lost. And the lake's bed must be lower than the lowest part of the rim or the water will run off elsewhere.

THE LARGEST OR DEEPEST LAKE

There are two main ways that a lake can be measured. The first is the area of its surface and the second is its depth. Lake Baykal in central Siberia, Russia is the deepest lake in the world. At its deepest point, the Olkhon Crevice, Lake Baykal is 1940 m deep, and 1485 m below sea level. The Great Lakes in North America are all linked and so could qualify as the largest by surface area.

STILL WATERS

Even though lakes seem still, few are completely stagnant. Water is at its densest at 4°C, so that in a cold winter, the lake may be covered with a sheet of ice, while the water at the bottom of the lake is warmer. In spring, the ice melts. As the temperature of the surface water rises, it becomes denser and sinks. The water in the lake circulates until, once again, water at 4°C settles to the bottom. In summer, the surface waters warm and circulate but stay above the layer of cold water in the lower part of the lake. In autumn the lake's surface cools again and the water circulates once more.

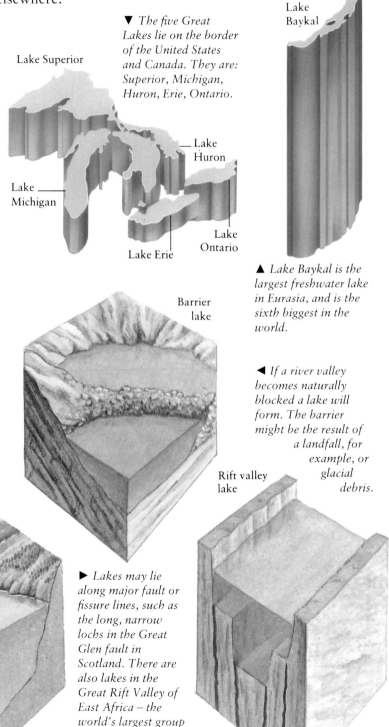

▼ *The five Great Lakes lie on the border of the United States and Canada. They are: Superior, Michigan, Huron, Erie, Ontario.*

Lake Superior

Lake Michigan

Lake Huron

Lake Erie

Lake Ontario

Lake Baykal

▲ *Lake Baykal is the largest freshwater lake in Eurasia, and is the sixth biggest in the world.*

Volcanic lake

◄ *A volcanic lake may fill up the crater of an extinct volcano. Lakes also form in places where hollow lava flows have collapsed.*

Barrier lake

◄ *If a river valley becomes naturally blocked a lake will form. The barrier might be the result of a landfall, for example, or glacial debris.*

Rift valley lake

Reservoir

Dam

▶ *Sometimes people create artificial lakes. If a dam is built across a river valley, the river waters build up behind it to form a lake. Eventually this will flood the valley. The lake may be used as a reservoir to store water, or as part of a hydroelectric scheme to generate electricity.*

▶ *Lakes may lie along major fault or fissure lines, such as the long, narrow lochs in the Great Glen fault in Scotland. There are also lakes in the Great Rift Valley of East Africa – the world's largest group of fault-created lakes.*

DISAPPEARING WATERS

Most lakes are quite shallow and are fed by rivers. A river brings with it a great deal of debris and sediment. The larger particles of sediment are dropped soon after the river enters the lake and a delta-like fan of material gradually spreads out into the water.

Very fine material may be carried quite a long way before it settles on to the lake's bed, slowly reducing the depth of water. At the same time, where the river leaves the lake, at the rim, it becomes worn away, and the lake is partly drained.

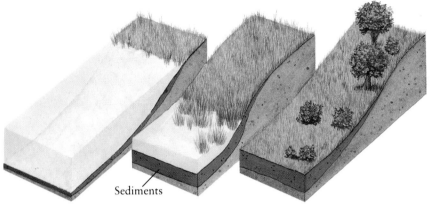

Sediments

▲ A fan of sediment builds up where the river feeds the lake and deposits material.

▲ Marsh plants colonize the waterlogged soil and trap more sediment.

▲ Eventually, the land dries out and other, less marshy, kinds of plants move in.

SWAMPS AND BOGS

In shallow lakes surrounded by plants, leaves and flowers fall into the water. A layer of peat-like ooze may build up. The ooze accumulates, becoming a bog or swamp.

▼ To the west of the Uinta Mountains in Utah, USA, is the Great Salt Lake. This is an inland salt lake about 120 km long and 4 m deep. It is the remains of a much larger lake which geologists call Lake Bonneville. The Great Salt Lake is getting larger without getting any less salty.

▲ The biggest inland water in the world is the Caspian Sea in Asia. It is 1225 km long. Estimates suggest that its total surface area is between 360,000 and 440,000 sq km. The Caspian Sea is known to be shrinking, despite this it is getting less salty. At its deepest point, the Caspian is about 1000 m deep.

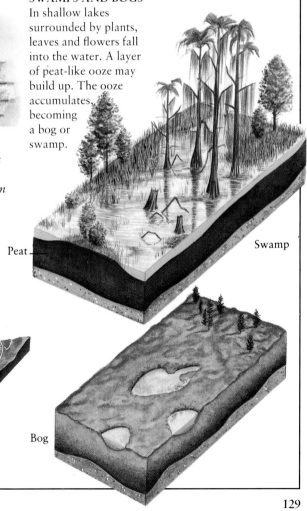

Peat

Swamp

Great Salt Lake

Extent of Lake Bonneville

Bog

WEATHER AND CLIMATE

The Atmosphere

The atmosphere is the envelope of air that surrounds the Earth. It has four layers: the lowest layer is the troposphere, above this are the stratosphere, the mesosphere and then lastly the thermosphere. The atmosphere extends upwards to a height of about 500km. Above this, the air merges with the particles streaming constantly from the Sun. There is no clear boundary where the Earth's atmosphere ends and that of the Sun begins. Air has weight, and the atmosphere nearest the Earth is pressed down, or compressed by the weight of the air above it. At sea level, the atmosphere presses down on every square centimetre of the Earth's surface with a weight of about 1kg. This pressure is called 'one bar', or 1000 millibars (mb). Atmospheric pressure decreases with height, until it falls to about one millibar at a height of 30km above sea level.

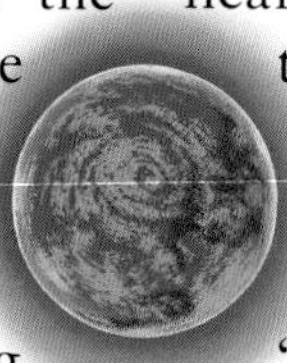

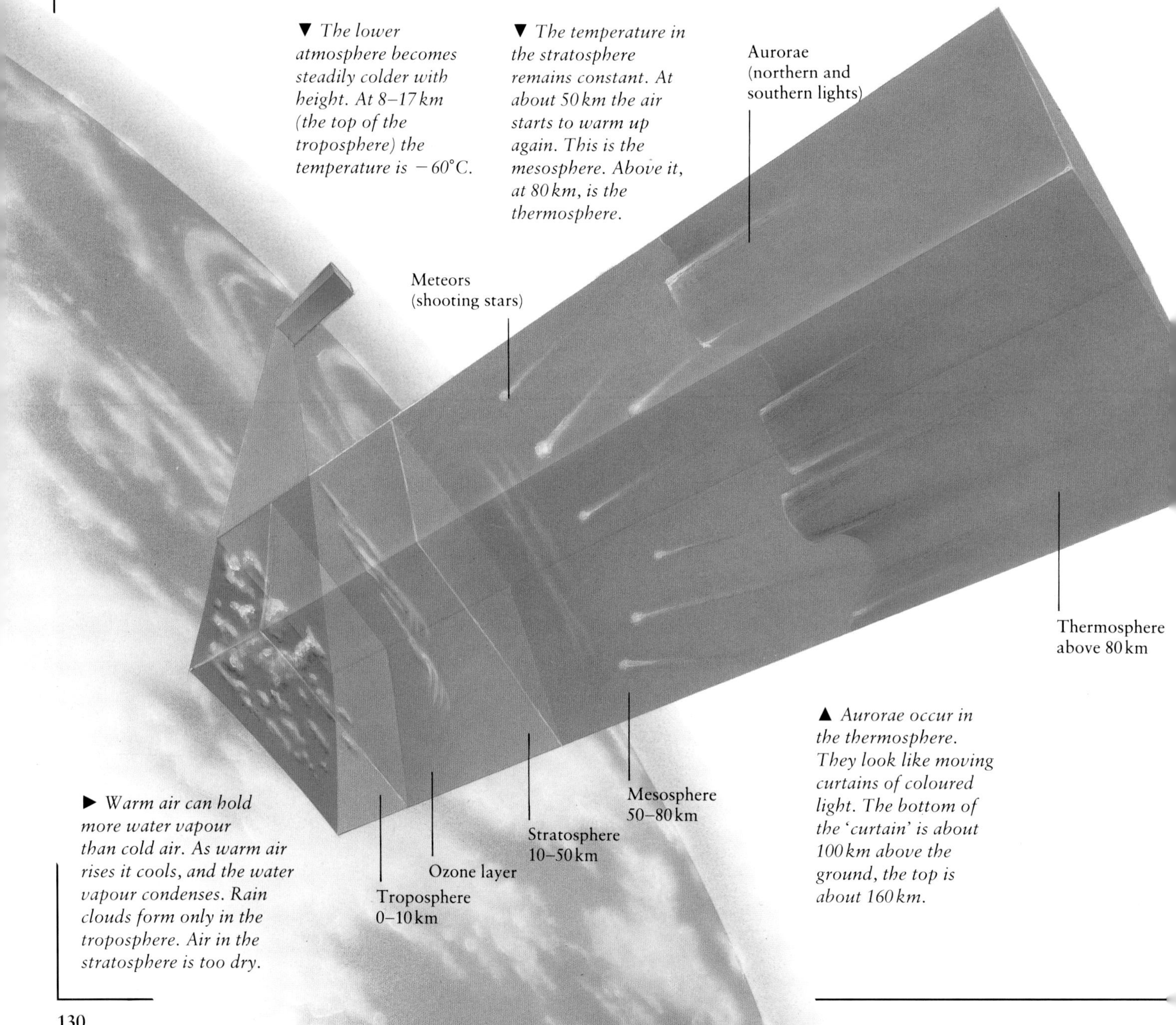

▼ *The lower atmosphere becomes steadily colder with height. At 8–17 km (the top of the troposphere) the temperature is −60°C.*

▼ *The temperature in the stratosphere remains constant. At about 50 km the air starts to warm up again. This is the mesosphere. Above it, at 80 km, is the thermosphere.*

Aurorae (northern and southern lights)

Meteors (shooting stars)

Thermosphere above 80 km

▶ *Warm air can hold more water vapour than cold air. As warm air rises it cools, and the water vapour condenses. Rain clouds form only in the troposphere. Air in the stratosphere is too dry.*

Mesosphere 50–80 km

Stratosphere 10–50 km

Ozone layer

Troposphere 0–10 km

▲ *Aurorae occur in the thermosphere. They look like moving curtains of coloured light. The bottom of the 'curtain' is about 100 km above the ground, the top is about 160 km.*

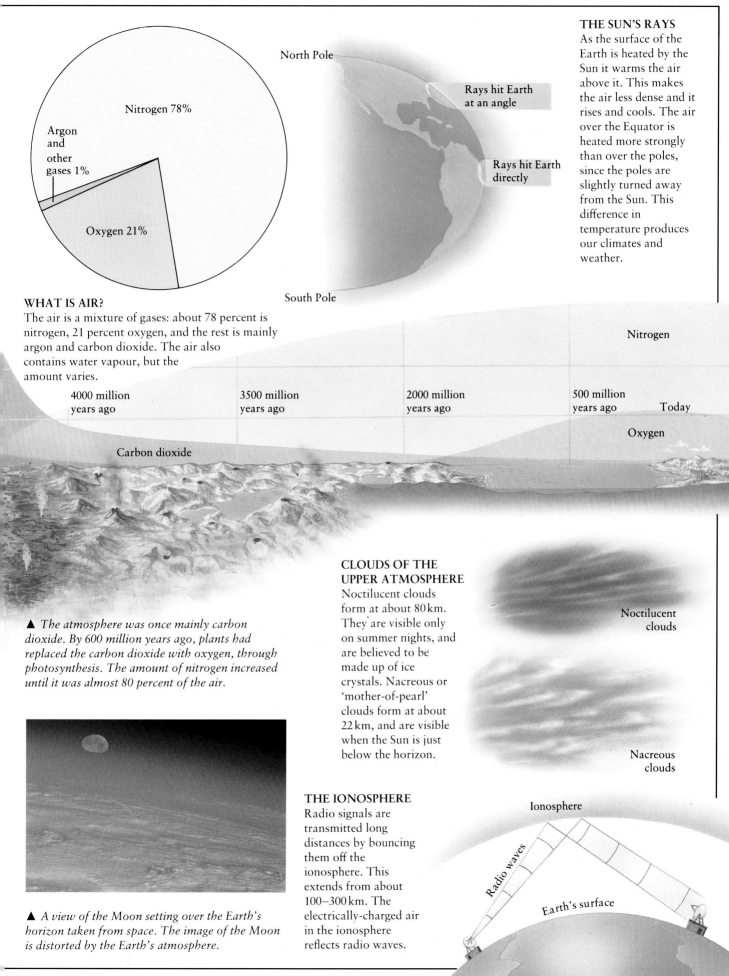

Nitrogen 78%

Argon and other gases 1%

Oxygen 21%

North Pole

Rays hit Earth at an angle

Rays hit Earth directly

South Pole

THE SUN'S RAYS
As the surface of the Earth is heated by the Sun it warms the air above it. This makes the air less dense and it rises and cools. The air over the Equator is heated more strongly than over the poles, since the poles are slightly turned away from the Sun. This difference in temperature produces our climates and weather.

WHAT IS AIR?
The air is a mixture of gases: about 78 percent is nitrogen, 21 percent oxygen, and the rest is mainly argon and carbon dioxide. The air also contains water vapour, but the amount varies.

Nitrogen

4000 million years ago

3500 million years ago

2000 million years ago

500 million years ago

Today

Oxygen

Carbon dioxide

▲ *The atmosphere was once mainly carbon dioxide. By 600 million years ago, plants had replaced the carbon dioxide with oxygen, through photosynthesis. The amount of nitrogen increased until it was almost 80 percent of the air.*

CLOUDS OF THE UPPER ATMOSPHERE
Noctilucent clouds form at about 80 km. They are visible only on summer nights, and are believed to be made up of ice crystals. Nacreous or 'mother-of-pearl' clouds form at about 22 km, and are visible when the Sun is just below the horizon.

Noctilucent clouds

Nacreous clouds

▲ *A view of the Moon setting over the Earth's horizon taken from space. The image of the Moon is distorted by the Earth's atmosphere.*

THE IONOSPHERE
Radio signals are transmitted long distances by bouncing them off the ionosphere. This extends from about 100–300 km. The electrically-charged air in the ionosphere reflects radio waves.

Ionosphere

Radio waves

Earth's surface

Climate

The Sun warms the surface of the Earth more strongly near the Equator than at the poles. The warm, tropical air rises and cooler, denser air from higher latitudes moves in to replace it. Water evaporates into warm air and condenses in cool air. This constant movement of the air, driven by the warmth of the Sun, produces the world's climates and the weather we experience from day to day. It is called the 'general circulation' of the atmosphere. It is influenced by the rotation of the Earth and the oceans.

GLOBAL WINDS

Warm air rises and moves away from the Equator, cooling and losing moisture as it does so. The trade winds bring cold air in from higher latitudes to replace it. The dry tropical air eventually sinks in the subtropics (about 30° latitude). When it reaches the surface, some of the sinking air is drawn back to the Equator, forming the trade winds, and some blows towards the poles. This circulation of the air near the Equator is called the Hadley cell. It is named after George Hadley, the meteorologist who described it in 1735.

WORLD CLIMATES

The world can be divided into several climate zones. The main factors that affect the climate of a particular place are its distance from the Equator (latitude) and its distance from the ocean. Climates are cooler further away from the Equator, and drier in places far from the ocean.

Mountain
Tropical wet and dry
Tropical wet
Desert   Oceanic moist
Subtropical dry summer   Subarctic
Continental moist   Polar

JET STREAMS

There is a sharp change in temperature between warm tropical air and the cooler air north and south of the tropics, and between this mid-latitude air and polar air. In these two regions, at about 10 km, westerly winds blow at speeds of about 200 km/h. These fast-moving winds are the jet streams.

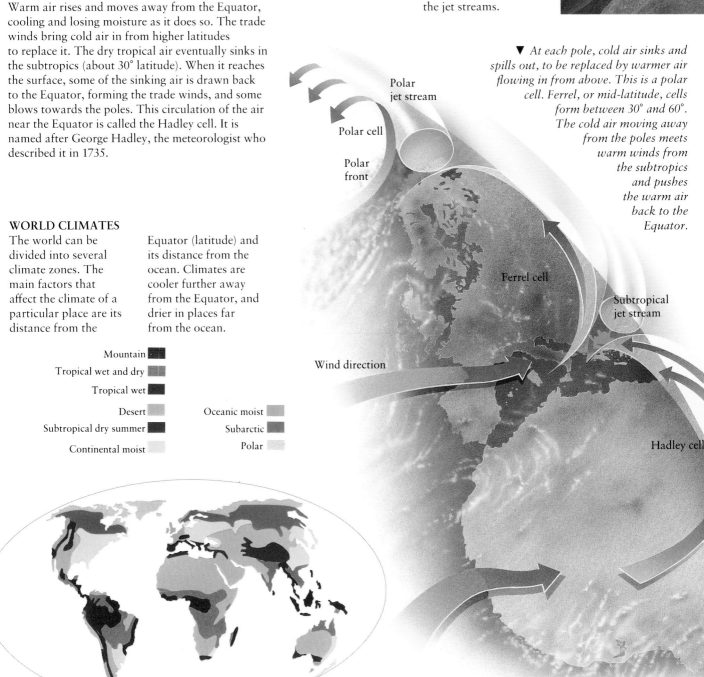

Polar jet stream

Polar cell

Polar front

Ferrel cell

Subtropical jet stream

Wind direction

Hadley cell

▼ At each pole, cold air sinks and spills out, to be replaced by warmer air flowing in from above. This is a polar cell. Ferrel, or mid-latitude, cells form between 30° and 60°. The cold air moving away from the poles meets warm winds from the subtropics and pushes the warm air back to the Equator.

THE CORIOLIS EFFECT

The Earth rotates to the east, the surface and air moving faster at the Equator. Warm air rises and is replaced by cooler air which is moving eastward more slowly, so the surface overtakes it. This creates the northeasterly and southeasterly trade winds, and is called the Coriolis effect.

▲ *Jet streams are often revealed by long narrow bands of cirrus cloud.*

MONSOONS

In June, differences in air pressure over land and sea bring thunderstorms and heavy rain to India and southern Asia. The parched ground revives and farm crops flourish. The rainy season is called the monsoon. It lasts until September and in some places 85 percent of the annual rain falls during this period. Monsoon seasons also occur in West Africa and northern Australia.

AIR MASSES

An air mass is a large body of air that has the same temperature and moisture. Depending on where it forms, it is called 'polar' or 'tropical', and 'maritime' or 'continental'. Continental air (forming over land) is dry and cool if it is polar, and warm if it forms at the tropics. Maritime air (forming over sea) is moist. As the air mass crosses the land it loses moisture, bringing rain. The weather usually changes when one air mass is replaced by another. The boundary between two air masses is a front.

▼ *In winter, the sea is warm relative to the land. The air above the sea is heated and rises, and cold, dry winds from the northeast blow towards the Indian Ocean.*

January

Himalayas

Cold dry winds

India

Indian Ocean

July

Torrential rain (monsoon)

India

Indian Ocean

Warm moist winds

▲ *In summer, the air over northern India becomes very hot and dry. Its pressure falls, causing warm moist air to move to the north, bringing heavy rain to southern Asia.*

FACTS ABOUT CLIMATES

• The winds drive the ocean currents, which also carry warmth from the Equator to cooler regions.
• The ocean currents affect climates by bringing warm or cool water to the shores of continents.
• The climate of western Europe is warmed by the waters of the Gulf Stream and North Atlantic Drift.
• The climate of the northwest coast of North America is cooled by the California Current, which flows south from the Arctic.
• Water warms and cools more slowly than land. A continental air mass that crosses the ocean will be warmed by the water in winter, and cooled in summer.
• The greatest amount of rain ever recorded in a single year was at Cherrapunji in India. It received 20.647 m of rain in the monsoon season of 1861.

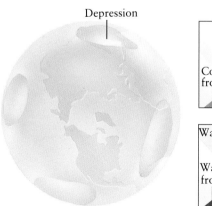

▲ *An area of low air pressure is called a depression. As the air rises its moisture condenses, layers of cloud form, and it rains.*

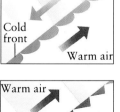

◀ *A cold front has cooler and often drier air behind it.*

◀ *A warm front brings cloud and rain. Cold air pushes beneath the warm air and lifts it.*

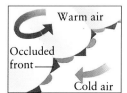

◀ *Where cold and warm air mix, the fronts are 'occluded'. They weaken and disappear.*

Winds and Storms

Air moves from areas of high atmospheric pressure to areas of low pressure, causing winds. It does not flow directly but moves around the centres of high or low pressure because of the Coriolis effect *(see page 133)*. In the Northern Hemisphere, air moves anticlockwise around low pressure and clockwise around high pressure. In the Southern Hemisphere the opposite occurs. The wind always moves 'downhill' from high to low pressure. Its speed depends on the difference in pressure.

WINDS OF THE WORLD

Because the Earth spins to the east, the winds either side of the Equator are from the northeast and southeast. They are the 'trade winds'. Between the trade wind belts lie the 'doldrums', where winds are light. In middle latitudes (30°–50°), winds are more often from the west than from the east. Easterly winds prevail in the Arctic and Antarctic.

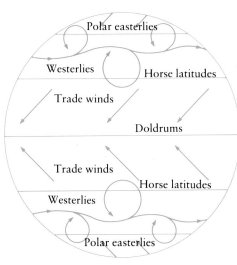

Polar easterlies
Westerlies
Horse latitudes
Trade winds
Doldrums
Trade winds
Horse latitudes
Westerlies
Polar easterlies

(see page 133)

THE BEAUFORT WIND SCALE

In 1806, Sir Francis Beaufort, an English admiral, devised a scale for measuring wind force. It is still used today.

Force	Speed	Definition
0	<1 km/h	calm
1	1–6.3 km/h	light air
2	6.4–12.7 km/h	light breeze
3	12.8–20.8 km/h	gentle breeze
4	20.9–30.5 km/h	moderate breeze
5	30.6–40.1 km/h	fresh breeze
6	40.2–52.4 km/h	strong breeze
7	52.5–61.6 km/h	moderate gale
8	61.7–75.5 km/h	fresh gale
9	75.6–88.4 km/h	strong gale
10	88.5–102.9 km/h	whole gale
11	103.0–120.7 km/h	storm
12	>120.7 km/h	hurricane

Wind speed is measured by an 'anemometer' *(see page 140)*. It has small cups, mounted on horizontal arms, which spin around on an axis. A wind vane is a flat blade that indicates wind direction.

(see page 140)

▶ *The strong upcurrents of air in heavy rainstorms have been known to lift up objects as large as fish and frogs, which then appear to rain down from the sky.*

THUNDER AND LIGHTNING

In a large storm cloud, as water droplets collide, water becomes electrically charged. Positive charges collect at the top of the cloud and negative charges at the bottom. The negative charge creates a positive charge on the ground surface, which builds until lightning sparks from the cloud to the ground and back again.

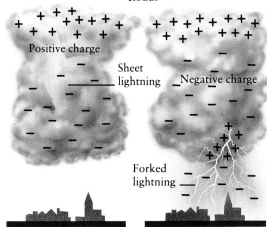

Cumulonimbus clouds

Positive charge
Sheet lightning
Negative charge
Forked lightning

▲ *Sheet lightning flashes inside or between clouds, forked lightning flashes to the ground. Thunder is the sound of hot air exploding.*

FACTS ABOUT WIND

● A warm, dry, 'föhn' or 'chinook' wind is caused by air flowing down the side of a mountain range.
● In southern Europe, the valleys of the Rhône and other rivers funnel the 'mistral', a cold, northerly wind.
● In West Africa, a dry, easterly wind is called the 'harmattan', or 'doctor', because it brings relief from very humid conditions.
● Winds in Commonwealth Bay, Antarctica, reach speeds of 320 km/h.

TORNADOES

A tornado is a twisting funnel, a few hundred metres across, in which wind speeds can reach 350 km/h. Tornadoes move in a straight line and can cause terrible destruction. The pressure inside is so low that it can cause nearby buildings to explode.

▶ *A hurricane is a tropical storm, usually about 650 km across. It brings heavy rain and winds of speeds up to 200 km/h. In the northwest Pacific they are called typhoons, and those in the Indian Ocean and north of Australia are called cyclones.*

▶ *Hurricanes form in late summer and autumn over warm water in the Atlantic, Pacific, and Indian Oceans. They then move westwards, along coasts.*

Typhoons
Apr–Dec

Cyclones
Dec–Apr

Hurricanes
Aug–Oct

Cyclones
May–Dec

Hurricanes
June–Oct

Direction of storm

Eye

Dry air
sinks

Strong
spiral
winds

Strong
upcurrents

Cumulonimbus
clouds

Warm
moist air

Low pressure
at core

Inward
flowing winds

Prevailing
wind direction

Warm sea

Rain

INSIDE A HURRICANE

In the eye of a hurricane, winds are light and the sky is clear. The descending air is warm and the pressure is very low. Fierce winds bring air swirling around the eye. The air is swept upwards by huge cumulonimbus clouds. As air in the clouds rises and cools, the water vapour it carries condenses. This releases heat, which warms the air again, sending it upward into a region of high pressure above the clouds. The big clouds cause heavy rain. Away from the centre, cirrus and cirrostratus clouds trace the storm's outline.

The Types of Cloud

Clouds form when water vapour condenses into tiny droplets. The conditions under which this happens vary, producing clouds of different types and shapes. White, puffy clouds are often seen on fine days. If they grow bigger, rain showers may fall from them. High above them, there may be small, wispy clouds made from ice crystals. Very large, dark clouds bring thunderstorms. Layers of cloud, like flat sheets covering the sky, bring dull weather or steady, sometimes heavy, rain.

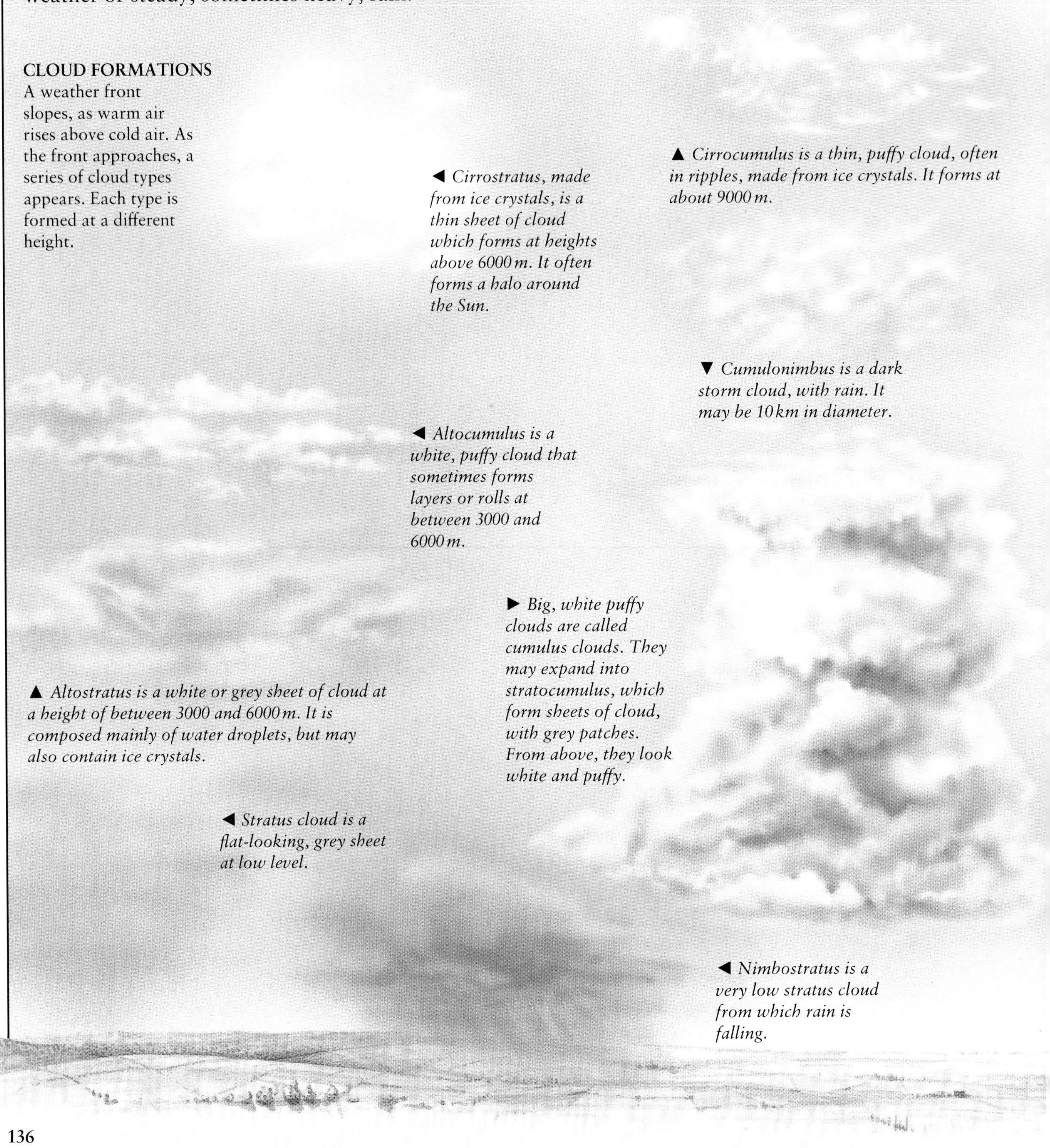

▲ *Cirrus, made from ice crystals, forms long, thin wisps of cloud aligned with the wind at about 12,000 m. Sometimes, the wisps separate at the ends, to form 'mare's tails'.*

CLOUD FORMATIONS
A weather front slopes, as warm air rises above cold air. As the front approaches, a series of cloud types appears. Each type is formed at a different height.

◀ *Cirrostratus, made from ice crystals, is a thin sheet of cloud which forms at heights above 6000 m. It often forms a halo around the Sun.*

▲ *Cirrocumulus is a thin, puffy cloud, often in ripples, made from ice crystals. It forms at about 9000 m.*

▼ *Cumulonimbus is a dark storm cloud, with rain. It may be 10 km in diameter.*

◀ *Altocumulus is a white, puffy cloud that sometimes forms layers or rolls at between 3000 and 6000 m.*

▶ *Big, white puffy clouds are called cumulus clouds. They may expand into stratocumulus, which form sheets of cloud, with grey patches. From above, they look white and puffy.*

▲ *Altostratus is a white or grey sheet of cloud at a height of between 3000 and 6000 m. It is composed mainly of water droplets, but may also contain ice crystals.*

◀ *Stratus cloud is a flat-looking, grey sheet at low level.*

◀ *Nimbostratus is a very low stratus cloud from which rain is falling.*

▶ *The Sun heats some parts of the ground, such as rock or bare soil, more than others. On warm days, bubbles of hot air form over these areas, and rise up through the cooler air around them.*

HOW CLOUDS FORM

The amount of water vapour air can hold depends on the temperature of the air. If warm, moist air is cooled, its water vapour will condense. This is why water condenses on a cold window. Clouds form when the water vapour condenses around tiny solid particles.

▲ *At night, fog forms as warm air is chilled by contact with a cold valley floor. As the ground warms again the fog lifts to form low cloud.*

▶ *The warm air rises into low pressure air and expands and cools. The air cools so much that the water vapour condenses into droplets, and a small cumulus cloud is formed.*

FOG

Fog is cloud that forms close to the ground. The different types of fog are named after the ways in which they are formed. Advection fog forms when warm moist air passes over cold ground or water. Radiation fog forms at night, as the land cools and the air above it is chilled.

▼ *Advection fogs are common in San Francisco, rolling in from the Pacific to envelop the Golden Gate Bridge. They form when warm, moist air from the south meets cold ocean currents from the Arctic. In the daytime, the air over the warm land is at low pressure and a sea breeze carries the fog ashore.*

▶ *The cloud grows if it is fed by a series of air bubbles, and the wind detaches it. Fair-weather cumulus looks like cotton wool. It does not carry enough water to cause rain.*

▼ *Moist air that rises over a mountain and then sinks again may set up waves in the air downwind of the mountain. As the air rises to the crest of a wave, it cools and clouds are formed in the shape of a lens. They are called 'lenticular' clouds.*

FACTS ABOUT CLOUDS

Cloud names are easy to remember:
● Those that begin with **alto-** form at medium height, between 2000 m and 6000 m.
● Those beginning **cirr-** form above 6000 m. If the name has neither of these prefixes, the cloud forms below 2000 m.
● **Strat-** clouds form flat-looking layers; those with **cumu-** form heaps.
● **Nimb-** means a rain cloud.

● The highest standard cloud formation is cirrus, which may reach 12,000 m, but nacreous cloud may form at a height of almost 24,000 m.
● Sea-level fogs on the Grand Banks, Newfoundland, Canada, persist on average for 120 days of the year.
● Aircraft often produce trails of cloud at high altitudes, when water vapour from the hot engine exhaust condenses.

Rain and Snow

Water that falls from a cloud is called 'precipitation' and may take the form of rain, drizzle, hail, sleet or snow. Not all precipitation reaches the ground. In warm weather, rain may fall from a cloud only to evaporate again in mid-air.

Whether precipitation falls as water, ice, or a mixture of the two, depends on the conditions inside the cloud and the temperature of the air outside it. In summer most of the ice that forms inside a cloud melts as it falls, except during the occasional hailstorm.

SNOW CRYSTALS

When water freezes, its molecules bind together into flat, six-sided crystals with four long sides and two short ones. The crystal grows as other water molecules attach themselves to its six sides. Each snow flake is unique.

RAIN AND SNOW

There are two main types of rain. In the tropics, rain is formed when air currents cause the tiny water droplets in a cloud to bump into each other and join together to form larger drops which fall as rain. Most rain outside the tropics is caused by snowflakes melting as they fall. The height at which water freezes as it condenses out of a cloud is called the 'freezing level'. The ice crystals grow rapidly into snowflakes as water droplets freeze on to them. If the freezing level is below 300 m the ice crystals will not have time to melt before reaching the ground, and will fall as snow.

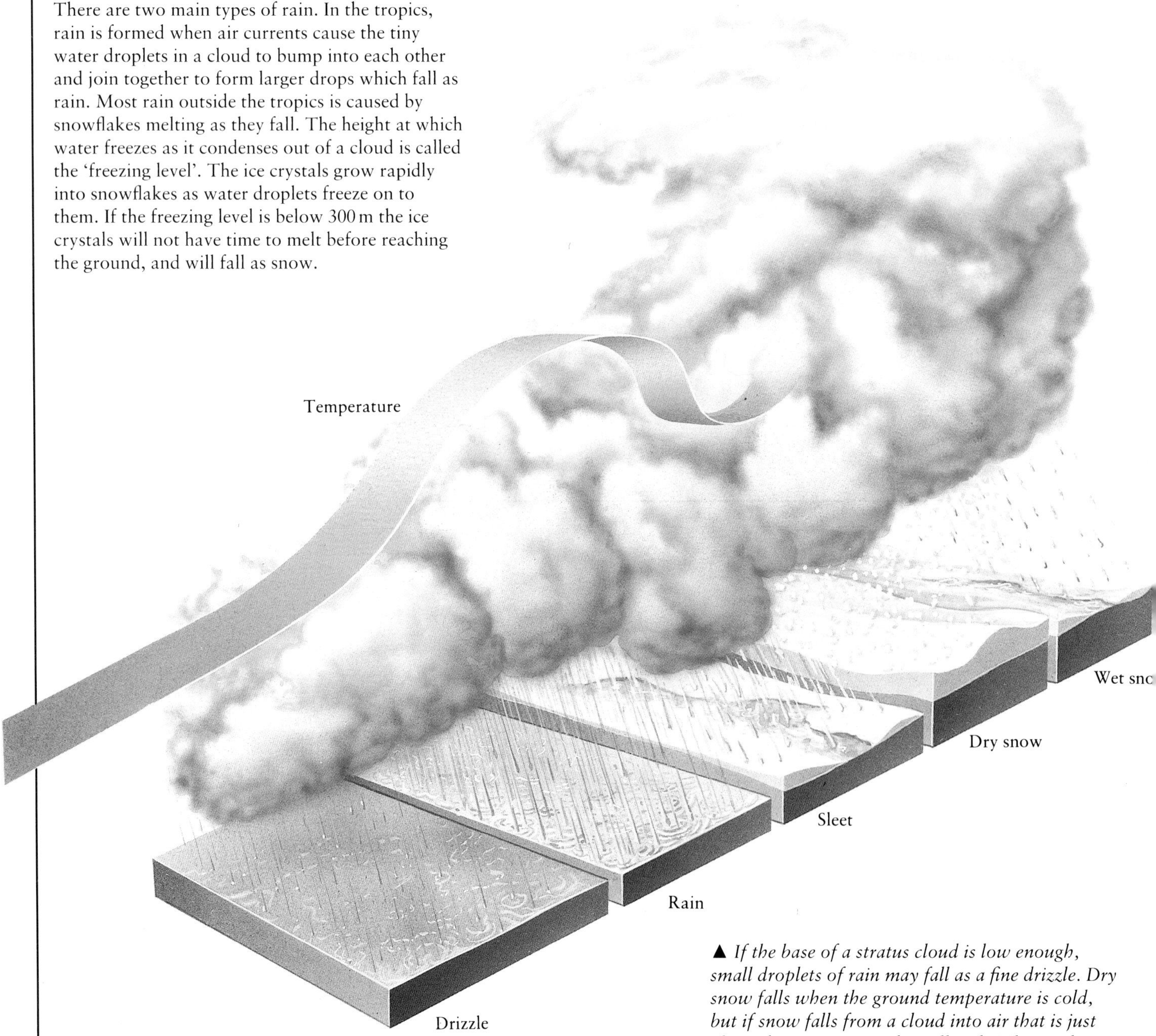

Temperature

Wet snow

Dry snow

Sleet

Rain

Drizzle

▲ *If the base of a stratus cloud is low enough, small droplets of rain may fall as a fine drizzle. Dry snow falls when the ground temperature is cold, but if snow falls from a cloud into air that is just above freezing, some of it will melt. The resulting mixture of snow and rain is called 'sleet'.*

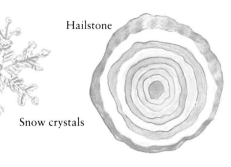

Hailstone

Snow crystals

HAILSTONES

Hailstones form around a small ice crystal. Alternate layers of clear and milky ice build up as the hailstones are swept up and float down inside the cloud.

▶ *Some very cold clouds can be made to release rain by dropping crystals of silver iodide or dry ice into them. Water then freezes onto the crystals. This is called 'seeding' the cloud, and has been used to end droughts.*

FACTS ABOUT RAIN AND SNOW

- Cherrapunji, India is one of the world's wettest places, receiving nearly 11,000 mm of rain a year. The South Pole is the driest, with only 40 mm.
- Libreville, in Gabon, Africa, receives more than 2500 mm of rain a year, with a short dry season in summer. Chicago, USA, has about 840 mm, and London has about 600 mm.
- As maritime air crosses mountains it loses moisture. The area on the far side of the mountains may lie in a 'rain shadow', with relatively little rain. The annual rainfall in Vancouver, Canada, is 1440 mm. In Calgary, on the other side of the Canadian Rockies, it is 440 mm. Calgary lies in a 'rain shadow'.
- Floods happen when heavy rain makes rivers overflow their banks.

SUN'S HALO

When a thin veil of cloud partly covers the Sun, light rays may be refracted (bent) by the ice crystals. This creates a 'halo', a ring of white light around the Sun, sometimes with a faint tinge of red on the inside and violet on the outside. Small water droplets in such clouds as altocumulus can also refract light, making a coloured 'corona', usually blue on the inside and red on the outside. A white halo can also occur when cirrus clouds obscure the Moon.

RAINBOWS AND FOGBOWS

A rainbow is caused by sunlight, or even moonlight, shining on a screen of water droplets. Rays are refracted as they enter a droplet, reflected from the back of the droplet, and then refracted a second time. Light of different wavelengths is refracted by different amounts, which splits the white light into its rainbow colours. A secondary rainbow, with the order of its colours reversed, may appear outside the primary rainbow. A fogbow is similar, but its colours overlap and mix to produce white.

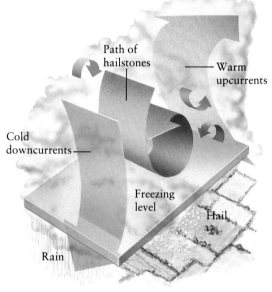

Path of hailstones

Warm upcurrents

Cold downcurrents

Freezing level

Hail

Rain

HOW HAIL IS FORMED

Inside a storm cloud, raindrops may be carried up by air currents and frozen high in the cloud. An opaque layer of ice builds up as water vapour freezes onto them. They fall to warmer levels, where the outside melts and is then refrozen into a clear layer of ice as the hailstone is carried up again. The hailstone rises and falls until it is heavy enough to fall out of the cloud.

▶ *In 1970, hailstones weighing 760 g fell in Kansas, USA. In 1928, a hailstone measuring 14 cm across, and weighing 700 g fell in Nebraska, USA.*

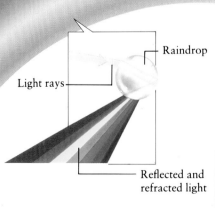

Light rays

Raindrop

Reflected and refracted light

Rainbow

Weather Forecasting

We all like to know what the weather will be like over the next few hours or days. Indeed, it is very important for some people to know. Farmers must know when to plough or harvest their crops. Fishermen must know whether it is safe for them to leave port, aircraft pilots must know what weather they will encounter during a flight, so that they can avoid dangers such as large thunderstorms. Scientists who study the weather are called meteorologists and much of their work involves preparing weather forecasts.

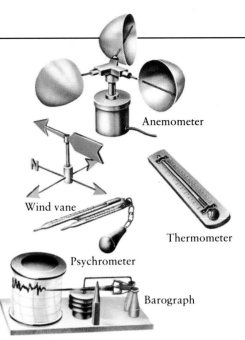

Anemometer

Wind vane

Thermometer

Psychrometer

Barograph

WEATHER SYMBOLS

Weather maps summarize conditions at a particular time. They are called 'synoptic charts' and use standard symbols. The most prominent of these are 'isobars', the lines connecting places where air pressure is the same. Winds flow roughly parallel to the isobars. The closer together the isobars are, the stronger the wind. The chart also shows warm and cold fronts (*see page 133*).

WEATHER INSTRUMENTS

Meteorologists use a barograph, a barometer linked to a pen and paper drum, to record atmospheric pressure. A thermometer records temperature, and a wind vane and anemometer record wind direction and speed. Wet- and dry-bulb thermometers (psychrometers) measure humidity.

▲ *A weather map may show the pressure (in millibars) on isobars and at centres of low and high pressure.*

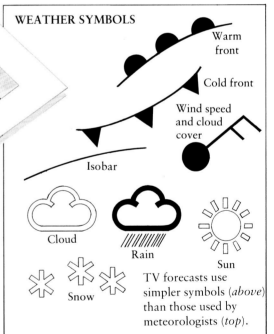

WEATHER SYMBOLS

Warm front

Cold front

Wind speed and cloud cover

Isobar

Cloud

Rain

Sun

Snow

TV forecasts use simpler symbols (*above*) than those used by meteorologists (*top*).

COLOURS IN THE SKY

There is a scientific explanation for much weather lore. If the wind is from the west, a red sky at sunset means the air to the west is dry and the next day is likely to be fine. If it is dull red with cloud, there may soon be rain. A red sky in the morning means clouds are arriving and the day may be rainy.

WEATHER TRACKING

Forecasters know the kind of weather associated with different cloud types. Cloud patterns often indicate areas of high and low pressure. By tracking weather systems, from surface reports and satellite images, meteorologists can predict their movements and speeds, and the ways they will change. It is essential that the path of a hurricane is predicted accurately, so that people in threatened areas can be evacuated. Unfortunately, hurricane systems are so complicated that this is not always possible.

▲ *Weather planes monitor conditions in the upper atmosphere, using instruments attached to the aircraft's long nose. Conditions at sea are reported by specially equipped ocean weather ships (left). These are towed to positions far from shipping lanes where they are anchored, and send reports up to eight times a day.*

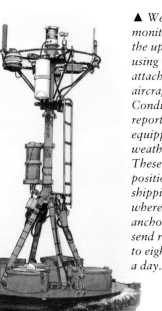

Meteosat

▲ *Weather satellites (left) transmit photographs of cloud patterns, back to Earth, allowing scientists to study their type and movement. Satellites travelling in geostationary orbit remain above one point on the surface. Others orbit from pole to pole.*

▶ *Balloons called 'radiosondes' carry instruments that are able to measure the temperature, pressure and humidity of the upper atmosphere. The readings are sent by radio from the balloon to ground weather stations. The flight of some balloons, called 'rawinsondes', is tracked. The balloons are filled with helium, and expand as they rise into less dense air. Their path reveals the speed and direction of winds at high altitudes.*

▼ *In temperate climates, a piece of dry seaweed will absorb moisture from damp air. It becomes wet as humidity increases, indicating the approach of a warm front and, therefore rain. It dries as the warm air passes.*

Kelp

CHAOS THEORY

Meteorologists are able to prepare a weather forecast for only a few days ahead. Long-range forecasts proved so unreliable that meteorologists no longer do them. The problem is that local differences in conditions, which are too small to record, can greatly alter the way a weather system moves and develops. So, for example, a small change in the air over the Arctic could cause a hurricane in the tropics. Scientists use a theory known as the 'chaos' theory to describe this unpredictable behaviour.

Helium balloon

Secondary balloon

Instrument package

LANDSCAPES

The Changing Scene

The world's different landscapes have been made mainly by the action of the weather on rocks. Over thousands of years, mountains are worn away by wind, ice and rain, until they become gently rolling hills and, eventually, level plains. As the rocks are broken into tiny fragments, living organisms can obtain the substances they need from them, providing that they also have water. This action converts the mineral particles into soil. Larger plants grow in the soil, and animals can feed on the plants. Farmers may clear away the natural vegetation to plough fields and grow crops, where the soil and climate are suitable. Climate variations are recorded in the landscapes they have formed. The hills, valleys and soils of a desert are different from those of a forest, but plants may grow in soils that formed millions of years ago in a desert.

WORLD VEGETATION

The Earth can be divided into regions that have roughly the same climate. On land, it is mainly the climate that determines the kinds of plants growing naturally. Similar types of vegetation cover vast areas. These are called 'biomes'.

The tropical rainforest biome forms a belt to either side of the Equator. Sub-tropical grasslands give way to scrub and semi-arid grassland, then to hot deserts, just outside the tropics. Beyond the tropics, temperate grasslands give way to temperate then conifer forest, tundra, and permanent ice.

Tundra	Grassland	Tropical rainforest
Temperate woodland	Desert	Boreal forest

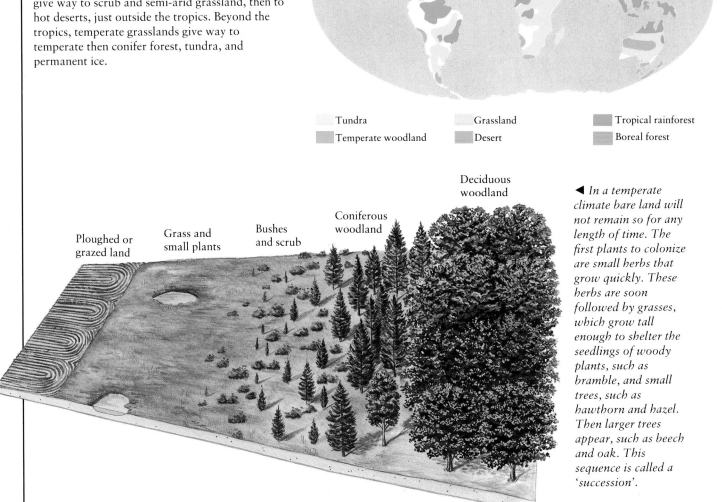

Ploughed or grazed land — Grass and small plants — Bushes and scrub — Coniferous woodland — Deciduous woodland

◄ *In a temperate climate bare land will not remain so for any length of time. The first plants to colonize are small herbs that grow quickly. These herbs are soon followed by grasses, which grow tall enough to shelter the seedlings of woody plants, such as bramble, and small trees, such as hawthorn and hazel. Then larger trees appear, such as beech and oak. This sequence is called a 'succession'.*

LAND USE

In Europe, the first villages were built near rivers, which supplied fish and fresh water. Later, forests were cleared to make fields for crops and grazing animals. The early farms grew until most of the valleys were cultivated. By the 11th century most of the original forest had disappeared and many riverside settlements became large towns. Rock and metal ores were mined before Roman times.

Prehistoric

Medieval

◀ *Until people settled down and began to clear the land for fields and cut trees for houses, they had little impact on the landscape.*

▶ *In the 18th–19th centuries as industry grew, so did the towns and the demand for raw materials and coal. The countryside became dirty and ugly. Today development continues, but we are aware of the damage we can do.*

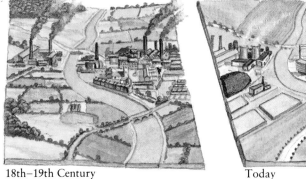

18th–19th Century

Today

SOIL

The rate at which rock is changed into soil depends mainly on the climate. In places where the ground is frozen for most of the time, soil forms very slowly. The soils in the far north of America and Asia are said to be 'young', because their formation has barely begun. Near the Equator, where the climate is warm and wet, soils form rapidly and are said to be 'ancient'.

Scientists group different soil types into 10 orders. The very young ones are called Inceptisols, the ancient ones are Oxisols or Ultisols. Desert soils, also called 'Aridisols', are poorly developed, because of the shortage of water and the lack of decomposed remains of plants (humus), which help make a soil fertile.

The best farm soils are the Mollisols of the prairies and steppes, and the Spodosols of temperate forests, found in Britain and northeastern North America.

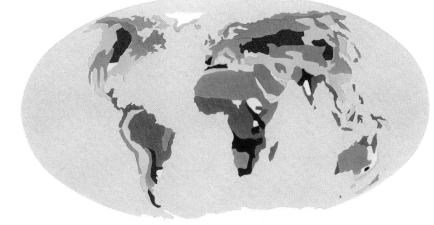

- Tundra soils
- Podzols (Spodosols)
- Podzols and Brown Earths (Spodosols and Inceptisols)
- Podzols (Spodosols)
- Chernozems (Mollisols)
- Alfisols
- Grumusols (Vertisols)
- Desert soils (Aridisols)
- Ferralsols (Oxisols)
- Montane soils

Zonal soil types (shown above) were based on climatic factors. New names are given in brackets.

SOIL PROFILES

Once a soil has developed it forms layers, called 'horizons'. Beneath a surface layer of plant remains, the A horizon is rich in decomposed organic plant and animal matter. The B horizon is mainly mineral particles, with much less organic material. The C horizon is mainly small stones, and beneath them all lies the bedrock.

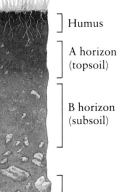

- Humus
- A horizon (topsoil)
- B horizon (subsoil)
- C horizon (fragmented rock and bed rock)

Blocky

Prismatic

Platy

Crumb

▲ *The amount of air and water found in a soil depends on the particles from which it is made. A platy structure packs into watertight layers. A blocky structure drains well, a prismatic one less well. A crumb structure is best of all.*

143

Polar Regions and the Tundra

Within the Arctic and Antarctic Circles there is at least one day a year when the Sun does not rise, and at least one when it does not set. The Arctic and Antarctic are lands of midnight Sun in summer, and noon darkness in winter. The polar regions are the coldest on Earth, and among the driest because there is little liquid water. Most of Greenland lies beneath ice 1500 m thick, that fills valleys and buries hills. The average thickness of the Antarctic ice sheet is more than 2000 m.

ICEBERGS

An iceberg is a large block of floating ice. It is much larger than it looks because some nine-tenths of the ice floats below the surface. This concealed ice can be dangerous to ships. Some Antarctic icebergs are more than 100 km long.

THE ARCTIC AND THE ANTARCTIC

Most of Greenland and the northern parts of Alaska, Canada, Scandinavia and Siberia lie within the Arctic Circle, but there is no land close to the North Pole itself.

Antarctica is the world's fifth largest continent, divided into two parts by the Transantarctic Mountains. Beneath the ice, the land of East Antarctica is mainly rugged, in places rising to more than 4000 m above sea level. West Antarctica is lower. Much of it is made up of a peninsula and island archipelago. In places, the land around the South Pole is up to 2500 m below sea level.

THE TUNDRA

Around the Arctic Circle, between the conifer forests further south and the region of permanent ice to the north, the tundra extends as a vast, treeless plain across all the northern continents. In summer the ground thaws for just a few weeks, triggering frantic activity for the region's animals and plants.

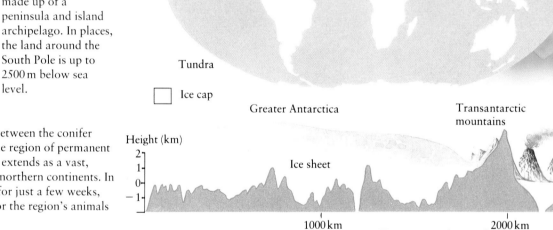

Tundra

☐ Ice cap

Greater Antarctica

Transantarctic mountains

Height (km)

2
1
0
−1

Ice sheet

1000 km

2000 km

▼ Geese, waders and sea birds live on the tundra. Tundra mammals include polar and grizzly bears, musk ox, caribou, voles and shrews.

Dwarf birch

Lichen

◄ Tundra plants are small, as their roots can only grow to a depth of 30 cm before they reach frozen ground. There are heaths, dwarf birch trees, sedges and rushes, mosses and lichens. Many plants flower in the brief summer.

FACTS ABOUT POLAR LANDS

• During the dark nights, plant nutrients accumulate in the sea. As the light returns, marine plants multiply rapidly providing food for small and larger animals, such as fish, sea birds, seals and whales.
• Each year, more than 7000 icebergs are carried south from Greenland in the Labrador Current.

Sea level

Glacier or ice sheet

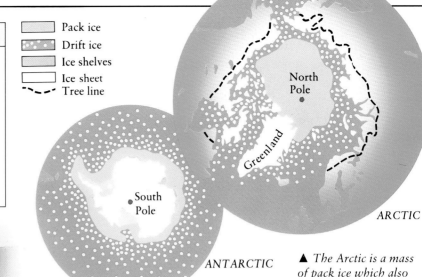

Pack ice
Drift ice
Ice shelves
Ice sheet
--- Tree line

North Pole

Greenland

South Pole

ANTARCTIC

ARCTIC

▲ Where a glacier enters the sea, the ice floats on the water. The end of the glacier snaps off to form an iceberg. Ice shelfs also break, forming much larger icebergs.

Lesser Antarctica

▼ Under the Antarctic ice sheet, unlike the Arctic, there is land. Near the coasts some glaciers have retreated, leaving dry, rocky valleys, called 'oases'. Inland, high mountain peaks project above the ice, as 'nunataks'.

▲ The extent of the Antarctic ice sheet varies with the changing seasons. In winter the drift ice extends out to the southern tip of South America. The Antarctic is home to a few plants and some insects. In summer, penguins, sea birds and seals visit it.

▲ The Arctic is a mass of pack ice which also changes with the seasons. In winter, its ice covers all of Greenland and its drift ice reaches as far south as Iceland and northern Russia. The presence of the ice and tundra lands limits the growth of trees to areas south of the line through northern Canada, Norway, Sweden and Russia.

Ross Ice Shelf

Ice sheet

3000 km　　4000 km　　5000 km

PERMAFROST
In winter, in the Arctic and Antarctic, all the moisture in the soil freezes, but in some areas the top few centimetres of the soil thaws in summer. During the summer thaw, the ground turns to mud, with pools in the hollows. The subsoil and deeper layers remain permanently frozen. They are called 'permafrost'. If the permafrost thaws, for example, because of the heating effect of a house or oil pipeline, then the land will subside.

Soil thaws in summer

Permafrost

POLAR RESOURCES
Long ago, the polar regions lay in lower latitudes and had warmer climates. In Antarctica, there are deposits of coal up to 6 m thick, formed more than 250 million years ago. Alaska also has vast coal reserves, and, in 1968, one of the world's largest oil fields was discovered at Prudhoe Bay.

▼ Oil travels south from Alaska to ports by the Trans-Alaska Pipeline. The pipeline was built on supports above the ground, to prevent it thawing the permafrost.

Temperate Woodland

During the last Ice Age, most of the northern latitudes, higher than 50°, lay beneath ice. When the ice retreated, it left bare rock and debris. As the climate warmed up, groups of plants spread north, until most of the landscape was covered by forest. Trees in far northern regions have to survive the equivalent of a dry season, when water is frozen. Deciduous trees save water by shedding leaves, conifers have needle-like leaves from which little water evaporates. Both types form large areas of forest.

SOIL
Soils of conifer forests have a light-coloured, rather acid upper layer. Some soil minerals dissolve and drain into the subsoil. Broadleaved forests develop very fertile soil with an even, brown surface layer.

WOODLAND AREAS
Broadleaved evergreen forests grow around the Mediterranean and in those regions of the southern United States, China, South America, South Africa and southern Australia, where temperatures rarely fall below freezing. Broadleaved deciduous forests grow further north. Southern Chile is the only place they are found in the Southern Hemisphere. Most of Canada, northern Europe and Asia is covered by coniferous, or boreal forest. There is no boreal forest in the Southern Hemisphere.

Temperate woodland

THE FOREST ECOSYSTEM
The trees of the broadleaved evergreen forest include holm oak, cork oak and a few species, such as holly, that also grow in mild, moist regions further north. These species are usually mixed with pines and cedars. The deciduous forests have a wider variety of species. They are often dominated by oak, beech and maple, with different species in Europe and North America. Coniferous forest is made up entirely of pines, spruces, firs, and larches. Each type of forest has its own type of wildlife. The evergreen forests have fewer animal species than the others. Species found in the conifer forests include moose, bears and wolves.

◀ *Near the edges of the temperate deciduous forest area, conifers grow side by side with broadleaved trees. This mixed forest of aspens and larch is in the Nevada Rockies. American woodlands contain more tree species than European woodlands. The richest deciduous forests are in the Appalachians, in the east. The species include tulip trees and oaks, and basswood and buckeye.*

Mixed woodland

WOODLANDS

• Today, about 10 percent of Britain is forested, mainly with conifer plantations, but more broadleaved trees are now being grown. The average in the EC is 24 percent and in the United States it is 29 percent.
• All the paper we use comes from conifers grown in temperate regions.

DEFORESTATION IN EUROPE

Most of the original forest that once covered Europe was cleared long ago to provide farmland. In Britain, this clearance was well advanced by the end of the Roman occupation. By the 11th century, trees covered a smaller area than they do today. The woodlands that remained were made up of species that had established themselves naturally. Some of these survive as 'ancient woodlands'. These are woods where trees have grown since before the forest plantations were begun in the 18th century. Scientists identify them from historical records, and also by the type of plant species they contain.

Natural extent of forest

Present extent of forest

▲ The New England forests in the United States are famous for their autumn colours. As leaves die, they lose their green chlorophyll, revealing many shades of red and yellow.

Deciduous woodland

▲ A European broadleaved forest typically contains oak, ash, beech and chestnut. The trees provide shelter and food for many species of birds, insects and small mammals. For example, the common European oak (Quercus robur) is said to support more than 300 animal species.

THE NITROGEN CYCLE

Nitrogen is constantly being recycled. All proteins contain atoms of nitrogen. The nitrogen is taken from the air by soil bacteria and made into soluble nitrate ('fixed') which is absorbed by plants. Other bacteria decompose organic matter, releasing nitrate and returning some nitrogen to the air.

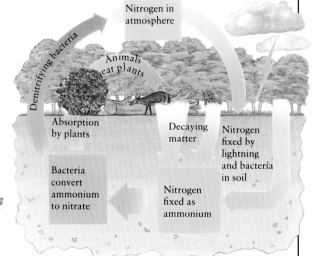

Nitrogen in atmosphere

Denitrifying bacteria

Animals eat plants

Absorption by plants

Decaying matter

Nitrogen fixed by lightning and bacteria in soil

Bacteria convert ammonium to nitrate

Nitrogen fixed as ammonium

▲ Nitrogen passes from air to soil, to plants, to animals which eat plants, and eventually back into the air. The energy of lightning also fixes some nitrogen, by making the gas react with oxygen to form nitrogen oxides. These dissolve in rain. Some nitrate drains from the soil into rivers and then into the sea. This supplies nitrogen for freshwater and marine plants, and the animals which feed on them.

Grasslands

There are regions where, for most of the year, the rate at which water can evaporate is greater than the amount of rainfall. Such regions would be deserts, were it not for the rain that falls during one season of the year. Just beyond the edges of the deserts, rain falls in the summer. In the dry interior of continents it falls in winter. The rain allows plants to grow, turning the dry, brown landscape green. Few trees can survive in these conditions, but flowering herbs and grasses abound. These regions are the grasslands.

SOIL

Grassland soils have a deep, dark-coloured, surface layer rich in humus. They are among the most fertile of all soils and are often farmed. The lower layers vary from place to place.

GRASSLANDS OF THE WORLD

The middle of continents are dry, because of their distance from the sea. The temperate, continental grasslands are called 'steppe' in Europe and Asia, 'prairie' in North America, and 'pampas' in South America. Temperate grassland is also found in eastern Australia. The subtropical grasslands of South America, Africa, India and northern Australia are called 'savanna'.

Grassland vegetation is mainly made up of drought-resistant grasses. In parts of the steppe these grasses are short, but they can be up to 2 m tall. Grass leaves grow from the base and can survive and grow even if it is grazed.

Grasslands

THE LANDSCAPES

In the rainy season, grasses and herbs grow rapidly. The land turns green or is blanketed by a mass of brightly coloured flowers. The flowers set seed quickly and then die, with nutrients stored in their roots. As the rains stop, the plants turn brown. The dry vegetation burns easily and fires are common.

The fires nourish the soil with ash, which encourages new growth next time it rains. The plants have deep roots.

In Europe, the climate and geography have led to forests as the natural landscape, and almost any grassland will have been reclaimed from forest.

▼ *Much of the South American pampas is covered by tussocks or humps of feather grass. Elsewhere there is scrub. Underneath the plants the ground is hard.*

Prairie

Pampas

Prairie grass

◄ *The prairies were once home to large herds of bison. Today, most of the prairie is used to grow wheat and corn (maize).*

◀ *The grasslands differ mainly in the species in each location. In Australia, the grasslands cover a wide range of soils and feature tough grasses and scattered acacia and gum trees. These grasslands are home to kangaroos, koalas, emus and kookaburras.*

SLASH AND BURN

People have extended grasslands by setting fire to vegetation during the dry season. This encourages new growth, but destroys woody plants. Livestock also destroy tree seedlings by trampling them.

THE DUST BOWL

The grassland climate is dry and sometimes there are long droughts. One in the prairies of the central United States lasted from 1933 to 1939. Severe dust storms in 1934 and 1935 turned the area into what came to be known as the 'Dust Bowl'. The situation had been made worse by years of overgrazing and poor farming.

▲ *On the African savanna, domed rock formations called 'bornhardts' stand above the plateau. These are made of granite or similar rock. The round shape results from curved sheets of rock that are separating from the solid rock below. There are other small, isolated hills about 10 m tall which are formed from exposed rock. They are called castle 'kopjes' (pronounced koppies).*

Kopje

Bornhardt

Savanna

Umbrella tree

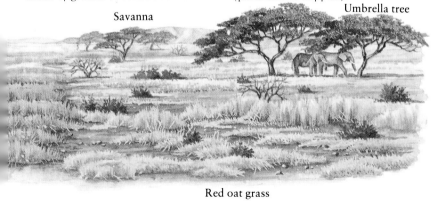

Red oat grass

▲ *African savanna is found on both sides of the Equator. It is home to many species of grazing animals, such as wildebeest which move in large herds. Each species feeds differently, so they do not compete with each other. The grazers provide food for lions, cheetahs, hyenas, dogs and other carnivores. Not all African grasslands are tropical savanna, the South African 'veld' is temperate grassland.*

FACTS ABOUT GRASSLANDS

● Grasslands are cultivated in North America and to a limited extent in Europe, but farming is restricted by the dry climate.
● In South America and Australia the grasslands are used for cattle ranching.
● The southern part of the African savanna is farmed, but over most of the area people live mainly by herding cattle. In the dry season people and cattle move around in search of pasture, as do all grazing animals.
● Wheat is grown on the Indian savanna.
● There are nearly 8000 species of grasses. Some have roots that can reach water 5 m below ground.

Deserts

When rain falls on the ground some of it evaporates. If the amount of water that evaporates is greater than the rainfall, a desert will form. Any region where the annual rainfall is less than 250 mm is a desert. Deserts are usually windy, but not necessarily hot. The polar regions are deserts, and temperatures in the Gobi Desert are below freezing for six months of every year. Most deserts are rocky not sandy. Sand covers about two percent of the North American desert, and only 11 percent of the Sahara.

▶ Many plants survive in the desert by having a very fast life cycle. Their seeds can lie dormant for many years. On the rare occasions of rainfall, these plants, such as this African grass, germinate, flower, set seed and die, all in a matter of days.

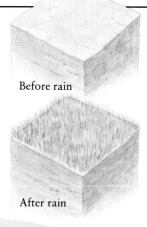

Before rain

After rain

ARID LANDS

Deserts are also known as arid or dry lands. Desert soils contain almost no plant or animal (organic) matter. They are made up of dry sand grains and stones, often with gravel, because wind blows away smaller particles. Some desert soils can be cultivated, if water is provided. Most of the world's hot deserts are spreading, mainly due to a change in climate, bringing drier weather to bordering lands. Overgrazing may make this worse by removing vegetation, causing soil erosion.

Arid areas

DESERT ECOSYSTEMS

Few plants can grow in shifting sand. There are two main types of desert plants. Shrubs and small trees, such as the Joshua trees, saguaro cactus trees and sagebrushes of North America, and the acacias and tamarisks of the Sahara, store water. Others lie dormant waiting for rain.

Joshua tree

▶ The constant sand-laden wind sculpts rocks into strange shapes. The rocks are also heated by the Sun, expanding, and then cooling and shrinking. This strain splits them.

Stony desert

Saguaro

Prickly pear

Dry river bed

Rock pavement

SAND DUNES

Many different types of sand dunes are formed in sandy deserts. They are shaped by the wind. A 'barchan' has a crescent-shaped front and a long tail made from sand blown by the wind. They form long series. 'Linear dunes' are created in strong steady winds, which cut troughs in the desert floor. The sand is piled up into long, rounded dunes. A 'seif' dune is a long, sharp ridge lying parallel to the wind direction. A ridge that is formed at right angles to the wind is an 'aklé' dune. It is formed where there are cross currents. Star dunes, with several sharp ridges, occur where the wind direction is constantly changing.

Barchan

Linear dune

FACTS ABOUT DESERTS

● In some hot deserts, a 'sand sea' may form, called an 'erg'. The biggest is the Grand Erg Oriental, covering 196,000 sq km in Algeria and Tunisia. Some dunes in the Grand Erg are more than 300 m high.
● Death Valley, in the Mojave Desert of California, is the hottest place in North America. Summer temperatures often exceed 50°C, and 57°C has been recorded. Temperatures are similar in the Libyan Sahara, where 58°C has been recorded. Desert nights are cool, and in winter temperatures often fall below freezing.
● The coldest place in the world is in Antarctica, which is also a desert. The winter temperature can fall to −90°C. It is also the largest desert at 14.2 million sq km.

▼ *High, rocky Saharan plateaux ('hammada') are cut through by deep canyons.*

Hammada

Sand dunes

Salt pan

Oasis

Sandy desert

▼ *Oases are natural desert features, but people can make them. In places where water lies close to the surface wells are dug, and the underground water from distant wetter regions is released under pressure from the aquifer.*

OASES

An oasis is a fertile place in a desert, where the water table reaches the surface. Sometimes water will fill an aquifer (a rock that holds water trapped between two impermeable layers). If there is a fault above the aquifer the water will be forced up it and an oasis will form.

◄ *A stony desert, or the surface of small, rounded pebbles, is called 'reg'.*

Oasis

Saturated sand

Fault

Impermeable rock

Aquifer

Impermeable rock

Tropical Rainforests

The ice sheets have advanced and retreated many times over land near the poles. But in a belt of land around the Equator the temperature has never fallen below freezing. As the climate changed near the poles, so did the forests. But in the tropics, forest of one kind or another has grown in some places for millions of years. In this time, species have evolved to fill every corner and use every source of food. This is why tropical rainforests contain a greater variety of plant and animals species than any other forests.

SOILS

Tropical soils are red or yellow in colour, and up to 10 m deep. They lie on top of clay. Most nutrients have been lost from the surface layers. Plants feed on the rapidly recycled organic matter.

HUMID HABITATS

The Equatorial climate is warm, with heavy rainfall. Plants grow rapidly and, in order to expose their leaves to sunlight, trees grow very tall. The tops of the trees form a continuous canopy, at a height of about 40 m, shading the ground. Most of the trees have shallow roots. They obtain their nutrients from the uppermost layer of soil. Many support themselves with roots that grow outwards as stilts or props. Smaller trees and seedlings form a lower layer of forest and shrubs grow near ground level.

Tropical rainforest

THE ECOSYSTEM

Rainforest grows in lowland areas, including shallow swamps. But much of the Equatorial region is mountainous. As you go higher, the lowland forest changes into forest with smaller trees. There is more abundant undergrowth often with palms, and many more plants growing at ground level. This is called 'montane' forest. Higher still, the forest becomes more open. The trees are shorter and covered in epiphytes and climbers. Mosses, ferns and herbs blanket the ground. This is called 'cloud' forest because it is often shrouded in low cloud, from which it obtains moisture.

FACTS ABOUT RAINFORESTS

- When tropical forest is cleared, new growth often forms a dense 'jungle'.
- Because of the shade in a rainforest, the air temperature may not be high. But the lack of wind and high humidity make it feel hotter.
- Despite the high rainfall, in most places the ground dries out quickly.
- Tropical forests are being cleared mainly to provide land for farming and plantation forestry. This is often successful on richer soils in valleys, but elsewhere crops soon fail as surface nutrients are removed.

Inselberg

EROSION

When trees are cleared from a hillside the soil may be left bare. Rain can then wash away topsoil, which is carried down the slope. Sometimes it falls into a river, causing pollution.

◀ *In Colombia, as elsewhere in the tropics, isolated hills with steep, smooth sides rise 400 m or more above the plains. These 'inselbergs' or 'sugar-loaf mountains' are made from layers of rock that have separated and are peeling away.*

▲ *In Madagascar, most of the original rainforest has been cut down to provide land for growing crops. Removing the protective forest cover has caused severe soil erosion.*

◀ *The tops, or crowns, of trees in the rainforest merge to form an interlocking canopy of leafy vegetation about 44 m from the ground. Food is more abundant here than on the ground and many of the snakes, lizards, frogs, birds, mammals and insects living here never visit the ground.*

MANGROVE SWAMPS

Mangrove forests form dense thickets in coastal swamps. The trees produce stilt roots which then develop more roots of their own. Some of these roots stick out above the mud in which they grow. The roots trap shifting sediment, gradually extending the land seaward. Snails and other small animals live among the roots.

PAST, PRESENT, FUTURE

Natural Resources: Energy

Substances we use to make the things we need are called 'resources'. To prepare a meal, for example, we need food, water, pots and pans, cutlery, a cooker and a source of heat. The food and water, the metals from which the cooker and utensils are made, and the fuel that is burned to produce heat are all resources. They are called natural resources because we obtain them from the world around us. If using a resource does not reduce the amount of it available to us, it is called a 'renewable' resource. River water is a renewable resource, provided we take no more of it than is replaced by the rain. Food is a renewable resource because farmers can grow more. Most of our energy resources are 'non-renewable', because either the amount of the resource is fixed and cannot be replaced, or because it is replaced, but only very slowly.

FOSSIL FUELS

'Fossil' is from a Latin word, meaning 'dug from the ground'. Coal, oil and natural gas are called fossil fuels because they are made from the remains of ancient plants or animals. They were formed very slowly over millions of years and are non-renewable.

▶ *Coal formed from trees and other plants which grew beside water. When the trees died, they could not rot away fully, because the ground was waterlogged. They accumulated as peat, and were eventually buried. The peat was squashed by its own weight and the weight of the rocks above it, making it harder, and turning into 'lignite' or 'brown coal'.*

Movements of the rocks underneath then squashed some of the coal even more and heated it, forming a hard black coal called anthracite. Anthracite burns better than lignite as it contains more carbon.

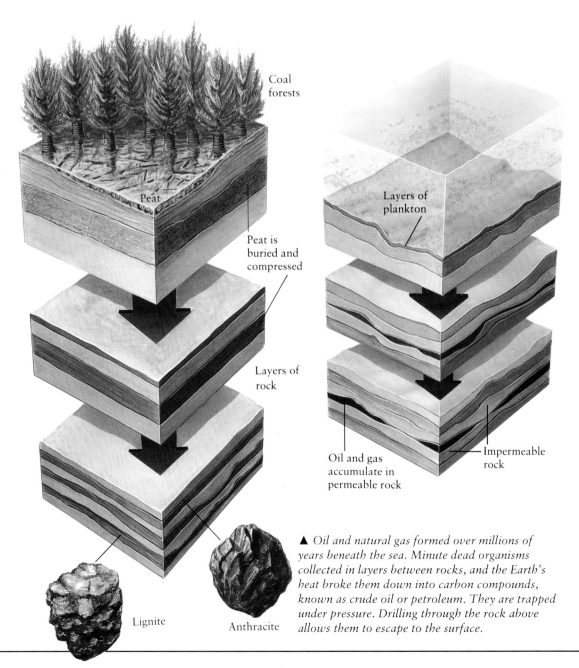

Coal forests

Peat

Peat is buried and compressed

Layers of rock

Layers of plankton

Oil and gas accumulate in permeable rock

Impermeable rock

Lignite

Anthracite

▲ *Oil and natural gas formed over millions of years beneath the sea. Minute dead organisms collected in layers between rocks, and the Earth's heat broke them down into carbon compounds, known as crude oil or petroleum. They are trapped under pressure. Drilling through the rock above allows them to escape to the surface.*

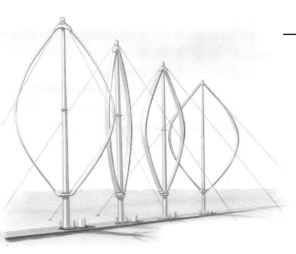

WIND POWER

Wind generators convert the motion of wind into electrical power. Wind is a renewable energy source, but it takes thousands of very large, costly machines to obtain useful amounts.

GEOTHERMAL POWER

If a mass of rock or water below ground is hotter than its surroundings, the heat can be recovered as 'geothermal energy'. Drilling into the rock allows the hot water to flow to the surface. If the rock is dry, water is pumped down one hole, heated, and recovered from another. This resource is non-renewable, because the rock is cooled, or the hot water is removed.

▲ *In some places, the pressure of water heated below ground forces it to the surface as a geyser (see page 101). The geyser can be capped and the steam is used to drive a turbine to produce electrical power.*

HYDROELECTRIC POWER

Hydroelectric power is generated by turbines driven by falling water. A dam is built across a river to form a lake. Gates in the dam wall allow the water to fall to the level of the river below, flowing past turbines inside the wall as it does so.

◀ *On the La Rance estuary, France, and in Fundy Bay, Canada, the ebb and flow of the tides turns turbines in a tidal barrier.*

NUCLEAR POWER

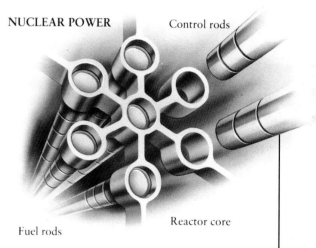

Control rods

Fuel rods

Reactor core

In the core of a nuclear reactor, uranium atoms are split to produce heat. The heat is used to boil water for steam to drive turbines. Uranium is mined from rocks.

HOW LONG WILL IT LAST?

No one knows how much of the non-renewable resources remain. Uranium and coal will last several centuries, but oil and gas are less abundant and may soon run out.

Oil 45 years

Gas 76 years

Coal 521 years

SOLAR POWER

Solar panels absorb heat from the Sun, which warms water flowing through pipes beneath the surface of the panels. The pipes pass inside the building to the hot water tank, and heat up the water. Solar cells convert sunlight into electricity. They work in warm or cold weather.

Natural Resources: Metals, Land and Water

Metals are extremely valuable resources. Many of the everyday articles in our homes are made from metal. A few metals, such as gold and copper, occur in the Earth's crust in pure form, as 'native elements'. But most are found as minerals called ores, which are chemical compounds containing a high proportion of the metal. Some of our mineral resources are non-metals. Paper is made whiter by adding kaolin, a clay mineral. Land and water are also valuable resources.

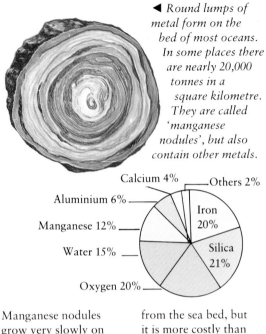

◄ *Round lumps of metal form on the bed of most oceans. In some places there are nearly 20,000 tonnes in a square kilometre. They are called 'manganese nodules', but also contain other metals.*

Calcium 4% — Others 2%
Aluminium 6% —
Manganese 12% —
Iron 20%
Water 15% —
Silica 21%
Oxygen 20% —

UNDERWATER RICHES

Mineral resources are non-renewable, although many can be recycled and used again. We obtain many minerals from quarries and mines, but the sea bed and sea water itself are rich in minerals.

Manganese nodules grow very slowly on deep sea beds. They contain enough of some metals to supply us for centuries. The nodules are dredged from the sea bed, but it is more costly than mining the metals on land. Phosphorus also forms nodules, and they are mined off the coast of California.

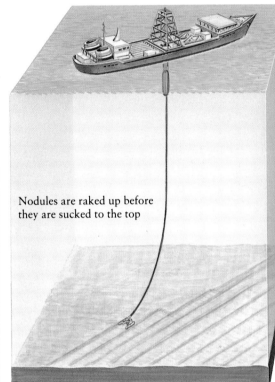

Nodules are raked up before they are sucked to the top

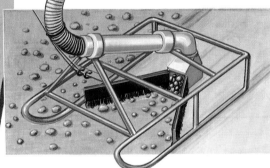

METALS

We use metals in widely differing amounts. Some, such as aluminium, iron and magnesium, are abundant, but tin, silver and platinum are already scarce. New deposits may be discovered, or new technology might allow existing resources to be mined more efficiently, but the costs will rise, and substitutes for some metals will be needed. The graph shows how long the known stocks of some metals may last, given the present rate of consumption.

DATAFILE

Amount of metal produced each year worldwide (tonnes):
● **Iron:** 740 million
● **Bauxite (aluminium ore):** 77 million
● **Manganese:** 22 million
● **Zinc:** 6 million
● **Lead:** 3 million
● **Nickel:** 689,000
● **Copper:** 8000
● **Gold:** 1500
● About 15 percent by weight of the uppermost 16 km of the Earth's crust is aluminium oxide.
● Sixty percent of the world's gold is mined in South Africa. The mines are up to 3700 m deep.

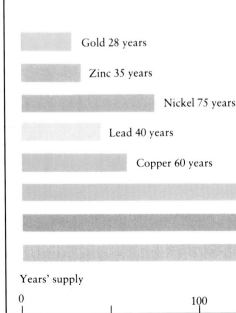

Gold 28 years
Zinc 35 years
Nickel 75 years
Lead 40 years
Copper 60 years
Manganese 180 years
Iron ore 400 years
Bauxite (aluminium ore) 255 years

Years' supply

0   100   200   300

Opencast mine

MINING ORES

Metal ores are cut or blasted from the surrounding rock. The ore is crushed, and the worthless rock removed. Many metal ores contain oxygen or sulphur. The pure metal can be separated by heating.

RARE METALS

Gold is usually found as small grains or nuggets of the pure metal. Where there is gold there may also be platinum, either pure or mixed with ores of copper, nickel, lead or other metals. Silver occurs as a pure metal, or as silver sulphide, with the sulphides of other metals.

DRINKING WATER

In regions where rainfall is low, drinking water can be obtained by purifying sea water. The process is called 'desalination' and there are two methods. The most common is distillation. Sea water is boiled and the vapour, which contains very little salt, is condensed and collected. The process is repeated until the water is fit to drink. The other method is to force water through a membrane that allows water molecules to pass through, but traps the salts.

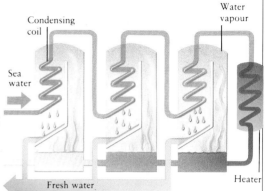

▲ *Some metals can be obtained from sands. Titanium is extracted from the rich sands on the Australian coasts.*

► *Land in the Netherlands has been reclaimed from the sea for nearly 1000 years. About a quarter of the present land area has been created in this way.*

RECLAIMING LAND FROM THE SEA

Since medieval times, earth banks or dikes were built to protect the reclaimed Dutch 'polders' from flooding. In the 1920s, a large part of the Zuider Zee in the Netherlands was reclaimed by enclosing it with a dam 29 km long. The fertile polders are valuable farmland, and can eventually be settled. Parts of England, Italy and Japan have also been reclaimed.

Dams
Land reclaimed :
before 1900   after 1900

▲ *The windmills, for which the Netherlands is famous, were used to pump water from the polders into drainage channels. Continous pumping is needed as the water seeps back in.*

Air Pollution

Technology makes our lives easier, but factories, cars and power stations also pollute the air we breathe. Burning fuel to produce power, and incinerating waste releases millions of tonnes of gases such as carbon dioxide, sulphur dioxide and nitrogen oxides into the air every year, together with ash, dust or soot particles. Air pollution damages human health and harms wildlife, but can also alter the finely balanced atmospheric processes of the Earth, with potentially serious consequences.

BURNING

Although some air pollution is caused by natural sources, such as volcanic eruptions, which release sulphur dioxide, most is caused by waste gases released by burning fuels and incinerating waste from homes and factories. Some of the waste contains toxic (poisonous) chemicals such as mercury which are then released into the air. Tiny particles of solids and liquids are also given off, which can cause breathing problems.

THE OZONE LAYER

Ozone is a form of oxygen in which the molecule is made up of three atoms (O_3), rather than the usual two (O_2). It forms in the stratosphere. Ultraviolet (UV) radiation from the Sun splits oxygen molecules into free oxygen atoms. Each oxygen atom joins an oxygen molecule to form ozone. UV radiation also splits ozone molecules. So ozone is constantly forming, splitting and reforming. The UV radiation absorbed by this process cannot reach Earth. UV radiation causes sunburn, skin cancer and eye problems, and affects plant growth.

THE HOLE OVER THE ANTARCTIC

1979

1987

1991

◀ Chlorine (Cl) reacts with ozone to form chlorine monoxide (ClO) and oxygen (O_2). The chlorine is then released to go round the cycle again.

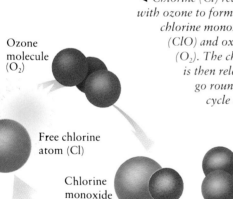

Ozone molecule (O_2)

Free chlorine atom (Cl)

Chlorine monoxide (ClO)

Oxygen molecule (O_3)

Free oxygen atom (O)

▶ Every spring (October) the ozone layer over Antarctica thins by up to 50 percent. This 'hole' disappears in summer, but reappears every year. In 1987 it covered an area the size of the United States. No 'hole' has been detected over the Arctic, but the ozone decreases slightly in January and February.

CFCs

Ozone is destroyed by compounds such as chlorofluorocarbons (CFCs). CFCs are used in some refrigerators and packaging materials. They drift up into the stratosphere, where they break down and release chlorine. Each chlorine atom can destroy hundreds of thousands of ozone molecules. Many scientists are concerned that as the ozone layer is damaged, a greater amount of harmful UV radiation will reach the Earth's surface.

▲ Photochemical smog is a health hazard in many major cities. It is the result of chemical reactions caused by the action of sunlight on nitrogen oxides and unburnt fuel from car exhaust fumes.

SMOG

Earlier this century, in London and other European cities, a mixture of fog and smoke caused choking smogs, known as 'pea-soupers'. Today, in places where there is a lot of sunshine, such as Los Angeles, USA, traffic fumes cause 'photochemical smog'.

ACID RAIN

Cloud droplets are naturally acidic, because the carbon dioxide in air dissolves to form a weak acid. But sulphur dioxide and nitrogen oxides produced by burning fossil fuels form stronger acids. The moisture reaches the ground as acid mist, snow, or rain. Acid rain damages forests and acidifies lakes, harming aquatic animals.

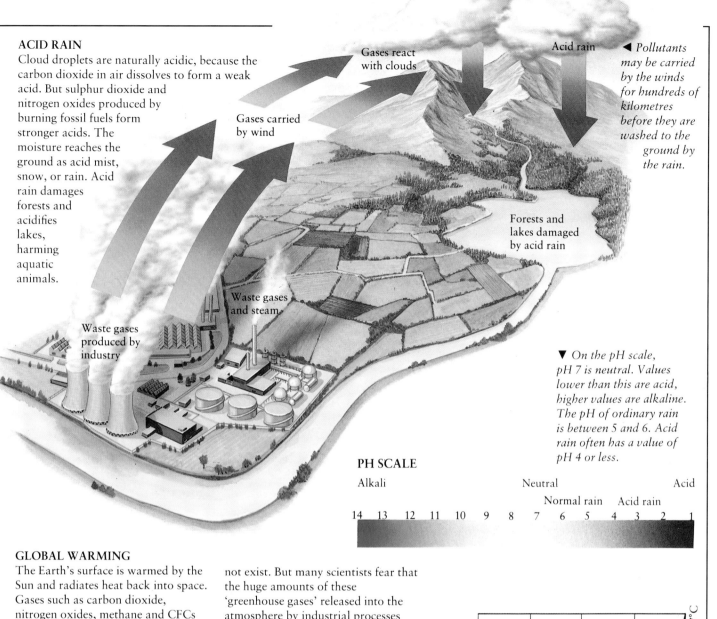

Gases react with clouds

Gases carried by wind

Acid rain

◄ *Pollutants may be carried by the winds for hundreds of kilometres before they are washed to the ground by the rain.*

Forests and lakes damaged by acid rain

Waste gases and steam

Waste gases produced by industry

▼ *On the pH scale, pH 7 is neutral. Values lower than this are acid, higher values are alkaline. The pH of ordinary rain is between 5 and 6. Acid rain often has a value of pH 4 or less.*

PH SCALE

Alkali   Neutral   Acid

Normal rain   Acid rain

| 14 | 13 | 12 | 11 | 10 | 9 | 8 | 7 | 6 | 5 | 4 | 3 | 2 | 1 |

GLOBAL WARMING

The Earth's surface is warmed by the Sun and radiates heat back into space. Gases such as carbon dioxide, nitrogen oxides, methane and CFCs in the atmosphere trap some of this heat, and warm the lower atmosphere. The atmosphere radiates heat back to Earth. This is called the 'greenhouse effect', and without it the Earth would be so cold that life could not exist. But many scientists fear that the huge amounts of these 'greenhouse gases' released into the atmosphere by industrial processes and burning fossil fuels are warming the Earth so much that they will eventually upset the world's climate, and cause sea levels to rise.

► *Some scientists predict that the Earth's temperature could rise 3°C by 2070. After this, the rise will level off and the temperature will stabilize. If the Antarctic ice sheet melted, sea levels could rise, threatening low-lying areas such as the US coast (left).*

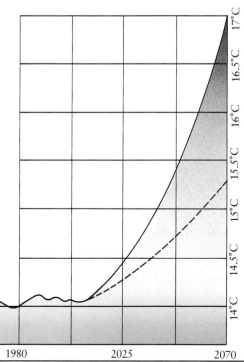

New York

Charleston

17°C

16.5°C

16°C

15.5°C

15°C

14.5°C

14°C

1980   2025   2070

Environmental Problems

Every living organism changes the world around it, including humans. We clear massive areas of land to grow food and to build homes, cities and roads. We quarry and mine for building stone, minerals and fuels, and manufacture the things that improve our lives. When we are careless we harm the environment in many ways: poor people are forced to farm using methods that damage the land; we dirty water with our waste; and we harm wildlife by destroying its food and shelter.

LAND AT RISK

Land bordering all deserts is at risk. As the deserts expand, people are forced onto smaller grazing areas, increasing the risk of soil erosion. The problem is most severe in the Sahel, south of the Sahara Desert.

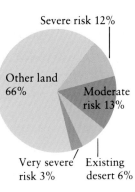

Severe risk 12%

Other land 66%

Moderate risk 13%

Very severe risk 3%

Existing desert 6%

MARCHING SAND

Much of the world's grazing land is in semi-arid areas. From time to time there are severe droughts lasting several years. During these droughts the ground dries, plants disappear and wind-blown sand and dust may bury more fertile soil and destroy crops. Many people in the semi-arid areas are nomadic, moving with the seasons in search of pasture for their animals. When the pasture fails, they are crowded into the small areas that remain. This leads to overgrazing, which causes soil erosion.

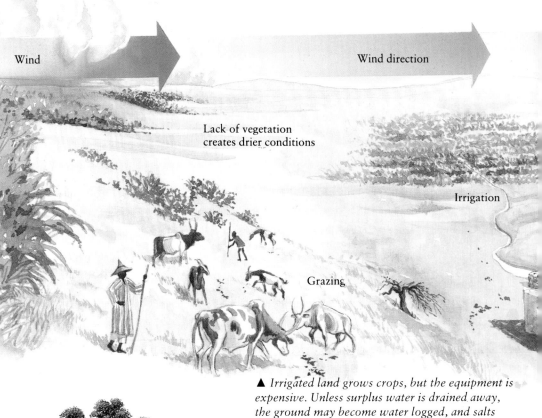

Wind

Wind direction

Lack of vegetation creates drier conditions

Irrigation

Grazing

▲ *Irrigated land grows crops, but the equipment is expensive. Unless surplus water is drained away, the ground may become water logged, and salts accumulate, so that crops cannot grow.*

DEFORESTATION

In the tropics, forests are cleared to provide timber. Some of the land is replanted as plantation forest and some is converted into farms and cattle ranches. Forest valleys are also flooded to make lakes for hydroelectric schemes. Plant and animal species disappear. Those found nowhere else become extinct.

▼ *Soil is washed into rivers, causing them to silt up.*

◄ *Clearing plants from high ground may cause flooding on low ground, as rain water quickly runs off the surface. In the dry season, exposed, infertile soils may be baked hard and crack.*

► *The soil in many parts of the rainforests is poor. The land can only support a few harvests before farmers have to move to a new area.*

RIVERS IN PERIL

Small quantities of waste do not usually cause serious harm if they are dumped into a river, because the river quickly purifies itself. But if many factories dump their waste into the same river, it cannot cope, and the water becomes very polluted.

Oil pipeline
5 days
9 days
50 days

Spread of oil slick

EXXON VALDEZ

On 24 March, 1989, the tanker *Exxon Valdez* ran aground in Alaska, releasing about 32 million litres of crude oil. The oil formed a slick covering more than 3600 sq km and about 1700 km of shoreline was badly polluted.

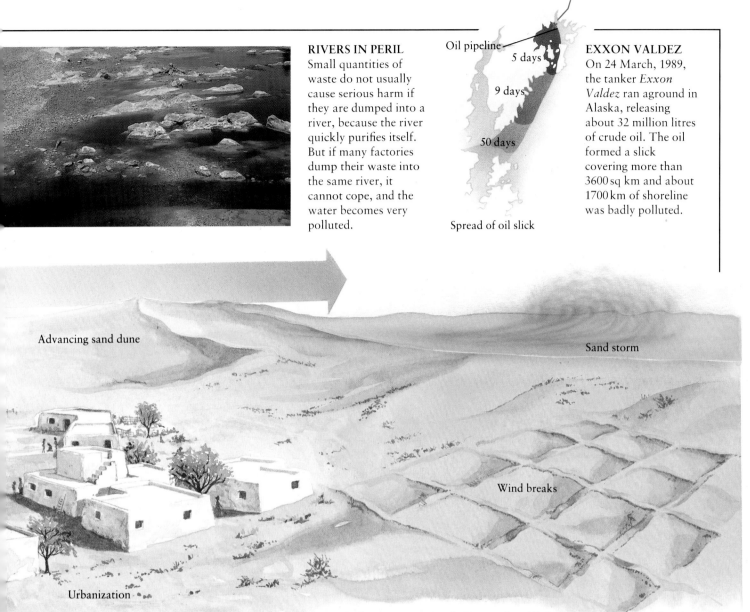

Advancing sand dune

Sand storm

Wind breaks

Urbanization

▲ As the deserts spread, many people are forced to leave their homes and try to make a living elsewhere. Settlements grow larger, increasing pressure on the land.

▲ Dry sand and light soil can be held in place by nets or by spraying a protective film over it, to stop the processes of erosion.

▶ Nuclear waste remains dangerous for several centuries. It must be stored deep underground.

WASTE DISPOSAL

We produce millions of tonnes of waste every year from mines, factories and homes. Most of the waste is buried in landfill sites. Although new sites are strictly controlled to ensure they are safe, toxic chemicals have leached from some old sites, contaminating the land and water supplies.

◀ The base of a landfill site is lined to prevent dirty liquids leaking into nearby water. At the end of each day, the rubbish is levelled and covered with topsoil.

Pollutants leach into water table

Steel containers

Concrete lining

Conservation

Over the last 30 years, we have become aware of the damage we do to the environment. People have begun to find ways to reduce the amount of waste released into the air and water, and strict laws are applied by many governments. Ecologists and conservationists have found ways to help wildlife. Recycling has encouraged new uses for things that we used to throw away as rubbish. Many problems remain, but progress has been made, and there have been many important improvements.

RECYCLED PAPER

About half of our domestic waste is paper which could be recycled. Recycling paper causes less pollution and protects the natural habitats cleared to plant the softwoods used to make new paper.

Symbol for recycled paper

GLASS AND ALUMINIUM RECYCLING

Processing raw materials uses energy and causes pollution. Recycling often saves energy and resources, and reduces domestic waste as well as pollution. Old glass jars and bottles can be crushed and melted to make new glass objects. Extracting aluminium from its ore uses a great deal of energy, so recycling aluminium cans saves energy. It used to be expensive to recycle the cans, because they contained steel, which had to be separated from the aluminium. Cans are now made from aluminium only.

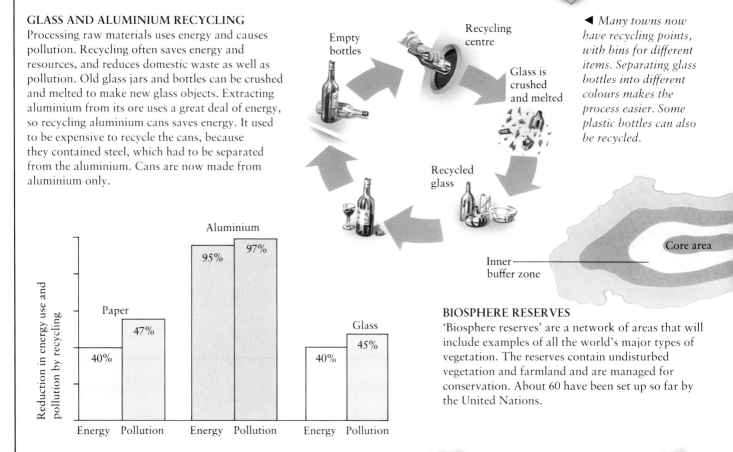

Empty bottles

Recycling centre

Glass is crushed and melted

Recycled glass

◄ *Many towns now have recycling points, with bins for different items. Separating glass bottles into different colours makes the process easier. Some plastic bottles can also be recycled.*

Core area

Inner buffer zone

BIOSPHERE RESERVES

'Biosphere reserves' are a network of areas that will include examples of all the world's major types of vegetation. The reserves contain undisturbed vegetation and farmland and are managed for conservation. About 60 have been set up so far by the United Nations.

Reduction in energy use and pollution by recycling

Paper: Energy 40%, Pollution 47%
Aluminium: Energy 95%, Pollution 97%
Glass: Energy 40%, Pollution 45%

LANDSCAPE PRESERVATION

Attempts are now being made to reclaim land that has been used for mining or industry. Opencast pits can be flooded, and turned into lakes for watersports and wildlife. Old industrial sites and rubbish tips can be covered with a thick layer of soil and turned into recreational land.

Old industrial site

CONSERVING HABITATS

International agreements exist to protect endangered species and to preserve their habitats. The habitats of migratory water birds are protected by the Ramsar Convention on Wetlands of International Importance. Other places are recognized by the United Nations as World Heritage Sites.

World Heritages Sites Protected

Wetlands of International Importance Protected

Wetlands and World Heritage Sites Protected

COUNTRIES WITH AGREEMENTS TO PROTECT WORLD HERITAGE SITES AND WETLANDS OF INTERNATIONAL IMPORTANCE

Outer buffer zone

▲ *The reserve has a protected core, and an inner 'buffer' zone for research. Local people live in an outer buffer zone, which tourists are allowed to visit.*

BIOLOGICAL CONTROL

Pesticides are expensive and can cause pollution. 'Biological control' uses natural enemies to control pests and weeds. For example, geese eat the weeds in fruit orchards, at the same time fertilizing the ground. Ladybirds are used to control aphids. Ducks are used by farmers in China to eat the insects that damage crops.

THE EARTH SUMMIT

In June 1992, the UN Conference on Environment and Development (the 'Earth Summit') took place in Rio de Janeiro. Agreements were signed by many countries to limit climate change, and to protect species and habitats ('biodiversity'), sustainable development and forest management. A programme to achieve these aims was outlined.

FAST-GROWING TIMBER

Tropical timber can be produced in plantations of fast-growing native species, to prevent rainforests being destroyed. One such tree, *Kadam*, is grown in Indonesia. It reaches 3 m in its first year after planting out, then adds 2–3 m a year for up to eight years. Another Asian species, *Erima*, can grow to 25 m in four years and 50 m in 60 years.

◀ *Industrial wasteland can become a park with lakes and trees or playing fields.*

Reclaimed land

GLOSSARY

Words in **bold** indicate an entry elsewhere in the Glossary.

Abrasion: Process of **erosion** in which particles of rock are worn away, and wear away a surface by being dragged over it or thrown against it.

Abyssal plain: Flat area of the ocean where depths exceed 2000 m. Oozes (mud and other sediments) are deposited on the abyssal plain.

Active margin: Margin of a continent which is also a **plate** margin, and is associated with earthquake and volcanic activity, and ocean trenches.

Agglomerate: **Igneous rock** made up of sharp fragments of different sizes. These may result from a volcanic explosion.

Alluvium: Sediment transported by a river or stream and deposited in its floodplain.

Amber: Fossilized sap of conifers. It hardens to a clear, brownish resin and may contain trapped insects.

Amethyst: Purple form of **quartz**.

Ammonites: Extinct **invertebrate** group related to squid and octopuses. The fossilized shell resembles a ridged catherine wheel. Ammonites are found in rocks from the Devonian to the Upper Cretaceous ages.

Andesite: Fine-grained volcanic rock.

Anthracite: Hard, jet-black form of **coal** which has a high carbon content.

Anticline: Arch-shaped **fold** in rocks with the oldest rocks in the core.

Anticyclone: Area of high **atmospheric pressure.**

Antiform: An arch-shaped **fold** in the rocks where the oldest rocks may not be in the centre.

Aquifer: Mass of rock that is **permeable** to water and in which a large quantity of water may be stored.

Archipelago: Group of islands.

Artesian well: Well from which water flows without being pumped, because the head of the water in the **aquifer** lies above the level of the well head.

Asthenosphere: Weak zone in the upper **mantle** of the Earth which lies beneath the **lithosphere.**

Atmosphere: Layer of air, which surrounds the Earth. The atmosphere is about 500 km thick.

Atmospheric pressure: Downward force exerted by the weight of the air; 1013 millibars at sea level.

Atoll: Ring-shaped coral **reef**, which surrounds a lagoon. It is often built on a submerging **volcano.**

Aurora: Phenomenon of bright lights in the **atmosphere** caused by the **solar wind** entering the **ionosphere.**

Avalanche: Sudden, rapid fall of rock or snow.

Badlands: Area of barren country where occasional heavy rainfall and little plant cover leads to severe **erosion.**

Barometer: Instrument for measuring **atmospheric pressure.**

Barrier reef: Coral **reef** which runs roughly parallel to a shoreline and is separated from the land by a **lagoon.**

Basalt: Blackish, fine-grained, **igneous rock** formed from the hardened **lava** from a volcanic **eruption.**

Basin: Large depression in the Earth's **crust.**

Batholith: Large igneous **intrusion** which occurs at great depths.

Beaufort Scale: Scale of whole numbers from 0 to 12 used to describe wind strength.

Bedding: Sheet-like layers in which **sedimentary rocks** are deposited.

Belemnites: Extinct **invertebrate** group related to squid and octopuses. They have hard internal parts which, when found as fossils, resemble bullets. Belemnites are found in rocks from the Jurassic to the Upper Cretaceous.

Biosphere: Part of the Earth in which life is found.

Black smoker: Fissure in the sea bed through which hot fluids flow into the sea water and mix with it to produce black, smoke-like plumes.

Brachiopod: Also known as lampshell. Marine **invertebrate** with the body contained in a pair of hinged shells.

Breaker: Sea wave that is collapsing as it approaches the shore.

Breccia: Coarse-grained **sedimentary rock** made up of angular fragments of rock held together by some kind of mineral **cement.**

Calcite: Common rock-forming mineral (calcium carbonate). It is the main mineral in **limestones.**

Carbon cycle: Movement of the element carbon (C) through the interior, surface and **atmosphere** of the Earth.

Caldera: Large, circular depression in the Earth's crust formed when the roof over a large mass of molten **igneous rock** collapses.

Cast: Replica of a **fossil** formed when the fossil itself is dissolved away to leave a **mould**, which is then filled in by sediment.

Cement: Material such as **calcite**, which passes into the spaces between sediments and then crystallizes out of solution to bind the sediment together.

Chalcopyrite: Common ore of copper. Because of its brassy yellow colour and metallic **lustre**, it is sometimes confused with gold, and is one of the minerals known as 'fool's gold'.

Chalk: Porous, fine-grained **sedimentary rock** which is hard when dry, and soft and clay-like when saturated with water. It is composed of the **calcite** skeletons of tiny sea creatures called coccolithophores and foraminiferids.

Chert: Form of **silica** which lacks a **crystal** structure.

Cirque: Armchair-shaped depression in a mountainous region, which is formed by the scouring action of a **glacier**. Also known as a corrie (Scotland) or cwm (Wales).

Cirrus: Type of cloud seen as wispy streaks high in the sky.

Clay: **Sedimentary rock** in which the particles are less than 4 micrometres in diameter.

Cleavage: The way a **crystal** splits along a plane of weakness caused by the mineral's atomic structure.

Clint: Block of hard, horizontally bedded **limestone** which is isolated from its neighbours by **joints** known as grikes.

Coal: Rock-like deposit, rich in carbon and used as a fuel, which is formed from the remains of fossil plants.

Composite volcano: **Volcano** in which the cone is built up of alternating layers of **lava** and ash.

Conglomerate: Coarse-grained **sedimentary rock** made up of rounded fragments.

Constructive margin: Boundary zone between two **crustal plates** where new crust is being formed. The mid-Atlantic ridge is a constructive margin.

Contact metamorphism: Type of **metamorphism** caused by heat resulting from contact with a large body of **magma.**

Continental crust: **Crust** that lies underneath the continents. It is composed mainly of **granite.**

Continental drift: Idea put forward in 1910 that, throughout geological time, the Earth's continents have been moving in relation to one another.

Continental margin: Zone between the shoreline and the deep ocean floor. It includes the **continental shelf**, the **continental slope** and the **continental rise**.

Continental rise: Ridge of sediment which forms at the bottom of the **continental slope**.

Continental shelf: Gently sloping zone between the shoreline and the top of the **continental slope**, which usually begins at a depth of about 150 m.

Continental slope: Steeply sloping zone between the bottom of the **continental shelf** and the beginning of the **continental rise**. It is usually cut by **submarine canyons** through which sediment from the land passes.

Convection current: Current within a fluid caused by temperature changes. Hot fluids are less dense than cool fluids and tend to rise. They then cool and fall again causing a continuous current. Convection currents within the **asthenosphere** may lead to the processes of **plate tectonics**.

Core: Centre of the Earth; it is divided into a solid inner core and a liquid outer core. The core is made mainly from nickel and iron at high pressures and temperatures.

Corrie: *see* **cirque**

Corundum: Hard mineral; sapphire and ruby are gem-quality forms of corundum.

Creep: Slow downhill movement of soil and subsoil caused by gravity.

Crust: Earth's outermost layer. It varies in thickness between about 5 km under some parts of the ocean and 50 km under mountain ranges.

Crystal: Solid body with a characteristic atomic structure, a definite chemical composition, regularly arranged plane faces and a shape which reflects the internal structure.

Cuesta: Landform which resembles a long, low ridge that has a steep slope on one side (the **scarp**) and a gentler slope on the other (the **dip** slope).

Cumulonimbus: Large cloud that towers up in a series of billowing cells, or smaller clouds, until it eventually flattens out to form an anvil shape. This a typical rain cloud.

Cumulus: Bulging, dome-shaped cloud with a flattened base, which resembles a cauliflower.

Cwm: *see* **cirque**

Cyclone: Region of low **atmospheric pressure**. Also called a depression.

Deep-sea trench: Deep, steep-sided trench more than 300 m deeper than the neighbouring ocean floor. Deep-sea trenches usually form at **destructive plate margins**.

Delta: Accumulation of sediments at the mouth of a river which resembles the shape of the Greek letter delta (Δ).

Depression: *see* **cyclone**.

Desert: Region in which the annual rainfall is less than 250 mm. Deserts may be either hot or cold.

Desertification: Spread of desert conditions, often as a result of human interference, for example by cutting down large areas of forest.

Destructive margin: Boundary between two crustal **plates** that are moving towards one another, where one plate is diving beneath the other and destroying **oceanic crust**. **Earthquakes** and volcanic activity occur at destructive margins.

Diamond: Crystalline form of carbon; the hardest naturally occurring material.

Dip: Angle formed between **beds** of rock and the horizontal.

Doldrums: Region close to the Equator where winds are light.

Dolerite: Dark-coloured, medium-grained **igneous rock** commonly found in **dykes**.

Dolomite: **Sedimentary rock** consisting of the rock-forming mineral also called dolomite.

Drainage pattern: Arrangement of the rivers and streams in an area. It is usually related to the geology of the area as well as its age.

Drift: Sediment deposited by a **glacier**.

Drumlin: Smooth, rounded, oval-shaped mound which is tapered at one end and blunt at the other. It may be made of glacial **drift** or of solid rock and is found in glaciated valleys.

Dry valley: Landform which resembles a river valley but contains no permanent stream.

Dune: Accumulation of wind-blown sand.

Dyke: Wall-like **intrusion** of **igneous rock**, which cuts through the bedding of the surrounding rocks.

Earthquake: Movement within the Earth's **crust** that sends out shock waves when brittle rocks suddenly fracture.

El Niño: Current of warm water which, from time to time, flows southwards along the coast of Ecuador and affects the climate throughout the Pacific.

Epicentre: Point on the Earth's surface immediately above the **hypocentre** of an **earthquake**.

Erosion: Wearing down of rocks and land surfaces through the movement of soil and rock debris by running water, wind, ice and gravity.

Erratic: Boulder which has not come from the local rocks but has been transported to its present position by moving ice.

Eruption: Outpouring of gas, **lava**, ash and other material from within the Earth, from a volcano or other opening, on to the surface, into the sea, or into the **atmosphere**.

Esker: Long, snake-like ridge of **drift** which has been laid down by the meltwater from a **glacier**.

Extinction: Complete death and therefore disappearance of a whole species of animals or plants.

Extrusion: Eruption of **magma** from a vent in the Earth's **crust**. A **volcano** is an extrusion.

Fault: Fracture or break in a body of rock which is too brittle to **fold**.

Feldspar: Important group of rock-forming minerals which includes orthoclase and plagioclase.

Fetch: Length of a stretch of water over which the wind is blowing to generate waves. The longer the fetch, the bigger the waves will be.

Fjord: (also fiord) Deep, narrow, U-shaped coastal inlet formed from a drowned glacial valley.

Flint: Variety of **chert** which often occurs as knobbly lumps in **chalk**.

Fog: Condition in which the air near the Earth's surface is almost saturated. The air contains suspended droplets of water that obscure vision.

Fold: Bend in the beds of rock.

Fossil: Remains or trace of an animal or plant preserved in the rocks. It is usually more than 10,000 years old.

Fracture: Clean break in a rock or mineral which is not caused by **cleavage** and is not related to the atomic structure of the mineral.

Front: Boundary between two different air masses.

Fumarole: Volcanic vent through which steam and gas are emitted.

Gabbro: Dark, coarse-grained **igneous rock** formed deep within the Earth.

Gaia hypothesis: Theory, developed by James Lovelock, suggesting that once life has begun on a planet, living things modify the conditions on the planet so that life is likely to be maintained.

Geological timescale: System that divides into named units all time since the Earth was formed.

Geyser: Vent in the Earth's crust which spouts a fountain of boiling water at intervals.

Glaciation: Covering of a large area of land by ice; an **ice age**.

Glacier: Large mass of moving ice. The effects of a glacier on, for example, a river valley can be easily recognized once the ice has retreated.

Gondwanaland: Supercontinent that existed in the Southern Hemisphere before continental drifting divided it into South America, Africa, India, Australia, New Zealand and Antarctica.

Graben: Trough-like structure which results from the downward movement of a block of **crust** between two almost vertical **fault** lines.

Granite: Coarse-grained, pale-coloured **igneous rock** consisting mainly of the minerals **quartz, feldspar** and **mica**.

Graptolites: Extinct group of sea-dwelling animals which lived in small colonies. Each individual was contained in a tube-like structure. Some colonies resemble tuning forks in shape. Graptolites lived between the Middle Cambrian and Lower Carboniferous Periods.

Greenhouse effect: Process in which the lower **atmosphere** is warmed. Clouds and gases such as carbon dioxide absorb and reradiate the sunlight reflected from the Earth's surface.

Grike: Widened **joint** separating one **clint** from another.

Guyot: Flat-topped, undersea mountain.

Gyre: Circular or spiral current of water.

Hail: Irregular pellets or rounded balls of ice that fall from the clouds like frozen rain.

Hanging valley: Valley formed by a **tributary** stream to a main valley that has been deepened by a **glacier**. The floor of the hanging valley is much higher than that of the main valley, and the tributary may flow into the larger river via a waterfall.

Hawaiian eruption: Volcanic **eruption** in which the basalt lavas are very fluid and where there are often fire fountains. Volcanic cones formed by Hawaiian eruptions have gently sloping sides.

Hematite: Important iron **ore**.

Hog's back: Landscape feature; a long narrow ridge formed where the **bedding** of the underlying rocks **dips** at an angle of 40° or more.

Hornblende: Important rock-forming mineral.

Horst: Block of rock thrust upwards between two nearly vertical **faults**.

Hot spot: Area of volcanic activity that is more or less stationary. It may form where there is a rising **convection current** in the **mantle**.

Humus: Decayed remains of plant material found in soil.

Hurricane: Violent tropical storm which occurs in the Caribbean area and on the north-eastern coast of Australia. It is caused by a deep **cyclone**.

Hydrological cycle: Water cycle; the flow of water through the **atmosphere**, land, oceans, seas, rivers, lakes and living things.

Hydrosphere: All of the water that occurs at the Earth's surface.

Hygrometer: Instrument for measuring humidity – the amount of moisture in the **atmosphere**.

Hypocentre: Centre or focus of an **earthquake**.

Ice age: Period during the Earth's history when the polar ice caps have expanded to cover large parts of other continents. There is also a fall in the average global temperature.

Igneous rock: Rock, such as **granite** or **basalt**, which has formed by crystallization from a hot **magma**.

Impermeable: Describes rocks that water or other liquids cannot pass through.

Impervious: Describes rocks that do not allow water, oil or gas to flow through them.

Inorganic: Substances that do not have a living origin, for example, minerals.

Intrusion: Body of **igneous rock**, such as a **batholith**, which has been thrust into existing or 'country' rocks.

Invertebrate: Animal which lacks a backbone. The great majority of the Earth's animals are invertebrates.

Ionosphere: Part of the Earth's **atmosphere**, above a height of about 80 km, where there are more free charged particles (ions and electrons).

Island arc: Group of volcanic islands situated close to a **deep-sea trench** where one crustal **plate** is being pulled beneath another.

Isobar: Line on a weather map which links points of equal **atmospheric pressure**.

Jet stream: High-speed flow of air that travels for great distances at heights of between 10–12 km and 12–15 km.

Joint: Break in a rock where there has been little movement along the line of the joint.

Karst: Area of **limestone** country with characteristics such as cavern systems, **sink holes**, and limestone **pavements**.

Kettle hole: Depression, sometimes filled with water, in an area of glacial **drift**. It is formed by melting ice.

Laccolith: Igneous **intrusion**, shaped like a lens, with a domed roof and flattened base, which has been thrust between the layers of other rocks.

Lagoon: Area of shallow water at the coast on the landward side of a reef or group of islands.

Laurasia: Supercontinent that existed in the Northern Hemisphere before **continental drifting** separated it into North America, Europe and Asia.

Lava: Hot, molten rock erupted from a **volcano**.

Limestone: Sedimentary rock made up mainly of **calcite** or **dolomite**.

Lithosphere: Upper, rocky layer of the Earth which includes the **crust** and the upper region of the **mantle**.

Longshore drift: Drifting of sand and shingle along a beach. Longshore drift results from sea currents caused by **prevailing winds**.

Lopolith: Saucer-shaped igneous **intrusion** thrust between the layers of surrounding rock.

Lustre: Describes the way **minerals** reflect light.

Magma: Body of molten rock.

Magnetic poles: Two points on the Earth's surface (north and south) to which a compass needle points. At the poles themselves a magnetized needle will point vertically downwards.

Magnetite: Magnetic **ore** of iron, also known as lodestone.

Mantle: Layer of the Earth lying between the **core** and the **crust**. It is hot and the lower part is thought to be in a semi-**plastic** state.

Marble: **Metamorphic rock** which is formed when **limestone** or **dolomite** are subjected to heat and/or pressure.

Meander: Turn or winding of a stream or river.

Meltwater: Water that has melted from a **glacier** or other body of ice.

Mercalli scale: Scale, from 1 to 12, for measuring the intensity of an **earthquake** based on its observed effects.

Mesa: Flat-topped hill formed by river action on horizontal beds of rock.

Mesosphere: Part of the Earth's **atmosphere**, between about 50 and 80 km in height.

Metamorphic rock: Rock which has been formed by the effects of heat and/or pressure on an existing rock so that the minerals have **recrystallized** – a changed rock.

Metamorphism: Process by which a rock changes through heat and/or pressure.

Meteorite: Small body of rocky or metallic material which enters the Earth's **atmosphere** from space and hits the ground.

Micas: Rock-forming minerals with a sheet-like structure found in many **metamorphic** and **igneous rocks**.

Mid-ocean ridge: Long ridge of active **volcanoes** in the middle of the ocean floor, where new **crust** is being created, and two **plates** are being forced apart through **sea-floor spreading**. The mid-Atlantic ridge is an example.

Mineral: Naturally occurring substance with a crystalline structure and definite chemical composition. Rocks are composed of minerals.

Mohorovičić discontinuity: Boundary between the **crust** and **mantle**, defined by the effects on **earthquake** waves.

Mohs' scale of hardness: Scale devised by the German scientist Friedrich Mohs (1773–1839) to estimate the hardness of **minerals** by their ability to scratch a set of standard minerals. Talc is very soft and is the mineral used to define 1 on the scale. It can be scratched by gypsum and other minerals of hardness 2. The other

minerals in the series are calcite 3; fluorite 4; apatite 5; orthoclase 6; quartz 7; topaz 8; corundum 9; diamond 10.

Monsoon: Seasonal change in the **prevailing wind** direction which may bring a dramatic change in weather, such as the rainy season in India.

Moraine: Ridge of **drift** left behind by a melting **glacier**.

Native element: Element, such as gold, which occurs in its pure form in the Earth's crust.

Oasis: Area in a desert where a regular supply of water, often from an underground source, enables a lush vegetation to thrive in fertile soils.

Oceanic crust: Rocks beneath the ocean bed and above the **Mohorovičić discontinuity**. Oceanic crust is composed mainly of **basalt**.

Olivine: Important rock-forming mineral found in **basalts** and **gabbros**.

Oolite: Type of **limestone** made up of rounded particles of calcium carbonate called ooliths.

Ore mineral: Mineral from which economically important amounts of a metal can be obtained.

Organic: Anything which has a living origin, for example, plants, animals, and their remains.

Outcrop: Rock exposed at the Earth's surface.

Ozone layer: Layer in the **atmosphere** at a height of 15–30 km where the form of oxygen called ozone (O_3) occurs in higher concentrations than usual. Ultraviolet (UV) light from the Sun is absorbed by ozone, converting it into the normal form of oxygen (O_2). This process therefore reduces the amount of potentially harmful UV radiation that reaches the Earth's surface.

Pack-ice: Area in the seas of polar regions where large blocks of ice are tightly packed together and move with the winds or currents.

Palaeontology: Science in which fossils are studied.

Pangaea: Single supercontinent from which all the current continents evolved by splitting up and slowly drifting apart.

Passive margin: Margin of a continent that is not the margin of a crustal **plate**.

Pavement: Area of bare, relatively flat rock resembling a road.

Peat: Black soil type with little or no structure, formed by the breakdown of plant material in wet, airless conditions.

Pegmatite: Very coarse-grained **igneous rock**.

Peléan eruption: Violent volcanic **eruption** where the **lavas** are very thick and clouds of gas-charged material are emitted.

Peridotite: Coarse-grained **igneous rock** rich in **olivine**. Much of the **mantle** is composed of this rock.

Permafrost: Permanently frozen ground.

Permeable: Describing rock through which water or other liquids can seep.

Petroleum: Naturally occurring crude oil.

Petrology: Scientific study of rocks.

Phaccolith: Igneous **intrusion** which follows the **folds** of rock layers.

Phyllite: Fine-grained **metamorphic rock** formed from **mudstones** and **shales**; it has a layered structure and silky sheen.

Pillow lava: Formation of **lavas** which resembles a pile of pillows, caused by the lavas erupting underwater.

Pitchstone: Solidified glassy **lava** with a waxy appearance.

Plastic: Describes rock material in the **asthenosphere**, which, because of the temperature and pressure, can be deformed very slowly.

Plate: Major portion of the **lithosphere** with little volcanic or earthquake activity, which is bounded by **active margins** with other **plates**. It is the movement of the Earth's crustal plates in relation to one another that causes **continental drift**.

Plate tectonics: Single model of how the outer part of the Earth works; it explains **continental drift, sea-floor spreading**, and volcanic and earthquake activity.

Polar reversal: Reversal of the Earth's **magnetic poles**. It occurs about every 20–50 million years.

Precipitation: All forms in which water falls from the **atmosphere** to the ground; including rain, **sleet, hail** and snow.

Prevailing wind: Commonest wind direction over a period of time in a given area.

Pumice: Volcanic rock that has been so strongly charged with gas that it has a frothy appearance and floats on water.

Pyrite: Yellow mineral also called iron pyrites or fool's gold.

GLOSSARY

Pyroxene: Important group of rock-forming minerals, such as augite.

Quartz: Silica, the important rock-forming mineral used to make glass.

Quartzite: Metamorphic rock composed mainly of quartz and formed from the metamorphism of quartz sandstones.

Rainbow: Arc-shaped spectrum of colours which forms in the sky when sunlight is split up by moisture in the atmosphere.

Raised beach: Beach from an earlier period which is now above the level of the shoreline, either because the sea level has fallen or the land has risen.

Recrystallization: Growth of new crystals in a rock as a result of the effects of heat and/or pressure.

Reef: Narrow, wall-like ridge of rock, usually limestone, which builds up in the sea as a result of the activity of animals such as corals.

Richter scale: Scale (from 1 to 10) that measures the intensity of earthquakes, based on the size of the shock waves.

Regional metamorphism: Type of metamorphism that occurs where plates are moving together.

Rift valley: Major trough in the Earth's crust bounded by faults.

Roche moutonné: Hump-shaped rock which has been smoothed on one side by a moving glacier and is rough and shattered on the opposite side.

Rock: Mass of minerals which may or may not be cemented together.

Salinity: Measure of the solids, including common salt, dissolved in the sea in parts per thousand. The salinity of sea water is about 35 parts per thousand.

Salt lake: Lake with a salinity of about 100 parts per thousand or more.

Sandstone: Sedimentary rock made up of grains of sand cemented together.

Savanna: Area on the edge of the tropics where rainfall is seasonal; typically, it is a region of coarse grassland with scattered trees.

Scarp: Steep slope or cliff associated with an almost flat tract of land. It results from the erosion of horizontal or gently sloping rocks by a river valley. Also called escarpment.

Schist: Medium-grained metamorphic rock with a layered structure and a sheen caused by mica minerals. Schists result from regional metamorphism.

Scree: Broken and shattered pieces of rock which accumulate down the slope of a rock face. It is caused by weathering and erosion of the rock.

Sea-floor spreading: Process by which new oceanic crust is created at plate margins marked by mid-ocean ridges.

Sedimentary rock: Type of rock, such as sandstone or limestone, formed from the accumulation and hardening of fragments of other rocks, organic material or minerals deposited from solution.

Seismic wave: Shock wave from an earthquake.

Seismology: Study of seismic waves from an earthquake.

Seismometer: Instrument used to detect seismic waves.

Shale: Fine-grained sedimentary rock with a sheet-like (platy) structure.

Silica: Silicon dioxide, which commonly occurs as quartz.

Sill: Shelf-like body of igneous rock which has been thrust between the bedding of the country rocks.

Sink hole: Steep-sided depression in a limestone area, formed by acid water dissolving away the limestone where two vertical joints have crossed.

Slate: Fine-grained metamorphic rock with a leafy or sheet-like structure.

Sleet: Mixture of falling rain and melting snow.

Smog: Mixture of smoke and fog.

Solar wind: Stream of protons, electrons and other high-energy particles that stream from the Sun.

Spit: Arm of sand and/or gravel which juts out into the sea from the shore.

Stack: Pillar of rock formed by the erosion of an arch that has been worn out of a cliff by the sea.

Stalactite: Column of limestone hanging from the roof of a cavern where there is a constant dripping of lime-rich water. It is formed as calcium carbonate comes out of solution.

Stalagmite: Column of limestone standing up from the floor of a cavern where lime-rich water drips.

Steppe: Vast, usually treeless plain where temperatures vary greatly between night and day, winter and summer.

Stratocumulus: Type of cloud consisting of flattened, greyish white layers.

Stratosphere: Layer of the atmosphere between about 10–50 km.

Streak: Colour of a mineral in its fresh, powdered form.

Strombolean eruption: Volcanic eruption in which there are frequent, medium-sized eruptions and small explosions.

Submarine canyon: Deep valley that cuts through the continental shelf.

Syenite: Coarse-grained igneous rock.

Syncline: Trough-shaped fold with younger rocks in the centre.

Synform: Trough-shaped fold in which younger rocks are may not always be in the centre.

Thermal: Rising air current caused by heating from below.

Throw: Vertical movement along a fault.

Tide: Rise and fall of the world's oceans, caused by the gravitational attraction mainly of the Moon but also the Sun.

Tornado: Twisting column of air where the wind speeds are very high.

Trade winds: Prevailing winds that blow in the tropics from about 30° north to 30° south. They blow from the northeast in the Northern Hemisphere and from the southeast in the Southern Hemisphere.

Transpiration: Process in which moisture is taken up from the soil through the roots of plants, moves up the stem and evaporates through pores in the leaves.

Trilobite: Extinct sea creature related to insects, with a body divided longways into three sections. Trilobites lived from Cambrian to Permian times.

Troposphere: Layer of the atmosphere from the Earth's surface to a height of about 10 km, where weather occurs.

Tsunami: Large sea wave caused by an earthquake or volcanic explosion. It is often wrongly called a tidal wave.

Typhoon: Powerful cyclone that occurs in the western Pacific and China Sea.

Unconformity: Surface between two beds of rock, which represents a break in the deposition of sediments.

Vein: Mineral deposit in a rock fracture.

Vesuvian eruption: Volcanic eruption where explosions take place after long quiet periods.

Volcanic bomb: Lump of lava that is thrown out of a volcano and takes on a characteristic shape during its flight.

Volcano: Vent in the Earth's crust through which lava, gas, ash and fragments of solid rock are ejected.

Weathering: Breakdown of rocks at the Earth's surface, for example, through heating and cooling, frost shattering and dissolving by acid rainwater.

THE
LIVING
WORLD

T *he Living World* is an illustrated guide to the living things that inhabit the Earth. In order to appreciate the rich variety of animals and plants that make up the world's natural communities we first need to understand how life on Earth evolved, how the different species are classified and how they have adapted to specific environments.

Plants make the Earth's atmosphere breathable; without plants there would be no animal life on Earth as we know it. We look at the fascinating world of the Plant Kingdom, from the simplest mosses to the more complex flowering plants. An equally astonishing variety of animals has evolved over the past three billion years. Each major animal group is treated separately, together with such specialized topics as animal homes, migration, relationship with people and conservation.

Finally, *The Living World* gives a guided tour of the human body's amazing structure. We find out how the body works, and how it grows and ages. To fully appreciate the complex web of life, a wide range of essential facts and figures are provided.

Brian Williams

THE LIVING EARTH

Life on Earth

The story of life on Earth begins many millions of years before the appearance of the first human beings. From dating the rocks, we can estimate the age of the Earth at around 4.5 billion years. How life began is uncertain. It may have been due to a chemical reaction, a haphazard coming together of lifeless molecules to form a tiny organism able to reproduce itself. The oldest known forms of life are the fossils of simple bacteria and algae, over 3.5 billion years old. Today there are more than 2 million living things on our planet. Many are so microscopically tiny that they are invisible to the naked human eye. Others are giants, such as the redwood tree and the blue whale. All the kinds, or species, of plants and animals have evolved as the result of gradual adaptation to the widely differing environments the Earth offers its inhabitants.

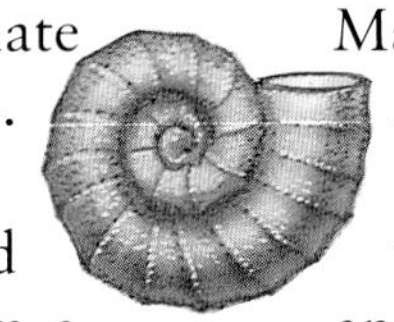

EVOLUTION

We mark the prehistory of the Earth by eras lasting many millions of years: the Precambrian, Paleozoic, Mesozoic, and Cenozoic. Life began in the oceans over 3.5 billion years ago. The first living things were simple, single-celled organisms. Scientists are still working out the relationship between these early groups. The Paleozoic Era brought an enormous expansion of life with some animals coming out of the warm, shallow seas onto the land. The evolution of species has shaped the "family tree" of life. Many plant and animal species died out. Other species developed new forms to create the diversity of animals and plants of today.

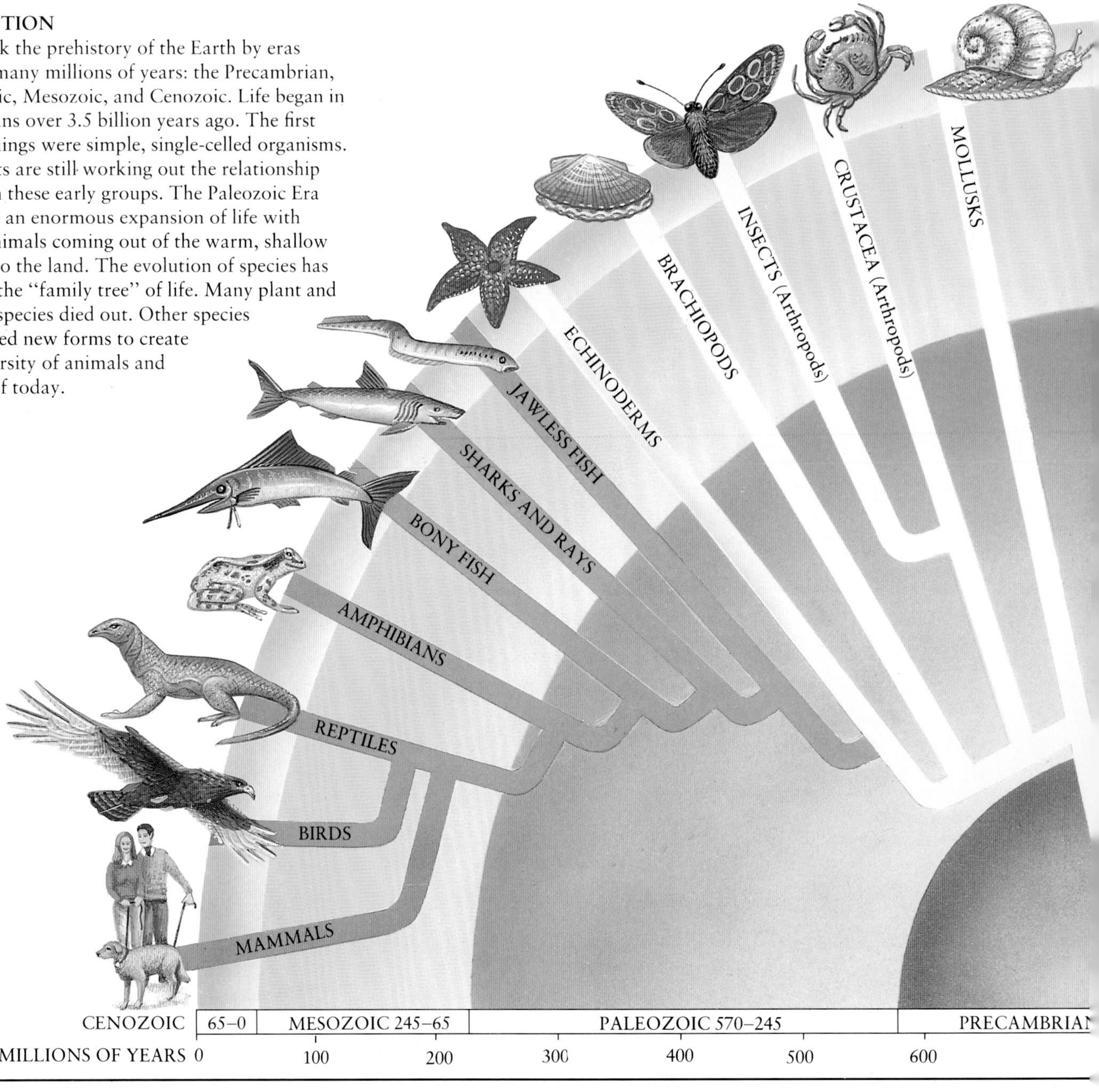

MOLLUSKS

CRUSTACEA (Arthropods)

INSECTS (Arthropods)

BRACHIOPODS

ECHINODERMS

JAWLESS FISH

SHARKS AND RAYS

BONY FISH

AMPHIBIANS

REPTILES

BIRDS

MAMMALS

CENOZOIC	65–0	MESOZOIC 245–65		PALEOZOIC 570–245		PRECAMBRIA
MILLIONS OF YEARS 0		100	200	300	400	500	600

FOSSILS: THE EVIDENCE

Fossils like this trilobite *(left)* are the hardened remains of dead animals and plants. Fossils are found in rocks millions of years old. The earliest soft-bodied animals left no fossils. By 600 million years ago, larger and more advanced animals and plants lived in the warm seas *(above)*. These animals, which had hard shells and skeletons, left fossil remains. Dating the rocks where fossils are found fills in the calendar of life.

WORMS

COELENTERATES

SPONGES

SINGLE-CELLED ORGANISMS

SINGLE-CELLED ORGANISMS

BACTERIA

FUNGI

ALGAE

MOSSES

HORSETAILS

FERNS

CYCADS

CONIFERS

FLOWERING PLANTS

PRECAMBRIAN	PALEOZOIC 570–245	MESOZOIC 245–65	65–0

600   500   400   300   200   100   0

Animal and Plant Classification

Classification, grouping living things together by similarities, shows how one group is related to another and how modern organisms may have evolved from earlier forms. The science of classifying plants and animals is called taxonomy, and Greek and Latin scientific names are used to identify each species, or kind, of living thing. Each species can be classed in levels: by kingdom (the largest group), then by phylum, class, order, family, genus, and lastly by species.

HOW MANY LIVING THINGS?
No one knows how many living things there are. About 2 million species have been named. But perhaps four times as many species remain unknown to science. Of the species we know about, 75 percent are animals (mostly insects), 18 percent are plants and 7 percent are 'in-betweens' – things that do not fit easily into either animal or plant groups.

ANIMAL CLASSIFICATION

KINGDOM
All animals belong to the kingdom Animalia. The other four kingdoms are plants, protoctists, bacteria and fungi.

PHYLUM
Within the animal kingdom are 20 or more phyla. All animals with backbones belong to the phylum Chordata.

CLASS
Animals with hair on their bodies that feed their young with milk are mammals, members of the class Mammalia.

ORDER
Mammals that eat meat such as bears, dogs (including foxes) and cats, belong to the order Carnivora.

FAMILY
Dogs, foxes and wolves look similar. These animals all belong to the same family, the Canidae.

GENUS
Animals of the same genus may not interbreed. Several foxes belong to the genus *Vulpes*.

SPECIES
Members of a species can interbreed. All fennec foxes belong to the fox species *Vulpes zerda*.

▲ *The fennec is a small fox of North Africa and Arabia. Its 'family tree', from kingdom to species, is illustrated here.*

FIVE KINGDOMS

Three groups of living things are classed separately from animals and plants. Some of the simple cells are claimed to be plants and some of them are claimed to be animals. Bacteria and blue-green algae-like cells form the kingdom Bacteria. These organisms are tiny single cells. Fungi (mushrooms and toadstools, for example) are like plants in some ways but have no chlorophyll and so cannot make their own food. Protoctists are the third 'outsiders'; they contain species claimed by both botanists and zoologists and some groups with no clear relationship to any species. Some are single-celled (such as diatoms and amoebas) and some are groups of cells such as red and brown seaweeds.

PLANT CLASSIFICATION

KINGDOM
Every multicellular green plant, from the tiniest to the tallest, belongs to the plant kingdom.

PHYLUM
All seed plants which reproduce themselves by flowers making covered seeds are Angiosperms.

CLASS
The Angiosperms are divided into two classes, Monocotyledons and Dicotyledons (right).

ORDER
Oak trees, along with their close relatives beeches and chestnuts, belong to the order Fagales.

FAMILY
Some 900 species of tree including beeches, chestnuts and oaks, belong to the family Fagaceae.

GENUS
All oaks belong to the genus *Quercus*. There are more than 600 species; some trees are tall, others shrubby.

SPECIES
The evergreen holm oak is *Quercus ilex*. The English oak tree is *Quercus robur*, the American white oak is *Quercus alba*.

Turkey oak

Red oak

English oak

Oaks vary in size and the way they grow and each species of oak has a distinctive leaf, flower and fruit.

Scarlet oak

Animal and Plant Habitats

Animals and plants live in places, or habitats, which provide the food and shelter they need. For example, giraffes (Africa), kangaroos (Australia) and prairie dogs (North America) are animals of the grasslands. Nature has equipped them to survive in this particular habitat. The Earth's regions offer many habitats, from freezing polar wastes to hot tropical rainforests. Animals and plants live together in biological communities. Ecology is the study of how living things interact within such communities.

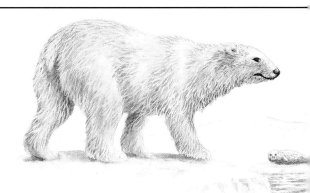

WORLDWIDE NATURAL REGIONS

▲ Oceans and seas form the marine habitat. The seashore, continental shelf, coral reefs and deep, cold ocean depths all have their own communities of plants and animals.

▶ Rivers and wetlands (marshes and swamps) are usually rich in plant and animal life. Animals can include fish, amphibians, reptiles and birds such as cranes.

▶ Plant and animal communities are grouped worldwide into 'biomes' – natural regions with similar climates and vegetation that provide similar habitats. The map shows the main land biomes. The oceans form a vast biome of their own.

◀ In tropical rainforest, plants thrive and animals (such as monkeys, birds, snakes and insects) live in the different layers of the forest canopy.

▲ Desert plants and animals must conserve water and keep cool. Reptiles such as lizards seek shade in the midday heat. Many desert animals are small and nocturnal.

▶ In hot climates savanna grasslands support herds of grazing animals, as well as the carnivores (such as African lions) that prey on these grass-eaters.

◄ *Polar bears and seals live in the cold Arctic. On the tundra plains, plants grow quickly in the brief summer warmth.*

► *Some plants are adapted to life on alpine slopes. Mountain animals include sheep, goats and soaring birds.*

▼ *The cold northern forests of evergreen conifer trees are home to animals as varied as owls, beavers, porcupines, moose, bears and wolves.*

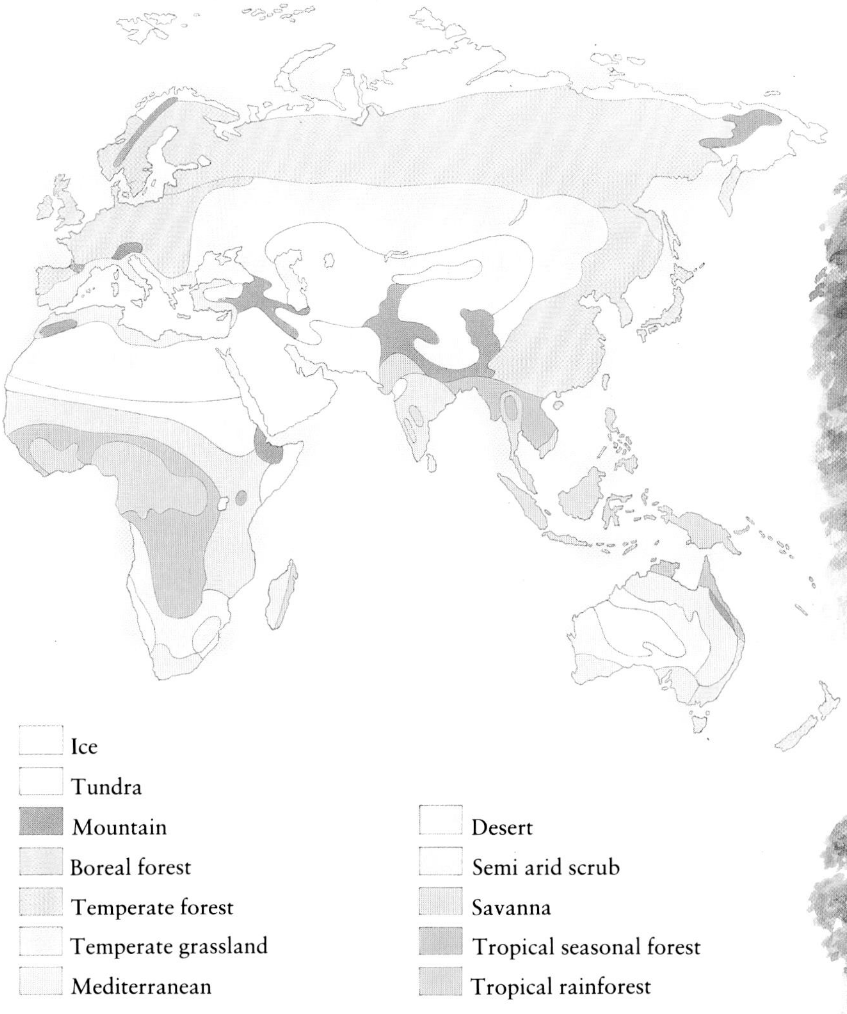

▼ *Temperate regions have warm summers and cool winters. In mixed forest and farmland small and large mammals are found, as well as birds such as woodpeckers.*

☐ Ice

☐ Tundra

☐ Mountain

☐ Boreal forest

☐ Temperate forest

☐ Temperate grassland

☐ Mediterranean

☐ Desert

☐ Semi arid scrub

☐ Savanna

☐ Tropical seasonal forest

☐ Tropical rainforest

THE PLANT KINGDOM

The World of Plants

Without plants, our planet would be a lifeless world. Plants give off the oxygen all animals need to breathe; they provide much of our food, materials such as timber and cotton, as well as many health-restoring drugs. Scientists have named more than 375,000 kinds of plants, ranging from simple algae to trees. There could be the same number of undiscovered plants growing in remote forests and on mountains. Even so, there are far fewer plants than there are animals. Some plants are widespread; others grow only in one place. Plants form the largest and longest-living things on Earth. All true plants are made up of many cells containing a material called cellulose. They develop from embryos (tiny forms of the adult plant). Most plants make their own food from water and carbon dioxide by a chemical process called photosynthesis which requires sunlight.

PLANT CLASSIFICATION
The system for naming plants and animals was drawn up by the Swedish naturalist Carl von Linné (Linnaeus) in 1735. The different groups of plants have been arranged in various ways since this time. Modern classification allows for many different phyla of which the main ones are the ones shown here.

NEITHER ANIMALS, OR PLANTS
The Protoctists, the Bacteria and the Fungi are not considered plants because they do not make their own food and their cells are different from those of animals and plants.

Protoctists include large algae, the seaweeds, as well as organisms that can live in either fresh or sea water.

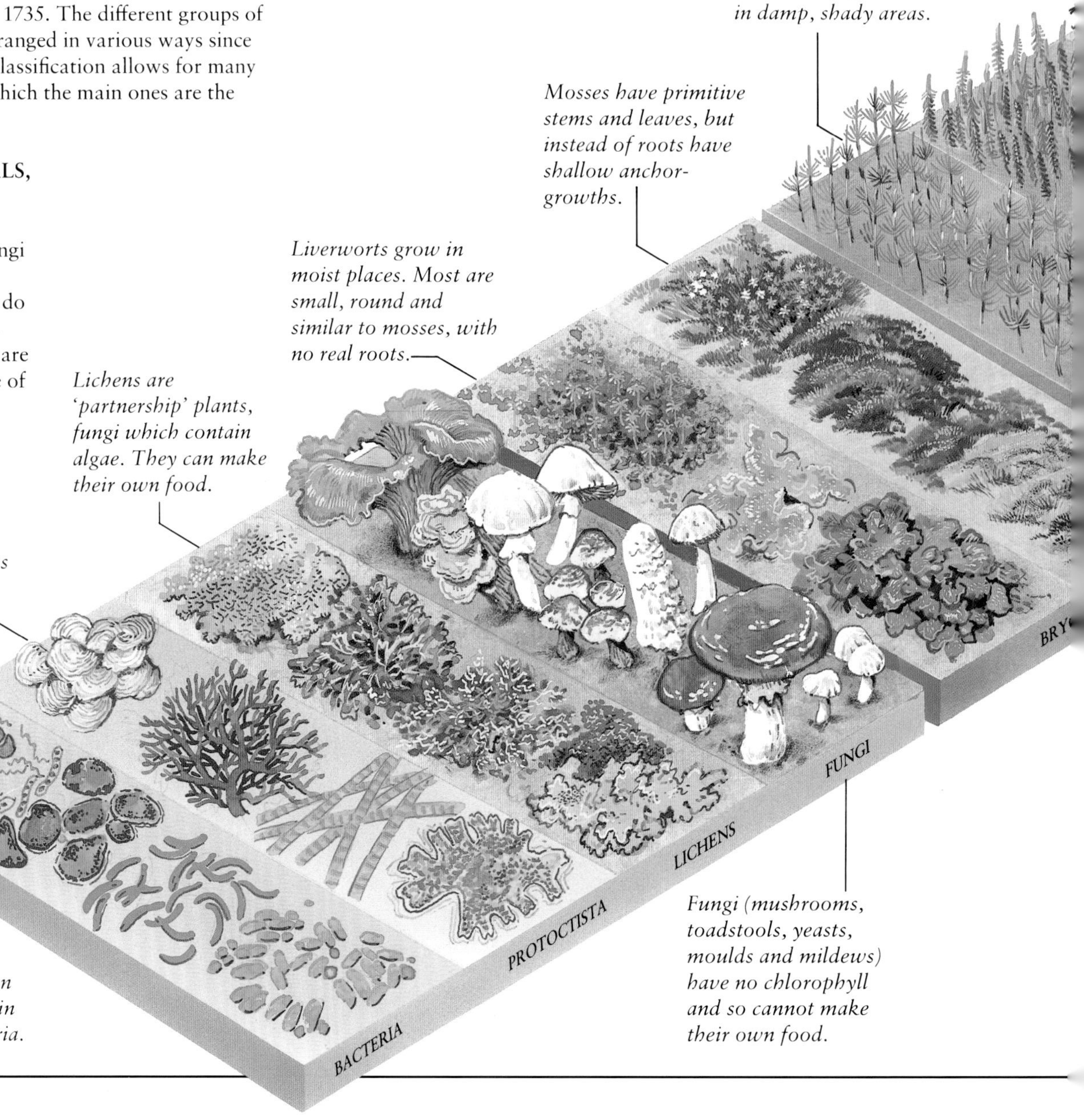

Lichens are 'partnership' plants, fungi which contain algae. They can make their own food.

Liverworts grow in moist places. Most are small, round and similar to mosses, with no real roots.

Mosses have primitive stems and leaves, but instead of roots have shallow anchor-growths.

Horsetails have small leaves and hollow stems. They grow best in damp, shady areas.

Bacteria are tiny, simple single-celled organisms. They and blue-green algae are classified in the kingdom Bacteria.

Fungi (mushrooms, toadstools, yeasts, moulds and mildews) have no chlorophyll and so cannot make their own food.

BACTERIA

PROTOCTISTA

LICHENS

FUNGI

BRY

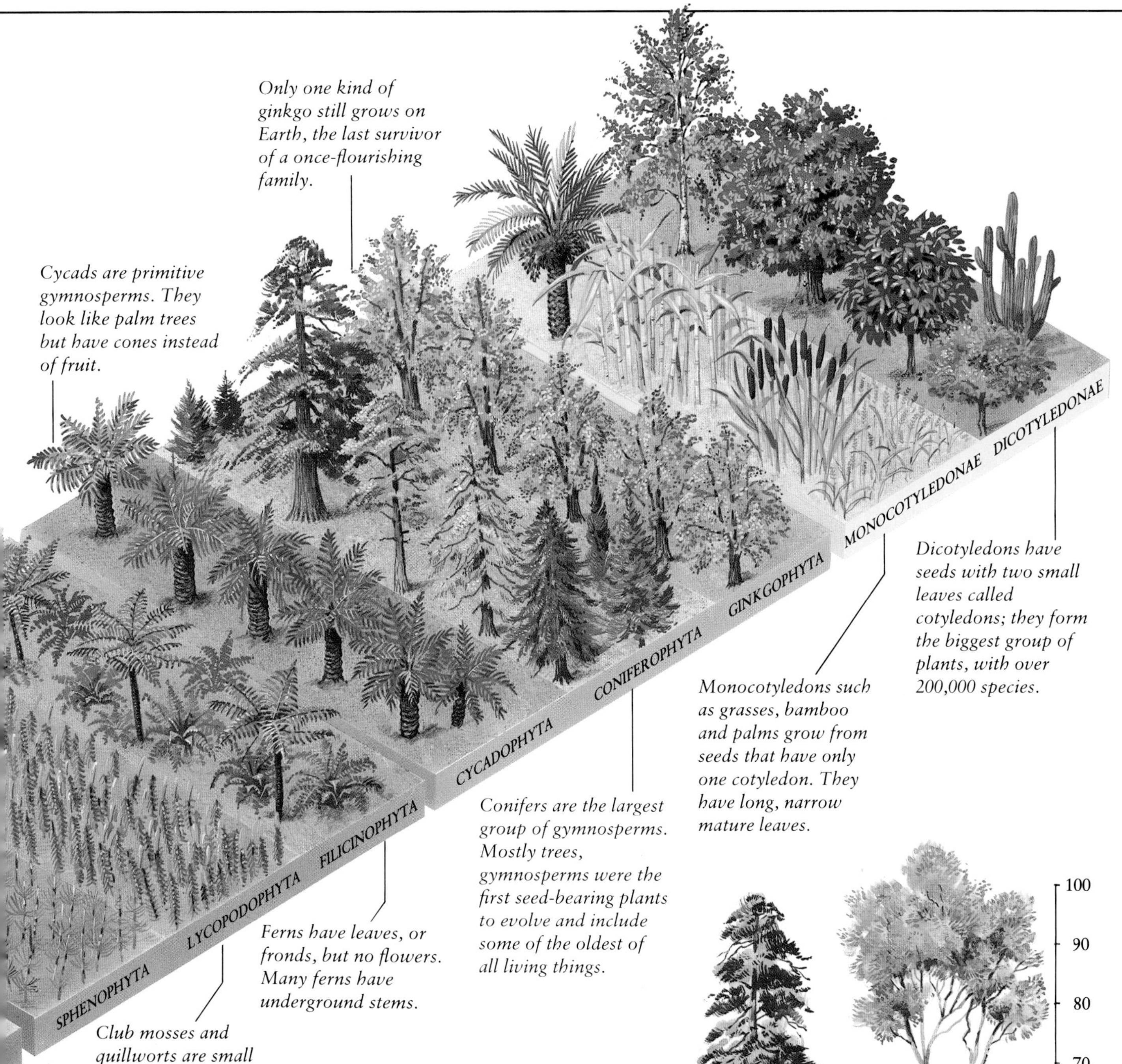

Only one kind of ginkgo still grows on Earth, the last survivor of a once-flourishing family.

Cycads are primitive gymnosperms. They look like palm trees but have cones instead of fruit.

SPHENOPHYTA

LYCOPODOPHYTA

FILICINOPHYTA

CYCADOPHYTA

CONIFEROPHYTA

GINKGOPHYTA

MONOCOTYLEDONAE

DICOTYLEDONAE

Dicotyledons have seeds with two small leaves called cotyledons; they form the biggest group of plants, with over 200,000 species.

Monocotyledons such as grasses, bamboo and palms grow from seeds that have only one cotyledon. They have long, narrow mature leaves.

Conifers are the largest group of gymnosperms. Mostly trees, gymnosperms were the first seed-bearing plants to evolve and include some of the oldest of all living things.

Ferns have leaves, or fronds, but no flowers. Many ferns have underground stems.

Club mosses and quillworts are small modern relatives of the first land plants.

PLANT HEIGHT RECORDS

Callie grass grows 15 cm a day. The tallest grass is bamboo, the tallest cactus the saguaro, and the biggest fern the Norfolk Island tree fern of the Pacific. The biggest seaweed is the Pacific giant kelp. The biggest trees are American sequoias weighing 2500 tonnes. The tallest tree on record was an Australian eucalyptus (132 m).

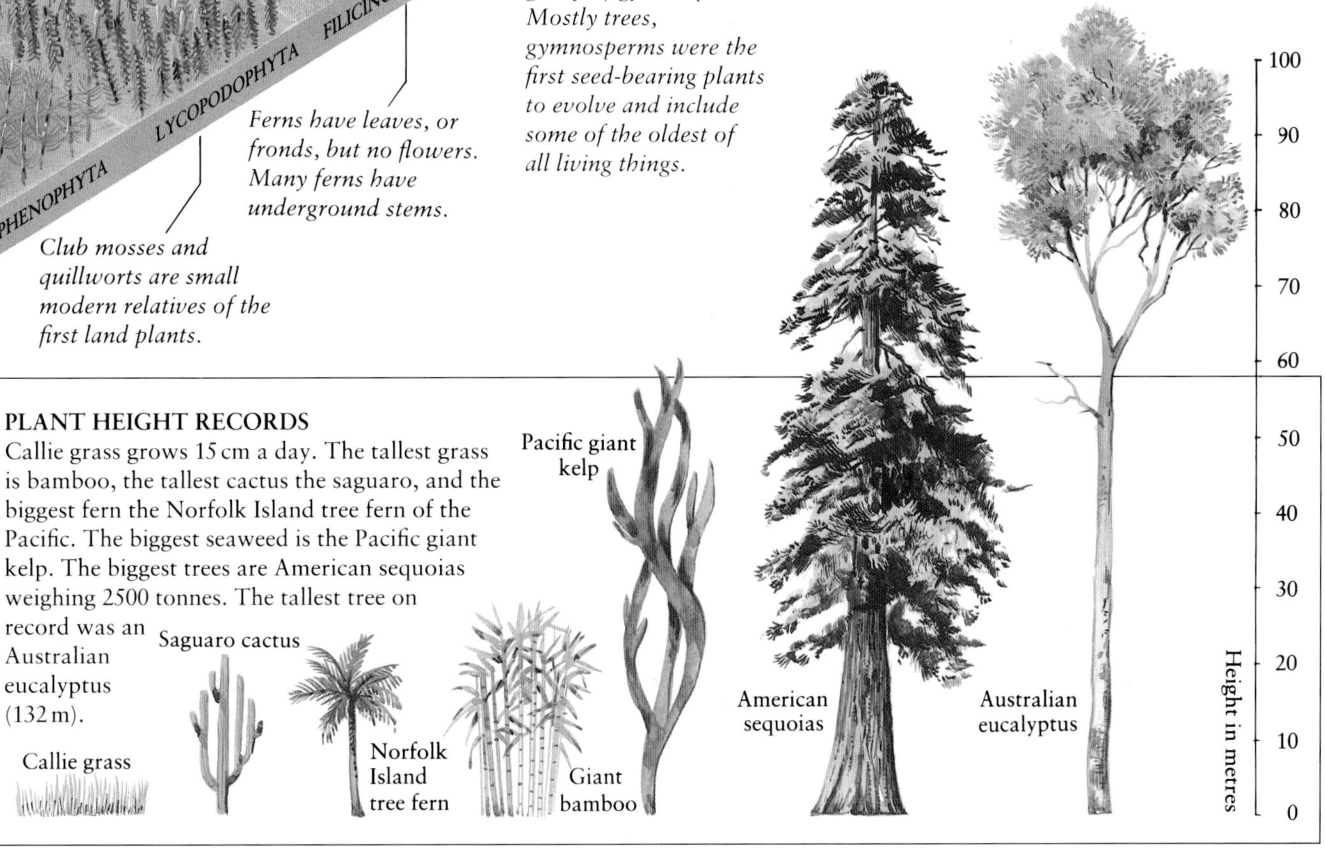

Callie grass

Saguaro cactus

Norfolk Island tree fern

Giant bamboo

Pacific giant kelp

American sequoias

Australian eucalyptus

100
90
80
70
60
50
40
30
20
10
0

Height in metres

Bacteria, Algae, Lichens and Fungi

These organisms are no longer classified as plants. Bacteria are tiny and single-celled, and were probably the first living things on Earth. They, and the microscopic blue-green algae, are widespread on land and in water. Other algae, classed separately as Protoctists, include the seaweeds, many of which more closely resemble plants. Fungi (mushrooms and toadstools, mildews, yeasts and moulds) are simple nongreen organisms without leaves, roots or stems; they are grouped on their own.

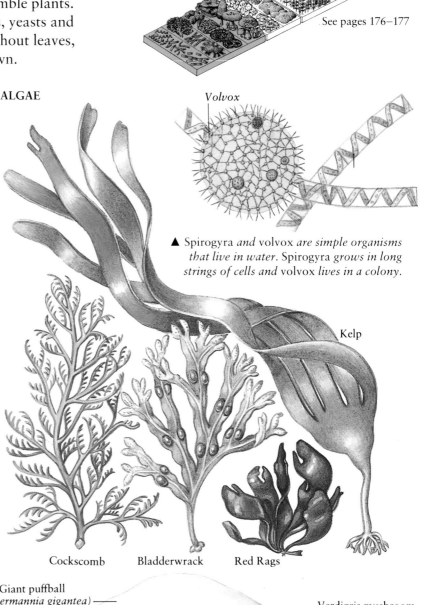

See pages 176–177

ALGAE

Volvox

▲ Spirogyra *and* volvox *are simple organisms that live in water.* Spirogyra *grows in long strings of cells and* volvox *lives in a colony.*

Kelp

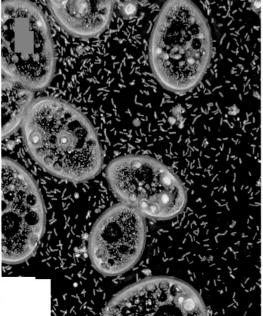

BACTERIA
Most bacteria can be seen only through a microscope. They have a simple structure, usually with a cell wall that stops them drying out. Huge numbers of bacteria live in the soil. They help to break down dead plant and animal matter.

▶ *Algae include the diatoms and the seaweeds. Classed by colour (green, brown and red), the 7000 kinds of seaweeds are plants of ocean and shore. Some have air bladders to help them float. Others cling to the sea bed.*

Cockscomb   Bladderwrack   Red Rags

Giant puffball
(*Langermannia gigantea*)

Verdigris mushroom
(*Stopharia aeruginosa*)

Shaggy ink cap
(*Coprinus comatus*)

Conical slimy cap
(*Hygrocybe conica*)

Fly agaric
(*Amanita muscaria*)

Rosy earthstar
(*Geastrum rufescens*)

Fairy ring mushroom
(*Marasmius oreades*)

Field mushroom
(*Agaricus campestris*)

Saw-gilled leptonia
(*Leptonia serrulata*)

Parasol mushroom
(*Lepiota procera*)

LICHENS

Alga

Fungal strands

Fungal mat

◀ *A lichen is made up of two living things in symbiosis, or partnership. Within the lichen is a single-celled alga enclosed in a fungus. Using photosynthesis, the alga makes food both for itself and for the fungus, which cannot survive on its own.*

▶ *Some lichens grow in soil, but most grow on rocks, walls or tree bark. Lichens are low-growing, but can live for over 4000 years, enduring extremes of heat and cold.*

FACTS ABOUT FUNGI

● A field mushroom produces 16,000 million spores in just under a week.
● Raindrops help to disperse the spores of puffballs. The paper-thin outer wall of the ball encloses the powdery spores. When a raindrop hits the wall of the ball, it bulges inwards and puffs out a cloud of spores.
● The most deadly fungus is the yellowish-green death cap *Amanita phalloides* which is commonly found with beech and oak trees. If eaten, it can kill in 6 to 15 hours.

THE LIFE CYCLE OF A FUNGUS

The mushrooms and toadstools we see are the 'fruiting bodies' of fungi. The hidden part of the fungus, growing under the soil or in the wood of trees, consists of thousands of thread-like cells which form a tangled mass, the mycelium. The fruiting body appears when the fungus is ready to produce spores which develop into new plants.

Mature mushroom disperses spores

Spores

Spore

Button forming

Spore

Mycelium

Button

MUSHROOMS AND TOADSTOOLS

Most fungi produce fruiting bodies in autumn – a good time to spot colourful mushrooms and toadstools. Some are good to eat, but others are poisonous. Never pick or eat a mushroom until you are certain it is not poisonous.

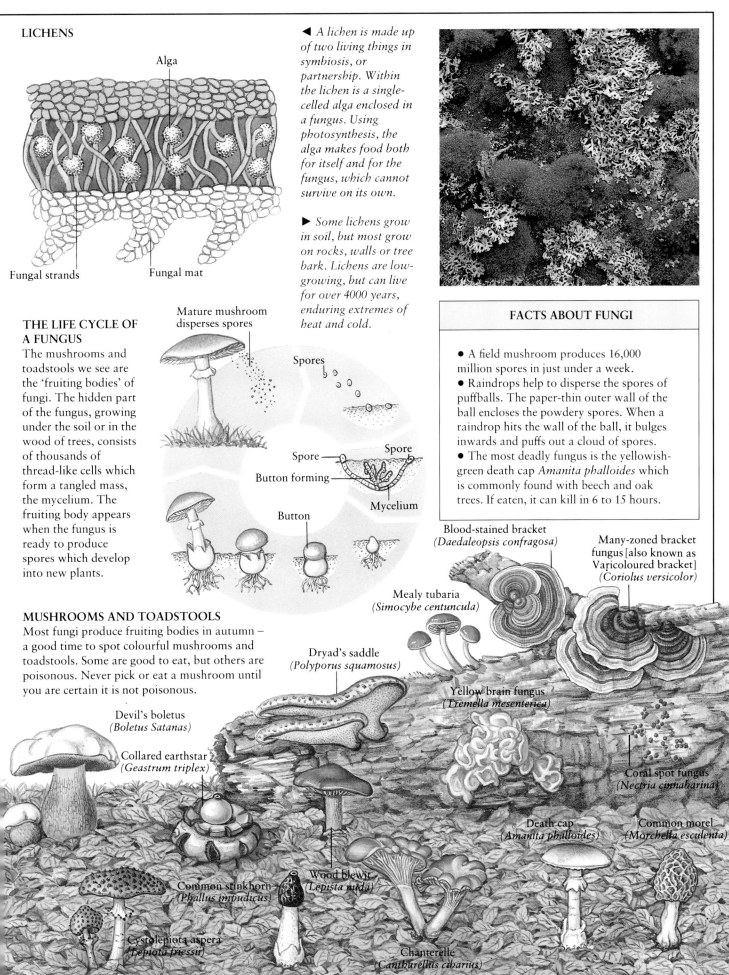

Blood-stained bracket
(*Daedaleopsis confragosa*)

Many-zoned bracket fungus [also known as Varicoloured bracket]
(*Coriolus versicolor*)

Mealy tubaria
(*Simocybe centuncula*)

Devil's boletus
(*Boletus Satanas*)

Dryad's saddle
(*Polyporus squamosus*)

Yellow brain fungus
(*Tremella mesenterica*)

Coral spot fungus
(*Nectria cinnabarina*)

Collared earthstar
(*Geastrum triplex*)

Death cap
(*Amanita phalloides*)

Common morel
(*Morchella esculenta*)

Common stinkhorn
(*Phallus impudicus*)

Wood blewit
(*Lepista nuda*)

Cystolepiota aspera
(*Lepiota friessir*)

Chanterelle
(*Cantharellus cibarius*)

Liverworts, Mosses, Horsetails and Ferns

Mosses and liverworts are classified as the phylum Bryophyta. They are small and instead of roots they have thread-like anchors called rhizoids. Horsetails, club mosses and ferns were once grouped as Pteridophytes but now are three separate phyla, Sphenophyta, Lycopodophyta and Filicinophyta. Instead of making flowers and seeds, ferns send out spores. A spore falls to the ground and grows into a 'prothallus', a tiny plant that makes male and female sex cells which in turn produce the new fern plant.

See pages 176–177

Marchantia polymorpha

Pellia epiphylla

◀ *Liverworts grow in damp places. Some have a flat body, or 'thallus'. Others look more leafy, with rows of leaves growing on a stem. There are about 8000 species of liverworts, found in both hot and cold climates.*

MOSS FACTS

- Millions of years ago, ferns, horsetails and club mosses forested the Earth.
- Peat moss is so absorbent it can be used to dress wounds.

MOSSES

Mosses are small and usually grow in clumps or dense mats, often clinging to a rock or a stone wall. As part of their complicated reproduction cycle, many mosses send out stalks with a pod at the tip. The pod releases thousands of spores to form new plants.

Leucobryum glaucum

Sphagnum papillosum

Racomitrium lanuginosum

Parts of a moss

Spore pod capsule

Stalk

Simple leaves

FORMATION OF A PEAT BOG

Peat mosses are often called sphagnum mosses. They may float on top of a lake, forming a thick green carpet. This is how a peat bog starts.

The submerged parts of the moss plants die. Dead and decaying matter sinks to the bottom of the lake, forming a mat below water level.

In time, the mat of decaying vegetation builds up into a dense mass. The plant matter absorbs water and gradually turns the lake into a bog.

The lower layers are squashed by the matter above, and slowly turn into mud-like peat. The bog dries out and new plants colonize the surface.

Trees take root

Water

Dead matter falls to bottom

Moss spreads and absorbs water

Mud-like peat formed

CLUB MOSSES
Club mosses are not true mosses.
They are related to ferns. Club
mosses have an underground root
from which grows a stem with
branches and small leaves. Club-
like cones which contain the
spores (from which new plants
grow) form at the tips of these
branches.

Stags horn
moss

HORSETAILS
Horsetails are small
plants with hollow,
jointed stems and
stalks that often look
like miniature trees.
They have no flowers
and can be found in
damp places.

Marsh
horsetail

New fern

HOW A NEW FERN GROWS
Ferns have fronds. Under
each frond are spore cases,
or 'sporangia', lined with
hundreds of spores.

The sporangia burst and
spores are blown away.
Fern spores survive best
in shaded, moist soil. In
suitable ground, a spore
grows into a prothallus.

The prothallus has male
and female cells from
which a young fern
develops; it feeds on the
prothallus until it roots
and can live on its own.

Fern

Sporangia

Prothallus

Young sporophyte

TYPES OF FERN
There are about 10,000 kinds of ferns on the
Earth today. Tree ferns grow in the Tropics. The
leaves or fronds of many ferns are long and lacy.
Other ferns have simple oval or round leaves.

Tree ferns

Maidenhair
spleenwort

Adder's tongue

Kidney ferns

Ginkgos, Cycads and Conifers

Ginkgos and cycads are the survivors of a group of plants that were growing over 300 million years ago when the first amphibians crawled onto the land. The sole surviving ginkgo is the Maidenhair tree. Only nine kinds of Cycads remain today. Both these plants are gymnosperms – plants that bear seeds in cones. The most successful gymnosperms are the conifers (Coniferophyta), which include the pines, spruces, larches, cedars, firs and cypresses. All except the larch and swamp cypress are evergreen trees.

See pages 176–177

GINKGOS

Leaves clustered

Stalked fruit

◀ *The Maidenhair tree* Ginkgo biloba *from China has fan-shaped leaves. The seed has a hard nut-like centre.*

CONIFERS

▼ *The* Welwitschia *is a gymnosperm, found in Africa, that lives for over 100 years. Two large woody leaves with a cone in the middle grow from its short stem.*

◀ *The Maidenhair tree is a 'living fossil', the only survivor of an ancient family of trees. Fossil leaves of ginkgos show how little this plant has changed over millions of years.*

CYCADS

Giant cone

◀ *Cycads first grew on Earth in the Triassic period (from 225 million years ago). Cycads resemble palm trees and some are very long-lived (up to 1000 years). The fern-like leaves sprout from the top of the stem. The seeds are inside a large cone that forms in the middle of the leaf cluster.*

Silver fir

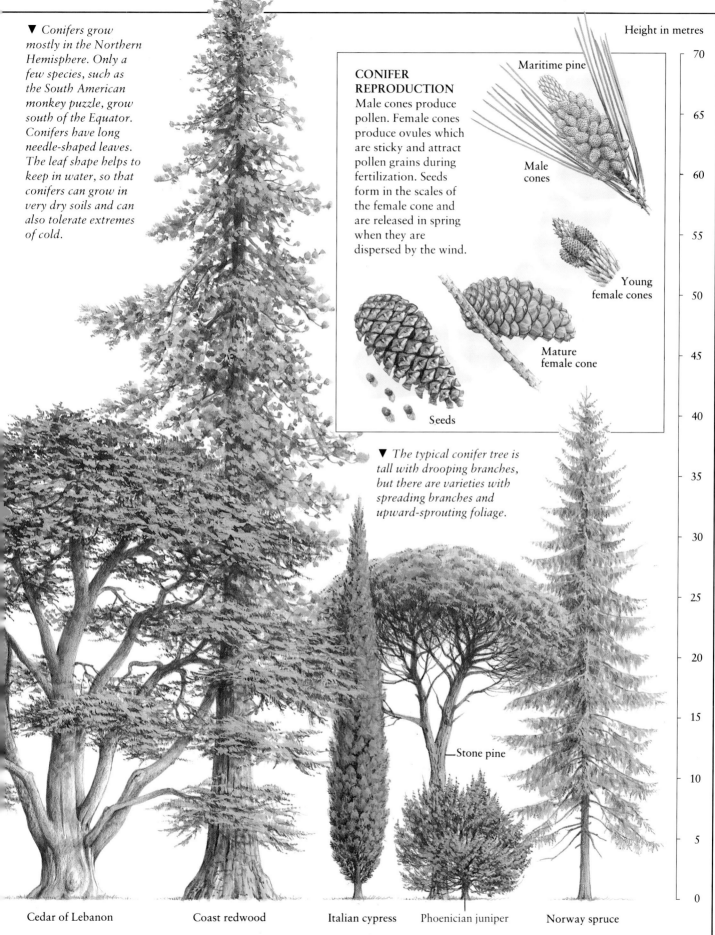

▼ *Conifers grow mostly in the Northern Hemisphere. Only a few species, such as the South American monkey puzzle, grow south of the Equator. Conifers have long needle-shaped leaves. The leaf shape helps to keep in water, so that conifers can grow in very dry soils and can also tolerate extremes of cold.*

Height in metres

CONIFER REPRODUCTION
Male cones produce pollen. Female cones produce ovules which are sticky and attract pollen grains during fertilization. Seeds form in the scales of the female cone and are released in spring when they are dispersed by the wind.

Maritime pine

Male cones

Young female cones

Mature female cone

Seeds

▼ *The typical conifer tree is tall with drooping branches, but there are varieties with spreading branches and upward-sprouting foliage.*

Stone pine

70

65

60

55

50

45

40

35

30

25

20

15

10

5

0

Cedar of Lebanon   Coast redwood   Italian cypress   Phoenician juniper   Norway spruce

183

Monocotyledons and Dicotyledons

Monocotyledons and dicotyledons are the two classes of flowering plants. They are the most diverse of all plants, with the most efficient reproductive system in the plant world. The basic difference, which gives the two classes their names, is in the number of cotyledons, or seed leaves. Monocots have one, dicots have two. There are also differences in the mature leaves. Monocots usually have long narrow leaves. Grass is a good example. Dicot leaves are usually broad, with smooth, rounded or toothed edges.

See pages 176–177

◀ *The cotyledon is the leaf part of a plant embryo, from which a new plant grows. Dicot seeds have two cotyledons.*

▶ *Monocot leaves are smooth-edged with parallel veins. The leaves grow from the base so, for example, grass keeps growing even when mowed or nibbled by animals.*

MONOCOTS	DICOTYLEDONS
The 40,000 species of monocotyledons include: **Grasses** **Cereals** such as rice, wheat and maize **Bulb plants** such as tulips and lilies **Orchids** **Bananas** **Bulrushes and reeds** **Palm trees**	Most flowering plants are dicots. Typical examples include: **Foxgloves** **Rhododendrons** **Deciduous trees** such as oak, beech, maple **Roses, grapes,** **Carrots, cucumbers** **Potatoes, beans** and peas

▶ *Typical plants of the cool temperate forest include deciduous trees (ones that shed their leaves in autumn) such as oak, maple and beech, and woodland flowers such as bluebells, which bloom in spring.*

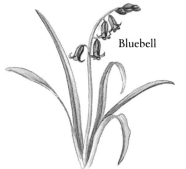

Bluebell

◀ *Grasslands are divided into three types: prairies, steppes or savannas. Prairies have longer grasses than steppes, while savannas have trees such as palm and acacia as well as grass.*

Pampas grass

◄ *Plants such as mosses, shrubs and flowers survive the wind and cold on high mountains by growing near to the ground and having long clinging roots. Conifers are the trees best adapted to alpine conditions.*

Alpine forget-me-not

▶ *Tropical forests contain half the known plant species. Most tropical forest trees are evergreen. Plants requiring little light such as ferns grow at ground level, while vines and orchids grow high on the trees.*

Rafflesia

◄ *Wetland plants include water plants such as lilies, reeds and willow and mangrove trees. Some wetland plants live completely under water; others have air spaces in their stems, and leaves that carry air to their roots and so keep them afloat in the water.*

Giant waterlily

▶ *Plants can survive in hot deserts, although some deserts have only sand dunes. Many desert plants – cactuses, palm trees, yuccas – have spiny leaves and fleshy stems for storing water. They flower quickly after rain.*

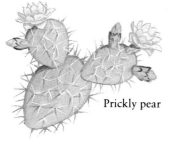

Prickly pear

Monocotyledons and Dicotyledons

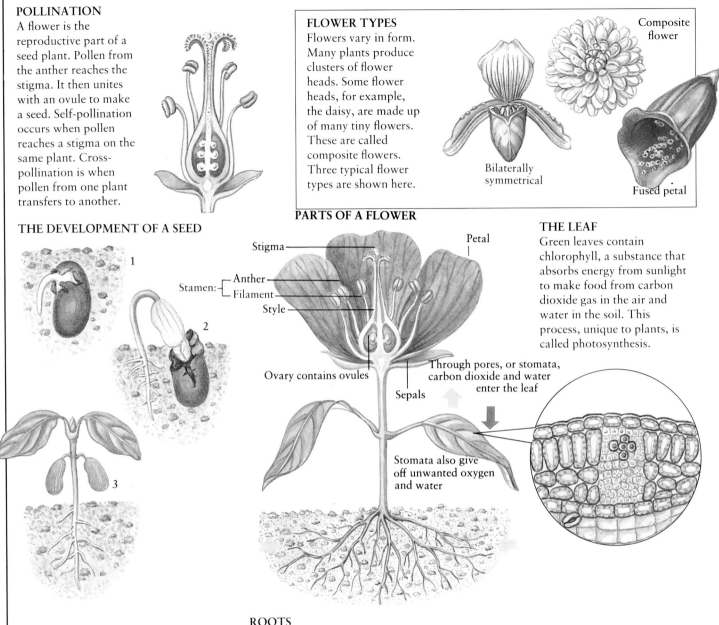

POLLINATION

A flower is the reproductive part of a seed plant. Pollen from the anther reaches the stigma. It then unites with an ovule to make a seed. Self-pollination occurs when pollen reaches a stigma on the same plant. Cross-pollination is when pollen from one plant transfers to another.

FLOWER TYPES

Flowers vary in form. Many plants produce clusters of flower heads. Some flower heads, for example, the daisy, are made up of many tiny flowers. These are called composite flowers. Three typical flower types are shown here.

Composite flower

Bilaterally symmetrical

Fused petal

THE DEVELOPMENT OF A SEED

1

2

3

PARTS OF A FLOWER

Stigma

Stamen: Anther Filament

Style

Ovary contains ovules

Sepals

Petal

THE LEAF

Green leaves contain chlorophyll, a substance that absorbs energy from sunlight to make food from carbon dioxide gas in the air and water in the soil. This process, unique to plants, is called photosynthesis.

Through pores, or stomata, carbon dioxide and water enter the leaf

Stomata also give off unwanted oxygen and water

▲ *First the seed absorbs water, swells and splits. It sends out an embryo root, or radicle, which pushes downwards into the soil. The shoot then pushes upwards, bending towards the sunlight. Finally, the first leaves sprout.*

ROOTS

A plant's roots anchor it in the soil, and absorb water and minerals. Plants such as grass have a fibrous root system, with slender spreading roots; plants such as carrots have a taproot system, where one root is much larger than the rest.

▼ *Plants have other organs than roots under the ground. Bulbs, tubers, corms and rhizomes store food to help the plant survive, and produce whole new plants without sexual reproduction as runners also do on the surface.*

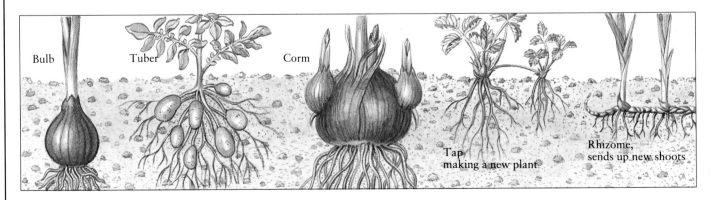

Bulb   Tuber   Corm

Tap making a new plant

Rhizome, sends up new shoots

DISPERSAL

When a bee or hummingbird collects nectar from a flower, pollen is brushed on to its body and then rubbed off on the next flower. Certain plants have fruits, good to eat but with indigestible seeds that pass through an animal's body. Some fruits cling to an animal's fur, while other plants rely on the wind to disperse their seeds.

◀ *Some plants, the legumes (peas, beans and clover), have bacteria living in nodules in their roots. These bacteria can convert nitrogen compounds which the plants need. This relationship between any two unrelated species is called symbiosis, which is from the Greek word for 'living together'.*

PARASITIC PLANTS

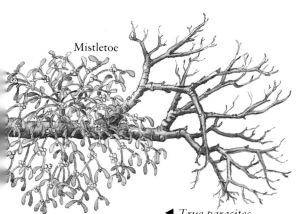

Mistletoe

Dodder plant

◀ *True parasites cannot make their own food. Some fasten on to other plants; examples are broomrape, dodder and the world's biggest flower, Rafflesia arnoldii. Semiparasites, such as mistletoe, take some food from their host but also make their own by photosynthesis.*

CARNIVOROUS PLANTS

Venus fly trap

Pitcher plant

A few plants prey on insects. Many carnivorous plants use their leaves to trap prey, and they secrete special chemicals in order to digest their prey. The Venus fly trap's hinged leaves snap shut when an insect lands on them. At the bottom of the pitcher plant's smooth-sided funnel is a liquid which dissolves its catch.

Fruits or Vegetables?

People have many uses for plants which are most valuable as a source of food. Prehistoric people first gathered seeds, berries and roots. About 10,000 years ago people began to grow cereals (such as wheat) and other crops. To the modern shopper, 'fruit' means a juicy food, such as apples, oranges or currants, grown on a bush or tree. These foods provide minerals, sugar and vitamins. As a rule, vegetables are less sweet-tasting. The part of the plant that we eat may be its leaf, stem, root, seed or fruit.

WHAT PARTS DO WE EAT?

BULB	Onion, garlic
TUBER	Potato, Jerusalem artichoke, yam, cassava
ROOT	Carrot, parsnip, beet, radish, turnip, swede, sweet potato
LEAF	Brussels sprouts, cabbage, chard, Chinese leaves, cress, endive, kale, lettuce, spinach
FLOWER	Broccoli, cauliflower
FRUIT	Cucumber, courgette, aubergine, apple, pepper, squash, tomato, watermelon
NUT	Coconut, almond, chestnut, hazelnut, pistachio, pine nut, cashew
SEED	Brazil nut, peanut, bean, pea, lentil, sweet corn, rice, oats, wheat, sunflowers
STEM	Asparagus, kohlrabi, bamboo shoots, onions. Celery and rhubarb are leaf-stalks

INFINITE VARIETY

The fruits and vegetables we enjoy are the result of cross-breeding from wild plants. There are many varieties, from all over the world. The familiar foods on the table come from a fascinating variety of plants.

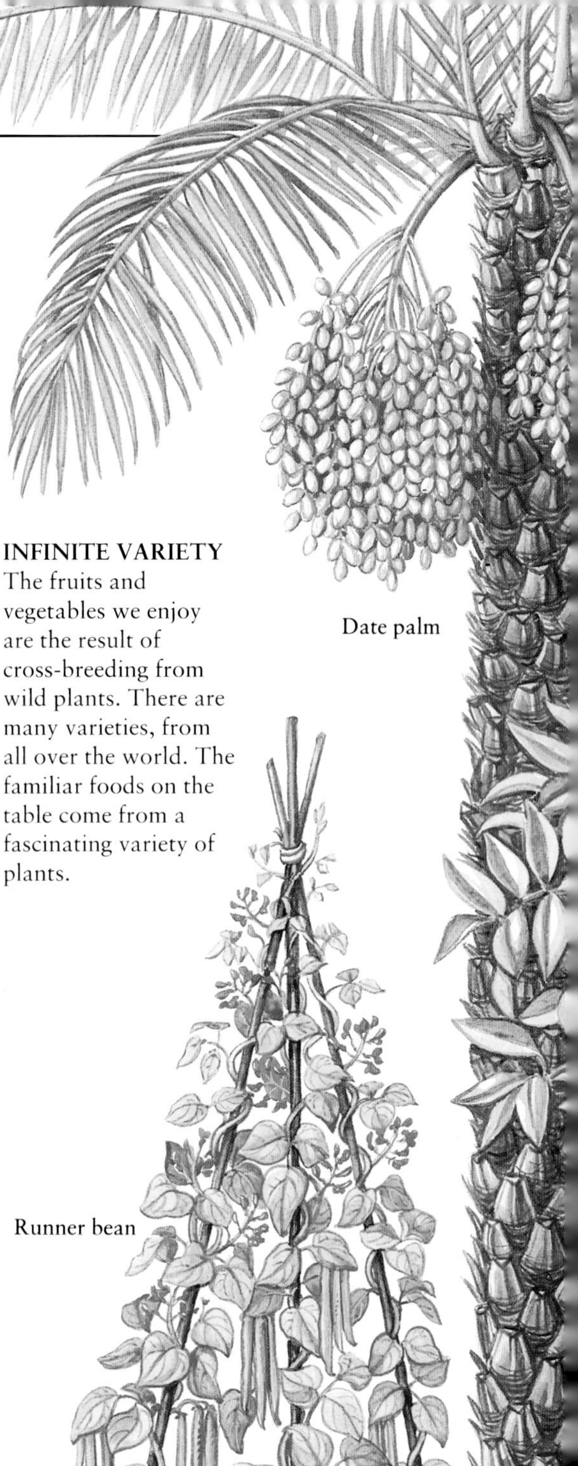

Date palm

Runner bean

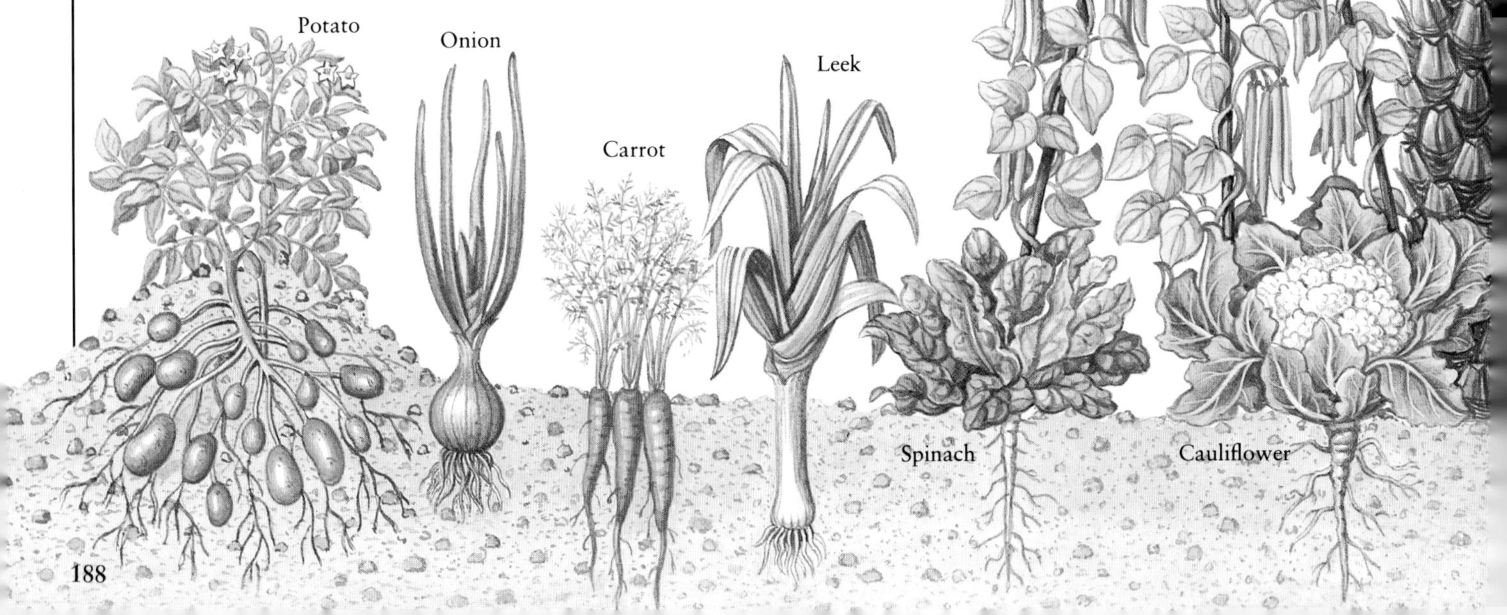

Potato

Onion

Carrot

Leek

Spinach

Cauliflower

TYPES OF FRUIT

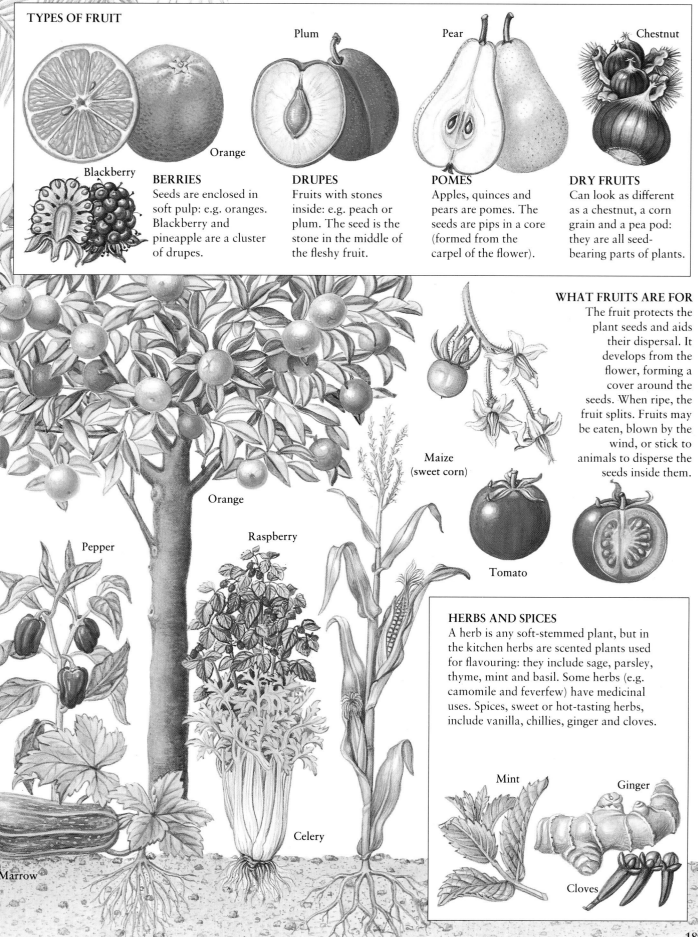

Plum

Pear

Chestnut

Orange

Blackberry

BERRIES
Seeds are enclosed in soft pulp: e.g. oranges. Blackberry and pineapple are a cluster of drupes.

DRUPES
Fruits with stones inside: e.g. peach or plum. The seed is the stone in the middle of the fleshy fruit.

POMES
Apples, quinces and pears are pomes. The seeds are pips in a core (formed from the carpel of the flower).

DRY FRUITS
Can look as different as a chestnut, a corn grain and a pea pod: they are all seed-bearing parts of plants.

WHAT FRUITS ARE FOR
The fruit protects the plant seeds and aids their dispersal. It develops from the flower, forming a cover around the seeds. When ripe, the fruit splits. Fruits may be eaten, blown by the wind, or stick to animals to disperse the seeds inside them.

Maize
(sweet corn)

Orange

Raspberry

Pepper

Tomato

HERBS AND SPICES
A herb is any soft-stemmed plant, but in the kitchen herbs are scented plants used for flavouring: they include sage, parsley, thyme, mint and basil. Some herbs (e.g. camomile and feverfew) have medicinal uses. Spices, sweet or hot-tasting herbs, include vanilla, chillies, ginger and cloves.

Celery

Mint

Ginger

Marrow

Cloves

189

Trees

There are two main groups of trees, conifers (softwoods) and broad-leaved trees (hardwoods). Conifers carry their leaves all year round, as do many tropical trees. Broad-leaved trees in cooler climates are deciduous: they shed their leaves in autumn. Trees need more internal stiffening than smaller plants. In trees the tubes called xylem that carry water through the stem (or trunk) from the roots are thick and stiffened. Thinner-walled tubes called phloem carry food made in the leaves to other parts of the plant.

▼ *Most deciduous trees have broad, flat leaves. They may be oval, with smooth or toothed edges. Others are narrow (peach), pinnate – compound – (acacia or ash) and forked (horse chestnut or sycamore).*

Horse chestnut

Sycamore

False acacia

Peach

Silver birch

FALLING LEAVES

Losing their leaves in autumn helps deciduous trees to conserve water through winter. Food 'pipes' to the stem are sealed: food has been stored for next year's bud. The leaf is sealed off from the stem; the chlorophyll that makes the leaf green breaks down and hidden colours are seen.

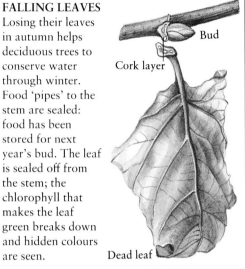

Bud

Cork layer

Dead leaf

DEEP ROOTS

Roots take in water and minerals. Some trees have long roots, with as much growth below the ground as above it. Others have massive trunks, but shallow roots.

Fig tree

⌐ 10 m

0

120 m

Judas tree

DECIDUOUS TREES

Most broad-leaved trees are deciduous, although some tropical broadleaves are evergreen. A typical broadleaf tree has spring flowers, which develop into fruits, and a spreading crown and roots.

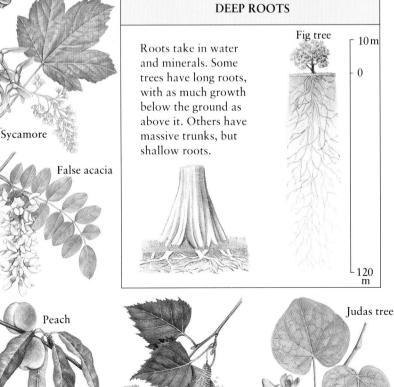

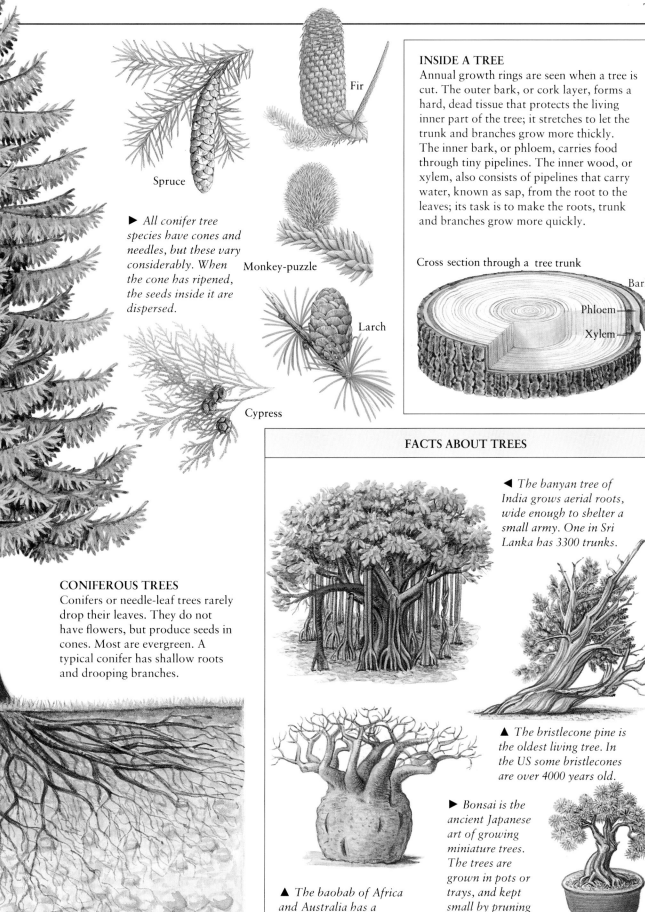

Spruce

Fir

▶ *All conifer tree species have cones and needles, but these vary considerably. When the cone has ripened, the seeds inside it are dispersed.*

Monkey-puzzle

Larch

Cypress

INSIDE A TREE

Annual growth rings are seen when a tree is cut. The outer bark, or cork layer, forms a hard, dead tissue that protects the living inner part of the tree; it stretches to let the trunk and branches grow more thickly. The inner bark, or phloem, carries food through tiny pipelines. The inner wood, or xylem, also consists of pipelines that carry water, known as sap, from the root to the leaves; its task is to make the roots, trunk and branches grow more quickly.

Cross section through a tree trunk

Bark

Phloem

Xylem

CONIFEROUS TREES

Conifers or needle-leaf trees rarely drop their leaves. They do not have flowers, but produce seeds in cones. Most are evergreen. A typical conifer has shallow roots and drooping branches.

FACTS ABOUT TREES

◀ *The banyan tree of India grows aerial roots, wide enough to shelter a small army. One in Sri Lanka has 3300 trunks.*

▲ *The bristlecone pine is the oldest living tree. In the US some bristlecones are over 4000 years old.*

▶ *Bonsai is the ancient Japanese art of growing miniature trees. The trees are grown in pots or trays, and kept small by pruning and shaping them.*

▲ *The baobab of Africa and Australia has a bottle-shaped trunk.*

Plants and People

Plants are important to us, both as sources of food and as raw materials. About 10,000 years ago people began to grow plants, rather than simply collecting them from the wild. The basic food crops, such as cereals, were developed in this way by selective breeding from wild plants. Today, cultivated plants may look very different from their wild ancestors, and genetic engineering is making it possible to develop plants that yield large crops, resist pests and grow in unfavourable conditions.

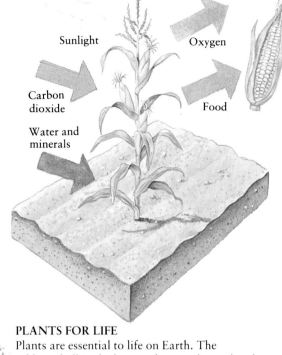

Sunlight

Oxygen

Carbon dioxide

Food

Water and minerals

THE USES OF PLANTS

Many different parts of plants can be used. The sap of the rubber tree is tapped to give the latex from which natural rubber is made. Cotton comes from the ripe fruit, or 'bolls', of the cotton plant. Inside the boll is a mass of fibres enclosing the seeds. Cork comes from the bark of the Mediterranean cork oak. The cork is stripped from the tree once every nine or ten years.

Tyre

Rubber tree being tapped

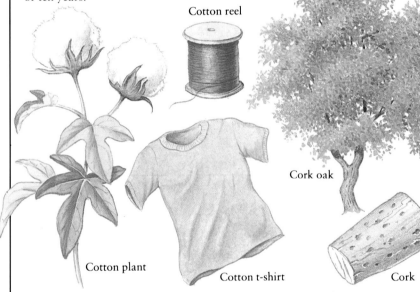

Cotton reel

Cork oak

Cotton plant

Cotton t-shirt

Cork

PLANTS FOR LIFE

Plants are essential to life on Earth. The chlorophyll in the leaves of green plants absorbs light energy from the Sun. Water is drawn up through the roots and carbon dioxide gas taken in from the air by the leaves, combining to make glucose (sugar) and oxygen. The plants use the sugar for food, releasing the oxygen into the air.

▶ All animals depend on plants for their food in some way. The most important food crops grown by people include wheat, maize, rice, potatoes, beans, cassava, fruits and vegetables.

FACTS ABOUT PLANTS AND PEOPLE

- The pain-killing drug morphine is made from the opium poppy.
- Quinine, used for treating malaria, comes from the cinchona tree.
- The drug digitalis, a treatment for heart disease, comes from the leaves of the foxglove.
- The first antibiotic drug effective against infections was penicillin. It was developed in the 1940s from a mould found in 1928 growing in a dish that contained bacteria. The mould killed the bacteria.

Cinchona tree (flower of)

HOW PEOPLE CHANGE PLANTS

There are thousands of varieties of apples, developed over the past 2000 years. Most apple trees are grown from a bud of one variety grafted on to the roots of another. Plant-breeders have also cross-bred flowers such as roses to give them better colours or perfumes.

Cox apple

Golden Delicious apple

Hy[rose

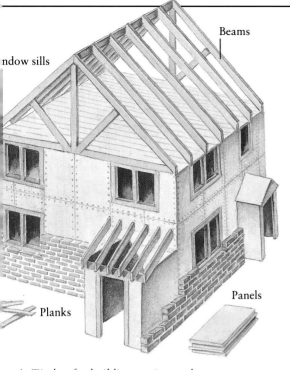

Beams

ndow sills

Panels

Planks

▲ *Timber for building use is mostly sawn softwood planking or factory-made laminate (such as plywood) and chipboard. Softwoods are far easier to saw, plane and bore than hardwoods making them ideal for the frame of a house. However, hardwoods such as oak or maple are often used for a house's interior panelling and for finished floors.*

HARDWOODS AND SOFTWOODS

These terms refer to the trees from which timber comes, not to its hardness. Softwood comes from conifer trees such as pine and cedar. Hardwood comes from broad-leaved trees growing either in cool regions (trees such as oak and ash) or in the Tropics (trees such as mahogany and ebony).

THE USES OF HARDWOOD	THE USES OF SOFTWOOD
Hardwoods can be very strong. Oak, for example, was used to make sailing ships. Beech is hard-wearing and elm is water-resistant. Furniture made from tropical hardwoods has an attractive colour.	Softwoods grow quickly, and are easy to cut and shape by hand or on machines. They are used for making boxes, furniture, toys, and for building materials such as planks, frames, doors, posts and beams.

▶ *Fine furniture is made from woods with a distinctive grain, such as cherry and walnut.*

▶ *Reeds and grasses have been used for thousands of years as materials for house-building and in basket-making.*

▲ *Most paper is made from the pulp of trees such as beech, fir, pine and oak, although other plant fibres can also be pulped to make paper.*

PLANTS AND LANDSCAPE

People have changed complete landscapes by cutting down forests *(above)*, ploughing prairies, and by introducing new kinds of plants. Plants are a vital ingredient of our landscape. Planting trees makes cities more pleasant to live in, and screens busy roads or factories.

DANGEROUS PLANTS

Some food plants have parts that are dangerous to eat – rhubarb and potato leaves, for example. Certain mushrooms are harmful if eaten. Poison ivy contains an irritant oil. Every part of azalea, deadly nightshade, foxglove, oleander and rhododendron is poisonous. Yew and laburnum seeds are poisonous, as are the berries of mistletoe and the bulb of a hyacinth.

Smooth lepiota
Leucoagaricus naucinus
(poisonous)

Field mushroom
Agaricus campestris

Hemlock

Rhubarb leaves

THE ANIMAL KINGDOM

The World of Animals

What makes an animal? A general rule is that animals move (plants are anchored by their roots). Unlike most plants, which make their own food, animals must eat either plants or other animals. Some live on dry land, others in water. Some have two legs, others have four, six, eight or hundreds. Some are constantly warm-blooded; others have body temperatures which vary with their surroundings. Animals with similar body characteristics are grouped together. Scientists do this to identify each distinct species, and also to show how species are related within larger groups.

Common features reveal how animal species have evolved over millions of years. An elephant looks very different from a dog, yet both are mammals and they share with birds, reptiles, fish and amphibians an important body feature – a backbone of vertebrae.

THE ANIMAL KINGDOM
There are over one million animal species, classified into 20 or more phyla. For example, all animals with backbones (vertebrates) belong to the phylum Chordata. This includes all reptiles, birds and mammals, but even so the chordates make up only a small part of the vast animal kingdom. Only major phyla are shown here.

Protozoans are single-celled organisms. They move by floating or waving hair-like organs on their bodies. Protozoans are now usually classed in the separate kingdom Protoctists.

Sponges are the most primitive of multi-cellular animals; the 5000 species make up the phylum Porifera. Sponges live in either fresh water or oceans; like most animals, they eat their food but they cannot move from place to place.

Flatworms, flukes and tapeworms belong to the phylum Platyhelminthes. These animals have soft, thin, flat bodies. Most flatworms live as parasites in other animals.

Nematodes are thin, round worms. Some are too small to be seen without a microscope. There are more than 15,000 species, living in soil and water. Many, such as hookworms, are parasites.

Worms with long bodies made up of segments are annelids. They are all soft-bodied, without hard skeletons. This phylum includes earthworms, leeches and lugworms.

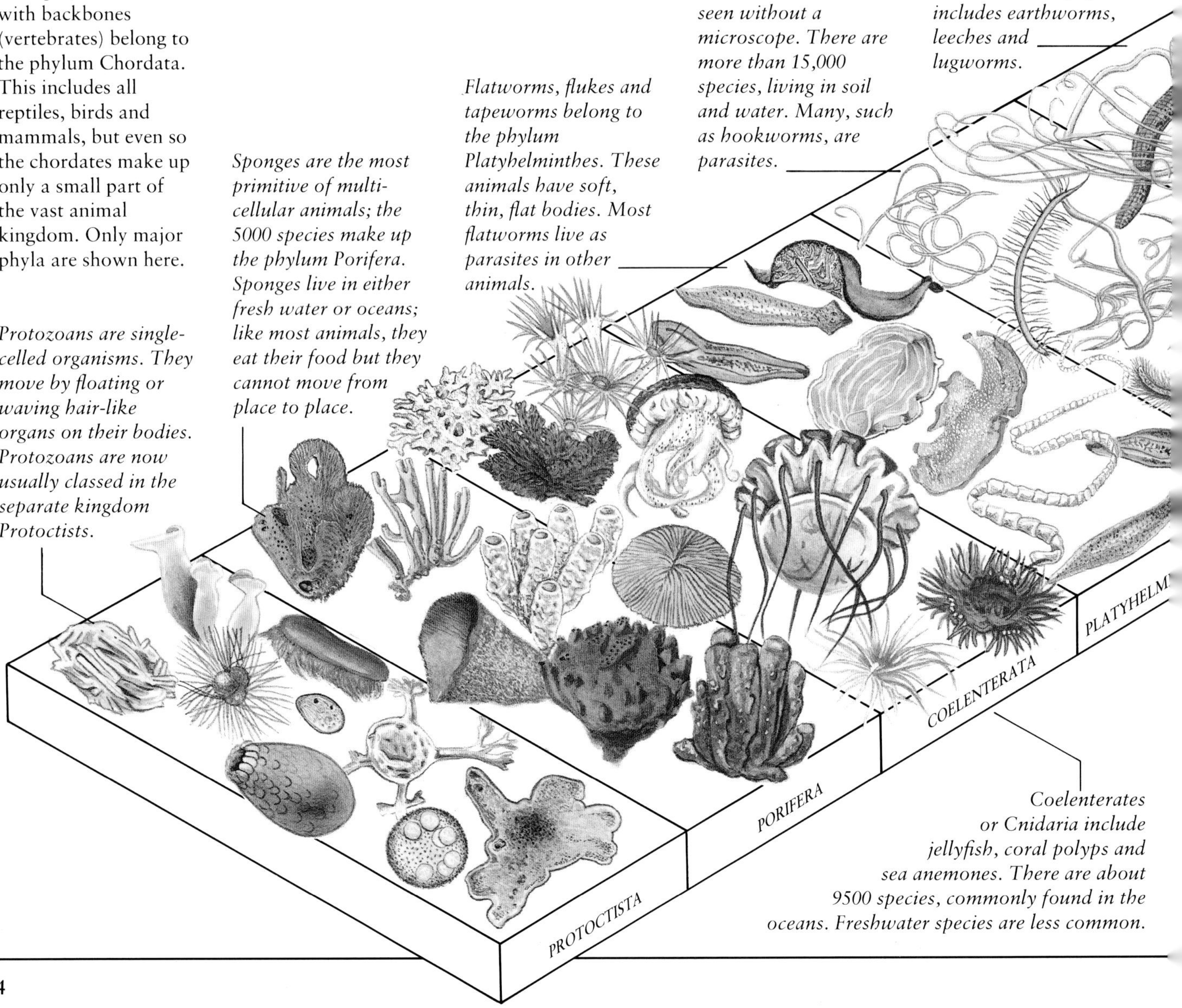

Coelenterates or Cnidaria include jellyfish, coral polyps and sea anemones. There are about 9500 species, commonly found in the oceans. Freshwater species are less common.

PROTOCTISTA

PORIFERA

COELENTERATA

PLATYHELM

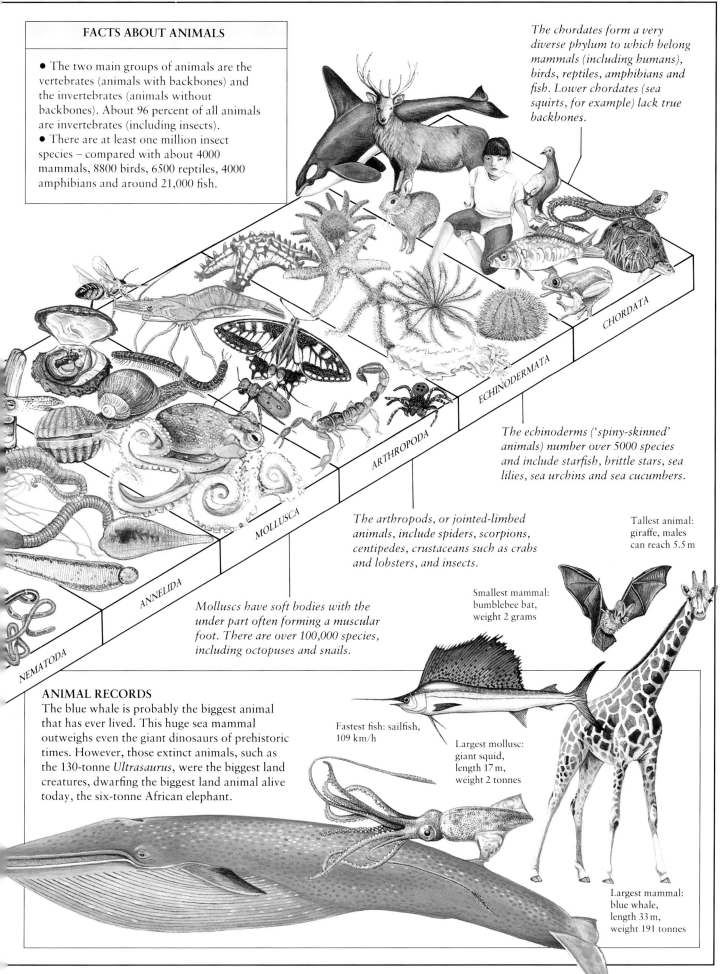

FACTS ABOUT ANIMALS

• The two main groups of animals are the vertebrates (animals with backbones) and the invertebrates (animals without backbones). About 96 percent of all animals are invertebrates (including insects).

• There are at least one million insect species – compared with about 4000 mammals, 8800 birds, 6500 reptiles, 4000 amphibians and around 21,000 fish.

The chordates form a very diverse phylum to which belong mammals (including humans), birds, reptiles, amphibians and fish. Lower chordates (sea squirts, for example) lack true backbones.

CHORDATA

ECHINODERMATA

The echinoderms ('spiny-skinned' animals) number over 5000 species and include starfish, brittle stars, sea lilies, sea urchins and sea cucumbers.

ARTHROPODA

The arthropods, or jointed-limbed animals, include spiders, scorpions, centipedes, crustaceans such as crabs and lobsters, and insects.

MOLLUSCA

Tallest animal: giraffe, males can reach 5.5 m

Smallest mammal: bumblebee bat, weight 2 grams

ANNELIDA

Molluscs have soft bodies with the under part often forming a muscular foot. There are over 100,000 species, including octopuses and snails.

NEMATODA

ANIMAL RECORDS

The blue whale is probably the biggest animal that has ever lived. This huge sea mammal outweighs even the giant dinosaurs of prehistoric times. However, those extinct animals, such as the 130-tonne *Ultrasaurus*, were the biggest land creatures, dwarfing the biggest land animal alive today, the six-tonne African elephant.

Fastest fish: sailfish, 109 km/h

Largest mollusc: giant squid, length 17 m, weight 2 tonnes

Largest mammal: blue whale, length 33 m, weight 191 tonnes

Marine Invertebrates, Worms, Snails and Slugs

The first multi-celled animals were sea-living invertebrates, creatures without backbones that swam and crawled in the oceans millions of years before the first backboned animals (fish). Their modern descendants include worms, corals, clams, snails, starfish and squid. Even without the arthropods (for example, insects, spiders and crabs), these 'lower' animals are enormously successful: there are more than 100,000 molluscs ranging from tiny snails to giant squid, and several thousand kinds of worms.

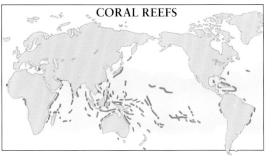

See pages 194–195

FACTS ABOUT MARINE INVERTEBRATES

- The bootlace worm of the North Sea can grow up to 55 m long.
- Sea cucumbers (echinoderms) force out their own insides to confuse enemies, while they crawl to safety.
- The venom of a sea wasp jellyfish can kill a person in 1 to 3 minutes.
- The biggest snail is the African giant snail, weighing 900 grams.
- The quahog clam of the Atlantic Ocean may live for 220 years.
- Squids, cuttlefish and octopuses are the most active molluscs. They are carnivores, and swim rapidly by squirting out jets of water behind them.

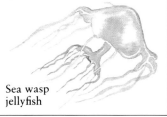

Sea wasp jellyfish

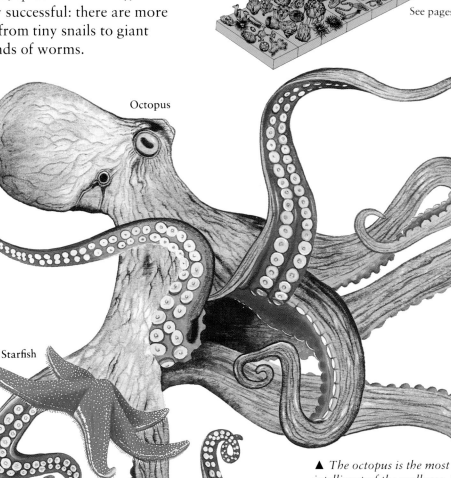

Octopus

Starfish

Limpet

▲ *A starfish hunts by smell; it digs out a mussel, oyster or clam and uses its tube feet to pull the two halves of the shell apart.*

▲ *The octopus is the most intelligent of the molluscs. It uses its sucker arms to seize prey and kills with a bite.*

◄ *Limpets cling to rocks. A force 2000 times the limpet's weight is needed to dislodge its sucker-like foot.*

► *Coral reefs are only found in tropical seas as the corals that form the reefs cannot live in cold water. Coral is made of limestone formed by millions of tiny marine animals.*

◄ *Small fish feed and shelter among the colourful branches and fronds of coral.*

CORAL REEFS

Coral reefs

20°C (coral cannot survive below this temperature)

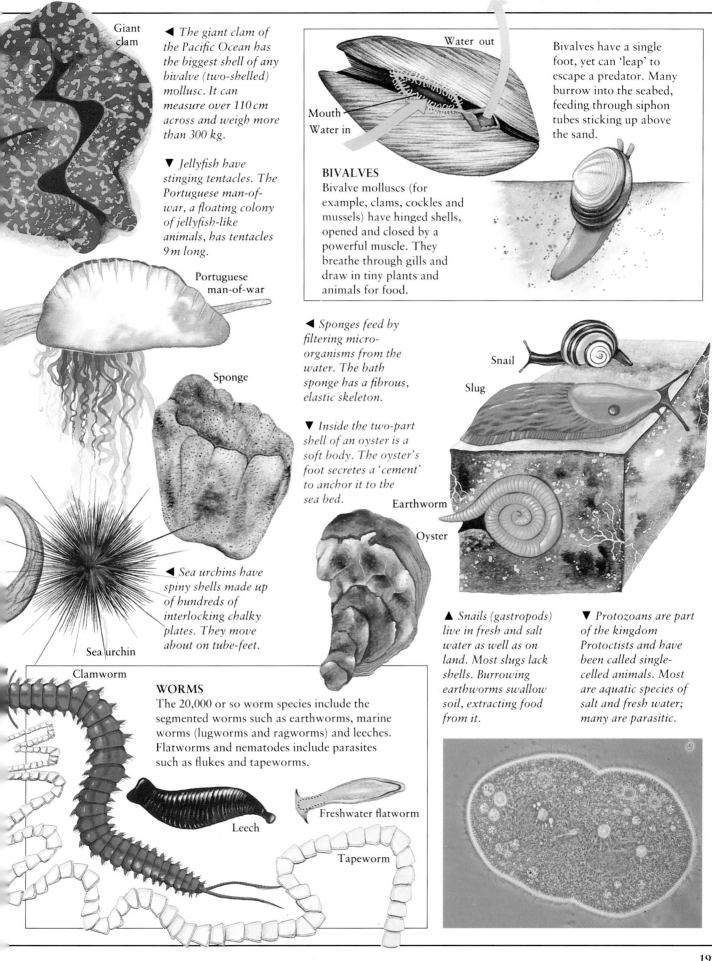

Giant clam

◄ *The giant clam of the Pacific Ocean has the biggest shell of any bivalve (two-shelled) mollusc. It can measure over 110 cm across and weigh more than 300 kg.*

▼ *Jellyfish have stinging tentacles. The Portuguese man-of-war, a floating colony of jellyfish-like animals, has tentacles 9 m long.*

Water out

Mouth
Water in

Bivalves have a single foot, yet can 'leap' to escape a predator. Many burrow into the seabed, feeding through siphon tubes sticking up above the sand.

BIVALVES
Bivalve molluscs (for example, clams, cockles and mussels) have hinged shells, opened and closed by a powerful muscle. They breathe through gills and draw in tiny plants and animals for food.

Portuguese man-of-war

◄ *Sponges feed by filtering micro-organisms from the water. The bath sponge has a fibrous, elastic skeleton.*

Sponge

▼ *Inside the two-part shell of an oyster is a soft body. The oyster's foot secretes a 'cement' to anchor it to the sea bed.*

Snail

Slug

Earthworm

Oyster

◄ *Sea urchins have spiny shells made up of hundreds of interlocking chalky plates. They move about on tube-feet.*

Sea urchin

Clamworm

WORMS
The 20,000 or so worm species include the segmented worms such as earthworms, marine worms (lugworms and ragworms) and leeches. Flatworms and nematodes include parasites such as flukes and tapeworms.

Leech

Freshwater flatworm

Tapeworm

▲ *Snails (gastropods) live in fresh and salt water as well as on land. Most slugs lack shells. Burrowing earthworms swallow soil, extracting food from it.*

▼ *Protozoans are part of the kingdom Protoctists and have been called single-celled animals. Most are aquatic species of salt and fresh water; many are parasitic.*

Millipedes, Crabs and Spiders

Like insects, these animals are arthropods, members of the largest animal phylum. All arthropods have jointed limbs and most have a plated body-covering, which the animal moults, or sheds, as it grows. Centipedes and millipedes are worm-like, with a pair of limbs on almost every segment of their bodies. Crustaceans (for example, crabs, lobsters and woodlice) number more than 30,000 species. The biggest group, with over 50,000 species, is the arachnids: spiders, scorpions and mites.

See pages 194–195

FACTS ABOUT ARTHROPODS

- The first true arthropods lived in the sea. They were the trilobites, now extinct.
- Millipedes use chemical defences. Stink glands in their bodies secrete a venom capable of killing or repelling insects.
- Most crabs live in the oceans and seas, but robber crabs are so adapted to life on land that they drown if kept under water.

◀ Millipedes have even more legs than centipedes: as many as 375 pairs. They live in soil and leaf litter, feeding on decaying vegetation.

▼ The horseshoe or king crab is closer to spiders than to true crabs. Up to 60 cm long, it has a horny shield.

Centipede

Millipede

◀ Not all centipedes have 100 legs; some have as few as 30, others as many as 177. They are all fast-moving hunters with poisonous claws.

▼ Lobsters are the heaviest crustaceans (weighing up to 20 kg). Spiny lobsters migrate in columns across the sea floor.

Horseshoe crab

Lobster

LIFE CYCLE OF A SHRIMP

Marine crustaceans such as shrimps lay eggs, often carried by the female until they hatch. The tiny larvae look very different from the adults. The larvae drift through the water, gradually changing body shape until fully developed.

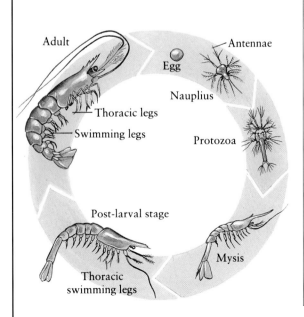

Adult
Egg
Antennae
Nauplius
Thoracic legs
Swimming legs
Protozoa
Post-larval stage
Mysis
Thoracic swimming legs

CARING PARENTS

Few arthropods are caring parents. The arthropods that show most concern for their young are those with the fiercest reputations as killers: spiders and scorpions. A female scorpion gives birth to live young. She carries the babies about on her back until after their first moult.

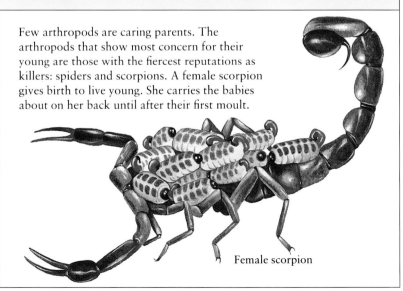

Female scorpion

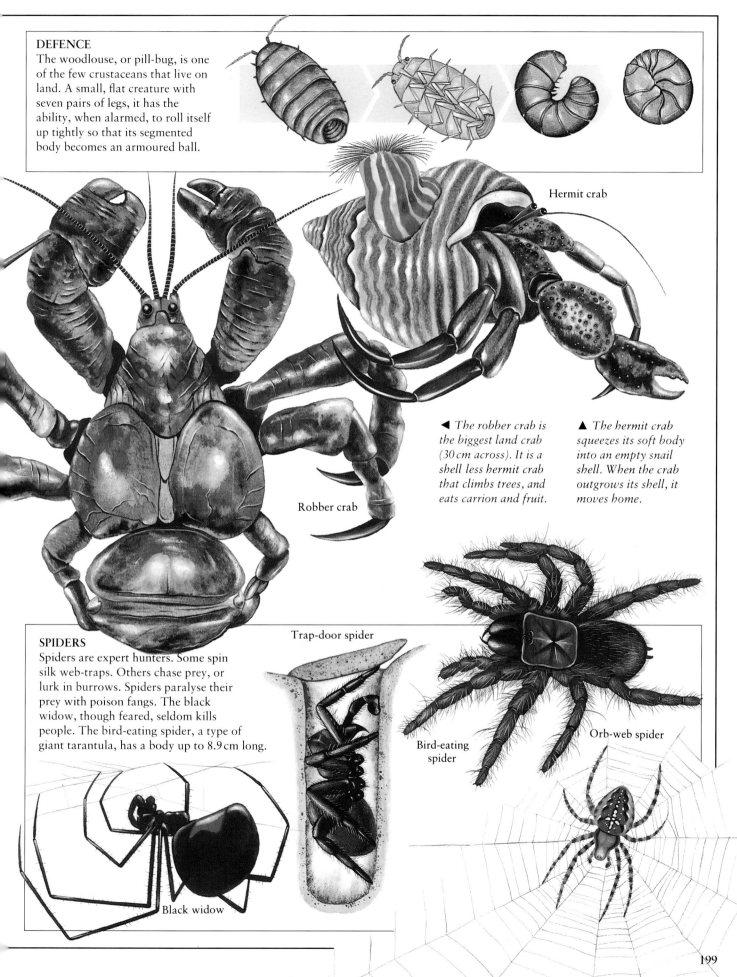

DEFENCE

The woodlouse, or pill-bug, is one of the few crustaceans that live on land. A small, flat creature with seven pairs of legs, it has the ability, when alarmed, to roll itself up tightly so that its segmented body becomes an armoured ball.

Hermit crab

◀ The robber crab is the biggest land crab (30 cm across). It is a shell less hermit crab that climbs trees, and eats carrion and fruit.

▲ The hermit crab squeezes its soft body into an empty snail shell. When the crab outgrows its shell, it moves home.

Robber crab

SPIDERS

Spiders are expert hunters. Some spin silk web-traps. Others chase prey, or lurk in burrows. Spiders paralyse their prey with poison fangs. The black widow, though feared, seldom kills people. The bird-eating spider, a type of giant tarantula, has a body up to 8.9 cm long.

Trap-door spider

Bird-eating spider

Orb-web spider

Black widow

Insects

There are about one million known species of insects, and millions more are probably still to be identified; about 80 percent of all known animals are insects. Some scientists believe there could be as many as 10 million insect species. The secret of the insect's success is their adaptability. Although they are limited in size by their body design, they have conquered all environments, from the hottest to the coldest places. Evolution has also equipped them to eat an astonishing variety of foods.

See pages 194–195

FACTS ABOUT INSECTS

- Insects breathe through tiny holes called 'spiracles' along the sides of their bodies. Each hole allows air to pass into a system of tubes branching all around the insect's body. These tubes carry oxygen to the cells and carry away carbon dioxide.
- Many insects can lift or drag an object 20 times their own weight. A caterpillar has from 2000 to 4000 muscles – six times as many as a human.
- Botflies and horseflies can fly at 39 km/h. A tiny midge holds the record for fast wing beats: more than 62,000 times a minute.

Midge

THE BODIES OF INSECTS

All insects, like this honey bee, have three pairs of legs. An insect's body has three parts: a head, a middle, or thorax, where the legs are attached, and an abdomen. Most adult insects have wings and a pair of antennae. But while the majority of insects (like the bee) have four wings, flies only have two.

▼ *Hornets are large social wasps. They build nests of paper made from chewed-up plant matter. Hornets sting if disturbed, and hunt flies and caterpillars.*

▶ *Dragonflies are the fastest insects, with a top speed of over 55 km/h when hunting.*

Hornet

Two pairs of wings

THORAX

ABDOMEN

HEAD

Compound eye

Antenna

Six jointed legs

▲ *The largest insect is the Queen Alexandra birdwing butterfly of Papua New Guinea. It measures 28 cm from wingtip to wingtip.*

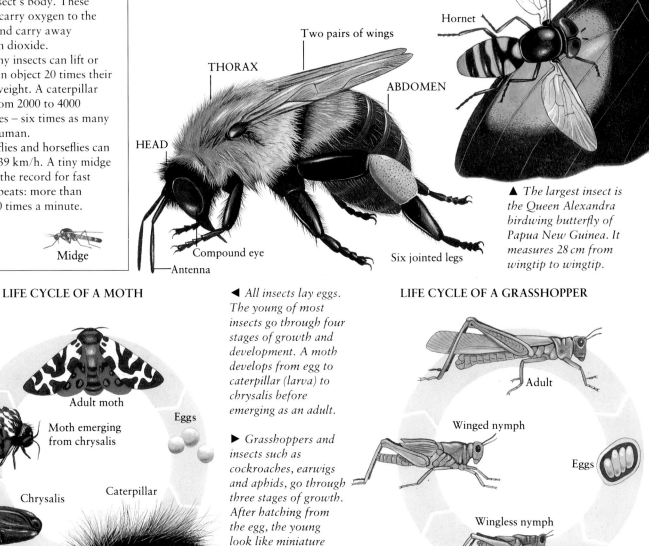

LIFE CYCLE OF A MOTH

Adult moth

Moth emerging from chrysalis

Eggs

Chrysalis

Caterpillar

◀ *All insects lay eggs. The young of most insects go through four stages of growth and development. A moth develops from egg to caterpillar (larva) to chrysalis before emerging as an adult.*

▶ *Grasshoppers and insects such as cockroaches, earwigs and aphids, go through three stages of growth. After hatching from the egg, the young look like miniature adults, though at first they lack wings.*

LIFE CYCLE OF A GRASSHOPPER

Adult

Winged nymph

Eggs

Wingless nymph

Dragonfly

Queen Alexandra
birdwing butterfly

◀ *The male Goliath
beetle of Africa is the
world's heaviest insect.
It can be more than
110 mm long and can
weigh 100 g.*

▼ *Ladybirds are
helpful predators as
both larvae and adults
kill aphids. Many
beetles are pests,
eating crops or trees.*

Ladybird

Flea

Goliath beetle

▼ *Houseflies will eat
fresh or rotting food,
and often lay their
eggs in dung.*

Silverfish

▲ *Insects are
astonishing athletes. A
flea can jump 130
times its own height.*

◀ *Shieldbugs have
specialized piercing
beaks for sucking the
juices of plants or
other animals.*

▲ *Silverfish are
primitive wingless
insects. Household
pests, they eat food,
paper and clothes.*

Housefly

◀ *To escape their
enemies some insects
have developed clever
camouflages. The
cryptic mantid can
escape predators
because of its close
resemblance to a leaf.
Other insects are
mimics, with similar
colouring to a
distasteful or
dangerous insect.*

Shieldbug

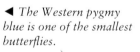
◀ *The Western pygmy
blue is one of the smallest
butterflies.*

PESTS AND PARASITES
Insects such as mosquitoes spread disease;
other pests eat crops and human food.
Parasitic wasps paralyse and lay eggs on their
prey, which then feeds the wasp larvae.

SOCIAL INSECTS
Social insects, such as ants, function only as
colony members. The colony's activities centre on
the egg-laying queen. Most of her eggs hatch into
female workers or soldiers. Males exist solely to
fertilize new queens, after which they die. Some
wasps and bees are also social insects.

Cockroach

Mosquito

Parasitic wasp

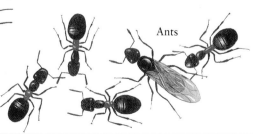
Ants

Fish

The first fish appeared in the oceans some 540 million years ago. By breathing through gills, fish have always been fully adapted to life in water. About 60 percent of all fish species live in salt water; a few kinds can live in either salt or fresh water. There are three main groups of fish: Agnatha or jawless fish (lampreys and hagfish), Chondrichthyes or fish with a skeleton of cartilage (sharks, chimaeras and rays) and Osteichthyes, a group that includes some 20,000 species of fish with a bony skeleton.

See pages 194–195

FISH RECORDS

- The biggest freshwater fish is the giant catfish at 5 m long (a record set in the 1800s).
- The longest bony fish is the oarfish, which grows up to 15 m long.
- The smallest fish is the dwarf goby of the Pacific Ocean. Few grow more than 9 mm long.
- Largest of all fish is the whale shark: 18 m long and weighing 15 tonnes. It eats only plankton.

Whale shark

- Coelacanths live deep in the Indian Ocean. Scientists believed they had died out 70 million years ago – until one was caught in 1938.
- Fish known to attack people include some sharks (whites, blues, hammerheads), barracudas and moray eels. Venomous fish include stonefish, with poisonous spines.

Coelacanth

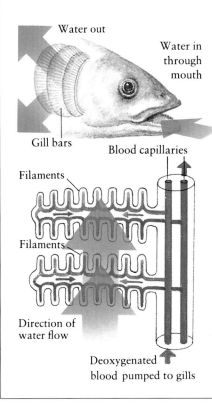

HOW FISH BREATHE
Fish breathe oxygen from water by means of gills; water contains amounts of dissolved oxygen. The fish gulps in water through its mouth. The water passes across the gills and out again. Blood flows through the gills in tiny filters that take oxygen in, and release waste carbon dioxide.

Water out

Water in through mouth

Gill bars

Blood capillaries

Filaments

Filaments

Direction of water flow

Deoxygenated blood pumped to gills

▼ *Sting rays have whip-like tails armed with poisonous spines. They are ocean bottom-dwellers with flattened bodies.*

Sting ray

▶ *A mako shark, is about 3.5 m long. Makos prey on fish but sometimes attack human bathers and small boats.*

Mako shark

▼ *The alligator gar is a large (3 m) freshwater hunter of North America. It has an alligator-like snout.*

▼ *The saltwater herring is an important North Atlantic food fish. Members of the herring family include shad and sardine.*

Alligator gar

Saltwater herring

▶ *Flying fish glide rather than fly. To escape predators they take off, using their long pectoral fins as wings.*

Flying fish

Lamprey

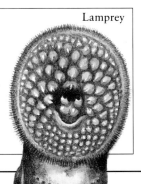

JAWLESS FISH
Lampreys and hagfish lack true jaws, but have sucking mouths with horny teeth. They clamp on to a victim and tear its flesh with file-toothed tongues.

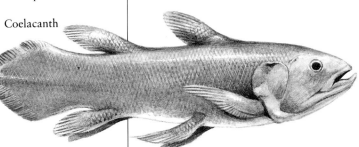

▶ *Puffer fish keep away their enemies by doubling their size; by quickly taking in water or air they inflate their stomachs.*

▼ *Chub are freshwater fish related to carp. Like most jawed fish, they have scales.*

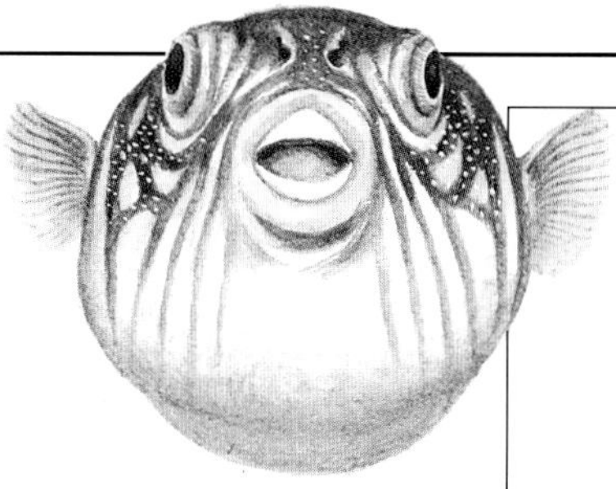

Puffer fish

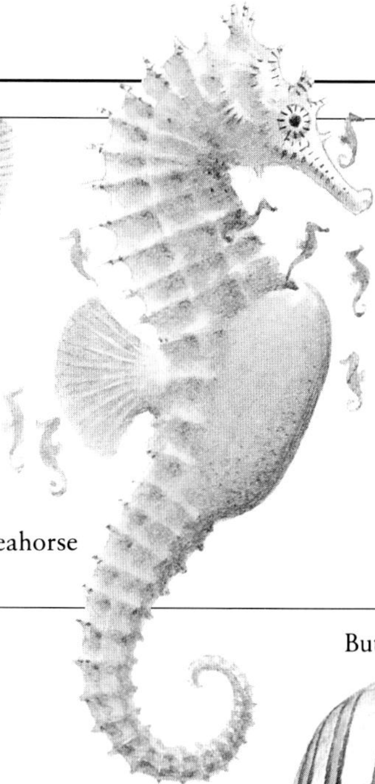

Seahorse

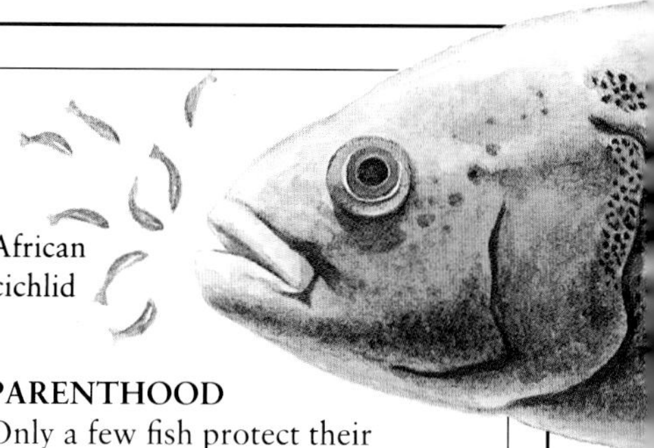

African cichlid

PARENTHOOD
Only a few fish protect their young. Some cichlids shelter their young in their mouths. Baby seahorses hatch and develop in a pouch on their father's body.

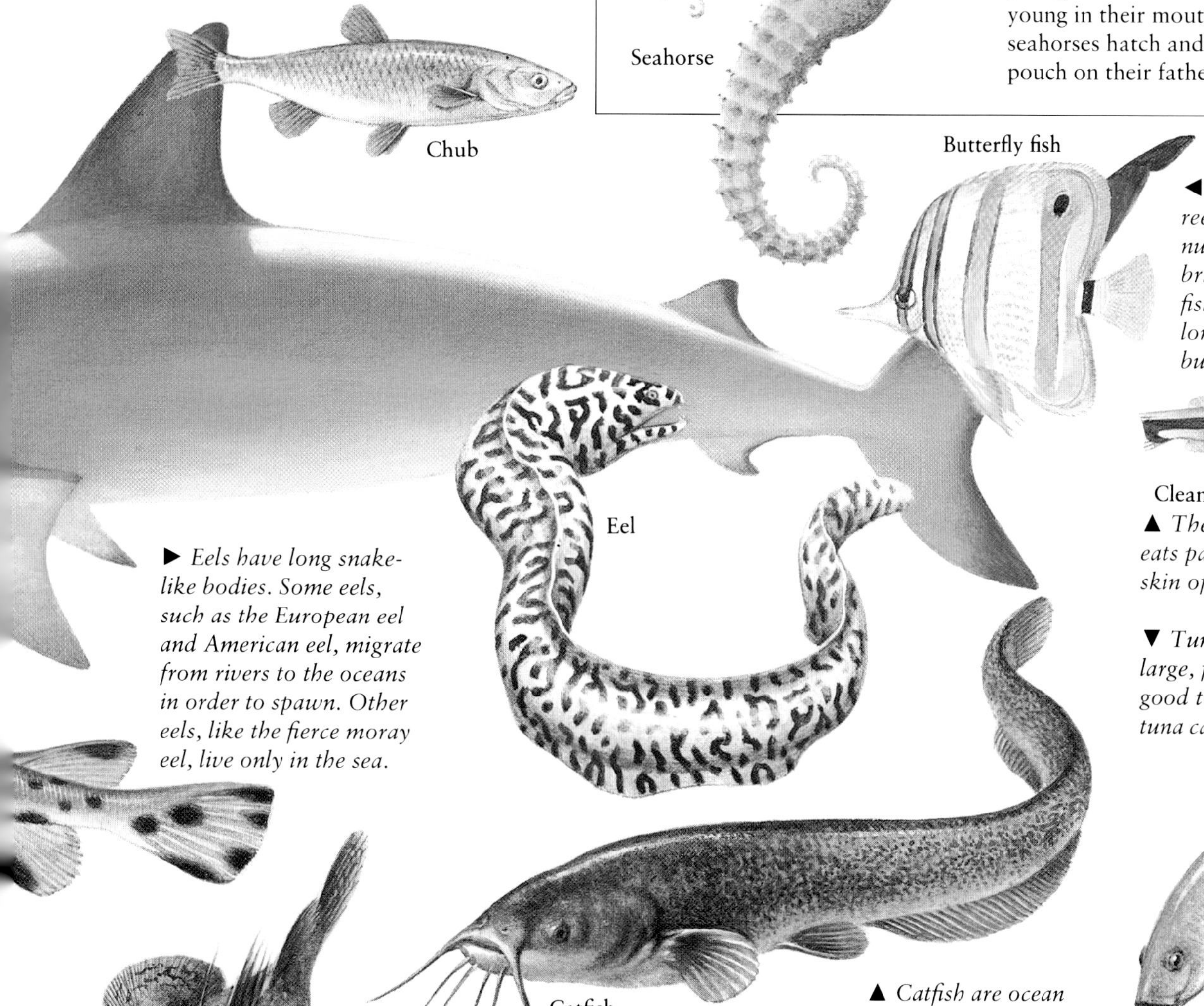

Chub

Butterfly fish

◀ *Tropical coral reefs shelter great numbers of brightly coloured fish, like this long-nosed butterfly fish.*

Cleaner wrasse

▲ *The cleaner wrasse eats parasites from the skin of larger fish.*

Eel

▶ *Eels have long snake-like bodies. Some eels, such as the European eel and American eel, migrate from rivers to the oceans in order to spawn. Other eels, like the fierce moray eel, live only in the sea.*

▼ *Tuna or tunny are large, fast fish that are good to eat. A blue fin tuna can weigh 900 kg.*

Catfish

▲ *Catfish are ocean bottom-feeders, using their whisker-like barbels to feel in mud.*

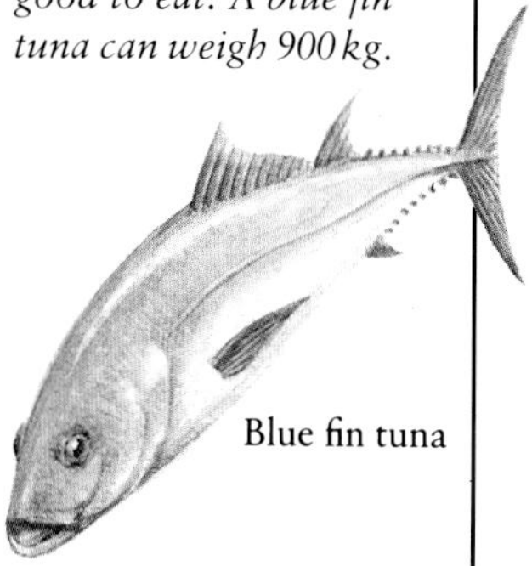

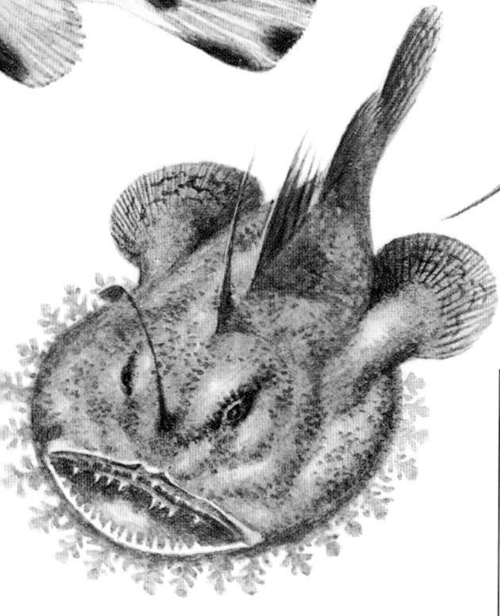

Blue fin tuna

▲ *The angler-fish has on its head rod-like growths with a fleshy tip. This wormlike 'bait' lures smaller fish within snapping range of its jaws.*

A FISH OUT OF WATER
Lungfish breathe through air bladders as well as gills. During a drought the fish survives by burying itself in the mud, motionless and barely breathing, until the rains come.

Lungfish

Burrow

Amphibians

Amphibians are a relatively small group of cold-blooded vertebrate animals: about 3000 species. Many are water creatures. Others live on land, in trees and even in deserts. Most amphibians need water (a river, pond or even a droplet on a leaf) to lay their eggs. There are three orders: worm-like caecilians (Apoda); newts and salamanders (Urodela) with long tails and usually four legs; and toads and frogs (Anura), tailless and four-legged. Amphibians are most common in warm climates.

See pages 194–195

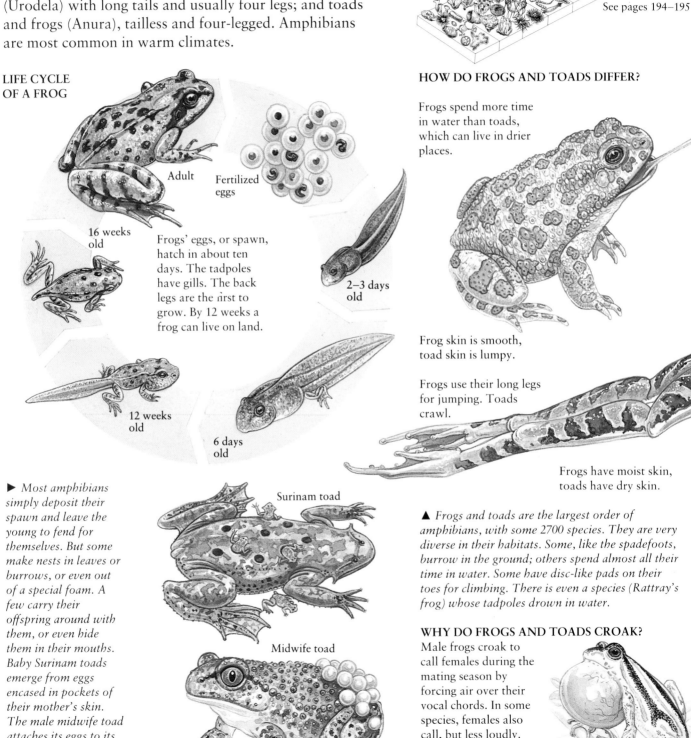

LIFE CYCLE OF A FROG

Adult

Fertilized eggs

16 weeks old

Frogs' eggs, or spawn, hatch in about ten days. The tadpoles have gills. The back legs are the first to grow. By 12 weeks a frog can live on land.

2–3 days old

12 weeks old

6 days old

► *Most amphibians simply deposit their spawn and leave the young to fend for themselves. But some make nests in leaves or burrows, or even out of a special foam. A few carry their offspring around with them, or even hide them in their mouths. Baby Surinam toads emerge from eggs encased in pockets of their mother's skin. The male midwife toad attaches its eggs to its hind legs and carries them for about three weeks until they hatch.*

Surinam toad

Midwife toad

HOW DO FROGS AND TOADS DIFFER?

Frogs spend more time in water than toads, which can live in drier places.

Frog skin is smooth, toad skin is lumpy.

Frogs use their long legs for jumping. Toads crawl.

Frogs have moist skin, toads have dry skin.

▲ *Frogs and toads are the largest order of amphibians, with some 2700 species. They are very diverse in their habitats. Some, like the spadefoots, burrow in the ground; others spend almost all their time in water. Some have disc-like pads on their toes for climbing. There is even a species (Rattray's frog) whose tadpoles drown in water.*

WHY DO FROGS AND TOADS CROAK?

Male frogs croak to call females during the mating season by forcing air over their vocal chords. In some species, females also call, but less loudly. The loudest croakers are species with an expanding vocal sac.

Tree frog

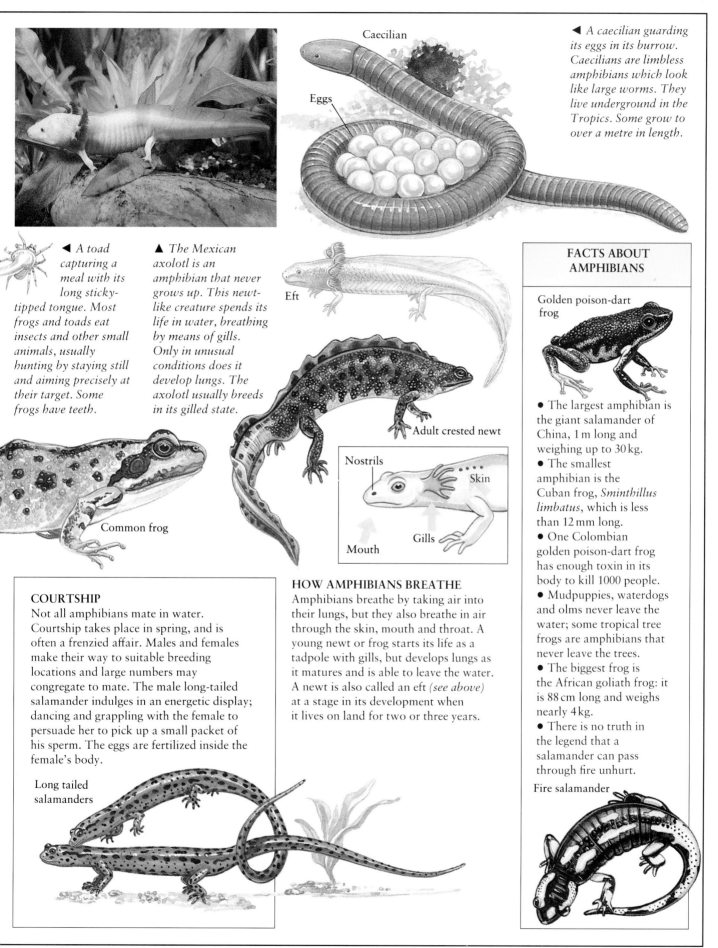

Caecilian

Eggs

◀ *A caecilian guarding its eggs in its burrow. Caecilians are limbless amphibians which look like large worms. They live underground in the Tropics. Some grow to over a metre in length.*

◀ *A toad capturing a meal with its long sticky-tipped tongue. Most frogs and toads eat insects and other small animals, usually hunting by staying still and aiming precisely at their target. Some frogs have teeth.*

▲ *The Mexican axolotl is an amphibian that never grows up. This newt-like creature spends its life in water, breathing by means of gills. Only in unusual conditions does it develop lungs. The axolotl usually breeds in its gilled state.*

Eft

Adult crested newt

Common frog

Nostrils

Skin

Gills

Mouth

FACTS ABOUT AMPHIBIANS

Golden poison-dart frog

● The largest amphibian is the giant salamander of China, 1 m long and weighing up to 30 kg.
● The smallest amphibian is the Cuban frog, *Sminthillus limbatus*, which is less than 12 mm long.
● One Colombian golden poison-dart frog has enough toxin in its body to kill 1000 people.
● Mudpuppies, waterdogs and olms never leave the water; some tropical tree frogs are amphibians that never leave the trees.
● The biggest frog is the African goliath frog: it is 88 cm long and weighs nearly 4 kg.
● There is no truth in the legend that a salamander can pass through fire unhurt.

Fire salamander

COURTSHIP

Not all amphibians mate in water. Courtship takes place in spring, and is often a frenzied affair. Males and females make their way to suitable breeding locations and large numbers may congregate to mate. The male long-tailed salamander indulges in an energetic display; dancing and grappling with the female to persuade her to pick up a small packet of his sperm. The eggs are fertilized inside the female's body.

Long tailed salamanders

HOW AMPHIBIANS BREATHE

Amphibians breathe by taking air into their lungs, but they also breathe in air through the skin, mouth and throat. A young newt or frog starts its life as a tadpole with gills, but develops lungs as it matures and is able to leave the water. A newt is also called an eft (*see above*) at a stage in its development when it lives on land for two or three years.

Reptiles

There are more than 6500 species of reptiles: some 250 kinds of tortoises and turtles (order Testudinidae); 25 species of crocodiles and alligators (order Crocodilia); about 2800 species of snakes (order Squamata); 3700 species of lizards (order Squamata); and the unique tuatara (order Rhynchocephalia). Like amphibians, reptiles are cold-blooded. Most live in the Tropics, though a few snakes and lizards live in cooler climates. Reptiles have scaly skins and most lay leathery-shelled eggs.

See pages 194–195

SNAKES

▶ *Poisonous snakes bite with grooved fangs which inject venom from sac-like glands in the head. Many venomous snakes are brightly coloured as a warning.*

Coral snake

Cobra

Venom sac

Fang

◀ *Male rattlesnakes wrestle for mates, but do not use their poison fangs. The rattle is formed by horny plates at the tip of the tail. Rattlesnakes detect prey with heat-sensing organs.*

▲ *Vipers, which include copperheads and rattlesnakes, have long fangs that unfold from the roof of the mouth as the snake strikes. Cobras and sea snakes have short, fixed fangs. Poisonous snakes can bite as soon as they have hatched.*

◀ *Snakes can swallow objects larger than their heads. The egg-eating snake swallows the egg, then crushes the shell.*

LIZARDS

▶ *The little gecko has sucker-like pads on its feet. It can run across the ceiling of a room with ease when hunting insects.*

▲ *The Gila monster is a poisonous lizard from the southwest USA. Like all lizards, this desert-dweller is most active when warmed by the Sun; being cold-blooded animals their bodies are as warm or as cool as their surroundings.*

◀ *The chameleon's colour-changes are the result of hormone activity triggered by a change of light or temperature, or by fear or anger. Chameleons catch insects by shooting out their long, sticky tongues.*

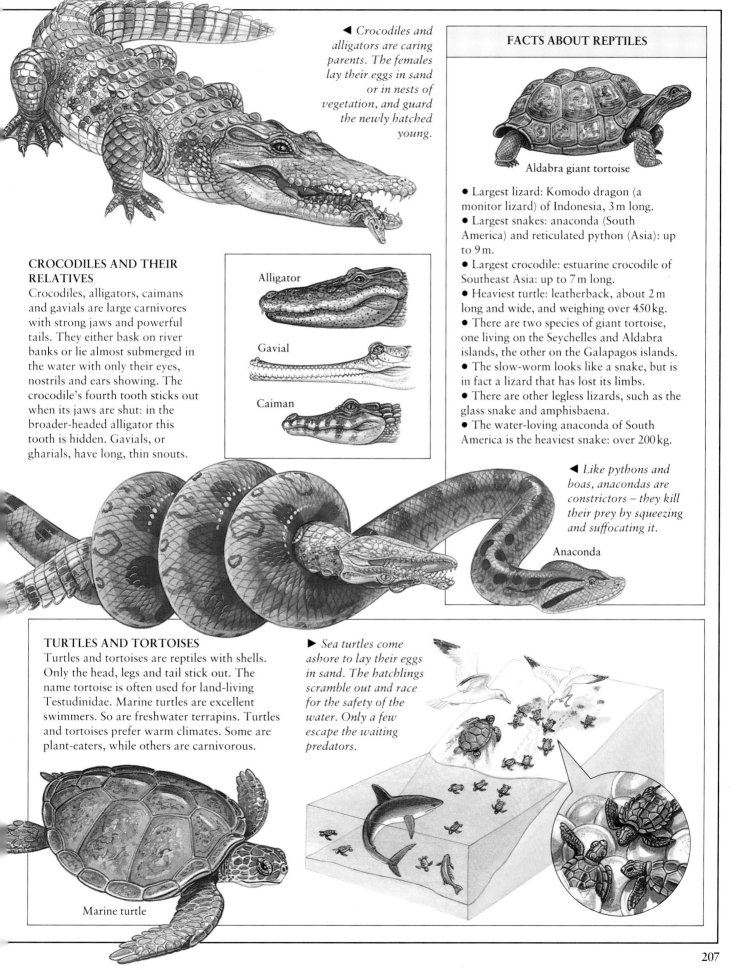

◀ *Crocodiles and alligators are caring parents. The females lay their eggs in sand or in nests of vegetation, and guard the newly hatched young.*

FACTS ABOUT REPTILES

Aldabra giant tortoise

- Largest lizard: Komodo dragon (a monitor lizard) of Indonesia, 3 m long.
- Largest snakes: anaconda (South America) and reticulated python (Asia): up to 9 m.
- Largest crocodile: estuarine crocodile of Southeast Asia: up to 7 m long.
- Heaviest turtle: leatherback, about 2 m long and wide, and weighing over 450 kg.
- There are two species of giant tortoise, one living on the Seychelles and Aldabra islands, the other on the Galapagos islands.
- The slow-worm looks like a snake, but is in fact a lizard that has lost its limbs.
- There are other legless lizards, such as the glass snake and amphisbaena.
- The water-loving anaconda of South America is the heaviest snake: over 200 kg.

CROCODILES AND THEIR RELATIVES

Crocodiles, alligators, caimans and gavials are large carnivores with strong jaws and powerful tails. They either bask on river banks or lie almost submerged in the water with only their eyes, nostrils and ears showing. The crocodile's fourth tooth sticks out when its jaws are shut: in the broader-headed alligator this tooth is hidden. Gavials, or gharials, have long, thin snouts.

Alligator

Gavial

Caiman

◀ *Like pythons and boas, anacondas are constrictors – they kill their prey by squeezing and suffocating it.*

Anaconda

TURTLES AND TORTOISES

Turtles and tortoises are reptiles with shells. Only the head, legs and tail stick out. The name tortoise is often used for land-living Testudinidae. Marine turtles are excellent swimmers. So are freshwater terrapins. Turtles and tortoises prefer warm climates. Some are plant-eaters, while others are carnivorous.

▶ *Sea turtles come ashore to lay their eggs in sand. The hatchlings scramble out and race for the safety of the water. Only a few escape the waiting predators.*

Marine turtle

Birds

Some prehistoric reptiles jumped or glided from tree to tree and, over millions of years, reptile scales became feathers. Birds are the only animals with feathers – they keep a bird warm, even in sub-zero temperatures, and they make flight possible. There are 28 orders and about 8600 species of birds. These include water birds (wildfowl, waders and seabirds), birds of prey (eagles, hawks and owls) and 'passerine' or perching birds, most of which live among trees or other high places when not flying.

See pages 194–195

THE 28 ORDERS OF THE CLASS AVES (BIRDS)

1 **Struthioniformes**: large, flightless birds, one species survives; ostrich.

2 **Rheiformes**: two species of flightless birds of South America; rhea.

3 **Casuariiformes**: large flightless birds of Australia, New Guinea; cassowary, emu.

4 **Apterygiformes**: nocturnal, flightless birds of New Zealand; kiwi.

5 **Tinamiformes**: weak-flying ground birds of S and C America; tinamou.

6 **Sphenisciformes**: flightless swimming birds with erect posture; penguin.

7 **Gaviiformes**: web-footed diving birds of Asia, America, Europe; diver, loon.

8 **Podicipediformes**: diving birds with long toes with flaplike lobes; grebe.

9 **Procellariiformes**: ocean birds with tubelike noses; petrel, shearwater, albatross.

10 **Pelecaniformes**: fully webbed feet, beak, pouch; pelican, cormorant, gannet.

11 **Ciconiiformes**: long-legged waders; heron, egret, stork, spoonbill, ibis.

12 **Anseriformes**: water birds; duck, goose, swan, screamer.

17 Pin-tailed sandgrouse

19 Macaw

22 Whip-poor-will

28 Eurasian robin

20 Yellow-billed cuckoo

15 Black crowned crane

2 Rhea

12 Black swan

10 Pelican

16 Caspian tern

4 Kiwi

13 Bald eagle

13 Falconiformes: birds of prey; eagle, buzzard, hawk, falcon, vulture.

14 Galliformes: fowl-like birds; quail, chicken, peacock, pheasant, turkey.

15 Gruiformes: marsh and land birds; rail, crane, coot, moorhen, bustard, trumpeter.

16 Charadriiformes: waders and water-birds; gull, sandpiper, plover, curlew, tern, oystercatcher, auk.

17 Pteroclidiformes: medium-sized birds with long, pointed wings; sandgrouse.

18 Columbiformes: medium-sized short-legged birds; pigeons, doves.

19 Psittaciformes: seed and fruit-eaters with grasping claws; parrots, lories, cockatoos.

20 Cuculiformes: tree and ground-dwelling; cuckoo, touraco, road-runner.

21 Strigiformes: mostly night-time silent birds of prey with large heads; owl.

22 Caprimulgiformes: night-time insect-eaters; nightjar, oilbird, frogmouth.

23 Apodiformes: weak-footed, strong wings, spend most of their lives flying; swift, hummingbird.

24 Trogoniformes: long-tailed forest birds with small, weak feet; trogon.

25 Coliiformes: small, long-tailed African fruit-eaters with four toes; coly, mousebird.

26 Coraciiformes: long bills, short legs; kingfisher, bee-eater, roller, hoopoe.

27 Piciformes: woodland birds that nest in holes; toucan, woodpecker, barbet.

28 Passeriformes: 60 families, over 5000 species; broadbills, all songbirds (crow, lark, finch, thrush, tit, etc).

23 Alpine swift

1 Ostrich

24 Resplendent quetzal

18 Turtle dove

9 Shearwater

25 Mousebird

3 Emu

26 Kingfisher

21 Barn owl

27 Toco toucan

11 Great blue heron

6 Adelie penguin

14 Lady Amherst's pheasant

8 Great crested grebe

5 Tinamou

7 Red-throated diver

Bird Behaviour

To call someone 'bird-brained' should be a compliment, for bird behaviour is amazingly complex, a mixture of learned skills – such as a pigeon getting food from a bird feeder – and instinct, as in the territorial aggression of a European robin. Flight enables birds to be extraordinary travellers and some species migrate across oceans and continents. Finding food in all kinds of habitats, mating and nest-building; birds around the world demonstrate a remarkable range of adaptations and techniques.

▶ *Depending on its species, a bird has between 940 and 25,000 feathers. In most species, the male has more colourful feathers than the female.*

Siberian jay

Osprey

Corn bunting

Teal

BIRDS' FEET
Most birds have four, clawed toes, adapted to suit different ways of life. Perching birds (for example, the corn bunting) have three forward-pointing toes and one backward-pointing one. Ducks have webbed feet, for swimming. The osprey's talons seize and clasp prey.

FEATHERS
Feathers are replaced (moulted) once or twice a year. A flight feather (*right*) has a central rod or quill. In close-up, the thread-like barbs can be seen; these are held together by smaller hooked fibres called barbules.

Barbule

Quill

WING SHAPES
Long slender wings like those of the albatross are best for effortless gliding flight. Fast fliers, such as hawks, have narrow, pointed wings. Game birds like the partridge have stubby wings; good for quick take-offs and brief dashes.

Albatross

Hobby

Partridge

BIRDS' BILLS
Many water birds use their bills as probes or sieves. Woodpeckers' bills are wood-drills. Seed- and nut-eaters have bills for cracking hard outer shells. Birds of prey have hooked bills for tearing flesh.

| Woodpecker (drill) | Crossbill (nutcracker) | Kestrel (tearing) | Spoonbill (detector/sieve) | Oystercatcher (probe) |

NESTS

Some birds, such as the plover, lay eggs in a scrape on the ground among sand or stones. Water birds, such as grebes, nest on or beside the water. Swallows are mud-builders, often nesting against walls of buildings. Many songbirds, such as the thrush, nest in trees or bushes, building a nest from twigs, leaves and grass in which to lay their eggs.

Plover's scrape

Grebe's nest

Swallow's nest

American robin's nest

FACTS ABOUT BIRDS

- The ostrich is the biggest bird (2.7 m tall, weighing 156 kg) and lays the biggest egg, weighing about 1.7 kg.
- The smallest bird is the bee hummingbird of Cuba, less than 60 mm long and weighing only 1.6 grams.
- The wandering albatross has the biggest wingspan: over 3 m.
- Bird song is a signal, usually telling other birds to stay off the singer's territory. Parents and chicks can recognize each other's voices.
- The peregrine falcon is credited with a top diving speed of more than 300 km/h, making it the world's fastest living animal.

▼ *Eider ducks are valued for the soft down on their breasts, used in bedding; they are also one of the world's fastest flying birds.*

COURTSHIP

Many birds have elaborate courtship behaviour, in which males dance or display colourful plumage to attract females. The Australian lyrebird has long tail feathers which it displays during its courtship.

Lyrebird

MIGRATION

Many birds make amazingly long migrations. Different species may be seen in flight along favoured routes, often in large flocks. The Arctic tern makes the longest migratory journey of any animal. It flies up to 36,000 km in a year, journeying south from its Arctic breeding grounds to the Antarctic summer, before returning once more to the Arctic.

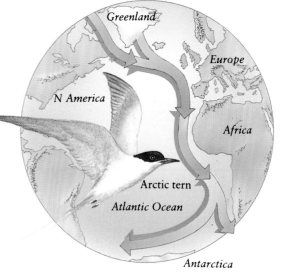

Greenland

Europe

N America

Africa

Arctic tern

Atlantic Ocean

Antarctica

Mammals

Mammals are one of the eight classes of vertebrate (backboned) animals. There are far fewer species of mammals than other groups of animals – but mammals have adapted to a wider range of habitats. Mammals live on land, in hot or cold climates, in the sea and have even taken to the air. Mammals feed their young on the mother's milk, they protect their young, they have hair, they maintain a constant body temperature, and they have relatively larger brains than other animals.

See pages 194–195

14 African elephant

16 Dugong

2 Koala

8 Pangolin

11 Dolphin

12 Lion

15 Hyrax

1 Echidna

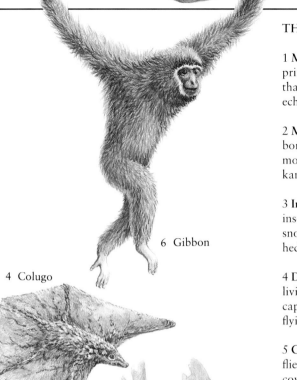

6 Gibbon

4 Colugo

THE 18 ORDERS OF MAMMALIA (MAMMALS)

1 **Monotremata:** primitive mammals that lay eggs; echidna, platypus.

2 **Marsupialia:** young born tiny, develop in mother's pouch; kangaroo, koala.

3 **Insectivora:** small insect-eaters with snouts; shrew, hedgehog, mole.

4 **Dermoptera:** tree-living Asian mammals capable of gliding; flying lemur.

5 **Chiroptera:** true fliers, with skin-covered forelimbs adapted as wings; bat.

6 **Primates:** uniquely grasping hands and feet; lemur, ape, monkey, human.

7 **Edentata:** no or few teeth, diggers and climbers; anteater, armadillo, sloth.

8 **Pholidota:** insect-eaters with no teeth and scaly bodies; pangolin.

9 **Lagomorpha:** small plant-eaters with nibbling teeth; pika, hare, rabbit.

10 **Rodentia:** gnawers, with chisel-like upper incisors; beaver, rat, squirrel, porcupine.

11 **Cetacea:** Aquatic, flat tail, paddle-like front limbs; whale, dolphin, porpoise.

12 **Carnivora:** meat-eaters, with claws; bear, raccoon, seal, cat, dog, wolf, weasel.

13 **Tubulidentata:** burrowing insect-eater with long, sticky tongue; aardvark.

14 **Proboscidea:** large, thick-skinned plant-eaters with trunks and tusks; elephant.

15 **Hyracoidea:** small and rodent-like with hoof-like claws and short tails; hyrax.

16 **Sirenia:** aquatic, with paddle-like front limbs, flat noses: dugong, manatee.

17 **Perissodactyla:** hoofs (one or three toes); horse, tapir, rhinoceros.

18 **Artiodactyla:** hoofs (two or four toes): pig, antelope, deer, camel, giraffe, cattle, sheep.

5 Horseshoe bat

18 Fallow deer

10 Red squirrel

17 Rhinoceros

3 Hedgehog

13 Aardvark

7 Armadillo

9 Arctic hare

Mammal Senses

Mammals are constantly receiving messages from their senses, on which their next meal or their lives may depend. Many mammals have senses far more acute than our own: keener eyesight and hearing, for example, as well as others (like the bat's sonar or the mole's sensitive whiskers) which we simply do not need. The variations in mammal body design are the result of millions of years of evolution and adaptation. So too is mammal behaviour, either as individuals or in co-operating groups.

Loris

ANATOMY OF A MAMMAL
SKELETON OF A HORSE

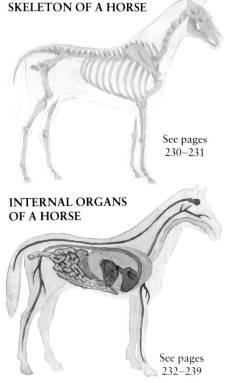

See pages
230–231

INTERNAL ORGANS OF A HORSE

See pages
232–239

◀ *The skeleton of a mammal acts as a framework for its body and protects vital organs such as the heart and stomach; also, the muscles that enable it to move are attached to its skeleton. An adult mammal – whether a mouse or an elephant – has over 200 bones.*

◀ *The main internal body systems of a mammal, such as a horse, are concerned with digestion and waste disposal, and reproduction. The skull protects the brain and houses important sense organs such as the eyes, ears, nose and mouth linked to the nervous system.*

SIGHT
In most mammals the two eyes are set either side of the head. So each eye gives a different image. A few have binocular vision, with the eyes set in the front of the head and able to work together to focus on one image. This enables the mammal to judge distance more accurately – an important aid for tree climbers, like the loris (a primate), and for hunters, such as cats.

Wild dogs

HIBERNATION
Some species of mammals hibernate: they sleep through all or part of the cold winter when food is scarce. Before hibernating, the animal stores fat in its body. It becomes chilled and its heartbeat slows. A hibernating dormouse will not wake up even if it is touched. Other animals, such as squirrels and badgers, emerge in mild weather to seek food.

Dormouse

TOUCH
In many mammals the sense of touch is highly developed. They use sensitive hairs or whiskers and inquisitive snouts to investigate their surroundings when either burrowing underground or moving about in darkness. Moles have weak eyes, but rely on touch and smell to find their way through their tunnels.

Mole

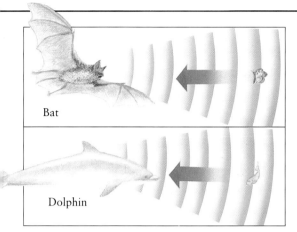

Bat

Dolphin

TASTE
Taste is situated in the taste-buds of the tongue. A dog has about 8000, a cow four times as many. Anteaters use their long tongues to raid ants' nests.

Anteater

HEARING
Some animals can hear much better than people. Bats in flight and dolphins swimming send out sound waves to detect prey by echo-location. The bat's sonar makes it an aerobatic flier even in the dark, though its eyesight is poor.

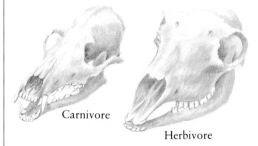

Carnivore

Herbivore

TEETH
Almost all mammals have teeth. Carnivores have sharp incisors and canines for tearing flesh. Herbivores nibble with their front teeth and use grinding molars to crush fibres.

◄ *Carnivores kill for food, but some also feed on dead animals, that they have seen or smelt.*

Hyena

Vulture

SMELL AND SCENT
Smell is an important sense for many mammals. Some deposit scent-messages to mark territory. Hunting animals, especially dogs (wild dogs, wolves and foxes) track prey by smell. Hunting lions approach a herd of zebras from downwind, so that their smell is not carried towards the prey, alerting them to the danger.

ANIMAL INTELLIGENCE
Chimpanzees are the most intelligent apes. Inquisitive and perservering, they will imitate human actions and can solve simple problems. Only dolphins rival chimps in intelligence. Rats, dogs and pigs also perform well in animal intelligence tests.

Dolphin

Dog

Chimpanzee

Rat

Pig

Animal Homes

Most animals need homes only to shelter their young. Birds build nests, a female bear seeks a den, a vixen (a female fox) takes over a burrow. Some social animals live in large colonies, used for many generations. The colony's home may be a structure of remarkable size – like a prairie dog town or a termite nest. Most hunting and grazing animals have no fixed homes, but wander territories in search of food. Each individual or group may fiercely defend its territory against rivals of the same species.

◀ *The water spider is the only spider that can live under water. It builds a 'diving bell' of silk which it fills with bubbles of air carried down from the surface. Inside the air-filled bell, the spider lives, mates and lays its eggs.*

◀ *Carmine bee-eaters, African birds related to kingfishers, nest in holes in river banks. The nest protects the young until they are old enough to fly. Birds' nests vary from complex woven or mud structures to holes or simple scrapes in the ground.*

▶ *Most bats are active at night. By day they shelter in caves, trees or the roofs or cellars of buildings. Large numbers may roost together, hanging upside down by their feet and huddled close for warmth.*

A BEAVER'S LODGE
Beavers build island homes in rivers. They use chisel-like teeth and strong claws to build a log dam. The dam creates a pond in which they build a lodge, a mound of sticks and mud with dry inner chambers and underwater entrances.

PRAIRIE DOG TOWN

Prairie dogs are burrowing rodents of the grasslands of North America. Hundreds may live together in a colony or town. Family groups dig territorial burrows, as deep as 5 m. Sentries keep watch above ground for predators.

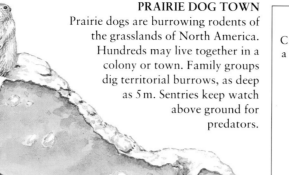

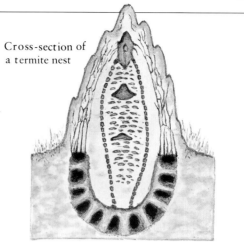

Cross-section of a termite nest

TERMITE NEST

Termites have the most amazing homes; these social insects build mud-mounds 9 m high. Some termite nests have sloping roofs to deflect rain. Australian compass termites align their narrow nests north-south to escape too much hot sun.

TERRITORY

Many animals are territorial. They will fight rivals for an area that is big enough to provide its occupants with food, breeding space and shelter. Territorial limits are respected. A rabbit will retreat, even when being chased, if it reaches a territorial 'no-go' zone.

SAFETY IN NUMBERS

Many grazers and browsers (cattle, sheep, deer, antelope, horses) live in herds, sometimes hundreds strong. Deer form groups of females and young, each led by a strong male. Herd living has advantages. Every animal is a lookout, alert for danger. The strongest animals will often defend the herd. Females may help one another with young. By being one of a crowd, an individual has a smaller chance of being singled out for attack by predators and more chance of escaping in the confusion as the herd runs away.

Animal Movement

All animals move at some time in their lives – even the limpet clinging to its rock began life as a free-swimming juvenile. Fast movement is essential for many animals, to hunt and to escape when hunted. To conserve energy, fast-moving animals usually sprint only when they have to, in bursts. Some have no need of speed, relying on other strategies such as camouflage or armour for protection. Other animals are marathon athletes, travelling immense distances during seasonal migrations.

FAST AND SLOW-MOVERS

The quickest land animals are slower than the fastest sea animals. A lion (80 km/h) can outsprint a racehorse (65 km/h). The garden snail crawls about 80 cm in a minute. This is about half the speed of a sloth on the ground (it moves a little faster when it is hanging upside-down from the branches of trees).

ANIMALS ON LAND

Legs act like props and levers. In motion, the legs push against the ground, propelling the animals forwards.

◄ *Gazelles are among the fastest four-legged animals; at top speed they only have one foot on the ground and may even lift all four legs in the air during each stride.*

▼ *Squids and octopuses swim by taking water in and then squirting it out through a tube; the expelled water causes them to shoot backwards.*

◄ *Arachnids (spiders and scorpions) have eight legs which move rather like the oars in a rowing boat.*

Water in

WITHOUT LEGS

Not all animals need legs to move quickly. The fastest snake, the black mamba, can reach over 30 km/h. Many snakes move on land or in water with a wriggling motion *(top)*. Burrowing snakes move in concertina-like contractions *(below)*.

▼ *Snails and slugs have a single foot used for clinging and motion. The animal moves in rhythmic muscular waves, by extending and withdrawing its foot. Slime helps the snail move, and leaves the familiar glistening trail.*

ANIMAL SPEEDS

Animal speeds are difficult to measure accurately. The fastest fish, the sailfin, narrowly outsprints the fastest land animal, the cheetah. But in flight, an eider duck in level flight would be overtaken by a diving peregrine falcon.

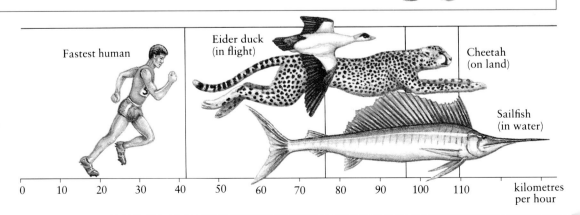

Fastest human

Eider duck (in flight)

Cheetah (on land)

Sailfish (in water)

| 0 | 10 | 20 | 30 | 40 | 50 | 60 | 70 | 80 | 90 | 100 | 110 | kilometres per hour |

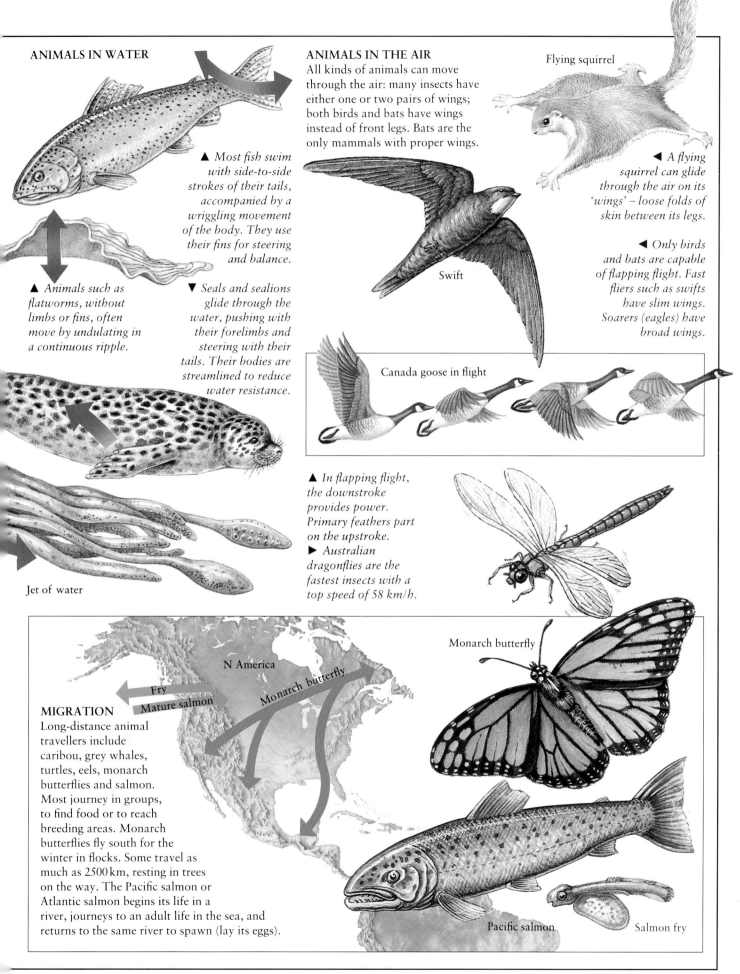

ANIMALS IN WATER

▲ *Most fish swim with side-to-side strokes of their tails, accompanied by a wriggling movement of the body. They use their fins for steering and balance.*

▲ *Animals such as flatworms, without limbs or fins, often move by undulating in a continuous ripple.*

▼ *Seals and sealions glide through the water, pushing with their forelimbs and steering with their tails. Their bodies are streamlined to reduce water resistance.*

Jet of water

ANIMALS IN THE AIR

All kinds of animals can move through the air: many insects have either one or two pairs of wings; both birds and bats have wings instead of front legs. Bats are the only mammals with proper wings.

Swift

Canada goose in flight

▲ *In flapping flight, the downstroke provides power. Primary feathers part on the upstroke.*
▶ *Australian dragonflies are the fastest insects with a top speed of 58 km/h.*

Flying squirrel

◀ *A flying squirrel can glide through the air on its 'wings' – loose folds of skin between its legs.*

◀ *Only birds and bats are capable of flapping flight. Fast fliers such as swifts have slim wings. Soarers (eagles) have broad wings.*

Monarch butterfly

MIGRATION

Long-distance animal travellers include caribou, grey whales, turtles, eels, monarch butterflies and salmon. Most journey in groups, to find food or to reach breeding areas. Monarch butterflies fly south for the winter in flocks. Some travel as much as 2500 km, resting in trees on the way. The Pacific salmon or Atlantic salmon begins its life in a river, journeys to an adult life in the sea, and returns to the same river to spawn (lay its eggs).

Fry
Mature salmon
N America
Monarch butterfly

Pacific salmon

Salmon fry

Animals and Their Young

An animal's life span is determined chiefly by the time it needs to reproduce. Wild animals face many hazards and few survive to extreme old age. Most records for longevity have been set by captive animals. Reproduction in animals takes two forms: asexual, when only one parent produces the young (such as budding in sponges or corals), and sexual (when male and female sex cells combine to form a new animal). Some animals can regenerate parts of their bodies; for example, a crab can grow a new claw.

LIFESPANS

Turtle

Elephant

Chimpanzee

Starling

Squirrel

Wasp

▲ Animals live much shorter lives than plants. Over 20 is old for most mammals. The potential lifespan of animals ranges from over 60 years (elephant, killer whale) to a few weeks or even a single day (adult mayfly).

| 0 | 10 | 20 | 30 | 40 | 50 | 60 | 70 | 80 | 90 | 100 yrs |

COURTSHIP

Mating involves pairing of males and females. Courtship rituals often involve elaborate behaviour, especially in birds. Egrets grow long plumes during the mating season and display these feathers as part of their courtship dance. Some animals pair for life, others mate and then part.

LIVING TOGETHER

Mammal babies take months or even years to develop. A female bear, by nature a solitary hunter, guards her young with care and teaches the cubs to catch fish. Bears are carnivores, but they also eat other kinds of food including grubs, birds' eggs and berries. The cubs are energetic and playful: through play they learn the skills necessary to survive. Usually the cubs will stay with their mother for one or two years.

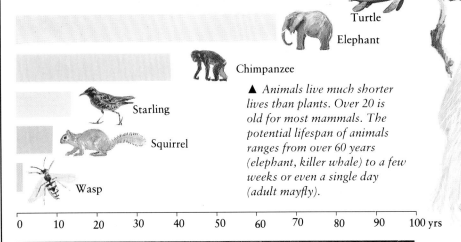

— Males follow behind

Dominant female elephant (matriarch) leads herd

▶ Elephants are sociable animals. They move in herds, feeding as they go. The herd is led by a dominant older female. A female giving birth is watched over by other female 'midwives'. If one elephant is trapped or wounded, other herd members will come to its aid.

▲ Male elephants (bulls) usually stay behind the herd. Rogues are aggressive males that live apart from a herd.

MAMMAL REPRODUCTION

Placental mammals

Most mammal species have a placenta, a two-way filter that joins the unborn baby to its mother's body. Through the placenta the baby gets food and oxygen from the mother's blood. After birth, it suckles on her milk.

Zebra with foal

Red kangaroo

Marsupials

Pouched mammals or marsupials give birth to live young, but the young are born only partially developed. The tiny baby crawls into a pouch on its mother's body. Inside the pouch, it feeds on milk from her body, and will return to the pouch for shelter even when big enough to emerge.

Monotremes

These are the most primitive mammals, found only in Australia and New Guinea. The female lays eggs, but when the young hatch they are fed on milk from her body.

Duck-billed platypus

LOOKING AFTER THE YOUNG

King penguin

Trout

◀ *A male king penguin of the Antarctic keeps its egg warm beneath a flap of skin on its feet. The chick is sheltered in the same place.*

▲ *Fish, with few exceptions, simply deposit their eggs and swim away. The young hatch and must look after themselves.*

▶ *Many baby mammals are born hairless, blind and helpless. Fox cubs are dependent on their mother for warmth and food for the first weeks of life.*

Fox with cubs

Macaque

◀ *Parents teach by example. Many animals have complex behaviour patterns which the young inherit. Monkeys, for example, exhibit learned skills – such as specialized food-gathering techniques. By watching its mother, this baby macaque learns to copy her behaviour.*

GESTATION PERIODS

Gestation is the time between fertilization and birth. Incubation is the time between fertilization and the hatching of an egg. A female elephant's pregnancy lasts 20–22 months. A fruit fly takes less than a day to change from egg to larva.

0   0.25   0.5   0.75   1.0   1.25   1.5   1.75   2.0

years

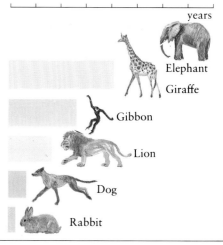

Elephant

Giraffe

Gibbon

Lion

Dog

Rabbit

FACTS ABOUT ANIMAL LIVES

- The longest-lived sea creature is the quahog clam (150 years).
- A queen ant may live for 18 years, some spiders for as long as 25 years.
- A mayfly emerges from the larval stage, breeds and dies in a few hours.
- Sturgeon (80 yrs) and carp (50 yrs) are among the longest-lived fish.
- Record litters are 19 (cat), 23 (dog), 34 (mouse). These records were all set by pet animals.

Mayfly

Animals and People

People first hunted animals, then domesticated some species for food or wool or as beasts of burden. Today domestic animals still carry goods and provide us with food, textiles and other materials. Through selective breeding people have changed animals. The growth of population has destroyed many animal habitats. Wild animals live alongside people in town and country. Some thrive (pigeons, cockroaches, rats, fleas). Many others face an uncertain future, possibly extinction.

ANIMALS THAT ARE USEFUL TO PEOPLE

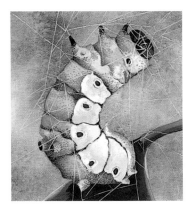

▲ *One of the most unusual animal providers is the silkmoth larva, which produces a cocoon from which natural silk is obtained. One type of silkworm is raised on silk farms; wild silk comes from silkworms living wild in China and India.*

LOAD CARRIERS
The dog was probably the first domestic animal. Native Americans used dogs as pack animals. Over 5000 years ago horses, donkeys and camels were tamed for riding and for carrying loads. Oxen pulled heavy ploughs and carts.

Horse
Donkey
Camel

◄ *The animals that are most useful to people provide fur, skin or wool as well as meat and milk; they include sheep, cattle, llamas and camels. Other animals are useful because they can help people to hunt or get about; while some animals can carry loads or messages.*

DAIRY FOODS
Milk, butter, yoghurt, cheese: from cows, sheep, horses, goats, reindeer and camels.

MEAT AND FISH
Beef (cattle), pork and bacon (pigs), lamb and mutton (sheep), goats, poultry, fish.

LEATHER
Hides from cattle, sheep, goats, even farmed alligators, for making leather.

TEXTILES
Wool from sheep, goats, camels, llamas. Silk from silkworms. Down from ducks.

ANIMAL COMPANIONS

The first pets were probably baby animals (wolf cubs, goat kids, birds) brought back by prehistoric hunters for children to play with. For thousands of years, and in every society, people have valued animals as companions. To the lonely and elderly a dog or cat can be both a friend and a comfort; pets can sometimes have a beneficial effect on people who are ill.

◄ *People have kept dogs as pets and helpers since prehistoric times. No dog is more valued than the guide dog, trained as the 'eyes' of its blind or partially sighted human owner.*

► *Bees not only provide us with honey, they also help to pollinate many plants, including fruit trees and garden flowers. People have kept bees for centuries as honey used to be the only sweetener for foods.*

DANGEROUS ANIMALS

Few animals attack people unless provoked and genuine man-eaters are rare. Venomous insects and spiders and disease-carrying flies are more likely to cause people harm than are sharks, tigers, alligators or snakes.

Brazilian wandering spider

White shark

▲ *The most venomous spider is a species of Brazilian wandering spider. It can hide in clothing or shoes, and give a fatal bite.*

Crocodile

▲ *Sharks have a worse reputation than they deserve, but white sharks can be very dangerous.*

▲ *Crocodiles and alligators occasionally attack people, dragging them under the water.*

Tsetse fly

◀ *The tsetse fly feeds on blood and spreads the disease sleeping sickness.*

Snapping turtle

◀ *Snapping turtles protect themselves with their strong jaws; these American freshwater turtles can give a painful bite to unwary swimmers.*

FACTS ABOUT PETS

● The best 'talkers' among pet birds are African grey parrots, budgerigars and mynahs.
● Cats usually live longer than dogs. The oldest cat on record lived to 36 (years).
● Cats kept ancient Egypt's granaries rat-free. People worshipped the cat-goddess Bastet (Bubastis), mourned cats' deaths, and often mummified their bodies.
● Guinea-pigs are descendants of wild South American rodents called cavies. Hamsters come from Syria; all pet hamsters are descended from a pair brought to England in 1930.

SELECTIVE BREEDING

The many breeds of dog, from Great Danes to chihuahuas, share a common wolf-like ancestor. Domestic cats are thought to be descended from African wildcats that were originally tamed by the ancient Egyptians. Since the 1800s, the increasing popularity of cats has resulted in much specialist breeding.

▲ *Breeding changed wild horses into strong war horses, the ancestors of the heavy cart and farm horses.*

▼ *A sheepdog obeys the calls of the shepherd as it drives sheep. The dog is carefully trained so that it chases but does not attack the sheep.*

ANIMALS AS PETS

Favourite pets include hamsters, gerbils, goldfish, birds such as budgerigars, parrots and canaries, rabbits, guineapigs, cats and dogs. Only animals bred in captivity should be kept as pets. Wild animals do not make good pets as a rule.

Endangered Animals

Animal species become extinct or die out usually because they cannot adapt to changing conditions. The problem for wildlife today is lack of living space. People compete with wild animals for space, and win. Even prehistoric hunters were efficient enough to wipe out animal populations. The rate of extinctions has accelerated since the 1600s. Many species are in danger; some are being hunted, some are losing their habitat, some are being overrun by other animals, introduced by people.

EXTINCT ANIMALS

Species with no natural enemies are defenceless. The dodo, a flightless pigeon from Mauritius, was extinct by 1680, victim of sailors, cats and rats who had landed on the island. The great auk of the Atlantic was slaughtered for its feathers. The last two were killed in 1844.

Dodo

Great auk

VANISHING ANIMALS

Animals close to extinction include the Javan rhino and South China tiger (about 50 left), kakapo of New Zealand (40 or so) and Southeast Asian kouprey or wild ox (about 300). The European bison or wisent, nearly extinct by 1920, survives in Polish reserves.

European bison

▲ *Habitat destruction can cause rapid extinction. Forest animals of the tropics are endangered as forests shrink before the chainsaw and bulldozer. Forest monkeys like South America's bearded sakis have only slim chances of survival without protection.*

Margay

THE SKIN TRADE

Fashion and vanity has brought about the decline of many animal species. Birds such as the egret were hunted for their feathers. Snakes and alligators are killed and skinned to make bags and shoes. The fur trade, though declining, still takes its toll, especially of spotted cats such as the margay.

Snake

Egret

RIVER POLLUTION
Animals, like people, need clean water. River and lake animals are sensitive to any change in their environment. In the past 50 years farm pesticides, fertilizers, and chemical waste from factories have steadily poisoned many rivers. The European otter *(left)* is no longer seen in most of the rivers in Britain where it was once commonly found.

▲ *Even when protected in game reserves, rare animals are not safe from poachers. In Africa, poachers have killed most of the rhinos, for their horns. In Indian nature reserves, tigers are poisoned for their skins and bones, which are made into a medicine drunk by Chinese and Koreans.*

◄ *In the 19th century collectors took large numbers of insects, such as butterflies, and birds' eggs for display in their homes. Big game hunters shot animals for trophies, to be similarly displayed. Such activities are frowned on today.*

ZOOS
Since the 1600s the number of human beings has risen from 450 million to over 5000 million. For many people, seeing a bear at the zoo or a lion in a game reserve is the nearest they get to seeing an animal in the wild. Zoos have a role to play in conservation, through education and schemes to save endangered species. However, many people no longer want to stare at lonely animals penned in unsuitable cages.

WOLVES AND PEOPLE
Wolves have survived centuries of persecution, often unjust, by people. These intelligent and adaptable predators were once widespread, as the map shows *(right)*, but now their distribution is greatly reduced. There are now only small numbers of wild wolves in the United States and a few in Europe.

Worldwide distribution of wolves [

▨ Past distribution of wolves

▨ Present distribution of wolves

Prehistoric Animals

Our knowledge of most prehistoric animals comes from their fossil remains, mostly bones and shells. No humans observed the mighty dinosaurs, as the last of these prehistoric reptiles died out 65 million years ago. Prehistoric mammmals then became the dominant animals, and from about 4 million years ago mammals such as sabre-toothed cats and woolly mammoths shared the Earth with prehistoric humans. By about 10,000 years ago these early mammals had died out or evolved into new species.

BEFORE DINOSAURS

By 350 million years ago, when *Ichthyostega* became the first four-legged animal to invade the land, many types of animals had evolved in the seas; they included early true fish and crustaceans.

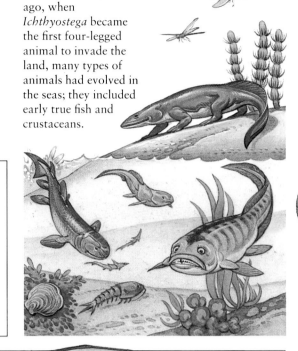

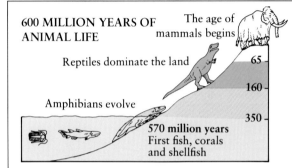

600 MILLION YEARS OF ANIMAL LIFE

The age of mammals begins

Reptiles dominate the land — 65

Amphibians evolve — 160

— 350

570 million years First fish, corals and shellfish

Evolution is a natural process of gradual change. Some species are better fitted to life in changing surroundings. They survive. Other, less adaptable species, die out.

DINOSAUR RECORDS

Tallest and heaviest dinosaur: (complete skeleton) *Brachiosaurus*, 22 m, 70 tonnes; an incomplete skeleton of a *Brachiosaurus*, named *Ultrasaurus*, estimated at 25 m long and 130 tonnes.

Longest: *Diplodocus*, almost 27 m long.

Smallest: chicken-sized *Compsognathus*.

Fiercest carnivore: *Tyrannosaurus rex* (14 m long, 12 tonnes).

Most intelligent?: *Stenonychosaurus* was dog-sized, large-eyed and large-brained.

Most stupid?: *Stegosaurus* had a walnut-size brain in an elephant-size body.

OTHER ANIMALS

There were animals just as remarkable as the dinosaurs – flying and swimming reptiles, such as *Pteranodon* and *Plesiosaurus*, lobe-finned fish like *Osteolepis*, and a reptilian ancestor of birds, *Archaeopteryx*.

Pteranodon

Archaeopteryx

Plesiosaurus

Osteolepis

Brachiosaurus

Diplodocus

Tyrannosaurus rex

Stegosaurus

Compsognathus

Stenonychosaurus

Duck-billed dinosaur

Corythosaurus

◀ *Like all reptiles, dinosaurs laid eggs. Some skeletons have been found with complete nests. Females may have incubated eggs with their bodies, like some snakes, or buried them as turtles do. The young were born as miniature versions of their parents.*

Deinonychus

AFTER THE DINOSAURS

When the dinosaurs vanished mammals and birds took over the land. *Diatryma* was a large flightless bird, *Smilodon* a sabre-toothed big cat. The woolly mammoth was closely related to the modern elephant. All three are extinct.

Woolly mammoth

Diatryma

HUNTERS AND HUNTED

The largest dinosaurs were plant-eaters. Some species lived in herds for safety. Others like *Stegosaurus* relied on armour for defence against predators. The agile, scythe-clawed *Deinonychus* was among the most efficient of dinosaur killers. It may have hunted in groups to kill larger prey.

Smilodon

FACTS ABOUT EXTINCT ANIMALS

- The giant Steppe mammoth that once roamed central Europe, (*Mammuthus trogontherii*), 4.5m tall, was the biggest elephant that has ever lived.
- *Thylacosmilus* looked like the sabre-toothed *Smilodon* but was not a cat at all.
- Why dinosaurs vanished is still being debated; climatic changes or an asteroid hitting the Earth are possible causes.
- The earliest ancestor of the horse was the dog-sized *Hyracotherium*, a forest animal of 50 million years ago.
- The Cretaceous pterosaur *Quetzalcoatlus* had wings as long as a bus; these flying reptiles probably had hair rather than feathers on the skin that formed their wings.

REPTILE SURVIVORS

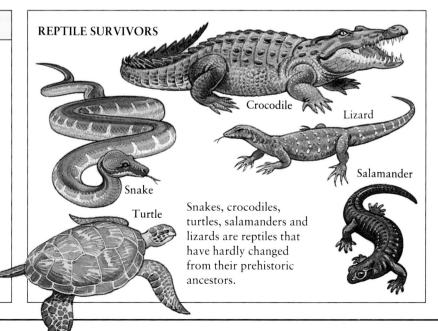

Crocodile

Lizard

Salamander

Snake

Turtle

Snakes, crocodiles, turtles, salamanders and lizards are reptiles that have hardly changed from their prehistoric ancestors.

THE HUMAN BODY

Systems of the Body

Human beings have more advanced brains than any other living thing. Human brainpower has given us abilities beyond those of any other animal – such as language and the transfer of knowledge from generation to generation. Human beings are primates, members of the species *Homo sapiens sapiens*. We share many characteristics with apes but unlike apes we walk erect on two legs. The body has parts and systems, like a machine, yet it can do things beyond the ability of any machine. It can grow, rebuild and fight off diseases. The brain is the control centre of our bodies; it receives information from our senses and then sends out commands that affect our development, movements and sensations as well as the involuntary actions of our internal organs. The brain also stores information and is the source of all our feelings, speech and thoughts.

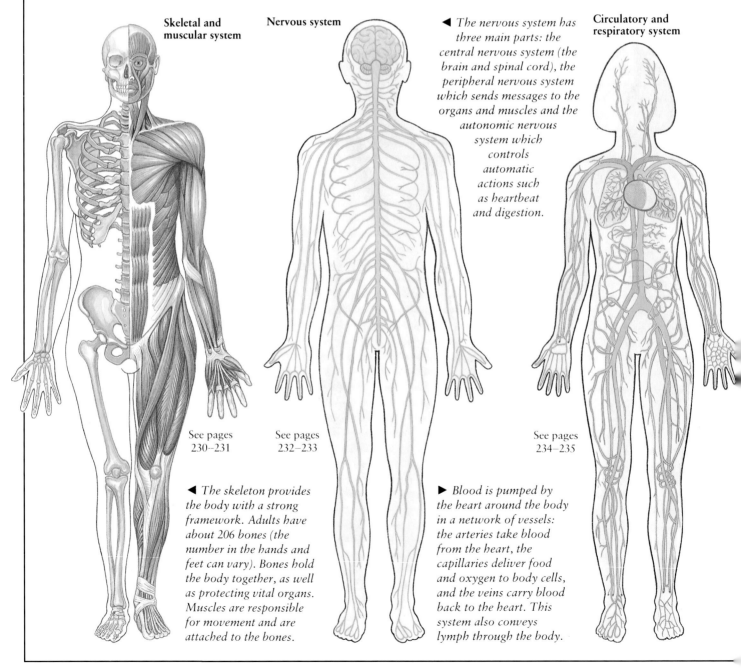

Skeletal and muscular system

Nervous system

Circulatory and respiratory system

◀ *The nervous system has three main parts: the central nervous system (the brain and spinal cord), the peripheral nervous system which sends messages to the organs and muscles and the autonomic nervous system which controls automatic actions such as heartbeat and digestion.*

See pages 230–231

See pages 232–233

See pages 234–235

◀ *The skeleton provides the body with a strong framework. Adults have about 206 bones (the number in the hands and feet can vary). Bones hold the body together, as well as protecting vital organs. Muscles are responsible for movement and are attached to the bones.*

▶ *Blood is pumped by the heart around the body in a network of vessels: the arteries take blood from the heart, the capillaries deliver food and oxygen to body cells, and the veins carry blood back to the heart. This system also conveys lymph through the body.*

FACTS ABOUT THE BODY

- The tallest recorded human was Robert Wadlow of the USA (1918–1940) who was 2.72 m (8ft 11.1 in).
- The oldest human (with an authenticated birth-date) was a Japanese, Shigechiyo Izumi, who died in 1986 aged 120 years 237 days.
- The strongest muscles are the masseters on each side of the mouth, which are used for biting; the most active muscles move the eye.
- An adult's body contains about five litres of blood. To pump blood around the body, the heart beats about 70 times a minute.

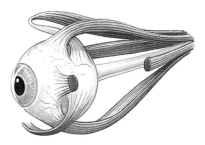

▲ *About 80 percent of the eyeball is made up of a jelly-like substance. Six muscles move the eye about in its socket.*

- The fastest nerve signals travel at 400 km/h.
- A person takes about 23,000 breaths each day.
- Children have more bones than adults – about 300. As a child grows, some bones fuse together.
- Each of a woman's ovaries contains about 400,000 eggs. Only about 400 mature during her child-bearing years.
- The eyeball measures about 25 mm across and is set into a socket in the skull, cushioned by fatty tissue.
- There are about 50 million cells in the body and 100,000 km of blood vessels.

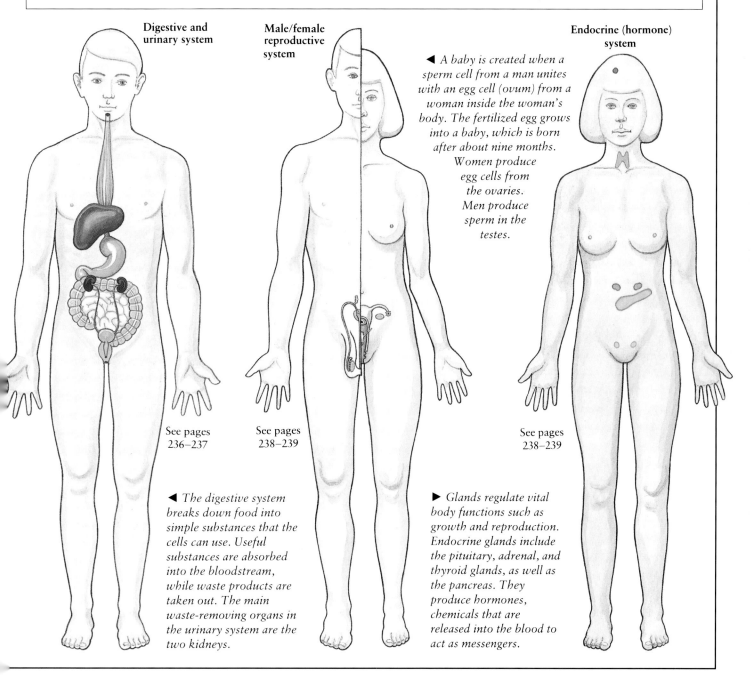

Digestive and urinary system

Male/female reproductive system

Endocrine (hormone) system

◄ *A baby is created when a sperm cell from a man unites with an egg cell (ovum) from a woman inside the woman's body. The fertilized egg grows into a baby, which is born after about nine months. Women produce egg cells from the ovaries. Men produce sperm in the testes.*

See pages 236–237

See pages 238–239

See pages 238–239

◄ *The digestive system breaks down food into simple substances that the cells can use. Useful substances are absorbed into the bloodstream, while waste products are taken out. The main waste-removing organs in the urinary system are the two kidneys.*

▶ *Glands regulate vital body functions such as growth and reproduction. Endocrine glands include the pituitary, adrenal, and thyroid glands, as well as the pancreas. They produce hormones, chemicals that are released into the blood to act as messengers.*

Skeleton and Muscles

Bones are made of living cells. The largest bone in the body is the femur or thigh bone. The smallest is a bone in the ear, the stirrup. The ribs form a cage to protect the heart and lungs; the skull similarly encloses the soft brain. Where bones meet, they form a joint. Joints are held together by elastic ligaments and soft tissue called cartilage. Muscles are attached to the bones by tendons. When the brain orders muscles to contract, the muscles pull the bones – this is how we move.

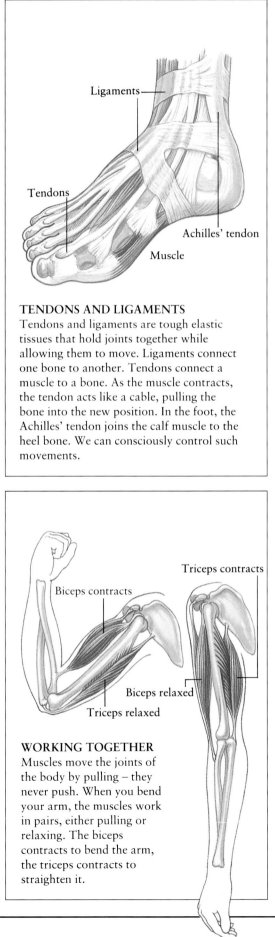

TENDONS AND LIGAMENTS

Tendons and ligaments are tough elastic tissues that hold joints together while allowing them to move. Ligaments connect one bone to another. Tendons connect a muscle to a bone. As the muscle contracts, the tendon acts like a cable, pulling the bone into the new position. In the foot, the Achilles' tendon joins the calf muscle to the heel bone. We can consciously control such movements.

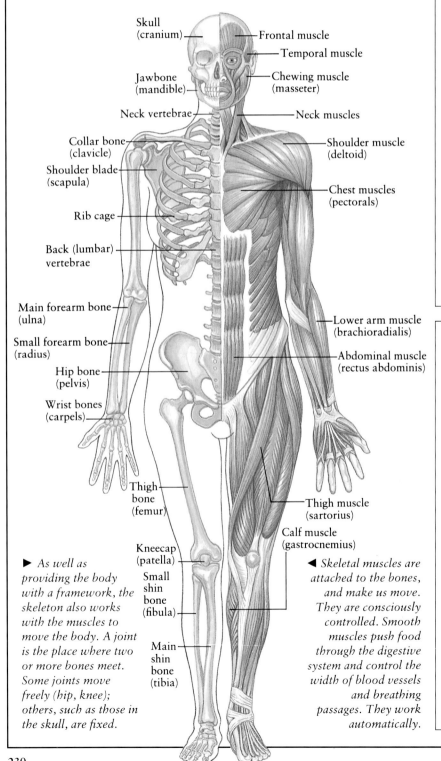

Skull (cranium)
Frontal muscle
Temporal muscle
Jawbone (mandible)
Chewing muscle (masseter)
Neck vertebrae
Neck muscles
Collar bone (clavicle)
Shoulder muscle (deltoid)
Shoulder blade (scapula)
Chest muscles (pectorals)
Rib cage
Back (lumbar) vertebrae
Main forearm bone (ulna)
Lower arm muscle (brachioradialis)
Small forearm bone (radius)
Abdominal muscle (rectus abdominis)
Hip bone (pelvis)
Wrist bones (carpels)
Thigh bone (femur)
Thigh muscle (sartorius)
Calf muscle (gastrocnemius)
Kneecap (patella)
Small shin bone (fibula)
Main shin bone (tibia)

▶ *As well as providing the body with a framework, the skeleton also works with the muscles to move the body. A joint is the place where two or more bones meet. Some joints move freely (hip, knee); others, such as those in the skull, are fixed.*

◀ *Skeletal muscles are attached to the bones, and make us move. They are consciously controlled. Smooth muscles push food through the digestive system and control the width of blood vessels and breathing passages. They work automatically.*

Biceps contracts
Triceps contracts
Biceps relaxed
Triceps relaxed

WORKING TOGETHER

Muscles move the joints of the body by pulling – they never push. When you bend your arm, the muscles work in pairs, either pulling or relaxing. The biceps contracts to bend the arm, the triceps contracts to straighten it.

MUSCLE

The interior of a muscle looks like bundles of cables (*far right*). Skeletal muscle is made up of long cells. Each cell has many nuclei. Smooth muscle and heart (cardiac) muscle both have shorter cells, each with only one nucleus.

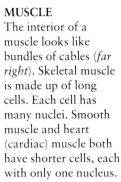

Skeletal muscle

Smooth muscle   Cardiac muscle

Muscle fibre

Muscle fibril

Nuclei

Nucleus

Bundle of muscle fibres

Connective tissue

JOINTS

Hinge joints (elbow, knee) allow movement in one direction only. The hip and shoulder are swivelling ball and socket joints. Other joints allow a range of movement: the saddle joint at the base of the thumb, the pivot that allows the forearm to twist, or the plane that allows sideways movement.

Hinge joint

Ball and socket joint

Plane joint

Saddle joint

Pivot joint

INSIDE A BONE

The outer layer of a bone is made up of hard compact bone, that forms rings around the Haversian canals. Inside each canal are blood vessels carrying food and oxygen to the bone cells. The compact bone is covered with an even tougher layer, the periosteum. The inner part of a bone is often called the spongy bone, but it is very strong. Bone strength comes from a protein called collagen. The hardness comes from phosphorus and calcium. The soft, fatty core of many bones is called the marrow.

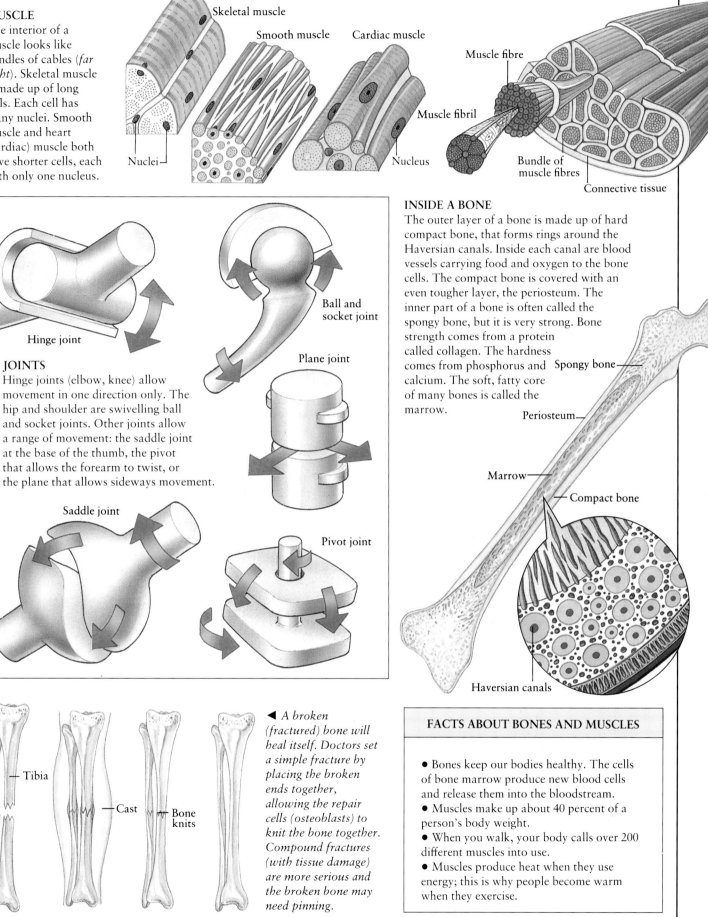

Spongy bone

Periosteum

Marrow

Compact bone

Haversian canals

◄ A broken (fractured) bone will heal itself. Doctors set a simple fracture by placing the broken ends together, allowing the repair cells (osteoblasts) to knit the bone together. Compound fractures (with tissue damage) are more serious and the broken bone may need pinning.

Tibia

Cast

Bone knits

FACTS ABOUT BONES AND MUSCLES

- Bones keep our bodies healthy. The cells of bone marrow produce new blood cells and release them into the bloodstream.
- Muscles make up about 40 percent of a person's body weight.
- When you walk, your body calls over 200 different muscles into use.
- Muscles produce heat when they use energy; this is why people become warm when they exercise.

The Nervous System

The nervous system is a complex network of nerves – bundles of long fibres made up of nerve cells. The nerves collect information from inside and outside the body and send messages to the brain. These messages are signals produced by sensory cells and passed to nerve fibres in the brain or spinal column; signals can also be sent from the brain to the body's organs. The part of the nervous system that controls such automatic body processes as breathing and digestion is called the autonomic nervous system.

▶ *The central nervous system – the brain and spinal cord – carries messages between the brain and body. The peripheral nervous system consists of sensory and motor nerve cells, linked with the central nervous system by special connector cells.*

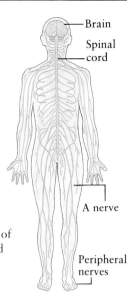

Brain

Spinal cord

A nerve

Peripheral nerves

THE BRAIN

The cortex is in the cerebrum. It receives sense-messages and sends out nerve impulses to the muscles. It is also responsible for conscious feelings, thought, memory and learning ability. The areas of the brain responsible for conscious thought and speech are at the front of the cortex. The left-hand side of the cortex controls activities on the right of the body; the right side controls the left of the body. The speech, reading and writing of a right-hander is directed by the left side of the cortex; the right side controls the actions of a left-handed person.

Broca's area sends instructions to the motor cortex to give orders for the speech organ muscles to move.

The motor cortex sends out signals to the skeletal muscles. Each area controls a different movement.

Interpretations of touch from all areas of the body are received by zones within the sensory cortex.

The sounds we hear are interpreted by the sensory area of the cortex. Other zones receive impulses of taste and smell.

The images that we see through the eyes are interpreted by the visual cortex, a sensory area at the back of the brain.

CEREBRUM

BRAIN STEM

CEREBELLUM

The cerebellum is concerned with balance and co-ordination. The medulla controls involuntary actions such as breathing.

MEDULLA

The brain is the most important part of the nervous system. It uses large amounts of energy and needs a constant supply of blood. Brain cells die if starved of oxygen for as little as five minutes. The brain has three main parts: the cerebrum (about 85 percent of brain weight), the cerebellum and the brain stem.

EYES AND SIGHT

The eye is a ball of fluid with a transparent window in the front, the cornea. Light rays are bent so that they pass through the pupil, a hole in the iris. The rays are bent again through the lens and focused on to the retina at the back of the eye, forming an upside-down image.

Muscle

Retina

Iris

Lens

Pupil

Cornea

Optic nerve

Muscle

So our eyes actually see everything upside down and it is the brain which processes the information to form an upright image.

ANIMAL VISION

Some animals have much better eyesight than humans. These include cats, who have a mirror-like organ in the eye that reflects light on to the retina. This is why a cat's eyes seem to glow in the dark. Some birds have exceptional vision: a flying vulture can spot a carcase on the ground from a height of 4000 m.

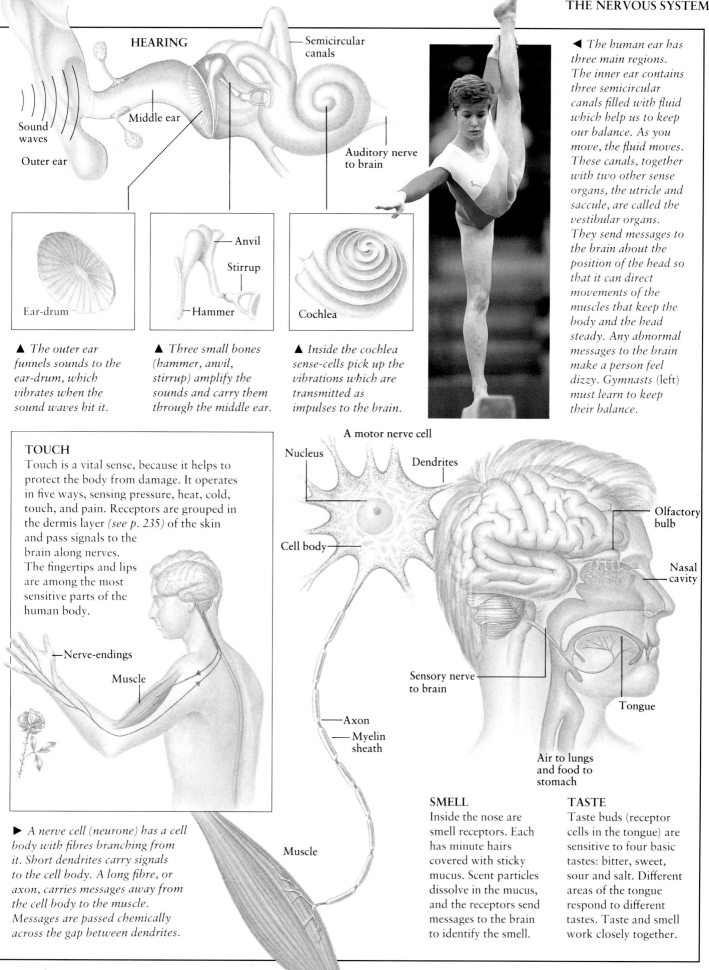

HEARING

Sound waves

Outer ear

Middle ear

Semicircular canals

Auditory nerve to brain

Ear-drum

Anvil

Stirrup

Hammer

Cochlea

▲ The outer ear funnels sounds to the ear-drum, which vibrates when the sound waves hit it.

▲ Three small bones (hammer, anvil, stirrup) amplify the sounds and carry them through the middle ear.

▲ Inside the cochlea sense-cells pick up the vibrations which are transmitted as impulses to the brain.

◀ The human ear has three main regions. The inner ear contains three semicircular canals filled with fluid which help us to keep our balance. As you move, the fluid moves. These canals, together with two other sense organs, the utricle and saccule, are called the vestibular organs. They send messages to the brain about the position of the head so that it can direct movements of the muscles that keep the body and the head steady. Any abnormal messages to the brain make a person feel dizzy. Gymnasts (left) must learn to keep their balance.

TOUCH

Touch is a vital sense, because it helps to protect the body from damage. It operates in five ways, sensing pressure, heat, cold, touch, and pain. Receptors are grouped in the dermis layer (see p. 235) of the skin and pass signals to the brain along nerves. The fingertips and lips are among the most sensitive parts of the human body.

Nerve-endings

Muscle

A motor nerve cell

Nucleus

Dendrites

Cell body

Olfactory bulb

Nasal cavity

Sensory nerve to brain

Tongue

Axon

Myelin sheath

Muscle

Air to lungs and food to stomach

▶ A nerve cell (neurone) has a cell body with fibres branching from it. Short dendrites carry signals to the cell body. A long fibre, or axon, carries messages away from the cell body to the muscle. Messages are passed chemically across the gap between dendrites.

SMELL
Inside the nose are smell receptors. Each has minute hairs covered with sticky mucus. Scent particles dissolve in the mucus, and the receptors send messages to the brain to identify the smell.

TASTE
Taste buds (receptor cells in the tongue) are sensitive to four basic tastes: bitter, sweet, sour and salt. Different areas of the tongue respond to different tastes. Taste and smell work closely together.

Heart, Blood and Skin

The heart works continuously to pump blood around the body, through the arteries and veins. The blood carries oxygen from the lungs and food-energy from the food we eat through the arteries to the rest of the body. The veins carry away waste products and return 'exhausted' blood from the body to the heart, for the cycle to begin again. The skin acts as a waterproof protective layer, shielding the body from infection and injury; it also keeps the body's internal temperature to a normal level.

FACTS ABOUT BLOOD

- There are four blood groups: A, B, AB and O. Someone who is given a blood transfusion must be given blood that matches their own type.
- One microlitre (millionth of a litre) of blood normally contains up to six million red blood cells, up to 10,000 white blood cells, and as many as 500,000 platelets.

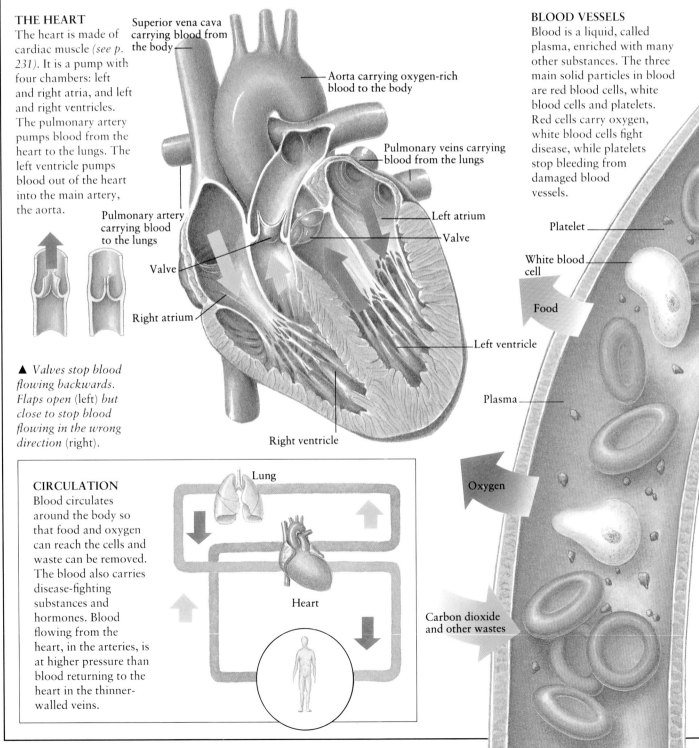

THE HEART
The heart is made of cardiac muscle (see p. 231). It is a pump with four chambers: left and right atria, and left and right ventricles. The pulmonary artery pumps blood from the heart to the lungs. The left ventricle pumps blood out of the heart into the main artery, the aorta.

Superior vena cava carrying blood from the body

Aorta carrying oxygen-rich blood to the body

Pulmonary veins carrying blood from the lungs

Pulmonary artery carrying blood to the lungs

Left atrium

Valve

Valve

Right atrium

Left ventricle

▲ Valves stop blood flowing backwards. Flaps open (left) but close to stop blood flowing in the wrong direction (right).

Right ventricle

BLOOD VESSELS
Blood is a liquid, called plasma, enriched with many other substances. The three main solid particles in blood are red blood cells, white blood cells and platelets. Red cells carry oxygen, white blood cells fight disease, while platelets stop bleeding from damaged blood vessels.

Platelet

White blood cell

Food

Plasma

Oxygen

Carbon dioxide and other wastes

CIRCULATION
Blood circulates around the body so that food and oxygen can reach the cells and waste can be removed. The blood also carries disease-fighting substances and hormones. Blood flowing from the heart, in the arteries, is at higher pressure than blood returning to the heart in the thinner-walled veins.

Lung

Heart

Lymphocyte

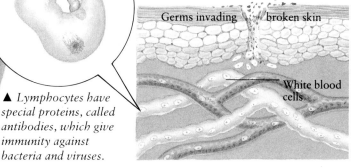

Germs invading — broken skin

White blood cells

▲ *Lymphocytes have special proteins, called antibodies, which give immunity against bacteria and viruses.*

◄ *The lymph or immune system is a network of vessels throughout the body. They carry the lymph fluid and white blood cells called lymphocytes which defend the body against infection.*

▼ *The comparative sizes of blood vessels are shown below. Blood leaves the left side of the heart through the aorta. The smallest arteries feed into the capillaries, which exchange food and oxygen for carbon dioxide and waste from individual cells.*

Red blood cell

Aorta

Large Artery

Small Artery

Arteriole

Capillary —

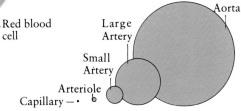

NAILS

Nails are made of dead cells containing a tough protein called keratin: which also makes up hair and the outer skin. Each nail grows about 0.5 mm a week.

Half moon (not firmly attached to skin below)

Round follicle — straight hair

Flat follicle — curly hair

Oval follicle wavy hair

SKIN

Skin keeps out germs, and is sensitive to heat, cold, touch and pain. The skin has an outer layer, or epidermis. The inner layer, or dermis, contains blood vessels, sweat glands, nerves and the roots of hairs.

HAIR

Each hair grows from a follicle and the type of hair depends on the shape of the follicle. The colour of hair depends on the amount of melanin (the pigment that determines skin colour) it contains.

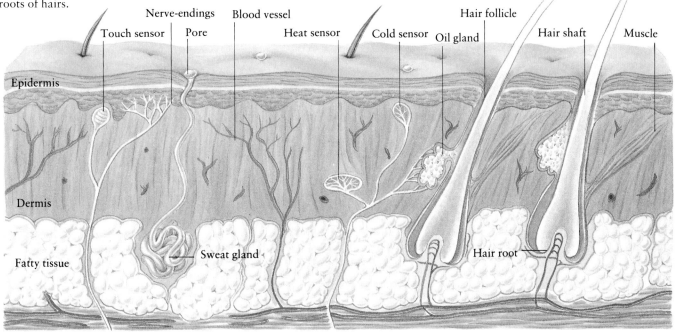

Nerve-endings

Touch sensor   Pore

Blood vessel

Heat sensor

Cold sensor

Oil gland

Hair follicle

Hair shaft

Muscle

Epidermis

Dermis

Fatty tissue

Sweat gland

Hair root

Digestion and Respiration

The digestive system breaks down food into simple substances for the body cells to use. These substances are absorbed into the bloodstream and waste matter is passed out of the body as urine or faeces. Cells need oxygen to break down and release the energy in food. The oxygen is taken into the body through the respiratory system – the nose, windpipe, or trachea, and two lungs. You take in oxygen from the air when you breathe in and release waste carbon dioxide when you breathe out.

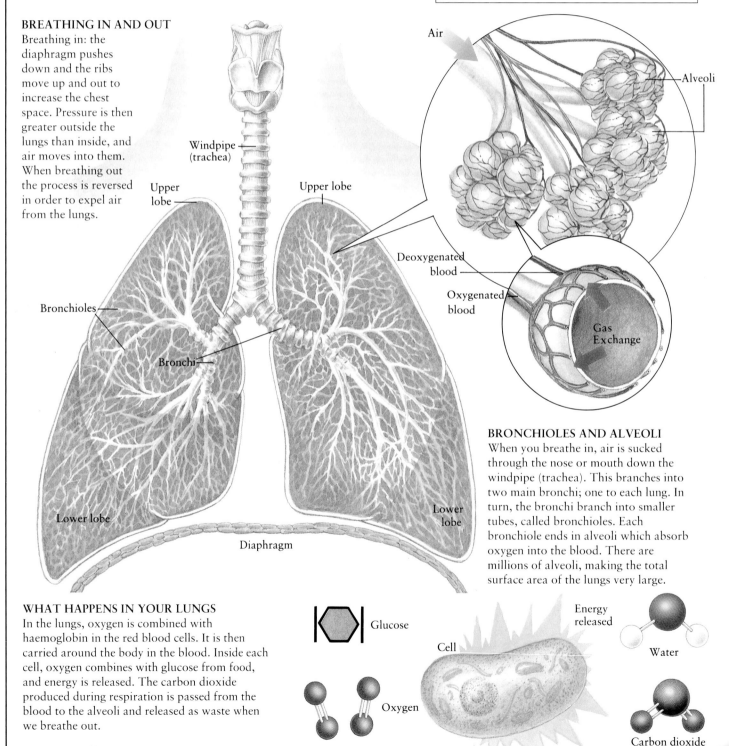

FACTS ABOUT BREATHING

- A baby is born with pink lungs. As we get older, our lungs darken from breathing in polluted air.
- The voice box, or larynx, is at the upper end of the trachea. Sounds are made when air is forced through the vocal cords, two bands of cartilage stretched across the opening into the larynx.

BREATHING IN AND OUT
Breathing in: the diaphragm pushes down and the ribs move up and out to increase the chest space. Pressure is then greater outside the lungs than inside, and air moves into them. When breathing out the process is reversed in order to expel air from the lungs.

Windpipe (trachea)

Upper lobe

Upper lobe

Bronchioles

Bronchi

Lower lobe

Lower lobe

Diaphragm

Air

Alveoli

Deoxygenated blood

Oxygenated blood

Gas Exchange

BRONCHIOLES AND ALVEOLI
When you breathe in, air is sucked through the nose or mouth down the windpipe (trachea). This branches into two main bronchi; one to each lung. In turn, the bronchi branch into smaller tubes, called bronchioles. Each bronchiole ends in alveoli which absorb oxygen into the blood. There are millions of alveoli, making the total surface area of the lungs very large.

WHAT HAPPENS IN YOUR LUNGS
In the lungs, oxygen is combined with haemoglobin in the red blood cells. It is then carried around the body in the blood. Inside each cell, oxygen combines with glucose from food, and energy is released. The carbon dioxide produced during respiration is passed from the blood to the alveoli and released as waste when we breathe out.

Glucose

Energy released

Cell

Water

Oxygen

Carbon dioxide

236

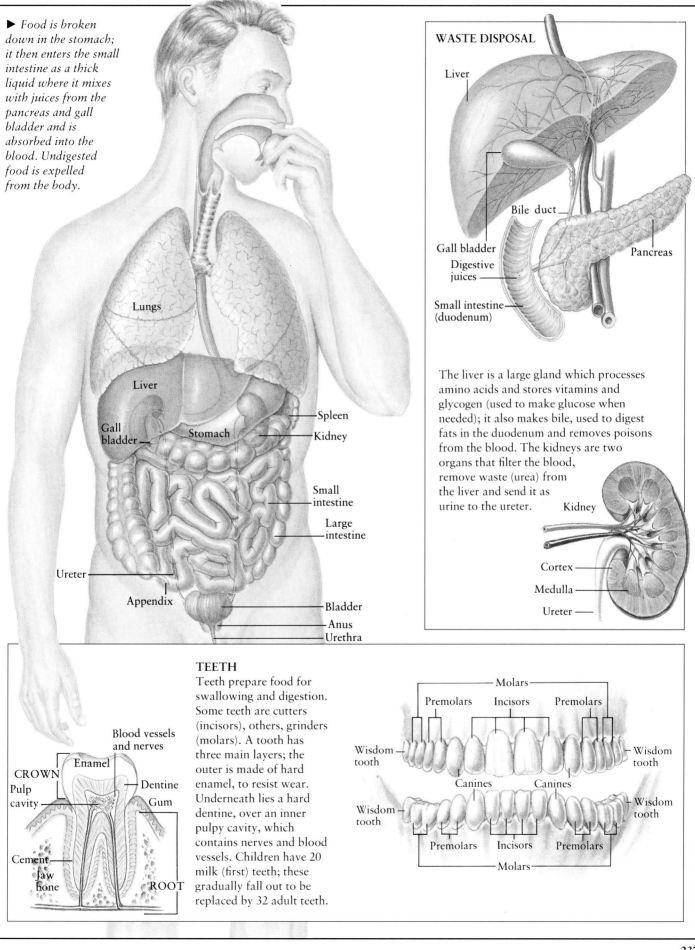

▶ *Food is broken down in the stomach; it then enters the small intestine as a thick liquid where it mixes with juices from the pancreas and gall bladder and is absorbed into the blood. Undigested food is expelled from the body.*

Lungs

Liver

Gall bladder

Stomach

Spleen

Kidney

Small intestine

Large intestine

Ureter

Appendix

Bladder

Anus

Urethra

WASTE DISPOSAL

Liver

Bile duct

Gall bladder

Digestive juices

Small intestine (duodenum)

Pancreas

The liver is a large gland which processes amino acids and stores vitamins and glycogen (used to make glucose when needed); it also makes bile, used to digest fats in the duodenum and removes poisons from the blood. The kidneys are two organs that filter the blood, remove waste (urea) from the liver and send it as urine to the ureter.

Kidney

Cortex

Medulla

Ureter

TEETH

Teeth prepare food for swallowing and digestion. Some teeth are cutters (incisors), others, grinders (molars). A tooth has three main layers; the outer is made of hard enamel, to resist wear. Underneath lies a hard dentine, over an inner pulpy cavity, which contains nerves and blood vessels. Children have 20 milk (first) teeth; these gradually fall out to be replaced by 32 adult teeth.

Blood vessels and nerves

Enamel

CROWN

Pulp cavity

Dentine

Gum

Cement

Jaw bone

ROOT

Molars

Premolars

Incisors

Premolars

Wisdom tooth

Wisdom tooth

Canines

Canines

Wisdom tooth

Wisdom tooth

Premolars

Incisors

Premolars

Molars

Reproduction

Humans reproduce sexually, like other mammals. The process of reproduction begins with conception – when sperm from a man fertilizes the egg of a woman. Both egg and sperm contain genetic information in chromosomes, and this information programmes the development of the embryo. After about two months the embryo has most of its internal organs. It is now a foetus. At four months, it can move, and after about nine months, a new human being is ready to be born.

The DNA molecule

▲ In the nucleus of each human cell are 23 pairs of chromosomes, made chiefly of proteins and the chemical deoxyribonucleic acid (commonly known as DNA). The DNA molecules contains coded instructions (genes) that control the workings of the cells. These genes also control how the cells develop into a body and carry the code for inherited chacteristics.

Pituitary

Parathyroids

Thyroid

Adrenals

Pancreas

Ovaries (female only)

Testes (male only)

GROWTH DURING PREGNANCY

▼ A human pregnancy typically lasts 38–40 weeks. At 12 weeks the baby is about 9 cm long and weighs 14 g.

5 weeks

8 weeks

12 weeks

Placenta

Umbilical cord

Womb

◀ For 9 months the baby grows inside the uterus or womb, a hollow organ in the mother's abdomen. Cells form the umbilical cord joining the growing foetus to the placenta. The cord provides the baby with air and food.

FACTS ABOUT REPRODUCTION

● The greatest number of children born in a single birth was 8 girls and 2 boys to a Brazilian woman in 1946.
● The mother who has given birth the most times in recent decades was a woman in Chile who in 1981 produced a final total of 55 children; they included 5 sets of triplets.

▲ The endocrine glands produce hormones. The pituitary hormone regulates growth. Testes produce the male hormone testosterone; ovaries produce the female hormones oestrogen and progesterone.

REPRODUCTIVE SYSTEMS

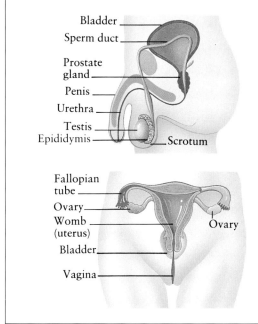

Bladder
Sperm duct
Prostate gland
Penis
Urethra
Testis
Epididymis
Scrotum

Fallopian tube
Ovary
Womb (uterus)
Bladder
Vagina
Ovary

◄ *The male sex organs (genitals) produce the sexual cell or sperm. Millions of sperm are made in the male's testes. During sexual intercourse, the sperm move through the urethra and out of the penis and then into the woman's body.*

◄ *An adult woman usually produces one egg a month from her ovaries. The egg passes into the fallopian tubes, and to the uterus. The lining of the uterus thickens, ready to nourish a fertilized egg.*

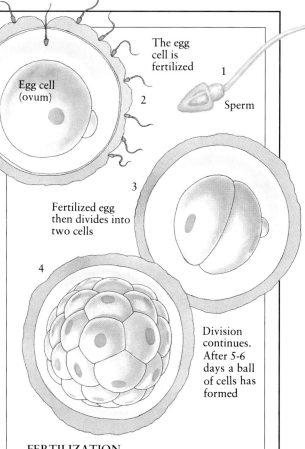

Egg cell (ovum)

The egg cell is fertilized

Sperm

1

2

3

Fertilized egg then divides into two cells

4

Division continues. After 5-6 days a ball of cells has formed

FERTILIZATION

During intercourse, millions of sperm pass from the man's body into the woman's, through the vagina. Only a few hundred reach the fallopian tubes, and only one will fertilize the egg. The nuclei of the two cells (male and female) merge, and the cell begins its journey down the fallopian tubes to the uterus. On the way, it grows by dividing: one cell becomes 2, 4, 8, 16 and so on.

▼ *By 4 months, the baby has doubled in size. It has well-developed features such as fingers and toes.*

▼ *At 7 months, the baby's lungs and most of its other body organs are working properly. This means that with modern care, the baby will usually survive if it is born prematurely.*

▼ *From 6 to 9 months of a mother's pregnancy, substances in her bloodstream are passed through the placenta that will help the baby to fight off diseases after its birth. At 9 months, the baby is ready to be born.*

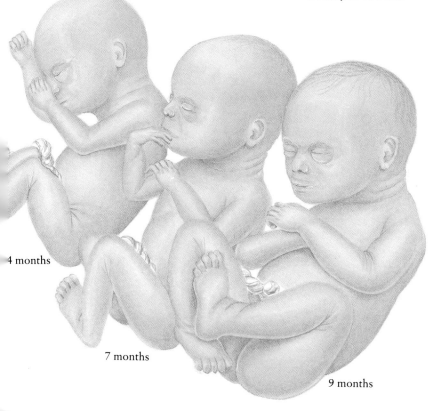

4 months

7 months

9 months

▲ *If the fertilized cell separates into two cells, two babies grow. Identical twins (above) have the same chromosomes, are the same sex and look alike. Two eggs fertilized at the same time by two sperm cells produce non-identical twins, with different chromosomes.*

Growth and Ageing

The rate at which children grow never ceases to astonish parents. Humans grow from conception (before birth) until after puberty (about 18–20 years old). Although our bodies do not usually grow taller after that, they do go on changing – putting on or losing weight, for example. Between the ages of 20 and 30 people are at their strongest. As people get older, their body cells renew themselves more slowly, their senses become less acute and they may suffer loss of memory.

AVERAGE NORMAL GROWTH FOR BOYS AND GIRLS

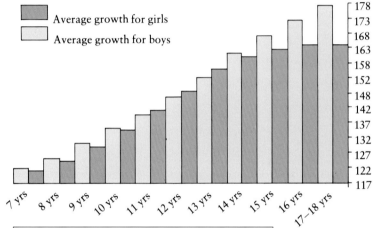

■ Average growth for girls
□ Average growth for boys

Height in centimetres: 178, 173, 168, 163, 158, 152, 148, 142, 137, 132, 127, 122, 117

7 yrs, 8 yrs, 9 yrs, 10 yrs, 11 yrs, 12 yrs, 13 yrs, 14 yrs, 15 yrs, 16 yrs, 17–18 yrs

◀ *This chart shows the differences in growth between girls and boys. Girls are on average only heavier and taller than boys around the age of 12 when they start their adolescent growth spurt. By the age of 18 boys are both taller and heavier.*

▲ *Small babies learn to do many things by copying older people; By the time they are 12 months they have begun to stand and say a few words. By 18 months, infants have learned to walk, and play with simple toys such as balls and building blocks.*

GROWING UP

Humans develop slowly compared to other animals. At birth an average baby is about 50 cm long and weighs 3.5 kg. The infant cannot move and depends on its mother for food, which at first is milk. By the age of two it has tripled in weight. Its hair has grown and it can walk and climb stairs. The baby has teeth and eats solid foods. It can talk and is learning rapidly. In growth, girls outstrip boys briefly around the age of 12, but after that boys grow taller and heavier. Puberty starts later in boys than in girls.

Day 1: Uterus lining shed – period begins

Day 5: Uterus lining starts to build up, ready to receive a fertilized egg

Day 14–28: Most likely time for ovum to be fertilized

Day 14: Mature ovum released from ovary

MENSTRUATION

The changes to girls that occur at puberty (usually 9–14) are activated by sex hormones. A girl begins to have periods (a loss of blood). Every month the ovaries of most women of childbearing age release an egg cell. If the egg is not fertilized, it is discharged with some blood and other cells through the vagina; this period of time (3–7 days) is called the menstrual period.

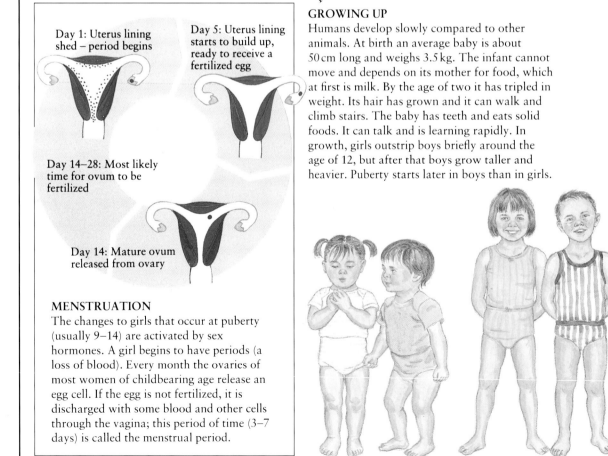

Age two   Age six   Age 10–12

Single cell

Cell grows
larger and prepares
to divide

Cell dividing
into two

SIGNS OF AGEING

In boys, one visible sign of developing sexual
maturity is the growth of hair on the face (a
beard or moustache). This happens any time
after the age of 12. Hair also grows around the
sexual organs and elsewhere on the body. The
voice becomes deeper. With advancing age,
other body changes are common. Hair becomes
grey, thins or falls out. The skin wrinkles and
muscles begin to sag.

Age 1

Age 30

CELL RENEWAL

New cells are made by other cells dividing. The
two grow to full size and divide again, and so
on. This is how all living things grow and repair
themselves. In our bodies, more than two million
blood cells are made every second to replace old
ones dying at the same rate. As we get older,
cells renew themselves more slowly, and brain
and nerve cells that die are not replaced.

Division complete:
now two identical
cells

Age 70

FACTS ABOUT GROWTH

- The average life span in the
West and Japan is over 70.
Women tend to live longer
than men.
- At the age of four a boy is
59 percent adult height, a
girl about 64 percent. Boys
may carry on growing until
they are 23, most girls are
fully grown by the age of 20.
- The ovum (female egg cell)
is the biggest cell in the
body: it is about the size of
a full stop.
- The heaviest human ever
weighed was an American,
Jon Minnoch, (1941–1983)
who weighed an estimated
635 kg in 1978. He slimmed
to 216 kg by 1979.
- Only one in five people
over 100 years old is a man.
- The first 'test-tube' baby
(conceived outside the
mother's body) was Louise
Brown, born in Oldham,
England, in 1978.

Age 20–22

Age 30–34

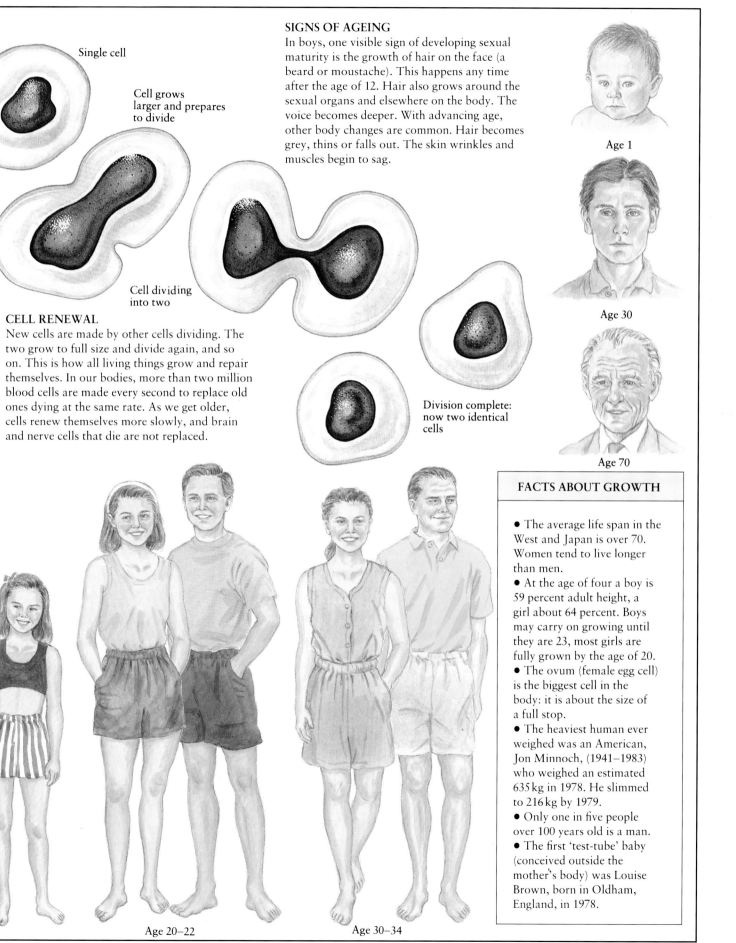

Looking After Your Body

The body can look after itself – it has powerful defences against disease and amazing powers of repair. But it needs sensible maintenance. Keeping healthy is mostly common-sense. Eat a balanced diet of different foods, including fresh fruit and vegetables. Take exercise to keep your body fit and trim (and to enjoy yourself). Avoid harmful habits, such as smoking. Follow basic rules of hygiene (brushing your teeth, washing, taking baths and showers) to keep your whole body clean and healthy.

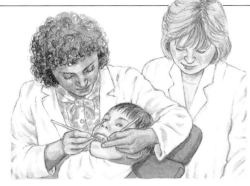

▲ *Regular checks at the dentist's should ensure your teeth need only minor repairs – such as filling a small cavity.*

NUTRITION

Fibre: aids digestion; bread, cereals, vegetables.

Carbohydrates: provide fuel; sugars, starches; bread, cereals, potatoes.

▲ *Nutrition is the process by which the body takes in and uses food. Our diet is the food and drink we eat. A balanced diet should contain some of each of the above foods.*

Fats: provide energy; butter, milk, cheese, eggs, meat, fish, vegetable oils, nuts.

Proteins: provide amino acids; meat, fish, eggs, milk, nuts, bread, potatoes, beans, peas.

FIGHTING TOOTH DECAY

Brushing teeth and gums regularly gets rid of tiny scraps of food sticking to them. This helps to stop tooth decay or cavities, which can cause toothache. Sugars in food and bacteria cause the tooth enamel to decay. Small holes can be filled by the dentist, but badly decayed teeth may have to be taken out.

Cavity

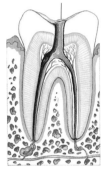

WHY WE NEED SLEEP

When you sleep, your heartbeat and breathing slow down, but the brain stays active. Most adults sleep between seven and eight hours a night although children need more sleep. During sleep, you have periods of dreaming and often change body position.

During sleep the pattern of brain waves records dream-periods

▼ *A fit, healthy body has the stamina to run and play without getting tired quickly.*

Baseball

Rapid eye movement (dreaming)

Football

HYGIENE AND DISEASE

◀ *Following simple rules of hygiene can help to ward off illness – especially infectious disease. Remember to wash your hands before eating and don't share food and drink. Keep food protected from flies or mice, which leave harmful bacteria.*

DON'T POISON YOUR BODY

Putting poisonous or harmful substances into your body is not a good idea. Smoking cigarettes is known to be a cause of lung cancer. Drinking too much alcohol can seriously damage your body. Taking harmful, habit-forming drugs such as narcotics, barbiturates, tranquillizers, amphetamines or hallucinogens can damage your health and spoil your enjoyment of life.

▶ *This sign on a bottle or container is a warning that a substance is poisonous and should never be eaten or drunk.*

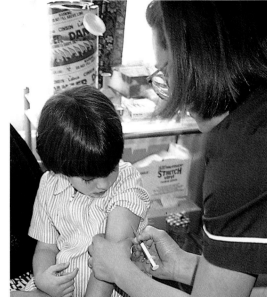

VACCINATION

Vaccination or immunization works by injecting into the body either a harmless form of a poison produced by a disease-bacterium, or a weak form of the bacterium or virus itself. The body's immune system makes antibodies to fight the invading 'disease', and these are stored until a real attack by the disease.

Netball

▼ *The energy from food builds the strong muscles you need to ride a bike.*

▼ *Keeping fit makes the body supple for energetic movements such as jumping.*

Tennis

Gymnastics

Cycling

KEEPING FIT

You can keep fit in all sorts of enjoyable ways. Take regular exercise, rather than exhausting yourself in one outburst of energy a week. A brisk walk is good for people of all ages. Running, cycling and swimming are other good ways to keep fit. So is dancing (but not in a smoke-filled room). Some people enjoy gymnastics, or a game of tennis, softball or football, while others prefer activities such as canoeing, abseiling, sailing or climbing.

PLANT GLOSSARY

Algae: Simple plants like **organisms**, including single **cells**, giant seaweeds.

Angiosperm: Flowering plant; includes grasses, **herbaceous plants**, most trees.

Annual: Plant which completes its life cycle in a season and then dies.

Anther: Part of the **stamen** (of a flower) that contains **pollen**.

Bark: Tough outer layer of trunk or branch of trees or shrubs.

Berry: Fleshy fruit with no hard inner layer, usually with several seeds; for example, date, orange, raspberry.

Biennial: Plant which completes its life cycle in two seasons, and then dies.

Botany: Scientific study of plants.

Bud: Undeveloped shoot.

Calyx: Protective outer ring of **sepals** of a flower in bud; often greenish, leaflike structures.

Carpel: Flower's female reproductive organ, made up of **stigma**, **style** and **ovary**.

Cellulose: Tough carbohydrate substance making up the cell walls of plants, formed by chains of **glucose** (sugar) molecules.

Chlorophyll: Green pigment (colouring matter) that enables green plants to use the energy in sunlight to make their food (in **photosynthesis**).

Clone: Plants, such as clusters of bulbs, with identical genetic features produced by **vegetative reproduction**.

Conifers: Cone-producing tree or shrub, usually evergreen.

Corm: Fleshy underground stem in which food is stored.

Cotyledons: Seed leaves forming part of the embryo in a seed.

Cycads: Fernlike tropical plants of the order Cycadales that have existed since prehistoric times; only nine kinds still grow today.

Deciduous: Shedding leaves at the end of each growing season.

Dehiscent fruit: Fruit that bursts open to release seeds; for example, poppies.

Dicotyledon: Member of the class of flowering plants with two **cotyledons** in each seed.

Drupe: Fruit with a fleshy outer layer and a hard inner layer (stone or pit); for example, peach, plum, cherry.

Embryo: Young plant within the seed.

Enzymes: Organic compound produced by plant or animal **cells** that causes chemical reactions in living cells; consists of protein alone or combined with nonprotein organic molecule.

Epidermis: Outer cell layer of a leaf, stem or root.

Epiphytes: Plants that grow on other plants, but do not feed from them.

Evergreen: Shrub or tree that bears leaves all year round.

Fertilization (in plants): Combining the male reproductive cell with the female ovule to form a seed.

Fruit: Ripe **carpel** or group of carpels, which protects seeds and helps to disperse or spread them.

Fungi: Simple plants without **chlorophyll**; for example, mould, **mushroom**, **yeast**.

Germination: Beginning of growth of a seed or **spore**.

Ginkgos: Plant phylum dating from prehistoric times, now reduced to one species, the **ginkgo** (Maidenhair tree).

Glucose: Simple sugar produced in **photosynthesis** and stored as a food reserve by some plants.

Gymnosperm: Term used for plants with seeds unprotected by an **ovary**; collectively **conifers**, **ginkgos**, **cycads**.

Heartwood: Tough wood (with no living **cells**) at the centre of a tree that gives the tree its strength.

Herbaceous plant: Plant without a woody stem; part above ground dies down each year but its roots survive.

Humus: Decaying organic matter in the soil.

Hybrid: *See* **Animal Glossary**

Legume: Pod or dry fruit produced from a single **ovary**, which splits when ripe; examples include peas, beans, laburnum, clover, acacia.

Lichen: Symbiotic association of **algae** and **fungi**.

Monocotyledon: Flowering plant which has only one **cotyledon** in each seed.

Mushroom: Name used for fruiting bodies of certain **fungi**. Toadstool is another name for mushroom; there is no real difference between them.

Nectar: Liquid made by a flower's nectaries that attracts insects to a flower.

Nut: Fruit containing one seed, within a tough woody shell.

Order: *see* **Animal Glossary**

Organic: Having organs or organized physical structure.

Ovary (in flower): Part of the **carpel**, contains the ovules that bear the female reproductive cells.

Parasite: Plant that lives by feeding from another (**host**) plant.

Perennial: Plant that lives for several years.

Petal: Part of flower that attracts pollinators such as birds or insects.

Phloem: Tissue that conducts food and other materials through a plant.

Photosynthesis: Process by which plants use sunlight to convert water and carbon dioxide into food (sugar).

Pistil: Another word for the female part of a flower (the **carpel**).

Pollen: Mass of grains made in the **stamens** of a flower, carrying male reproductive cells.

Pollination: Transfer of **pollen** from **stamen** to **stigma**.

Respiration: Taking in oxygen from the air to 'burn' food to provide energy, releasing carbon dioxide.

Rhizoid: Hair-like structure anchoring a moss to the ground.

Runner: Creeping stem by which plants such as strawberries reproduce.

Saprophyte: Organism that feeds on chemicals from decaying plants or animals; many **fungi** are saprophytes.

Sepal: Outermost parts of a flower, usually green; they protect **petals** before flower opens.

Shrub: Woody plant with many branches.

Species: *see* **Animal Glossary**.

Spore: Single or multi-celled structure formed during reproductive process in many plants; for example, ferns, **mushrooms**.

Stamen: Male reproductive part of a flower, made up of **anther** and supporting stalk or filament.

Starch: Carbohydrate made up of sugars, the main food storage compound in plants; potato tubers store starch.

Stigma: Tip of the **carpel** of a flower, receives the **pollen**.

Style: Stalk-like part of the **carpel**, with **stigma** at its tip.

Succulents: Plants with swollen leaves, for storing water.

Symbiosis: *see* **Animal Glossary**.

Taproot: Main root of a plant.

Tendril: Modified stem, leaf or leaflet used by some climbing plants to coil around any support.

Thallus: Simple plant body not divided into root, stem and leaves.

Transpiration: Loss of water by evaporation from a plant's leaves.

Tuber: Swollen stem used to store food.

Vegetative reproduction: Process in which a whole new plant is produced from part of a plant with sexual reproduction; for example, a bulb.

Xylem: Woody tissue.

Yeasts: Single-celled **fungi**, many of which can cause fermentation (used in baking, brewing and wine-making).

ANIMAL GLOSSARY

Albino: Animal lacking pigment from its skin, hair, feathers or eyes.

Amphibian: Animal that lives partly in water and partly on land.

Anatomy: Study of the internal structure of living organisms.

Antenna: Sense-organ on the head of an **arthropod**.

Arthropod: Animal with hard external skeleton, segmented body and jointed limbs; includes insects, **arachnids**, **crustaceans**, centipedes, millepedes.

Aquatic: Living in water.

Arachnid: Arthropod, normally with four pairs of walking legs, no antennae and a pair of grasping appendages on the head; for example spiders, scorpions.

Bacterium (plural bacteria): Microscopic single-celled organism. Most are harmless, but some cause disease. **Bacteria** help to break down dead plant and animal remains.

Barbel: Slender sensory **organ** that grows from the jaws of some fishes.

Benthic: Living on the sea bed.

Biome: Major community of plants and animals, characterized by a particular type of vegetation (for example, savanna, rainforest) and climate.

Biological control: Control of pests by use of natural predators or diseases; for example, use of **bacteria** to control grain weevils and use of fish to control mosquitoes.

Biosphere: Part of the Earth and atmosphere that is inhabited by living **organisms**.

Blubber: Thick layer of fat under the skin of a whale or seal.

Camouflage: Disguise, produced by colour, pattern or shape, that makes an animal hard to see.

Carnivore: Animal that lives by eating meat rather than plants.

Carrion: Remains or flesh of an animal that has died.

Cartilage: Tough, elastic gristle in animal bodies; a layer of cartilage makes joints work smoothly. In sharks and rays, the skeleton is made of cartilage rather than bone.

Caterpillar: Soft-bodied **larva** that is a stage in the development of certain kinds of insect; for example, moths and butterflies.

Cell: Structural and functional unit that makes up all living things. There are many types of cell; for example, bone cells, skin cells, nerve cells.

Class: Grouping of living things, the next major rank below **phylum**.

Classification: Way in which animals and plants are divided into groups and sub-groups.

Clutch: Set of eggs laid by a bird.

Cold-blooded: Animal that cannot automatically keep its body at operating temperature by burning fuel (sugar) stored in the body. A cold-blooded animal remains at about the same temperature as its surroundings.

Colony: Large number of animals living together; ants, rabbits, seals and gulls all live in colonies.

Convergence: Resemblance between animals of different species that has developed because they adapted to the same kind of life in different parts of the world; examples are the Australian spiny anteater and the European hedgehog.

Coral: Small sea animals called polyps that grow in a hard, chalky skeleton. They often live in a **colony** and their remains form coral reefs.

Courtship: Behaviour that leads up to two animals pairing and mating.

Crustacean: **Arthropods** such as crabs and shrimps; they almost all live in water and most have a shell.

Dinosaur: Prehistoric reptile known only from **fossils**. Dinosaurs of many kinds were the major land animals between 205 and 65 million years ago.

Display: Any kind of animal behaviour that has a particular meaning. For example, **courtship** display is used to attract a mate; threat display is used to frighten off an enemy.

Diurnal: Animal active by day, rather than by night. *See also* **nocturnal**

Dorsal: Of or close to the back of an animal; for example, the dorsal fin of a fish.

Echinoderm: Marine **invertebrates**, symmetrical in shape, often with spiny skins; they have 'tube feet' for movement or feeding. They include starfish and sea urchins.

Ecology: Study of the relationship between plants and animals.

Ecosystem: Community of **organisms** and the **habitat** in which they live.

Embryo: Immature **organism** developing in the egg or in the womb of its mother.

Evolution: Changes that take place in animal and plant **species**, over millions of years, that change them from simpler to more complex forms.

Exoskeleton: External **skeleton** or outer body that covers the body of animals such as **arthropods**.

Extinct (of animals or plants): **Family** or **species** that has died out.

Family: Grouping used in the **classification** of animals and plants. Similar families are grouped together in an **order**.

Fauna: Animal population of a particular area or period in time.

Feral: Animals (such as cats) that have escaped from homes or captivity and are living wild.

Food chain: Natural links between animals and what they eat. A simple example is cat-bird-spider-fly – each one eats the next one down the chain.

Fossil: Remains of an animal or plant left in rocks. The best fossils are found in limestone and mudstone.

Genus (plural genera): Grouping used in the **classification** of living **organisms**. Similar genera are grouped together in a **family**. A genus is divided into **species**.

Gill: Breathing organ of animal, such as a fish, that lives in water; it takes oxygen from the water just as animals with lungs takes oxygen from air.

Habitat: Natural living place of an animal or plant. Examples are lakes, forests, grassland, deserts.

Herbivore: Plant-eating animal.

Hibernate: To spend the winter in a deep sleep; the animal slows down its heartbeat and other body systems and lives off stored body fat until spring.

Host: Animal or plant that is used by another animal or plant as a source of food. The **parasite** lives on, or in some cases inside, the host.

Hybrid: Plant or animal produced from the mating of parents of different species or varieties; hybrids between species are usually sterile. A mule, for example, is the offspring of a horse and a donkey that have mated.

Insectivore: Insect-eating animal; many insectivores eat other **invertebrates** as well as insects.

Instinct: Built-in ability to do certain things without having to learn them; for example, baby turtles always go to the sea as soon as they hatch out.

Invertebrate: Animal that does not have a backbone; for example, **arthropods**.

Kingdom: Largest grouping used in the classification of living **organisms**.

Larva: Grub of an insect; the insect is a larva from when it hatches from the egg until it turns into a **pupa**.

Life cycle: Series of stages through which an **organism** passes from **fertilization** to death.

Mammal: Warm-blooded **vertebrate** with a larger brain and greater intelligence than other types of animal; all mammals suckle their young and have a covering of hair.

Marsupial: Mammal whose young are born in an undeveloped state. The young complete their development inside their mother's pouch.

Mating season: Time of year when male and female animals pair off, or gather in groups, in order to breed.

Metamorphosis: Means 'change of shape' and describes the changes in an insect's life from egg to **larva** to **pupa** to adult. At each change, the insect grows a new kind of body.

Migrate: To make a regular journey to a particular place in order to breed and raise young, or in some cases to search out better food supplies.

Mollusc: Large group of **invertebrate** animals that usually have hard shells; includes snails, slugs, squids and octopuses.

Monotreme: Egg-laying mammal with other reptilian features; includes platypus and echidna.

Natural selection: Natural process in which the animals best equipped for a particular set of living conditions will be the most successful breeders.

Nocturnal: Animals active at night. *See also* **diurnal**

Nucleus: Central part of an animal or plant **cell** that acts as a command centre and controls all the chemical processes the cell carries out.

Nymph: Immature insect, resembling the adult but without wings.

Omnivore: Animal that has wide diet including meat and plants.

Order: Grouping used in the **classification** of plants and animals. Similar orders are grouped together in a **class**. Order is divided into **families**.

Organism: Any living thing, plant or animal.

Parasite: Plant or animal that depends completely on another plant or animal in order to stay alive.

Pelagic: Living in the upper regions of the ocean.

Phylum: In animal and plant **classification** a group below **kingdom**.

Placental mammals: Mammals whose young are well developed inside the mother before they are born. The placenta is the organ that supplies the unborn baby with food.

Plankton: Tiny animals that drift in salt or fresh water.

Predator: **Carnivore** that gets food by hunting and killing other animals.

Prehistoric: Something that dates from before history, or before the invention of writing.

Primary feathers: Flight feathers on the parts of a bird's wing that correspond to the human wrist, palm and fingers.

Primate: Mammal of the group that includes monkeys, apes and humans; called the primate or 'first' because it is the highest **order** of mammals.

Protein: Any of a group of complex compounds of hydrogen, oxygen and nitrogen, and sometimes other elements. Proteins are essential parts of all living **cells**.

Protozoan: Simple single-celled **organisms** considered to be animal-like; currently classified in the kingdom Protoctista.

Pupa: Stage between the **larva** and adult in the development of some insects.

Raptor: Predatory bird adapted for seizing prey; for example, hawk, owl.

Regeneration: When living thing regrows or replaces lost **organs** or tissues.

Reproduction: Process of making new members of the same animal or plant species. Some species reproduce asexually by growing an additional replica of the parent, or by splitting into two identical copies. Others reproduce sexually by joining together an egg from a female parent and sperm from the male parent.

Reptile: Cold-blooded scaly animals that lay eggs on land; a few give birth to live young. Reptiles include snakes, lizards, crocodiles, turtles, tortoises.

Rodent: Mammals with big, chisel-like front teeth used for gnawing tough plant food. Rodents include mice, squirrels, beavers, porcupines.

Ruminant: Animal such as cow, goat or sheep that has a four-chambered stomach that enables it to process tough plant food. Ruminants feed, then later bring up the food into their mouths and chew it a second time.

Scavenger: Animal that feeds on refuse or the flesh of dead animals (**carrion**); for example, jackals, vultures, beetles.

Skeleton: Framework of bone that supports the body of a bird, **mammal**, fish, **amphibian** or **reptile**. *See also* **exoskeleton**

Spawn: Eggs without hard shells that are laid in large quantities by fish, **amphibians** or **molluscs**.

Species: Group of animals or plants of the same kind that breed and produce more of their own kind. Species of the thrush family, for example, are quite different from species of the heron family.

Symbiosis: Association between two dissimilar living organisms from which both partners benefit.

Terrestrial: Living on land.

Territory: Area of land that animal (usually the male) takes over and defends against other animals of the same species.

Thorax: Middle section of an insect's body, between the head and the abdomen. The thorax carries three pairs of legs and two pairs of wings.

Tundra: Arctic region of level, treeless, land; has thin soil that is always frozen, apart from the surface layer, which melts in summer so that a carpet of grass and lichen can grow.

Ungulate: **Herbivores** with hooves such as horses and cows.

Vertebrate: Animal with a backbone; vertebrates have an internal **skeleton** of bone and **cartilage**, or just cartilage, a spinal cord, a brain enclosed in a cranium, a **heart** with 2–4 chambers and a maximum of 4 limbs. *See also* **invertebrate**

Warm-blooded: Animal that maintains its body at full operating temperature by burning fuel (food) to create chemical energy; warm-blooded animals keep themselves warm in cold weather (within certain limits) and cool in hot weather.

Wattles: Fleshy parts on the chin or throat of a bird such as a turkey.

Zoo: Public or private grounds where animals are kept for study and/or exhibition to the public.

Zoogeography: Study of the geographical distribution of animals.

Zoology: Study of animals.

HUMAN BODY GLOSSARY

Abscess: Painful, red, swollen area, inside the body, caused by **bacteria**.

Acne: Spots, blackheads or whiteheads caused by inflammation of the oil glands in the skin.

Acupuncture: Chinese medical treatment, relying on the pricking of skin with needles in the parts of the body where the Chinese believe the life forces flow.

Adenoids: Small **glands** at the back of the nasal passages.

Allergy: Reaction such as a running nose, rash or wheezing caused when people are sensitive to certain substances such as dust or pollen.

Anaesthetic: Substance that makes a person insensitive to pain. A general anaesthetic puts a person to sleep before an operation. A local anaesthetic numbs only the area of the body where the drug was applied.

Antibiotics: Drugs that can kill **bacteria**. Antibiotics do not kill **viruses** and so cannot cure viral diseases such as the common cold.

Antibodies: Substances produced by the body's immune system. They destroy harmful **bacteria** and **viruses**.

Antiseptics: Substances used to clean wounds and sterilize doctors' instruments; they prevent the growth of disease carrying micro-organisms.

Artery: Any blood vessel which carries blood away from the heart to the rest of the body.

Asthma: Difficulty in breathing, usually caused by an **allergy** or infection.

Autonomic nervous system: Part of the nervous system that controls 'automatic' actions such as breathing and heartbeat.

Backbone: Another word for the spine or vertebral column.

Bile: Green liquid produced by the **liver** that helps to digest fat. Bile is stored in the **gall bladder**.

Bladder: Muscular bag that collects urine produced by the **kidneys**.

Blood pressure: Measured using a sphygmomanometer. The results are shown as two figures given in millimetres of mercury – a person's blood pressure should range from 100–140 mm when their heart contracts, 60–90 mm when it relaxes.

Brain: **Organ** of mass of nerve **tissue**; in humans, the centre of the nervous system, occupying the entire skull.

Bruise: Mark on the skin caused by a bang or by pressure; blood vessels under the skin are damaged.

Cancer: Disease that begins when some abnormal or malignant **cells** begin to grow uncontrolledly and form a tumour or swelling.

Capillary: Blood vessel connecting the small branches of **arteries** with small branches of **veins**.

Carbohydrates: With **protein** and fats, one of the three main groups of foods. Foods which contain a lot of carbohydrate are bread, cereals, potatoes and rice.

Cartilage: *See* **Animal Glossary**

Cholesterol: A fatty substance made by the **liver** and adrenal **glands**.

Chromosome: One of the 46 structures in the nucleus of every **cell**. Chromosomes are made of **DNA**; they carry the genes that determine inherited characteristics.

Coronary: Referring to the blood vessels that supply the **heart**.

Corpuscle: Another name for a red or white blood cell.

Cortex: Outer layer of the **brain** or 'grey matter', responsible for all thinking processes.

Cramp: Pain in a **muscle** caused when it contracts and goes into a spasm.

Dermis: Lower living layer of the skin – just below the epidermis.

Diabetes: Illness in which a person does not produce enough **insulin** and so cannot control the level of sugar (**glucose**) in their blood.

DNA: Deoxyribonucleic acid is the chemical that makes up our chromosomes and carries – as **genes** – all the information which we inherit from our parents.

Ear-drum (**tympanum**): Thin membrane at the end of the ear canal.

Eczema: Inflammation of the skin (itchy rash and blisters).

Eustachian tube: Tube that connects the middle ear with the throat; it helps to keep the pressure inside the ear the same on both sides of the **ear-drum**.

Faeces: Waste material that leaves the body after food has been digested.

Femur: Thigh bone – the longest, strongest bone in the body.

Fertilization (in animals): Union of two unlike sexual **cells** or **gametes** (**sperm** and **ovum**). In humans, this may happen between the 13th and 15th day of a woman's **menstrual cycle**, in one of the Fallopian tubes; after it has been fertilized the ovum can begin to develop into a baby.

Fingerprints: No two people have the same fingerprints which is why police use them as a means of identification.

Foetus: Unborn baby from two months until it is born. From **fertilization** to two months it is called an embryo.

Follicle: Pocket in the skin from which hair grows.

Gall bladder: Sac, about 8–10 cm long, under the **liver**, that releases **bile**.

Gamete: Mature **cell** that can unite with another in sexual reproduction.

Genes: Combinations of fundamental **DNA** units that make up the **chromosomes** in each **cell**.

Glands: The body has two types of glands: exocrine produce substances that are carried away in ducts, endocrine produce **hormones** that are secreted into the blood.

Haemoglobin: Red pigment found in **red blood cells** that gives blood its colour. Haemoglobin carries oxygen from the **lungs** around the body to the **cells**.

Heart: Muscular organ that keeps blood circulating through the body.

Hormones: The body's chemical messengers – substances produced in tiny amounts in the endocrine **glands**; they control many body processes.

Hypothermia: Especially low body temperature that occurs when a person is too cold for too long.

Immunization: Way of preventing certain diseases, usually by giving injections.

Incisors: Flat front teeth that cut food.

Insulin: **Hormone** produced by the **pancreas** that controls the level of **glucose** (sugar) in the blood.

Intestine: Long tube, beginning at the stomach and ending at the anus, in which food is digested.

Iris: Coloured part of the eye that surrounds the pupil.

Joint: Place where two bones meet; lined with **cartilage** and held in place by **ligaments**.

Keratin: Hard substance found in nails, hair and skin.

Kidneys: **Organs** that filter waste from the blood and produce urine which collects in the **bladder**.

Larynx (**voice box**): Located at the top of the **trachea**, it is made of **cartilage** and has the vocal cords inside it.

Ligament: Tough elastic band of **tissue** that holds bones together at a **joint**.

Liver: The body's largest **gland** is found in the abdomen of **vertebrates**; an adult's liver weighs about 1500 g. The liver's functions include the secreting of **bile**.

Lungs: **Organs** that enable air-breathing vertebrates to breathe.

Lymph: Clear liquid that contains **white blood cells.**

Marrow: Soft jelly-like substance in the hollow centres of some bones.

Membranes: Thin layers of **cells** that line or cover various parts of the body. Membranes line the nose, mouth and **intestine**, and cover the **heart, lungs** and other **organs.** Many lining membranes produce mucus to protect the body – in particular its openings – from infection.

Menstruation (or periods): Bleeding from the **vagina** as the lining of the **uterus** breaks down during the female menstrual cycle. *See also* **fertilization**

Muscle: Tissue that effects movement of the body. There are three types of muscles in the body: skeletal or striped muscle allows for movement; heart muscle pumps blood around the body; smooth muscle in the intestine moves food.

Nerves: Bundles of the long fibres of nerve cells that carry electrical messages to and from the brain and **spinal cord.**

Oesophagus: Tube that carries food from the mouth to the stomach.

Organ: Group of different tissues that work together to perform a special job in the body. For example, the **kidneys, heart** and **lungs.**

Ovaries: Two female **organs** that produce ova (egg cells). Usually one is released each month from puberty to menopause (about 11 years to between 45–55 years).

Pancreas: **Gland** behind the stomach; it produces **insulin,** and pancreatic juice, which helps to digest food in the duodenum (small intestine).

Pelvis: Hip bones.

Pituitary gland: Endocrine **gland** at the base of the brain.

Plasma: Liquid part of blood that remains when **red** and **white blood cells** and platelets are removed.

Plastic surgery: Surgery, usually for repairing or rebuilding parts of the body that have been damaged or scarred.

Proteins: Body-building chemicals that are part of every living **cell.** Proteins are made of units called amino acids.

Puberty: When reproductive system becomes active; begins between 12–15 years for a boy and between 10–14 years for a girl.

Pulse: Throbbing that can be felt in arteries as the heart pumps. For adults pulse rate is 65–80 beats per minute, for a 10 year old about 90 beats per minute and for a baby about 140 beats per minute.

Red blood cells: Small disc-shaped cells in the blood that carry oxygen to all cells.

Renal: Referring to the **kidneys.**

Retina: Inner lining of the eyeball that is sensitive to light.

Saliva: Liquid produced by three pairs of **glands** in the mouth. Saliva moistens food so that it can be swallowed easily and it contains an enzyme (ptyalin) that digests starch.

Siamese twins: Identical twins who are joined together when they are born.

Sinuses: Hollow cavities inside the skull; there are two sets in the forehead, one behind the nasal passages and one in the cheeks.

Sneeze: Reflex action that forces air out of the **lungs** through the nose in order to clear an irritation in the nasal passages.

Sperm: Male sex cells that are produced in the **testes.**

Spinal cord: Thick cord of nerves that extends from the base of the **brain** to the bottom of the back.

Spleen: Soft **organ** on the left side of the body between the stomach and diaphragm. In adults it is part of the **lymph** system and helps fight infection.

Tendons: Bands of **tissue** that connect **muscles** to bones.

Testes: Two male sex glands that produce **sperm** cells and male **hormones.**

Thyroid: **Gland** in the neck, on both sides of the **trachea,** that produces the growth **hormone** thyroxine.

Tissues: Groups of similar **cells** that form various parts of the body.

Tonsils: Oval structures found at the entrance to the throat. Together with the **adenoids** they guard against the **bacteria** that may enter through the mouth and nose.

Trachea (windpipe): Leads from the **larynx** in the throat to the two main bronchi in the chest.

Tumour: Swelling caused by the abnormal growth of cells without a useful function. There are two kinds of tumour: malignant (invading normal tissue; cancerous) or benign (non-malignant).

Ulcer: Open sore on the skin or on a membrane inside the body.

Umbilical cord: Cord that connects a developing baby to the placenta inside its mother's **uterus.**

Ureters: Tubes that carry urine from the **kidneys** to the **bladder.**

Urethra: Tube that leads from the **bladder** to the outside of the body.

Uterus (womb): Part of a woman's body, inside her abdomen, where a baby develops.

Vaccination: Injecting a person with weakened or dead disease-causing micro-organisms to make them immune from one or several diseases.

Vagina: Passageway from the **uterus** to the outside of a female mammal's body. During childbirth it stretches to let the baby out.

Vein: Any blood vessel that carries blood towards the **heart.**

Villi: Tiny projections from the lining of the small intestine that absorb digested food.

Virus: Infectious agent capable of causing illness in plants and animals; infectious diseases include measles, mumps, poliomyelitis and smallpox.

Vitamins: Group of substances found in food that are essential for health. An average person needs small amounts of about 15 different vitamins.

Vocal cords: Two ligaments stretched across the **larynx,** controlled by **muscles** that allow speech.

White blood cells: Colourless **cells** in blood that help to fight disease; they are larger than **red blood cells** and are made in the bone **marrow.**

Zygote: **Cell** that results from the fusion of two **gametes;** a fertilized egg before it begins to divide

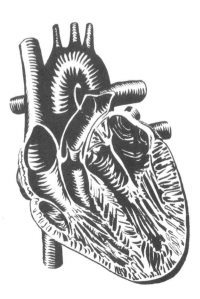

SCIENCE
AND
TECHNOLOGY

S cience makes discoveries; technology puts the discoveries to use. From earliest times, prehistoric people observed the weather, the behaviour of animals and the growth of plants; their observations marked the beginnings of science. The first sciences to develop were counting (mathematics), healing (medicine), the rising and setting of the Sun (astronomy), and tools (mechanics). When people first picked up stones to use as tools or weapons, the long march of technology had begun.

In modern times scientists have learned to rely on *method* as well as observation to acquire knowledge. They try and find out how things happen through a series of experiments. The scientists can then predict what ought to happen, given certain conditions. If the experiments show that his or her theory is correct, the scientist may be able to state a new principle or rule.

Science and Technology first deals with the different branches of science, including matter and energy, force and motion, space and time, light and sound, and electromagnetism. The technology section covers engineering, transport, materials, farming, medicine and modern communications.

Brian Williams

DISCOVERING SCIENCE

The Branches of Science

Science means knowledge (from the Latin word *scientia*), and therefore covers every field of human inquiry. The desire to find out is one of humankind's most distinctive qualities. Science has given people power, for example, to make their lives more comfortable and to change their environment. It has also given people technology – the ability to make tools, to build with materials and to harness sources of energy.

Science has various branches, concerned with different areas of knowledge. They include the physical sciences, such as astronomy, chemistry, physics and geology; mathematics; life sciences (biology, botany, zoology); and the social sciences such as anthropology, economics and psychology. The pages that follow concentrate on the ways in which science and technology have shaped the modern world.

◄ *Astronomy began thousands of years ago when people first peered at the stars. The study of the Universe is called cosmology. Modern ideas about cosmology date from the 1500s, when Copernicus showed that the Earth and other planets orbit the Sun. The Universe began about 15 billion years ago, almost certainly with the Big Bang.*

The Sun

The Solar System

Mars Jupiter Saturn Uranus Pluto

Venus

Mercury Earth

Neptune

(Distances not shown to scale)

▶ *The steam engine changes heat energy into mechanical energy. James Watt perfected his steam engine in the 1780s; the first steam railway to carry passengers on a regular schedule opened in 1830.*

Ancient scientists thought there were only four 'elements'

Earth

Air

Water

Fire

CHEMISTRY
Modern chemistry has its origins in alchemy, a mixture of science and superstition. The Egyptians, Chinese and Arabs were masters of alchemy. Early chemists made important discoveries (such as gunpowder) and identified a number of elements, while vainly seeking a magical method to turn lead into gold.

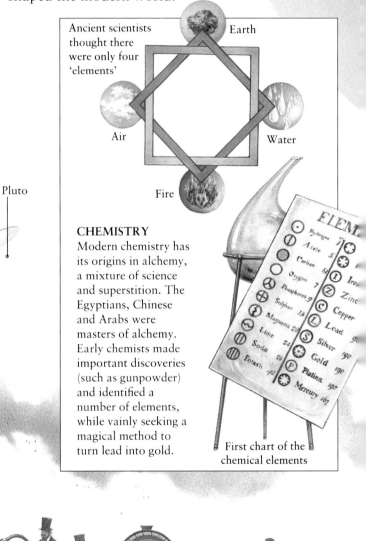

First chart of the chemical elements

◄ Theories about the nature of the atom date back to ancient Greece. By 1913 Ernest Rutherford and Niels Bohr had described a 'model' of the atom. Nuclear fission, or 'splitting the atom', was first achieved in 1938 and led to the development of the first nuclear reactor in 1942.

MATHEMATICS

Mathematics has its roots in India, China, Arabia and Greece. From the abacus, a beads-on-a-frame calculator invented 5000 years ago, we have moved to computers, with their microchip technology. Computers have the ability to process data at fantastic speeds using codes based on the binary system (which counts in 0s and 1s).

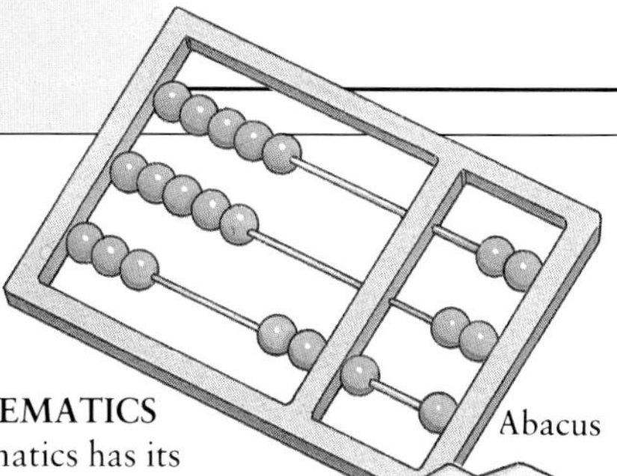

Abacus

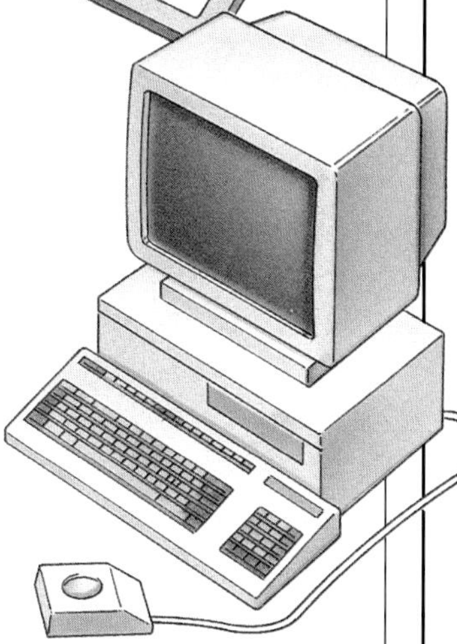

Computer

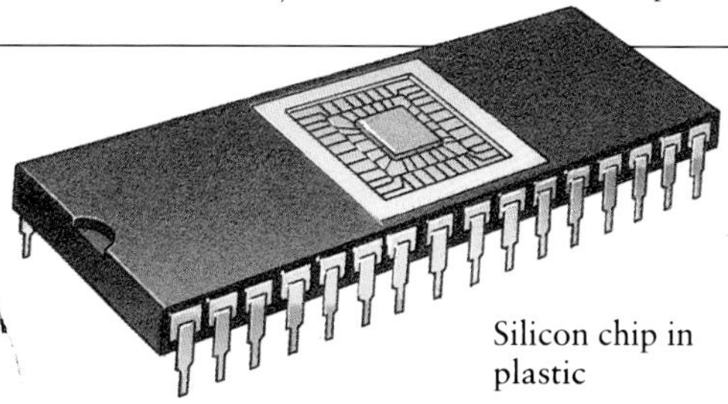

◄ Our understanding of how living things replicate themselves stems from the discovery of the DNA molecule in every cell, which carries genetic information.

▼ The Renaissance in Europe (1400s–1500s) was an age of discovery. Artists such as Leonardo da Vinci, who drew this anatomical drawing, were also scientists.

Silicon chip in plastic

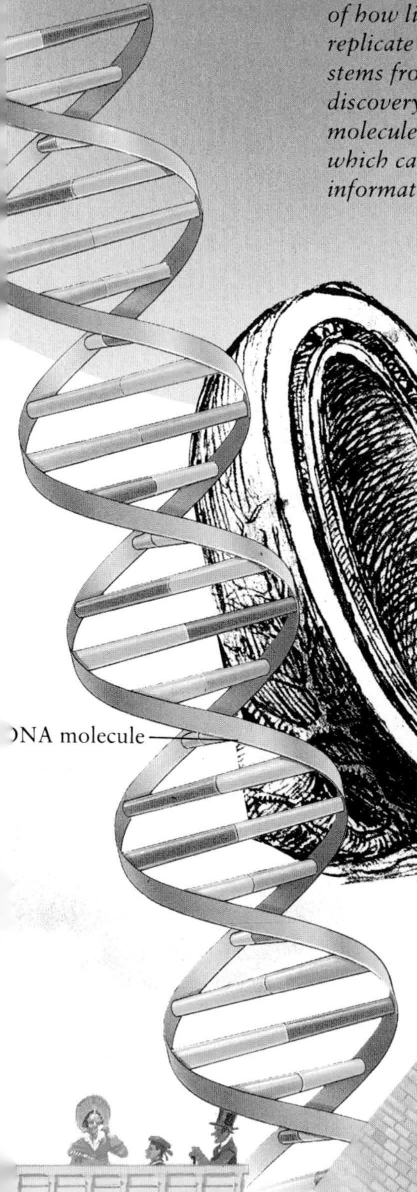

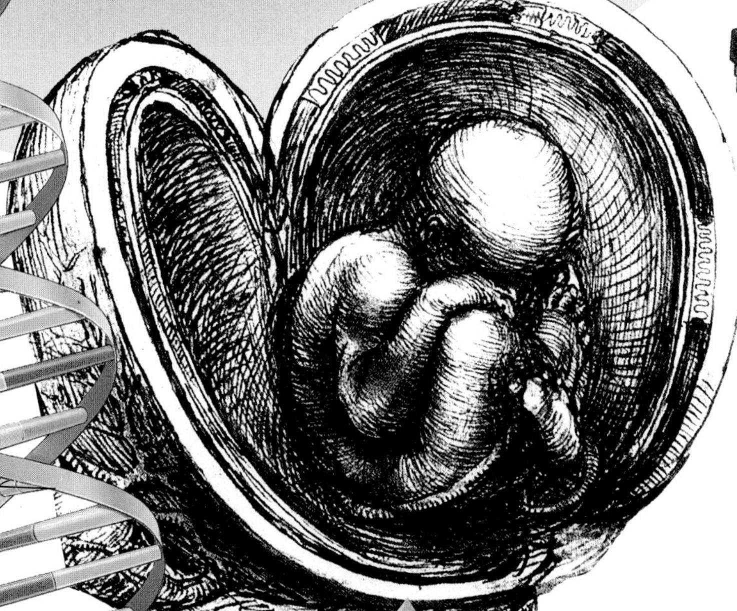

▼ The first people to use geometry were the Babylonians, and Egyptian pyramid-builders (about 5000 years ago). The Greek mathematician, Pythagoras, devised his right-angled triangle theorem in the 500s BC. Pythagoras proved that in this kind of triangle (shown below) the larger square has the same area as the sum of two smaller ones.

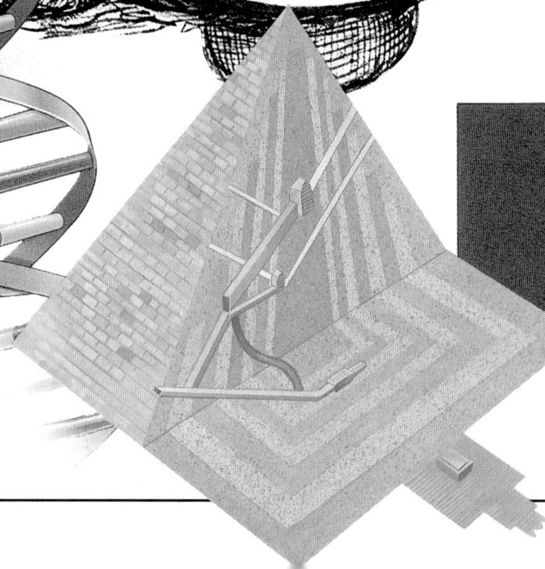

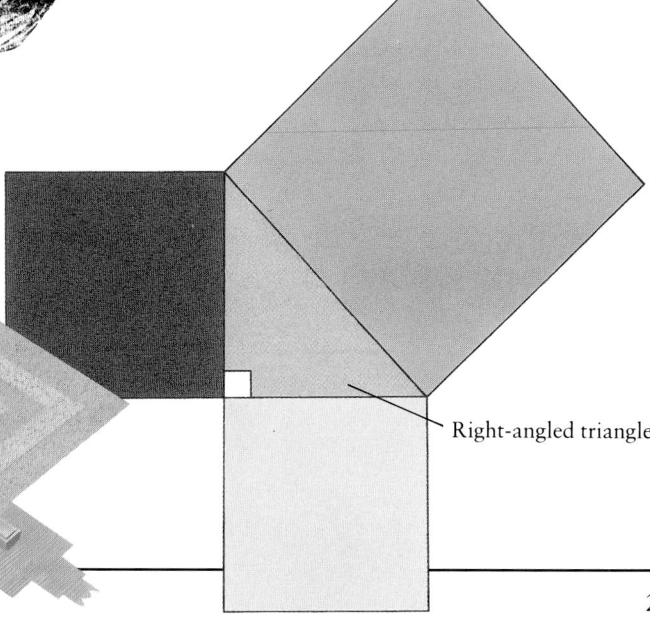

DNA molecule

Right-angled triangle

251

MATTER AND ENERGY

Atoms and Molecules

Matter is all the material in the Universe – animals, plants, rocks, air, water. Matter can exist in three familiar states – solid (ice), liquid (water) and gas (steam). A fourth state, plasma, is formed at very high temperatures – for example, within stars. In all its states, matter is made of the same basic units, atoms. The smallest piece of a substance that can exist on its own is called an atom. An element is a substance made up of only one kind of atom. Atoms are made of even smaller particles, called electrons, moving around a centre called a nucleus made up of neutrons and protons, in much the same way as the planets orbit the Sun. Within the atom is immense energy, which can be released by splitting the atom to produce a chain reaction, called nuclear fission. Atoms can combine with other atoms to form molecules.

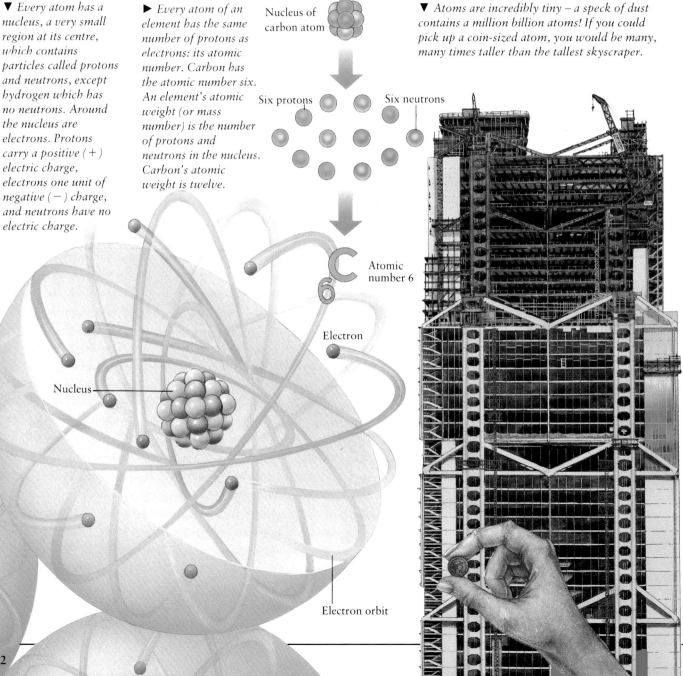

▼ *Every atom has a nucleus, a very small region at its centre, which contains particles called protons and neutrons, except hydrogen which has no neutrons. Around the nucleus are electrons. Protons carry a positive (+) electric charge, electrons one unit of negative (−) charge, and neutrons have no electric charge.*

▶ *Every atom of an element has the same number of protons as electrons: its atomic number. Carbon has the atomic number six. An element's atomic weight (or mass number) is the number of protons and neutrons in the nucleus. Carbon's atomic weight is twelve.*

Nucleus of carbon atom

Six protons

Six neutrons

C
6

Atomic number 6

Electron

Nucleus

Electron orbit

▼ *Atoms are incredibly tiny – a speck of dust contains a million billion atoms! If you could pick up a coin-sized atom, you would be many, many times taller than the tallest skyscraper.*

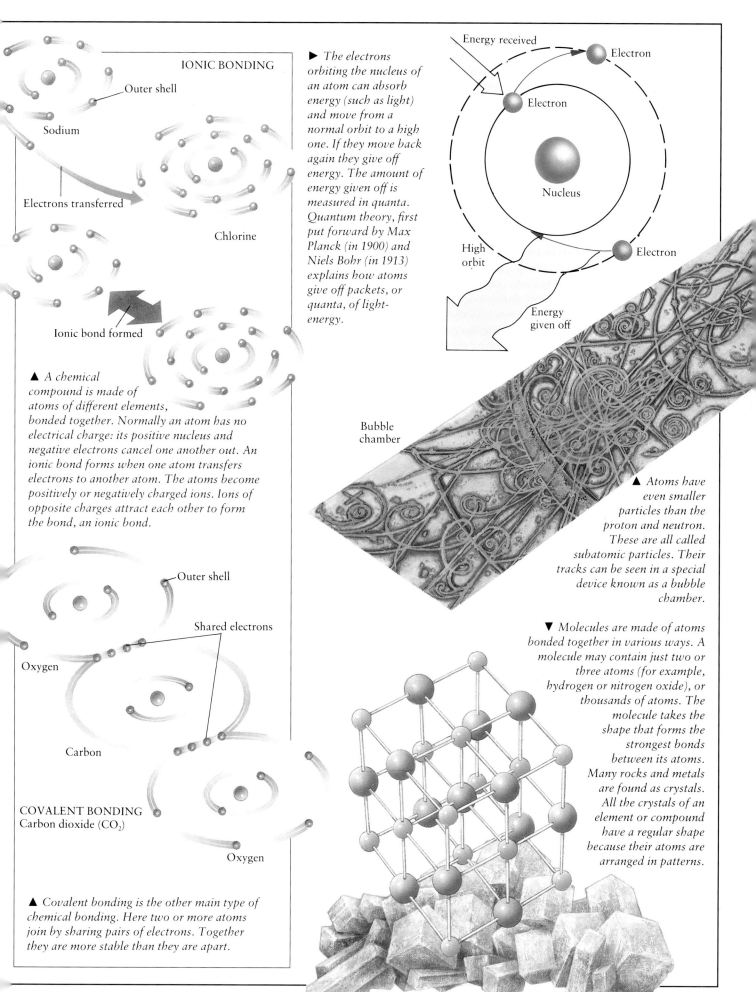

IONIC BONDING

Outer shell

Sodium

Electrons transferred

Chlorine

Ionic bond formed

▲ *A chemical compound is made of atoms of different elements, bonded together. Normally an atom has no electrical charge: its positive nucleus and negative electrons cancel one another out. An ionic bond forms when one atom transfers electrons to another atom. The atoms become positively or negatively charged ions. Ions of opposite charges attract each other to form the bond, an ionic bond.*

Outer shell

Shared electrons

Oxygen

Carbon

COVALENT BONDING
Carbon dioxide (CO_2)

Oxygen

▲ *Covalent bonding is the other main type of chemical bonding. Here two or more atoms join by sharing pairs of electrons. Together they are more stable than they are apart.*

Energy received

Electron

Electron

Nucleus

High orbit

Electron

Energy given off

▶ *The electrons orbiting the nucleus of an atom can absorb energy (such as light) and move from a normal orbit to a high one. If they move back again they give off energy. The amount of energy given off is measured in quanta. Quantum theory, first put forward by Max Planck (in 1900) and Niels Bohr (in 1913) explains how atoms give off packets, or quanta, of light-energy.*

Bubble chamber

▲ *Atoms have even smaller particles than the proton and neutron. These are all called subatomic particles. Their tracks can be seen in a special device known as a bubble chamber.*

▼ *Molecules are made of atoms bonded together in various ways. A molecule may contain just two or three atoms (for example, hydrogen or nitrogen oxide), or thousands of atoms. The molecule takes the shape that forms the strongest bonds between its atoms. Many rocks and metals are found as crystals. All the crystals of an element or compound have a regular shape because their atoms are arranged in patterns.*

What Are Things Made Of?

Every substance is either a chemical element or a combination of elements. The atoms in a substance are held together by chemical bonds that form molecules. Different elements can bond together to make compounds. As bonds form or break, a chemical reaction takes place. Carbon is found in all living things. It combines freely with hydrogen, nitrogen and oxygen. Organic chemistry concentrates on substances that have carbon-to-carbon bonds: there are over one million organic compounds.

HYDROGEN BONDS

In water, hydrogen and oxygen atoms join by sharing pairs of electrons – an example of covalent bonding. Water molecules are also held together by hydrogen bonds. These weak bonds are important in building large molecules such as DNA (deoxyribonucleic acid) and protein structures.

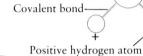

Non-bonding pairs of electrons

Oxygen atom

Hydrogen bond

Covalent bond

Positive hydrogen atom

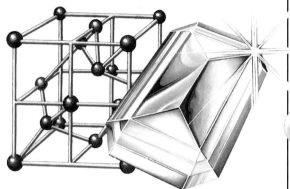

► *Diamond is a form of pure carbon. The atoms in diamond are arranged in a dense lattice framework. This is why diamond is so hard. Carbon makes up less than 0.03 percent of the Earth's crust. Most of this carbon is combined with other elements.*

◄ *Graphite, once called plumbago, is another form of pure carbon. Its atoms are arranged in layers which slide easily over one another. Graphite is one of the softest solids. It is also greasy and makes a useful lubricant. The 'lead' in a pencil is a mixture of graphite and clay.*

Synthetic rubber gloves

Vinyl disc

Plastic cassette case

Toothbrus

Detergent

Plastic bucket

Racquet

THE USES OF HYDROCARBONS

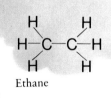

H–C–C–H (Ethane, with H atoms)

Ethane

Benzene

Balls

▲ *Hydrocarbons are compounds made only of hydrogen and carbon atoms. They are found in petroleum and natural gas. Hydrocarbons found in nature also provide the raw material for making plastics, solvents and other synthetic materials. In hydrocarbons, carbon atoms are arranged either in chains (as in ethane) or rings (as in benzene).*

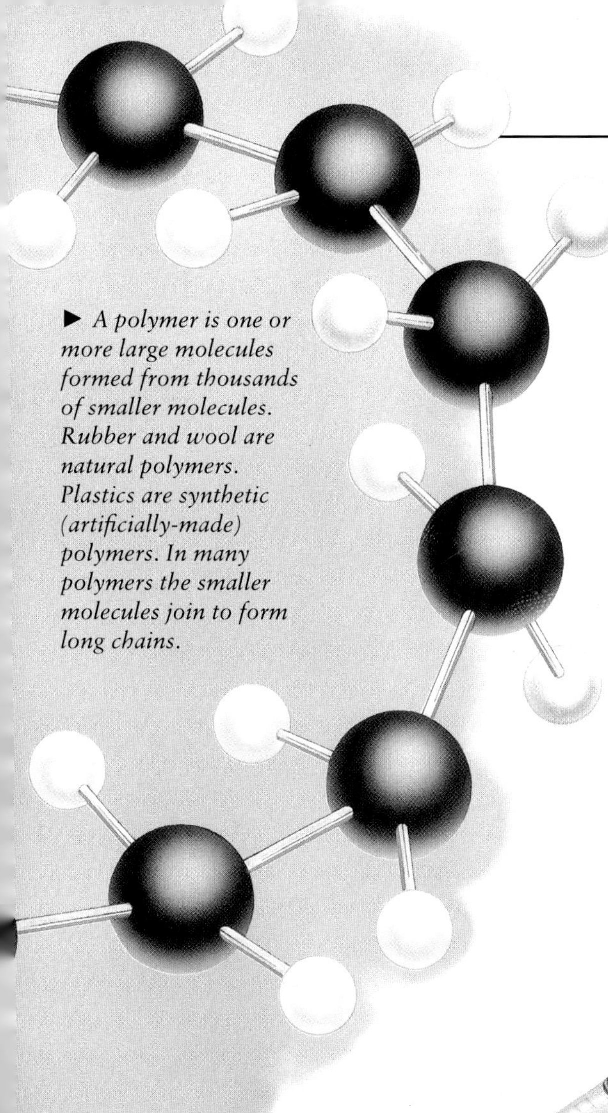

► A polymer is one or more large molecules formed from thousands of smaller molecules. Rubber and wool are natural polymers. Plastics are synthetic (artificially-made) polymers. In many polymers the smaller molecules join to form long chains.

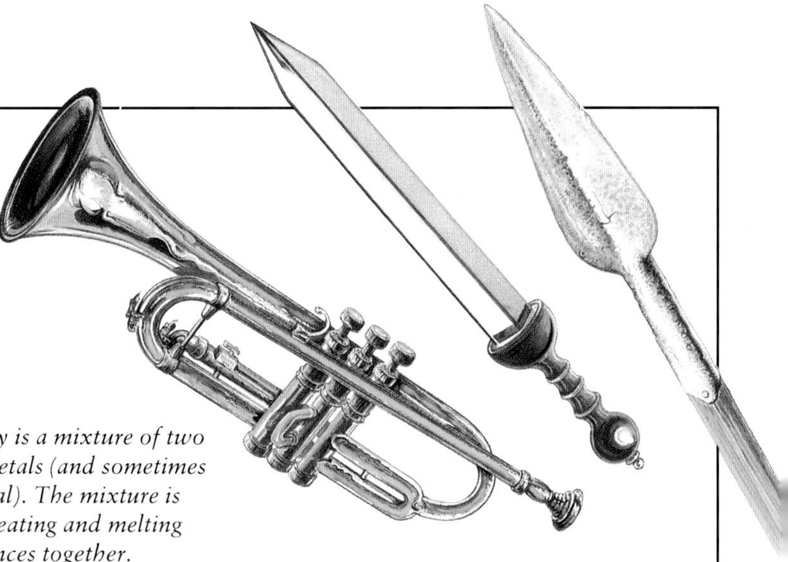

► An alloy is a mixture of two or more metals (and sometimes a non-metal). The mixture is made by heating and melting the substances together. Examples of alloys are bronze (copper and tin), brass (copper and zinc) and steel (iron and carbon). Aluminium alloys are used in aircraft. Jet engines and parts of spacecraft are made of 'super-alloys' containing nickel, cobalt and other elements.

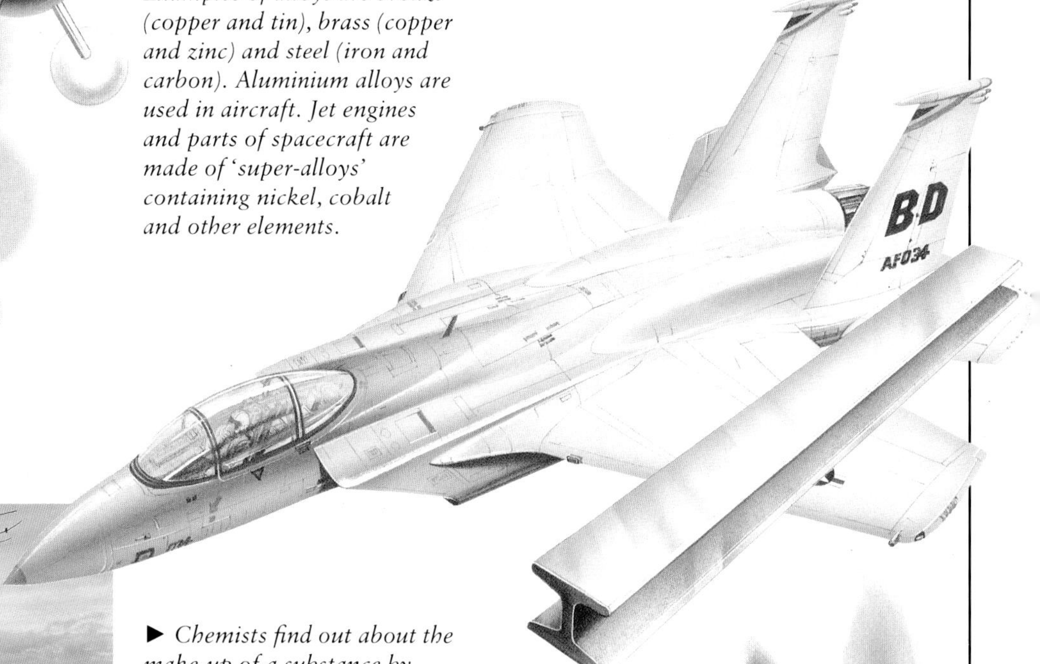

► Chemists find out about the make-up of a substance by analysis. Qualitative analysis shows what elements a substance contains. Quantitative analysis shows how much of a substance it contains. A flame test is one way of identifying elements in compounds. The compound is burned at the end of a platinum wire in a Bunsen burner. Different elements burn with distinctive colours.

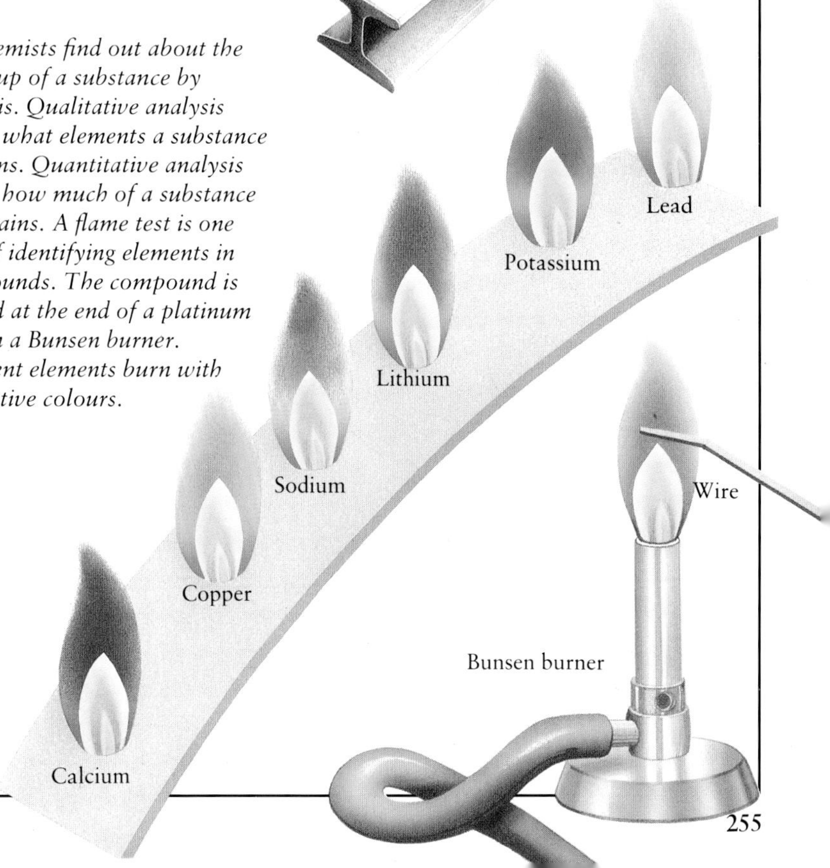

▲ An acid is a compound of hydrogen and at least one other element. Solutions of acid are usually sour-tasting and corrosive. Acids dissolve many metals and turn blue litmus paper red. Acid rain (rain polluted by acids in the atmosphere by the burning of industrial waste gases) has damaged trees and crops, and polluted rivers and lakes, in many countries.

Lead

Potassium

Lithium

Sodium

Copper

Wire

Bunsen burner

Calcium

The Periodic Table

In all, 103 elements have been officially named. Ninety-two elements occur naturally on the Earth and others have been made in laboratories. Scientists claim to have discovered a further six elements, known as 104 to 109. Twelve elements were known to the ancient world (before AD 1000). Seventy-six more were identified between the 1500s and 1920s. Each element from 1 (Hydrogen: H) to 103 (Lawrencium: Lr) has a symbol. Chemists use these symbols when writing formulas for compounds.

► *The Periodic Table presents information about the elements: their name, atomic number and similarities with other elements. The elements are arranged in rows, or periods, in order of increasing atomic number. Groups of elements share certain characteristics because of the way the electrons in their atoms are arranged in shells. Elements with the same number of electrons in their outermost shells behave similarly. There are two main groups: the non-metals and the metals; certain similar elements fall into families, e.g. alkali metals, transition metals and inner transition metals.*

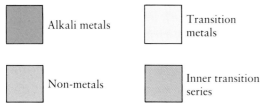

☐ Alkali metals

☐ Transition metals

☐ Non-metals

☐ Inner transition series

▼ *Water is a molecule made of two atoms of hydrogen (H) and one atom of oxygen (O). Hydrogen is the simplest and most abundant element in the Universe. Methane gas is a hydrocarbon made of one atom of carbon and four atoms of hydrogen. Carbon dioxide is made of two atoms of oxygen to one of carbon.*

DOWN
Going down, the size of atoms increases; elements in the same group behave similarly.

Carbon dioxide (CO_2)

Water (H_2O)

Methane (CH_4)

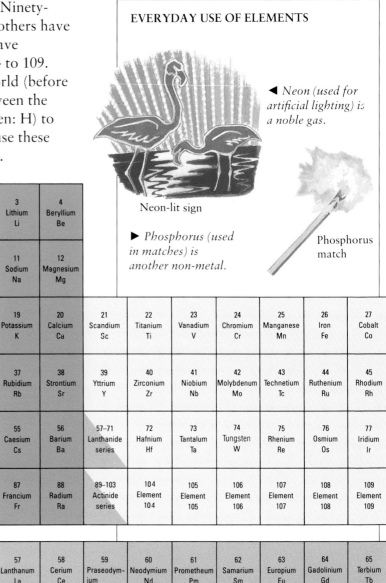

Neon-lit sign

◄ *Neon (used for artificial lighting) is a noble gas.*

► *Phosphorus (used in matches) is another non-metal.*

Phosphorus match

3 Lithium Li	4 Beryllium Be							
11 Sodium Na	12 Magnesium Mg							
19 Potassium K	20 Calcium Ca	21 Scandium Sc	22 Titanium Ti	23 Vanadium V	24 Chromium Cr	25 Manganese Mn	26 Iron Fe	27 Cobalt Co
37 Rubidium Rb	38 Strontium Sr	39 Yttrium Y	40 Zirconium Zr	41 Niobium Nb	42 Molybdenum Mo	43 Technetium Tc	44 Ruthenium Ru	45 Rhodium Rh
55 Caesium Cs	56 Barium Ba	57–71 Lanthanide series	72 Hafnium Hf	73 Tantalum Ta	74 Tungsten W	75 Rhenium Re	76 Osmium Os	77 Iridium Ir
87 Francium Fr	88 Radium Ra	89–103 Actinide series	104 Element 104	105 Element 105	106 Element 106	107 Element 107	108 Element 108	109 Element 109

| 57 Lanthanum La | 58 Cerium Ce | 59 Praseodymium Pr | 60 Neodymium Nd | 61 Prometheum Pm | 62 Samarium Sm | 63 Europium Eu | 64 Gadolinium Gd | 65 Terbium Tb |
| 89 Actinium Ac | 90 Thorium Th | 91 Protactinium Pa | 92 Uranium U | 93 Neptunium Np | 94 Plutonium Pu | 95 Americium Am | 96 Curium Cm | 97 Berkelium Bk |

► *Gold is a metallic element. It is soft but heavy, and forms few compounds.*

Gold bar

◄ *Uranium exists in several varieties, or isotopes. It is used as a nuclear fuel and in weapons.*

Nuclear explosion

▼ *By using the Periodic Table we can predict the properties of elements (or compounds of two or more elements), from what is known about neighbouring elements in the table. For example, on the far right, the noble gases (helium, neon, argon and others) are gases that do not combine easily with other elements to form compounds. They are all 'inert'. The first periodic table was drawn up by the Russian chemist Dmitri Mendeleyev (1834–1907). He charted the known elements and predicted the existence of undiscovered ones.*

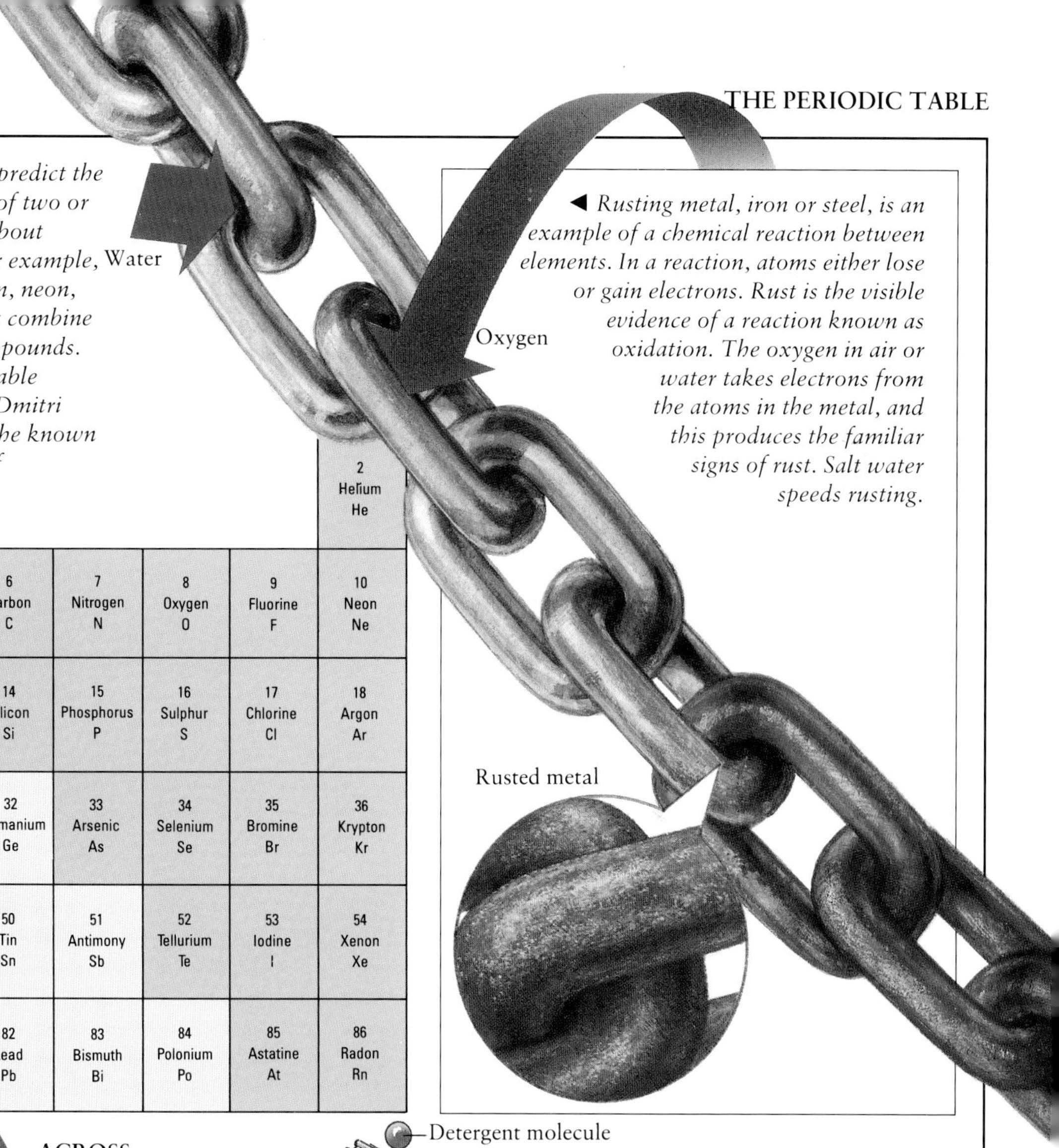

◄ *Rusting metal, iron or steel, is an example of a chemical reaction between elements. In a reaction, atoms either lose or gain electrons. Rust is the visible evidence of a reaction known as oxidation. The oxygen in air or water takes electrons from the atoms in the metal, and this produces the familiar signs of rust. Salt water speeds rusting.*

Water

Oxygen

Rusted metal

2 Helium He							

1 Hydrogen H		5 Boron B	6 Carbon C	7 Nitrogen N	8 Oxygen O	9 Fluorine F	10 Neon Ne
		13 Aluminium Al	14 Silicon Si	15 Phosphorus P	16 Sulphur S	17 Chlorine Cl	18 Argon Ar
28 Nickel Ni	29 Copper Cu	30 Zinc Zn	31 Gallium Ga	32 Germanium Ge	33 Arsenic As	34 Selenium Se	35 Bromine Br	36 Krypton Kr
46 Palladium Pd	47 Silver Ag	48 Cadmium Cd	49 Indium In	50 Tin Sn	51 Antimony Sb	52 Tellurium Te	53 Iodine I	54 Xenon Xe
78 Platinum Pt	79 Gold Au	80 Mercury Hg	81 Thallium Tl	82 Lead Pb	83 Bismuth Bi	84 Polonium Po	85 Astatine At	86 Radon Rn

ACROSS

Going across, the size of atoms increases; elements change from metals through metal-like elements to non-metals.

66 Dysprosium Dy	67 Holmium Ho	68 Erbium Er	69 Thulium Tm	70 Ytterbium Yb	71 Lutetium Lu
98 Californium Cf	99 Einsteinium Es	100 Fermium Fm	101 Mendelev-ium Md	102 Nobelium No	103 Lawrencium Lr

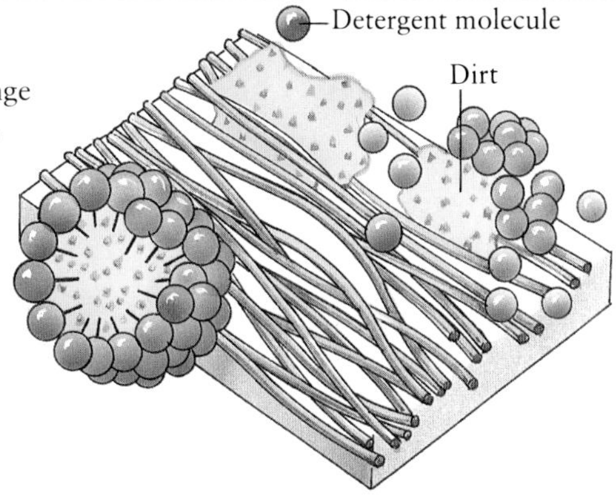

Detergent molecule

Dirt

◄ *Detergents are compounds of elements. They weaken the surface tension of the water, so that fabrics get thoroughly wet. The detergent molecules dislodge dirt particles by sticking to them and squeezing them out of the fibres.*

Half life of radon 222 = 4 days

Polonium 218 formed

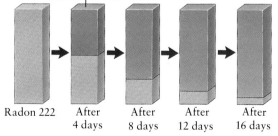

Radon 222   After 4 days   After 8 days   After 12 days   After 16 days

▲ *Certain kinds of atom give out radioactivity (alpha, beta and gamma radiation). A radioactive element decays into another element. The time taken for half of it to decay (from seconds to millions of years) is called its 'half-life'.*

▼ *Certain elements, such as uranium, are radioactive. The three forms of radioactivity are alpha, beta and gamma radiation. Their penetrating abilities are illustrated in the diagram below.*

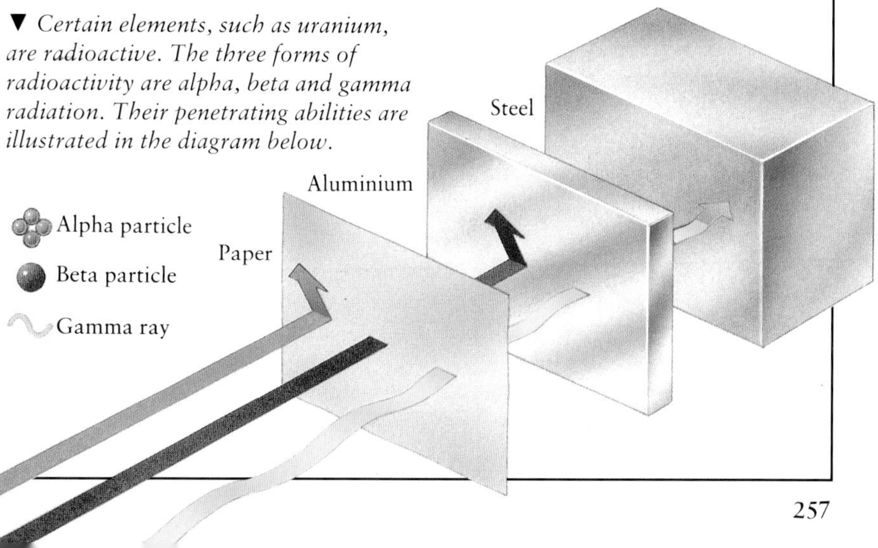

Alpha particle

Beta particle

Gamma ray

Steel

Aluminium

Paper

Solids, Liquids and Gases

The three states in which matter can exist under normal conditions are solid, liquid and gas. Solids have both shape and volume: their molecules are squashed together tightly. Liquids also have volume, but no shape. Their molecules are held together less tightly, so that a liquid will flow into a container. A gas has neither volume nor shape. Its molecules are spread very thinly and a gas will fill any container that encloses it. Many substances change their state when cooled or heated.

GAS
Because the molecules are only loosely held together, they move around faster than in liquids or solids.

CHANGES OF STATE

Most matter can exist as solid, liquid or gas. When matter is heated, it can change its state or 'phase'. The heat and pressure beneath a volcano *(below)* turn solid rock within the Earth into liquid lava or gases.

▲ *When a liquid is heated, it changes to a vapour or gas. This is evaporation. Steam from a volcano or boiling kettle is an example of water vapour.*

LIQUID
Molecules are more mobile than in a solid, less mobile than in a gas.

Warm air rises and cools

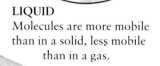
Condensation

SOLID
A solid is hard and rigid; atoms and molecules cluster in a regular pattern.

▲ *As a solid such as a rock is heated, its atoms vibrate more and move apart. The rigid structure breaks down and it melts. Nearly all solids melt eventually.*

▶ *Sublimation is a direct change from solid to gas, without a liquid stage between. Solid iodine does this when heated. Sublimation is part of the process of making freeze-dried coffee.*

▲ *Condensation is the process by which a gas or vapour becomes liquid when cooled. Clouds form when air containing water vapour cools: the water condenses into droplets.*

MIXTURES

Mixtures are different from compounds because the substances in them are not chemically bonded. For example, iron filings mixed with sulphur can be separated using a magnet. But heating them produces a compound, iron sulphide, from which a magnet cannot pick out the iron. Solutions and colloids (aerosols, emulsions and foams) are all mixtures.

▲ *An aerosol is a cloud of fine liquid or solid particles suspended in a gas.*

▼ *Milk and paint are emulsions; colloids of two liquids whose particles are evenly mixed without being in solution.*

◄ *Colloids are liquids or gases containing larger particles than solutions. Butter, foam and toothpaste are all examples of colloids.*

THE THREE GAS LAWS

1 Gas pressure doubles if its volume is halved and its temperature stays constant (unchanged). The molecules are squashed together.
2 Gas volume doubles if its temperature doubles and the pressure stays the same. The molecules move faster but in more space.
3 Gas pressure doubles if the volume stays the same and the temperature doubles. The molecules move faster in the same space.

Temp.

Pressure

▼ *Most liquids contract as they cool and freeze. Water is unusual in contracting until it reaches 4°C, and then expanding as it freezes, at 0°C.*

DISTILLATION

A solution is a liquid mixture. One substance, called the solute, dissolves in a liquid, the solvent. When a solution (for example, salt and water) is boiled in a flask, vapour is given off.

▼ *In a condensing vessel, the vapour cools and becomes a liquid. Salt crystals are left in the flask. This apparatus is called a still; the process is distillation.*

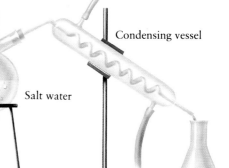

Condensing vessel

Salt water

Distilled water

Energy

Energy is all around us. We can sometimes see it as light, hear it as sound and feel it as heat. All these are forms of energy. Energy is the ability to do work. The spring in a toy car provides energy to drive the car. A torch battery gives the energy needed to light the bulb. All living things on the Earth depend on the Sun for their energy. Energy comes from matter. It is everywhere in the Universe. It can be neither created nor destroyed; it can only be changed into a different form.

THE ENERGY CYCLE

Energy from the Sun is absorbed by the sea and land. Plants use light energy to grow, and animals that eat plants convert energy for their own use. Decaying plants and animals became fossil fuels; we use the energy from these fuels for light and power.

▼ The Sun is powered by the energy from nuclear fusion in which hydrogen atoms combine to form helium.

Nuclear fusion

Radiant light energy from the Sun is absorbed by living things

We turn the energy from food into the energy of movement

▲ Kinetic energy is the energy of movement. Any moving body, such as a child on a swing, has kinetic (moving) energy. By the time she has reached position A the child has maximum potential (stored) energy; gravity then swings her to B, the point at which she has maximum kinetic energy.

Fossil fuels store the chemical energy of ancient plants and animals

JOULES

The joule is the SI unit of measurement of work or energy. One joule of work is done when a force of one newton moves through a distance of one metre. The joule is named after the English scientist James Joule (1818–1889).

▶ Coal, oil and natural gas store energy that came originally from the Sun. Coal stores the chemical energy of the ancient plants that lived and died in the prehistoric coal-forests; oil and gas store energy from the bodies of tiny dead sea creatures.

1 joule effort

1 metre

1 newton

Energy and matter are never destroyed. Energy released into space may one day help form a new star.

THE CONSERVATION OF ENERGY

The law of conservation of energy says that energy is never created or destroyed. Energy is constantly changing its state, from one form to another. Every time it is used, energy is converted. For example, steam from water heated in a boiler can be released as the kinetic energy of a spinning turbine, which can be changed into electrical energy in a generator; this energy, in turn, can power devices that produce sound, heat and light.

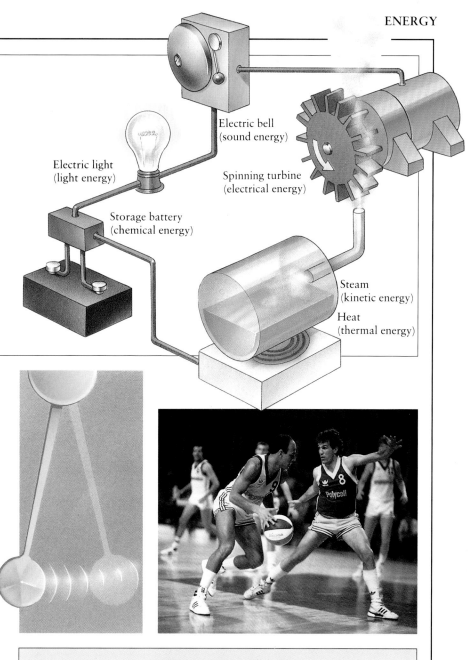

Electric bell (sound energy)

Electric light (light energy)

Spinning turbine (electrical energy)

Storage battery (chemical energy)

Steam (kinetic energy)

Heat (thermal energy)

Chemical energy

Radiant energy

...r ...ns ...coal, ...erting heat energy ...ctrical energy

▶ *Potential energy is stored energy as in a pendulum weight at the top of its swing. Gravity makes it swing, work is done, and potential energy becomes kinetic energy. A simple pendulum takes the same time to swing, no matter how heavy its weight. A basketball about to be thrown has potential energy. When the player passes the ball, it has kinetic energy.*

◀ *Chemical energy is released in a chemical reaction, such as burning. Our digested food releases chemical energy for use by the body. Heat is thermal energy. The hotter an object is, the faster its molecules move around. Heat is also a form of kinetic energy. Radiant energy is transmitted as electromagnetic radiation, such as light from the Sun or a light bulb.*

FACTS ABOUT ENERGY

• The Sun is an immense source of energy. Scientists calculate that every year the Earth receives from the Sun an amount of energy equal to burning 227 thousand billion tonnes of coal.

• Energy always ends up as heat energy. A bouncing ball (with kinetic energy) slowly rolls to a standstill. But the energy that made it bounce has not been lost. Kinetic energy changes to heat energy as the ball rubs against the air and the ground (friction).

• Most energy loss is through heat escaping. Even the most efficient car engine wastes about 60 percent of the energy in the fuel it burns. An electric lamp is even less efficient; it turns only about 20 percent of the electricity it uses into light. The rest is 'lost' as heat.

• Every year we consume energy equivalent to burning two billion tonnes of coal. Fossil fuels (coal, oil, gas) will eventually run out. Alternative energy sources (wind, tide, solar power) may not be able to replace them. Just 135 tonnes of deuterium (found in the oceans), one of the hydrogen-like fuels used in nuclear fusion, would give the same amount of energy as two billion tonnes of coal.

Heat

Scientists once believed that heat was an invisible fluid. Not until the late 1700s did Benjamin Thompson show that heat is a form of energy. To make atoms move faster you have to add energy, often in the form of heat. A large pan of boiling water contains more heat than another pan with only a little boiling water, though the water in each is at the same temperature: 100°C. Heat can move from one substance to another in one of three ways: by convection, by radiation and by conduction.

100°C   373 K   212°F
   350 K
50°C
  37°C   309 K   100°F / 98.6°F
  300 K
0°C   273 K   32°F

▲ *Temperature measures how hot a substance is. There are three main temperature scales: Fahrenheit, Celsius (centigrade) and Kelvin. Here the three are compared at normal (human) body temperature.*

Convection

◄ *Convection takes place only in liquids (for example, water in a kettle) and gases (for example, air warmed by a heat source such as a fire or radiator). When a liquid or gas is heated, it expands and becomes less dense. Warm air above the radiator rises and cool air moves in to take its place, creating a convection current.*

Radiation

◄ *Radiation is the movement of heat through the air. Heat from a match sets molecules of air moving and rays of heat spread out around the heat source.*

Radiator

Conduction

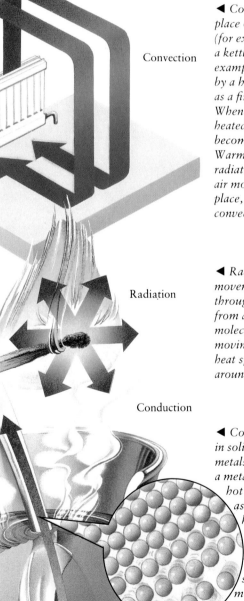

◄ *Conduction occurs in solids such as metals. The handle of a metal spoon left in hot liquid warms up, as molecules at the heated end move faster and collide with their neighbours, setting them moving. The heat travels through the metal, which is a good conductor of heat.*

Metal spoon conducts heat

▲ *Insulation keeps heat in houses during cold weather, and out during hot weather. Plastic, wood and air-filled spaces are good insulators.*

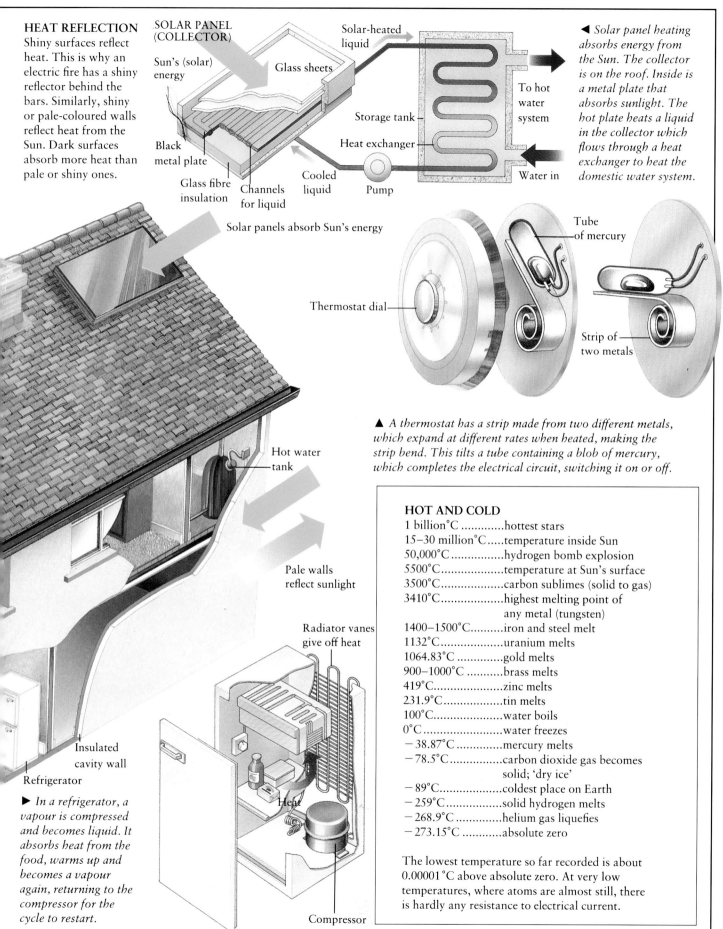

HEAT REFLECTION

Shiny surfaces reflect heat. This is why an electric fire has a shiny reflector behind the bars. Similarly, shiny or pale-coloured walls reflect heat from the Sun. Dark surfaces absorb more heat than pale or shiny ones.

SOLAR PANEL (COLLECTOR)

Sun's (solar) energy

Glass sheets

Black metal plate

Glass fibre insulation

Channels for liquid

Cooled liquid

Pump

Solar-heated liquid

Storage tank

Heat exchanger

To hot water system

Water in

◀ *Solar panel heating absorbs energy from the Sun. The collector is on the roof. Inside is a metal plate that absorbs sunlight. The hot plate heats a liquid in the collector which flows through a heat exchanger to heat the domestic water system.*

Solar panels absorb Sun's energy

Hot water tank

Insulated cavity wall

Refrigerator

▶ *In a refrigerator, a vapour is compressed and becomes liquid. It absorbs heat from the food, warms up and becomes a vapour again, returning to the compressor for the cycle to restart.*

Pale walls reflect sunlight

Radiator vanes give off heat

Heat

Compressor

Thermostat dial

Tube of mercury

Strip of two metals

▲ *A thermostat has a strip made from two different metals, which expand at different rates when heated, making the strip bend. This tilts a tube containing a blob of mercury, which completes the electrical circuit, switching it on or off.*

HOT AND COLD

1 billion°C	hottest stars
15–30 million°C	temperature inside Sun
50,000°C	hydrogen bomb explosion
5500°C	temperature at Sun's surface
3500°C	carbon sublimes (solid to gas)
3410°C	highest melting point of any metal (tungsten)
1400–1500°C	iron and steel melt
1132°C	uranium melts
1064.83°C	gold melts
900–1000°C	brass melts
419°C	zinc melts
231.9°C	tin melts
100°C	water boils
0°C	water freezes
−38.87°C	mercury melts
−78.5°C	carbon dioxide gas becomes solid; 'dry ice'
−89°C	coldest place on Earth
−259°C	solid hydrogen melts
−268.9°C	helium gas liquefies
−273.15°C	absolute zero

The lowest temperature so far recorded is about 0.00001°C above absolute zero. At very low temperatures, where atoms are almost still, there is hardly any resistance to electrical current.

Fuels

Fuels are materials with energy stored in them. Burning the fuel releases the energy as heat. This heat is used to drive machines. Burning (combustion) is a chemical action. Carbon and hydrogen in the fuel combine with oxygen in the air, releasing energy as heat and light. The fuels we burn include coal, oil, gas and wood. Their energy was originally absorbed from the Sun. Nuclear reactors use a different fuel – by splitting atoms of unstable substances such as uranium and plutonium, energy is released.

▼ *Until the 1950s many millions of people, particularly in Europe, burned coal on household fires. Coal is no longer such an important domestic fuel. Most of the world's coal is now burned in power stations that generate electricity.*

▼ *Coal mining is a worldwide industry. Most coal is either dug from close to the surface (drift or open-cast mining), or brought up from deep seams, or layers, hundreds of metres under the ground.*

▼ *An offshore oil platform. Oil and gas are found beneath the desert, under ice and in the ocean. Oil reserves may last for only 30 years, gas for 40 to 50 years.*

▲ *Burning waste could be an alternative energy source. A power station in California generates electricity by burning old tyres. The station's fuel supply is 40 million tyres, enough to provide heat to drive the generators for ten years.*

OIL, or petroleum, is found as crude oil, which is refined to produce fuels such as petrol and diesel oil. Also the raw material for petrochemicals and plastics.

COAL occurs as lignite or brown coal, bituminous, sub-bituminous and anthracite. Bituminous is used most. Anthracite gives most heat but burns slowly.

GAS: natural gas is mostly methane, but also contains butane and propane. These gases become liquid when pressurized and are usually stored in liquid form.

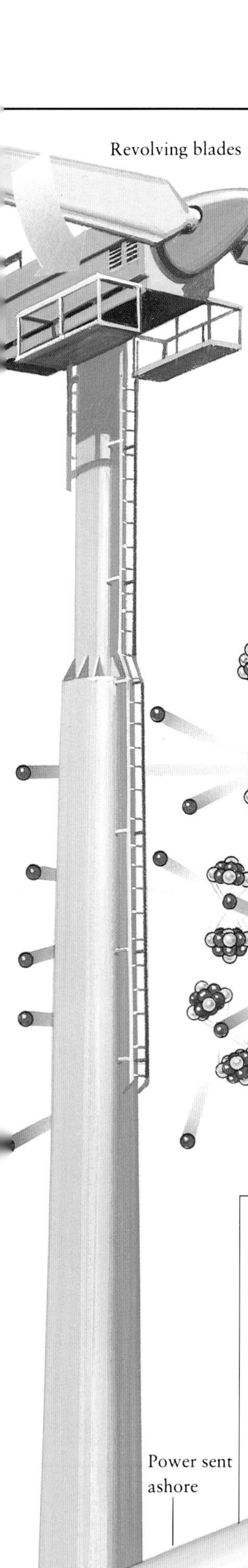

Revolving blades

Direction of wind

Negative terminal

Sunlight

Light causes electrons to move through layers of solar cells, creating an electric current

▲ *The wind can provide a free and constant source of energy. The modern wind turbine generator, often grouped in a wind 'farm', is much more efficient than its ancestor, the windmill.*

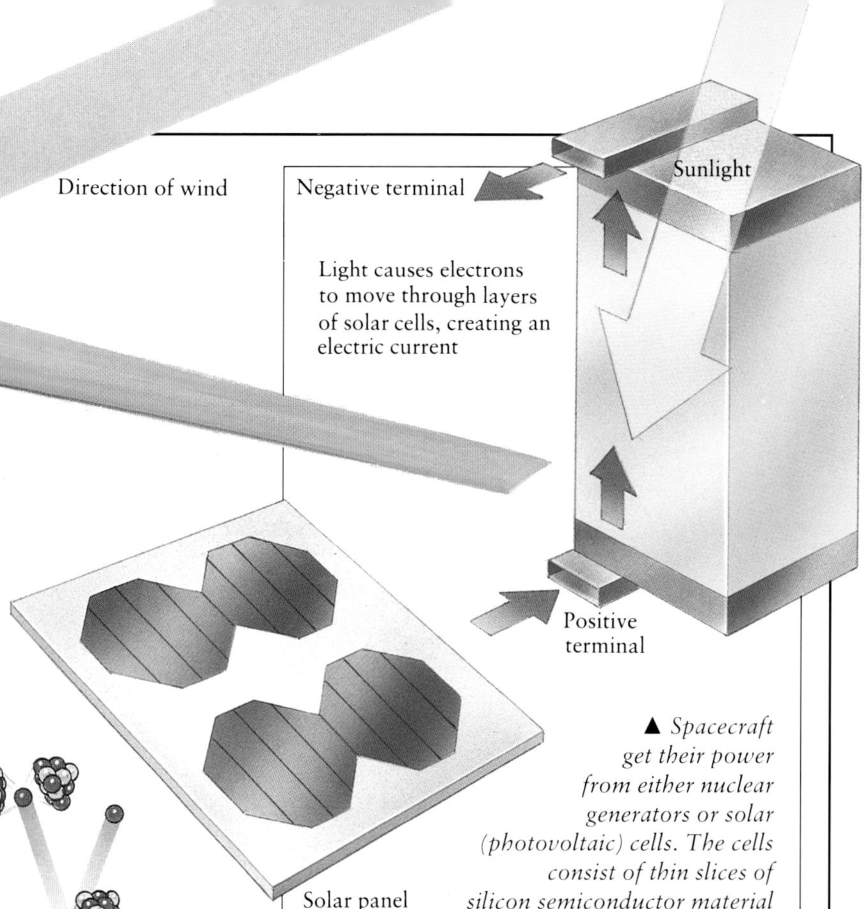

Positive terminal

▲ *Spacecraft get their power from either nuclear generators or solar (photovoltaic) cells. The cells consist of thin slices of silicon semiconductor material which converts the energy in the Sun's rays into electrical energy.*

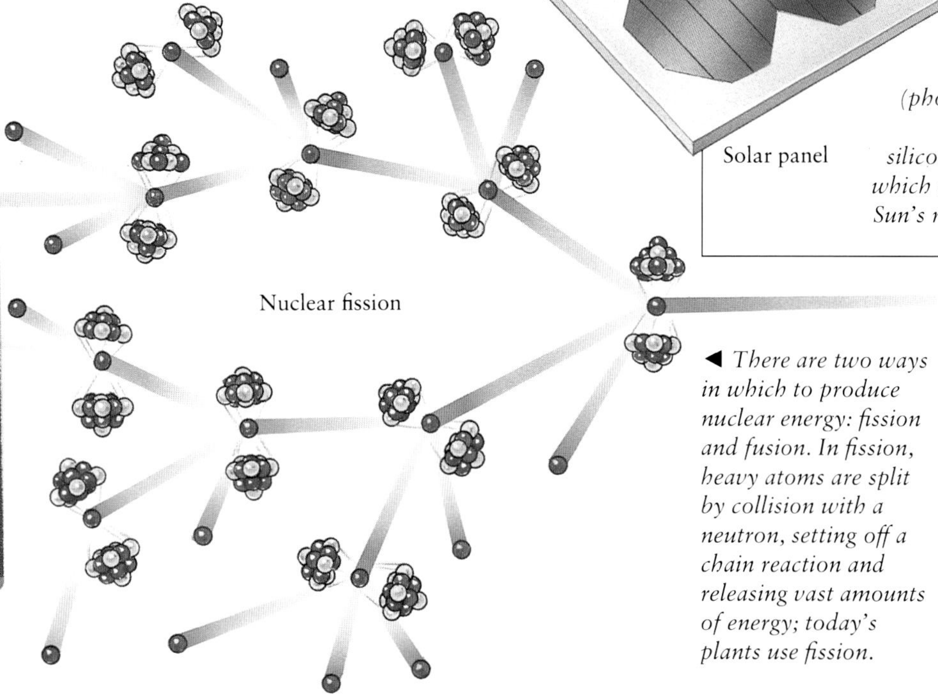

Solar panel

Nuclear fission

◄ *There are two ways in which to produce nuclear energy: fission and fusion. In fission, heavy atoms are split by collision with a neutron, setting off a chain reaction and releasing vast amounts of energy; today's plants use fission.*

Fusion technology mimics the Sun itself, joining or fusing together two light atomic nuclei. The result is a release of energy, far greater than from fission.

'Ducks' nod up and down

▼ *The daily movement of the tides and the motion of ocean waves offer other alternative energy sources. This type of wave-generator converts the bobbing motion of the 'ducks', or floats, into mechanical energy to drive electricity generators.*

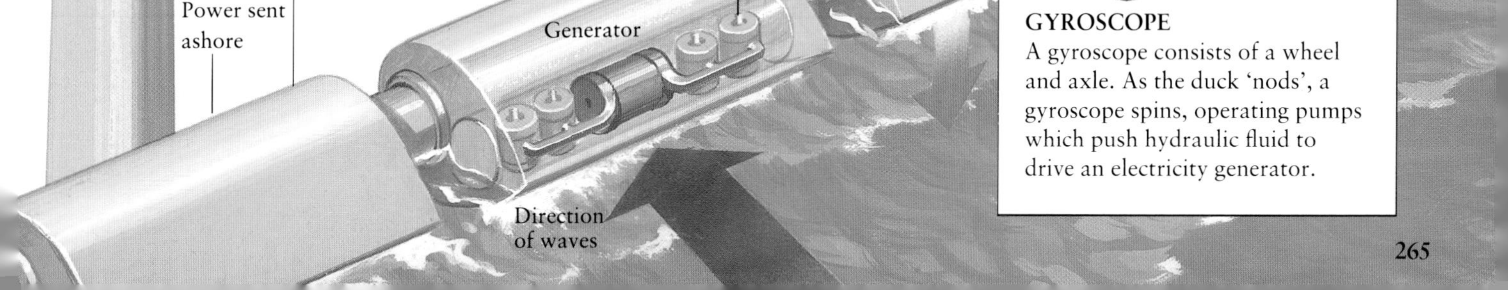

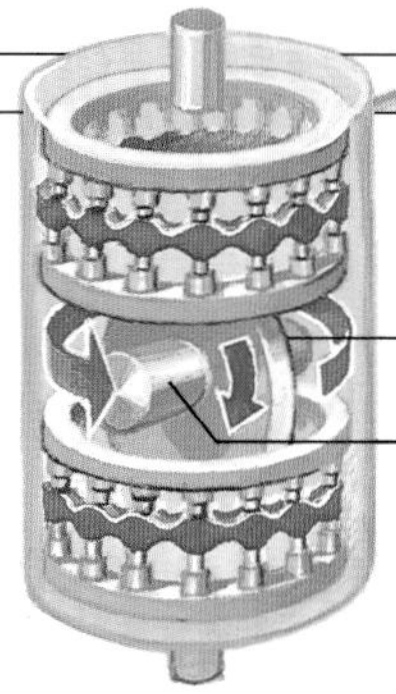

Gyroscopes with hydraulic motors

Wheel

Axle

Power sent ashore

Generator

GYROSCOPE
A gyroscope consists of a wheel and axle. As the duck 'nods', a gyroscope spins, operating pumps which push hydraulic fluid to drive an electricity generator.

Direction of waves

FORCE AND MOTION

Gravity and Mass

There are four basic forces that control how everything in the Universe behaves. They are gravity, electromagnetism, and two subatomic forces (strong and weak) that control the atoms of which all matter is made. Everything in the Universe is either at rest or in motion. Motion is change of position, and a force is needed either to start an object moving or to stop it. A force pushes or pulls an object in a particular direction. The most obvious forces, known as mechanical forces, act directly on an object (for example, a person pushing a barrow, or a nail holding a picture on a wall). Other forces, such as magnetism and gravity – the force that pulls objects downwards towards the Earth – act at a distance. The force that presses evenly on a surface is pressure; the air exerts a pressure of one kilogram per square centimetre all over the Earth's surface.

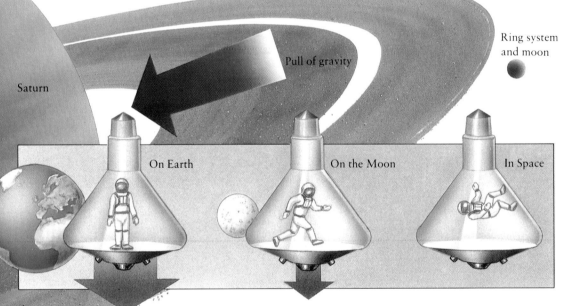

Saturn

Pull of gravity

Ring system and moon

On Earth

On the Moon

In Space

◀ Gravity is the force that pulls everything on Earth towards the ground and makes things feel heavy. Gravity keeps the rings of Saturn in orbit around the planet.

◀ As they escape the influence of the Earth's gravity, astronauts become weightless. On the Moon the pull of gravity is weaker than on Earth, so an astronaut there would seem to weigh less.

FACTS ABOUT GRAVITY AND MASS

• When the Moon and Sun pull together on the same side of the Earth, ocean tides are highest (spring tides).
• The mass of an object is the amount of material it contains. A body with greater mass has more inertia; it needs a greater force to accelerate. That is why a bus is harder to push than a car.
• Weight depends on the force of gravity, but mass does not.

▶ When an object spins around another (for example, a satellite orbiting the Earth) it is pushed outwards. Two forces are at work here: centrifugal (pushing outwards) and centripetal (pulling inwards). If you whirl a ball around you on a string, you pull it inwards (centripetal force). The ball seems to pull outwards (centrifugal force) and if released will fly off in a straight line.

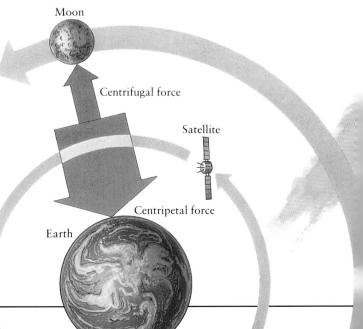

Moon

Centrifugal force

Satellite

Centripetal force

Earth

NEWTON'S LAWS

In 1687, the English scientist, Isaac Newton *(left)*, published three rules about force and motion. He realized that forces act on one another. His laws of motion are set out below.

1 Every object remains stopped or goes on moving at a steady rate in a straight line unless acted upon by another force. This is the inertia principle.

2 The amount of force needed to make an object change its speed depends on the mass of the object and the amount of acceleration or deceleration required.

3 To every action there is an equal and opposite reaction. When a body is pushed one way by a force, another force pushes back with equal strength.

▶ *Acceleration means increasing speed. Gravity produces a standard acceleration of 1 G. Jet fighters and spacecraft subject pilots to greater acceleration. At 2 G pilots feels twice as heavy as normal. At 5 G they may pass out.*

▲ *A rocket motor is an example of Newton's third law of motion in action. The burning fuel forces gas backwards (action). The spacecraft is forced in the opposite direction (reaction).*

▲ *A spacecraft accelerates to a high speed after its launch. To escape the Earth's gravity a spacecraft must reach a speed of 11.2 km/s (about 40,000 km/h). This is called the 'escape velocity'.*

▶ *Ocean tides are caused by the gravitational pull of the Sun and Moon on the Earth. The land is also pulled, but the water movement is more apparent.*

Earth

Pull of Moon causing tides

Moon

GRAVITY

Gravity makes all falling bodies accelerate at a constant 9.8 m/s. In the Earth's atmosphere air resistance slows acceleration. Only on the airless Moon would a feather and a hammer fall to the ground together.

Motion

All motion is relative. So when a car passes a house it is not strictly true to say that only the car is moving; the house is moving too, as the Earth itself moves. The car is moving relative to the Earth. The Earth is moving relative to the Sun. To move at all, the car must overcome the forces of gravity (holding it down) and friction – the force that resists the movement of surfaces in contact. Only in space, where there is no air, is there no friction to slow down a moving object.

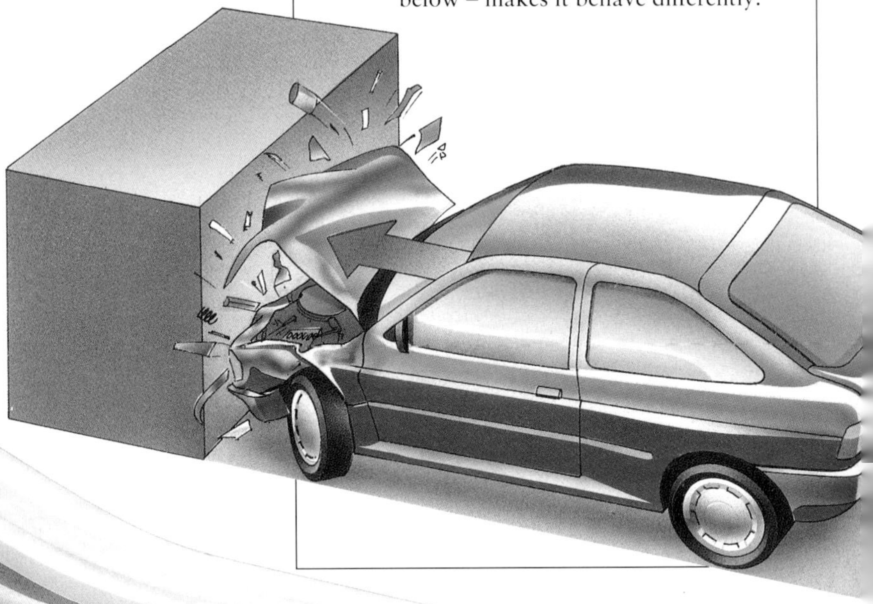

▼ *Wind resistance is a form of friction. Any vehicle must push aside the air in front of it. Car designers aim for a smooth, or streamlined, body shape so that airflow created by the forward motion slips easily over and around the vehicle. Streamlined vehicles use less fuel.*

Airflow over
streamlined vehicle

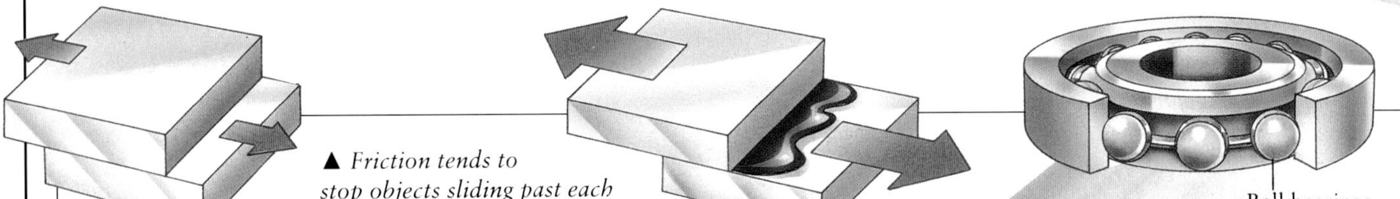

INERTIA
A body with a large mass is harder to start and also harder to stop. A heavy truck travelling at 50 km/h needs more powerful brakes to stop its motion than a car travelling at the same speed. Inertia is the tendency of an object either to stay still or to move steadily in a straight line, unless another force – such as the brick wall stopping the vehicle in the illustration below – makes it behave differently.

▲ *Friction tends to stop objects sliding past each other. Lubrication (oil or grease) reduces friction. Ball or roller bearings in machines ensure that moving surfaces are not in direct contact.*

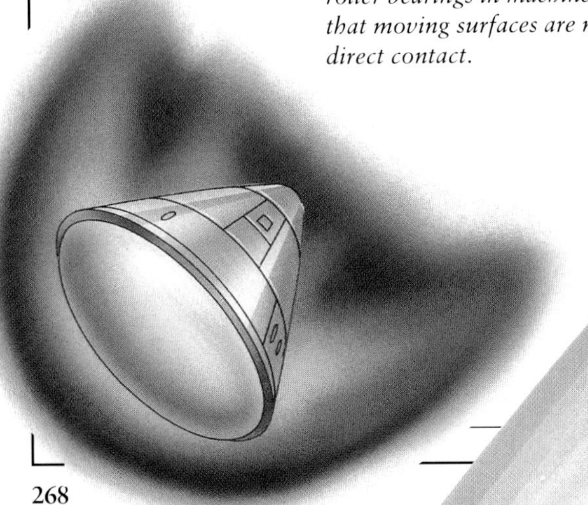

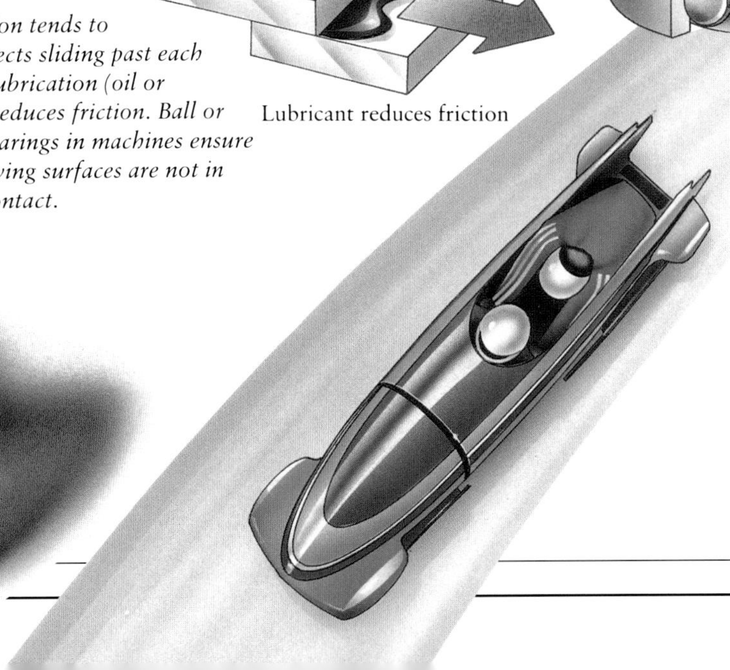

Lubricant reduces friction

Ball bearings

◄ *Friction produces heat. A spacecraft glows red-hot as it re-enters the thick atmosphere of the Earth. Without friction, our feet would not grip the ground. The runners of a sledge slide by melting the ice beneath them, reducing friction.*

► Speed is the rate at which a moving object changes position – how far it moves in a fixed time. Velocity is speed in a particular direction. If either speed or direction changes, velocity changes too. Riders on a fairground ride travel at a constant speed, but their velocity changes continually because they keep pointing in a different direction.

FACTS ABOUT MOTION

- The study of the effects of moving objects on gases, liquids or solids at rest or in motion is called mechanics.
- According to the theories of relativity, the greatest possible velocity is the velocity of light, about 300 million metres per second.
- A car travelling at 50 km/h needs about 23 m to come to a stop. A car travelling at 80 km/h needs 53 m to stop. The faster car has greater momentum.
- A perpetual motion machine is supposed to run for ever. So far, no one has invented one that works. All machines need energy input to keep them working and overcome friction. Even an orbiting satellite in space (where there is no friction) is eventually brought down from orbit by the pull of the Earth's gravity.

► Momentum is the sum of a moving object's mass (its weight on Earth) multiplied by its velocity (speed and direction). You may hardly feel a softball thrown gently at you; but a ball hit hard by a softball bat moves faster and gains momentum – so you feel it! One pool ball hitting another transfers momentum to the target ball and sets it moving.

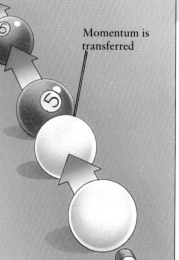

Momentum is transferred

Machines

Machines are devices that make work easier either by reducing the effort needed, or making it simpler to use effort. A machine need not have moving parts – an earth ramp is a machine, and so is a wedge used to split logs. The oldest known machines are the simplest. There are six basic kinds. The lever, the pulley, and the wheel and axle form one group; the inclined or sloping plane, the wedge and the screw make up the other group. These were the keys that unlocked the marvels of technology.

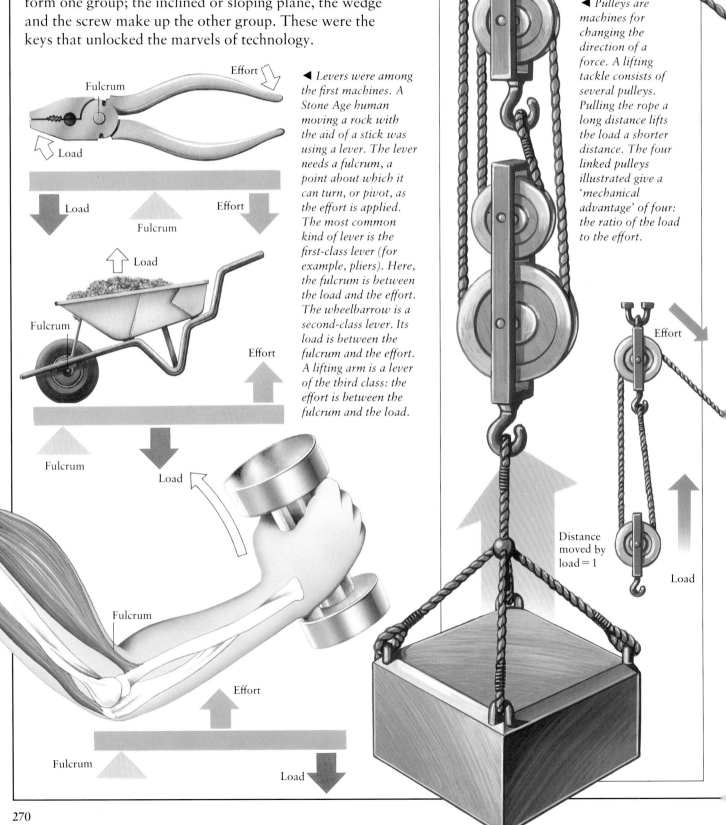

Effort

Fulcrum

Load

Load

Effort

Fulcrum

Load

Fulcrum

Effort

Load

Fulcrum

Fulcrum

Load

Effort

Fulcrum

Load

◀ *Levers were among the first machines. A Stone Age human moving a rock with the aid of a stick was using a lever. The lever needs a fulcrum, a point about which it can turn, or pivot, as the effort is applied. The most common kind of lever is the first-class lever (for example, pliers). Here, the fulcrum is between the load and the effort. The wheelbarrow is a second-class lever. Its load is between the fulcrum and the effort. A lifting arm is a lever of the third class: the effort is between the fulcrum and the load.*

Distance moved by effort = 4

Mechanical advantage = 4

◀ *Pulleys are machines for changing the direction of a force. A lifting tackle consists of several pulleys. Pulling the rope a long distance lifts the load a shorter distance. The four linked pulleys illustrated give a 'mechanical advantage' of four: the ratio of the load to the effort.*

Effort

Distance moved by load = 1

Load

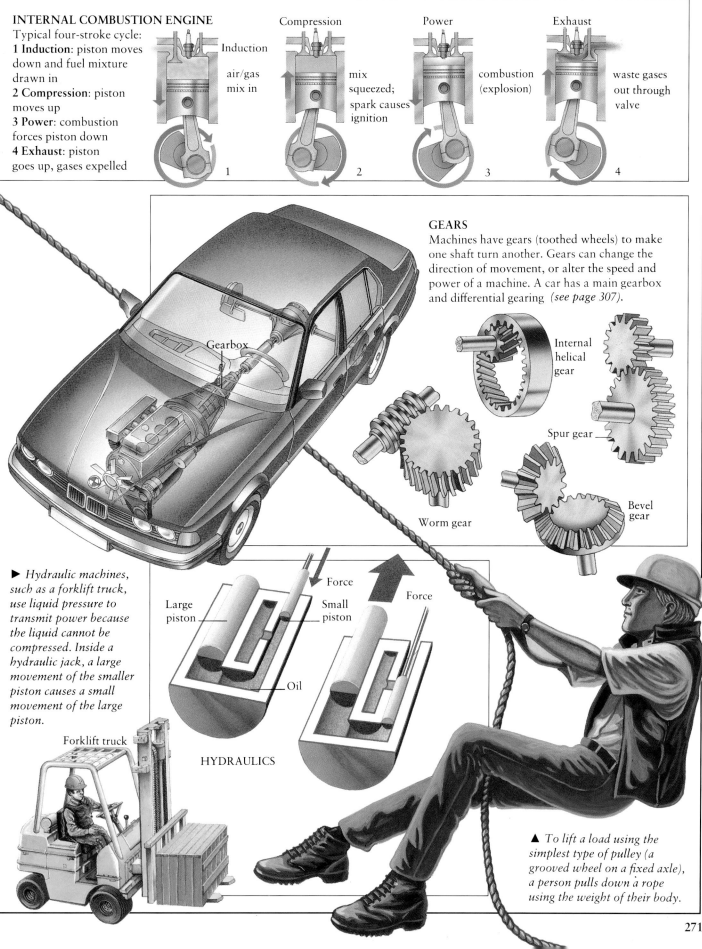

INTERNAL COMBUSTION ENGINE

Typical four-stroke cycle:
1 Induction: piston moves down and fuel mixture drawn in
2 Compression: piston moves up
3 Power: combustion forces piston down
4 Exhaust: piston goes up, gases expelled

Induction
air/gas mix in
1

Compression
mix squeezed; spark causes ignition
2

Power
combustion (explosion)
3

Exhaust
waste gases out through valve
4

Gearbox

GEARS

Machines have gears (toothed wheels) to make one shaft turn another. Gears can change the direction of movement, or alter the speed and power of a machine. A car has a main gearbox and differential gearing *(see page 307)*.

Internal helical gear

Spur gear

Worm gear

Bevel gear

► *Hydraulic machines, such as a forklift truck, use liquid pressure to transmit power because the liquid cannot be compressed. Inside a hydraulic jack, a large movement of the smaller piston causes a small movement of the large piston.*

Force

Force

Large piston

Small piston

Oil

HYDRAULICS

Forklift truck

▲ *To lift a load using the simplest type of pulley (a grooved wheel on a fixed axle), a person pulls down a rope using the weight of their body.*

Flying and Floating

A balloon rises because the gas inside it is less dense than the air around it. A bird and an airliner are both heavier than air. To fly, they produce an upward force, called lift, to overcome their weight. They also need to generate a forward thrust to overcome the drag or resistance of the air. A ship floats in water because (being hollow and filled with air) it has a lower density than the water. Any floating object displaces its own weight of the fluid it is floating in.

Thrust

Drag

Lift

Gravity

Airflow faster

Airflow slower

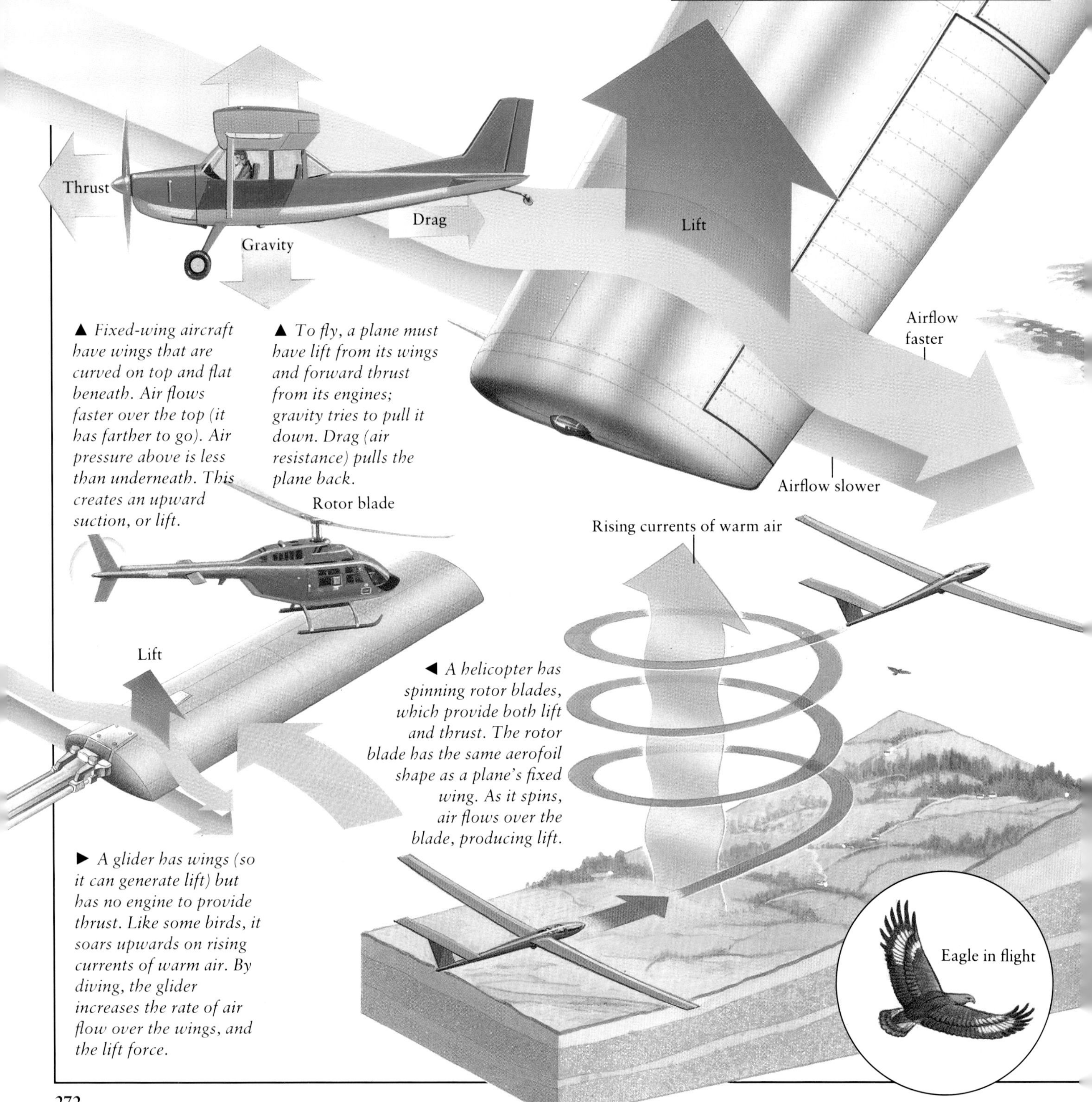

▲ Fixed-wing aircraft have wings that are curved on top and flat beneath. Air flows faster over the top (it has farther to go). Air pressure above is less than underneath. This creates an upward suction, or lift.

▲ To fly, a plane must have lift from its wings and forward thrust from its engines; gravity tries to pull it down. Drag (air resistance) pulls the plane back.

Rotor blade

Rising currents of warm air

Lift

◀ A helicopter has spinning rotor blades, which provide both lift and thrust. The rotor blade has the same aerofoil shape as a plane's fixed wing. As it spins, air flows over the blade, producing lift.

▶ A glider has wings (so it can generate lift) but has no engine to provide thrust. Like some birds, it soars upwards on rising currents of warm air. By diving, the glider increases the rate of air flow over the wings, and the lift force.

Eagle in flight

▲ *Airships are power-driven balloons filled with a lighter-than-air gas such as helium. They are slow but can lift considerable loads.*

► *There are two kinds of balloon: filled with a lighter-than-air gas, or with hot air. In a hot-air balloon, a gas burner warms the air inside the balloon. The hot air is less dense than the surrounding air, so the balloon rises.*

Hot-air balloon

Weight of ship

Upthrust of water (buoyancy)

◄ *A ship floats because the buoyancy (the upward force of the water around it) balances the ship's weight. All floating objects displace or push aside their own weight of water. A huge metal ship floats because it has so much light air inside its hull.*

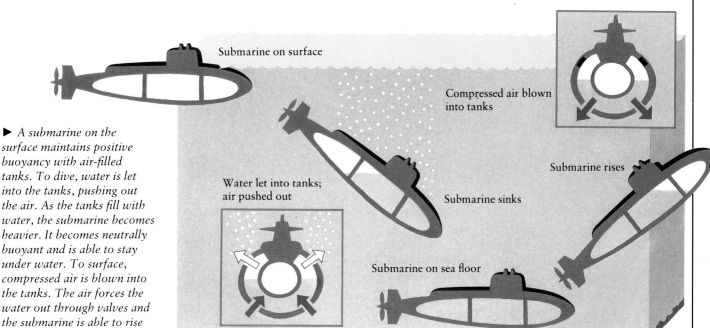

Submarine on surface

Compressed air blown into tanks

Submarine rises

Water let into tanks; air pushed out

Submarine sinks

Submarine on sea floor

► *A submarine on the surface maintains positive buoyancy with air-filled tanks. To dive, water is let into the tanks, pushing out the air. As the tanks fill with water, the submarine becomes heavier. It becomes neutrally buoyant and is able to stay under water. To surface, compressed air is blown into the tanks. The air forces the water out through valves and the submarine is able to rise to the surface.*

273

SPACE AND TIME

Counting and Measuring

Human curiosity about space and time began when our earliest human ancestors gazed at the stars and wondered about the daily miracle of sunrise. Cave paintings made by prehistoric hunters show animals hit many times by spears. The artist knew the difference between 'one' and 'many'. Keeping count of things became important when people became farmers. From counting on fingers and toes, people progressed to tally-sticks (sticks with notches cut in them) and eventually to number-systems, with which people could record measurements and calculate. The numbers we use today came from the Arabs, who in turn developed them from the Hindus of India. The system for writing numbers that we take for granted, based on powers of 10, is known as the base 10 or decimal system and did not become widespread in Europe until after about AD 1100.

Spring – sowing

Summer – growth

Winter – plough in stubble

Autumn – harvest

◀ *Early farmers recorded the changing seasons, and in this way made the first calendars, based on either the seasons or the phases of the Moon.*

DEVELOPMENTS IN COUNTING
4000 BC: Babylonians wrote numbers from left to right, grouping them in tens
Before 3000 BC: Egyptians used measuring rods and balance scales for weighing things
1400 BC: Decimals used in China
300 BC: Euclid's *Elements* summarized Greek geometry
AD 600: Zero (0) used in China and India
700: First mechanical clocks in China
1500s: Negative (−) numbers first used in Europe
1789: France adopted the metric system
1960: Modern SI units adopted

▼ *The Babylonians (who lived in what is now Iraq) used these standard weights and notched tally-sticks (for counting). As trade developed, people needed accurate measurements to make sure that buyer and seller agreed. Surprisingly accurate scales were used for weighing.*

MEASURING

Over 5000 years ago, the builders of the pyramids in Egypt had to measure length, to know how many stones they needed, and how to drive shafts accurately through the huge structures. The Egyptians also used delicate weighing scales, to weigh gold and precious stones.

Length

Weight

Standard Babylonian weights

Notched tally-stick

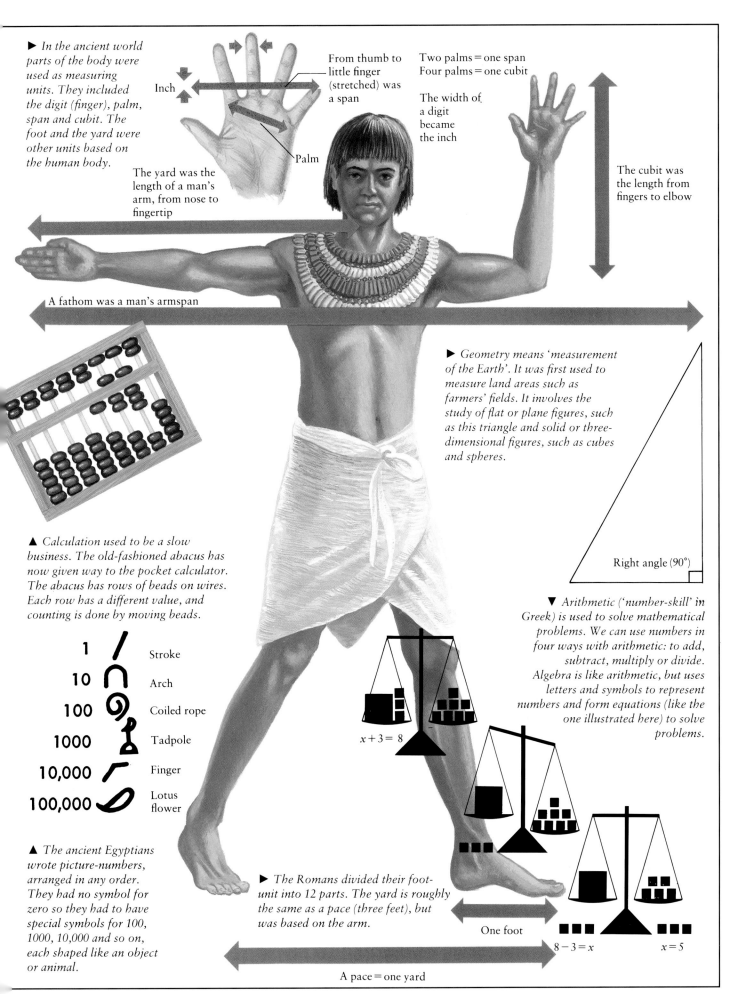

► In the ancient world parts of the body were used as measuring units. They included the digit (finger), palm, span and cubit. The foot and the yard were other units based on the human body.

Inch

From thumb to little finger (stretched) was a span

Palm

Two palms = one span
Four palms = one cubit

The width of a digit became the inch

The yard was the length of a man's arm, from nose to fingertip

The cubit was the length from fingers to elbow

A fathom was a man's armspan

► Geometry means 'measurement of the Earth'. It was first used to measure land areas such as farmers' fields. It involves the study of flat or plane figures, such as this triangle and solid or three-dimensional figures, such as cubes and spheres.

Right angle (90°)

▲ Calculation used to be a slow business. The old-fashioned abacus has now given way to the pocket calculator. The abacus has rows of beads on wires. Each row has a different value, and counting is done by moving beads.

1	/	Stroke
10	∩	Arch
100	ϱ	Coiled rope
1000		Tadpole
10,000		Finger
100,000		Lotus flower

▲ The ancient Egyptians wrote picture-numbers, arranged in any order. They had no symbol for zero so they had to have special symbols for 100, 1000, 10,000 and so on, each shaped like an object or animal.

▼ Arithmetic ('number-skill' in Greek) is used to solve mathematical problems. We can use numbers in four ways with arithmetic: to add, subtract, multiply or divide. Algebra is like arithmetic, but uses letters and symbols to represent numbers and form equations (like the one illustrated here) to solve problems.

$x + 3 = 8$

$8 - 3 = x$

$x = 5$

► The Romans divided their foot-unit into 12 parts. The yard is roughly the same as a pace (three feet), but was based on the arm.

One foot

A pace = one yard

Mathematics

People have found mathematics useful for thousands of years, ever since the Egyptians and Babylonians used it to work out a calendar (as a guide to crop-sowing). The peoples of Asia were the first masters of mathematics, developing key branches of mathematics such as arithmetic, geometry and algebra. 'Pure' maths has to do with theory; 'applied' maths deals with problems in engineering, science, business or any other activity when we need to calculate, measure and predict.

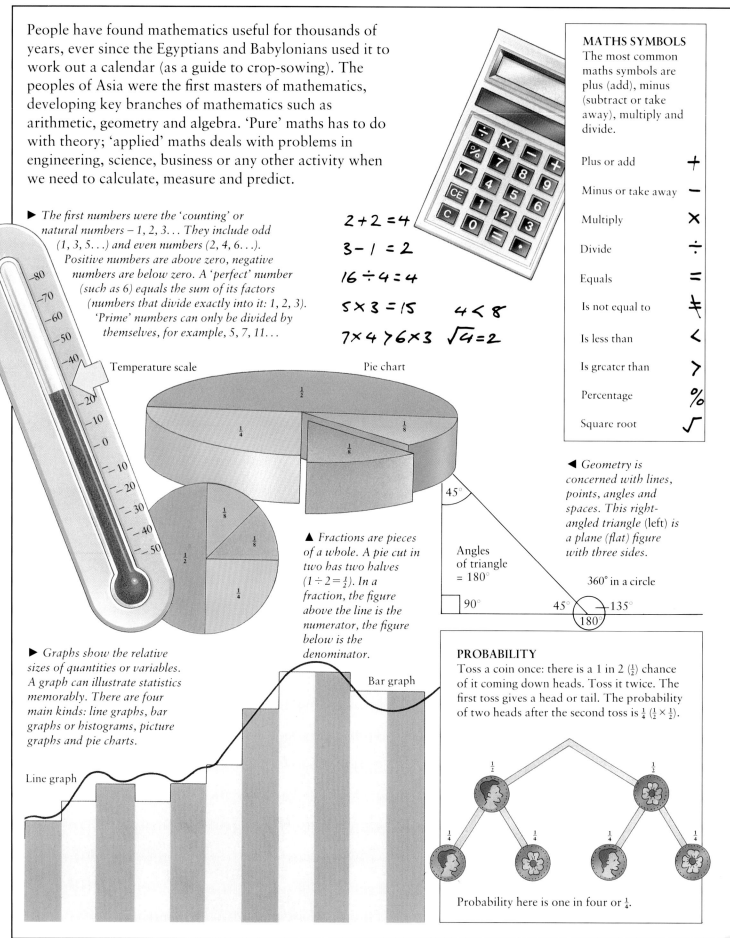

▶ The first numbers were the 'counting' or natural numbers – 1, 2, 3... They include odd (1, 3, 5...) and even numbers (2, 4, 6...). Positive numbers are above zero, negative numbers are below zero. A 'perfect' number (such as 6) equals the sum of its factors (numbers that divide exactly into it: 1, 2, 3). 'Prime' numbers can only be divided by themselves, for example, 5, 7, 11...

$2 + 2 = 4$

$3 - 1 = 2$

$16 \div 4 = 4$

$5 \times 3 = 15$

$7 \times 4 > 6 \times 3$ $\sqrt{4} = 2$

$4 < 8$

MATHS SYMBOLS
The most common maths symbols are plus (add), minus (subtract or take away), multiply and divide.

Plus or add	$+$
Minus or take away	$-$
Multiply	$\times$
Divide	$\div$
Equals	$=$
Is not equal to	$\neq$
Is less than	$<$
Is greater than	$>$
Percentage	$\%$
Square root	$\sqrt{}$

Temperature scale

Pie chart

◀ Geometry is concerned with lines, points, angles and spaces. This right-angled triangle (left) is a plane (flat) figure with three sides.

Angles of triangle = 180°

45°

90°

45°

135°

180°

360° in a circle

▲ Fractions are pieces of a whole. A pie cut in two has two halves $(1 \div 2 = \frac{1}{2})$. In a fraction, the figure above the line is the numerator, the figure below is the denominator.

▶ Graphs show the relative sizes of quantities or variables. A graph can illustrate statistics memorably. There are four main kinds: line graphs, bar graphs or histograms, picture graphs and pie charts.

Bar graph

Line graph

PROBABILITY
Toss a coin once: there is a 1 in 2 ($\frac{1}{2}$) chance of it coming down heads. Toss it twice. The first toss gives a head or tail. The probability of two heads after the second toss is $\frac{1}{4}$ ($\frac{1}{2} \times \frac{1}{2}$).

Probability here is one in four or $\frac{1}{4}$.

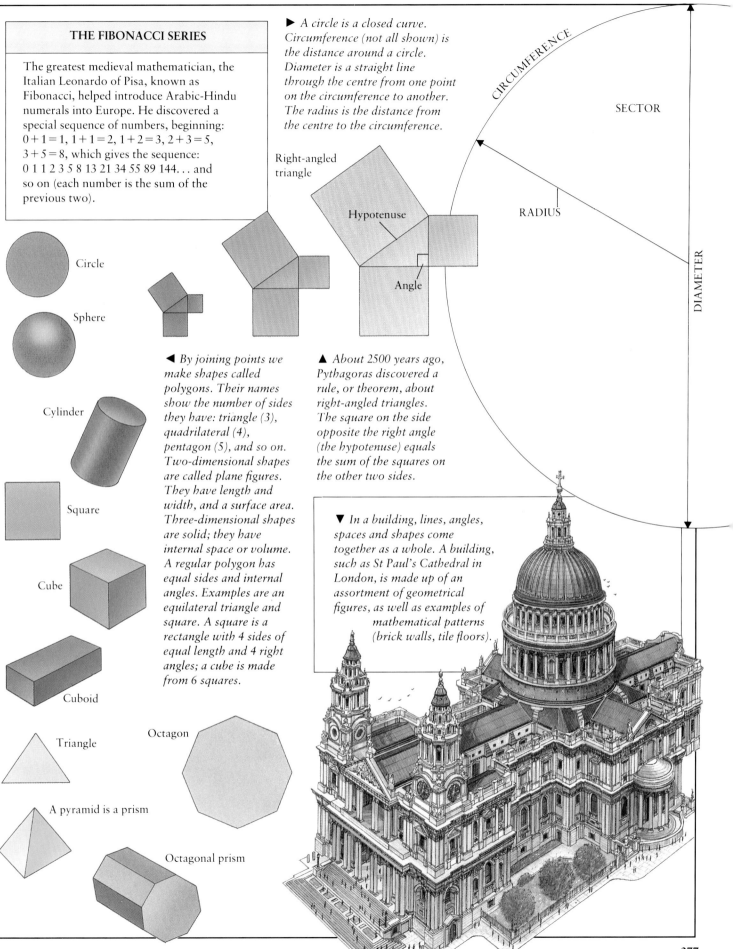

THE FIBONACCI SERIES

The greatest medieval mathematician, the Italian Leonardo of Pisa, known as Fibonacci, helped introduce Arabic-Hindu numerals into Europe. He discovered a special sequence of numbers, beginning: $0+1=1$, $1+1=2$, $1+2=3$, $2+3=5$, $3+5=8$, which gives the sequence: 0 1 1 2 3 5 8 13 21 34 55 89 144. . . and so on (each number is the sum of the previous two).

▶ *A circle is a closed curve. Circumference (not all shown) is the distance around a circle. Diameter is a straight line through the centre from one point on the circumference to another. The radius is the distance from the centre to the circumference.*

Right-angled triangle

Hypotenuse

Angle

CIRCUMFERENCE

SECTOR

RADIUS

DIAMETER

Circle

Sphere

Cylinder

Square

Cube

Cuboid

◀ *By joining points we make shapes called polygons. Their names show the number of sides they have: triangle (3), quadrilateral (4), pentagon (5), and so on. Two-dimensional shapes are called plane figures. They have length and width, and a surface area. Three-dimensional shapes are solid; they have internal space or volume. A regular polygon has equal sides and internal angles. Examples are an equilateral triangle and square. A square is a rectangle with 4 sides of equal length and 4 right angles; a cube is made from 6 squares.*

▲ *About 2500 years ago, Pythagoras discovered a rule, or theorem, about right-angled triangles. The square on the side opposite the right angle (the hypotenuse) equals the sum of the squares on the other two sides.*

▼ *In a building, lines, angles, spaces and shapes come together as a whole. A building, such as St Paul's Cathedral in London, is made up of an assortment of geometrical figures, as well as examples of mathematical patterns (brick walls, tile floors).*

Triangle

Octagon

A pyramid is a prism

Octagonal prism

Measuring Time

Long ago, people counted the days from sunrise to sunset, either as 'suns' or 'nights'. They measured the phases of the Sun, and the Babylonians worked out that in a year there were twelve equal parts. The Babylonians and Egyptians then calculated the year's length at 365 days and 6 hours, astonishingly accurate, since it is in fact 365 days 6 hours 41 minutes and 59 seconds! The first clocks were not very precise. However, the latest atomic clock is accurate to a second in 1.6 million years.

Perpetual calendar, 18th century

Calendar of feast days, 18th century

▲ Calendars are systems by which the length of the year is fixed. Perpetual calendars show the day of the week for any year that may be wanted.

▶ A solar day starts at midnight, and lasts for the time it takes the Earth to spin once on its axis. The time when our part of the Earth faces the Sun we call 'day'; the time it is turned away from the Sun is 'night'. The length of day and night varies; at the North Pole a midwinter day is 24 hours of darkness. When the North Pole faces the Sun the South Pole is always dark. A month is the time it takes for the Moon to orbit the Earth. A year is the time it takes the Earth to travel around the Sun.

▼ The interval between one New Moon and the next is 29.5 days. The New Moon waxes (gets larger) and halfway through its cycle, we see the whole face of the Moon lit by sunlight.

Gibbous

Last quarter

New Moon

First quarter

Waxing gibbous

Full Moon

Phases of the Moon

Full Moon

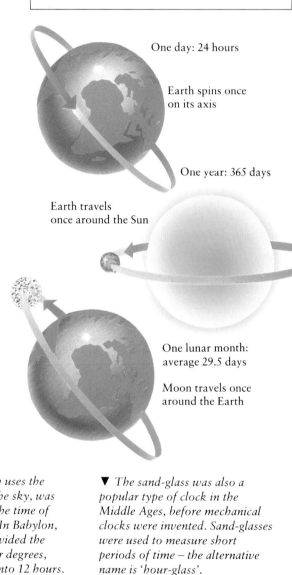

One day: 24 hours

Earth spins once on its axis

One year: 365 days

Earth travels once around the Sun

One lunar month: average 29.5 days

Moon travels once around the Earth

▼ Candle clocks were common in the Middle Ages. The candle was marked down its side to show the passing of the hours.

▼ In a water clock of ancient Egypt, water dripped slowly from one vessel to another. Some water clocks had floats fixed to pointers.

▼ The sundial, which uses the Sun's motion across the sky, was first used to indicate the time of day in ancient Egypt. In Babylon, where astronomers divided the circle into 360 parts or degrees, the dial was marked into 12 hours.

▼ The sand-glass was also a popular type of clock in the Middle Ages, before mechanical clocks were invented. Sand-glasses were used to measure short periods of time – the alternative name is 'hour-glass'.

Water clock

Candle clock

Sundial

Sand-gla

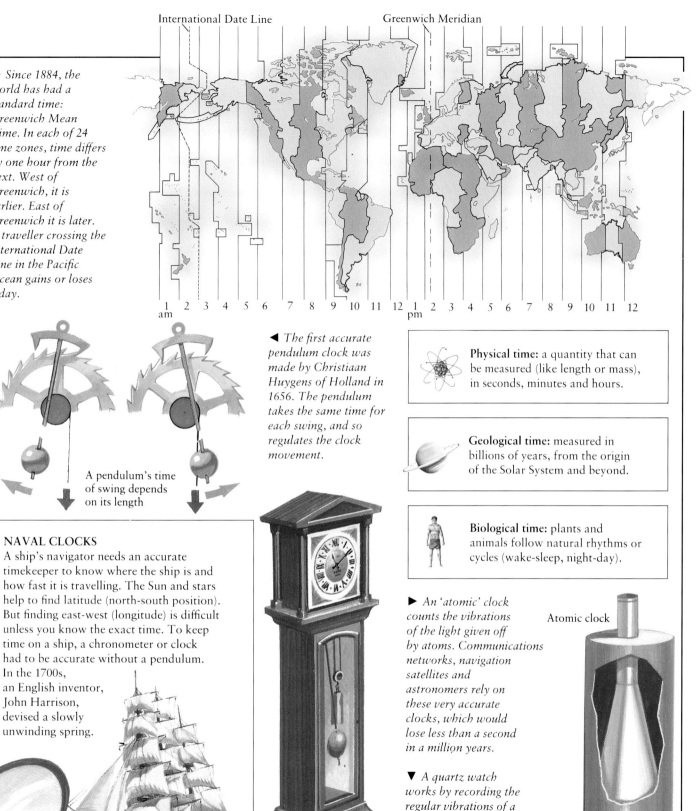

International Date Line

Greenwich Meridian

► Since 1884, the world has had a standard time: Greenwich Mean Time. In each of 24 time zones, time differs by one hour from the next. West of Greenwich, it is earlier. East of Greenwich it is later. A traveller crossing the International Date Line in the Pacific Ocean gains or loses a day.

| 1 | 2 | 3 | 4 | 5 | 6 | 7 | 8 | 9 | 10 | 11 | 12 | 1 | 2 | 3 | 4 | 5 | 6 | 7 | 8 | 9 | 10 | 11 | 12 |
| am | | | | | | | | | | | | pm | | | | | | | | | | | |

A pendulum's time of swing depends on its length

◄ The first accurate pendulum clock was made by Christiaan Huygens of Holland in 1656. The pendulum takes the same time for each swing, and so regulates the clock movement.

Physical time: a quantity that can be measured (like length or mass), in seconds, minutes and hours.

Geological time: measured in billions of years, from the origin of the Solar System and beyond.

Biological time: plants and animals follow natural rhythms or cycles (wake-sleep, night-day).

NAVAL CLOCKS

A ship's navigator needs an accurate timekeeper to know where the ship is and how fast it is travelling. The Sun and stars help to find latitude (north-south position). But finding east-west (longitude) is difficult unless you know the exact time. To keep time on a ship, a chronometer or clock had to be accurate without a pendulum. In the 1700s, an English inventor, John Harrison, devised a slowly unwinding spring.

► An 'atomic' clock counts the vibrations of the light given off by atoms. Communications networks, navigation satellites and astronomers rely on these very accurate clocks, which would lose less than a second in a million years.

Atomic clock

▼ A quartz watch works by recording the regular vibrations of a quartz crystal.

Pendulum clock

◄ Without this, Cook might not have found his way to Australia.
Harrison's chronometer

▲ The pendulum of this 19th-century clock controls its speed.

Quartz watch

LIGHT AND SOUND

The Spectrum

We live in a world in which light and sound constantly convey information to our senses. Light and sound are both forms of energy that travel in waves. Light comes originally from the Sun. It can travel through space, whereas sound can only travel through a substance that has molecules which are able to move around. Sound travels far more slowly than light – between 330–340 m per second (m/s) in air. Light travels very quickly, at 300,000 km per second. Light rays are a form of electromagnetic radiation; the only type we can see. Other rays making up the electromagnetic spectrum are invisible. At the red end of the spectrum are infrared rays, microwaves, radar, television and radio waves. At the other (violet) end of the spectrum are ultraviolet, X-rays, gamma rays and cosmic rays.

ELECTROMAGNETIC SPECTRUM

Spectrum

Microwaves

Glass prism

▲ *The electromagnetic spectrum is made up of waves of different lengths, forming bands. Radio waves are very long, as much as thousands of metres long. Microwaves have wavelengths of only a few millimetres and cosmic rays are only a tiny fraction of a millimetre in length.*

Light wave

Radar waves

10^{-3}

Long wavelength

10^{-2}

Television waves

▲ *The frequency of a wave is its rate of vibration. The length of a wave is the distance between its top and the tops of the neighbouring waves. Waves with long wavelengths have low frequencies. Waves with short wavelengths have high frequencies. Visible light forms the middle band of the spectrum. On either side, but invisible to our eyes, are ultraviolet and infrared waves.*

10^{-1}

Radio waves

1

10^{1}

◀ *Light behaves both as a wave and as a particle. In an atom, an electron moved to a higher energy level gives off photons.*

Photon

▲ *Light is a kind of electromagnetic radiation. It travels in a wave made up of an electric field and a magnetic field at right angles to each other, and to the direction of the wave's travel. Nothing travels faster than light.*

◀ *A rainbow shows the colours of the visible spectrum. Sunlight is bent or refracted by raindrops in the air, and the white light is split into red, orange, yellow, green, blue, indigo and violet.*

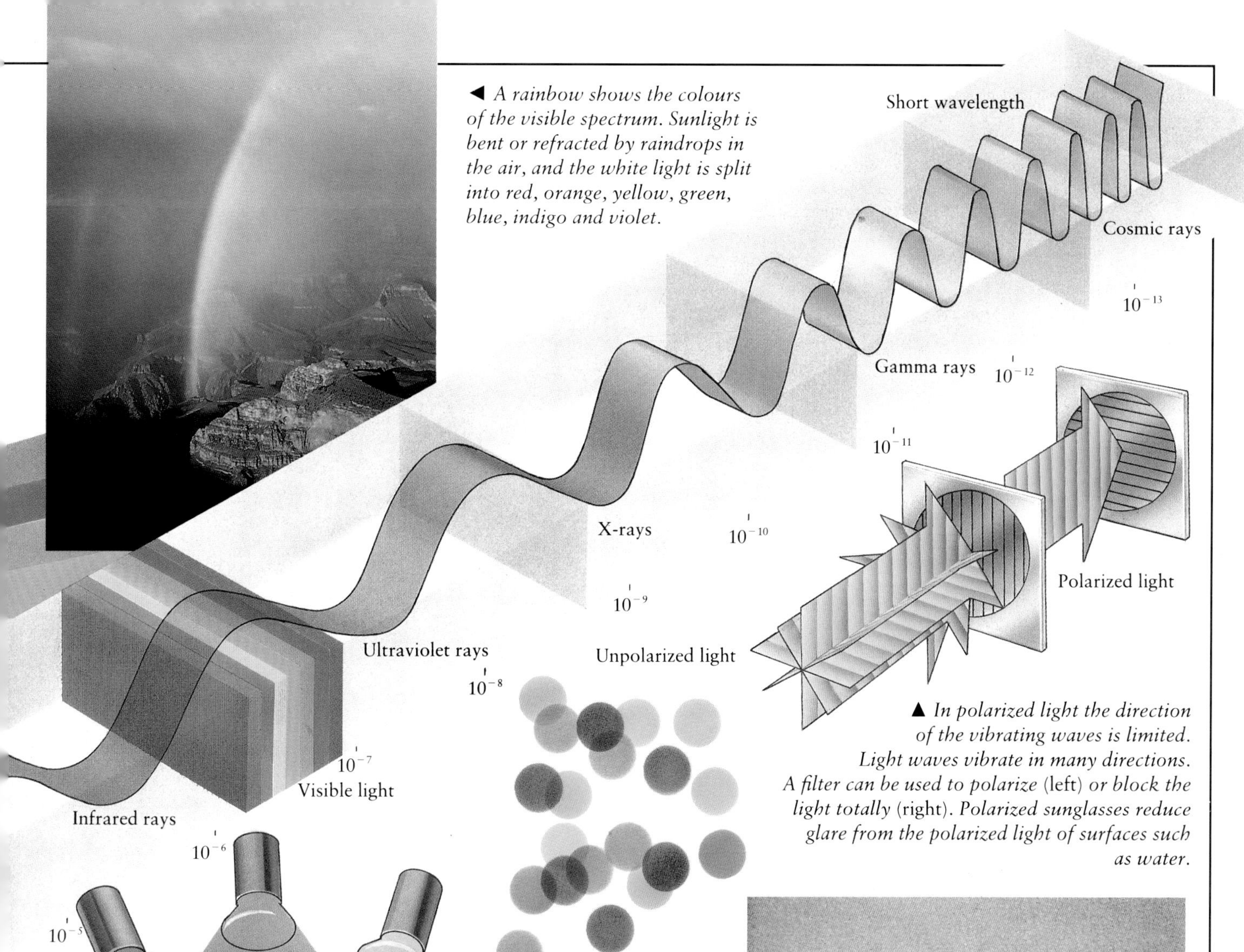

Short wavelength

Cosmic rays

10^{-13}

Gamma rays 10^{-12}

10^{-11}

X-rays 10^{-10}

10^{-9}

Ultraviolet rays 10^{-8}

Unpolarized light

Polarized light

10^{-7}

Visible light

Infrared rays

10^{-6}

10^{-5}

▲ *In polarized light the direction of the vibrating waves is limited. Light waves vibrate in many directions. A filter can be used to polarize (left) or block the light totally (right). Polarized sunglasses reduce glare from the polarized light of surfaces such as water.*

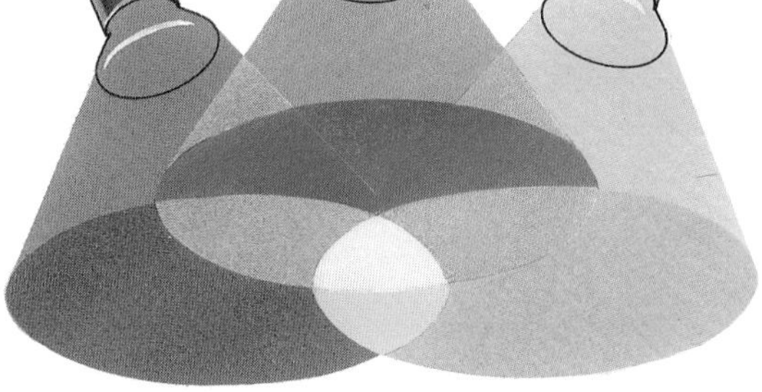

▲ *The three primary colours when mixing light are red, green and blue. Added together, the primary colours make white light.*

▼ *Paint pigments mix differently. The primary colours are yellow, blue and red. All three added together make brown.*

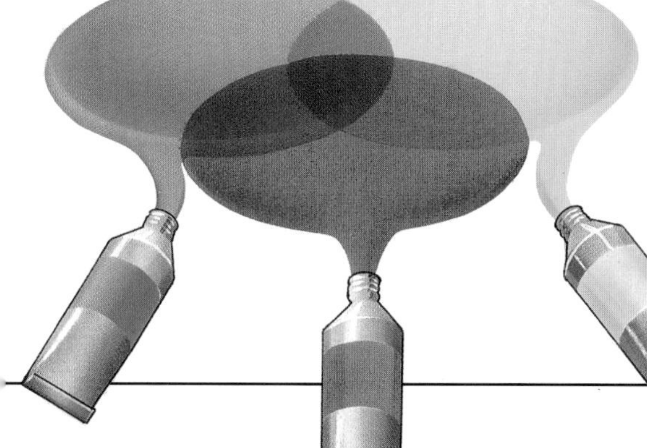

▶ *Pointillism is a painting technique developed by the Neo-Impressionists in the late 1800s. In this picture by Maximilien Luce, the artist has covered the canvas with tiny dots of colour which blend when viewed from a distance.*

▶ *When light rays pass from one substance to another at any angle except a right angle (in this illustration from air to water), they are bent. This bending, called refraction, distorts the image (here straws) seen by the eye.*

Refraction

Light

Light is as vital to our existence on Earth as oxygen or water. Without light we could not see. Without sunlight the Earth would be a frozen and lifeless planet. Without light, there would be no green plants. The energy in the fuels we burn came originally from sunlight. Ever since people discovered how to make fire, they have found ways to make their own light – candles, oil lamps, gas and electric lights. Today, light is used in areas as diverse as entertainment, surgery and telecommunications.

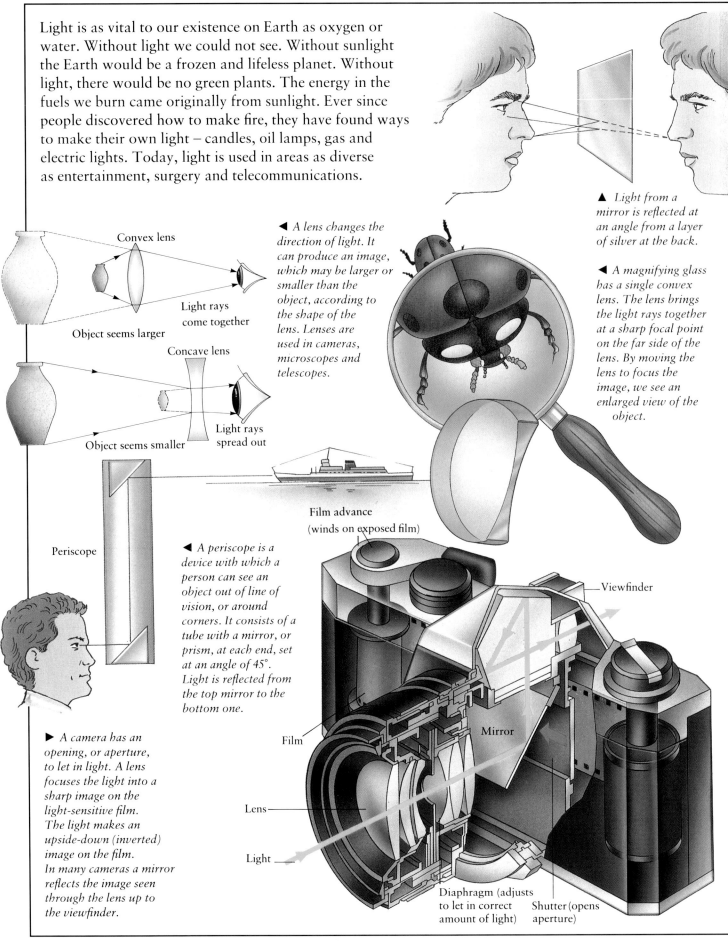

▲ *Light from a mirror is reflected at an angle from a layer of silver at the back.*

◀ *A magnifying glass has a single convex lens. The lens brings the light rays together at a sharp focal point on the far side of the lens. By moving the lens to focus the image, we see an enlarged view of the object.*

Convex lens

Light rays come together

Object seems larger

Concave lens

Object seems smaller

Light rays spread out

◀ *A lens changes the direction of light. It can produce an image, which may be larger or smaller than the object, according to the shape of the lens. Lenses are used in cameras, microscopes and telescopes.*

Periscope

◀ *A periscope is a device with which a person can see an object out of line of vision, or around corners. It consists of a tube with a mirror, or prism, at each end, set at an angle of 45°. Light is reflected from the top mirror to the bottom one.*

Film advance (winds on exposed film)

Viewfinder

Film

Mirror

Lens

Light

Diaphragm (adjusts to let in correct amount of light)

Shutter (opens aperture)

▶ *A camera has an opening, or aperture, to let in light. A lens focuses the light into a sharp image on the light-sensitive film. The light makes an upside-down (inverted) image on the film. In many cameras a mirror reflects the image seen through the lens up to the viewfinder.*

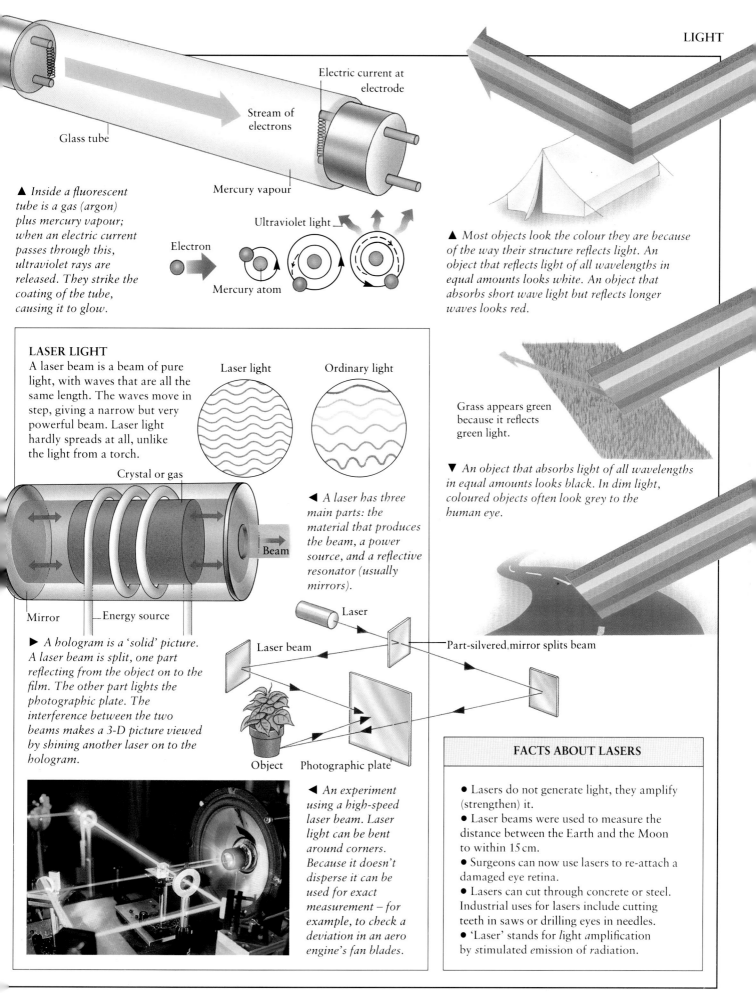

▲ *Inside a fluorescent tube is a gas (argon) plus mercury vapour; when an electric current passes through this, ultraviolet rays are released. They strike the coating of the tube, causing it to glow.*

Glass tube

Stream of electrons

Electric current at electrode

Mercury vapour

Ultraviolet light

Electron

Mercury atom

▲ *Most objects look the colour they are because of the way their structure reflects light. An object that reflects light of all wavelengths in equal amounts looks white. An object that absorbs short wave light but reflects longer waves looks red.*

Grass appears green because it reflects green light.

▼ *An object that absorbs light of all wavelengths in equal amounts looks black. In dim light, coloured objects often look grey to the human eye.*

LASER LIGHT

A laser beam is a beam of pure light, with waves that are all the same length. The waves move in step, giving a narrow but very powerful beam. Laser light hardly spreads at all, unlike the light from a torch.

Laser light

Ordinary light

◄ *A laser has three main parts: the material that produces the beam, a power source, and a reflective resonator (usually mirrors).*

Crystal or gas

Beam

Mirror

Energy source

▶ *A hologram is a 'solid' picture. A laser beam is split, one part reflecting from the object on to the film. The other part lights the photographic plate. The interference between the two beams makes a 3-D picture viewed by shining another laser on to the hologram.*

Laser

Laser beam

Part-silvered mirror splits beam

Object

Photographic plate

◄ *An experiment using a high-speed laser beam. Laser light can be bent around corners. Because it doesn't disperse it can be used for exact measurement – for example, to check a deviation in an aero engine's fan blades.*

FACTS ABOUT LASERS

- Lasers do not generate light, they amplify (strengthen) it.
- Laser beams were used to measure the distance between the Earth and the Moon to within 15 cm.
- Surgeons can now use lasers to re-attach a damaged eye retina.
- Lasers can cut through concrete or steel. Industrial uses for lasers include cutting teeth in saws or drilling eyes in needles.
- 'Laser' stands for *l*ight *a*mplification by *s*timulated *e*mission of *r*adiation.

Sound

All sounds are made by vibrations of objects. When an object moves backwards and forwards, or vibrates, it produces sound. The molecules around it vibrate and set up a sound wave. Sound can travel through air, water, metal or other materials. Unlike light waves, sound waves cannot travel through a vacuum (airless space), so there is no sound in space or on the Moon. Sound travels faster through water (1400 m/s) than through the air (around 330–340 m/s), because water is more dense.

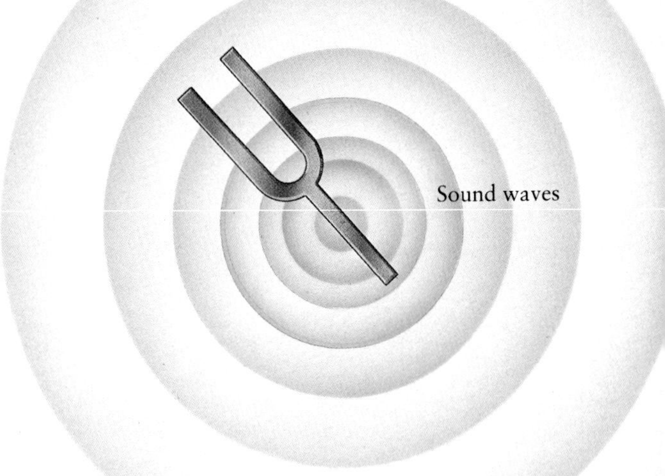

Sound waves

▼ Pitch (how high or low a sound is) depends on the frequency of waves: the number of air vibrations per second.

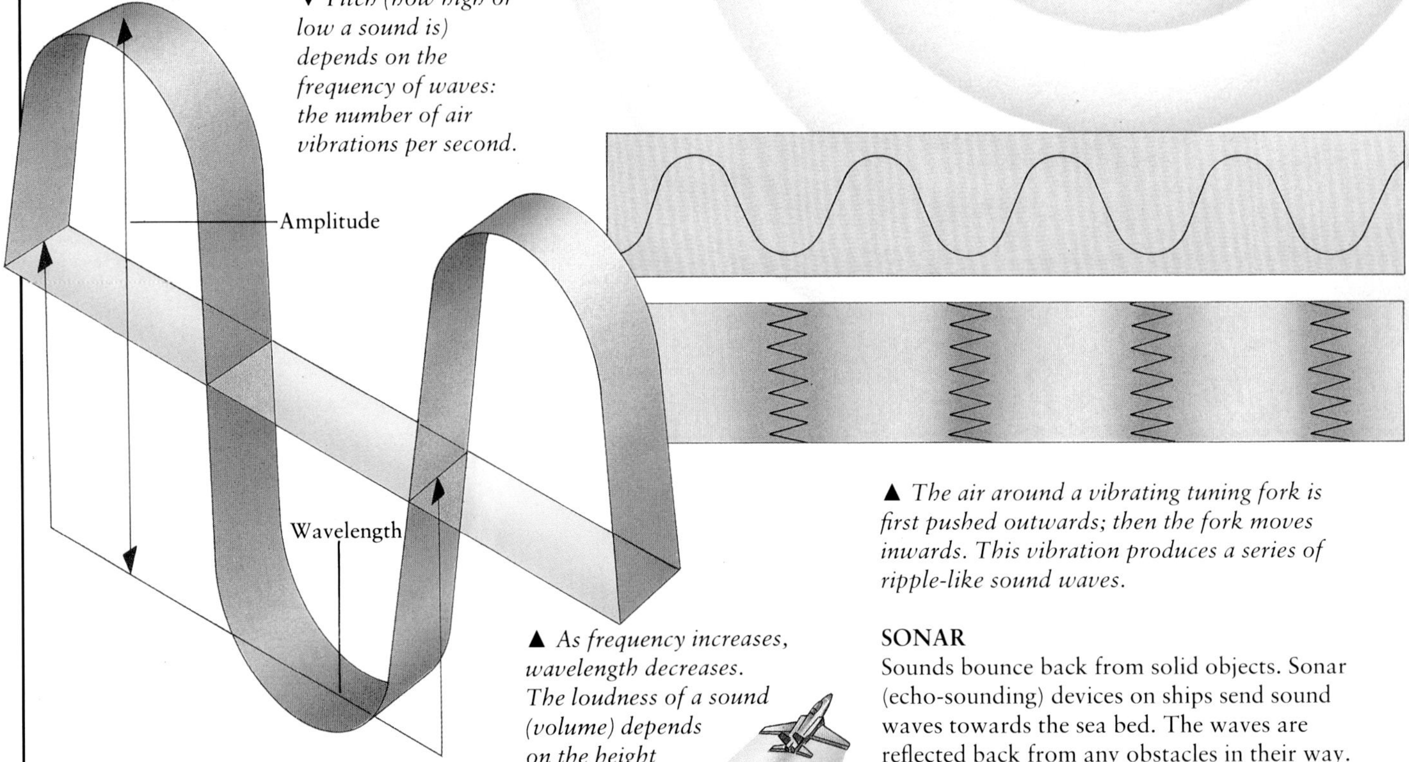

Amplitude

Wavelength

▲ The air around a vibrating tuning fork is first pushed outwards; then the fork moves inwards. This vibration produces a series of ripple-like sound waves.

▲ As frequency increases, wavelength decreases. The loudness of a sound (volume) depends on the height of the wave (amplitude).

SONAR
Sounds bounce back from solid objects. Sonar (echo-sounding) devices on ships send sound waves towards the sea bed. The waves are reflected back from any obstacles in their way. The time it takes for the sound to come back indicates the depth of the obstacle.

THE SONIC BOOM
An aircraft flying at the speed of sound (Mach 1) flies inside a pattern of pressure waves caused by its movement through the air. Above Mach 1 a supersonic jet overtakes the pressure waves, creating a cone-shaped shock wave.

Shock wave

▶ Fishing vessels use sonar to locate shoals. Survey ships use sonar to chart the seabed.

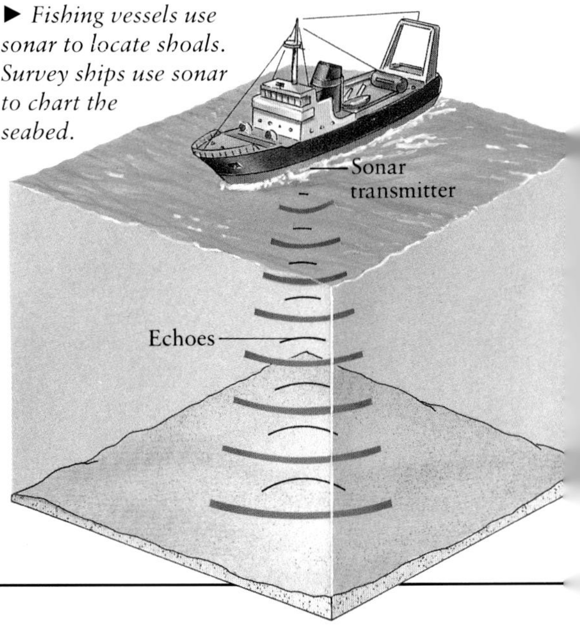

Sonar transmitter

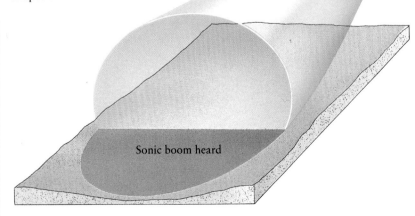

Sonic boom heard

Echoes

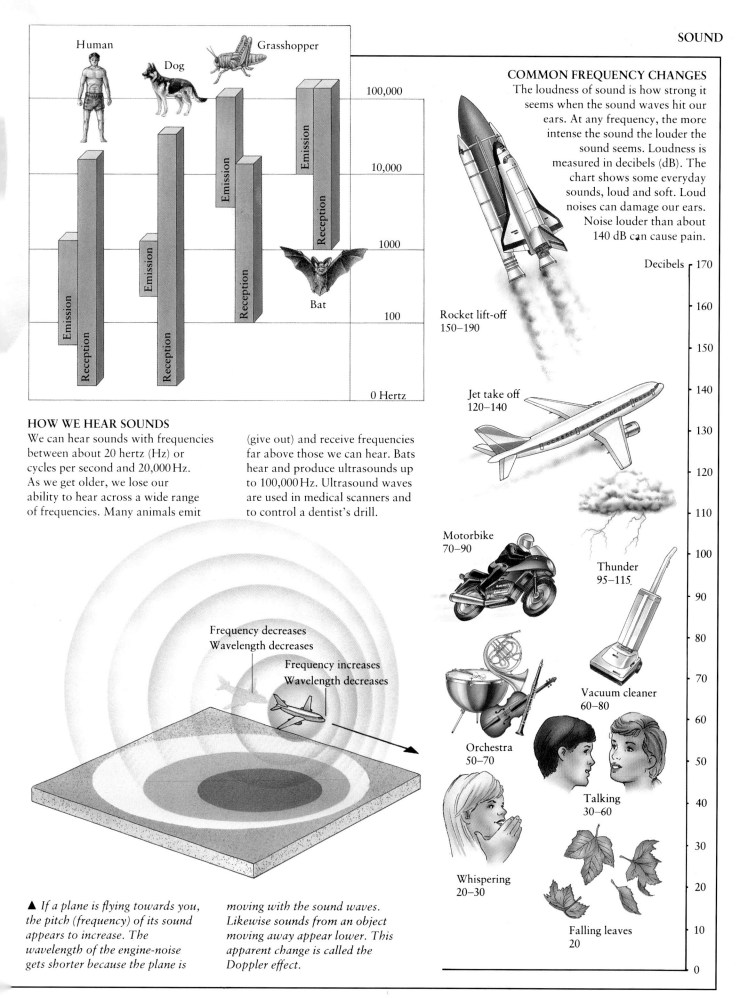

100,000

10,000

1000

100

0 Hertz

Human

Dog

Grasshopper

Emission

Reception

Emission

Reception

Emission

Reception

Emission

Reception

Bat

COMMON FREQUENCY CHANGES

The loudness of sound is how strong it seems when the sound waves hit our ears. At any frequency, the more intense the sound the louder the sound seems. Loudness is measured in decibels (dB). The chart shows some everyday sounds, loud and soft. Loud noises can damage our ears. Noise louder than about 140 dB can cause pain.

Decibels — 170

— 160

— 150

— 140

— 130

— 120

— 110

— 100

— 90

— 80

— 70

— 60

— 50

— 40

— 30

— 20

— 10

— 0

Rocket lift-off
150–190

Jet take off
120–140

Motorbike
70–90

Thunder
95–115

Vacuum cleaner
60–80

Orchestra
50–70

Talking
30–60

Whispering
20–30

Falling leaves
20

HOW WE HEAR SOUNDS

We can hear sounds with frequencies between about 20 hertz (Hz) or cycles per second and 20,000 Hz. As we get older, we lose our ability to hear across a wide range of frequencies. Many animals emit (give out) and receive frequencies far above those we can hear. Bats hear and produce ultrasounds up to 100,000 Hz. Ultrasound waves are used in medical scanners and to control a dentist's drill.

Frequency decreases
Wavelength decreases

Frequency increases
Wavelength decreases

▲ *If a plane is flying towards you, the pitch (frequency) of its sound appears to increase. The wavelength of the engine-noise gets shorter because the plane is moving with the sound waves. Likewise sounds from an object moving away appear lower. This apparent change is called the Doppler effect.*

Sound Applications

Sound has many uses – as entertainment, as a means of communication, and as a tool in industry and scientific research. From ancient times, music and the different kinds of instruments used to make music have played a key role in human expression. From the 1870s it became possible to record sounds, and from the early 1900s sound broadcasting opened up new worlds of communication. The microphone, radio, tape player and compact disc have become part of our everyday lives.

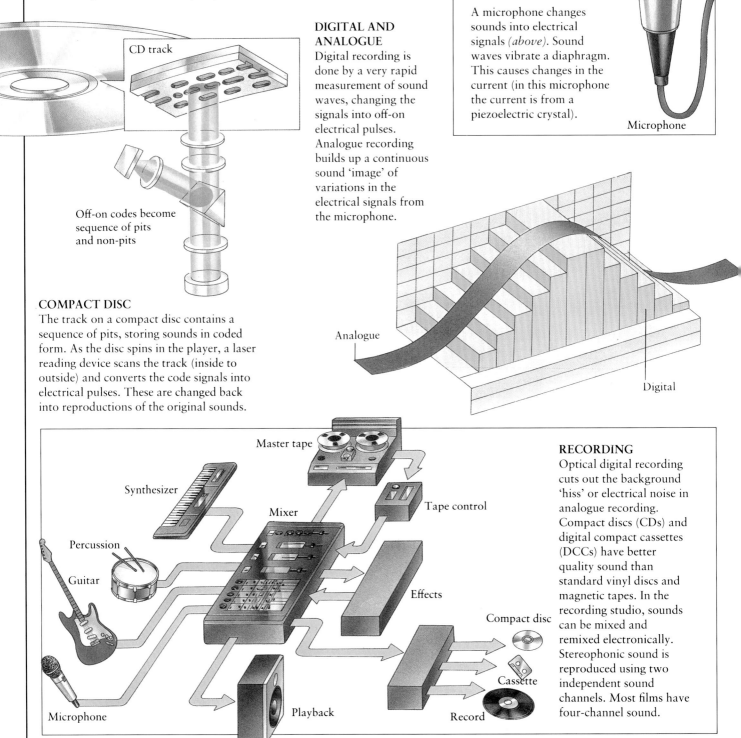

Diaphragm

Crystal

A microphone changes sounds into electrical signals *(above)*. Sound waves vibrate a diaphragm. This causes changes in the current (in this microphone the current is from a piezoelectric crystal).

Microphone

DIGITAL AND ANALOGUE

Digital recording is done by a very rapid measurement of sound waves, changing the signals into off-on electrical pulses. Analogue recording builds up a continuous sound 'image' of variations in the electrical signals from the microphone.

CD track

Off-on codes become sequence of pits and non-pits

COMPACT DISC

The track on a compact disc contains a sequence of pits, storing sounds in coded form. As the disc spins in the player, a laser reading device scans the track (inside to outside) and converts the code signals into electrical pulses. These are changed back into reproductions of the original sounds.

Analogue

Digital

Master tape

Synthesizer

Mixer

Tape control

Percussion

Guitar

Effects

Compact disc

Microphone

Playback

Cassette

Record

RECORDING

Optical digital recording cuts out the background 'hiss' or electrical noise in analogue recording. Compact discs (CDs) and digital compact cassettes (DCCs) have better quality sound than standard vinyl discs and magnetic tapes. In the recording studio, sounds can be mixed and remixed electronically. Stereophonic sound is reproduced using two independent sound channels. Most films have four-channel sound.

LOUDSPEAKER

Loudspeaker

Diaphragm

To change the electrical signals back into sounds, they pass through a loudspeaker. The signals cause a diaphragm in the loudspeaker to vibrate and this motion reproduces the original sounds.

MUSICAL INSTRUMENTS

Musical instruments make sounds by vibrating the air in different ways. A violin's strings are bowed or plucked. As the string vibrates, the hollow body and the air around the instrument vibrate. We hear a musical tone.

Holes

◀ *In a woodwind instrument, the longer the column of air inside, the lower the note. Fingering the holes alters the note.*

Valves

◀ *A trumpet has valves that change the length of the air column. The player pushes a valve open to open up extra loops of tube.*

Sound waves

◀ *When a drummer taps the drum skin with a stick, the skin vibrates. The resulting sound resonates (increases) inside the hollow drum body.*

Record playback head

Iron oxide particles

SYNTHESIZED SOUNDS

An electronic synthesizer stores and reproduces sounds digitally. The keyboard controls the frequency of the signals. The sounds are made by circuits called oscillators, and blended or shaped by other circuits called filters. Synthesized sound emerges from a loudspeaker. A synthesizer can produce an amazing range of musical and other sounds, including special effects.

Keyboard

Waveforms

Oscillator circuit

Filter circuit

Low-pass filter (low-pitched sounds)

High-pass filter (only high-pitched sounds pass)

Amplifier

CASSETTE

The plastic tape inside most cassettes is coated with iron oxide. The iron oxide particles normally lie in a random pattern. The recording process magnetizes them to form a regular pattern. When the tape is played, it passes through the recording head where the magnetized particles produce signals that are amplified to reproduce sounds.

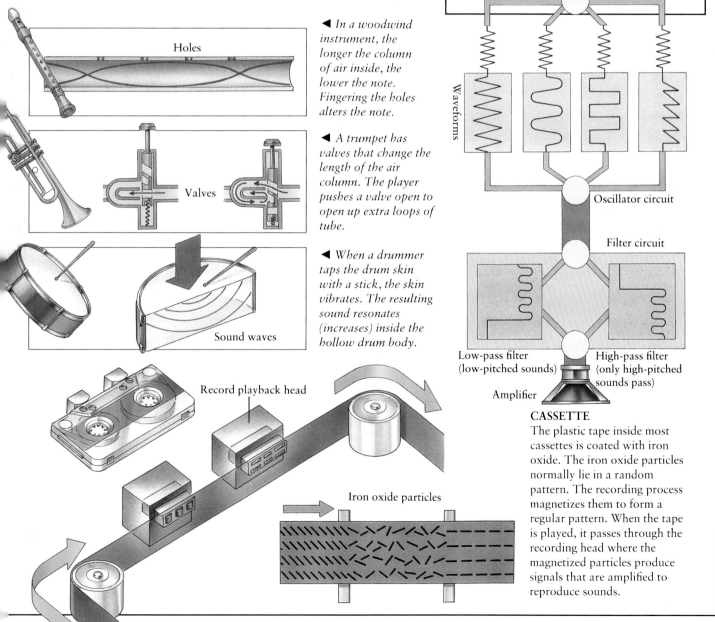

ELECTRICITY

Electromagnetism

Electromagnetism is one of the most influential forces shaping our world. Human life changed dramatically from the late 1700s when science opened the way to the widespread use of the enormous power of electricity. Magnetism had been known about for thousands of years. But it was not until 1820 that the Danish scientist, Hans Christian Oersted, discovered what we now call the magnetic effect – that magnetism and electricity are closely connected and that one can produce the other. This discovery made possible the development of electric generators and motors. Later, radio and television communication and the use of X-rays became possible. Devices to control the motion of electrons (the elementary particles which make up electrical current) brought about the modern electronics revolution in both the home and at work.

▼ *Electromagnetic radiation travels as waves. A wave has two main properties: height, or amplitude, and length (the distance between two neighbouring waves). The number of waves that pass a certain point in a certain time gives the frequency.*

▶ *Radio and TV signals are transmitted on 'carrier' waves. In AM (amplitude modulation) the amplified signal from a microphone is made to modulate, or vary, the amplitude of a carrier wave. In FM (frequency modulation) the voice signal modulates the frequency of the carrier wave.*

RADIO WAVES
Radio waves with short wavelengths penetrate the atmosphere and are used to communicate with spacecraft. Long wave signals are reflected back from the ionosphere. In this way, radio waves can be 'bounced' around the world.

Long wave

Medium wave

Short wave (VHF/UHF)

Microwave

Amplified voice wave

Carrier wave

Combined voice and carrier wave

10^4 1 10^{-3} 10^{-6}

Radio waves

Infrared radiation

Visible light

Microwave

Ionosphere

Reflected sky wave

Long waves

High frequency waves transmitted to land aerials

Microwave receiver

Radio transmitter

◀ *A lightning flash – an example of electricity in nature – is a huge electrical spark in the atmosphere. A flash produces about 100 million volts of electricity.*

▼ *X-rays have a very high frequency, and a very short wavelength. Wilhelm Roentgen discovered X-rays in 1895. The rays pass easily through most living tissue, but not through material such as bone which contains heavier atoms. It is important to control doses of X-rays, since too many can cause cell damage.*

X-rays

Gas discharge tube

Ultraviolet rays   X-rays   Gamma rays

10^{-8} 10^{-9} 10^{-10} 10^{-11}

Communications satellite

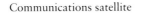

10^{-1} 10^{-2} 10^{-3}
Radar waves   Microwave waves   Infrared waves

Ionosphere

Microwave

Reflected sky wave

Microwave transmitter

MICROWAVES
Microwaves are a form of short-wave electromagnetic radiation. They are used for communications, since their wavelength is conveniently easy to direct. They are also used in microwave cookers, in which they are generated from a valve called a magnetron.

FACTS ABOUT ELECTROMAGNETISM

● In 1752 Benjamin Franklin proved that lightning is electric by flying a kite in a thunderstorm. Attached to the string was a metal key. As lightning struck the kite, a spark flashed as electricity passed down the string from the key.
● Wilhelm Roentgen, a German, was awarded the first Nobel Prize for Physics in 1901 for his discovery of X-rays. He photographed the bones of his wife's hand.

▼ *Ultraviolet radiation has a higher frequency than light we can see. Some insects can see ultraviolet light. A bee, for example, sees 'target' marks which attract it to the centre of the flower where the nectar is. Ultraviolet light can burn human skin. The ozone layer in the atmosphere absorbs most ultraviolet radiation in sunlight.*

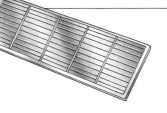

Visible light

10^{-6} 10^{-7} 10^{-8} 10^{-9}
Ultraviolet light

X-rays

Electricity in Action

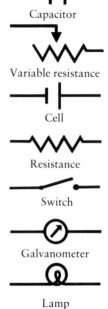

Electricity was long regarded as a mystery, because it is an invisible form of energy. It is produced when electrons, tiny atomic particles, move from one atom to another. Electrons carry negative electric charges; the nucleus of an atom carries a positive charge. An electric current is a flow of electric charges, pushed along by a force. There are two kinds of current. Direct current (DC) flows in only one direction. Alternating current (AC) changes its direction of flow at regular intervals – one hundred times a second.

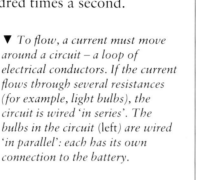

Capacitor

Variable resistance

Cell

Resistance

Switch

Galvanometer

Lamp

◄ *All circuits need a force to make the current flow. This force, the electromotive force (e.m.f.) has to overcome electrical resistance to make the current flow. Circuits with batteries work with direct current. Mechanical generators usually produce alternating current. Shown here are some symbols used when drawing a circuit.*

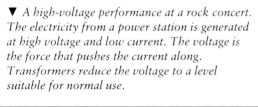

In parallel

Bulbs are brighter

In series

Bulbs share power

Light dim

▼ *To flow, a current must move around a circuit – a loop of electrical conductors. If the current flows through several resistances (for example, light bulbs), the circuit is wired 'in series'. The bulbs in the circuit (left) are wired 'in parallel': each has its own connection to the battery.*

▼ *A high-voltage performance at a rock concert. The electricity from a power station is generated at high voltage and low current. The voltage is the force that pushes the current along. Transformers reduce the voltage to a level suitable for normal use.*

Negative terminal

Positive terminal

Plates

WET BATTERY
A battery uses chemical energy to produce electricity. A car battery is a 'wet' battery (its metal plates are in acid). These lead-acid storage batteries store or accumulate electricity and can be recharged by a battery charger when exhausted. This type of battery can also provide vital emergency electricity in, for example, hospitals.

DRY BATTERY
A dry battery (the kind of battery used in a torch) contains a dry pastelike or jellylike chemical. The acid in a lemon may produce enough current to light a small bulb if wired to suitable terminals, such as a copper coin and a strip of aluminium foil.

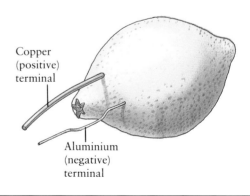

Copper (positive) terminal

Aluminium (negative) terminal

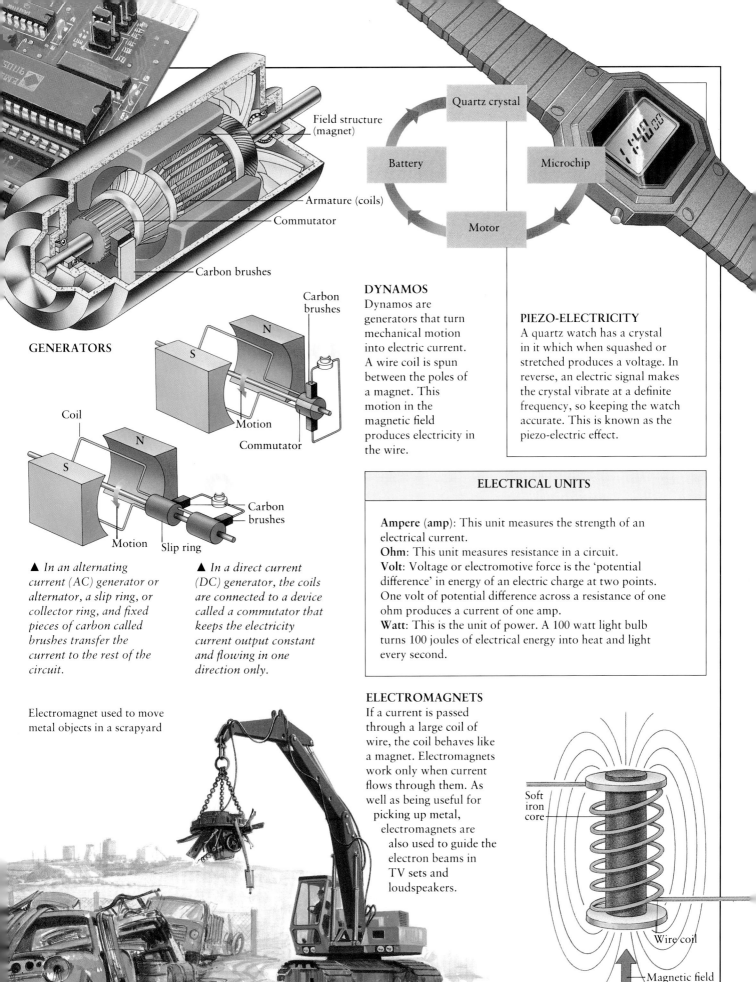

Field structure (magnet)

Armature (coils)

Commutator

Carbon brushes

Quartz crystal

Battery

Microchip

Motor

GENERATORS

Carbon brushes

N

S

Motion

Commutator

Coil

N

S

Carbon brushes

Motion

Slip ring

▲ *In an alternating current (AC) generator or alternator, a slip ring, or collector ring, and fixed pieces of carbon called brushes transfer the current to the rest of the circuit.*

▲ *In a direct current (DC) generator, the coils are connected to a device called a commutator that keeps the electricity current output constant and flowing in one direction only.*

DYNAMOS

Dynamos are generators that turn mechanical motion into electric current. A wire coil is spun between the poles of a magnet. This motion in the magnetic field produces electricity in the wire.

PIEZO-ELECTRICITY

A quartz watch has a crystal in it which when squashed or stretched produces a voltage. In reverse, an electric signal makes the crystal vibrate at a definite frequency, so keeping the watch accurate. This is known as the piezo-electric effect.

ELECTRICAL UNITS

Ampere (amp): This unit measures the strength of an electrical current.
Ohm: This unit measures resistance in a circuit.
Volt: Voltage or electromotive force is the 'potential difference' in energy of an electric charge at two points. One volt of potential difference across a resistance of one ohm produces a current of one amp.
Watt: This is the unit of power. A 100 watt light bulb turns 100 joules of electrical energy into heat and light every second.

Electromagnet used to move metal objects in a scrapyard

ELECTROMAGNETS

If a current is passed through a large coil of wire, the coil behaves like a magnet. Electromagnets work only when current flows through them. As well as being useful for picking up metal, electromagnets are also used to guide the electron beams in TV sets and loudspeakers.

Soft iron core

Wire coil

Magnetic field

Electronics

In our daily lives, we rely constantly on devices controlled by electronic circuits. These circuits are made up of components (such as diodes and resistors). Electronic components affect the way electrons, and therefore electric currents, flow through them. Complete electronic circuits can now be made small enough to fit on a single silicon chip (a wafer of silicon semiconductor material). Components, including silicon chips, are fitted together to make printed circuits.

◀ *Vacuum tubes or valves were the first devices for controlling the flow of an electric current. The diode (1904) and triode (1906) made radio and TV possible. Valves were replaced by the transistor, invented in 1948.*

▼ *Transistors are smaller and use less power than valves. They are made of semiconducting material. A microchip is an electronic circuit mounted on a single piece of silicon. It works at great speed.*

Transistor

Microchip

1930s valve radio

Vacuum tube

▼ *The silicon chip is sealed in a plastic block, with metal contacts to connect it to a printed circuit board. The most important chip is the microprocessor, the control centre of a computer.*

Silicon wafer with microchips

Chemical process etches program on to microchips

◀ *How do you make a microchip less than a centimetre square? The parts are too small to be stuck together like the pieces of a model. All the components and connections are made as layers in a complicated pattern, reproduced from larger-scale originals by a chemical process. The components are built on to a chip, cut from a wafer-thin slice of silicon.*

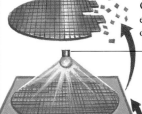

Silicon wafer cut from cylinder (about 0.25 mm thick)

◀ *A chip can control the flow of current through its miniature components. Each link in the pattern can carry out a function very quickly. There are so many links that the chip is capable of carrying out an amazing number of functions.*

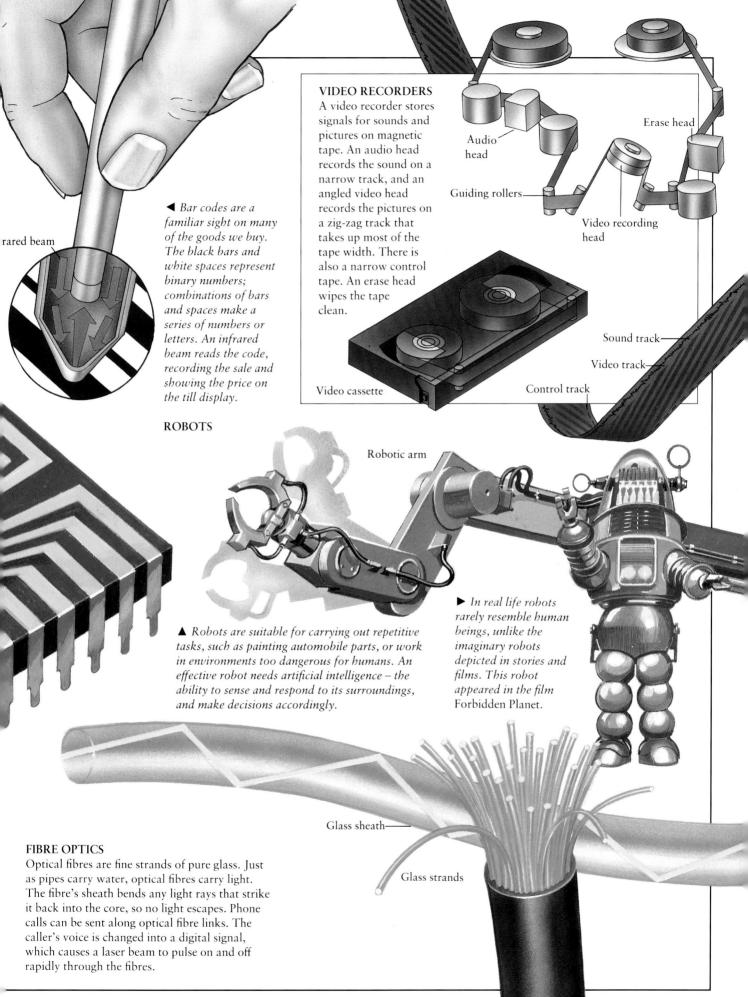

◀ *Bar codes are a familiar sight on many of the goods we buy. The black bars and white spaces represent binary numbers; combinations of bars and spaces make a series of numbers or letters. An infrared beam reads the code, recording the sale and showing the price on the till display.*

rared beam

VIDEO RECORDERS

A video recorder stores signals for sounds and pictures on magnetic tape. An audio head records the sound on a narrow track, and an angled video head records the pictures on a zig-zag track that takes up most of the tape width. There is also a narrow control tape. An erase head wipes the tape clean.

Erase head

Audio head

Guiding rollers

Video recording head

Sound track

Video track

Control track

Video cassette

ROBOTS

Robotic arm

▲ *Robots are suitable for carrying out repetitive tasks, such as painting automobile parts, or work in environments too dangerous for humans. An effective robot needs artificial intelligence – the ability to sense and respond to its surroundings, and make decisions accordingly.*

▶ *In real life robots rarely resemble human beings, unlike the imaginary robots depicted in stories and films. This robot appeared in the film Forbidden Planet.*

FIBRE OPTICS

Optical fibres are fine strands of pure glass. Just as pipes carry water, optical fibres carry light. The fibre's sheath bends any light rays that strike it back into the core, so no light escapes. Phone calls can be sent along optical fibre links. The caller's voice is changed into a digital signal, which causes a laser beam to pulse on and off rapidly through the fibres.

Glass sheath

Glass strands

Computers

The fastest computers can do billions of calculations every second. Their main ability is to do a lot of basic tasks quickly and accurately. We use computers at work, school, and play, even if we never tap a keyboard. When we buy goods in a supermarket, draw money from a bank, or ask for information about a vacation, we are making transactions that are now done with the aid of computers. A revolution that began in the 1940s with room-sized machines has today given us the laptop personal computer.

The English mathematician Charles Babbage (1792–1871) designed a large calculating machine which, in theory, could be programmed, like a computer. But the electronic age had not yet dawned, and there was no way to give Babbage's Analytical Engine the power it needed.

PERSONAL COMPUTERS

Small personal computers can be found in offices, schools, and homes all over the world. The machinery and electronics (screen, keyboard, disk drives, printer) are the hardware. Software programs stored on disks tell the computer what to do—in this illustration, a graphics program is being used to design a building.

Printer

◀ *The output from a computer can be in the form of a visual display on a screen, printed paper, a modem link, or a disk.*

Disk

Disk drive

◀ *A keyboard, a mouse, a modem linked to other computers, and a floppy disk input data and instructions.*

Screen

Keyboard

INSIDE A COMPUTER

A computer has four basic parts: input, processing, memory, and output. It also needs a program—instructions telling the processing unit how to do different tasks.

◀ *A mouse is a simple hand-controller. By moving the mouse, you direct the cursor around the screen to give the computer commands.*

Mouse

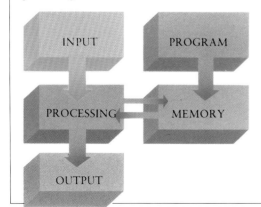

INPUT

PROGRAM

PROCESSING

MEMORY

OUTPUT

Across

Down

▲ *Computers are now used in almost every business. For these financial dealers, computers are vital for storing business data and analysing movements on the world's money markets, 24 hours a day. Computers in offices and laboratories all around the world are constantly exchanging information.*

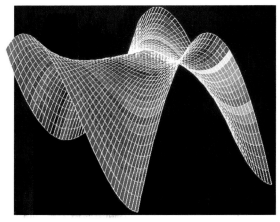

LARGE AND SMALL

The first fully electronic computers were the British Colossus (completed in 1943) and the American ENIAC – *Electronic Numerical Integrator And Computer* – (completed in 1946). Both needed teams of operators. These computers, called mainframes, were at first so big that they needed whole rooms to contain them. In the 1950s, smaller transistorized computers were developed. By the 1970s, the miniaturization of electronic equipment led to advances in computer technology such as the small, less expensive, personal computer (pc).

Mainframe computer

Laptop computer

Notebook computer

Computer software (program)

Light pen

Computer generated picture

◀ *Computer graphics are made by converting information into pictures. Computer-aided design programs allow engineers, architects and scientists to study and modify designs on screen. The operator can use a light-pen to alter the computer-made picture.*

USEFUL TERMS

Bit: Binary digit; a numeral in binary notation (0 or 1)
Byte: Space in a computer's memory occupied by one letter or numeral
Cursor: Highlighted area on screen
Data: Information processed by a computer
Hardware: The physical parts of a computer system
Network: Several computers connected, e.g. by a modem (telephone)
Software: Programs for a computer

VIRTUAL REALITY

Graphics programs are now so sophisticated that computers can interact with people to create 'virtual reality'. The computer generates sounds and images, creating a 'landscape', heard and seen inside a special helmet. The effect is to construct a seemingly real world that the person feels a part of. The possibilities for entertainment and education are endless.

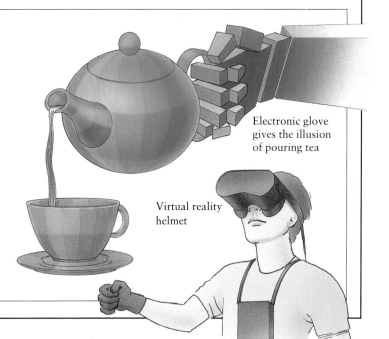

Electronic glove gives the illusion of pouring tea

Virtual reality helmet

TECHNOLOGY

Engineering

Science is knowledge. Technology is the process of applying knowledge to make work easier, to make our lives more comfortable, and to prevent and cure disease. Technology began when human beings first shaped tools and used fire. It remained very simple until about 10,000 years ago, when farming began. Key inventions quickly followed this shift to a settled way of life – for example, the wheel, metalworking, pottery and weaving. Industrial technology began in the late 1700s, with the steam engine and powered machinery. Engineers mastered new technologies – steel-making, electricity and the manufacturing of motor cars and aeroplanes. Technology has given us the power to control the environment. It has brought faster travel and communications. But it has also created problems which today's technology must solve for the sake of tomorrow.

Automatic tunnelling machine (mole)

DIGGING AND DRILLING

Some of the most advanced technology is used in mining, drilling and tunnelling. From Stone Age times, miners were pioneer technologists. Today, explosives, pneumatic drills and the automatic tunnelling machine, or mole, have replaced the pick and human muscle-power of the past.

Miners with picks

Canary

Simple mining tools

Electronic canary

Pneumatic drill

▼ *Production line assembly was an important step towards automation – the use of machines to do work previously done by people. Today, computer-controlled robots are used for routine assembly jobs. Before the assembly line was introduced (in the early 1900s, for car-making), most goods were made one at a time, just as potters have made pots by hand for thousands of years.*

FACTS ABOUT TECHNOLOGY

● Inventions can come too early. A spinning steam device was designed by an ancient Greek called Hero of Alexandria. It was thought of as a toy.

● Leonardo da Vinci's flying machine and Babbage's computer were also ahead of their time. But they were unworkable without a power source.

Punch press

Grinder

Borer

Press brakes

▲ *Machine tools are powered tools, used for shaping metal or other materials, by drilling holes, chiselling, grinding, pressing or cutting. Often the material (the workpiece) is moved while the tool stays still.*

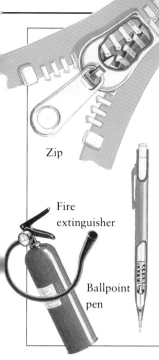

CLASSIC INVENTIONS

Commonplace but extremely useful inventions are often minor miracles of engineering. We take the zip and the ballpoint pen for granted – both were unknown 100 years ago. The chemical or foam fire-extinguisher is not particularly sophisticated, yet its technology would have baffled an 18th-century firefighter.

Zip

Fire extinguisher

Ballpoint pen

▲ *With submersibles and bathyscaphs, we can explore the depths of the oceans.*

▼ *Technology has given us the power to fight disasters, natural and human-made.*

▲ *Space technology has developed from the modest experiments of the 1930s to interplanetary probes.*

▼ *Technology keeps a deep sea diver alive in airless water, able to observe and work.*

▼ *Early people slowly mastered technological skills such as house-building, clothes- and fire-making, food preservation and water storage. They were using technology to adapt their environment, and make their lives easier. Domestic technology is still developing, though at different rates in different parts of the world.*

▼ *The modern Western house is far removed from the smoky huts of our ancestors. It has TV, radio and telephones, as well as electricity, gas, water and drainage.*

HOMES AND HOUSES

Modern technology can create a clean, comfortable and energy-efficient home. The house of tomorrow may well be computer-controlled, with all its systems (heating, lighting, water supply, security and communications) run by a small computer.

Television aerial

Solar panel on roof

Television satellite dish

Central heating radiator

Milling

Turning machine

Saw lathe

Broach

Sewage pipes

Water pipes

Buildings: Construction

The builders of the past used materials such as wood, stone and brick. Most of the work was done by hand, with hand-held tools. The construction of massive structures such as the pyramids of Egypt and Central America required thousands of workers, as well as skilful mathematics. There were some machines on the building sites of old – the Romans had cranes, for example. But not until the 1800s did the new steel and concrete construction techniques make it possible to build a skyscraper.

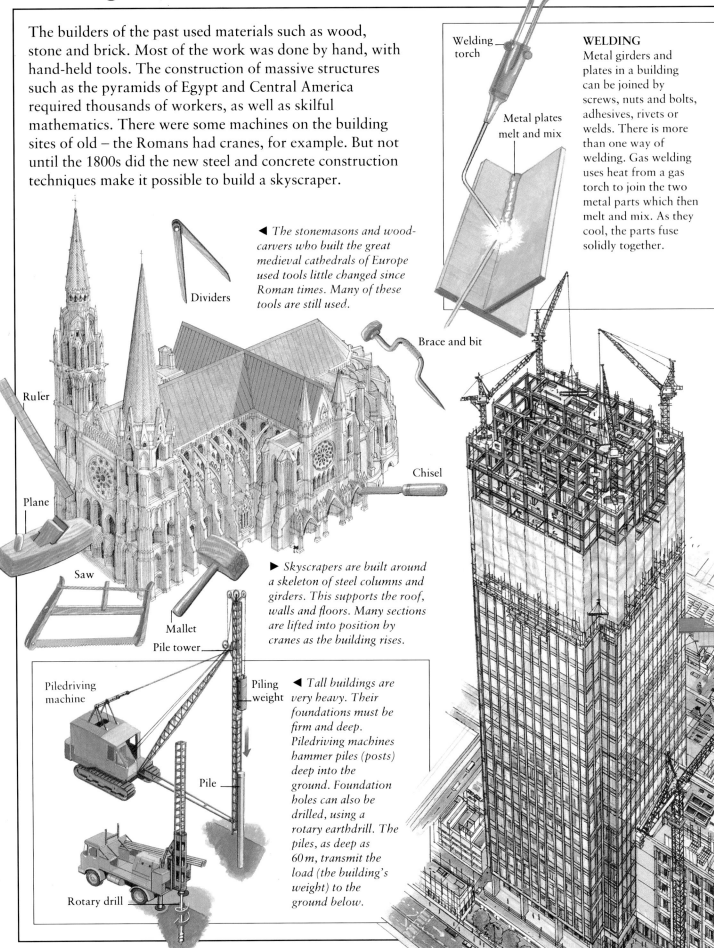

Welding torch

Metal plates melt and mix

WELDING
Metal girders and plates in a building can be joined by screws, nuts and bolts, adhesives, rivets or welds. There is more than one way of welding. Gas welding uses heat from a gas torch to join the two metal parts which then melt and mix. As they cool, the parts fuse solidly together.

◀ *The stonemasons and wood-carvers who built the great medieval cathedrals of Europe used tools little changed since Roman times. Many of these tools are still used.*

Dividers

Brace and bit

Ruler

Chisel

Plane

Saw

Mallet

▶ *Skyscrapers are built around a skeleton of steel columns and girders. This supports the roof, walls and floors. Many sections are lifted into position by cranes as the building rises.*

Pile tower

Piledriving machine

Piling weight

Pile

Rotary drill

◀ *Tall buildings are very heavy. Their foundations must be firm and deep. Piledriving machines hammer piles (posts) deep into the ground. Foundation holes can also be drilled, using a rotary earthdrill. The piles, as deep as 60 m, transmit the load (the building's weight) to the ground below.*

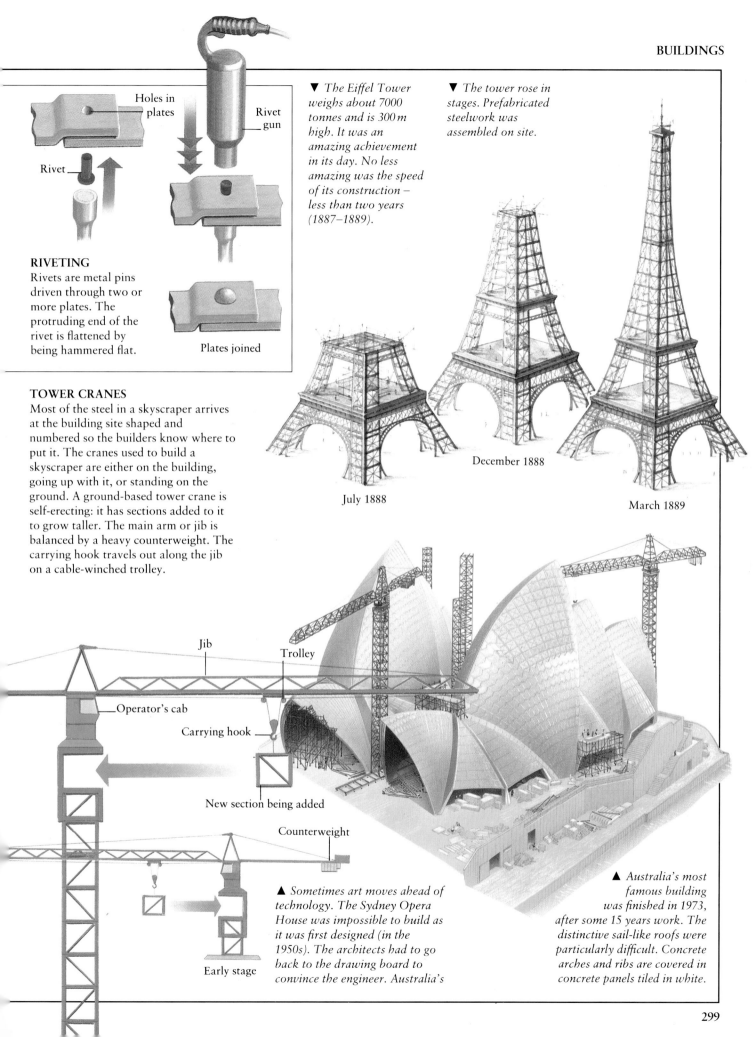

RIVETING

Rivets are metal pins driven through two or more plates. The protruding end of the rivet is flattened by being hammered flat.

Holes in plates

Rivet

Rivet gun

Plates joined

TOWER CRANES

Most of the steel in a skyscraper arrives at the building site shaped and numbered so the builders know where to put it. The cranes used to build a skyscraper are either on the building, going up with it, or standing on the ground. A ground-based tower crane is self-erecting: it has sections added to it to grow taller. The main arm or jib is balanced by a heavy counterweight. The carrying hook travels out along the jib on a cable-winched trolley.

▼ *The Eiffel Tower weighs about 7000 tonnes and is 300 m high. It was an amazing achievement in its day. No less amazing was the speed of its construction – less than two years (1887–1889).*

▼ *The tower rose in stages. Prefabricated steelwork was assembled on site.*

July 1888

December 1888

March 1889

Jib

Trolley

Operator's cab

Carrying hook

New section being added

Counterweight

Early stage

▲ *Sometimes art moves ahead of technology. The Sydney Opera House was impossible to build as it was first designed (in the 1950s). The architects had to go back to the drawing board to convince the engineer. Australia's*

▲ *Australia's most famous building was finished in 1973, after some 15 years work. The distinctive sail-like roofs were particularly difficult. Concrete arches and ribs are covered in concrete panels tiled in white.*

Buildings: Interiors

A building is an artificial environment. Its outside may look traditional or futuristic, but for the people who live and work in it, the inside is just as important. A building's internal systems must work efficiently for the comfort and safety of the people in it. The systems installed in many modern buildings include heating, air-conditioning, fire sprinklers, power and water supplies, waste disposal and communications. In multi-storey buildings, lifts and escalators are also important components.

CENTRAL HEATING

Different central heating systems use hot air, or hot water flowing through pipes and radiators. Gas-fired heating systems like this one, heat water in a boiler. Any water lost from the system is topped up from the header (or water supply) tank.

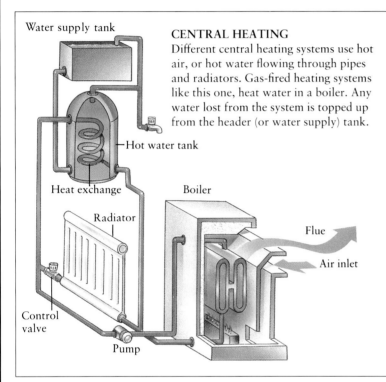

Water supply tank

Hot water tank

Heat exchange

Radiator

Boiler

Flue

Air inlet

Control valve

Pump

ROMAN CENTRAL HEATING

The Romans devised a method of heating their homes with hot air. This system was called a 'hypocaust'. The floors of their homes were raised on piers. The air was heated by burning fuel in a furnace. It then flowed through tiled flues in the walls into the space beneath the floors, heating the room above.

▲ *Modern building techniques can create huge interior spaces. In the Hong Kong and Shanghai Bank, in Hong Kong (47 storeys, opened 1986), the floors hang from steel masts. This unusual design creates a light and airy open space, called an atrium, inside the building.*

▼ *The Pompidou Arts Centre in Paris has its 'insides' on the outside. The pipes and tubes that carry essential services (the blue pipes are air-conditioning) are hidden in most buildings, but here they are on the outside. The lifts are also on the outside. This controversial design gave easy access to the services for maintenance and more room inside the building.*

▼ *Electric lifts are the kind of lift that serve high-rise offices and flats. Hydraulic lifts are driven by a hydraulic system. This type of lift is slower and usually serves buildings of fewer stories.*

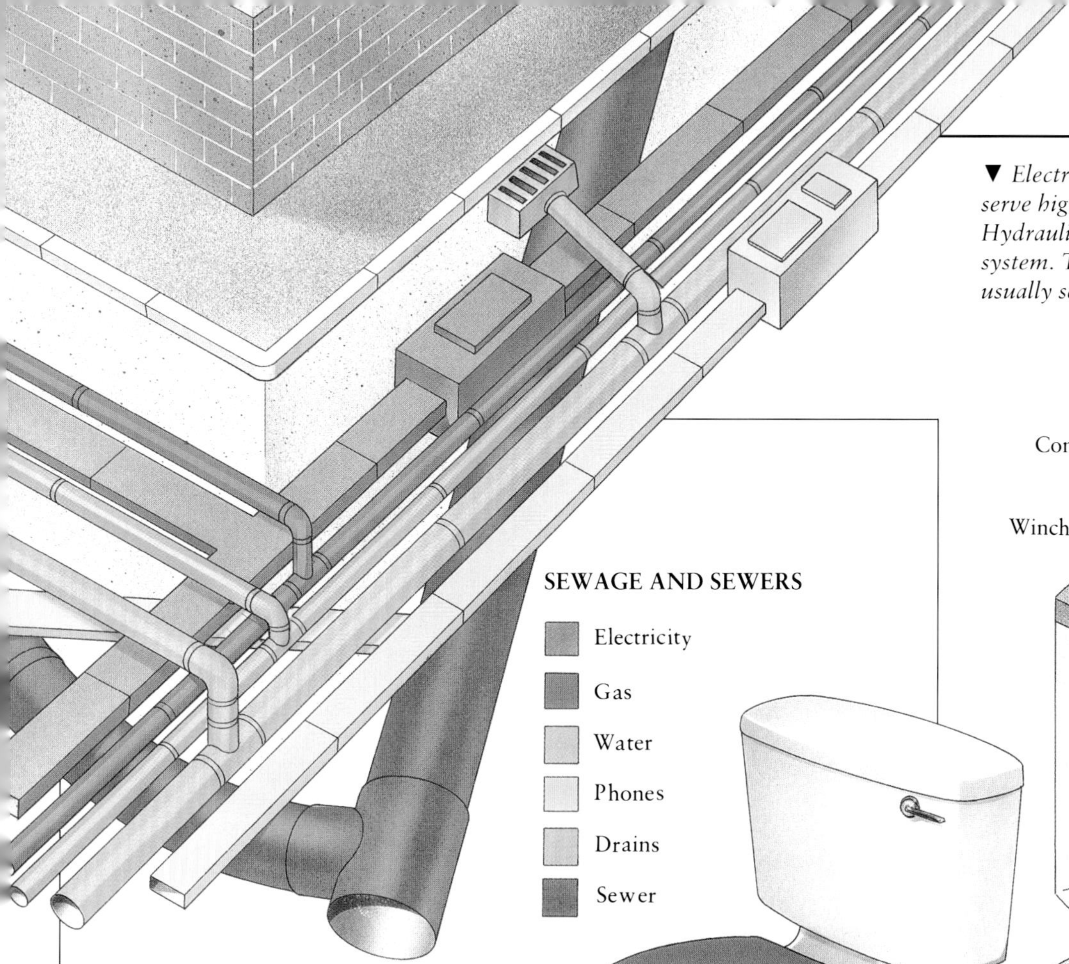

Lifting motor

Control gear

Winch

Main cable

Lift car

Safety brake

Guide rail

SEWAGE AND SEWERS

- Electricity
- Gas
- Water
- Phones
- Drains
- Sewer

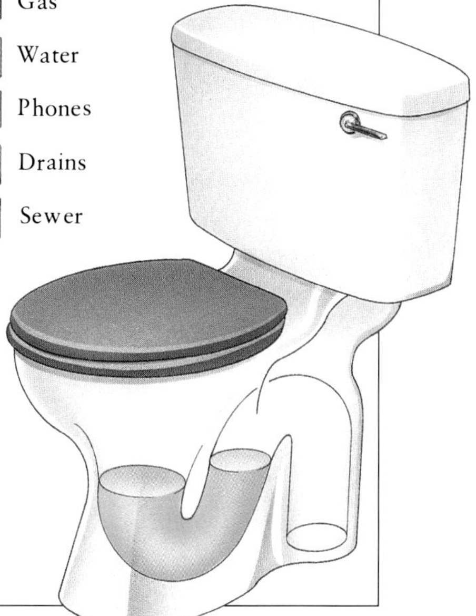

▲ *Beneath the city streets is a maze of drains, sewers, pipes and cables. These are the city's lifelines, bringing in water, gas and electricity – and removing the waste products from kitchens and bathrooms. Sewage plants remove harmful waste while clean water is recycled. Modern kitchen appliances and flushing lavatories use a lot of water!*

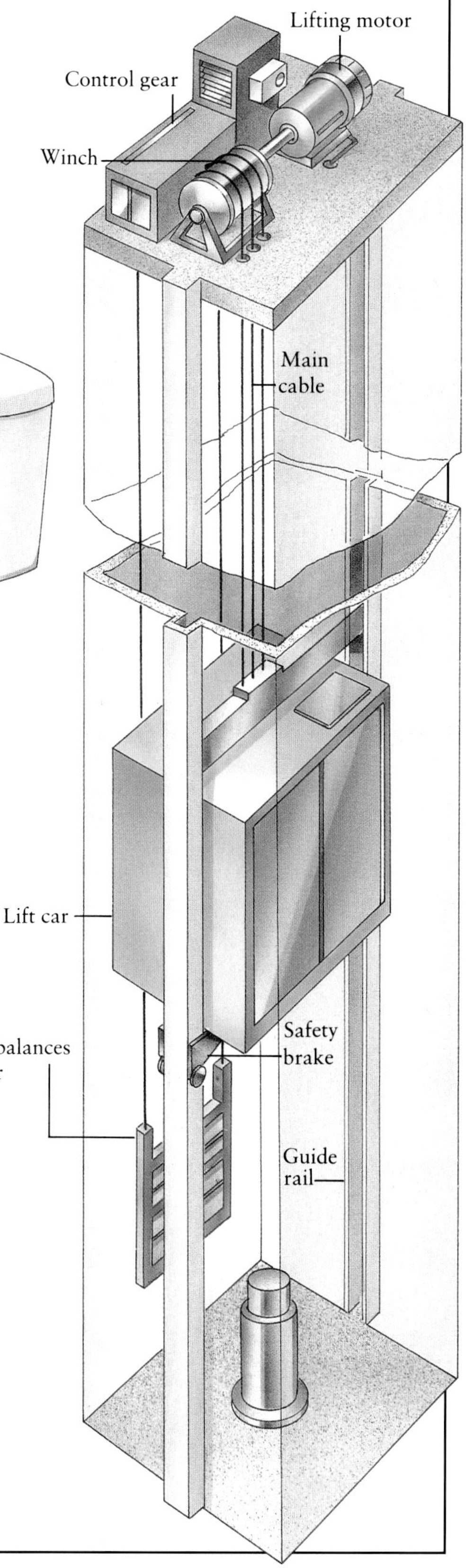

Counterweight balances weight of lift car

LIFTS

The lift was a 19th-century invention, and essential for high-rise living. Lifts are either electric or hydraulic. The lift runs up and down in a guide tower, or on guide rails. The motor does not have to raise the whole weight of the lift. A counterweight rises as the lift descends, and helps to pull the lift up again. If the cable snaps, the lift car is clamped against the tower or rails by a safety lock, or brake.

Bridges, Tunnels, Dams and Roads

Bridges were among the earliest structures. The simplest were log or rope bridges across rivers. The Romans spanned chasms with stone arches and built some of the most durable roads the world has seen. Dams were built 5000 years ago to control river waters and tunnels have a similarly long history. Methods of building were revolutionized in the 1800s by the use of steel-reinforced concrete, and by a more exact knowledge of the stresses and loads that such massive structures must withstand.

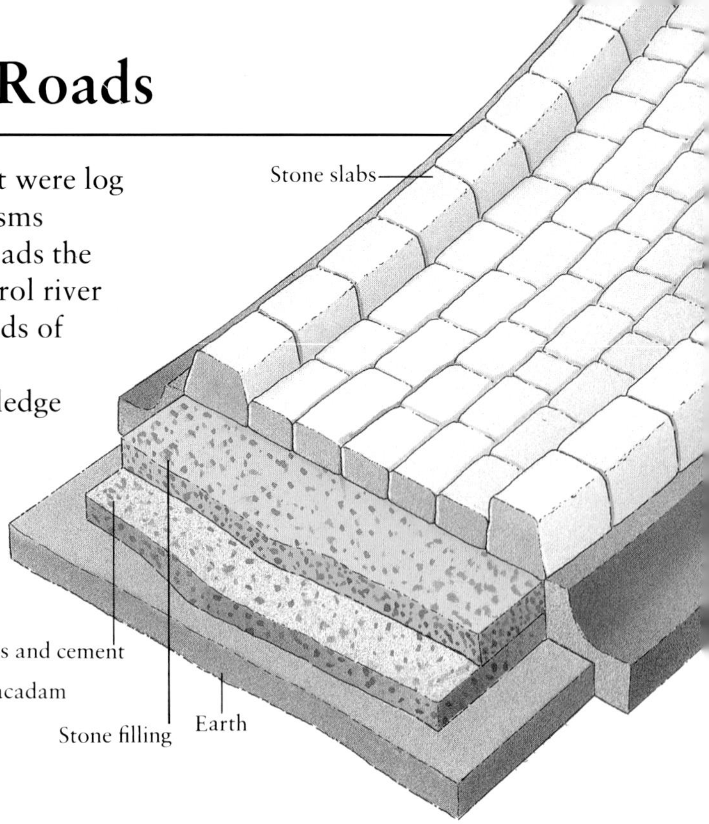

Stone slabs

Asphalt

Bitumen macadam

Stones and cement

Stone filling

Earth

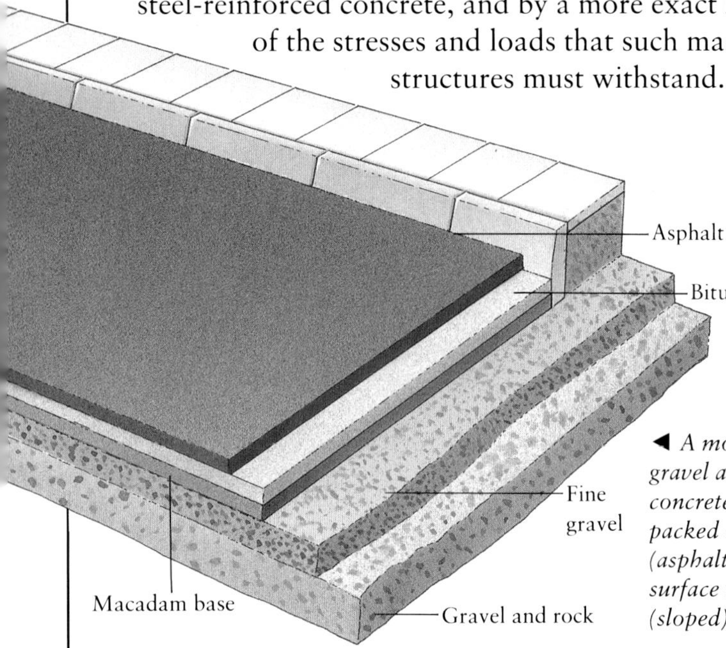

Fine gravel

Macadam base

Gravel and rock

◄ *A modern road has a bed of gravel and rock, topped with concrete or macadam – a hard-packed mixture of bitumen (asphalt and tar) and gravel. The surface is smooth, and cambered (sloped) to drain off water.*

▲ *A Roman road of 2000 years ago was made in layers: stones and cement, more stones or sand, and a top layer of larger slabs. The surface was sloped, so that water ran off into ditches at the sides. Roman roads were usually straight.*

DAMS

The two main kinds of modern dam are the embankment dam, a mass of earth and rock with a thin concrete skin, and the all-concrete dam. The embankment dam is more massive and cheaper: it does not need to be braced against the sides of a river valley.

The world's highest dams are embankment dams. A gravity dam is the simplest kind of concrete dam. The weight of concrete holds back the water. The arch dam is curved so that the weight of water is directed into the sides of the valley.

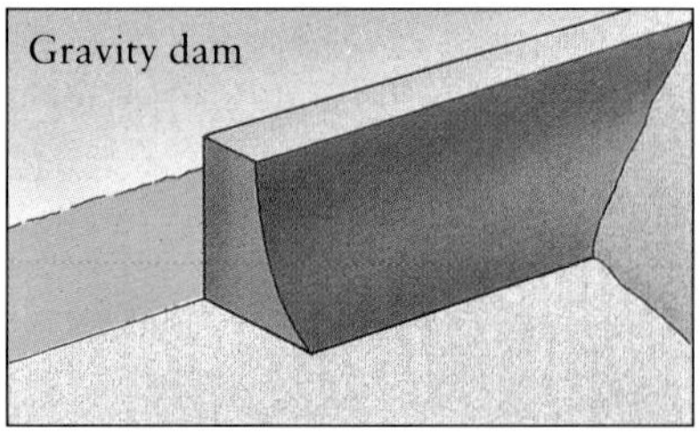

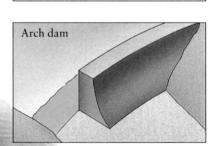

Gravity dam

Arch dam

Embankment dam

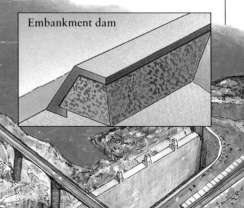

Cross-section of Channel Tunnel

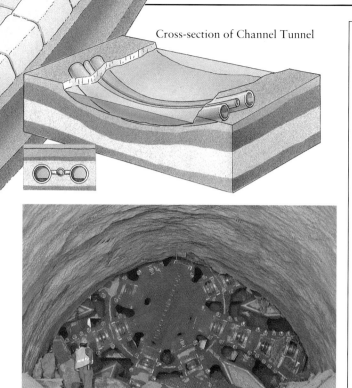

TYPES OF BRIDGES

▶ *A beam bridge is basically a giant 'log' placed across a stream. The beam (the roadway) stretches from bank to bank, and can be supported by pillars buried deep in the river bed.*

Beam bridge

▶ *Arch bridges may have one or more arches. The arch is immensely strong, so long as its ends are fixed. The roadway is built on top of the arch, which takes the weight of the whole structure.*

Arch bridge

▶ *Suspension bridges are hung by steel cables from tall towers. The cables can carry huge loads and a single span (distance from tower to tower) over 1000 m is possible.*

Suspension bridge

▲ *The Channel Tunnel, a rail link between England and France (top), was bored by tunnelling machines weighing 1300 tonnes each. Lasers kept the machines on course. The rotating cutting heads (above) were moved forwards by hydraulic jacks.*

▼ *A bridge must support its own weight, the weight of the traffic crossing it, and withstand stresses caused by high winds. A steel girder cantilever design was used for the rail bridge across the Firth of Forth in Scotland (completed in 1890).*

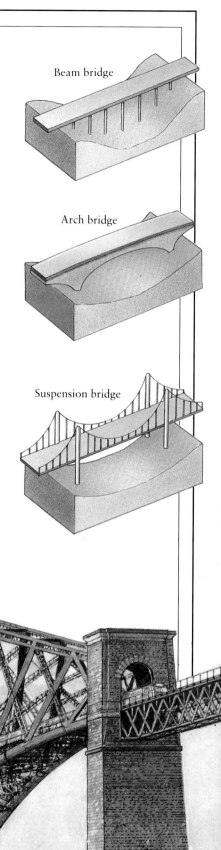

Transport

Transport developments have speeded every advance in civilization. Stone Age hunters dragged food home on wooden sledges or floated across streams on log rafts. By 3000 BC people had domesticated animals, fitted the wheel to the cart, and built the first sea-going ships. The horse and the sailing ship remained supreme until the late 1800s, when the railway, steamship and car brought undreamed-of speed and power. In the past 100 years, aeroplanes and spacecraft have transformed our world.

▼ *In 1804 Richard Trevithick developed the first steam locomotive.*

▲ *In the 1800s, people took coaches for long journeys.*

▶ *A powerfully-engined GMC 'dumper' truck.*

ROAD TRANSPORT

Trains now match some aeroplanes for speed. But most goods are carried by road in diesel trucks, and most people travel by car. The pedal bicycle (1839) offered cheap personal mobility. In the 1880s the motor car and motorcycle brought in the auto age, and a social and technological revolution. Horse cabs and horse-drawn carts lingered on into the early 1900s. By then electric trams running on rails laid in city streets were popular. Motor buses replaced the trams by the 1950s, but the 'environmentally friendly' tram is now making a comeback in some cities.

◀ *The Ferrari Dino was a classic sports car of the 1970s.*

▼ *American David Bushnell's submarine of 1775 was operated by hand-cranked screws.*

SEA TRANSPORT

The shape of sails was a key to the development of ships. The fully-rigged sailing ship – galleons and clippers – used a combination of square and triangular sails. Steam power was used first to drive paddlewheels, then screws or propellers.

In 1776 the tiny man-powered *Turtle* was the first submarine to go to war. Its modern counterpart is the nuclear submarine, able to cruise at a depth of 150 m and sail around the world without refuelling and without needing to surface.

▼ *Both the Americans and the British built fleets of clippers, the super-fast merchant ships of the mid-1800s.*

▼ *In ancient Egypt, ships were driven by oars and a single sail.*

304

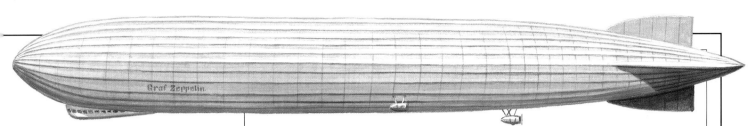

▼ With an average speed of 270 km/h, the French TGV (train à grand vitesse) is the world's fastest train; other fast electric trains include the Japanese bullet trains.

▲ A famous airship of the 1920s and 1930s was the German Graf Zeppelin.

▲ The SF-34 Delphin is a modern 2-seat training and sporting sailplane.

AIR TRANSPORT

Air transport began with the hot-air balloon pioneers of the late 1700s. Then came the great airships and the first epic flights across oceans and mountains in aeroplanes. Gliding and hang-gliding offer a chance for modern pilots to recapture the thrills of the early pioneer aviators.

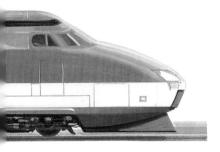

RAIL TRANSPORT

The steam railway combined medieval technology (wheels on metal rails) with the new power of steam. The world's first public steam railway opened in 1825. This was the Stockton and Darlington Railway in England. The first steam trains had a top speed of 20–40 km/h. Today's high-speed electric trains travel at 200 km/h.

▲ Octave Chanute (US) was one of the early pioneers of flight with his biplane glider.

▶ The German Fokker triplane was a successful World War I fighter plane.

▼ In the 1920s and 1930s, flying boats, like the Dornier Do X, defied wide oceans.

D-1929

DORNIER

▼ German U-boats sank many Allied boats in World War II.

▼ The great ocean liners are now usually used as cruise ships.

FRANCE

Land Transport

The wheel was probably the single most important invention in the history of transport. Its unknown inventor may have first used log rollers to move heavy stones. Together with the speed and muscle power of the horse, the wheel gave people new mobility. But for thousands of years, roads were usually terrible and few people actually travelled very far. Today, millions take to the roads every day. Cars and trucks fill the roads, causing traffic jams. The wheel's success has created a modern-day problem.

◄ *A wheel and axle together are a rotating lever, which increases force. A short movement of the axle produces a greater movement of the wheel. The wheel makes movement easier by reducing friction. Yet it needs friction, to push against the ground. Otherwise it would just spin round.*

WHEEL
The wheel was invented in the Middle East over 5000 years ago. The earliest land vehicles were four-wheeled carts. The wheels were made from wooden boards fixed together and roughly rounded. Spoked wheels appeared by 1500 BC. Wheel design then changed little until the 1800s when pneumatic (air-filled) tyres were developed.

◄ *Modern motorcycles have developed since the original wooden Daimler-Maybach Einspur (1885). The first bicycles had no pedals. The riders pushed against the ground with their feet. The modern bicycle dates from the 1860s.*

▼ *Spoked wheels were fitted to light chariots from about 1500 BC. The horse collar (invented c.AD 800), which did not choke the animal, allowed horses to pull much heavier wagons.*

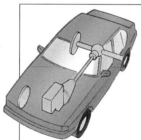

Rear wheel drive

Disc brake

DISC BRAKE
A car brake works by friction. There are two kinds of car brake, disc brakes and drum brakes. In a disc brake, pads press against both sides of a disc on the axle. Pressure from the brake pedal is increased by fluid hydraulics or by air pressure.

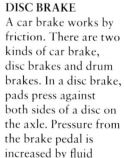

Brake grips disc

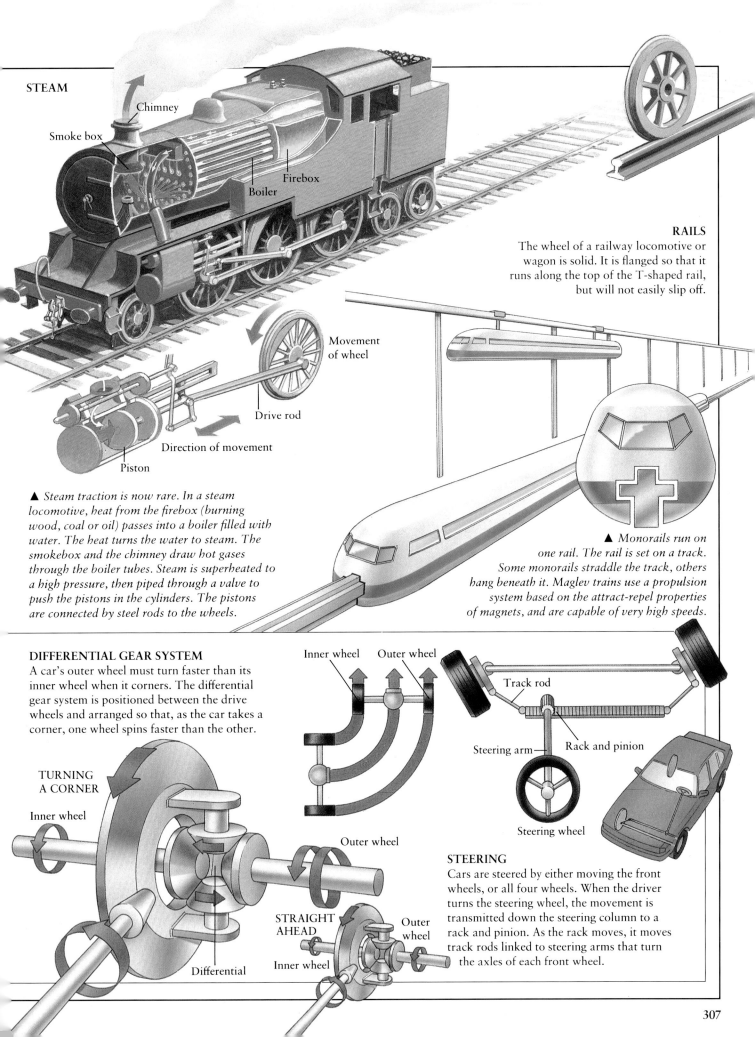

STEAM

Chimney

Smoke box

Boiler

Firebox

Movement
of wheel

Drive rod

Direction of movement

Piston

▲ *Steam traction is now rare. In a steam
locomotive, heat from the firebox (burning
wood, coal or oil) passes into a boiler filled with
water. The heat turns the water to steam. The
smokebox and the chimney draw hot gases
through the boiler tubes. Steam is superheated to
a high pressure, then piped through a valve to
push the pistons in the cylinders. The pistons
are connected by steel rods to the wheels.*

RAILS

The wheel of a railway locomotive or
wagon is solid. It is flanged so that it
runs along the top of the T-shaped rail,
but will not easily slip off.

▲ *Monorails run on
one rail. The rail is set on a track.
Some monorails straddle the track, others
hang beneath it. Maglev trains use a propulsion
system based on the attract-repel properties
of magnets, and are capable of very high speeds.*

DIFFERENTIAL GEAR SYSTEM

A car's outer wheel must turn faster than its
inner wheel when it corners. The differential
gear system is positioned between the drive
wheels and arranged so that, as the car takes a
corner, one wheel spins faster than the other.

Inner wheel   Outer wheel

Track rod

Rack and pinion

Steering arm

Steering wheel

TURNING
A CORNER

Inner wheel

Outer wheel

STRAIGHT
AHEAD

Outer
wheel

Inner wheel

Differential

STEERING

Cars are steered by either moving the front
wheels, or all four wheels. When the driver
turns the steering wheel, the movement is
transmitted down the steering column to a
rack and pinion. As the rack moves, it moves
track rods linked to steering arms that turn
the axles of each front wheel.

Sea Transport

The first boats were floating logs or rafts, driven by paddles. The development of sail took thousands of years, with sailors in different lands borrowing ideas from each other. The stern rudder, for example, came from China. Paddle-driven steamships were developed in the early 1800s, at about the same time as iron hulls began to be used instead of wooden ones. From the 1830s, the screw propeller replaced the paddle wheel. Ships grew larger and today the biggest are 500,000-tonne supertankers.

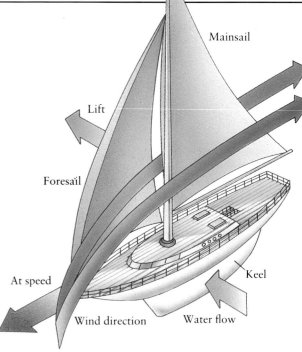

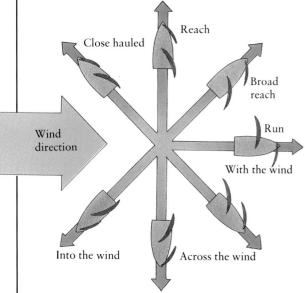

Reach
Close hauled
Broad reach
Run
With the wind
Wind direction
Into the wind
Across the wind

SAILING CRAFT
A sailing craft, such as a yacht, is dependent on the wind, but it can make headway in any direction – though at different rates. Sailing (running) with the wind is not the fastest. Sailing across the wind (reaching) is faster. To sail into the wind, a boat must tack or zig-zag at an angle of 45° to the wind direction. Sailing directly into the wind causes the sails to flap uselessly.

Mainsail
Lift
Foresaïl
At speed
Keel
Wind direction
Water flow

SAILS
When sailing into the wind, the sails act like a slotted wing, and a strong suction force (similar to an aerofoil's lift) is produced. This operates in two directions: a forwards thrust and a sideways push. The keel beneath the boat counteracts this sideways push and stops the boat capsizing.

MODERN SHIPS
Most modern ships are powered either by steam turbines or diesel engines. Both need oil as fuel. Nuclear power plants have been tried in naval ships, but not adopted for general use. The biggest ships afloat are oil tankers, bulk carriers and aircraft carriers. A big tanker may need 8 km to slow to a halt; at normal speed this can take as long as 20 minutes.

HOVERCRAFT
Air-cushion vehicles (ACVs) or hovercraft ride on a cushion of air, blown downwards by fans. The air is trapped inside the skirt of the craft. ACVs can travel over both land and water.

Air cushion

At rest

At speed

HYDROFOIL
A hydrofoil is faster than ordinary craft because its design reduces water resistance. It has wings beneath its hull. At rest, the hydrofoil floats low in the water. As it gains speed, the wings lift the craft so that it skims across the water.

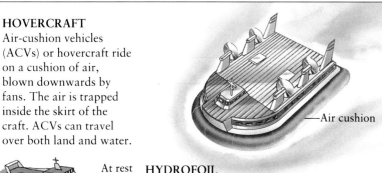

Lift

Water flow

Radar scanner

Fishing trawler

Crew's quarters

Cold storage of fish

4000 BC: Egyptians build reed boats
500 BC: Oared trireme galley
AD 1200s: Stern rudder replaces steering oar
1500: First galleons
1801: Fulton's submarine *Nautilus*
1802: First working steamship, Symington's *Charlotte Dundas*
1807: Fulton's steamboat *Clermont* first carries passengers
1818: First all-iron sailing ship
1830s: Screw propeller
1838: Steamer *Sirius* crosses Atlantic
1840s: First clippers
1872: First oil tanker with engines in the stern (as now)
1894: First turbine ship
1906: First hydrofoil
1954: First nuclear submarine

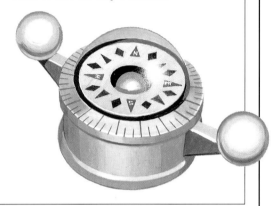

Horizon in view

Sun brought into view by mirrors

Mirrors adjusted so horizon and Sun align; altitude measured

Sextant

NAVIGATION
The sextant is an optical instrument with mirrors and a telescope. It measures the altitude of the Sun above the horizon, in order to find the ship's latitude.

▶ *The ship's compass has a compass card, with magnets beneath, floating in liquid inside a bowl. Navigators also use radar scanners and direction-finders, to receive signals from other ships, shore beacons and satellites. Echo-sounders measure the depth of water beneath the ship.*

PROPELLER BLADES
The blades of a ship's screw propeller force water backwards as they are turned by the engines. The water pushes back, with equal force, against the ship. This reaction force moves the ship forwards. The propeller blades are curved, like aerofoils, producing additional forward suction.

Screw propeller   Water forced backwards
Forward movement
Direction of spin

STEERING
The ship's rudder hangs in the water flow produced by the ship's forward motion. In straight motion, the water flows past the rudder. Moving the rudder left or right pushes water aside. The water pushes back with equal and opposite force. The effect of this reaction is to push the stern of the boat in the opposite direction to the rudder's movement.

▼ *A ship floats if it weighs less than the weight of water it displaces. Only warships are measured by displacement. Others are measured in deadweight tonnage (total weight) or gross tonnage (internal volume).*

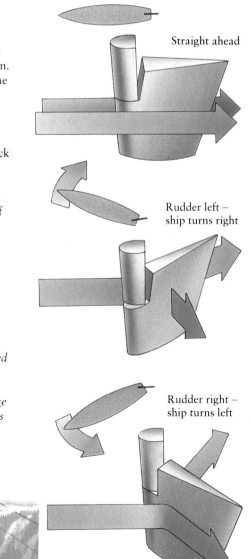

Straight ahead

Rudder left – ship turns right

Rudder right – ship turns left

ration of fish

l tanks   Diesel engines

Air Transport

The pioneers of air travel knew little about the forces acting on an object in flight. The Montgolfier brothers' hot-air balloons of the late 1700s were rumoured to contain a mysterious 'rising air'. During the 1800s, scientists began to work out the forces involved in flight, through experiments with gliders and airships. From 1903, when the Wright brothers flew their first flimsy aeroplane, to the jumbos and supersonic jets of today, air transport has developed with astonishing speed.

INSIDE AN AIRLINER
A modern airliner, such as the Airbus, has a wide body able to carry 300 or more passengers. The body is known as the fuselage, and houses crew, passengers and cargo. Major sections of the plane (wings, tail, engines) are often built in different factories.

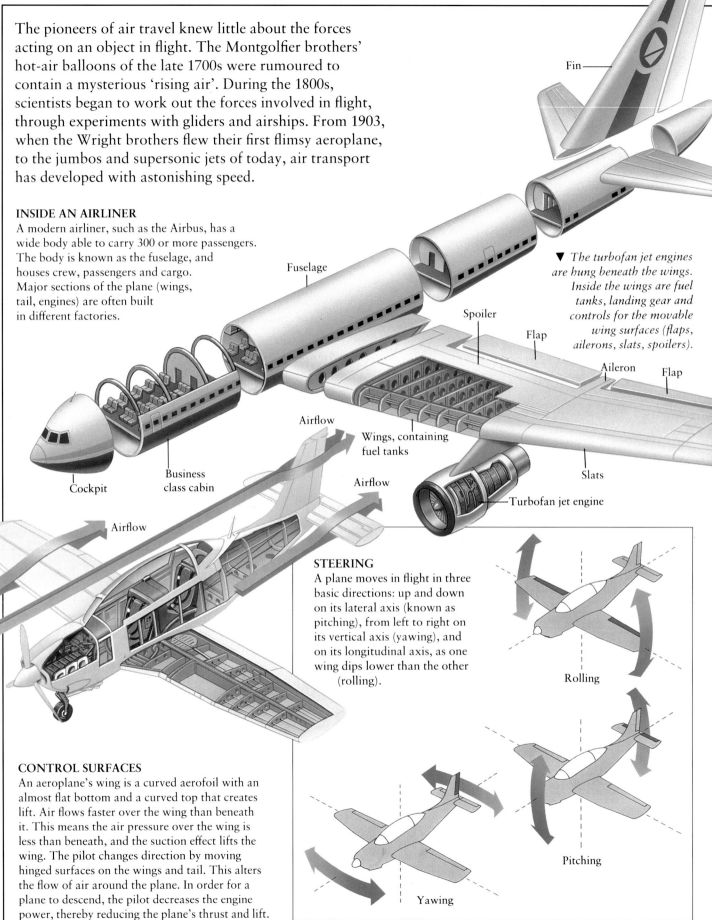

▼ *The turbofan jet engines are hung beneath the wings. Inside the wings are fuel tanks, landing gear and controls for the movable wing surfaces (flaps, ailerons, slats, spoilers).*

Fin

Fuselage

Spoiler

Flap

Aileron

Flap

Airflow

Wings, containing fuel tanks

Airflow

Slats

Turbofan jet engine

Cockpit

Business class cabin

Airflow

STEERING
A plane moves in flight in three basic directions: up and down on its lateral axis (known as pitching), from left to right on its vertical axis (yawing), and on its longitudinal axis, as one wing dips lower than the other (rolling).

Rolling

Pitching

Yawing

CONTROL SURFACES
An aeroplane's wing is a curved aerofoil with an almost flat bottom and a curved top that creates lift. Air flows faster over the wing than beneath it. This means the air pressure over the wing is less than beneath, and the suction effect lifts the wing. The pilot changes direction by moving hinged surfaces on the wings and tail. This alters the flow of air around the plane. In order for a plane to descend, the pilot decreases the engine power, thereby reducing the plane's thrust and lift.

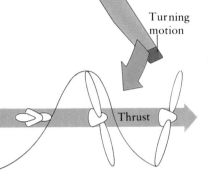

Engine

Propellers

Turning motion

Thrust

PROPELLERS

All aeroplanes had propellers until the 1940s. The shape of a propeller, or airscrew, is an aerofoil, similar to the wing. As it is spun by the engine, it bites into the air to produce thrust.

Compressor

Exhaust gases

Combustion chamber

Higher speed

Air sucked in

JET ENGINES

Jet engines were invented in the 1930s and first used in aircraft during World War II. In a simple jet engine, air is sucked in at the front by compressors into a combustion chamber where fuel is burned. Hot exhaust gases shoot out backwards, pushing the plane forwards. Modern turbofan engines have longer blades at the front of the compressor, to push in extra air.

Lower speed

▲ *A fast jet has a swept-back wing, to minimize drag. But at low speeds, straight wings fly better. The swing-wing aeroplane has movable wings. They stick out for take-off and landing, but are swept back for high speed.*

FACTS ABOUT FLIGHT

- The first jet-engine aircraft was the German Heinkel He 178; its first flight was in 1939.
- The first jet airliners were the De Havilland Comet and the Boeing 707, both introduced in the 1950s.

- The first plane to fly faster than sound and break the 'sound barrier' was the US Bell XS-1 in 1947.
- The world's fastest plane was the US X-15 rocket plane, which had a top speed of 7297 km/h. It was used for research in the 1960s.

HELICOPTERS

Helicopters are the most successful vertical take-off and landing aircraft (VTOL) and the most versatile of all air transport. Helicopters obtain lift and propulsion from engine-driven rotors. As they are able to hover at nearly zero ground speed, they can play vital roles in transporting ill people, air-sea rescue, sowing crops, or as military transportation. The CH-47 Chinook *(left)* is a medium transport helicopter with a tandem-rotor; it was originally developed for the US Army.

Normal flight

Nozzles rotate for acceleration

Thrust engines blast down for take-off

VERTICAL FLIGHT

The Harrier is one of the few fixed-wing planes able to rise straight into the air and hover in mid-air. It has four swivelling nozzles which direct exhaust gases from the jet engines. When the nozzles direct thrust downwards, the plane takes off or lands vertically, or hovers.

Materials

The materials we use are natural (wood, cotton, wool) or synthetic (glass, steel, plastic), or sometimes a mixture of the two. The first materials people used were natural. They learned to shape stones, to weave fibres, and to make pots and bricks from clay. They discovered how to extract metals from ores in the ground, and how to make metal objects. In the Bronze and Iron Ages, the Earth's resources seemed limitless. Now we must learn to conserve and recycle, and to make the best use of all materials.

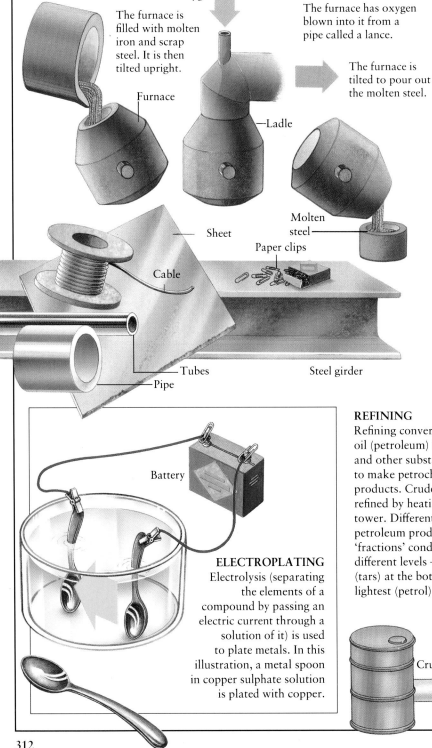

BASIC OXYGEN PROCESS Oxygen

The furnace is filled with molten iron and scrap steel. It is then tilted upright.

The furnace has oxygen blown into it from a pipe called a lance.

The furnace is tilted to pour out the molten steel.

Furnace

Ladle

Molten steel

Sheet

Paper clips

Cable

Tubes

Pipe

Steel girder

STEEL-MAKING
More than half the world's steel is made by the basic oxygen process. The raw material is about three parts melted iron and one part scrap steel. Blowing oxygen into the melted iron raises the temperature and gets rid of impurities. Two other processes (electric arc and open hearth) are also common.

USES OF STEEL
Solid lumps of steel (known as blooms, billets or slabs) are finished in various ways – by rolling them into sheets or bars, or by drawing them into thin wires, for example. Rust can be prevented by coating the steel with zinc (a process called 'galvanizing').

Battery

ELECTROPLATING
Electrolysis (separating the elements of a compound by passing an electric current through a solution of it) is used to plate metals. In this illustration, a metal spoon in copper sulphate solution is plated with copper.

REFINING
Refining converts crude oil (petroleum) into fuels and other substances used to make petrochemical products. Crude oil is refined by heating it in a tower. Different petroleum products, or 'fractions' condense at different levels – heaviest (tars) at the bottom, lightest (petrol) at the top.

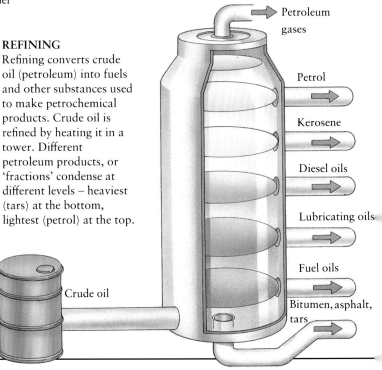

Petroleum gases

Petrol

Kerosene

Diesel oils

Lubricating oils

Fuel oils

Bitumen, asphalt, tars

Crude oil

GLASS

Glass is made by mixing and heating sand, limestone and soda ash. When these ingredients melt they turn into glass, which hardens as it cools. Glass is in fact not a solid but a 'supercooled' liquid. It can be shaped by blowing, pressing, drawing, casting into moulds, rolling, and floating across molten tin, to make large sheets.

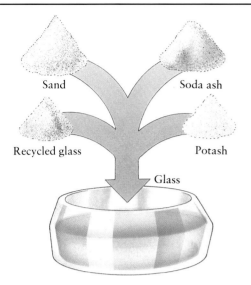

Sand
Soda ash
Recycled glass
Potash
Glass

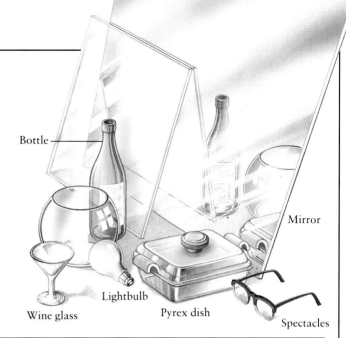

Bottle
Mirror
Wine glass
Lightbulb
Pyrex dish
Spectacles

MATERIAL BREAKTHROUGHS

- Stainless steel is an alloy of steel with chromium or nickel. It was first made by accident.
- All plastics are chemical compounds called polymers. The first synthetic plastic was bakelite (1908). Other important plastic breakthroughs were cellophane (1912), polystyrene (1930s) and PVC (1940s).
- The first synthetic fibre was nylon, developed in the 1930s as a cheap alternative to silk.
- Carbon fibres were first used by Edison as filaments in his light bulb (1879).

CERAMICS

Ceramic objects, such as pottery and porcelain, electrical insulators, bricks and roof tiles, are all made from clay. The clay is shaped or moulded when wet and soft, and heated or 'fired' in a kiln until it hardens.

TEXTILES

A textile is any cloth made from woven fibres. People first wove textiles nearly 8000 years ago. The first synthetic fibres, such as acrylics, were made from cellulose in the 1930s. Other synthetics, like nylon, come from oil. Most synthetic fibres are stronger than natural fibres and can be made crease-resistant.

WEAVING

In weaving, threads are joined in a crisscross pattern to make cloth. Fibres from plants (flax, cotton) or animals (wool) are first spun (twisted) into thread. Then the threads are woven on a loom. Lengthwise threads make up the warp; crosswise threads are the weft.

Weft

Warp

Teasing wires produce loose bundles of fibres (slivers)

Dividers

THE SPINNING PROCESS

Slivers stretched and spun into cotton yarn

Pressure rollers flatten cotton fibres

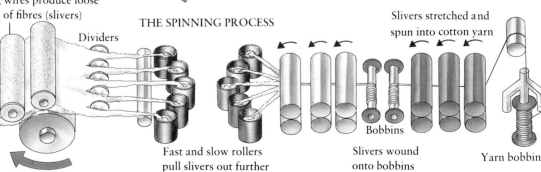

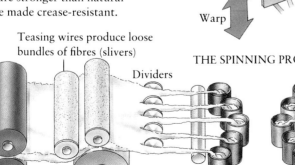

Fast and slow rollers pull slivers out further

Bobbins

Slivers wound onto bobbins

Yarn bobbin

Farming

Farming began about 10,000 years ago, probably in the Middle East. Farming technology developed slowly as iron tools replaced wooden sticks and flint sickles. Later, heavier ploughs, drawn by animals, came into use and crop rotation was developed. After the 1700s farms began to be mechanized. Two kinds of farming are now practised worldwide: subsistence (the farmer plants crops to eat) and cash (the farmer plants crops to sell). Science has helped boost crop yields and reduce losses from pests and disease.

CHANGES IN FARMING

8000–7000 BC: Sowing of cereals, domestication of animals
4000 BC: Irrigation of crops
500 BC: Iron tools, ox-drawn plough
100 BC: Romans practise rotation of crops
1400s: Farmers in Europe begin to enclose (hedge) their land. Enclosure meant bigger farms and improved methods
1500s: New plants (maize, tomato, potato) brought from America to Europe
1600s: European farmers start to grow clover and turnips to feed their animals in winter. Before this, most pigs and cattle were killed in the autumn
1700s: Scientific farming begins. Improved breeds of livestock. Tull's seed drill (1701)
1800s: Threshing and reaping machines McCormick's reaper-binder (1873). Steam power. Food canning and refrigeration
1900s: Tractors replace horses on many farms. Fewer but larger farms means fewer farmworkers. Chemical fertilizers, weedkillers and pesticides. Green revolution boosts crop yield. Genetically engineered disease-free plants. Intensive rearing of livestock

Shaduf

Canals

IRRIGATION

To bring water to their fields, farmers in the dry lands of the Middle East, Africa and Asia have always practised irrigation. Simple machines like the shaduf and screw-pump are used to lift water from a river into ditches. Canals are dug to bring water to dry areas.

▼ *Aerial crop spraying defends field crops against pests.*

PEST CONTROL

Anything that eats crops or causes disease is a pest. Insect pests (for example, locusts) are devastating. Chemicals can destroy pests, but biological control (for example, the sterilization of males, or finding a natural predator) does less harm to other living things.

Colorado beetle

THE PLOUGH

The modern tractor plough has a number of blades, or bottoms. In a typical plough, the share cuts a furrow through the soil; the mouldboard then turns the soil and breaks it up. There are also disc and rotary ploughs. The first ploughs were stick-ploughs, pulled and pushed by the farmers themselves.

Early ploughs

Modern plough

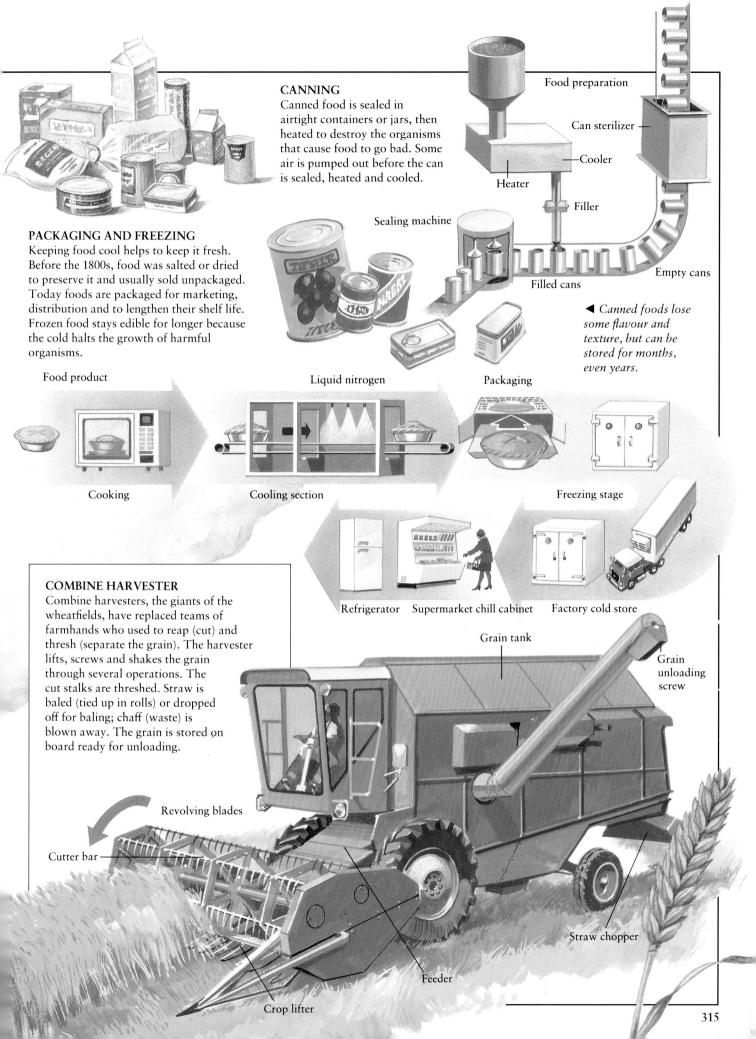

CANNING

Canned food is sealed in airtight containers or jars, then heated to destroy the organisms that cause food to go bad. Some air is pumped out before the can is sealed, heated and cooled.

Food preparation

Can sterilizer

Cooler

Heater

Filler

Sealing machine

Filled cans

Empty cans

◀ *Canned foods lose some flavour and texture, but can be stored for months, even years.*

PACKAGING AND FREEZING

Keeping food cool helps to keep it fresh. Before the 1800s, food was salted or dried to preserve it and usually sold unpackaged. Today foods are packaged for marketing, distribution and to lengthen their shelf life. Frozen food stays edible for longer because the cold halts the growth of harmful organisms.

Food product

Liquid nitrogen

Packaging

Cooking

Cooling section

Freezing stage

Refrigerator   Supermarket chill cabinet   Factory cold store

COMBINE HARVESTER

Combine harvesters, the giants of the wheatfields, have replaced teams of farmhands who used to reap (cut) and thresh (separate the grain). The harvester lifts, screws and shakes the grain through several operations. The cut stalks are threshed. Straw is baled (tied up in rolls) or dropped off for baling; chaff (waste) is blown away. The grain is stored on board ready for unloading.

Grain tank

Grain unloading screw

Revolving blades

Cutter bar

Straw chopper

Feeder

Crop lifter

315

Medicine

Doctors of the ancient world combined folklore, observation and philosophy to treat illness. They carried out surgery without anaesthetics, using techniques such as acupuncture. Scientific medicine began in the 1600s, with the discovery of microscopic bacteria, and with advances in anatomical knowledge. Surgery was made safer in the 1800s with anaesthetics and antiseptics. Today, doctors use antibiotics to kill bacteria. Surgeons can transplant organs, and scientists probe the secrets of the gene.

Stethoscope

Otoscope

Thermometer

▶ *Doctors use various tools to examine a patient. The stethoscope amplifies sounds made by the heart and lungs. The otoscope is used to examine the inner ear. The thermometer records body temperature.*

MICROSCOPE
The medical microscope dates from the mid-1600s, when bacteria were seen through lenses for the first time. The optical microscope, and the more powerful electron microscope (1930s), have enabled scientists to unravel the secrets of the cell.

Microscope

▲ *A patient having a body scan. CAT (computerized axial tomography) takes X-ray pictures, computerized into 'slice' images.*

▶ *Ultrasound scanners are used in the treatment of kidney or heart disease. A computer changes the data received from a transducer into an image of the organ.*

▼ *This HIV virus causes AIDS (acquired immune deficiency syndrome). Viruses live in other living things. They invade cells, causing disease. Drugs such as antibiotics do not work against viruses.*

◀ *Radioisotopes are used in medical detective work. A radioactive trace (a radioisotope attached to a carrier substance) is put into the patient's body. It is carried around the bloodstream to the target organ. As the radioisotope decays, it gives off radiation that forms a scanner image.*

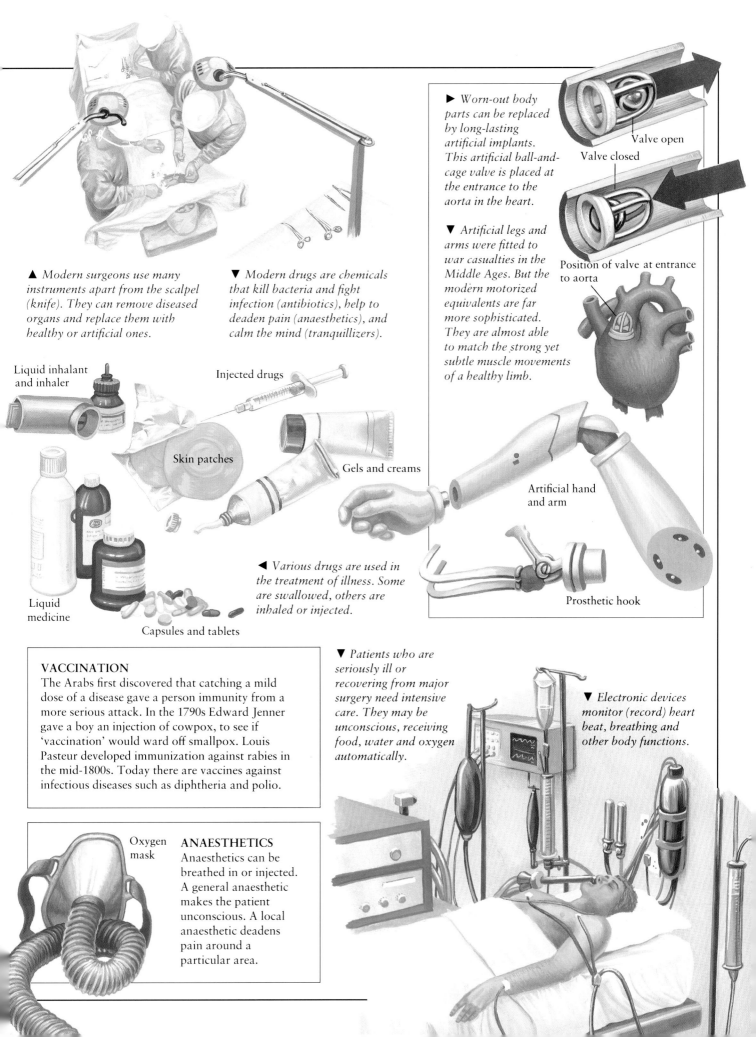

▲ Modern surgeons use many instruments apart from the scalpel (knife). They can remove diseased organs and replace them with healthy or artificial ones.

▼ Modern drugs are chemicals that kill bacteria and fight infection (antibiotics), help to deaden pain (anaesthetics), and calm the mind (tranquillizers).

► Worn-out body parts can be replaced by long-lasting artificial implants. This artificial ball-and-cage valve is placed at the entrance to the aorta in the heart.

Valve open

Valve closed

Position of valve at entrance to aorta

▼ Artificial legs and arms were fitted to war casualties in the Middle Ages. But the modern motorized equivalents are far more sophisticated. They are almost able to match the strong yet subtle muscle movements of a healthy limb.

Liquid inhalant and inhaler

Injected drugs

Skin patches

Gels and creams

Liquid medicine

Capsules and tablets

◄ Various drugs are used in the treatment of illness. Some are swallowed, others are inhaled or injected.

Artificial hand and arm

Prosthetic hook

VACCINATION
The Arabs first discovered that catching a mild dose of a disease gave a person immunity from a more serious attack. In the 1790s Edward Jenner gave a boy an injection of cowpox, to see if 'vaccination' would ward off smallpox. Louis Pasteur developed immunization against rabies in the mid-1800s. Today there are vaccines against infectious diseases such as diphtheria and polio.

▼ Patients who are seriously ill or recovering from major surgery need intensive care. They may be unconscious, receiving food, water and oxygen automatically.

▼ Electronic devices monitor (record) heart beat, breathing and other body functions.

Oxygen mask

ANAESTHETICS
Anaesthetics can be breathed in or injected. A general anaesthetic makes the patient unconscious. A local anaesthetic deadens pain around a particular area.

Communications

Communication is the exchange of ideas and information. It has developed from the beginnings of language in the Stone Age to modern methods of message-sending and storing, such as radio, television, recording and computers. The communications revolution began with the development of printing in the 1400s, allowing information to be copied and distributed easily for the first time. In this century, electronic telecommunications have given us almost instant communications with people and machines far apart.

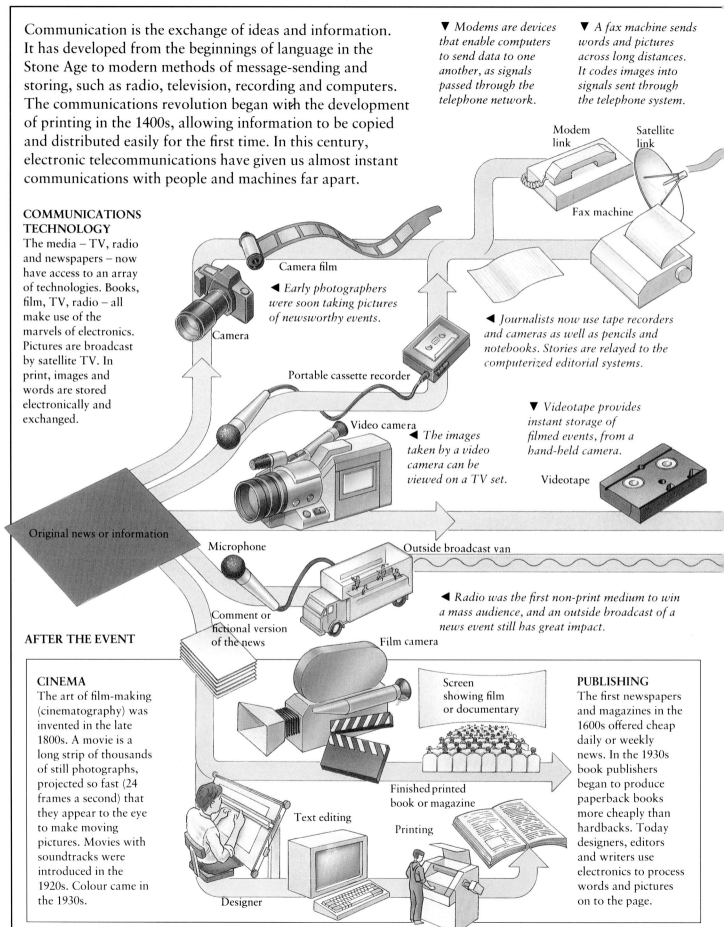

▼ *Modems are devices that enable computers to send data to one another, as signals passed through the telephone network.*

▼ *A fax machine sends words and pictures across long distances. It codes images into signals sent through the telephone system.*

Modem link

Satellite link

Fax machine

COMMUNICATIONS TECHNOLOGY
The media – TV, radio and newspapers – now have access to an array of technologies. Books, film, TV, radio – all make use of the marvels of electronics. Pictures are broadcast by satellite TV. In print, images and words are stored electronically and exchanged.

Camera film

Camera

◀ *Early photographers were soon taking pictures of newsworthy events.*

◀ *Journalists now use tape recorders and cameras as well as pencils and notebooks. Stories are relayed to the computerized editorial systems.*

Portable cassette recorder

Video camera

◀ *The images taken by a video camera can be viewed on a TV set.*

▼ *Videotape provides instant storage of filmed events, from a hand-held camera.*

Videotape

Original news or information

Microphone

Outside broadcast van

AFTER THE EVENT

Comment or fictional version of the news

◀ *Radio was the first non-print medium to win a mass audience, and an outside broadcast of a news event still has great impact.*

Film camera

CINEMA
The art of film-making (cinematography) was invented in the late 1800s. A movie is a long strip of thousands of still photographs, projected so fast (24 frames a second) that they appear to the eye to make moving pictures. Movies with soundtracks were introduced in the 1920s. Colour came in the 1930s.

Screen showing film or documentary

Finished printed book or magazine

Text editing

Printing

Designer

PUBLISHING
The first newspapers and magazines in the 1600s offered cheap daily or weekly news. In the 1930s book publishers began to produce paperback books more cheaply than hardbacks. Today designers, editors and writers use electronics to process words and pictures on to the page.

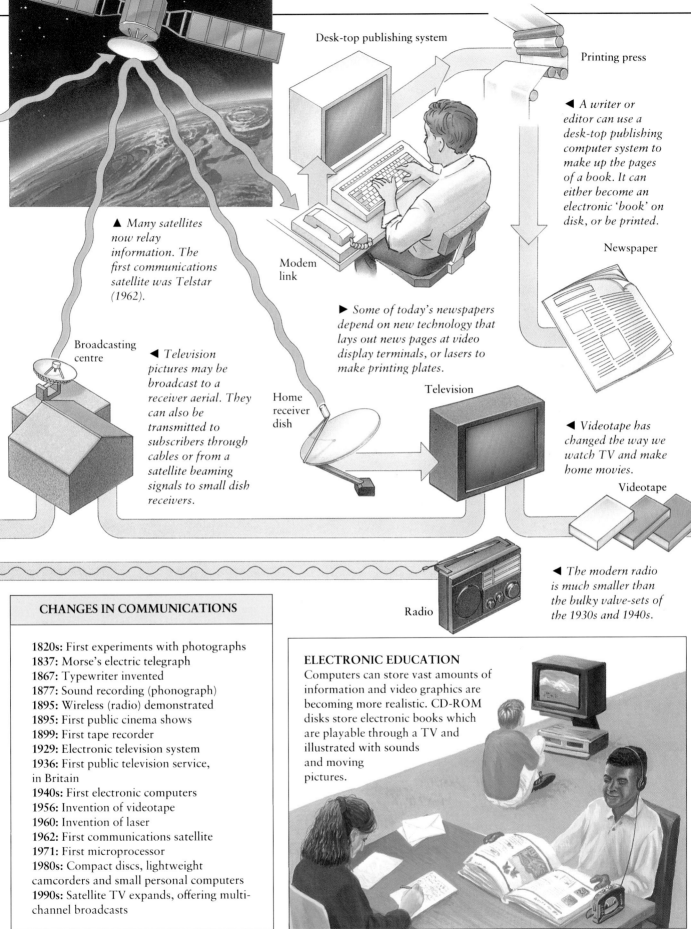

Desk-top publishing system

Printing press

▲ *Many satellites now relay information. The first communications satellite was Telstar (1962).*

Modem link

◀ *A writer or editor can use a desk-top publishing computer system to make up the pages of a book. It can either become an electronic 'book' on disk, or be printed.*

Newspaper

▶ *Some of today's newspapers depend on new technology that lays out news pages at video display terminals, or lasers to make printing plates.*

Broadcasting centre

◀ *Television pictures may be broadcast to a receiver aerial. They can also be transmitted to subscribers through cables or from a satellite beaming signals to small dish receivers.*

Home receiver dish

Television

◀ *Videotape has changed the way we watch TV and make home movies.*

Videotape

◀ *The modern radio is much smaller than the bulky valve-sets of the 1930s and 1940s.*

Radio

CHANGES IN COMMUNICATIONS

1820s: First experiments with photographs
1837: Morse's electric telegraph
1867: Typewriter invented
1877: Sound recording (phonograph)
1895: Wireless (radio) demonstrated
1895: First public cinema shows
1899: First tape recorder
1929: Electronic television system
1936: First public television service, in Britain
1940s: First electronic computers
1956: Invention of videotape
1960: Invention of laser
1962: First communications satellite
1971: First microprocessor
1980s: Compact discs, lightweight camcorders and small personal computers
1990s: Satellite TV expands, offering multi-channel broadcasts

ELECTRONIC EDUCATION
Computers can store vast amounts of information and video graphics are becoming more realistic. CD-ROM disks store electronic books which are playable through a TV and illustrated with sounds and moving pictures.

319

INVENTIONS

7000 BC: Pottery (Mesopotamia)

4000 BC: Iron smelting (origin unknown)

4000–3000 BC: Bricks (Egypt and Assyria)

*c.*3000 BC: Wheel (Asia)

*c.*3000 BC: Plough (Egypt and Mesopotamia)

3000 BC: Glass (Egypt)

2600 BC: Geometry (Egypt)

700 BC: Calendar (Babylon)

*c.*500 BC: Abacus (China)

200s BC: Screw (for raising water), Archimedes (Greece)

Early wheels

Screw pump

AD 105: Paper (from pulp), Ts'ai Lun (China)

250: Algebra, Diophantus (Greece)

*c.*1000: Gunpowder (China)

1100: Magnetic compass (China)

1100: Rocket (China)

1250: Cannon (China)

1440: Printing press (movable type), Johannes Gutenberg (Germany)

Early printing press

1520: Rifle, Joseph Kotter (Germany)

1589: Knitting machine, William Lee (England)

1590: Compound microscope, Zacharias Janssen (Netherlands)

1593: Thermometer, Galileo (Italy)

1608: Telescope, Hans Lippershey (Netherlands)

Lippershey's telescope

1614: Logarithms, John Napier (Scotland)

1636: Micrometer, William Gascoigne (England)

1637: Co-ordinate geometry, René Descartes (France)

1640: Theory of numbers, Pierre de Fermat (France)

1642: Calculating machine, Blaise Pascal (France)

1643: Barometer, Evangelista Torricelli (Italy)

1650: Air pump, Otto von Guericke (Germany)

1656: Pendulum clock, Christiaan Huygens (Netherlands)

1665–75: Calculus, Sir Isaac Newton (England) and Gottfried Leibniz (Germany), independently

1675: Pressure cooker, Denis Papin (France)

1698: Steam pump, Thomas Savery (England)

1712: Steam engine, Thomas Newcomen (England)

1714: Mercury thermometer, Gabriel Fahrenheit (Germany)

1725: Stereotyping (printing), William Ged (Scotland)

1733: Flying shuttle, John Kay (England)

1735: Chronometer, John Harrison (England)

1752: Lightning conductor, Benjamin Franklin (US)

1764: Spinning jenny, James Hargreaves (England)

1765: Condensing steam engine, James Watt (Scotland)

1768: Hydrometer, Antoine Baume (France)

1783: Parachute, Louis Lenormand (France)

1783: Hot-air balloon: Montgolfier brothers (France)

First hot-air balloon

1785: Power loom, Edmund Cartwright (England)

1793: Cotton gin, Eli Whitney (US).

1796: Lithography, Aloys Senefelder (Germany)

1800: Electric battery, Alessandro Volta (Italy)

1800: Lathe, Henry Maudslay (England)

1804: Steam locomotive, Richard Trevithick (England)

Early steam locomotive

1815: Miner's safety lamp, Sir Humphry Davy (England)

1816: Metronome, Johann Malzel (Germany)

1816: Bicycle, Karl von Sauerbronn (Germany)

1817: Kaleidoscope, David Brewster (Scotland)

1823: Digital calculating machine, Charles Babbage (England)

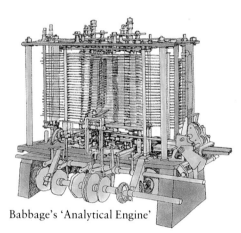

Babbage's 'Analytical Engine'

1823: Waterproof macintosh, Charles Macintosh (Scotland)

1824: Portland cement, Joseph Aspdin (England)

1825: Electromagnet, William Sturgeon (England)

1826: Photography, Joseph Niepce (France)

1827: Friction match, John Walker (England)

1828: Blast furnace, James Neilson (Scotland)

1831: Dynamo, Michael Faraday (England)

1834: Reaping machine, Cyrus McCormick (US)

1836: Revolver, Samuel Colt (US)

1837: Telegraph, Samuel Morse (US)

1839: Vulcanized rubber, Charles Goodyear (US)

1844: Safety match, Gustave Pasch (Sweden)

1846: Sewing machine, Elias Howe (US)

1849: Safety pin, Walter Hunt (US)

1852: Gyroscope, Léon Foucault (France)

1852: Passenger lift, Elisha Otis (US)

1855: Celluloid, Alexander Parkes (England)

1855: Bessemer converter, Henry Bessemer (England)

1855: Bunsen burner, Robert Bunsen (Germany)

1858: Refrigerator, Ferdinand Carre (France)

Washing machine (1850s)

1858: Washing machine, Hamilton Smith (US)

1859: Internal combustion engine, Jean-Joseph-Etienne Lenoir (France)

1859: Storage battery, which can be recharged again and again, Gaston Planté (France)

1861: Linoleum, Frederick Walton (England)

1862: Rapid-fire gun, Richard Gatling (US)

Gatling gun

Early typewriter

1865: Cylinder lock, Linus Yale Jr. (US)

1866: Dynamite, Alfred Nobel (Sweden)

1867: Typewriter, Christopher Sholes (US)

1868: Motorized bicycle, Michaux brothers (France)

1870: Margarine, Hippolyte Mège-mouriés (France)

1873: Barbed wire, Joseph Glidden (US)

1876: Telephone, Alexander Graham Bell (Scotland/US)

Bell's telephone

1876: Carpet sweeper, Melville Bissell (US)

1877: Phonograph, Thomas Edison (US)

1878: Microphone, David Edward Hughes (England/US)

1879: Incandescent lamp, Thomas Edison (US)

1879: Cash register, James Ritty (US)

1884: Fountain pen, Lewis Waterman (US)

1884: Linotype, Ottmar Mergenthaler (US)

1885: Motorcycle, Edward Butler (England)

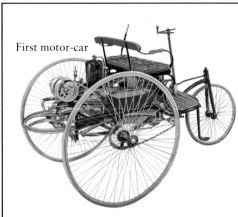

First motor-car

1885: Motor-car engine, Gottlieb
Daimler and Karl Benz (Germany)
independently

1885: Vacuum flask, James Dewar
(Scotland)

1885: Electric transformer, William
Stanley (US)

1886: Electric fan, Schuyler Wheeler
(US)

1886: Halftone engraving, Frederick Ives
(US)

1887: Gramophone, Emile Berliner
(Germany/US)

1887: Monotype, Tolbert Lanston (US)

1888: Pneumatic tyre, John Boyd
Dunlop (Scotland)

1888: Kodak camera, George Eastman
(US)

1890: Rotogravure printing, Karl Klie
(Czechoslovakia)

1892: Diesel engine, Rudolf Diesel
(Germany)

1892: Zip fastener, Whitcomb Judson
(US)

Early zip fastener

1895: Wireless, Guglielmo Marconi
(Italy)

1895: Photoelectric cell, Julius Elster
and Hans Geitel (Germany)

1895: Safety razor, King C. Gillette (US)

1898: Submarine, John P Holland
(Ireland/US)

1899: Tape recorder, Valdemar Poulsen
(Denmark)

1901: Vacuum cleaner, Hubert Booth
(England)

1902: Radio-telephone, Reginald
Fessenden (US)

1902: Air conditioner, Willis H. Carrier
(US)

1903: Aeroplane, Wilbur and Orville
Wright (US)

1904: Diode, John Fleming (England)

1906: Triode, Lee De Forest (US)

1908: Bakelite, Leo Baekeland
(Belgium/US)

1908: Cellophane, Jacques
Brandenberger (Switzerland)

1911: Combine harvester, Benjamin
Holt (US)

1913: Geiger counter, Hans Geiger
(England)

1914: Tank, Ernest Swinton (England)

First tank

Early Marconi
wireless set

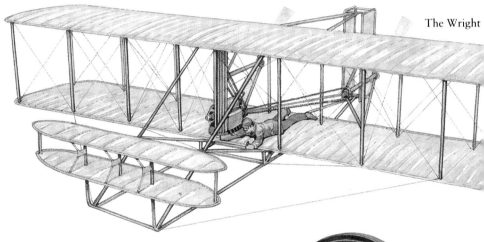

The Wright

Baird's televisor (1930)

1915: Tungsten filament lamp, Irving
Langmun (US)

1918: Automatic rifle, John Browning
(US)

1925: Television (mechanical system),
John Logie Baird (Scotland) and
others

1925: Frozen food process, Clarence
Birdseye (US)

1926: Rocket (liquid fuel), Robert H.
Goddard (US)

1927: First talking picture, *The Jazz
Singer* (US)

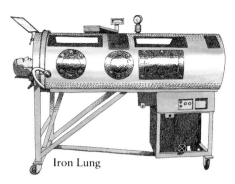

Iron Lung

1927: Iron lung, Philip Drinker and Louis Shaw (US)

1928: Electric razor, Jacob Schick (US)

1929: Television (electronic system, adopted as standard), Vladimir Zworykin (US)

1930: Jet engine, Frank Whittle (England)

1931: Cyclotron, Ernest Lawrence (US)

1935: Nylon, Wallace Carothers (US)

1935: Parking meter, Carlton Magee (US)

1936: First practical helicopter, Heinrich Focke (Germany)

1938: Ballpoint pen, Ladislao and Georg Biro (Hungary)

1939: Electron microscope, Vladimir Zworykin and others (US)

1940: Penicillin as an antibiotic, Howard Florey (Australia) and Ernst Chain (Germany/England)

1940: Xerography photocopier, Chester Carlson (US)

1942: Nuclear reactor, Enrico Fermi (Italy) and others, in Chicago (US)

1944: Automatic digital computer, Howard Aiken (US)

1946: Electronic computer, J. Presper Eckert and John W. Mauchly (US)

1947: Polaroid camera, Edwin Land (US)

1948: Transistor, John Bardeen, Walter Brattain and William Shockley (US)

1948: Long-playing record, Peter Goldmark (US)

1954: Maser, Charles Townes (US)

1954: Solar battery, D. Pearson, C. Fuller, G. Pearson (US)

1955: Hovercraft, Christopher Cockerell (England)

1955: Contraceptive pill, Gregory Pincus and others (US)

1956: Rotary engine (car), Felix Wankel (Germany)

The Gloster E 28/39 aircraft first flew with a Whittle jet engine in May 1941

Sputnik 1, the first artificial Earth satellite

1956: Videotape recording, A. Poniatoff (US)

1957: Artificial Earth satellite (USSR)

1959: Fuel cell, Francis Bacon (England)

1959: Microchip, Fairchild Semiconductors Corp (US)

1960: Laser, Theodore Maiman (US)

1962: Industrial robot, Unimation (US)

1965: Holography (an idea conceived in 1947 and subsequently developed using laser), Dennis Gabor (Hungary/England)

1971: EMI-Scanner, Godfrey Hounsfield (England); developed from his invention of computerized tomography in 1967

Polaroid camera

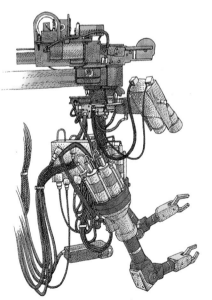

Japanese automated 'arm'

A computer, aiding design

1971: Microprocessor, Intel (US)

1973: Teletext, British Broadcasting Corporation and Independent Television (UK)

1979: Compact disc, Sony (Japan) and Philips (Netherlands)

1981: Space shuttle (US)

1984: Macintosh PC, Apple Corp (US)

DISCOVERIES

1543: Sun as centre of Solar System, Copernicus (Poland).

1590: Law of falling bodies, Galileo (Italy).

1609–1619: Laws of planetary motion, Johannes Kepler (Germany).

1660: Relation between gas pressure and volume, Robert Boyle (Ireland).

1669: Phosphorus, Hennig Brand (Germany).

1675: Measurement of speed of light, Olaus Romer (Denmark).

1678: Wave theory of light, Christiaan Huygens (Holland).

1687: Laws of gravitation and motion, Isaac Newton (England).

1751: Nickel, Axel Cronstedt (Sweden).

1766: Hydrogen, Henry Cavendish (England).

1772: Nitrogen, Daniel Rutherford (Scotland).

1774: Oxygen, Joseph Priestley (England), Karl Scheele (Sweden).

1774: Chlorine, Karl Scheele (Sweden).

1781: Uranus (planet), William Herschel (England).

1783: Tungsten, Fausto and Juan José d'Elhuyar (Spain).

1789: True nature of combustion, Antoine Lavoisier (France).

1797: Chromium, Louis Vauquelin (France).

1803: Atomic structure of matter, John Dalton (England).

1808: Magnesium, Sir Humphry Davy (England).

1811: Molecular hypothesis, Amadeo Avogadro (Italy).

1817: Cadmium, Friedrich Stromeyer (Germany).

1820: Electromagnetism, Hans Christian Oersted (Denmark).

1824: Silicon, Jons Berzelius (Sweden).

1826: Bromine, Antoine Balard (France).

1826: Laws of electromagnetism, André Ampère (France).

1827: Law of electric conduction, Georg Ohm (Germany).

1827: Aluminium, Hans Christian Oersted (Denmark).

1831: Electromagnetic induction, Michael Faraday (England); discovered previously, but not published, by Joseph Henry (US).

1839: Ozone, Christian Schönbein (Germany).

1841: Uranium, Martin Klaproth (Germany).

1846: Neptune (planet), Johann Galle (Germany), from predictions of others.

1864: Electromagnetic theory of light, James Clerk Maxwell (Scotland).

1868: Helium, Sir William Ramsay (Scotland).

1869: Periodic Table of elements, Dmitri Mendeleyev (Russia).

1886: Electromagnetic waves, Heinrich Hertz (Germany).

1886: Fluorine, Henri Moissan (France).

1894: Argon, Sir William Ramsay (Scotland) and Lord Rayleigh (England).

1895: X-rays, Wilhelm Roentgen (Germany).

1896: Radioactivity, Antoine Becquerel (France).

1897: Electron, Sir Joseph Thomson (England).

1898: Radium, Pierre and Marie Curie (France).

1900: Quantum theory, Max Planck (Germany).

1905: Special theory of relativity, Albert Einstein (Switzerland).

1913: Hertzsprung-Russell diagram (star pattern), Henry Russell (US) and Enjar Hertzsprung (Denmark).

1913: Atomic number, Henry Moseley (England).

1915: General theory of relativity, Albert Einstein (Switzerland/US).

1919: Proton, Ernest Rutherford (NZ/GB).

1924: Wave nature of electron, Louis de Broglie (France).

1926: Wave mechanics, Erwin Schrödinger (Austria).

1927: Uncertainty principle, Werner Heisenberg (Germany).

1928: Penicillin, Alexander Fleming (Scotland)

1930: Pluto (planet), Clyde Tombaugh (US), from prediction by Percival Lowell (US) in 1905.

1931: Possibility of neutrino (mass-less atomic particle), predicted by Wolfgang Pauli (Germany).

1931: Deuterium (heavy hydrogen), Harold Urey (US).

1932: Neutron, James Chadwick (England).

1932: Positron, Carl Anderson (US).

1935: Mesons (subatomic particles), predicted by Hideki Yakawa (Japan).

1940: Plutonium, G T Seaborg and others (US).

1948: Theory of continuous creation of matter, Fred Hoyle (England).

1950: Unified field theory, Albert Einstein (Switzerland/US).

1953: DNA/double helix, F Crick (England), J Watson (US) and M Wilkins (England).

1955: Antiproton, Emilio Segre and Owen Chamberlain (US).

1958: Radiation belts surrounding Earth, James Van Allen (US).

1963: Quasars, Thomas Matthews and Allan Sandage (US).

1964: Omega particle, Brookhaven Laboratory, New York (US).

1967: Pulsars, Radio Astronomy Group, University of Cambridge (England).

1977: Chiron: distant asteroid orbiting between Saturn and Uranus, Charles Kowal (US).

1992: First 'map' of human chromosome, Daniel Cohen and others (France, GB, US).

1992: Evidence for birth of the Universe and Big Bang, NASA (US).

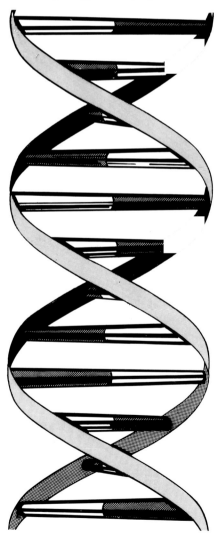

FAMOUS INVENTORS AND SCIENTISTS

Aristotle (384 BC–322 BC): Greek philosopher, whose thinking dominated Western science for many centuries.

Arkwright, Richard (1732–1792): English inventor of the spinning-frame, which revolutionized the textile industry.

Avicenna (**Ibn Sina**) (980 BC–937 BC): Persian physician whose book *The Canon of Medicine* contains all the medical work of **Aristotle** and Galen.

Bacon, Roger (1214–1292): English monk who made magnifying glasses and experimented with gunpowder.

Baird, John Logie (1888–1946): Scottish engineer who demonstrated a mechanized television system in the 1920s.

Becquerel, Antoine-Henri (1852–1908): French scientist who discovered that uranium gives off radiation; shared the 1903 Nobel Prize with the **Curies**.

Bell, Alexander Graham (1847–1922): Scottish-born American inventor of the telephone.

Bessemer, Henry (1813–1898): English inventor of the 'converter' process for making steel from molten iron.

Bohr, Niels (1885–1962): Danish scientist who increased our understanding of the structure of the atom.

Boyle, Robert (1627–1691): Irish-born scientist, the 'father of modern chemistry'; defined an element and has a law about behaviour of gases named after him.

Brunel, Isambard Kingdom (1806–1859) and **Marc Isambard** (1769–1849): Son (born in England) and father (born in France, later lived in US and England), engineers who designed tunnels, bridges, steamships and railways.

Celsius, Anders (1701–1741): Swedish scientist who invented the Celsius scale (centigrade).

Copernicus, Nicolas (1473–1543): Polish astronomer who proved that the Earth spins in orbit around the Sun.

Curie, Marie (1867–1934): Polish physicist who discovered radium; she won the Nobel Prize for Physics with her husband **Pierre** in 1903, and the Nobel Prize for Chemistry in 1911.

Daguerre, Louis (1789–1851): French physicist and scene painter who invented the first practical photographic process, the daguerrotype.

Darwin, Charles (1809–1882): English naturalist whose studies of animals and plants during a round-the-world voyage helped to formulate his theory of evolution by natural selection (that characteristics enabling a species to survive are passed on from generation to generation).

Descartes, Rene (1596–1650): French mathematician, famous for his saying 'I think, therefore I am'.

Edison, Thomas Alva (1847–1931): American inventor of, among other things, the electric light bulb and sound recording.

Einstein, Albert (1879–1955): German-born physicist who changed our view of the Universe, famous for his General Theory of Relativity (1915); he won the Nobel Prize for Physics in 1921.

Euclid (*c*.330 BC–260 BC): Greek mathematician whose *Elements* remained a standard textbook on mathematics for 2000 years.

Faraday, Michael (1791–1867): English physicist and chemist, pioneer of electricity, whose work made possible the dynamo and the electric motor.

Fermi, Enrico (1901–1954): Italian nuclear physicist who helped design the first nuclear reactor.

Freud, Sigmund (1856–1939): Austrian neurologist and psychotherapist, who founded psychoanalysis as both a theory and a therapeutic practice.

Fulton, Robert (1765–1815): American inventor of steam boats and submarines.

Galilei, Galileo (1564–1642): Italian astronomer and physicist whose discoveries include pendulum law and falling body behaviour; invented thermometer and used telescope to observe the Moon and planets.

Goddard, Robert Hutchings (1882–1945): American engineer who pioneered liquid-fuelled rockets.

Harvey, William (1578–1657): English physician who showed that the heart pumps blood around the body.

Hertz, Heinrich (1857–1894): German physicist who proved that light is a form of electromagnetism.

Kepler, Johannes (1571–1630): German astronomer who explained the motion of the planets.

Lavoisier, Antoine (1743–1794): French chemist who categorized the elements and discovered how combustion works; helped introduce metric system in France.

Leonardo da Vinci (1452–1519): Italian artist, engineer and scientist; investigated anatomy, built canals, designed futuristic machines.

Marconi, Guglielmo (1874–1937): Italian electrical engineer, the first person to transmit long-distance radio signals.

Maxwell, James Clerk (1831–1879): Scottish physicist who worked on electromagnetic theory.

Mendel, Gregor (1822–1884): Austrian monk who researched heredity, using pea plants.

Newton, Sir Isaac (1642–1727): English mathematician who devised laws of motion, theorized about gravity, showed nature of light and colour, and built first reflecting telescope.

Niepce, Joseph Nicéphore (1765–1833): French inventor, credited with taking the first photograph (1826).

Nobel, Alfred (1833–1896): Swedish inventor of dynamite; his fortune founded the Nobel prizes.

Oersted, Hans Christian (1777–1851): Danish physicist who discovered the connection between electricity and magnetism.

Pasteur, Louis (1822–1895): French scientist who proved that bacteria cause decay and disease.

Planck, Max (1858–1947): German physicist who devised a quantum theory concerning the nature of energy.

Pythagoras (*c*. 550 BC): Greek mathematician and philosopher, best known for his geometry theories.

Rutherford, Sir Ernest (1871–1937): New Zealand-born physicist who worked on radioactivity and structure of the atom.

Scheele, Karl Wilhelm (1742–1786): Swedish scientist who discovered oxygen in 1772 (independently of the English chemist Joseph Priestley).

Stephenson, George (1781–1848): English engineer who developed the first successful railway locomotive.

Volta, Alessandro (1745–1827): Italian physicist who described electric currents for the first time and invented the battery.

Watt, James (1736–1819): Scottish engineer who improved the steam engine to make it a suitable power plant for all kinds of machinery.

Wright, Orville (1871–1948) and **Wilbur** (1867–1912): American engineers who built and flew the first powered aircraft (1903).

GLOSSARY

Words in **bold** indicate an entry elsewhere in the **Glossary**.

Absolute zero: Lowest temperature possible in theory; zero on absolute scale is $-273.15°C$ ($-459.67°F$).

Acceleration: Rate of change of **velocity**; measured in distance per second per second.

Acid: Chemical substance that produces hydrogen **ions** when dissolved in water. The hydrogen ions may be replaced by metals to form **salts**.

Aerodynamics: Science that deals with air moving against an object.

Aerosol: Cloud of fine particles suspended in a **gas**.

Alcohols: Liquid chemical compounds that contain atoms of carbon, hydrogen and oxygen. In industry, alcohols are commonly used as solvents.

Alkali: **Base** consisting of a soluble **metal** hydroxide.

Alpha particle: One of the three types of **radiation** emitted by some **radioactive** substances. It consists of two **protons** and two **neutrons**.

Alternating current: Electric **current** that rapidly goes from maximum in one direction through zero to maximum in the other direction.

Ampere: (A) Unit of electric current equivalent to a flow of 6×10^9 electrons per second (i.e. 6 million, million, million electrons).

Amplifier: Device for increasing the power of an electrical signal.

Amplitude: Maximum value (or maximum height of the waves) of anything that goes back and forth in a cycle, for example, **alternating current** or sound waves.

Analogue: Representation of numerical or physical quantities by means of physical variables such as voltage or resistance shown by pointer on a dial.

Anode: Positive **electrode** through which current enters an electrolytic cell or a vacuum tube.

Antimatter: Matter made up of subatomic particles that are exactly the same as the particles commonly found, except that they have the opposite charge.

Archimedes' principle: When a body is immersed or partly immersed in a fluid, the apparent loss in weight is equal to the weight of the fluid displaced.

Atmosphere: Layer of gases that surrounds the Earth (or any other planet, star or moon).

Atom: Smallest part of an **element** that can take part in a chemical reaction. It consists of a positively charged central nucleus surrounded by orbiting **electrons**. *See also* **isotope**

Base: Substance that reacts chemically with an **acid** to form a salt and water.

Battery: Device that converts chemical **energy** into electrical energy.

Beta particles: Fast-moving **electrons** emitted by some **radioactive** substances, more penetrating than **alpha particles**, but less penetrating than gamma rays.

Binary: Number system with base of two, using the digits 0 and 1.

Biotechnology: Use of organisms to make or change products (such as in the fermentation of beer, or using bacteria to consume household waste and produce methane gas as a fuel).

Bit: Smallest piece of information that a computer can process: formed from the words 'binary digit'. A bit can have one of two values, zero (0) or one (1).

Boiling point: Temperature at which liquid turns into **gas**.

Buoyancy: Upward force exerted on an object when it is in a **liquid** or **gas** (a **fluid**).

Byte: Eight **bits**, the usual length of a coded character, and the unit of measurement for computer storage.

Calorie: Unit of heat equal to the amount needed to raise the temperature of one gram of water through one degree centigrade.

Catalyst: Substance that improves the rate of a chemical reaction without itself being altered by it.

Cathode: Negative **electrode** through which an electric current leaves an electrolytic cell or a vacuum tube.

Cell: Smallest living unit able to carry out the basic functions of life: growth, metabolism, reproduction.

Celsius: Temperature scale on which 0°C is the melting point of ice and 100°C is the boiling point of water; often called centigrade.

Chip: Thin slice of semi-conducting material, usually **silicon**, that contains all the parts that make an electronic circuit.

Circuit, electrical: Complete path taken by an electric current.

Colloid: Chemical substance with large **molecules** suspended in a **fluid**. Gelatine, starch, foam and plastics are examples of colloids.

Combustion (burning): Chemical reaction in which a substance combines with oxygen and gives off heat and light.

Compound: Chemical substance that contains two or more elements combined together; for example, salt is a compound of sodium and chlorine.

Concave: Curving inwards. A concave **lens** is thinner in the middle than at the edges.

Condensation: Change of **vapour** into a liquid that takes place when pressure is applied to the **vapour**, or the temperature is lowered.

Conduction: Process that allows heat to be transferred from one part of a substance to another.

Conductor, electric: Substance that permits the flow of electricity, e.g. metal.

Convection: Movement of **molecules** from a warmer place to a cooler place in a fluid, i.e. a **liquid** or **gas**.

Convex: Curved outwards. A convex **lens** is thinner at the edges than in the middle.

Corrosion: Chemical process by which a material such as metal is tarnished or destroyed by the action of a **liquid** (**acid**, **alkali** or water) or a **gas** (usually oxygen).

Coulomb: **SI unit** used to measure electric charge. One **ampere** corresponds to one coulomb of charge passing each point in the **circuit** every second.

Crystal: Substance that has been solidified in a definite geometrical form. Some solids do not form crystals.

Current: Flow of **electrons** along a conductor.

Data: General term for basic elements of information for processing in computer.

Decibel: Unit for comparing power levels or sound intensities.

Density: How heavy a substance is for its size. It is calculated by dividing mass by volume.

Diffraction: Spreading out of waves, e.g. light when it passes through a narrow slit or past the edge of an obstacle.

Diode: Electronic component through which **electric current** can flow in one direction only.

Direct current: **Current** that always flows in the same direction.

Disks or discs: Used to store data on magnetized surface. Hard disks hold more information and are more expensive than floppy disks.

Distillation: Way of separating or purifying **liquids** by heating them until they boil, and then condensing the vapour back into a liquid.

Elasticity: Property of a material that makes it go back to its original shape after a force deforming it is removed.

Electrode: Metal plate through which **electric current** enters or leaves an electrolysis cell, **battery** or **vacuum** tube. *See* **anode** *and* **cathode**

Electrolysis: Passing electricity between two terminals (**electrodes**) through a liquid that contains **ions**, in order to produce a chemical change at the terminals.

Electromagnetic waves: Waves of **energy** that include a range of different wave-lengths from short cosmic rays to long radio waves.

Electron: Negatively charged subatomic particle. The number of electrons in an **atom's** outermost shell determines the atom's behaviour.

Element: Substance made up of exactly similar **atoms**.

Energy: Capacity for doing work.

Evaporation: Process by which a liquid turns into a **vapour** without necessarily reaching its boiling point.

Fission: (Splitting) in atomic or nuclear **fission**, the nuclei of heavy **atoms** split and release vast quantities of **energy**.

Fluid: Substance (**liquid** or **gas**) that takes the shape of part or all of the vessel that contains it.

Focus: Point at which converging rays of light meet.

Force: Anything that can act on a stationary body and make it move, or make a moving body change speed or direction.

Formula, chemical: Shorthand method of writing the ingredients of a chemical compound, using symbols and figures to show the proportions in which the **elements** combine to form the compounds.

Frequency: Of a wave motion; the number of oscillations, cycles, vibrations or waves per second.

Friction: **Force** that resists one surface sliding or rolling when in contact with another.

Fulcrum: Point at which a **lever** is supported when it is lifting something.

Fusion, nuclear: Joining together of the nuclei of light **atoms** with the resulting release of vast amounts of

energy; this is the process that occurs in stars.

Gamma radiation (or rays): Form of electromagnetic radiation, similar to **X-rays**. However, gamma rays are of a much shorter wavelength than **X-rays** and are given off by some radioactive substances.

Gas: **Fluid** that, no matter how little there, is always evenly distributed throughout the whole of the vessel containing it.

Geiger counter: Instrument for detecting and measuring **radioactivity**.

Gravitation: Force of attraction between any two objects because of their **masses**.

Half-life: Time it takes for the **radioactivity** of a substance to decrease to half of its original value.

Hardware: Mechanical and electronic units of a computer system.

Hertz: Unit used to measure **frequency**, equal to one cycle per second.

Hologram: Three-dimensional photograph.

Hydrocarbons: **Compounds** consisting of **atoms** of hydrogen and carbon only.

Inclined plane: Simple machine consisting of smooth plane sloping upwards; used for moving heavy loads with a relatively small **force**.

Inertia: Property of an object that makes it resist being moved or its motion being changed.

Infinity: A number, quantity or distance so large it cannot be counted or measured. In geometry, an unreachable distant point.

Infrared rays: Electromagnetic radiation of **wavelengths** just longer than those of visible light; invisible **heat radiation**.

Input: Section of computer that translates information into a code. Formerly done by punched tape and cards, now by keyboard, magnetic tape **disks** or optical scanners reading bar codes (e.g. shop goods).

Insulator: Substance that does not **conduct** electricity or a substance that does not **conduct** heat.

Integrated circuit: Electronic circuit on a **silicon chip** (roughly one centimetre square); may contain several hundred thousand components.

Ion: **Atom** or group of atoms carrying an electrical charge.

Isotope: One of two or more forms of an element with the same atomic number (i.e. number of **protons** in the

nucleus), but different relative atomic masses (due to different numbers of **neutrons** in the nucleus). *See also* **atom**

Joule (J): Unit of work or energy; the main **SI unit** for heat measurement.

Kinetic energy: Energy an object has because it is moving.

Laser: Device that produces an intense, thin beam of light; abbreviation for light amplification by stimulated emission of radiation.

Latent heat: Heat that is absorbed without a rise in temperature when a substance is changed from **solid** to **liquid**, or liquid to **gas**.

Lens: Device that affects light passing through it by converging (bringing together) or diverging (spreading apart) the rays.

Lever: Simple machine consisting of a rigid beam pivoted at one point, called the fulcrum; effort applied at one point on the beam can lift a load at another point.

Light pen: Photosensitive device that can communicate instructions to a computer via the screen of its terminal.

Liquid: Substance that, without changing its volume, takes up the shape of all, or the lower part of, the vessel containing it.

Magnetic field: Area around the poles of a magnet, in which the magnet can exert a force.

Mainframe: Largest-sized computer.

Mass: The amount of material a body contains. A body's mass never changes; its weight depends on the force of **gravity**.

Mechanics: That part of physics dealing with the way objects move in response to the forces between them.

Melting point: Temperature at which a **solid** turns to a **liquid**; equal to the freezing point of the liquid.

Metal: **Element** or **alloy** that is a good conductor of heat and electricity, and usually has a high density.

Metallurgy: Branch of chemistry that studies metals.

Mixture: More than one **element** or **compound** together, but not in chemical combination.

Molecule: Smallest amount of chemical substance that can exist alone; it is made up of two or more **atoms**.

Momentum: Product of the **mass** and **velocity** of a moving body.

Motion, Newton's laws of: (1) A stationary object remains still or a moving object continues to move in a straight line unless acted on by an external force. (2) The force producing acceleration in an object is proportional to the product of the object's mass and its acceleration. (3) Every action has an equal and opposite reaction.

Neutron: Uncharged atomic particle found in the nuclei of all **atoms** except hydrogen.

Newton: SI unit of force. One newton is force needed to increase or decrease velocity of 1-kilogram object by 1 m per second every second.

Nucleus, atomic: Positively-charged centre of an **atom**; consists of one or more **protons** and, except for hydrogen, one or more **neutrons**.

Ohm: SI Unit of electrical resistance: the resistance between two points on a **conductor** when a constant potential difference of one **volt** applied between the points produces a current of one **ampere** in the conductor.

Output: Section of a computer that turns code back into words. Information usually takes the form of a TV display, a high-speed paper print out or instructions to a robot.

Oxidation: Making a substance combine with oxygen.

Ozone: Form of oxygen containing three **atoms** in each **molecule**; O_3.

Periodic Table: Table of the elements in order of their atomic numbers.

Pitch: Quality of a musical sound that depends on the frequency of the vibrations which produce it. A note of high pitch has a high **frequency**, while a note of low pitch has a low frequency.

Polymer: Chemical **compound** with very large **molecules** made up of thousands of units of a smaller molecule.

Prism: A solid figure; a triangular glass or plastic prism bends light, splitting white light into its coloured **spectrum**.

Program: Complete sequence of instruction, or steps, for a job to be performed by computer.

Proton: Positively charged atomic **particle** found in nuclei of all **atoms**. Number of **protons** in the atom gives a substance its atomic number.

Radiation, heat: Transfer of heat by means of waves. *See* infrared rays.

Radioactivity: Emission of radiation, such as **alpha particles**, **beta particles** and **gamma rays**, from unstable elements by the spontaneous splitting of their atomic nuclei.

RAM (random access memory): Part of a computer's memory in which

programs and **data** are held temporarily. Programs and data in the RAM can be changed by the person using the computer.

Reflection: Bouncing back of a sound or light wave as it hits a surface.

Refraction: Bending of a light ray as it crosses the boundary between two substances of different optical densities, e.g. air and water.

Resistance: Way in which an **electrical circuit** opposes the flow of electric current through it. Resistance is measured in **ohms** and is equal to the voltage divided by the **current**.

ROM (read only memory): Part of a computer's memory that has its **program** permanently fixed, usually by the manufacturer. Users cannot program the computer to change this memory.

Salt: Chemical compound formed, with water, when a base reacts with an **acid**. A salt is also formed, often with the production of hydrogen, when a metal reacts with an **acid**.

Semiconductor: Material which can behave either as a conductor of electricity, or as an insulator.

SI units: Units of measurement used for scientific work, adopted in 1960. The base units are the metre (length), kilogram (mass), second (time), ampere (electric current), kelvin (thermodynamic temperature), candela (luminous intensity) and mole (amount of substance).

Silicon chip: Wafer of silicon that carries miniaturized **circuits**.

Software: **Programs** available with a computer to simplify programming and operations.

Solid: State of matter that has a definite shape and resists having its shape changed; a crystalline **solid** melts to a **liquid** when it is heated above its **melting point**.

Solubility: Quantity of a substance (solute) that will dissolve in a solvent to form a **solution**.

Solution: Liquid that contains a solid (or gaseous) substance completely dissolved in it.

Specific gravity: Of a material, its density compared with the density of water. Also called *relative density*

Spectrum: Total range of electromagnetic radiation.

Speed: Distance travelled by a moving object divided by the time taken. Speed in a particular direction is **velocity**.

Static electricity: Electricity at rest (not flowing), in contrast to an **electrical current**.

Storage: Any device – mechanical, electrical or electronic – capable of recording **data** and retaining it for future use.

Superconductor: Material that conducts **current** at very low temperatures with virtually no resistance.

Surface tension: Property of the surface of a **liquid** that makes it behave as though it were covered with a thin elastic skin.

Thermodynamics: Study of heat and the way it flows from one place to another.

Transistor: Semi-conducting electronic component that can amplify signals or turn AC into DC.

Ultrasonic waves: Sound waves beyond the range of human hearing.

Ultraviolet rays: Electromagnetic radiation of wavelengths just shorter than those of visible light. The Sun's radiation contains many ultraviolet rays.

Vacuum: A region in which pressure is considerably less than atmospheric pressure.

Valency: Combining power of a chemical **element**, telling how many bonds the element can form when it combines with other elements.

Vapour: **Gas** that can be turned into a **liquid** by compressing it without cooling.

VDU: Visual display unit, part of a computer that shows text and graphics on screen.

Velocity: Rate of change of an object's position equal to speed in a particular direction.

Volt (V): Unit of electromotive force.

Volume: Measurement of the space occupied by an object.

Watt (W): Unit of electrical power, defined as the rate of work done in **joules** per second; equal to the product of current in **amperes** (A) and voltage difference in **volts** (V).

Wavelength: Of a wave motion, the distance between crests (or troughs) of two consecutive waves.

Waves: Regular disturbances that carry **energy**. Light and radio travel as **electromagnetic waves**.

Word processor: Computer-based system used to store and process information; in its simplest form, the electronic typewriter with a memory.

X-rays: Electromagnetic radiation with a very short **wavelength**.

WORLD HISTORY

World History is an illustrated guide that highlights the most important topics and trends in world history and the people and the circumstances that helped to shape them. The eight sections each cover a distinct period in the story of humankind, from the earliest evidence of human activity to the complex world of the 1990s. A chronology of world events and a collection of brief biographies of notable men and women supplement the main text.

Areas as diverse as the arts, science and technology, religion and the lives of people, both extraordinary and ordinary, are used to illuminate the major events of the past.

Together, the text and illustrations suggest some of the conclusions to be drawn from the study of history. Wars it seems rarely settle anything; rather they breed future conflict. History does not repeat itself, however, situations that are similar continually recur. Nor does *World History* assume that the history of the world is solely the story of Western nations. It shows that the achievements of the great civilizations of America and Africa were substantial and that certain Asian civilizations have been more advanced than those of Europe.

Ken Hills

EARLY CIVILIZATIONS

Discovering the Past

History is not just the study of past events and famous people; it is also the story of human ideas and advancement. Until the 1800s, knowledge of history depended almost entirely on the study of written records. In the past two hundred years the science of archaeology has revealed much about the people who lived before writing was invented, about 5000 years ago. Archaeologists can reconstruct the lives of prehistoric people by studying the objects, buildings or bones that they left behind. Through these reconstructions we can learn about the first humans, who lived by hunting animals, as well as about those hunters who learned to plant their food and so became the first farmers. We can also find out about the lives of people who lived in the early civilizations of Europe, Africa, China, the Americas, India and the Middle East.

RADIOCARBON DATING
The age of an ancient object can be fixed through radiocarbon dating. Living things absorb two kinds of carbon atoms – ordinary carbon (carbon 12) and radio carbon (carbon 14). When a plant or animal dies, the ratio of carbon 14 to carbon 12 decreases at a known rate. An archaeologist uses an instrument, a particle accelerator, to work out the age of an object by measuring its radiocarbon content.

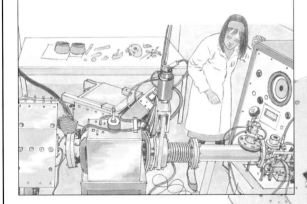

▶ The earliest humanlike creatures so far discovered are australopithecines (southern apes). Their remains have been found in southern and eastern Africa, where they lived between 4 million and 1 million years ago.

▼ Archaeologists find out about the lives of people who lived before the first written records were made (prehistory) by studying their bones, their tools and utensils and the remains of their buildings. A grid laid over the site is used to record exactly where each object was found.

Pottery

Stone knife

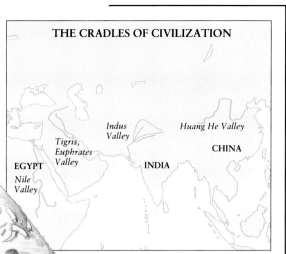

THE CRADLES OF CIVILIZATION

Huang He Valley

Indus Valley

CHINA

Tigris, Euphrates Valley

EGYPT

Nile Valley

INDIA

▲ The first centres of civilization grew up in the valleys of great rivers where there was plenty of water and soil was good for growing crops.

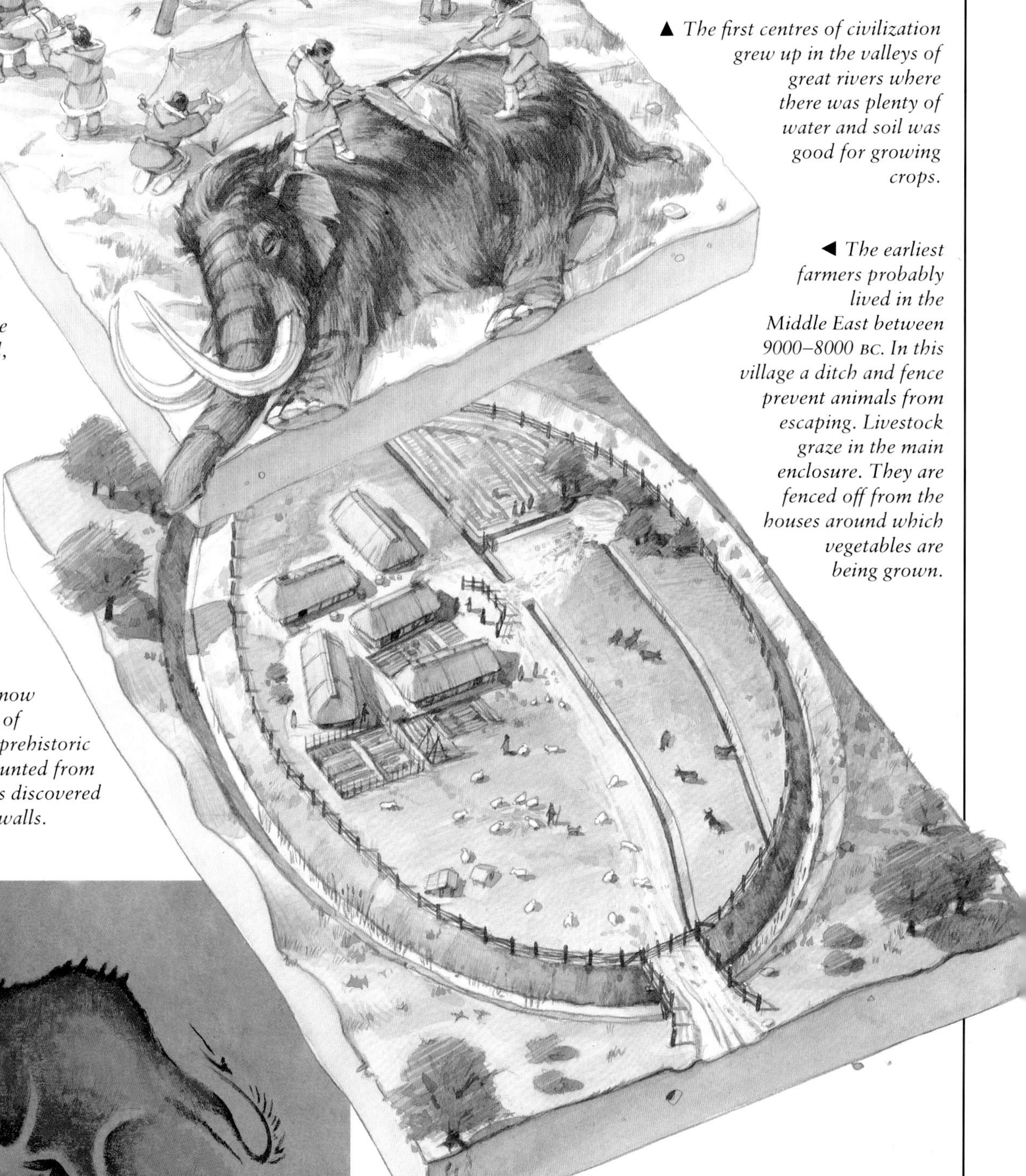

▶ The earliest humans to look like modern people, lived over 130,000 years ago in small groups. They were continually on the move in search of food, fishing, hunting wild animals and gathering berries and roots.

◀ The earliest farmers probably lived in the Middle East between 9000–8000 BC. In this village a ditch and fence prevent animals from escaping. Livestock graze in the main enclosure. They are fenced off from the houses around which vegetables are being grown.

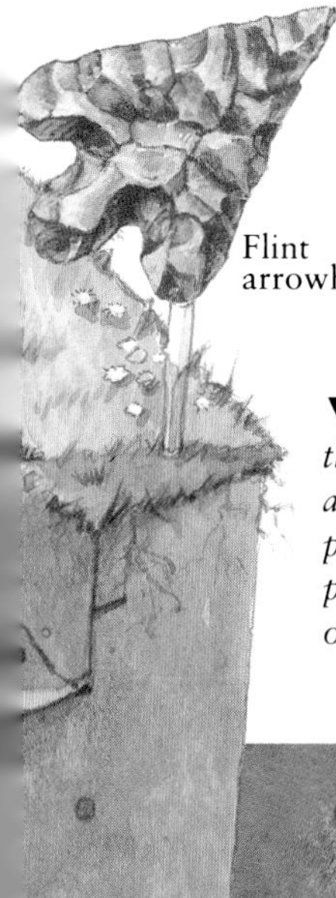

Flint arrowhead

▼ We know the kind of animals prehistoric people hunted from paintings discovered on cave walls.

331

The Birth of Civilization

About five thousand years ago, in four separate areas of the world – the Nile valley, the Tigris-Euphrates valley, the Indus valley and the Huang He valley – people in farming villages came together to establish towns. Later, they founded cities. The original farmers were compelled to work together in groups, to set up and manage the irrigation systems necessary to channel precious river water to the fields. This need for people to live together to control their environment may be the origin of civilization.

▼ *A huge desert to the west protected Egypt and enabled an early civilization to grow up there, free from attack by enemies.*

▶ *Between 2630 and 1640 BC, the pharaohs (rulers) of Egypt built themselves gigantic tombs in the shape of pyramids made of blocks of stone.*

*c.*2371 BC–2316 BC
Reign of Sargon, first ruler of Sumeria

1567 BC–1085 BC
Ancient Egypt at height of its power

30 BC
Romans conquer Egypt

THE FIRST WRITING

The cities of Sumer in the region we now call the Middle East formed the world's first civilization. The Sumerians invented cuneiform writing, a series of signs and pictures. Their writing tells us how the Sumerians lived.

The Rosetta stone has enabled scholars to read hieroglyphics, the picture writing used by the ancient Egyptians. This is because the stone's message is also in ancient Greek, a language scholars already knew.

▼ *A labour force of 84,000 men working for 20 years was needed to construct Egypt's largest pyramid at Giza. The workers were peasants made to work on the pharaoh's building projects every year between the harvest and sowing the next crop.*

Desert —

Worker's house

▶ *Criminals or prisoners of war built the tombs of the later pharaohs. Excavations show that they were housed in reasonable comfort. They lived with their families in cottages, consisting of an entrance hall, a living room, a kitchen and a bedroom. The houses were grouped in small settlements surrounded by high walls, patrolled by guards day and night.*

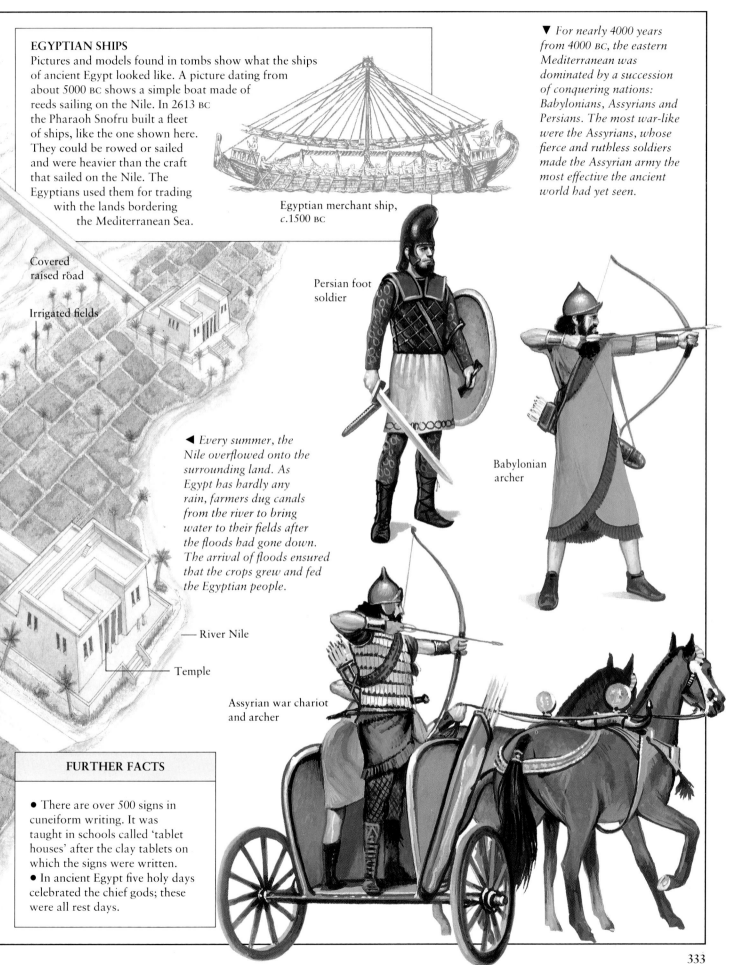

EGYPTIAN SHIPS

Pictures and models found in tombs show what the ships of ancient Egypt looked like. A picture dating from about 5000 BC shows a simple boat made of reeds sailing on the Nile. In 2613 BC the Pharaoh Snofru built a fleet of ships, like the one shown here. They could be rowed or sailed and were heavier than the craft that sailed on the Nile. The Egyptians used them for trading with the lands bordering the Mediterranean Sea.

Egyptian merchant ship, *c*.1500 BC

▼ *For nearly 4000 years from 4000 BC, the eastern Mediterranean was dominated by a succession of conquering nations: Babylonians, Assyrians and Persians. The most war-like were the Assyrians, whose fierce and ruthless soldiers made the Assyrian army the most effective the ancient world had yet seen.*

Covered raised road

Irrigated fields

Persian foot soldier

◄ *Every summer, the Nile overflowed onto the surrounding land. As Egypt has hardly any rain, farmers dug canals from the river to bring water to their fields after the floods had gone down. The arrival of floods ensured that the crops grew and fed the Egyptian people.*

Babylonian archer

— River Nile

— Temple

Assyrian war chariot and archer

FURTHER FACTS

• There are over 500 signs in cuneiform writing. It was taught in schools called 'tablet houses' after the clay tablets on which the signs were written.
• In ancient Egypt five holy days celebrated the chief gods; these were all rest days.

The Beginnings of Beliefs

Every human society has had some form of religion. That the earliest peoples believed in life after death is proved by the way corpses were buried with tools or pots for use in the afterlife. As the great civilizations developed in Asia, the Middle East, India and China, religious practices became more elaborate. Priests were appointed to ensure that religious ceremonies were properly observed. From 1500 BC to 500 BC many of the great religions of the world began to take shape within these civilizations.

c.1500–600 BC
Hindu religion develops in India

c.1200 BC
Beginning of Jewish religion, which worships one god, Yahweh

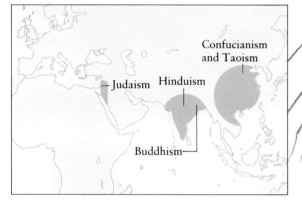

▲ Of the world's major religions, Hinduism and Buddhism started in India; Confucianism and Taoism in China. The Middle East was the birthplace of Judaism, and later of Christianity and Islam.

▼ A reconstruction of Solomon's temple. It is impossible to know exactly what it looked like as it was burnt down by the Babylonians in 586 BC.

Solomon's temple

Workers constructing the temple

Bronze bowl for the temple water

▲ The Hebrews or Israelites (later called the Jews) were 12 tribes who settled in Palestine. By the 900s BC Israel had become a wealthy nation; its king, Solomon, built a magnificent temple in Jerusalem as the centre of the Jewish religion.

EASTERN RELIGIONS

Of the two great Indian religions only Hinduism has no founder. It combines the beliefs of the Aryan tribes who invaded India in about 1500 BC with the religion of the people they conquered. Buddhism, India's other great religion, was founded in the 6th century BC. Three centuries later, Emperor Asoka was converted to Buddhism. By the end of his reign, Buddhism had spread throughout India and beyond into Sri Lanka. The two ancient religions of China are Taoism and Confucianism. The story of the founding of Judaism is told in the book known to Jews as the Hebrew Bible and to Christians as the Old Testament.

Siva

▶ Hinduism is the term used for the religious beliefs and practices of India. Among its most important gods is Siva, who is believed to be both creator and destroyer.

▶ Gautama, the Buddha, lived c.563–480 BC. He was a wealthy prince who gave up his life of luxury to become a poor wandering preacher in northern India.

The Buddha

Lao-Tzu

◀ Taoism came from ancient Chinese folk religions in about 500 BC. This statue is of a Taoist founder, Lao-Tzu, riding on a green ox.

▶ Confucius (c.551–c.479 BC) was a great Chinese philosopher or thinker. He was not a spiritual leader, but he taught the practical advantages of kindness, respect and personal effort.

Confucius

FURTHER FACTS

- The followers of early religions worshipped many gods. The Jews were the first people to believe in one god, whom they called Yahweh.
- Taoism has more gods than most other religions; some of these gods are famous people, others are ancestors.
- Another major ancient religion is Shinto, the native religion of Japan; Shinto developed from early folk beliefs.

The Greeks

Ancient Greece was not one state with its own government. It was made up of many independent communities called 'city-states', who all shared the same language and culture. Between 800 and 400 BC the people of these miniature countries, particularly those of the most successful city, Athens, established many of the ideas that underlie Western civilization. But although democratic government started in Greece, only men could become citizens and vote – women (and slaves) were excluded.

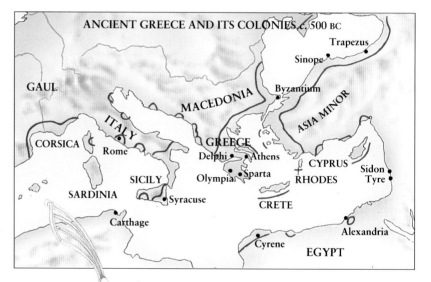

THE MINOANS
The Minoans were traders who, between 2000 and 1100 BC, established the first major civilization in Europe on the island of Crete. *(Above)* A decorated Minoan vase and a frieze depicting a religious or magical rite that involved leaping over bulls.

*c.*3000–1100 BC	*c.*800–338 BC	323 BC
Minoan civilization	Golden age of Greek civilization	Alexander's death ends great age of Greece

▶ *About 1000 BC many of the original Greek cities had become overcrowded. By 500 BC, groups of citizens had left the mainland and settled in other parts of the Mediterranean.*

◀ *Well-armed Greek hoplites (foot-soldiers) were almost unbeatable on land. At sea, powerful Greek triremes rowed by 150 oarsmen overcame all opposition.*

ANCIENT GREECE AND ITS COLONIES *c.* 500 BC

GAUL
ITALY
CORSICA
Rome
SICILY
SARDINIA
Syracuse
Carthage
MACEDONIA
GREECE
Delphi • Athens
Olympia • Sparta
CRETE
Cyrene
EGYPT
Trapezus
Sinope
Byzantium
ASIA MINOR
CYPRUS
RHODES
Sidon
Tyre
Alexandria

ALEXANDER THE GREAT
Alexander, king of Macedon, was one of the greatest generals of all time. When he died in 323 BC, aged only 32, he left behind an empire that extended from Greece to India. In 333 BC at Issus *(below)*, Alexander won a great victory when his troops defeated a much larger Persian army led by the Persian king Darius *(right)*. By 330 BC Alexander had conquered all of the Persian empire.

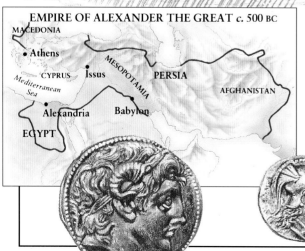

EMPIRE OF ALEXANDER THE GREAT *c.* 500 BC

MACEDONIA
• Athens
CYPRUS • Issus
Mediterranean Sea
MESOPOTAMIA
PERSIA
AFGHANISTAN
• Alexandria
Babylon
EGYPT

FURTHER FACTS

● In about 1500 BC, a volcanic eruption blew apart the island of Santorini (now Thera). The subsequent tidal wave destroyed many of the Minoan cities on Crete, 96 km away.

● The first Olympic Games were held at Olympia in western Greece in 776 BC. They were repeated every four years, and they originally also included musical and literary competitions, as well as running and gymnastics.

◀ The Greeks did not invent their alphabet. They adopted a set of signs used in Syria and modified them to form a simple alphabet of 24 letters.

▶ Greek plays were acted in open-air theatres. Some theatres seated over 10,000 people. Men wearing masks played all the parts.

▲ A bronze statue of a Spartan girl athlete. The city of Sparta was a powerful rival of Athens. Spartan women lived the freest lives of any women in ancient Greece.

▶ An 'acropolis' was a fortress on a hill where citizens took shelter in times of danger. The Acropolis in Athens is famous for its shrines and temples, such as the Parthenon.

▶ In Athens, all citizens over 30 served on juries. Each juror was given two bronze tokens. Tokens with a solid centre meant 'innocent'. Those with a hole meant 'guilty'.

▶ The Greeks told stories of their gods in which they behaved like ordinary people. On this decorated plate Hades, god of the underworld, drinks with his wife, the goddess Persephone.

The Rise of Rome

According to tradition, Rome was founded by Romulus and Remus in 753 BC. Until about 500 BC, Rome was one of several towns ruled by the kings of Etruria in the region now called Italy. After the Etruscans were overthrown the city of Rome became a republic. The Romans were a warlike people who sought to gain new territory. Their greatest rivals in southern Europe were the Carthaginians, whom they defeated in the three Punic Wars. By 44 BC the Romans controlled most of the Mediterranean lands.

c.500 BC
Founding of
Roman republic

264 BC–146 BC
Three Punic Wars
against Carthage

27 BC
Roman republic
ends; empire begins
under Augustus

▼ *In amphitheatres the Romans watched wild animals or gladiators fighting each other to the death.*

▲ *Legend says that Rome's founders, Romulus and Remus, were abandoned as babies but were found by a she-wolf who fed them on her milk.*

THE ROMAN CIRCUS

Rome's chariot-racing stadium, the Circus Maximus, was 550 m long by 180 m wide. The stands could hold up to 250,000 spectators; more than a quarter of the population of the city.

▼ *Most Roman shops were small. Jewellers, bakers, carpenters, shoe-makers, tanners and ironmongers made what they sold in workshops attached to their premises. In this smithy (left), the smith's tools are shown separately. Everyday objects such as keys, household lamps and coins (below) were all hand crafted.*

▼ *The Romans were greatly influenced by Greek drama and both plays and theatre were copied from the Greeks. In this mosaic from a house in Pompeii, Roman actors and musicians are preparing to perform in a Greek play.*

Key

Oil lamp

Coins

GLADIATORS

Gladiators were slaves or criminals who were trained in special schools to fight each other or wild animals in the amphitheatres.

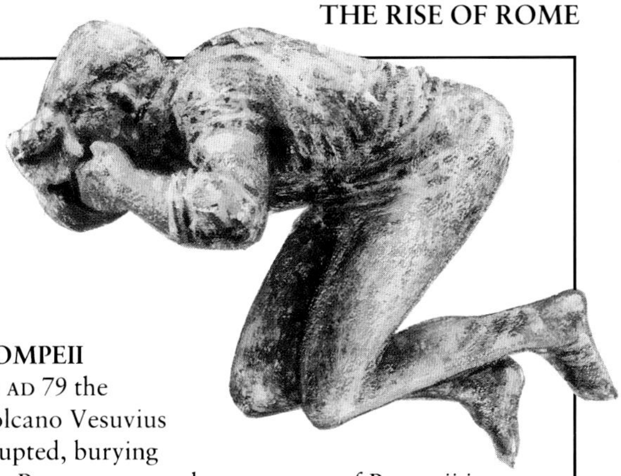

POMPEII

In AD 79 the volcano Vesuvius erupted, burying the Roman port and resort town of Pompeii in southern Italy. In 1748 the town was rediscovered. Volcanic ash and cinders had preserved the ruins and the shapes of the bodies of citizens, who were unable to get away in time. A baker (*above*) was found beside the loaf of bread he had just baked.

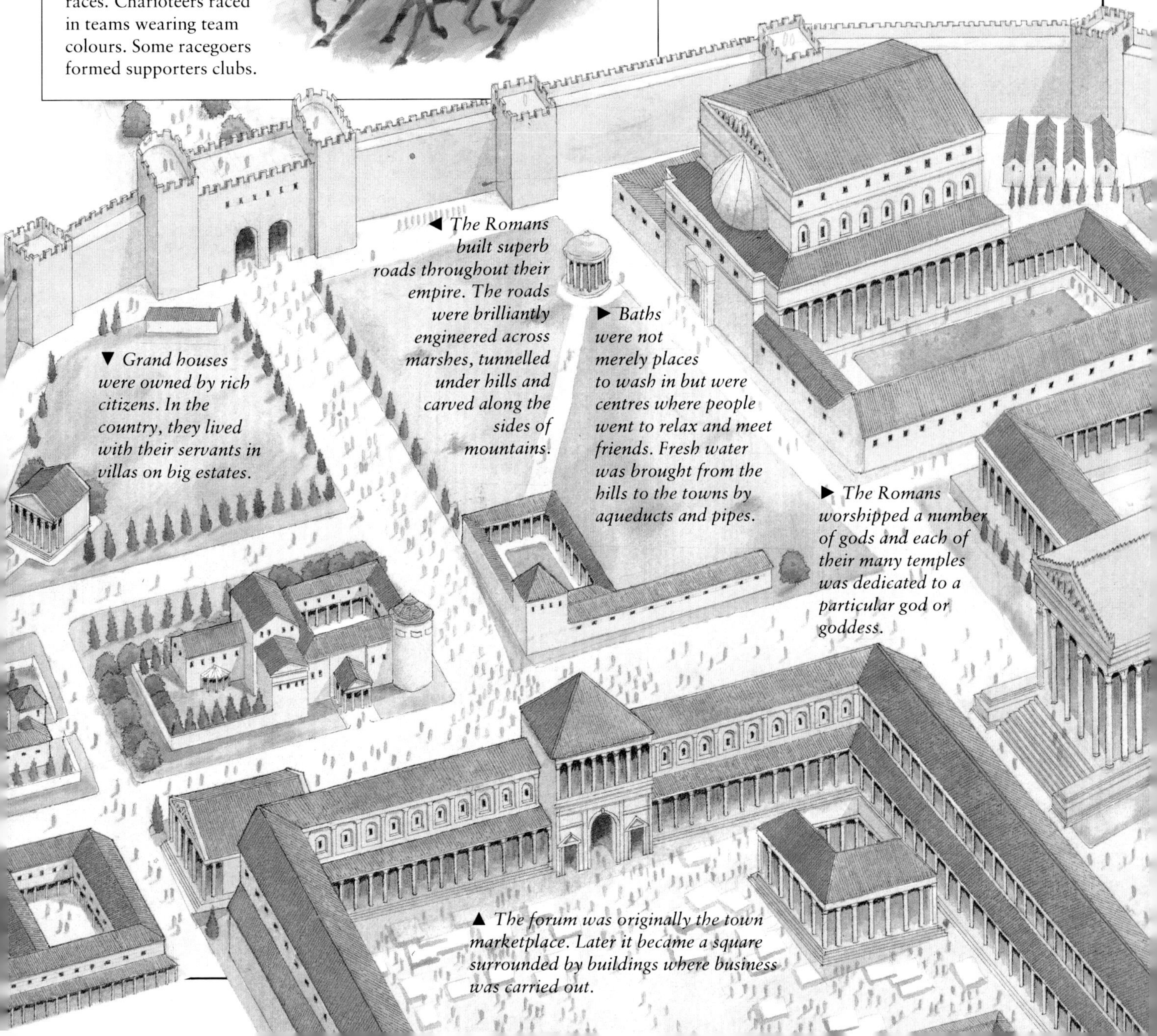

HORSE RACES

Vast crowds flocked to watch and bet on chariot races. Charioteers raced in teams wearing team colours. Some racegoers formed supporters clubs.

◄ *The Romans built superb roads throughout their empire. The roads were brilliantly engineered across marshes, tunnelled under hills and carved along the sides of mountains.*

► *Baths were not merely places to wash in but were centres where people went to relax and meet friends. Fresh water was brought from the hills to the towns by aqueducts and pipes.*

▼ *Grand houses were owned by rich citizens. In the country, they lived with their servants in villas on big estates.*

► *The Romans worshipped a number of gods and each of their many temples was dedicated to a particular god or goddess.*

▲ *The forum was originally the town marketplace. Later it became a square surrounded by buildings where business was carried out.*

The Roman Empire

The empire founded by emperor Augustus in 27 BC lasted for nearly 500 years. At its greatest territorial extent, about AD 100, it stretched from Spain in the west to the Persian Gulf in the east. For two hundred years, the Roman empire was relatively peaceful. But the 3rd century AD saw the beginnings of turmoil as migrating tribes attacked the empire's eastern frontiers. Eventually, the empire was split into an Eastern empire with its capital in Constantinople, and a Western empire ruled from Rome.

27 BC–AD 14
Reign of Augustus, first Roman emperor

AD 395
Roman empire split in two by Theodosius

AD 476
Romulus Augustus, last emperor of Western empire deposed

▲ *The senate was the governing council of the Roman republic. Its members were retired government officials, most of whom came from wealthy families. Under Augustus the senate gradually lost its power.*

▼ *A legion was an infantry unit of the Roman army. It was made up of ordinary soldiers called legionaries commanded by officers (centurians). Standard bearers carried the legion's emblem. The legions' victories built the Roman empire.*

Centurion

Legionary

Standard bearer

ROME'S ACHIEVEMENTS
Between about 27 BC and AD 200 the Roman empire was prosperous and peaceful. Travel was relatively quick and safe along the network of excellent roads which linked all parts of the empire.

A common coinage, language and legal system encouraged trade. Towns had fine public buildings and clean water. Outside the towns, irrigation and better tools led to more efficient farming methods.

▲ *The Roman empire was constantly under attack from invading tribes seeking land and plunder. Rome was finally overrun by Alaric, leader of the Visigoths, in AD 410.*

▶ *Roman legions were equipped with machines for attacking enemy strongholds. Catapults shot large arrows. The ballista was similar but fired stones.*

ARMOUR AND WEAPONRY

By the 1st century AD, the Romans had replaced chain-mail with plate-armour. Flaps on the helmet gave better protection to the head. The shield had become rectangular and stronger. Javelins were weighted with lead. Swords remained short for stabbing the enemy in the close-quarter fighting at which the legions excelled.

▲ *The testudo or 'tortoise' was a formation tactic used by Roman soldiers attacking a fortress. The men held their shields overhead, in front and at the sides. This cover was strong enough to protect them from any missiles hurled down by the defenders.*

SPREAD OF CHRISTIANITY

Despite periods of persecution, Christianity spread through the Roman empire in the 2nd and 3rd centuries AD. Christians used secret symbols, such as a fish, to symbolize their religion. In AD 391 the emperor Theodosius made Christianity the state religion of the empire.

Early Christian fish symbol

▶ *By the 3rd century AD the Roman empire was in serious decline. Rival emperors struggled for power; in AD 238 alone no fewer than six reigned and were overthrown. Trade declined and corruption grew. On the frontiers, attacks by Germanic tribes increased. In AD 395 the Roman empire was divided into eastern and western parts. As the Eastern Byzantine empire thrived, Rome lost its power until it eventually disintegrated. The Western empire ended when a Germanic tribe deposed the last emperor.*

Western empire

Eastern empire

BRITAIN
FRANCE
SPAIN
ITALY
Rome
Constantinople
Black Sea
ASIA MINOR
Athens
Carthage
Mediterranean Sea
EGYPT
Alexandria
Red Sea

▶ *The Emperor Constantine was converted to Christianity by a vision of a flaming cross. In AD 313 he issued an order allowing Christians to worship.*

THE MIDDLE AGES

Raiders and Invaders

The Middle Ages is the time in European history between ancient and modern times. The period is also known as the medieval period, from the Latin words *medium* (middle) and *aevum* (age). Early in the Middle Ages, western European civilization went through a period of upheaval and chaos as a succession of Germanic tribes surged through the former Roman empire. Meanwhile, the rise of Islam in the Near East gave birth to a dynamic and warlike culture which gradually spread into southern and northern Europe. Elsewhere, powerful empires and highly-developed civilizations prospered in Asia and the Americas. By the late Middle Ages, the increased power of the European kings and the civilizing force of the Christian Church helped Europe recover from centuries of invasion, lawlessness and economic breakdown.

1066	1218–1224
William of Normandy conquers England	Genghis Khan's Mongols reach southeast Europe

▲ *The Vikings were traders and warriors from Scandinavia who raided, and later settled, in parts of northern Europe between the 9th and 11th centuries.*

Thor

Odin

◀ *The Vikings believed in many gods, the most important of whom was Odin. Odin's son Thor was the god of thunder and war. Thursday (Thor's day) is named after him.*

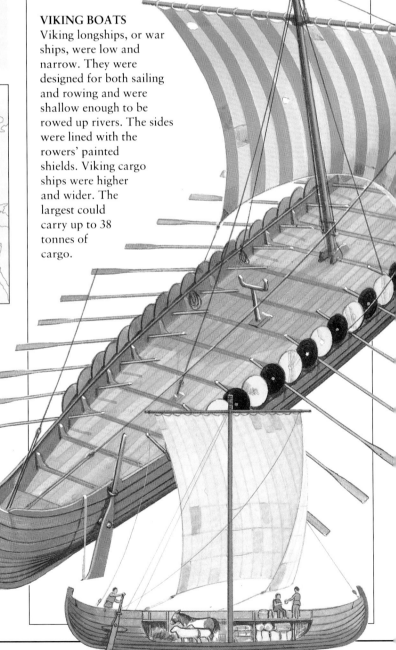

VIKING BOATS
Viking longships, or war ships, were low and narrow. They were designed for both sailing and rowing and were shallow enough to be rowed up rivers. The sides were lined with the rowers' painted shields. Viking cargo ships were higher and wider. The largest could carry up to 38 tonnes of cargo.

◀ *In the 1100s, tribes of nomadic peoples called Mongols, living in central Asia, united under a great warrior, Genghis Khan. The Mongols were to conquer a vast empire that stretched over China, and India, the Near East and into parts of Europe.*

THE DOMESDAY BOOK

In 1085, William the Conqueror decided to find out who owned land and property and how much tax they should pay on it. His officials toured England recording the names of landowners, their holdings and how much their possessions were worth. The survey was called the Domesday Book.

▶ *There are many romantic stories about the British king, Arthur, his court at Camelot and the knights of the Round Table. There may be some truth in the legends. One early chronicle tells of a leader named Arthur who led the British against Saxon invaders in the 800s.*

Arthur and the knights of the Round Table

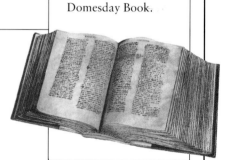

THE NORMAN CONQUEST

The Normans were descended from Vikings who had settled in northern France. In 1066 their leader, Duke William, invaded England to seize the throne from King Harold. The English were routed at the battle of Hastings and William became king.

▼ *The Bayeux Tapestry is a gigantic strip-cartoon recording the Norman conquest of England. It was woven on the orders of Bishop Odo, half-brother of William the Conqueror. The section shown depicts Harold's death in the battle of Hastings.*

After his successful invasion, William the Conqueror consolidated his rule by crushing any revolts by English rebels

Christianity and Islam

Christianity originated in Palestine, Islam arose in Arabia; both regions of the Middle East. Christianity grew out of Judaism, the religion of the Jews, in the 1st century AD. Six centuries later, the prophet Muhammad preached to the Arab people that a single god, Allah, should replace the many gods they had worshipped before. Both faiths spread rapidly. Christianity became the dominant religion of Europe, but was in peril of being overwhelmed by Arab armies until an Arab invasion was halted in France in 732.

▼ *During the early Middle Ages people who believed they were called to devote their lives to God, began the practice of living in private communities. They did not mix with the rest of society. Women entered convents as nuns. Men became monks and lived in monasteries.*

Illumination by monks in medieval book

*c.*4 BC–*c.*AD 30	*c.*570–*c.*632	732
Life of Jesus Christ, central figure of Christian religion	Life of Muhammad, founder of Islamic faith	Battle of Poitiers halts Arab advance in Europe

▲ *Monasteries fed the needy and provided rest and food for travellers. Food was grown by the monks and cooked in the monastery's bakery, kitchens and brewhouse.*

A MONK'S DAY
2.30 a.m. Get up
3.00 a.m. Prayers
6.00 a.m. Prayers
7.00 a.m. Study
8.00 a.m. Prayers
9.00 a.m. Meeting
10.00 a.m. Work
12.00 a.m. Communion Service
2.00 p.m. Dinner
3.00 p.m. Recreation or study
4.00 p.m. Evensong
5.30 p.m. Supper
7.00 p.m. Prayers
8.00 p.m. Bed

▲ *The monastic movement split into different groups or 'orders', following different ways of life. The Cistercian order emphasized prayer, study and physical labour. In the Middle Ages they were known as superb farmers.*

▲ *When a monk fell sick or became too old to work, he was moved to the infirmary. Many orders of monks and nuns also cared for local old and sick people.*

Islamic
conquests 633–945

SPAIN
Córdoba
• Tangiers Sardinia
Carthage Sicily
Berbers   Crete
• Poitiers
BYZANTIUM Constantinople
MESOPOTAMIA PERSIA
Kabul •
Khazars
Jerusalem
EGYPT
Medina •
NORTH AFRICA • Mecca

◀ *Muhammad founded the religion of Islam in Arabia. Within a century of his death his Arab followers had won an empire that stretched from Persia to Spain.*

▼ *The Dome of the Rock in Jerusalem covers the rock from where Muslims believe Muhammad ascended to heaven. It is one of Islam's holiest shrines. Delicate and intricate patterns, typical of Muslim art, cover almost every surface in what is probably Jerusalem's most beautiful building.*

IMAGES OF MUHAMMAD

Muslim law forbids the making of pictures or sculptures for religious purposes, and illustrations in which Muhammad appears are rare. This representation of him from an ancient book shows Muhammad's face hidden by a veil. The prophet's head is crowned with flames, not unlike a halo.

Spanish drug jar from the 15th century, decorated with Arabic writing

▼ *The Moors were Muslims from North Africa. In the 700s they invaded parts of Spain, which they ruled until the 1400s. The city of Córdoba was their capital. The Great Mosque in Córdoba is a fine example of Moorish art and culture.*

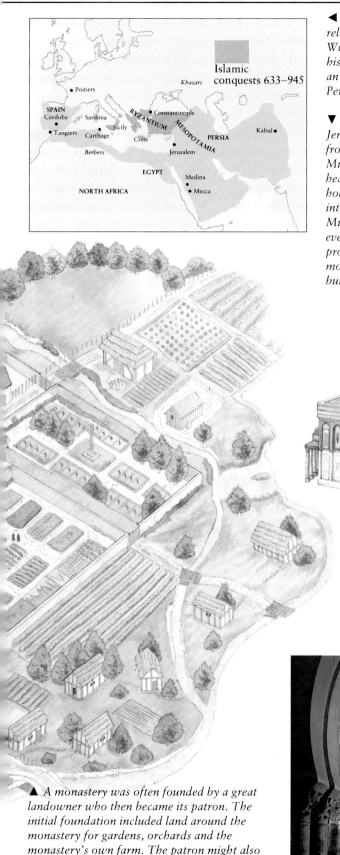

▲ *A monastery was often founded by a great landowner who then became its patron. The initial foundation included land around the monastery for gardens, orchards and the monastery's own farm. The patron might also give the monks the rights to build a mill, to catch fish in nearby rivers, and to receive gifts of food and produce from people who lived in nearby villages or towns.*

The Crusades

During the Middle Ages, many Christian pilgrims from Europe travelled to Palestine to worship at places associated with the life of Jesus Christ. In 1071 a Muslim people, the Seljuk Turks, conquered Palestine and brought these pilgrimages to an end. When Pope Urban II summoned European Christians to take up arms against the Muslims, thousands of knights and ordinary soldiers answered his call. For two centuries Christian armies strove to regain Palestine in wars called the Crusades.

▼ *During the Crusades Muslims were called 'Saracens' by the Christians. The Saracens were superb warriors on horseback.*

1095–1099
First Crusade captures Jerusalem. Four Christian kingdoms set up in Holy Land

1187
Saladin, Sultan of Egypt, re-captures Jerusalem

1217–1221
The Fifth and last major Crusade

▼ *During the Third Crusade Richard I of England won a major victory when his troops captured the Saracen fortress of Acre and defeated the army of the Muslim leader Saladin at Arsuf. This victory earned Richard the name of 'Lion-Heart'. Fighting in the Holy Lands or France, Richard seldom visited England. He is buried next to his mother, Queen Eleanor, at Fontrevault in France.*

▶ *Among the most feared Christian warriors were the Knights Templars. They were members of a religious military order who chose to serve God by fighting rather than through prayer.*

▲ *The Crusaders built castles to defend the lands they conquered. The largest and strongest Crusader castle was Krak des Chevaliers. It was built by the Knights Hospitalers (a military religious order) and lies in the desert of what is now Syria on a hilltop 750 m high. During* the Crusades it was garrisoned by up to 2000 men. It held out against many attacks but finally fell to the Saracens in 1271 when the defenders were starved into surrender after a year's siege.

Crusader castle of Krak des Chevaliers

THE ROUTES OF THE CRUSADES

First Crusade 1095–1099
Second Crusade 1147–1149
Third Crusade 1189–1192

HOLY ROMAN EMPIRE

Ratisbon
Vienna
Milan
Venice
Marseilles
Genoa
Rome
Belgrade
Adrianople
Durazzo
Constantinople
Lisbon
Cadiz
Jebel Tarik (Gibraltar)
Crete
Antioch
Acre
Tripoli
Jerusalem

SELJUK TURKS

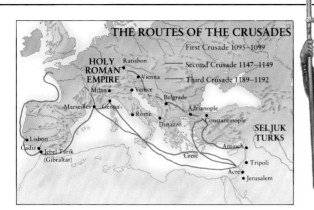

◀ *Pilgrimages are journeys to holy places. The men and women who went on pilgrimages to the Holy Land often brought back a palm tree branch to lay on the altar of their church at home.*

▲ *Apart from the major Crusades, expeditions from countries as far away as Norway went to fight in the Holy Land.*

FURTHER FACTS

The capture of Jerusalem made the First Crusade (1095–1099) the most successful Crusade for the Christians. In 1187 Muslim armies took Jerusalem. and the Christians never recaptured it. The last Christian stronghold at Acre in Palestine fell to the Muslims in 1291.

◀ *In 1212 thousands of children from France and Germany joined a Crusade. They were inspired by a French boy, Stephen, and a German boy, Nicholas. Neither group reached the Holy Land. Many died of hunger or disease. Some were sold as slaves.*

CHIVALRY, HERALDRY AND TOURNAMENTS

The ideal knight was brave in battle, loyal to his lord and protected women. These rules of behaviour were known as 'chivalry'. Fully-armed knights displayed a sign on their shields or on their surcoat in order to be recognized in battle. During the 1100s each design or 'coat of arms' became the property of a particular family, a system known as 'heraldry'. Knights fought mock battles called 'jousts' in tournaments *(right)*. They used blunted weapons and wore special armour. Each joust started with two knights charging each other with lances.

Jousting armour

War and Plague

The 1300s and 1400s were a disastrous period for Europe. The Hundred Years' War, fought when England tried to gain lands in France, was a calamity with parts of France laid waste by armies. In the mid-1300s, rich and poor alike died in the plague, known as the Black Death. Many peasants survived only to die of starvation as crops remained unpicked. About 25 million people may have died. Disorder became widespread. In France, Italy and England peasant revolts were crushed by the authorities.

1337–1453
The Hundred Years' War

1347–1353
The Black Death rages in Europe

1431
English burn Joan of Arc as a witch

Longbowman

Crossbowmen

▲ *Bows and arrows were key weapons of the Middle Ages. Crossbows needed less strength to fire than longbows but were slower. The English longbowmen won famous victories at Crécy and Agincourt against far stronger French armies.*

▼ *In the 1300s the thick walls of a besieged castle could often withstand siege weapons. In this siege of a French town the English are using early cannons. By the mid-1400s cannons had improved; it was the increased fire power of the French artillery that helped them win the final battles of the war.*

▼ *As the the Hundred Years' War was being fought in Europe, a Mongol warrior Timur (or Tamerlane), who claimed to be a descendant of Genghis Khan, was building an Asian empire. Between 1379 and 1402, Timur swept south from his base at Samarkand (where he is shown being entertained) to invade Persia, India and Turkey.*

▼ *Inspired by mysterious 'voices', a French peasant girl, Joan of Arc, persuaded the heir to the throne, Charles, to give her troops to fight the English. In 1429 the army she led saved the city of Orléans from an English siege. It was the turning point of the Hundred Years' War. Later that year Joan stood beside Charles as he was crowned king at Rheims; by 1453 England had lost all its conquests except the port of Calais. Joan herself was captured and executed by the English. She was made a saint in 1920.*

The Black Death came to Europe from Asia in 1347. It began in Italy, spreading like wildfire to the rest of the continent.

The Black Death was bubonic plague, a type of plague carried by the fleas living on black rats. The name came from a victim's black swollen lymph nodes; the disease was usually fatal.

Route of plague from Asia

ENGLAND AND SCOTLAND 1348
SCANDINAVIA 1349
NORTH RUSSIA 1349
SOUTH RUSSIA 1345
FRANCE 1347
From Asia
SPAIN 1348
ITALY 1347
OTTOMAN EMPIRE 1347
SICILY 1347

Black rat

THE BLACK DEATH

The Black Death was only one of the disasters to afflict Europe in the 14th century. Several bad summers and poor harvests brought starvation to many regions. Death became a frequent and familiar part of everyday life. Artists of the time depicted death in many forms, including a skeleton riding a horse.

People of the Middle Ages did not understand that disease thrives in dirt. It was usual to tip household rubbish onto the street and woe betide any unwary passer-by!

FURTHER FACTS

• Although the Black Death killed between one quarter and one-third of Europe's population, parts of Poland, Italy, Bohemia and France escaped altogether. Less terrible epidemics continued for three centuries.

• At the time, people believed that cats and dogs spread the Black Death – so they killed them. As a result the true carriers, black rats, only increased.

At night plague carts were loaded with corpses to be taken away for burial. People in towns and communities such as monasteries suffered particularly badly from the plague since close-packed houses were ideal breeding grounds for the disease-carrying rats and fleas.

THE MODERN WORLD

The Renaissance

The 1400s and 1500s saw a period of new learning – the Renaissance – that fundamentally changed the attitudes and ideas of educated people. This renewed scholarship and the questioning of established ideas which it fostered, marks the beginning of the modern world. News of advances in philosophy, arts and the sciences spread rapidly thanks to the development of the printed book. The new ideas also gave impetus to the Reformation – a movement that led to the division of western Christendom in the 1500s. An improved understanding of the Earth's geography encouraged Europe's seafarers and travellers to pioneer new routes in search of trade. At first European expansion hardly touched the empires of Asia but the civilizations of the Americas soon fell victim to the greed of the European invaders.

1300s
Birth of the
Renaissance in Italy

1400s–1600s
Renaissance spreads
from Italy to rest of
western Europe

1400s–1700s
Florence ruled by
the Medici family

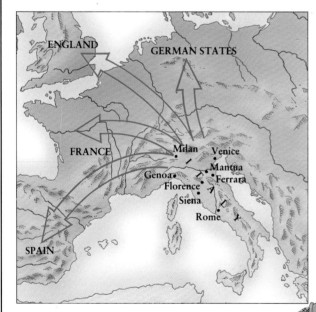

▲ *Italy in the late 1300s was the birthplace of the Renaissance. The development of printing in Europe in the 1450s helped to spread the Renaissance to other countries.*

▶ *A French nobleman travelling in Italy was impressed by the new architecture. Back in France he hired an Italian architect to build him this chateau in the same style. All over Europe, people were fascinated by the ideas and designs of the Italian Renaissance and copied them in their own countries.*

▶ *The new learning gave birth to humanism, a new way of thinking about human beings and their place in the universe. Humanists like the Dutch philosopher Erasmus rejected the belief that all actions are directed by God, in favour of the idea that people are responsible for their own lives.*

French chateau built
in Renaissance style

Merchant and his wife
in Renaissance Italy

PATRONAGE BY POWERFUL FAMILIES

During the Renaissance, many great works of art and architecture were made possible by the patronage of rich families. In Florence the Medici, a family of merchants and bankers, were generous patrons of the arts. In Venice, the painter Vittore Carpaccio was commissioned by wealthy patrons to paint the townscapes for which he is celebrated (*left*: 'The Arrival of the Ambassadors' by Carpaccio).

▼ *The great cities of the Italian Renaissance such as Rome, Venice, Siena and Florence (shown here), were governed as independent states. The powerful families who ruled them had become rich from banking, as well as from trading in Asia and Europe.*

▼ *Although people had used devices to tell the time for thousands of years, the first spring-driven clocks with a dial and hour hand, were not developed until the 1400s.*

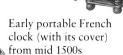

Early portable French clock (with its cover) from mid 1500s

◄ *The greatest thinkers of the Renaissance often anticipated future ideas. This sketch of a flying machine is by Leonardo da Vinci (1452–1519).*

▶ *The German Johannes Gutenberg introduced printing from moveable type into Europe in the 1450s. Books at once became relatively cheap and enabled the ideas of the Italian Renaissance to spread through the rest of Europe.*

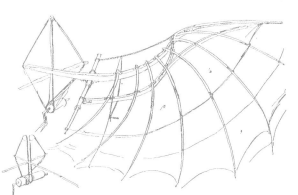

THE RENAISSANCE IN EUROPE

ITALY: Brunelleschi (1377–1446), architect; Michelangelo (1475–1564), artist, architect; Galileo (1564–1642), astronomer
FRANCE: Ronsard (1524–1585), poet; Rabelais (*c*.1494–*c*.1553), writer; Clouet (*c*.1485–1541), painter
GERMANY: Gutenberg (*c*.1400–1468), printer; Dürer (1471–1528), painter; Holbein (*c*.1497–1543), painter
SPAIN: Great age of Spanish exploration (*c*.1450–*c*.1550); El Greco (1541–1614), painter; Seville Cathedral (1517)
HOLLAND/BELGIUM: Erasmus (*c*.1469–1536), philosopher; Bruegel (*c*.1525–1569), painter
ENGLAND: Caxton (*c*.1421–*c*.1491), printer; More (1478–1535), scholar; Raleigh (*c*.1552–1618), poet, statesman

Reformation and Counter Reformation

During the Middle Ages, Christians of western Europe belonged to a single Church, whose centre was in Rome with the Pope at its head. The Reformation of the 1500s started out as an attempt to reform the Church. It grew into a movement which gave birth to a variety of Protestant Churches and led to a permanent split in the Christian community. The Counter Reformation was the attempt by the Roman Catholic Church to reform itself and win back the loyalty of those who had left it.

1517
Luther's criticisms begin the Reformation

1536
John Calvin founds Protestant centre in Geneva

1545–1563
The Council of Trent establishes the Counter Reformation

◀ In 1517 Martin Luther, a German monk and lecturer, nailed a list of 95 theses (statements) to the church door at Wittenberg. The theses challenged the authority of the Pope, who excommunicated Luther in 1521. His followers became known as 'Protestants' because they protested against the teachings of the Roman Catholic Church.

▶ For nearly 40 years Europe suffered from a series of religious wars. England, Holland and some German states fought on the Protestant side, while France and Spain supported the Roman Catholic cause. Massacres and the execution of dissenters occurred in several countries. In England many Catholics were executed in 1537, after an uprising during Henry VIII's reign.

St Bartholomew's Day Massacre

▶ Years of religious conflict between Catholics and Protestants followed the Reformation. The Catholic authorities burned Protestants to death for heresy. Protestants executed Catholics, sometimes with atrocious cruelty. On St Bartholomew's Day 1572, Catholic mobs in Paris killed about 3000 French Protestants.

◄ *The Reformation split Europe. The north became mainly Protestant, while southern countries remained faithful to the Church of Rome.*

◄ *The Spanish Inquisition was set up in 1478 to arrest and punish those who did not follow the Christian faith. Its first victims were Muslims and Jews. After the Reformation, it attacked all forms of Protestantism. The Inquisition executed those it found guilty in great public spectacles called* auto-da-fés.

HENRY'S BREAK WITH ROME

In 1525 the Pope refused to let the English king, Henry VIII, have a divorce from his wife, Catherine of Aragon, so that he could marry Anne Boleyn. In order to legalize the divorce he wanted, Henry decided to take personal control of religion in England. By threats and persuasion he caused the English Parliament to pass an Act breaking all ties with the Pope in Rome. Henry then became absolute head of the Church in England.

Henry VIII and Anne Boleyn

▼ *In 1588, the English fleet defeated a large Spanish fleet, the Armada, sent by Philip II to overthrow the Protestant Elizabeth I and re-establish the Catholic faith. The Armada was defeated as much by bad weather as by the English, and only half the fleet returned to Spain. This victory helped establish the English as a major world seapower.*

Damaged Spanish galleon after the defeat of the Spanish Armada

Queen Elizabeth I

FURTHER FACTS

● In Martin Luther's time nailing theses to a church door was the recognized way of starting a debate.
● Luther's ideas were developed by a French Protestant, John Calvin, who was exiled in Geneva. Calvin's teachings were followed by Protestants in Europe and the Puritans, who later settled in America.
● The Council of Trent of 1545 began the Counter Reform movement which revived and reorganized the Catholic Church.

American Civilizations

American Indians, or Native Americans, were the first people to live in the Americas. They came to America from Asia over 20,000 years ago and developed many different lifestyles. When the Spanish arrived in Central America in the 1500s, they marvelled at the civilizations of the Aztecs and the Incas. They found wealthy, well-ordered cities, connected by good road systems. Far to the north, in what is now North America, people usually lived as hunters and farmers in small villages or as bands of nomadic hunters.

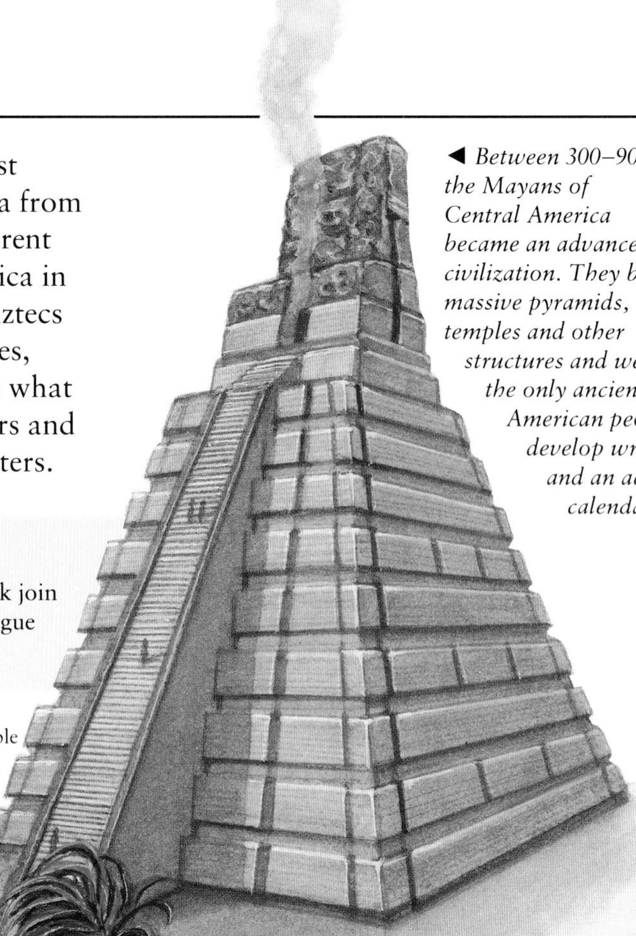

◀ *Between 300–900 the Mayans of Central America became an advanced civilization. They built massive pyramids, temples and other structures and were the only ancient American people to develop writing and an accurate calendar.*

c.300–c.900
Mayan civilization in Central America

1400s
Aztec civilization at its height

c.1570
The Mohawk join Iroquois League

Aztec sacrificial knife

Mayan temple

▲ *A warrior-tribe, the Aztecs, dominated Central America in the 1400s. Every night, priests ripped out the hearts of 100 human beings with a sacrificial knife to please their god of war. The Incas ruled an empire in Peru, South America. By the 1500s their civilization was at its peak, with great cities and beautiful works of art (below).*

Hollow wooden snake covered in turquoise

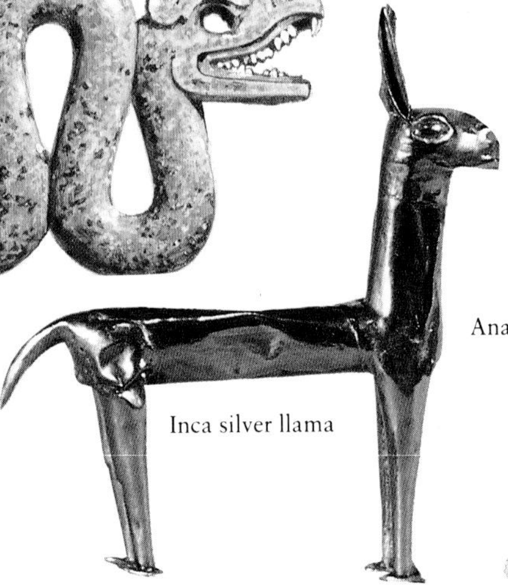

Inca silver llama

Anasazi pueblos

▶ *The Anasazi were Native Americans who lived in what is now the southwestern United States. They built villages called pueblos, where houses were joined together to form a single, large building. The Anasazi abandoned their pueblos soon after 1200, when the local climate became too dry to grow crops.*

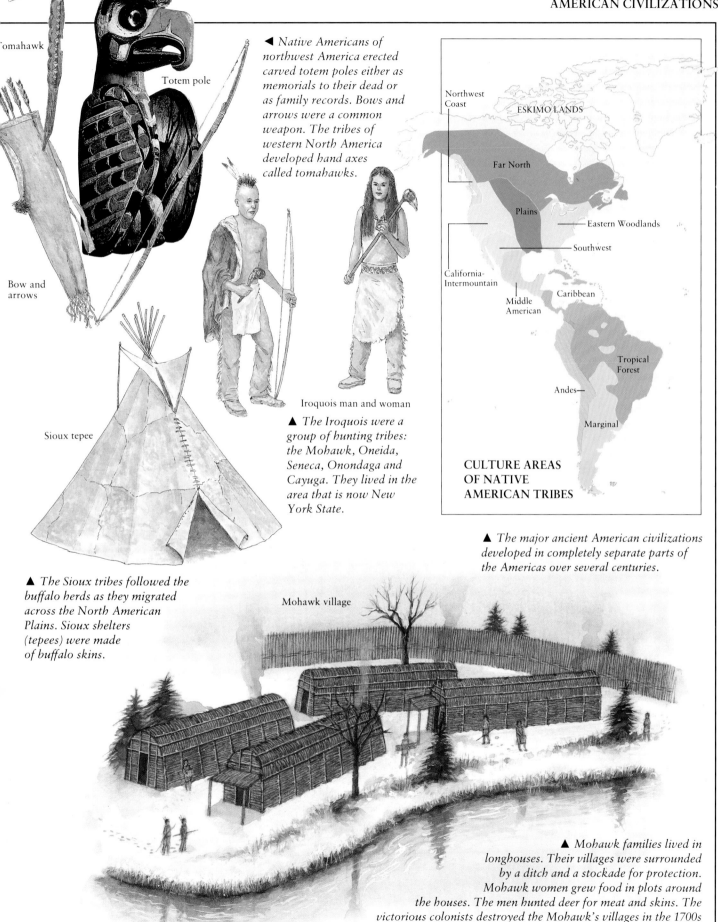

Tomahawk

Totem pole

Bow and arrows

Sioux tepee

◀ Native Americans of northwest America erected carved totem poles either as memorials to their dead or as family records. Bows and arrows were a common weapon. The tribes of western North America developed hand axes called tomahawks.

Iroquois man and woman

▲ The Iroquois were a group of hunting tribes: the Mohawk, Oneida, Seneca, Onondaga and Cayuga. They lived in the area that is now New York State.

Northwest Coast

ESKIMO LANDS

Far North

Plains

Eastern Woodlands

Southwest

California-Intermountain

Middle American

Caribbean

Tropical Forest

Andes

Marginal

CULTURE AREAS OF NATIVE AMERICAN TRIBES

▲ The major ancient American civilizations developed in completely separate parts of the Americas over several centuries.

▲ The Sioux tribes followed the buffalo herds as they migrated across the North American Plains. Sioux shelters (tepees) were made of buffalo skins.

Mohawk village

▲ Mohawk families lived in longhouses. Their villages were surrounded by a ditch and a stockade for protection. Mohawk women grew food in plots around the houses. The men hunted deer for meat and skins. The victorious colonists destroyed the Mohawk's villages in the 1700s because they had sided with the British in the War of Independence.

The Age of Discovery

The European navigators of the 1400s and 1500s sailed in search of profit; their discoveries were by-products of their voyages. Fortunes were to be made from the trade in ivory, jewels, perfumes, fabrics, and spices (which hid the taste of rotting food in the days before refrigeration). Many of the early voyages had a disastrous effect on the native populations. Whole tribes were slaughtered in the search for riches or wiped out by European diseases. Not until the 1600s did some explorers seek knowledge rather than gain.

1271–1295
Marco Polo's travels through Asia

1492
Columbus lands in America

1768–1779
Cook explores and charts the southern Pacific

THE AMERICAS
In 1492 the Italian Christopher Columbus sailed across the Atlantic from Spain to find a shorter trade route to China and India. He landed instead on Hispaniola in the Bahamas. The islanders thought the Spaniards were gods. Columbus believed that the islands were part of Asia and christened them 'The Indies'. Further explorations revealed the islands were not part of Asia but a totally new continent.

Columbus and islanders from Hispaniola

▶ The early Spanish and Portuguese voyagers chose boats called caravels for distant expeditions. Columbus's favourite ship, the Niña, was a caravel. She made at least five voyages to the New World. A caravel could be sailed by a 24-man crew. It was 21 m long, 6.5 m wide and could carry a cargo of 60 tonnes. Caravels were all-purpose craft. They were as dependable in ocean storms as when manoeuvring in shallow water close to uncharted coasts.

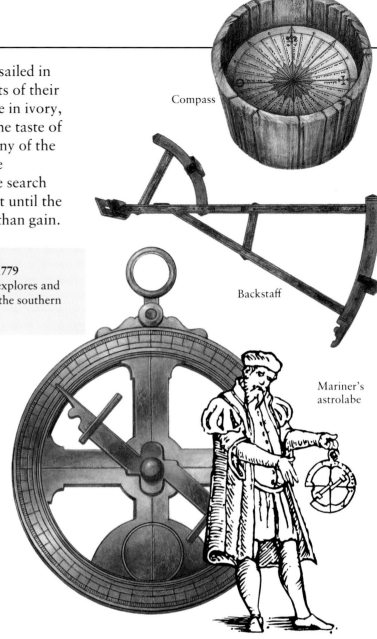

Compass

Backstaff

Mariner's astrolabe

▲ The simple navigation instruments of the 1400s were not very accurate. The compass, first used by the Chinese in the 1100s, was used to keep the ship on course. The backstaff and astrolabe helped the captain find the height of a star or the Sun so that he could work out the ship's latitude; they were difficult to use in bad weather.

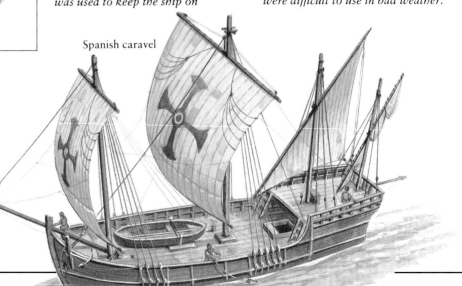

Spanish caravel

EXPLORER/DATES OF MAJOR JOURNEYS

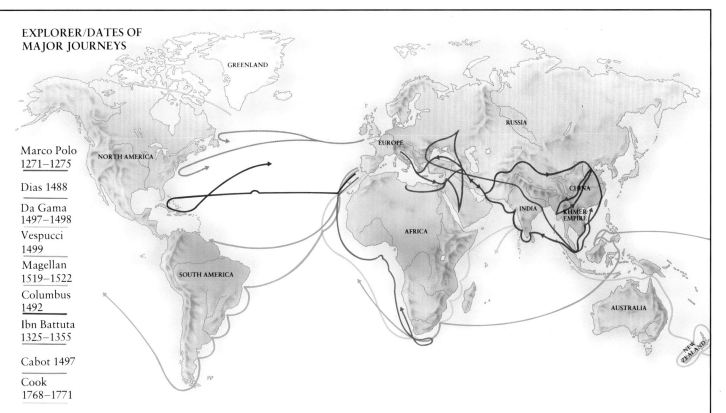

Marco Polo
1271–1275

Dias 1488

Da Gama
1497–1498

Vespucci
1499

Magellan
1519–1522

Columbus
1492

Ibn Battuta
1325–1355

Cabot 1497

Cook
1768–1771

▲ *Marco Polo's tales of China's wealth inspired the search for new trade routes to the East. Dias and da Gama pioneered the way around Africa. Columbus and Vespucci went west and found the route blocked by an unknown continent. Magellan's expedition was the first to sail round the world.*

▼ *Europeans knew little about the South Pacific until the three scientific voyages of the English explorer Captain James Cook in the mid-1700s. He charted Australia's east coast, claiming it for Britain. He later visited New Zealand. Cook was killed in Hawaii while looking for the Northwest Passage around North America.*

EARLY EXPLORERS

Marco Polo (Italy, *c*.1254–*c*.1324): Wrote of his 17-year stay in China
Ibn Battuta (Morocco, *c*.1304–1369): Travelled in E Africa, Arabia, China
Bartolomeu Dias (Port., d. 1500): First European to round Cape of Good Hope
Christopher Columbus (Italy, 1451–1506): Made four voyages to Caribbean
Amerigo Vespucci (Italy, 1451–1512): Sailed to Caribbean and S America
Vasco da Gama (Port., *c*.1469–1524): Pioneered eastern sea route to India
John Cabot (Italy, 1461–1498): Sailed across North Atlantic to Canada
Ferdinand Magellan (Port., *c*.1480–1521): Led first expedition round world

Captain Cook with the Maoris of New Zealand

FURTHER FACTS

- When Columbus landed on Hispaniola, about 300,000 Arawaks were living there. By 1548, European diseases, murder by the Spanish and death from work as slaves had reduced the islanders to about 500.
- The continent of America was named after Amerigo Vespucci, an Italian who sailed with the second expedition to visit northern South America in 1499.

The East: India, China and Japan

The most popular travel book in medieval Europe was Marco Polo's account of his years of service in the court of the Mongol ruler of China, Kublai Khan. The achievements of the great Asian empires were not mere traveller's tales. Cut off from most outside contact, the Japanese developed a unique civilization of their own. Inventions as diverse as gunpowder and the magnetic compass were used in China centuries before they were known in the West. In India the Moguls ruled a great empire half the size of Europe.

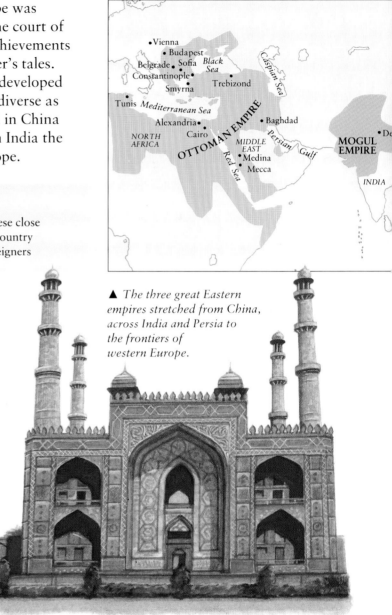

▲ The three great Eastern empires stretched from China, across India and Persia to the frontiers of western Europe.

1368–1644
Ming dynasty sees period of Chinese prosperity

1500s–1700s
Mogul period in India

1630s
Japanese close their country to foreigners

THE OTTOMAN EMPIRE

For 500 years the Ottoman empire was a great Islamic world power. It was founded in northern Turkey at the end of the 1300s. As devout Muslims, the Ottomans believed it their duty to fight to defend their religion against unbelievers. In a series of jihads (holy wars), they enlarged their empire in all directions. The chief victim of Ottoman aggression was the Christian empire of Byzantium. In 1483 the Ottomans captured Constantinople; it became the capital of their empire until the 1800s. The empire reached its greatest extent under Suleiman the Magnificent. His army overran the Balkans, and only his failure to capture the Austrian capital Vienna in 1529 (below) prevented an invasion of western Europe.

▲ In 1526 the Mogul leader Babar conquered northern India and founded an empire. His grandson was the Mogul emperor Akbar, who is buried in a superb tomb at Fatehpur Sikri.

◄ The Moguls were Muslims but Akbar (seen here in battle) won the loyalty of his Indian subjects, most of whom were Hindus, by allowing them to worship in peace. Akbar was also a generous patron of writers, artists and architects.

▼ *The architectural masterpiece of the Ming empire was the capital Peking (Beijing). At its heart lay the 'Forbidden City', forbidden to all except the emperor and his household.*

▶ *The Ming era of Chinese history, from the mid-1300s to mid-1600s, is renowned for its delicate blue and white porcelain.*

Ming vase

CHINA

Peking

JAPAN

MING EMPIRE

CATHOLIC MISSIONARIES
Catholic missionaries arrived in the East in the 1500s. They founded a community in China which lasted until modern times. Japanese Christianity was wiped out in 1638, when 30,000 converts were massacred near Nagasaki.

Seismograph

Chinese cannon

◀ *Paper, printing, guns, gunpowder, rockets, compasses, bridges made of cast iron, seed drills, seismographs, steel, umbrellas, paper money – all were invented in China long before they were first used in the West.*

Shogun

Samurai warrior

▶ *From 1339 to 1573 civil war raged in Japan. In spite of the disorder, the arts flourished. The Golden Pavilion was built (1394) in Kyoto, Japan's capital city from 794 until 1868.*

▼ *Japanese women practise the Tea Ceremony in the 1700s. Tea-drinking is an ancient Japanese ritual; it shows the formal behaviour of Japanese life.*

▲ *From the 1100s to the 1800s Japan was ruled by military dictators who bore the title of shogun. The samurai were the warrior class of Japan, whose code of bravery, loyalty and honour was known as bushido.*

The Colonization of America

Spaniards began to settle on the Caribbean island of Hispaniola in 1493, a year after Columbus's first landing. In 1496, a few Spanish soldiers slaughtered thousands of rebellious native Arawaks. This pattern of oppression and murder was repeated in Mexico and Peru on a far larger scale by the expeditions of the Spanish conquistadores under Cortés and Pizarro. A century later, the early settlers in New England gradually drove out groups of Native Americans in order to occupy their land.

1492–1504
Columbus's four voyages to America

1541–1542
Orellana first European to cross S America

1733
Foundation of Georgia, the last of the original 13 Colonies

▶ In 1519, Spanish soldiers led by Cortés landed in Mexico to plunder the fabled wealth of the Aztecs. Pizarro arrived in Peru in 1532 and within two years, he had overthrown the Inca empire. The first North American colonies (opposite page) were settled by immigrants from several European countries.

◀ In 1519 the Aztec ruler Montezuma welcomed Hernán Cortés to his capital of Tenochtitlán and showered him with gifts. The early goodwill soon turned to enmity and the Spaniards besieged the city. Aztec wood and stone weapons were no match for steel swords and crossbows. By 1521 the entire Aztec empire had fallen to the Spanish.

BRAZIL'S ORIGIN

In the 1400s Portuguese navigators travelling to India often sailed far across the Atlantic Ocean to pick up the currents that would sweep them round the Cape of Good Hope. In 1500, on one of these voyages, a fleet led by Pedro Cabral was swept too far west. They reached the coast of Brazil, which they claimed for Portugal.

▶ In 1532 Spanish conquistadores under Francisco Pizarro kidnapped the Inca emperor Atahualpa. Pizarro's plan was to terrify the Inca army that faced his tiny band of 159 men by capturing their emperor, who was also their god. The plot worked and the Spanish soldiers then killed more than 4000 unarmed Inca nobles. Within hours, Pizarro was master of the Inca capital, Cuzco. Atahualpa was executed in 1533.

Spanish conquistadores capture Atahualpa

EUROPEAN
SETTLEMENT
c.1775

- ■ Dutch
- · French
-   German
- ■ Mainly English
- ■ Scottish
- · Scotch-Irish

HUDSON'S BAY COMPANY

French fur-traders founded the first permanent European settlement in what is now Canada in 1604. In 1670 two French traders received the backing from a group of English noblemen to found a company to exploit the fur trade around the shores of Hudson's Bay. At the trading posts that the company set up Native Americans exchanged goods such as beaver and other animal skins for guns. After the English conquered Canada in 1763, the company gained control of the fur trade in the region.

Puritan settler

▼ *The Pilgrim Fathers, who sailed from England in 1620, founded the first permanent European settlement in what is now the USA at Plymouth, Mass.*

New England farmer

New England settlement

New England woman settler

▲ *Between 1620 and 1700 about 400,000 people of European stock, most of them from England or France, were living in North America. The English settled in far greater numbers because the area they settled in was more suitable for farming. Whole communities came out together from England. They cleared the land for cultivation and for raising farm animals. They soon produced most of the necessities of life and before long became independent of their homeland. A college was founded at Harvard in New England as early as 1636.*

European Society in the 1600s

At the beginning of the 1600s the new-found lands of the Americas were still a novelty to the people of Europe. Only the rich could afford its native vegetables and fruits, which later were to change the diet of much of the world. The gulf between the classes widened. The new-style houses of the wealthy were designed to afford a higher degree of comfort and luxury while the hovels of the poor remained dank, dark and insanitary. In England the one place where all classes mingled were the theatres.

SCIENTIFIC ADVANCES
The 1600s saw a scientific revolution with the invention of the telescope (1608), microscope (1618), thermometer (1641), and barometer (1644). Instruments such as these helped scientists gain an accurate picture of the natural world.

Englishman Isaac Newton's reflecting telescope (1668)

1582
Pope Gregory introduces modern calendar

*c.*1601
First performance of *Hamlet* by William Shakespeare

1665
Isaac Newton discovers force of gravity

▼ *In medieval England the ownership of land set the nobles apart from the rest of the population. But in the late 1500s rich merchants bought land as a way of becoming 'gentlemen'. The splendour of many of the larger houses built at this time demonstrates the growing wealth of the merchant classes.*

◄ *In most European countries, falconry was a popular sport with both kings and commoners.*

17th-century English manor house

▶ *Early visitors to America brought back many foods new to Europe, including maize, potatoes, tomatoes and French beans. Peaches and apricots were also introduced from Asia.*

▲ *Imported cotton from the new colonies was first woven in Europe in the 1600s.*

▲ *New spices such as mace, cloves, pepper and cinnamon were used to flavour food.*

▲ *The Spanish brought the potato to Europe, a food known in South America for 2000 years.*

▲ *Tobacco was first used in France in the 1560s by Jean Nicot.*

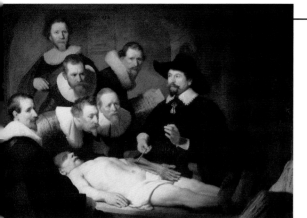

◄ *The Dutch artist Rembrandt painted* The Anatomy Lesson of Dr Tulp *in 1642. Anatomy was then quite a new science. A Belgian doctor, Andreas Vesalius, published the first accurate account of the human body's bones and nervous system in 1543.*

FURTHER FACTS

- In the 1600s the smoking of tobacco was thought to keep away the plague.
- Crops failed regularly in the years 1600–1720. The climate in Europe at that time was unusually severe and the period is known as 'The Little Ice Age'.
- Newspapers were started in the 1600s; among the earliest was the single-page *Antwerp Gazette* in Belgium.

▼ *For centuries peasant families had lived in single-roomed, windowless hovels, which they shared with any animals they might possess.*

▼ *About 90 percent of the population of Europe lived on the land. It was a hard life. Wind and water mills, animals and humans were the only sources of power.*

▲ *The harvest was the most important event of a peasant's year. A poor harvest meant hunger and misery.*

Globe theatre

ELIZABETHAN DRAMA

England was the first country to produce great drama after the Reformation. By 1600 London had five theatres, some of them large enough to hold a thousand spectators. Actors, who a few years earlier had been imprisoned as 'rogues and vagabonds' by the English authorities, were now patronized by Queen Elizabeth and her courtiers. The need for new plays to please the growing audiences was answered by young writers such as Marlowe, Johnson and Middleton. The most popular dramatist of them all was William Shakespeare.

▲ *William Shakespeare (1564–1616) is one of the greatest of English-language dramatists.*

◄ *Many of Shakespeare's plays were performed at the Globe theater, one of the first public theatres in London.*

Africa and the Slave Trade

Powerful, well-developed civilizations existed in Africa centuries before the Europeans arrived. Slavery was a recognized part of most of these societies and when the first Europeans arrived, slaves were among the goods exchanged in trade. At first, only a few slaves were taken but the number rose to millions when slaves began to be transported across the Atlantic to work on the plantations of the European colonies in America. The loss of so many people was a catastrophe for large regions of Africa.

GREAT ZIMBABWE

The ancient city of Great Zimbabwe lies in the modern country of Zimbabwe to which it gave its name. Prehistoric farmers were the first people to occupy Zimbabwe, but the ruins which remain today date from the middle of the 1300s. At that time the city was the centre of a powerful empire which traded as far afield as China. The present-day ruins of Great Zimbabwe consist of a tower, 9 metres high, surrounded by part of a dry stone wall, 240 metres around and 10 metres high.

Pre-1500s	1500s	1700s
Arabs capture and sell Africans as slaves	Europeans begin shipping slaves to New World	Height of transatlantic slave trade

Charles II guinea coin

▶ *The cities of Ife and Benin were the centres of two West African trading kingdoms dating from the 1200s. Both kingdoms produced superb sculptures in bronze, wood and terracotta.*

13th-century terracotta head from Ife

▲ *The kingdoms of West Africa were rich in gold. Arabs called the area 'Guinea' and Europeans borrowed the word. In 1663 a coin made of Guinea gold was struck in England by order of Charles II. By the mid-1600s the Guinea coast was supplying most of the New World's slaves.*

FURTHER FACTS

● Denmark first made the slave trade illegal (1792); the US made the trade illegal in 1808. William Wilberforce led the British anti-slavery movement; the trade was abolished in Britain in 1807.

● Desperate slaves sometimes mutinied; sailors were known to hold matches near the ships' cannons as a precaution when the slaves were above deck.

▶ *Europeans brought goods such as guns to coastal African rulers to exchange for slaves who had either been kidnapped or were prisoners of war. Many slaves did not survive the voyage to the Americas, often dying from disease, or suicide. After the slaves had been landed, the ships returned to Europe with cargoes of sugar and tobacco.*

► Zanzibar Island lies off the coast of present-day Tanzania on the east coast of Africa. Once Muslims from the Middle East had conquered large parts of North Africa in the AD 600s and 700s, they began to travel south, to trade south of the Sahara Desert. Africans in these regions sold slaves to the Arabs along with ebony and ivory. By the time the Portuguese arrived in Africa in the 1400s the slave trade had been established for hundreds of years.
In 1698 Arabs from the Middle East captured the Portuguese trading post on Zanzibar and made it into a base for slave-trading on the eastern mainland.

▼ In 1482 the Portuguese built a castle at El Mina (now in Ghana) to defend their trade with the gold mines inland. French, Dutch and British merchants soon built their own forts on the west African coast as warehouses for the slave trade.

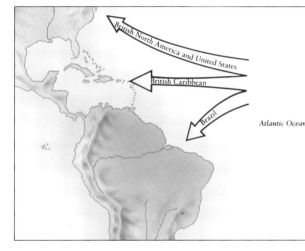

▼ The Slave Coast was the area between the Gold Coast (now Ghana) and the Niger River. The countries which controlled the slave trade – Britain, France, Holland – had no interest in going further into the interior of the continent. Portugal supplied slaves for Brazil from Angola.

THE GROWTH OF THE SLAVE TRADE, 1526–1810

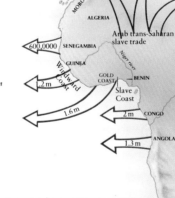

This painful device prevented the wearer lying down

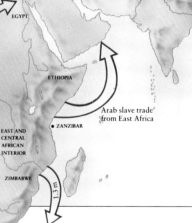

◄ Newly captured slaves were chained together by the neck or feet and marched in long rows called 'coffles' to the coast to await shipment abroad. Iron collars, sometimes with heavy weights attached, prevented slaves from running away. During the whole Atlantic crossing they were chained in the hold of the ship.

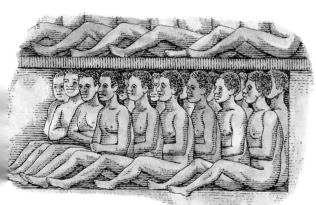

▲ Slave ships were terribly overloaded. Slaves were often packed so tightly that they could only sit or lie flat for the long voyage to the Americas.

Iron manacles

365

THE AGE OF KINGS

Kings and Commoners

The 1600s was the age of absolute rulers. Not only in Europe, but in India, China and Japan, power was wielded by kings, emperors or shoguns who had total authority over their subjects. Only in England was its king, Charles I, defeated in a civil war and executed by order of parliament. In Europe the most powerful monarchs were Louis XIV of France and Peter the Great of Russia. Peter forced drastic reforms on his backward country.

Louis's reign brought the French monarchy to its zenith, even while his financial extravagance contributed to its destruction less than 70 years after his death. In India, the Moguls built mosques, tombs, citadels and palaces of unparalleled splendour. The 1600s and 1700s also confirmed Europe's world leadership. The growth of their empires overseas was to bring nearly half the world under Europe's control.

▼ *Compared with western Europe, Russia was poor and backward when Peter the Great became tsar in 1682. Peter resolved to make Russia a great power. He toured Europe to recruit technicians and craftsmen. He reformed the government and modernized his army and navy. He also moved his capital to the new city of St Petersburg, which he called his 'window to the West'.*

A jewelled cup given by Peter the Great to his son Alexis

1643–1715	1649	1682–1725
Reign of Louis XIV of France	Charles I beheaded in England	Reign of Peter the Great of Russia

Peter the Great in England

Russian boyars

▲ *The boyars were a group of families who had been the ruling class in Russia since the Middle Ages. Peter abolished their powers and ordered that their beards be cut off as a symbol of their lost authority.*

FURTHER FACTS

● Louis XIV's absolute control of France is epitomized by his supposed remark '*L'état, c'est moi*' ('I am the state').
● After Charles I's execution, England became a commonwealth ruled by parliament. In 1653 Oliver Cromwell, a general in the civil war, became lord protector. The monarchy was restored in 1660 when Charles II returned to England.
● A brilliant general, Cromwell was also ruthless, as shown by his forced settlement of Protestants in Catholic Ireland after Ireland rebelled against English rule in 1649.

◀ *Under Peter, Russian labourers (serfs) continued to live in great poverty; in the countryside, people often starved in the harsh Russian winters.*

◄ Like his father James I, Charles I of England believed he had been appointed by God to rule his country. He refused to accept parliamentary control of his policies and imposed taxes without parliament's consent. For 11 years he governed on his own. In 1642 the quarrel between king and parliament developed into a civil war. Charles was supported by the nobles, Anglicans and Catholics. The parliamentary army was mostly made up of working men. After a series of victories by the parliamentarian general Oliver Cromwell, Charles surrendered in 1645. He was put on trial, found guilty of treason and executed in 1649.

▼ Louis XIV built the most magnificent palace in Europe for himself and his court at Versailles, near Paris. No cost was spared, and the finest artists were hired to decorate it with sculptures, carvings and paintings. It was surrounded by beautiful formal gardens. Versailles is considered to be the greatest architectural achievement of the 1600s.

Known as the 'Sun King', Louis XIV's emblem was a golden sun

LOUIS XIV'S EXTRAVAGANCE

Louis XIV doubled taxes to raise money for both the building of his palace at Versailles and to keep France in a series of European wars. But the wars brought France no gains and Louis's extravagance created an enormous strain on the country's resources. Six out of every 10 francs collected in taxes had to pay for the building and upkeep of Versailles alone.

◄ A tapestry of a scene at the world-famous Gobelins workshops. Louis XIV inspects furnishings intended for Versailles. Louis and his minister Colbert encouraged the establishment of French factories to provide tapestries and other luxurious items for his palaces.

The Age of Reason

The Age of Reason, or Enlightenment, was a period from about 1650 to 1750 when people in western Europe believed that everything in nature could be explained by scientific enquiry and reason. This led to a questioning of established beliefs and to support for religious tolerance in much of Europe and the British North American colonies (later the United States). Even despotic rulers such as Frederick the Great of Prussia tried to put the new social and political ideas into practice in their states.

1596–1650
Life of René Descartes. The Age of Reason grew from his ideas

1740
Prussia given freedom of press and worship by Frederick the Great

1751–1776
Denis Diderot publishes his multi-volume *Encyclopédie*

▼ *In 1735 a Swedish doctor, Carl von Linné (known as Linnaeus), produced the first logical system for naming and classifying plants and animals. He gave everything two names. The first part of the name is the* genus *(group), the second part the* species *(kind). In 1801, the French naturalist Jean-Baptiste Lamarck devised a system for classifying animals without backbones (invertebrates).*

◄ *The baroque was the name given to the style of European art in the 1600s. Its leading artist was Rubens, whose paintings for the French court included* The Marriage of Marie de Médicis to Henri IV. *In the 1700s a renewed interest in classical art caused many public buildings in Europe to be modelled on Greek temples (below).*

Old Museum, Berlin, Germany

BALLET AND OPERA

Ballet was developed as an entertainment in the French court of the 1600s. The first public performance was in France in about 1708. The first operas were composed in Italy in the 1590s, but the art form reached greater heights in the works of Gluck and Mozart in the 1700s. Elaborate sets and costumes dazzled the audiences with spectacular effects.

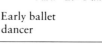

Early ballet dancer

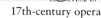

17th-century opera

► *Frederick II of Prussia, known as 'the Great', was perhaps the outstanding monarch of the Age of Reason. Frederick was a brilliant general in war and an able administrator in times of peace. He was a keen student of literature, philosophy and music and played the flute almost as a professional. A talented composer himself, he was a generous patron of other composers, notably of Johann Sebastian Bach. He also corresponded with Voltaire and other leading thinkers of the time.*

Frederick the Great playing the flute

▼ *In 1675, Charles II of England founded the Royal Observatory at Greenwich, near London. Its purpose was to provide aids to accurate navigation for ships on the high seas. The Greenwich system of geographical longitude and time-keeping has since become standard throughout the world.*

▼ *The great work that promoted the humanistic philosophy of the Age of Reason was the* Encyclopédie *(1747–1772), edited by a universal genius, the French philosopher Denis Diderot. The 35 volumes reviewed the arts and sciences of the time.*

JAPANESE ISOLATION

During the 1630s Japan's rulers decided that contact with the West must end. In particular, they feared that Christian missionaries might bring European armies to invade Japan. They therefore banned most foreigners from entering Japan and the Japanese from leaving their country. As a result, people in the West were unable to appreciate the great beauty of the Japanese art of this period until the late 1800s.

Japanese porcelain figures *c.* 1700

European Settlement Overseas

By the beginning of the 1600s, the heyday of Portuguese and Spanish expansion had passed. It was now the French, Dutch and British who built empires overseas. Most of their colonies were not established by governments but by groups of merchants organized into trading companies, such as the Dutch and British East India Companies. The company was granted the right to trade in the area by the local ruler. Later the trading companies were dissolved and their possessions became part of their country's empire.

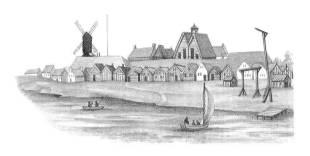

1600	1641	1763
British East India Company founded	Dutch seize Malacca from Portuguese	Peace of Paris ends Seven Years' War

▲ *The first Europeans to settle along the Hudson River Valley, in present-day New York state, were the Dutch. In 1625 they built a trading post on Manhattan Island which they had bought from the Native Americans. The British captured the colony in 1664 and renamed it New York.*

▶ *The Dutch East India Company was set up in 1602 to promote and defend Dutch trade with the East Indies. By 1641 the company had taken the place of the Portuguese as controllers of the valuable East Indian spice trade. In 1652 the company founded a base at the Cape of Good Hope as a staging post for Dutch ships on the voyage from Europe to the East Indies. This began Dutch settlement in South Africa.*

▲ *Samuel de Champlain (c.1570–1635) was one of the founders of the French colonies in North America. In 1603 he explored the St Lawrence River in Canada. In 1608 he built a fur-trading post on its shores which he called Quebec.*

▶ *The Seven Years' War (1756–1763) involved several European powers; France and Britain were in conflict because of a longtime rivalry for colonial supremacy in India and North America. The fate of the North American colonies was decided in 1759 when a British force led by General James Wolfe captured Quebec, the capital of New France (present-day Canada). Quebec's fall ensured that Britain gained all of France's lands in North America.*

EUROPEAN EMPIRES, c.1770

- Spanish
- Portuguese
- British
- Dutch
- French
- Russian (c.1763)

Musketeers aboard the British warship *Centurion*, 1752

▲ Spain and Portugal were the first European countries to build empires overseas. The Portuguese focused their efforts on Africa and Asia. The Spanish occupied all of South America except for Brazil. The English and French settled in North America. Dutch traders colonized the East Indies.

► *During the 1700s European colonial powers were frequently at war with each other. Since the colonies could only be reached by ship, many clashes took place at sea. A major objective in war was to interfere with the enemy's trade and to seize enemy ships. Here, British musketeers on the warship* Centurion *fire on the* Covadonga, *loaded with silver from the Spanish colony of Mexico.*

Tipu's tiger

◄ *In 1757 British East India Company troops defeated the ruler of Bengal at Plassey, northern India. With French influence in decline, the victory made Britain the dominant power in India. However, Indian rulers such as Tipu, ruler of Mysore, continued to defy the British. Tipu ('tiger') had a model made showing a tiger eating a British soldier.*

FURTHER FACTS

- In the 1600s and 1700s the term 'East Indies' was originally used to describe India; later it came to refer to southeast Asia, especially Indonesia.
- The only country in Asia never to be colonized by any European power was Siam (now Thailand).
- In 1756 a number of British prisoners were shut up in a small room during a battle between British and Indian troops. Several died in the suffocating heat. The British greatly exaggerated the size of the room and the number of deaths. The incident became known among the British as 'The Black Hole of Calcutta'.

THE AGE OF REVOLUTIONS

The American War of Independence

The colonists of the Thirteen Colonies of British North America were governed from London. They were treated as British subjects except that they did not have the vote and therefore nobody to represent their interests in parliament. When parliament passed laws which imposed new taxes, the colonies rebelled. In the revolution that followed the colonists won their independence from Britain and set up a republic. The success of the Americans in overthrowing a ruling authority was an inspiration to the peoples of Europe who lived under repressive regimes. Within a few years of the Americans' revolution, the French had risen against their king and ruling classes. After several years of violence and bloodshed they established a republic which in its turn became the model for revolutionaries throughout the world.

1775–1776
Early fighting around Boston

Sept. 1777
Americans win key battle of Saratoga

Sept. 1783
Britain recognizes independence of the United States

◀ *The 'Boston Tea Party' was a protest against taxation in Britain's North American colonies. The colonists objected to paying taxes on items such as tea, imposed by the British parliament without their consent. A small band of colonists dressed up as Mohawk Indians, boarded three ships in Boston harbour and dumped tea chests in the sea. The British reacted with a series of punitive laws known as the 'Intolerable Acts', which included the closure of the port of Boston until money was paid to the East India Company for the loss of the tea.*

▶ *The Declaration of Independence, adopted on 4 July 1776, is the foundation document of the United States of America. It proclaimed the separation of the American colonies (which now became states) from Britain. A lawyer, Thomas Jefferson (centre), was the principal author. The document was signed by 56 delegates of the Thirteen Colonies. Since 1776, 4 July has been a national holiday in the USA.*

The Liberty Bell in Philadelphia is a symbol of American independence

Draft of the Declaration of Independence

Quebec *
Montreal *
Saratoga *
Great Lakes
Lexington/ * Bunker Hill
Concord
Princeton *
Extent of American Colonies —
Yorktown *
Camden *
INDIAN TERRITORY
FLORIDA

* = battle

▲ *Early in the war the British captured New York (1776). The war ended with their surrender at Yorktown (1781). A turning point was the American alliance with the French in 1778.*

KEY DATES

● **April 1775:** The first shots of the war were fired at Lexington near Boston, when British troops arrived to destroy the arms store of the local militia.
● **June 1775:** George Washington becomes commander of the rebel American army.
● **March 1776:** The British evacuate Boston.
● **4 July 1776:** The Declaration of Independence is adopted by delegates of the 13 Colonies.
● **October 1781:** The British are besieged at Yorktown by the Americans and their French allies.
● **September 1783:** US and Britain sign final peace treaty in Paris.

▲ *George Washington became commander of the American forces in 1775. On Christmas night 1776, Washington crossed the Delaware river, before beating the British in the* battles of Trenton and Princeton. *Washington's greatest achievement was to keep 16,000 volunteer troops together during five years of conflict in which they suffered many reverses.*

▼ *The British victory at Bunker Hill (1775) cost them 1000 casualties against 400 American casualties. Their well-drilled troops trained for European wars stood in close-packed ranks firing volleys of shot in the direction of the enemy. The Americans, used to killing game and fighting on the frontiers with Native Americans, were skilled marksmen who could put a bullet through a man's head at 200 paces.*

American revolutionary soldier

British grenadier *c.* 1775

The French Revolution

The revolution in France of 1789 is one of the most important events in human history. It is important because it overthrew a powerful monarchy and introduced new principles of democratic government. The revolution was extremely violent, killing both the French king and thousands of citizens. France was in chaos as one group of revolutionaries after another failed to establish firm government. Eventually, the French army seized power, led by its most successful general, Napoleon Bonaparte.

July 1789
Mobs storm the Bastille; the revolution begins

July 1794
Robespierre executed; the Terror ends

November 1799
Napoleon overthrows the revolutionary government

▲ *Louis XVI was shy and stupid rather than bad or cruel. He preferred hunting to governing his country. He was also unfortunate in having an unpopular wife, the pleasure-loving Marie Antoinette. In 1793 he was to pay with his life for his indifference to the misery that heavy taxation was causing ordinary French people.*

▲ *By 1789 the States-General (a national parliament) had not met since 1614. In June the Third Estate (the commoners in the parliament) met in a tennis court where they took an oath not to disband until France had a new assembly and constitution. The Tennis Court Oath was the beginning of the revolution.*

▶ *Although Louis XVI gave in to the Third Estate and ordered that a new National Assembly should meet, rumours spread through Paris that the king would soon disband it. The rumours started riots both outside Paris and in the city itself, where on 14 July an angry mob captured the Bastille prison, a symbol to Parisians of royal power.*

◄ In 1789 many working men and women in Paris were jobless and hungry. On 14 July the price of bread was doubled. The unemployed joined shopkeepers and tradesmen to form the mob that stormed the Bastille.

Woman revolutionary with tricolor rosette in her hat

Revolutionaries were called *sans culottes* because they wore trousers rather than breeches (unlike the nobility)

UNITÉ INDIVISIBILITÉ DE LA RÉPUBLIQUE LIBERTÉ ÉGALITÉ FRATERNITÉ OU LA MORT

► Slogans such as 'unity, liberty, equality and fraternity or death' were seen on the revolutionary posters stuck up in Paris.

◄ The period from mid 1793 to mid 1794 is called the Terror. France was then ruled by the Jacobins, a group of extremist revolutionaries led by Maximilian Robespierre. The Jacobins ruled by fear. Thousands of innocent people from all classes were condemned for their opposition to the revolution. Large crowds watched the public executions on the guillotine.

Napoleon Bonaparte

Napoleon Bonaparte seized power in France when the government turned to the army for support. Napoleon was the army's most successful general. From 1799 Napoleon led a number of brilliant military campaigns that won him control of most of western Europe. His one major defeat was at Trafalgar in 1805, which gave Britain command of the seas. From 1812 Napoleon's fortunes declined. His armies retreated from Russia and he lost a series of battles in Germany. His defeat at Waterloo in 1815 ended his career.

▼ In 1799 Napoleon made himself first consul (a form of dictator). To confirm his position he took the title of Emperor of France in 1804. At his coronation Napoleon took the crown from the pope and placed it on his own head as a sign of his personal power. He followed this by crowning his wife, Josephine as empress. The first French republic was now ended.

1799
Napoleon becomes first consul of France

1812
French army retreats from Russia

1815
Napoleon finally beaten at battle of Waterloo

▶ The only force that continually foiled Napoleon's ambitions was the British navy. Under Horatio Nelson, the British won a number of key sea battles such as Trafalgar (1805), when Nelson was killed. At the time of the Napoleonic Wars, life on board naval ships was extremely harsh. Up to 24 lashes with a whip was the usual punishment for the often mutinous sailors. Even this painful ordeal was imposed by some captains as an act of mercy. The alternative was a court martial which might sentence a man to hundreds of lashes, or to death.

▲ One of Napoleon's most famous battles was at Eylau, now in Poland (1807), when in a snowstorm his army withstood heavy losses to hold off a far larger Russian army.

▲ By 1810 Napoleon controlled most of Europe, including several German states and much of Poland. He made members of his family the rulers of Spain, Italy and the Netherlands.

FURTHER FACTS

● By destroying the joint Franco-Spanish fleet at Trafalgar in 1805, the British navy saved Britain from invasion.

● In 1814 Napoleon was defeated by the armies of a European coalition at Leipzig. He abdicated and was exiled on the island of Elba. In March 1815 he escaped from Elba and raised a new army. He was finally defeated by the British and Prussians at the battle of Waterloo in June 1815.

▲ In 1812 Napoleon made the disastrous decision to invade Russia; the Russians were his only remaining rivals on mainland Europe. His army reached Moscow in September 1812 to find that the Russians had burned it down. The French army was not equipped to survive the harsh Russian winter which was just beginning. Napoleon ordered a withdrawal. As the French retreated, three quarters of the 500,000-strong army were killed by the Russians, or died of cold and hunger.

▲ After his final defeat at Waterloo, Napoleon gave himself up to the British to escape being executed by the Prussians. The British sent him to the remote Atlantic island of St Helena, where he died in 1821.

THE AGE OF IMPERIALISM

The Industrial Revolution

The Industrial Revolution is a term describing major changes in the economic and social structure of many western countries in the 1700s and 1800s. At the beginning of the 1700s most of Europe's people lived and worked on the land. By the time the 1800s ended, most Europeans were city dwellers, earning a living in factories or offices. As work became unavailable on the land huge numbers of Europeans migrated overseas, particularly to America. The political map of Europe was also redrawn during this period. Revolutions convulsed the continent from the 1820s to the 1870s. They swept away states ruled by hereditary families and replaced them with new nations based on shared history, culture and language. The European powers also strove to win new colonial territories in Africa and to extend their empires in Asia and the Pacific.

1787	1789–1815	1833
In US John Fitch demonstrates first workable steamboat	France's industrial revolution stopped by revolution and wars	British Factory Act bans children under nine working in factories

THE FIRST INDUSTRIAL REVOLUTION

Britain's industrial revolution was the period (1750–1850) when Britain's dominance of overseas markets through its empire, and the availability at home of coal and iron ore, transformed it from a farming to a manufacturing community. The harnessing of steam power and major new inventions led to cheap mass-manufacture of materials such as cotton. Iron, made by the new processes, was strong enough for building structures like bridges in a different way.

The world's first iron bridge, built in England, 1777

▶ *The transitions of Britain's industrial revolution were repeated elsewhere as other western countries became industrialized. Farmworkers moved to the towns, seeking work in the new factories. The densely-packed, low-quality houses built for them soon became unhealthy slums.*

New factory

Workers' housing

Eli Whitney's cotton gin

Canal

Canal barge

▶ *In Britain a system of canals linking the major rivers was built, providing the cheap transport the new factories needed to deliver raw materials and take away finished goods. The goods were loaded onto barges pulled by horses along tracks called towpaths. Canal-building reached its peak in Britain in the 1790s. Later in the Industrial Revolution, goods could be moved more easily on the newly-built railways.*

◀ Before the new machines led to manufacture in factories, cloth was made in homes. Women and children did the spinning. Weaving was traditionally men's work.

▼ George Stephenson opened the first public railway in 1825, between Stockton and Darlington in Yorkshire. In 1835 his son Robert built the engine for the first German train, Der Adler (The Eagle).

Early German train (1835)

▶ In the early 1800s, children as young as five years old worked underground in the mines. They often had to work shifts of 12 hours and more. Some toiled half-naked, chained to carts laden with coal which they pulled along dark passageways. Factories also used children. The usual shift was 15 hours a day. Many children were orphans; they lived in crowded, dirty hostels where the death rate could reach 60 percent.

▼ In the 1700s a revolution also took place in British farming. Jethro Tull's seed drill and improved ploughs raised the standard of cultivation. Animals that in an earlier age would have been slaughtered in the winter were now kept alive on root crops. Between 1700 and 1800, the yield of wheat doubled. Selective breeding meant larger, healthier livestock.

Jethro Tull's seed drill

Improved cattle and sheep

FURTHER FACTS

● Hargreaves introduced his 8-thread spinning machine, (called 'jenny' after his wife) in 1764. A later model was able to spin 120 threads.
● After Britain, the next western country to become industrialized was Belgium.
● By the 1840s France, Germany, Belgium and the US had all begun to build railways; the coming of the railways revolutionized travel as ordinary people were able to move about more easily.
● Towns grew rapidly: in Britain, in 1801 Manchester's population was 75,000. By 1851 it was 303,000.

The New Nationalism

Napoleon's domination of Europe at the beginning of the 1800s created a renewed desire for liberty and the pride in nationality which had inspired the French Revolution. Greece and Belgium were the first to throw off the old order and gain independence. In South America, after twenty years of uprisings and wars, independent states replaced the old empires of Spain and Portugal. By the 1870s, both Italy and Germany had become unified, and Germany had become a major new world power.

1821–1827
War of Greek
Independence

1848
Year of
revolutions
in Europe

1871
Germany united
under Prussian
leadership

▶ *The Ottoman Turks had conquered Greece in the 1500s but the Greeks never forgot they were a nation. In 1821 they rebelled against Turkish rule. In 1827 Russia, Britain and France agreed to use force if necessary to help the Greeks gain their independence. When Turkey refused to give up control of Greece, a joint French, Russian and British force defeated the Turkish fleet in Navarino Bay. The battle helped Greece become independent in 1832.*

19th-century
Greek soldier

Battle of Navarino

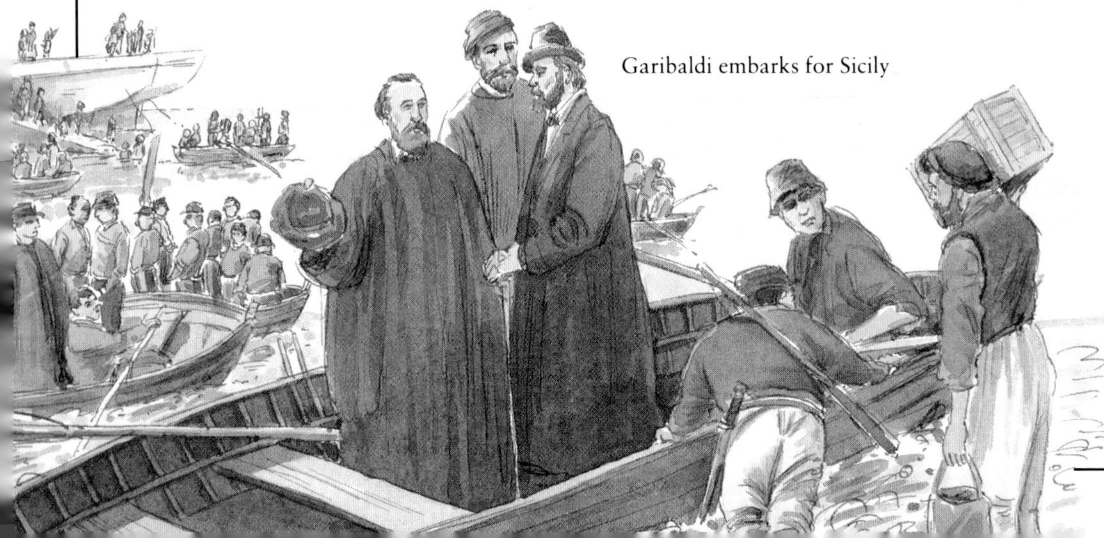

Garibaldi embarks for Sicily

◀ *Giuseppe Garibaldi was the hero of the Italian Risorgimento – the movement to replace Austrian and French rule with unification and independence. In May 1860 he landed in Sicily with a thousand red-shirted followers. In August he crossed to the mainland and captured Naples. Garibaldi's example inspired his fellow patriots to continue the struggle which was finally won when Rome became the capital of a united Italy in 1870.*

◄ *In Europe, 1848 was a year of revolutions. There were revolts in Germany, Italy, Poland and Hungary. The rulers of France and Austria gave up their thrones after major uprisings.*

▼ *In July 1870 France went to war with Prussia, the leading state of Germany. The war was a disaster for France. Its armies were destroyed and Paris came under siege. The city's defenders held out for four months but in January 1871 they were forced by starvation to surrender. The victory united the German states. In 1871 King Wilhelm of Prussia became emperor of all Germany.*

The Arc de Triomphe is protected as Parisians leave before the 1870 siege

KARL MARX

The ideas of the German philosopher Karl Marx inspired the worldwide communist movements of the 1900s. He wanted all political power to belong to the working class. Most of his writing and research was done in London, where he lived in exile from 1849. His most important works were the *Communist Manifesto* (published in Paris during the 1848 Revolution) and *Das Kapital*.

Simón Bolívar

INDEPENDENCE IN SOUTH AMERICA

The peoples of the Spanish South American empire were inspired by the French Revolution to fight for their freedom. Mexico won independence in 1821. Simón Bolívar's armies fought for the independence of Colombia and Bolivia. José San Martín liberated Chile and, with Bolívar, freed Colombia and Ecuador.

MEXICO 1821
CENTRAL AMERICAN FEDERATION 1821–1838
VENEZUELA 1830
British
Dutch
French colonies in Guyana
COLOMBIA 1819
ECUADOR 1830
BRAZIL 1822
PERU 1821
BOLIVIA 1825
PARAGUAY 1811
CHILE 1818
URUGUAY 1828
ARGENTINA 1810

FURTHER FACTS

● In 1830 the French deposed their king, Charles X. Louis Philippe became king until the 1848 revolution.
● The 1830 French uprising encouraged the Belgians to rebel against their Dutch rulers. Belgium became independent in 1833.
● In 1830 and 1863 Polish patriots rebelled against Russian rule. Both uprisings failed and many Poles were exiled to Siberia.

The American Civil War

In 1861 seven (later eleven) southern states of the USA declared themselves a separate nation, the Confederate States of America. The northern (Union) states then went to war with the South to preserve the country's unity. The cause of the row between the two regions was slavery. The agricultural South wished to retain it; the industrial North was determined to end it. The South lost the civil war as, despite early military success, it was overwhelmed by the superior forces and industrial might of the North.

1860
Abraham Lincoln elected United States' president

1865
The Union wins the American Civil War

1869
First American transcontinental railway completed

Abraham Lincoln in 1861

▲ *The Confederates rejected the Stars and Stripes and adopted their own flags. Their troops wore grey uniforms. The Union troops wore blue.*

Slaves picking cotton

◀ *The economy of the southern states was based on black slave labour. The new president, Abraham Lincoln, and his Republican party wanted to limit slavery. Afraid of being outvoted by northern non-slave states, the southern states under Jefferson Davis left the Union. War broke out in April 1861.*

▼ *New, more effective, long-range guns made the American Civil War one of the bloodiest wars in history. Three million men fought in it and over 600,000 died. However, twice as many died from disease as were killed in action.*

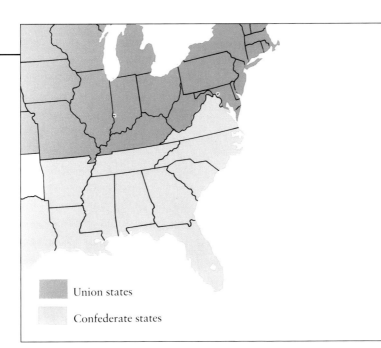

► The division of the United States at the beginning of the American Civil War. Eleven of the 34 US states made up the Confederacy. The civil war took place over a vast area. For the first time in history, railways played a vital part in warfare by moving troops and supplies swiftly over great distances.

Union states

Confederate states

FURTHER FACTS

● America's first railroad opened in South Carolina in 1830.
● The civil war began in April 1861, when Confederate artillery fired on Union troops at Fort Sumter. It ended in April 1865 when the Confederates surrendered at Appomattox, Virginia.
● A major turning point of the civil war was the Union victory at Gettysburg, Pennsylvania in July 1863; the South then abandoned its hopes of invading the Union.
● In 1869 the first railway to cross the US cut in two the buffalo herds on which the Plains tribes depended for food and clothing. By 1900 the tribes had all been moved to reservations.

WINNING THE WEST

In 1803, the United States bought France's claim to the lands west of the Mississippi river for $15 million and so doubled the new country's size. The purchase of this new land began a movement to the western territories of thousands of people, seeking their fortunes and a better life. The move west increased after the civil war in the 1860s. But the land was not empty. Native American tribes had lived on the Plains for many generations. The new settlers found they could only build and farm there if they first drove the local tribes away.

Wagon train, travelling to American West

SETTLER TRAILS ACROSS THE USA

CANADA

California

Utah

Pennsylvania

New Mexico

Texas

Georgia

Louisiana

MEXICO

► The first American railroad was opened in 1830. By 1880, America's rail network exceeded that of Europe. Rail transport overcame the great distances which had hindered the development of America. It made sending goods to markets cheap and easy. In return it brought back the factory-made equipment that the Midwestern farmers needed.

The Movement of Peoples

European migration to America gathered pace after the American War of Independence. During the 1800s, millions more crossed the Atlantic. Driven out by famine, the numbers of Irish emigrants overtook those from the rest of Britain. More emigrants came from Germany, Sweden and later Italy, Russia and eastern Europe. In its early years Australia had been a British prison colony. The discovery of gold in the mid-1800s increased the flow of people to both Australia and North America.

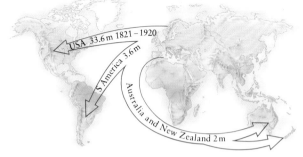

EMIGRATION FROM EUROPE, 1820s–1920s

USA 33.6 m 1821–1920

S. America 3.6 m

Australia and New Zealand 2 m

Arrows show numbers in millions

▲ *Most of the Europeans who emigrated during the 1800s went to the United States. Other favoured destinations were Australia and New Zealand and the countries of South America.*

1815–1914	1840s	1867
Main period of European migration	Potato famine begins in Ireland	Britain ends transportation to Australia

Sydney Harbour in the early 1800s

A CONVICT SETTLEMENT

In the 1700s convicted criminals in Britain were sometimes sentenced to hard labour in its colonies overseas. Most went to North America. After the US won independence in 1776, Britain established a new penal colony at Botany Bay in Australia. Convicts were shipped to parts of Australia until the 1860s.

▲ *New South Wales in eastern Australia was founded as a British prison colony. A group of convicts and guards arrived on the site of the future city of Sydney in 1788. Before then the people who lived there were Aborigines. From the 1820s free settlers were allowed to immigrate. The rearing of sheep in the rich pastures near the coasts created a profitable wool industry. By 1900 Sydney had a population of 400,000.*

FURTHER FACTS

- A penal colony was established on the island of Tasmania off the coast of mainland Australia in 1803; 65,000 convicts served their sentences there.
- By the 1870s every one of the Australian Aborigines who had lived on the island of Tasmania was dead. Some had perished from European diseases; white settlers had murdered the rest.
- European immigration into the US was at its height during 1901–1910, with 8,795,386 people admitted. Of those, over 6 million came from southern and eastern Europe.

Prospector panning for gold

◄ In 1848 gold was discovered in California. Within a few months a gold rush had started. The nearest port, San Francisco, grew from a small town to a city of 25,000 as prospectors and other people massed to seek their fortune. In the late 1800s there were also gold rushes in Canada, South Africa, New Zealand and Australia.

▶ Dawson, northeastern Canada, was typical of the towns that sprang up almost overnight in the newly discovered gold fields. At the height of the gold rush in the Yukon in the 1890s Dawson had about 25,000 residents.

THE IRISH POTATO FAMINE

The main food of the Irish people was the potato. Between 1845–1851 the crop failed. About a million people died of hunger and another million people emigrated, mostly to the US. Millions more have emigrated since. Today Ireland's population is about half the 8 million it was before 1845.

▼ Immigration into America between 1815 and 1914 was the largest peaceful movement of people in history. It is estimated that about 35 million people entered the US during that time. Thousands of Chinese landed in the west coast states until the US Congress restricted further entry in 1882. The overwhelming majority of the immigrants came from Europe. From 1892–1924 the chief entry point to the US was Ellis Island in New York Bay. Here, would-be immigrants (below) were interviewed by immigration officers.

Society in the 1800s

The taste and the standards of the prosperous middle class set the pattern of the West in the Victorian Age (named after Queen Victoria, who ruled from 1837 to 1901). They were highminded, for their education was dominated by Christian teaching; their life centred on the family and the home. A great many men and women were employed as domestic servants in the homes of the middle and upper classes. They received free food and lodging and a small wage but in return they worked up to 70 hours a week.

1837–1901
The 63-year reign of Queen Victoria

1860s
Victorian style in design reaches its peak

1890s
Reaction against Victorian style

▲ *Most of the servants of middle-class families lived on the premises in simply-furnished rooms in the attic or cellar.*

Middle-class Victorians

▼ *The upper middle classes in Victorian times enjoyed a highly privileged life-style. They lived in imposing villas set in large grounds in leafy suburbs. They did no housework. A staff of servants ranging from the lordly butler down to the lowly scullery maid attended to all their needs.*

Brass four poster bed

Butler serves tea in drawing room

19th-century house, Boston, US

Kitchen

◄ *Servants rose at six in summer and winter. In winter, grates had to be cleaned and blacked, and fresh fires lit. After the room had been dusted the family's breakfast was laid. Later, the mistress of the house might discuss with her cook what food needed to be bought for the day's main meals.*

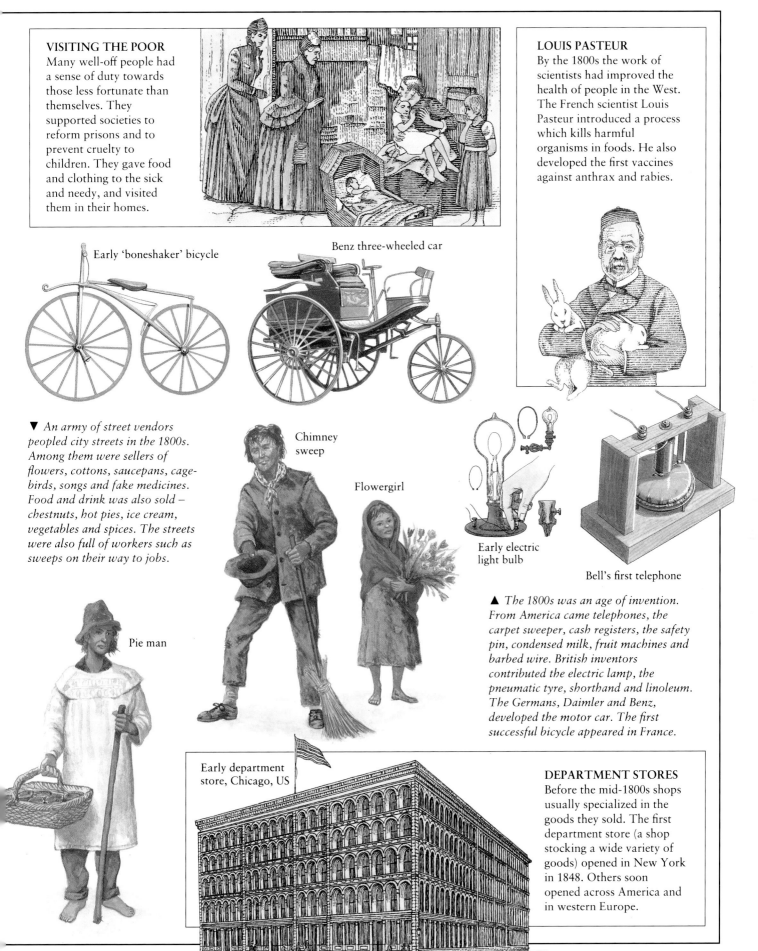

VISITING THE POOR

Many well-off people had a sense of duty towards those less fortunate than themselves. They supported societies to reform prisons and to prevent cruelty to children. They gave food and clothing to the sick and needy, and visited them in their homes.

LOUIS PASTEUR

By the 1800s the work of scientists had improved the health of people in the West. The French scientist Louis Pasteur introduced a process which kills harmful organisms in foods. He also developed the first vaccines against anthrax and rabies.

Early 'boneshaker' bicycle

Benz three-wheeled car

▼ An army of street vendors peopled city streets in the 1800s. Among them were sellers of flowers, cottons, saucepans, cage-birds, songs and fake medicines. Food and drink was also sold – chestnuts, hot pies, ice cream, vegetables and spices. The streets were also full of workers such as sweeps on their way to jobs.

Chimney sweep

Flowergirl

Early electric light bulb

Bell's first telephone

Pie man

▲ The 1800s was an age of invention. From America came telephones, the carpet sweeper, cash registers, the safety pin, condensed milk, fruit machines and barbed wire. British inventors contributed the electric lamp, the pneumatic tyre, shorthand and linoleum. The Germans, Daimler and Benz, developed the motor car. The first successful bicycle appeared in France.

Early department store, Chicago, US

DEPARTMENT STORES

Before the mid-1800s shops usually specialized in the goods they sold. The first department store (a shop stocking a wide variety of goods) opened in New York in 1848. Others soon opened across America and in western Europe.

The Colonial Age

The Industrial Revolution caused the new industrial powers to search for raw materials for their factories, mineral wealth such as gold for investment and new markets for their goods. European powers began to acquire many new colonies, especially in Africa, southeast Asia and the islands of the Pacific Ocean. From the 1870s to 1910, in the 'Scramble for Africa', almost the whole of that continent was colonized by Europeans who needed its abundant supply of raw materials.

1817–1818
The British dominance of India begins

1860
French begin expansion in West Africa

1898
Spain cedes Philippines to the US

Commodore Perry in Japan, 1853

▶ *In 1857 a mutiny by sepoys, the Indian soldiers in the British army in India, grew into a widespread revolt against British rule. The mutineers seized Lucknow and India's capital, Delhi. Cawnpore was captured and its British residents murdered. The British called up reinforcements and retook the captured cities, including Delhi (right). By July 1858 the rebels were defeated and the British were again in control of India.*

▲ *Japan had been isolated by its rulers from foreign contact, from the 1600s until the mid-1800s. The western powers tried, unsuccessfully, to gain admittance. In 1853 American warships under Commodore Matthew Perry anchored in Tokyo Bay. The threat of American naval power helped Perry persuade the Japanese to resume trading with the West.*

EUROPEAN COLONIES IN THE 1800s

As the 1800s ended, Britain, France and the Netherlands occupied most of south and southeast Asia. The British ruled India, Burma and Malaya. France had absorbed Vietnam. The United States had taken the Philippines from Spain in the war of 1898. The Dutch had ruled most of the East Indies ever since driving out the Portuguese in the early 1600s, but Germany occupied part of New Guinea and Britain controlled Brunei, Sarawak and North Borneo. Of all the south Asian countries, only the kingdom of Siam was not under foreign rule. By 1914 the whole of Africa with the exception of Ethiopia and Liberia, had either been colonized or was supervised by a European power (*see opposite page*). Territory controlled by Britain stretched almost unbroken from Egypt to South Africa. France possessed most of West and North Africa. Germany, Italy, Portugal and Spain held the rest of the continent.

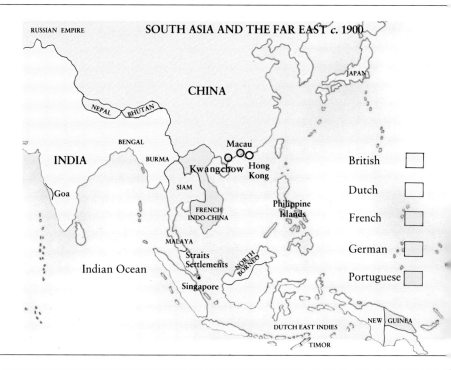

SOUTH ASIA AND THE FAR EAST c. 1900

RUSSIAN EMPIRE

CHINA

JAPAN

NEPAL BHUTAN

BENGAL

INDIA BURMA

Macau

Kwangchow Hong Kong

SIAM

Goa

FRENCH INDO-CHINA

Philippine Islands

MALAYA

Straits Settlements NORTH BORNEO

Indian Ocean

Singapore

DUTCH EAST INDIES NEW GUINEA

TIMOR

British ☐
Dutch ☐
French ☐
German ☐
Portuguese ☐

▼ *In the scramble for colonies, France claimed rights over Vietnam in SE Asia. French Catholic missionaries had been in Vietnam since the 1600s.*

After defeating the Vietnamese in a long series of wars the French made Vietnam a colony in 1887 (as French Indochina).

French soldiers fighting in North Vietnam, 1853

▶ *In 1839 the Chinese tried to stop the illegal importing of opium by the British. When they destroyed a large cargo of the drug, the British retaliated by landing troops and taking the city of Shanghai. Fighting only ended in 1856 with the seizure of Peking by an Anglo-French force; this opened Chinese ports to western trade.*

▼ *Throughout the 1800s European explorers and Christian missionaries travelled deep into Africa. In 1866 the Scottish missionary and explorer, David Livingstone, disappeared while seeking the sources of Nile. In a famous meeting, the American journalist H.M. Stanley met him by Lake Tanganyika.*

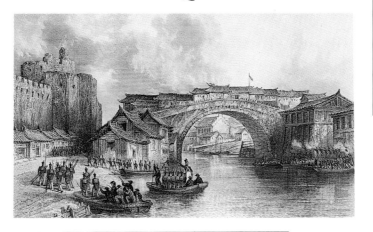

AFRICA IN 1914

Belgian colonies ☐

British colonies ☐

French colonies ☐

German colonies ☐

Portuguese colonies ☐

Spanish colonies ☐

Italian colonies ☐

Independent African state ☐

Part of the Ottoman empire but under British control ☐

THE TWO WORLD WARS

World War I

World War I (1914–1918) was the most destructive war in world history. Of the 65 million men who served in the different armies, an estimated 10 million died. Large parts of Europe were left in ruins. Some years after the war, in the late 1920s and 1930s, the world was hit by a severe economic crisis. The Great Depression began in the US, before spreading around the world. Thousands of businesses were ruined, and in the US alone 16 million people (a third of the workforce) were out of work. The crisis forced Western governments to reshape their policies. But there was no real improvement in employment until the military aggression of Germany, Italy and Japan created a need for more jobs in the defence and other industries in the 1940s. By then, the world had embarked on another terrible war.

August 1914
Germany invades
Belgium; France, Britain
declare war on Germany

1916
Battles of Verdun
and Somme create
2 million casualties

November 1918
After revolt in Germany,
armistice signed
ending the war

▶ *Many new weapons made their appearance in World War I. Aircraft were used for the first time. Tanks ended the long stalemate of trench warfare. Poison gas added to the terrors of the battlefield. At sea, no surface vessel, not even the new great battleships, were immune to attack by submarines.*

FURTHER FACTS

● In June 1914 a Serbian terrorist assassinated the heir to the Austrian throne in Sarajevo, Bosnia. Within six weeks Europe was at war – Germany and the Austro–Hungarian empire ranged themselves against France, Britain and Russia.
● The sinking of American merchant ships by German submarines brought the US into the war in 1917. The fresh troops, backed by the resources of the US, caused the final defeat of Germany.

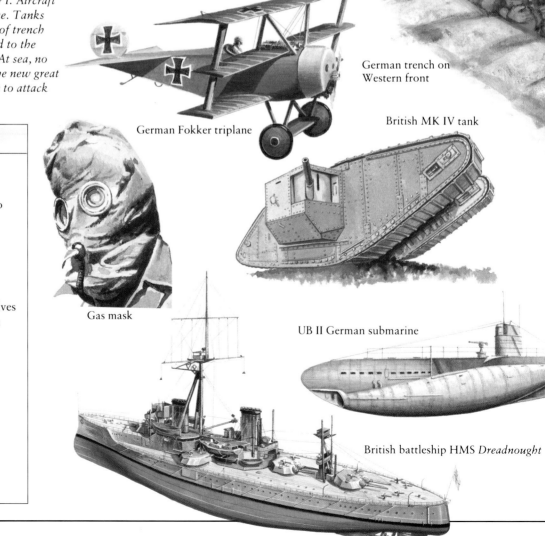

German trench on
Western front

German Fokker triplane

British MK IV tank

Gas mask

UB II German submarine

British battleship HMS *Dreadnought*

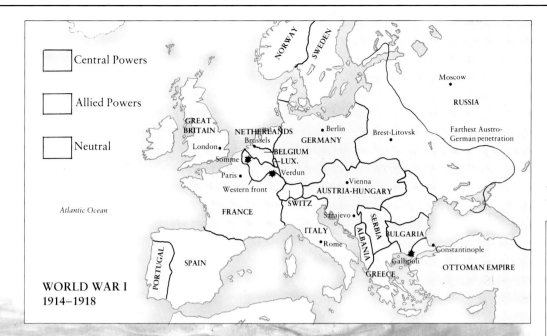

Central Powers

Allied Powers

Neutral

**WORLD WAR I
1914–1918**

◄ *World War I changed the map of Europe. In the east, Poland, Latvia, Lithuania and Estonia became independent states. Hungary become a separate republic from Austria. A new state, Czechoslovakia, was created in central Europe. Serbia, Croatia and Slovenia united under a king in an attempt to solve the long-term problems of the Balkan states.*

THE TREATY OF VERSAILLES

The treaty signed in June 1919 ended the war. The British, French and American statesmen who drew it up hoped it would make the world safe from future conflicts. It founded the League of Nations to solve future disputes between states. The League cleared up minor issues but failed to settle major problems. The Germans resented the harsh terms imposed on them and as they recovered from the war they became increasingly hostile towards the League and its members. Once more, Europe became divided into two armed camps.

◄ *Despite its casualties, World War I was fought without a single decisive battle on the Western front. For over four years, fighting centred around two lines of trenches, stretching across western Europe. As the war dragged on, life in the dirty, waterlogged trenches became intolerable for the soldiers who lived in them.*

THE RUSSIAN REVOLUTION

By the end of 1916 the better-equipped German army had brought the Russian army near to defeat. In order to reduce Russia to even further chaos, the Germans smuggled the marxist revolutionary Vladimir Lenin (depicted *right* in a 1930s painting) back into Russia from exile abroad. In November 1917 Lenin's Bolshevik (later Communist) party made an attempt to overthrow the Russian government. The troops sent to put down the uprising joined the rioting crowds. Strikes in Petrograd (St Petersburg) grew into a full-scale revolution which saw the downfall of the monarchy and the eventual establishment of a communist dictatorship in Russia.

The Great Depression

After World War I, democratic governments often seemed too weak and indecisive to handle the problems of peacetime, especially the economic crisis of the Depression. Both Italy and Germany became dictatorships under men who promised strong leadership and simple cures for their nation's woes. After a savage civil war, Franco emerged as Spain's leader. The USSR was governed by the tyrannical Joseph Stalin, who forced through a series of ruthless social policies in order to modernize his country.

January 1920
League of Nations'
first meeting

January 1933
Hitler becomes
German Chancellor

September 1939
German army
invades Poland

PARTITION OF IRELAND

Ireland had been dominated by Britain since the 1100s. At Easter in 1916, British troops crushed a revolt in Dublin by Irish nationalists seeking independence. In 1918 the nationalists declared Ireland an independent state and the Anglo-Irish treaty of 1921, recognized the independence of southern Ireland as the Irish Free State. The six mainly Protestant counties of Ulster remained part of the UK.

◀ *Dublin's post office was at the centre of the 1916 uprising.*

Queue of
unemployed
in 1930s

▲ *As world trade declined in the 1930s millions were thrown out of work throughout the West. Banks collapsed, and people lost their savings. The unemployed rioted and everywhere the job queues lengthened. In America, the man-made calamity of the slump was made worse by a natural disaster. In 1934 and 1935, the Midwest was stricken by severe drought. Intensive farming had exhausted the soil and, as the crops died, there was nothing to bind it together. Gales arose and blew the soil away. Thousands of farmers and their families were forced off the land, their livelihoods ruined (left).*

◄ In Europe the sacrifices of war had been followed by economic suffering. These difficult times provided opportunities for both the German Nazi Party under Adolf Hitler, and Benito Mussolini's Italian Fascist party. Both men came to power promising national recovery. Millions of their fellow-countrymen believed them. Soon both leaders were also seeking territorial expansion in Europe.

Hitler at Nazi rally

Republican poster in Spanish Civil War

◄ In 1936, officers of the Spanish army led by General Franco, rebelled against their government. The revolt swiftly developed into a civil war. Foreign states joined in. The fascist (extreme right-wing) powers, Germany and Italy, sent help to the army and its right-wing supporters. Communist Russia aided the government. By 1939 most of Spain had been overrun by the rebels and their leader General Franco was appointed head of state.

Voy a luchar por tu porvenir

Russian tractors in 1930s

▲ Lenin died in 1924 and Joseph Stalin succeeded him as head of the USSR. Stalin set out to strip farmers of their land in order to reorganize farming in larger state-owned units called collectives. His orders were brutally carried out by the army and secret police. Villages were burnt and the villagers killed. Millions of people were transported to labour camps in Siberia.

MASS CULTURE

The new means of communication and travel which appeared between the wars started to break down the old barriers between classes and nations. The first worldwide form of mass culture was the movies. Film actors like the comedian Charlie Chaplin became international idols. In travel, faster aircraft brought the countries of the world closer together, and mass-produced cars increased private travel. In the 1930s, radio and the first television services brought information and entertainment to millions in their own homes.

Charlie Chaplin

FURTHER FACTS

- **1919:** The German Nazi party and the Italian Fascist party were both founded.
- **1924:** The American Ford motor company produced its ten millionth car.
- **1935:** British publisher Allen Lane, launched mass-market paperbacks with Penguin Books.
- **1939:** Pan American Airlines began the first regular trans-Atlantic air service.

Early wireless

Handley Page HP42 airliner, 1931

Model 'T' Ford

World War II

American *Mustang P51* fighter plane

World War II was an even more destructive war than
World War I. Over 50 million people died, the great
majority of them innocent civilians. It was caused by the
military aggression of three countries – Italy, Germany
and Japan (the Axis Powers). At first the Axis won a string
of victories. But neither of the three countries had enough
resources for a long war. They were eventually defeated by
the superior numbers and technology of the Allies – the
British Commonwealth, France, USSR and the United States.

German *Tiger Tank*

September 1939
Britain and
France declare
war on Germany

April 1945
Hitler kills himself;
Germany surrenders
to Allies in May

August 1945
Japan accepts
Allied surrender
terms

Japanese battleship *Yomoto*

German V2 rocket

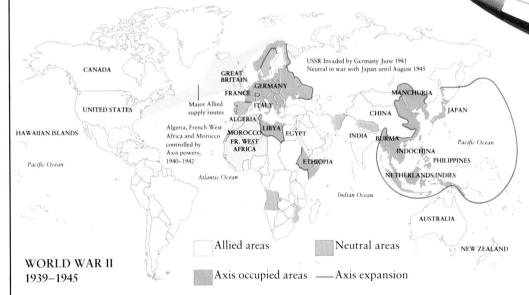

CANADA

GREAT BRITAIN

USSR Invaded by Germany June 1941
Neutral in war with Japan until August 1945

FRANCE
GERMANY
ITALY
MANCHURIA
JAPAN

UNITED STATES

Major Allied supply routes

CHINA

HAWAIIAN ISLANDS

ALGERIA
MOROCCO
LIBYA
EGYPT

Algeria, French West
Africa and Morocco
controlled by
Axis powers,
1940–1942

FR. WEST
AFRICA

INDIA
BURMA

Pacific Ocean

INDOCHINA

Pacific Ocean

ETHIOPIA

PHILIPPINES

Atlantic Ocean

NETHERLANDS INDIES

Indian Ocean

AUSTRALIA

NEW ZEALAND

**WORLD WAR II
1939–1945**

Allied areas Neutral areas

Axis occupied areas —— Axis expansion

▲ *World War II
produced a revolution in
armaments. Aircraft with
deadlier weapons flew
faster and higher.
Powerful tanks dominated
the battlefield. The aerial
strike-power of aircraft
carriers made battleships
obsolete. German V2
rockets gave a terrifying
foretaste of future wars.*

▲ *Both Germany and Japan
made huge gains early in the war.
Germany dominated the whole of
continental Europe. Japan overran
the western Pacific and conquered
southeast Asia and the East Indies.
As the war went on the Russians,
Americans, British and their allies
regained the lost territories and
forced the Axis Powers to surrender.*

▶ *In 1941 the Americans and the
Japanese were discussing peace in
the Pacific. On 7 December 1941
Japanese planes made a surprise
attack on ships of the US fleet
based at Pearl Harbor in Hawaii.
Within half an hour the US fleet
had been crippled. The next day,
the US president, Franklin D.
Roosevelt, declared war on Japan
and the other Axis Powers.*

THE HOLOCAUST

The most appalling aspect of the Nazi regime was the persecution and extermination of the Jews. Violent attacks on Jews in Germany began in the 1930s and were continued in all the countries the Germans occupied. Death camps were established for the sole purpose of eliminating the entire Jewish population. Altogether, nearly 6 million Jews were murdered.

▶ *Jewish families are herded by German guards onto cattle trucks for transportation to one of several European death camps.*

▶ *In August 1943 Hitler ordered his armies in Russia to capture Stalingrad. By November they had taken most of the city. Then the Russians counter-attacked. Cut off, short of food, and without warm clothing in the Russian winter, the German troops surrendered. The German defeat was a major turning point in the war.*

▼ *By the 1940s bombing raids meant that civilians far from the battlefields had become directly involved in wars. In German air attacks on Britain about 70,000 people died, and about a million Germans died from the Allied bombing raids. A million Japanese civilians were killed by American bombs.*

▼ *In July 1945 America's new president, Harry Truman, gave permission to drop the first atomic bombs on Japan. The bomb that fell on Hiroshima on 6 August killed about 130,000 people. Three days later a second bomb on the city of Nagasaki caused up to 750,000 deaths. The terror the bombs caused persuaded the Japanese to surrender.*

A mushroom cloud forms after the first atom bomb was dropped on Hiroshima

THE POSTWAR WORLD

The Cold War

After the war, world power became divided between two superpowers, the USSR and the United States of America. Instead of disarming, the former wartime partners became rivals in an increasingly dangerous arms race. The result was the so-called 'Cold War', in which a state of hostility existed for decades between the superpowers without actually leading to major conflict. The United Nations, set up at the end of World War II to keep the peace, was powerless to influence the conduct of its two most powerful members. China became communist under Mao Zedong, wars in Korea and Indochina followed, as the USA attempted to contain communist influence in southeast Asia. Superpower rivalry in space technology and travel also led to the race to be first on the Moon, a race won by the USA in 1969.

January 1946
First meeting
of the UN
General Assembly

1961
Berlin Wall built as
a barrier between
East and West

August 1963
US, USSR and Britain
sign nuclear test
ban treaty

EUROPE DURING THE COLD WAR
After World War II the wartime co-operation between the USSR and the Western allies collapsed. An 'iron curtain' of mistrust fell between them. By 1950 Europe was cut in two by a string of minefields and border posts which stretched from the Baltic in the north to the Black Sea in the south. In 1949 the Western powers formed a military alliance (North Atlantic Treaty Organization) to fight any Soviet attack.

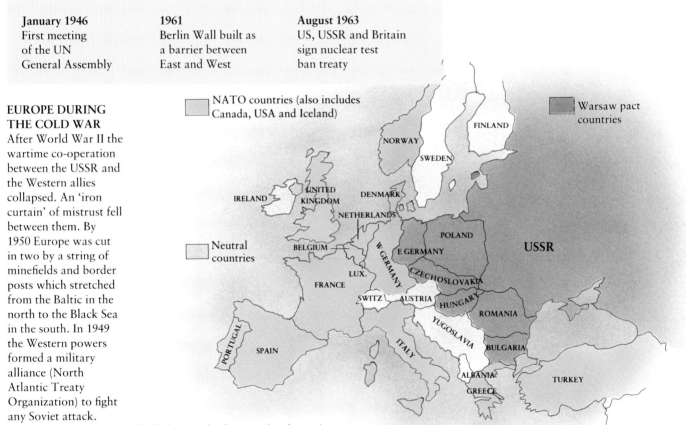

NATO countries (also includes Canada, USA and Iceland)

Warsaw pact countries

Neutral countries

Allied planes unloading supplies for Berlin, 1949

◄ In 1945, Germany and its former capital Berlin were divided into four Allied occupation zones. In 1948 the Soviets cut all land links between western Germany and the Allied sectors in Berlin. The Allies then airlifted goods into West Berlin. The Soviets allowed the flights to continue in case war broke out. In 1949 Germany split into two states, East and West Germany.

在毛澤東的勝利旗幟下前進

CHINA TURNS COMMUNIST

When the war in Asia and the Pacific ended, a struggle began between the nationalist government under Chiang Kai-shek and the communists led by Mao Zedong *(left)* to decide the future of China. Chiang's forces outnumbered the communists by ten to one but his regime was corrupt and his army poorly trained. His troops deserted in droves and city after city fell to the communists. In 1949 in the capital Peking (Beijing), Mao proclaimed the establishment of the People's Republic of China under communist control.

▼ *The United Nations was founded in 1945 by the wartime Allies. Its purposes are to maintain international peace and to solve problems through international co-operation. Since 1945 the UN's forces have been involved in several conflicts including Korea, the Middle East and Yugoslavia.*

UN Headquarters, New York

◄ *In 1950 North Korea's Soviet-trained army crossed into South Korea. The United Nations condemned the invasion. For the first time, a major international, although mainly American, force gathered under the UN flag. The UN army landed in South Korea and by 1953 North Korea and its Chinese allies were forced to recognize South Korea's independence.*

FURTHER FACTS

● **1948**: Organization for European Economic Cooperation (OEEC) founded. It has since developed into the European Community (EC).
● **1949**: North Atlantic Treaty Organization (NATO) formed – a military alliance between the US and her allies in western Europe.
● **1955**: USSR and her allies sign the Warsaw Pact, an East European defence treaty.

► *Cuba was the centre of a major international crisis in 1962. In 1961 a failed invasion of the island, backed by the USA, confirmed the alliance of Cuba's marxist ruler Fidel Castro with the USSR. During 1962, Soviet nuclear missiles, capable of hitting American cities, were installed in Cuba. US president John Kennedy ordered a naval blockade of Cuba. Nuclear war threatened but the Soviets withdrew their missiles while the US promised not to invade Cuba.*

Missile launchers in Cuba

The World Transformed

The greatest changes of the 1900s have been caused by the dramatic advances in science and technology. New forms of transport, entertainment, household appliances and medical advances are only a few of the areas that have improved the quality of life for most of us. In the past 50 years computers have enabled people to totally transform the world we live in. Used first in business, they are now found in almost every aspect of human life from medicine and education, to home entertainment.

1950s
Elvis Presley begins pop music revolution

1960s
High point of pop art and op art

1980s
Madonna's first album 'Madonna' released

► *In 1957 the USSR launched the first artificial satellite to stay up in space. Soviet scientists followed this success by putting the first person into orbit in April 1961. Americans were humiliated by the USSR's clear lead in space technology. In May 1961 President Kennedy committed the United States to landing an astronaut on the Moon before the end of the decade. Billions of dollars were poured into a US space program. On 20 July 1969, stepping from the lunar module Eagle, US astronaut Neil Armstrong became the first human being to set foot on the Moon.*

Fourth landing of American astronauts on the Moon, 1971

▼ *Buying cooked food to be eaten straightaway is not new. Hot pies, jellied eels and roast chestnuts have been sold for centuries. But it has grown enormously in recent decades, with more restaurants selling food that is prepared quickly and easily.*

▼ *Computers can perform millions of calculations in seconds. They help to design and manufacture many things, including cars, more quickly and cheaply and are becoming increasingly more important in business, education and the home.*

Eating fast food

Personal computer

Communications satellite

Television cameraman

▲ *Satellite television makes it possible to broadcast over vast distances and to several countries at the same time. The first such television broadcast took place in July 1964, when the American satellite Telstar relayed the Olympic Games around the world from Tokyo.*

▶ *Increased pollution is a price we pay for living in the late 1900s. Engine fumes pouring from thousands of vehicles stuck in city traffic jams not only poison human lungs but eat away the fabric of the buildings in which we work and live.*

Traffic jam in American city

FURTHER FACTS

- **1958**: Opening of Guggenheim Museum, New York, designed by Frank Lloyd Wright.
- **1958**: Niemeyer designs the president's palace in Brasília.
- **1985**: Pop singer Bob Geldof organizes 'Live Aid', the famous global pop concert, to help raise money for world famine.

TWENTIETH CENTURY CULTURE

Culture in the late 1900s cannot be readily classified into movements or schools. Much art and music is being produced by young people, for young people. Pop singers such as Elvis Presley, the Beatles and Madonna are transformed by clever promotion and image-making from mere entertainers into role models. American pop artist Roy Lichtenstein used comic strips, advertisements and other common images and made them subjects of art. The American author, Toni Morrison, writes prize-winning books that explore the subject of Black American relationships. New materials and technologies enable architects to design elegant structures of glass and metals. Englishman Henry Moore's sculptures seem to grow naturally from the landscape around them.

Blam by Roy Lichtenstein

Madonna, American entertainer

Reclining Figure by Henry Moore

Toni Morrison, American Pulitzer Prize winning writer

Itamaraty Palace, Brasília

Retreat from Empire

The old European empires were speedily dismantled in the years following World War II. The effort of fighting the war had weakened the European powers and they became incapable of resisting the various nationalist movements that had grown up in their overseas possessions. India's independence in 1947 began the break-up of the British empire. Between 1950 and 1980 more than 45 former African colonies became independent countries, as well as the majority of Asian and Middle Eastern colonies.

■ Countries that have become independent from 1950

▲ Between 1950 and 1980 most colonies became independent states. The majority were to be found in Africa, south of the Sahara.

1947
India, divided into India and Pakistan, becomes independent

1965–1980
Ruling white minority in Rhodesia (now Zimbabwe) refuses black majority rule

1954–1975
Wars in Vietnam, involving western powers of France and US

▲ Mohandas Gandhi known as 'Mahatma' (Great Soul) led India to independence from the British. He organized passive resistance to British rule on a mass scale and was imprisoned several times. India won independence in 1947 but Gandhi was assassinated in 1948 by a Hindu fanatic.

◄ Algeria had been French since 1848 and many French colonists had settled there. The refusal of the settlers to grant equal rights to the native Muslim population caused increasing unrest. In 1954 a major revolt led by the Front de Libération Nationale (FLN) resulted in seven years of savage fighting. Algeria became an independent republic in July 1962.

▶ *Vietnam became a united country in April 1975 when the communists of North Vietnam (the Vietcong) captured the southern capital of Saigon from the South Vietnamese and their American allies. Twenty years of war, including some of the heaviest bombing of all time, had devastated the country. As the Vietcong approached Saigon, and the Americans left, many of their South Vietnamese allies tried to flee the country.*

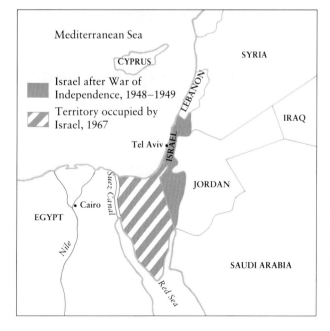

Arab soldiers during 1973 Arab-Israeli war

▲ *In 1947 the UN put forward a plan for separate Jewish and Arab states in the previously British administered territory of Palestine. However, as the British were leaving, the new state of Israel was proclaimed by the Palestine Jews. Since 1947 Israel has fought four wars with her Arab neighbours and Palestine has become divided between Israel, Egypt and Jordan.*

▶ *By the end of the war of 1948–1949 Israel occupied most of Palestine. Gains in the Six Day War (1967) trebled its size. But pressure from the US, and Israel's desire for peace, made it give up most of its gains. Israel signed a peace treaty with Egypt in 1979.*

Mediterranean Sea

CYPRUS

SYRIA

LEBANON

■ Israel after War of Independence, 1948–1949

▨ Territory occupied by Israel, 1967

ISRAEL

Tel Aviv •

IRAQ

JORDAN

Suez Canal

• Cairo

EGYPT

Nile

SAUDI ARABIA

Red Sea

FURTHER FACTS

● In 1945 the United Nations had 51 members. By 1992 the membership had grown to 179. Most new members had been colonies in the European empires.

● In 1957 Ghana (formerly the Gold Coast) became the first of many countries in Africa to gain independence.

● In the Belgian Congo (now Zaire), Angola and Mozambique there were years of warfare against the colonial power in each country to decide who should run the country after independence.

The New World Order

In the early 1990s the Cold War, which once divided the world into two armed camps, was replaced by conflict between states that had been part of the Soviet empire. Technology, which contines to make rapid advances, usually means a more agreeable life for those who can afford it. Yet pollution of land, sea and air seems to be the penalty for the prosperity of the world's richer nations. Meanwhile, population growth, wars and climatic change have brought severe famine to millions in Africa and Asia.

1960
Sharpeville, South Africa: troops kill 67 black demonstrators

1986
Chernobyl, USSR Nuclear disaster causes international pollution

1992
USSR splits into 15 independent republics

THE FALL OF COMMUNISM
After the war the Soviet Union imposed communism on the countries of eastern Europe that had fallen under its control. Any uprisings against the USSR were ruthlessly crushed. But nationalism in eastern Europe continued. In 1985 a new leader, Mikhail Gorbachev, came to power in the USSR. Gorbachev was committed to reform. He allowed more political freedom within Russia and its subject states. Popular democratic movements sprang up in eastern Europe and led to the overthrow of their communist governments. In 1989 the most hated symbol of communist repression, the wall that divided East and West Berlin, was torn down (*below*). By 1990 communism in Europe had collapsed.

▼ *Famine, caused by wars and climatic change, means that many millions of people in the world's poorer nations are kept alive only by foreign imported aid of food, medicines and clothing. In Asia, Bangladesh has suffered from catastrophic flooding, while several African countries south of the Sahara Desert are turning into desert wastelands, rife with starvation and disease.*

▼ *Improved farming methods, plants that give higher yields, scientific animal breeding and irrigation schemes have greatly increased the production of food in some developing countries.*

WORLD TRADE ASSOCIATIONS SET UP SINCE 1945

EFTA

EC

COMECON

ASEAN

OECD

LAIA

CACM

OPEC

See pages 485 and 486

▲ *Associations between groups of countries have grown up in many parts of the world. Their objectives vary. Some are merely agreements to cooperate in economic and social matters. The aim of the EC (European Community) is eventually to form complete political union between the nations concerned.*

THE END OF APARTHEID

The apartheid laws passed in 1948 in South Africa separated the population according to race and colour. White people became a privileged ruling class while non-whites were deprived of all civil rights. After 30 years of agitation in South Africa and world-wide condemnation, the apartheid laws began to be dismantled. The respected black leader Nelson Mandela was released after 26 years in prison. In 1991 the apartheid laws were repealed by the government.

Nelson Mandela

▶ *When a fully-laden oil-tanker is wrecked, marine and shore life may be wiped out. Local fishing is destroyed and pollution can remain for many years over a wide area. The risk of such a disaster is considerable, for at any given moment the world's combined tanker fleets are transporting a billion tonnes of crude oil across the high seas. The sinking of the tanker* Braer *off one of the Shetland Isles in northern Scotland in January 1993 has been a catastrophe, both for the people of the islands, and for the sea birds and animals that live there.*

FURTHER FACTS

● The first nuclear reactor for generating electricity opened at Obninsk, the USSR in 1954. In 1956 Britain started up the world's first large-scale nuclear power plant, at Calder Hall.

● The General Agreement on Tariffs and Trade (GATT) is an agency set up by the UN. Its purpose is to reduce tariffs and to remove barriers to trade world-wide.

GATT was established in 1958.

● The dismantling of the Berlin Wall was the most dramatic event of the end of the Cold War. On 9 November 1989 East German guards were told to let people pass freely through the checkpoints. The wall, which had stood since 1961, was pickaxed and bulldozed down.

Cleaning up coast after oil slick disaster

PEOPLE IN WORLD HISTORY

Words in **bold** indicate an entry elsewhere in People in World History and Key Dates in World History.

Akbar the Great (1542–1605): Mogul emperor of India (1556–1605). Conquered most of India. Supported writers and artists and allowed freedom of worship.

Alexander the Great (356–323 BC): King of Macedon and greatest soldier of ancient times. Conquests stretched from Egypt to India; introduced Greek ideas to other lands.

Augustus (63 BC–AD 14): First emperor of Rome (27 BC–AD 14). During his reign Rome was peaceful and prosperous.

Babar (1483–1530): First Mogul emperor. Descendant of **Tamerlane**; invaded northern India; began 200 years of Mogul rule.

Bach, Johann Sebastian (1685–1750): German composer. Wrote concertos, sacred cantatas, clavier works, *St Matthew Passion*, and *B Minor Mass*.

Beethoven, Ludwig van (1770–1827): German composer. Wrote sonatas, symphonies, chamber music, concertos and opera *Fidelio*, considered to be among finest written.

Bismarck, Otto von (1815–1898): German statesman, known as 'the Iron Chancellor'. Was instrumental in uniting Germany under Prussian crown in 1871.

Bolívar, Simón (1783–1830): South American revolutionary leader. Led resistance which freed several South American countries from Spanish rule in early 1800s.

Buddha (Siddhartha Gautama) (*c.* 563–*c.*480 BC): Founder of Buddhism. Son of a wealthy Indian ruler. Left a life of luxury to become a religious leader.

Castro, Fidel (1926–): Cuban marxist and revolutionary. President of Cuba (1959–). Supported revolutions in Africa and Latin America.

Catherine II ('the Great') (1729–1796): Russian empress. German princess, who married future Russian tsar Peter III. Became empress after his murder in 1762. During her reign Russia gained the Crimea and most of Poland.

Charlemagne (*c.* 742–814): King of the Franks and emperor of the West. Empire included Italy, France and most of Germany and Spain. Defended western Europe against Moors, Saxons and Norsemen.

Charles I (1600–1649): King of England (1625–1648). After defeat in Civil War (1642–1648) was tried by a parliamentary court and publicly executed.

Chiang Kai-shek (1887–1975): General and leader of Chinese Nationalist party. President of separate Chinese state of Taiwan (1950).

Churchill, Sir Winston (1874–1965): British statesman, soldier and author. Prime minister (1940–1945 and 1951–1955). Helped maintain British resistance to Nazi Germany. Won Nobel Prize for Literature (1953).

Columbus, Christopher (1451–1506): Italian explorer. 'Discovered' New World (actually Caribbean islands) by accident while seeking route to Asia.

Constantine I ('the Great') (*c.* 274–337): First Christian Roman emperor. Divided Roman empire into East and West. Founded Constantinople as capital of the Eastern empire.

Cook, James (1728–1779): English explorer and navigator. Explored coasts of Australia and New Zealand.

Cortés, Hernán (1485–1547): Spanish conquistador. Conquered Aztec empire and added Mexico to the Spanish empire.

Cromwell, Oliver (1599–1658): English soldier and statesman. General in parliamentary army in English Civil War. Lord Protector (1653–1658).

Eisenhower, Dwight D. (1890–1969): General and 34th president of the USA (1953–1961). Supreme commander of Allied invasion of Europe in World War II (1944).

Elizabeth I (1533–1603): Queen of England (1558–1603). Daughter of **Henry VIII**; reign saw England become important European power; also a golden age of English drama.

Franco, Francisco (1892–1975): Spanish general and statesman. Leader of fascist Falange party; led nationalist rebels to victory in Spanish Civil War (1936–1939). *Caudillo* (ruler) of Spain (1939–1975).

Frederick II ('the Great') (1712–1786): King of Prussia (1740–1786). Made Prussia a leading power in Europe. Patron of writers, philosophers and musicians.

Gama, Vasco da (*c.* 1469–1524): Portuguese navigator and explorer. Led first European expedition to reach India around the Cape of Good Hope (1497–1499).

Gandhi, Mohandas (1869–1948): Indian reformer and political leader, called 'Mahatma' (Great Soul). Led movement for Indian independence and sought to end caste system.

Garibaldi, Giuseppe (1807–1882): Italian freedom fighter and soldier. Leader in struggle (Risorgimento) that united Italy in 1860s.

Genghis Khan (*c.*1167–1227): Mongol leader. Conquered an empire stretching from China to Black Sea.

Gorbachev, Mikhail (1931–): President of USSR (1985–1991). Introduced policies of *glasnost* (openness) and *perestroika* (restructuring). Awarded Nobel Peace Prize (1990).

Hadrian (76–138): Roman emperor (117–138). Ordered building of Hadrian's Wall in northern England as a frontier against invading tribes.

Henry VIII (1491–1547): King of England (1509–1547). Removed English Church from papal control and became supreme head of Church of England. Ordered monasteries to close down and seized their wealth. Married six times.

Hitler, Adolf (1889–1945): German dictator. Founder of National Socialism (Nazi party). German chancellor (1933). Led Germany into war in 1939 by invading Poland. Committed suicide at end of war.

Ho Chi Minh (1890–1969): Vietnamese nationalist leader. Fought French colonial regime (1946–1954). First president of North Vietnam (1954–1969). Led struggle against US-supported South Vietnam.

Jesus Christ (*c.*4 BC–*c.*AD 30): Central figure of Christian religion. A Jew, born in Palestine. After three-year preaching mission, tried and crucified as a political agitator.

Joan of Arc (*c.*1412–1431): National heroine of France. Heard 'voices' telling her to free France from English invaders. After early successes, was captured by the English and burned at the stake as a witch.

Kennedy, John F. (1917–1963): 35th US president (1961–1963). Two major foreign policy crises during presidency were invasion of Cuba (1961) and Cuban Missile Crisis (1962). Assassinated in Dallas, Texas.

Lenin, Vladimir (1870–1924): Russian revolutionary. Founder of Bolshevik (later Communist) party. Led Russian Revolution (1917). Premier and virtual dictator of new communist state.

Leonardo da Vinci (1452–1519): Italian artist and scientist. Considered to be supreme example of Renaissance genius. Paintings include the *Last Supper* fresco and the *Mona Lisa*.

Lincoln, Abraham (1809–1865): 16th US president (1861–1865). Opposed extension of slavery. Led Northern states in American Civil War (1861–1865). Assassinated 1865.

Louis XIV (1638–1715): King of France (1643–1715). Known as 'the Sun King'. All-powerful, absolute monarch. Persecutor of French Protestants (Huguenots). Patron of arts; built palace at Versailles.

Luther, Martin (1483–1546): German religious leader. Prime mover in Protestant Reformation.

Magellan, Ferdinand (*c.*1480–1521): Portuguese navigator. Commanded first expedition to sail round the world (1519–1522). Was killed in Philippines on the return journey.

Mandela, Nelson (1918–): Leader of African National Congress in South Africa. Imprisoned 1962–1989. Has since campaigned for democratic, multiracial society.

Mao Zedong or Mao Tse-tung (1893–1976): Chinese Marxist revolutionary leader. Overthrew nationalist government after 20-year struggle. First chairman of Peoples' Republic of China (1949–1976).

Marx, Karl (1818–1883): German philosopher and economist. Co-author (with Friedrich Engels) of *Communist Manifesto* (1848). Exiled to England, wrote *Das Kapital*, key publication of communist philosophy.

Mozart, Wolfgang Amadeus (1756–1791): Austrian composer. Works include more than 40 symphonies, nearly 30 piano concertos, and several operas (*Don Giovanni, The Marriage of Figaro*).

Muhammad (*c.*570–632): Prophet and founder of Islamic faith. His sayings are collected in the Koran. Islam counts its dates from his flight to Yathrib (now Medina) after a plot to murder him (622).

Mussolini, Benito (1883–1945): Leader (*Il Duce*) of Italian fascism. Seized power (1922); allied with Hitler in World War II. Replaced after invasion of Italy by Allies (1943); executed by Italian partisans.

Napoleon I (Bonaparte) (1769–1821): Emperor of France (1804–1814).

Rose to power during French Revolution. After series of military victories, established French empire. Downfall began with invasion of Russia (1812). Final defeat at Waterloo (1815); exiled to St Helena.

Nelson, Horatio (1758–1805): English admiral. Victories during Napoleonic wars kept England safe from invasion; died commanding fleet at Trafalgar (1805).

Peter I ('the Great') (1672–1725): Tsar of Russia (1682–1725). Visited western Europe to study European industrial techniques. Reformed Russian armed forces, government, alphabet and calendar. Built city of St Petersburg as capital.

Philip II (1527–1598): King of Spain (1556–1598), husband of Mary, Catholic queen of England (1554-1558). Strongly anti-Protestant; attempted invasion of England during reign of **Elizabeth I**, Mary's sister, but Armada was defeated (1588).

Pizarro, Francisco (*c.*1478–1541): Spanish conquistador. Conquered Inca empire in Peru with less than 200 men (1532) and killed their emperor, Atahualpa.

Polo, Marco (*c.*1254–*c.*1324): Venetian traveller. Lived at court of Kublai Khan in China. Account of his travels (1271–1295) gave Europeans their first glimpse of life in Asia.

Rembrandt (Harmenszoon van Rijn) (1606–1669): Dutch painter. Greatest achievements are portraits which show deep insight into human character. Works include *The Night Watch, The Anatomy Lesson of Dr Tulp* and self-portraits.

Robespierre, Maximilien (1758–1794): French revolutionary. Lawyer who became leader of Jacobins, most extreme party in French Revolution. Removed rivals during Reign of Terror, but was later arrested and guillotined.

Roosevelt, Franklin Delano (1882–1945): 32nd president of the USA (1933–1945) for a record four terms. His 'New Deal' programme rescued America from Great Depression of 1930s. Co-ordinated Allied war effort after American entry in World War II.

Rubens, Peter Paul (1577–1640): Flemish painter, considered a master of the baroque style. Painted portraits, landscapes, religious and historical subjects.

Saladin (1137–1193): Sultan of Egypt and Muslim warrior. Recaptured Jerusalem and most of Palestine from the Crusaders. Renowned for his military prowess, religious tolerance and justice to his enemies.

Shakespeare, William (1564–1616): English dramatist and poet. Wrote tragedies (*Hamlet*), histories (*Richard III*) and comedies (*Twelfth Night*), generally regarded as among finest plays in the English language.

Stalin, Joseph (1879–1953): Russian communist dictator. Sole ruler of USSR from 1927. Led Russia during World War II. Ruthlessly wiped out any opposition to his rule.

Tamerlane or Timur (*c.* 1336–1404): Mongol conqueror and ruler of Turkistan. Seized large parts of central Asia and Near East.

Truman, Harry S (1884–1972): 33rd president of USA (1945–1953). Took decision to drop atomic bomb on Japan (1945). Established NATO (1949). Sent US troops to join UN forces resisting communist invasion of South Korea (1950).

Victoria (1819–1901): Queen of United Kingdom (1837–1901) and empress of India (from 1876). Reigned over British empire at height of its power; gave her name to the period.

Washington, George (1732–1799): General and 1st president of the USA (1789–1797). Commander-in-chief of Continental Army which fought British during American War of Independence (1775–1783).

Wilberforce, William (1759–1833): British statesman and reformer. As Member of Parliament campaigned for abolition of slavery. His Abolition Bill became law in 1807.

Wilhelm II (1859–1941): King of Prussia and emperor of Germany (1888–1918). Ruled personally after dismissing his chancellor **Bismarck** (1890). Abdicated after Germany lost World War I.

William I, 'the Conqueror' (*c.*1027–1087): First Norman king of England (1066–1087). Defeated Saxons under Harold at Hastings (1066). Ordered survey of England which became the Domesday book.

Wilson, Thomas Woodrow (1856–1924): 28th president of the USA (1913–1921). Took America into World War I (1917). After the war, championed League of Nations as means of keeping world peace.

KEY DATES IN WORLD HISTORY

BC

*c.*5 million–1 million: *Homo habilis*, early ancestors of modern humans live in tropical Africa.

*c.*1.5 million: *Homo erectus* learn to make better tools than *Homo habilis*. Move into parts of Europe and Asia.

*c.*9000–8000: First farmers, in the Middle East.

*c.*9000: Tribes of hunters cross from Asia into North America.

*c.*8500: Jericho founded, world's first walled town.

*c.*7000: Pottery produced in Iran.

*c.*5500: Farming begins in Egypt.

*c.*4000–3500: Plough, wheel and sail in use in Mesopotamia and Egypt.

*c.*3500: Mesopotamia: first writing appears in Sumer.

*c.*3000: First evidence of pottery in America.

*c.*2590: Egyptian pharaoh Khufu (or Cheops) builds pyramid at Giza.

*c.*2500–*c.*1628: Minoan civilization in Crete.

*c.*2000: Rise of Babylon.

*c.*2000–1000: Beginnings of Mayan culture in Central America.

*c.*1814–1754: First Assyrian empire.

*c.*1500–600: Hindu religion develops in India.

*c.*1300: Phoenicians develop alphabet to replace picture-writing.

*c.*1200: Beginning of Jewish religion.

776: First Olympic Games in Greece.

753: Legendary founding of Rome.

550: Persian empire founded by Cyrus II; Persia conquers Assyria.

530: Accurate calendar in use in Babylonia.

*c.*500–27: Roman republic.

*c.*480: Death of the **Buddha** (Siddhartha Gautama).

480: Battle of Salamis: Persian invasion of Greece defeated.

*c.*479: Death of Confucius; his teachings became basis of Confucianism.

479–338: Years of Greek civilization's greatest achievements.

336–323: Reign of **Alexander the Great**, king of Macedon.

146: Carthage becomes Roman province of North Africa.

*c.*100: Chinese merchant ships begin trade with India.

54: Roman general Julius Caesar invades Britain.

49: Caesar conquers Gaul (France).

30: Egypt falls to Rome after defeat of Queen Cleopatra at Actium.

27: **Augustus** becomes first Roman emperor – start of Roman empire.

AD

25–222: Han dynasty in China begins great age of Chinese culture.

*c.*30: **Jesus Christ** crucified.

79: Volcano Vesuvius erupts and destroys Pompeii and Herculaneum.

122–127: **Hadrian**'s Wall built as northern frontier of Roman Britain.

135: Palestine becomes Roman province of Judaea.

257: Goths invade Roman empire.

*c.*300: Yamato government established in Japan; Japanese clans practise Shinto religion.

313: **Constantine** ends persecution of Christians in Roman empire.

330: **Constantine** founds Constantinople on site of Byzantium.

391: Emperor Theodosius makes Christianity state religion.

410: Alaric the Goth captures Rome.

433: Attila becomes leader of the Huns.

470: Huns retreat from Europe.

476: End of Western Roman empire.

527–565: Justinian the Great emperor of Eastern Roman (Byzantine) empire.

529: St Benedict founds first Christian monastery, at Monte Cassino, Italy.

*c.*570–*c.*632: Life of **Muhammad**, founder of Islam.

*c.*600: High point of Mayan civilization.

624: Buddhism becomes official religion in China.

*c.*700–1200: Kingdom of Ghana, first West African trading empire.

711: Arabs conquer most of Spain.

732: Battle of Poitiers: Charles Martel checks Arab advance into Europe.

742–814: Life of **Charlemagne**, king of Franks; first Holy Roman emperor.

750: Moors found city of Granada.

*c.*793: First Viking raids in northern Europe.

900: Anasazi begin to build pueblos in southwestern North America.

1000: Viking Leif Ericson lands in North America.

1066: **William of Normandy** invades England; becomes William I.

1071: Muslim Turks stop Christian pilgrimages to Jerusalem.

1086: **William I** orders survey of England (the Domesday Book).

1095: Pope Urban urges Christians to undertake a Crusade to free Holy Land from Muslim rule.

1096: First Crusade begins.

1097: Crusaders capture Jerusalem. Foundation of the Order of Knights Hospitalers.

*c.*1100: Growth of Ife kingdom in Nigeria.

1147–1148: Second Crusade: Crusaders fail to take Damascus.

1187: Saracen leader **Saladin** captures Jerusalem from Christians.

1189–1192: Third Crusade: Crusaders capture Jaffa. Richard I of England signs peace with **Saladin**.

*c.*1200–1300: Early Inca period in Peru.

1202–1204: Fourth Crusade.

1211: **Genghis Khan** leads Mongols to invade northern China.

1212: Children's Crusade.

1215: English barons force King John to sign Magna Carta, basis of English constitutional practice.

1218: Mongols under **Genghis Khan** overrun Persia.

1234: Mongols overthrow Chin empire in China.

1237: Mongols capture Moscow.

*c.*1250: Berbers establish several states in North Africa.

1260: Kublai Khan becomes ruler of the Mongol Empire.

1264: Kublai Khan founds Yuan dynasty in China.

1275–1292: **Marco Polo** in the service of Kublai Khan in China.

1291: Muslims capture Acre; end of Christian rule in Palestine.

1293: First Christian missionaries in China.

*c.*1300: Rise of Aztecs in Mexico.

*c.*1300: Emergence of Benin empire in Nigeria, West Africa.

1337–1453: Edward III of England claims French throne; Hundred Years' War between England and France.

1347–1351: Black Death comes to Europe from Asia. Millions die.

1352: Ibn Battuta, Berber scholar, recounts visit to Mali in Africa.

1364: Aztecs begin building their capital Tenochtitlán.

1368–1644: Ming dynasty in China; period of stability and prosperity.

1401: **Tamerlane**, ruler of Turkistan, conquers Damascus and Baghdad.

1415: English under King Henry V defeat French at battle of Agincourt.

1429: French led by **Joan of Arc** defeat English at Orléans. Charles VII crowned king of France at Rheims.

1431: **Joan of Arc** burnt by English.

1445: German Johannes Gutenberg publishes *Gutenberg Bible*, first printed book in Europe.

1453: English lose all conquests in France except Calais. Ottoman Turks capture Constantinople; the end of Byzantine empire.

1474: William Caxton prints the first

book in English.

1462–1492: Rule of Lorenzo de Medici in city of Florence; patron of artists such as Michelangelo.

1480: Ivan III, grand prince of Muscovy, frees Russia from Mongols.

1487: Portuguese Bartolomeu Dias first European to round Cape of Good Hope, southern Africa.

1492: Christian Spaniards capture Granada, last stronghold of Moors in Spain. **Columbus** crosses Atlantic and reaches Caribbean islands.

1493: Pope divides New World between Spain and Portugal.

1493–1521: Reign of Huayna Capac, greatest Inca conqueror; founds a capital at Quito, Peru.

1497: Italian John Cabot sails from Bristol, England and reaches Newfoundland in North America.

1498: Vasco da Gama makes first European sea voyage to India.

*c.*1500: Aztec empire at greatest extent.

1507: The New World named America after Italian navigator Amerigo Vespucci.

1510: Spaniards first import Africans as slaves to work in their American colonies.

1516: Coffee first imported into Europe.

1517: Martin Luther challenges teachings of Catholic Church. Protestant Reformation begins.

1519–1521: Spanish conquistador **Hernán Cortés** conquers Aztec empire in Mexico.

1520–1566: Reign of Suleiman the Magnificent; great age of Ottoman empire.

1526: Babar wins battle of Panipat in India and founds Mogul dynasty.

1531: The Inquisition established in Portugal. Copernicus, Polish astronomer, circulates his theory that the planets move round Sun, not Earth (the Church's teaching).

1532–1534: Francisco Pizarro conquers Inca empire in Peru.

1533–1584: Reign of Ivan IV ('the Terrible'), first tsar of Russia.

1534: English king **Henry VIII** denies authority of the Pope and breaks with Roman Catholic Church. French expedition led by Jacques Cartier reaches Labrador, Canada.

1541: Frenchman John Calvin founds Protestant movement in Geneva.

1545: Council of Trent begins Counter Reformation.

1556–1605: Reign of **Akbar**, greatest of Mogul rulers in India.

1558–1603: Reign of **Elizabeth I** of England; England stays Protestant and becomes major European power.

1562: English start shipping slaves from West Africa to Caribbean.

1571: Turks defeated by alliance of European Christian powers at sea battle of Lepanto. Turkish power in the Mediterranean checked.

1572: Massacre of 20,000 French Protestants on St Bartholomew's Day.

1588: English defeat Spanish Armada.

1598: Edict of Nantes gives French Protestants equal rights with Catholics; ends French Wars of Religion.

1600: British East India Company founded. Tokugawa Ieyasu becomes shogun (ruler) of Japan. His descendants rule Japan for 250 years.

1602: Dutch East India Company founded.

1607: Colony of Jamestown, Virginia founded. The first permanent English settlement in North America.

1608: French traders found Quebec in Canada.

1618–1648: Thirty Years' War between Catholic and Protestant European powers.

1620: Pilgrim Fathers sail from Plymouth, England, in *Mayflower* to Massachusetts in North America.

1637: Japan begins a period of isolation from the rest of the world.

1642–1648: English Civil War.

1643–1715: Reign of **Louis XIV**; France becomes chief European power.

1644: Ming dynasty overthrown; Manchu dynasty founded in China.

1645: Dutchman Abel Tasman first European to reach Tasmania and New Zealand.

1649 King **Charles I** executed; England becomes republic until 1660.

1652: Dutch found colony at Cape of Good Hope (Cape Town).

1658–1707: Rule of Aurangzeb, last of great Mogul emperors.

1663–1699: Ottoman Turks invade central Europe.

1664: English capture New Amsterdam from Dutch. They re-name it New York.

1665: English scientist Isaac Newton discovers gravity.

1670: Hudson's Bay Company founded in England to acquire territory in Canada.

1682–1725: Reign of **Peter the Great** of Russia.

1697–1712: Dominance of Ashanti

empire in West Africa.

1700–1720: Great Northern War between Russia and Sweden.

1701–1714: War of the Spanish Succession; general European war fought over control of Spanish empire after death of Charles II of Spain.

1707: Union of England and Scotland. India: death of Aurangzeb begins decline of Mogul empire.

1733: Founding of Georgia, last of Thirteen Colonies in New England.

*c.*1750s–1850s: Many new advances in science and technology in Europe sees start of Industrial Revolution.

1756: The Black Hole of Calcutta – British civilians imprisoned by ruler of Bengal die in tiny prison.

1756–1763: Seven Years' War caused by rivalry of Austria and Prussia in Europe, and France and Britain in North America.

1757: British defeat combined French and Indian army at Plassey. Beginning of British supremacy in India.

1757–1843: China limits foreign trade to city of Canton.

1762–1796: Reign of **Catherine the Great** of Russia.

1768–1771: During round the world trip English navigator and explorer **James Cook** reaches Australia and New Zealand.

1775–1783: American War of Independence.

1776: American Declaration of Independence.

1782: Scot James Watt invents rotary steam engine.

1788: Britain sends first convicts to Australia; Sydney is first permanent British settlement.

1789: George Washington becomes the first president of United States of America.

1789–1799: French Revolution.

1793: Execution of Louis XVI; France a republic.

1799: Napoleon becomes first consul and disbands the ruling Directory.

1804: Napoleon crowns himself emperor of France.

1805: British defeat combined Franco-Spanish fleet at Trafalgar.

1807: Slave trade abolished within British empire.

1812: Napoleon's invasion of Russia ends in disaster for him and his army.

1815: British under Wellington and Prussians under Blucher defeat **Napoleon** at battle of Waterloo. **Napoleon** exiled to St Helena.

1818: Shaka forms Zulu nation in southern Africa.

1819: Singapore founded by British as a base for East India Company.

1821–1829: Greek War of Independence against Turkey.

1822: Brazil becomes independent from Portugal. State of Great Columbia (Venezuela, Colombia, Ecuador, and Panama) set up under Simón Bolívar; becomes independent from Spain.

1825: First passenger steam railway opens in England.

1835–1837: Great Trek when Boers leave Cape Colony in South Africa and found the state of Transvaal.

1837–1901: Reign of **Queen Victoria** of Great Britain.

1845: Texas and Florida become states of the USA.

1848: Year of revolutions, including Paris, Milan, Naples, Venice, Rome, Berlin, Vienna, Prague and Budapest. **Marx** and Engels issue *Communist Manifesto*. Californian gold rush.

1853: Gold rush in Australia.

1854: Perry forces Japanese to sign treaty agreeing to trade with USA.

1854–1856: Crimean War; Britain, France and Turkey against Russia.

1857–1858: Indian Mutiny.

1861–1865: American Civil War.

1861: Unification of Italy.

1865: Slavery abolished in USA.

1866: Prussia defeats Austria and wins leadership of Germany.

1867: USA buys Alaska from Russia. Canada becomes British dominion.

1870–1871: Franco-Prussian War.

1871: Germany united; Wilhelm I, king of Prussia, becomes first emperor.

1880–1881: First Boer War between Britain and Dutch settlers (Boers) in Transvaal, South Africa.

1886: Gold discovered in Transvaal; Johannesburg founded.

1890: Wounded Knee, last Native American uprising in USA.

1897: Pierre and Marie Curie discover radioactive element, radium.

1898: Spanish-American war. USA seizes Philippines, Guam and Puerto Rico.

1899–1902: Second Boer War.

1901: Commonwealth of Australia established.

1903: In USA Wright brothers make first powered aircraft flight.

1904–1905: Japan and Russia at war; Japan victorious.

1907: New Zealand becomes British dominion.

1910: Union of South Africa established as British dominion.

1911: Revolution in China. Sun Yat-Sen leads new Chinese republic (1912). Norwegian explorer Roald Amundsen first to reach South Pole.

1912: Henry Ford begins mass production of motor cars in USA.

1914–1918: World War I.

1917: Russian Revolution.

1919: Peace treaty of Versailles signed.

1920: League of Nations founded.

1922: **Mussolini** comes to power in Italy. Irish Free State proclaimed. Union of Soviet Socialist Republics (USSR) founded.

1924: **Lenin** dies; **Stalin** becomes dictator of Russia in 1927.

1927: Charles Lindbergh makes first solo flight across the Atlantic. Civil war in China after Chiang Kai-shek breaks with Chinese communists.

1929: Wall Street crash begins worldwide recession. In India, **Gandhi** begins campaign of civil disobedience against British.

1933: **Hitler** becomes German chancellor; becomes *Führer* (leader) and dictator (1934). US president **Roosevelt** introduces New Deal policy to end American depression.

1934–1935: **Mao Zedong** leads the Long March of Chinese communists in northern China; establishes him as leader of Chinese communist party.

1935: Nazis begin persecution of Jews in Germany. Italy invades Ethiopia.

1936–1939: Spanish Civil War.

1937: Japanese invade China.

1939: Germany invades Poland.

1939–1945: World War II.

1945: USA drops atom bombs on Hiroshima and Nagasaki. United Nations formed.

1946: Indochina: War between Vietnamese nationalists and French.

1947: India and Pakistan become independent. US aid speeds recovery of Europe (Marshall Plan).

1948: USSR blockades Berlin; the Berlin airlift. State of Israel declared. Arabs at war with Israel.

1949: NATO formed. Germany becomes two republics, East and West. **Mao Zedong** establishes communist rule in China. Apartheid laws introduced in South Africa.

1950–1953: Korean War: N Korea and China against S Korea, the USA and UN troops. US tests hydrogen bomb.

1953: Death of **Stalin**. Tito becomes president of Yugoslavia (until 1980).

1954: French leave Vietnam; Vietnam becomes two states, North (communist) and South.

1954–1962: Algerian war between France and Algerian nationalists.

1955: Communist states in East Europe sign Warsaw Pact.

1956: Britain and France, with Israeli help, fail to take control of Suez Canal, nationalized by Egypt's President Nasser.

1957: Treaty of Rome establishes European Common Market. Ghana (Gold Coast) becomes first British African colony to win independence.

1960: Africa: 17 former French and British colonies become independent.

1961: Berlin Wall built.

1962: Cuban Missile Crisis. Algeria becomes independent from France.

1963: President **Kennedy** assassinated.

1964–1975: Vietnam War: civil war in Vietnam with US forces supporting South Vietnam; ends with victory of communist North Vietnam.

1967: Six Day Arab-Israeli War.

1969: American Neil Armstrong first human on Moon. Violence between Protestant majority and Catholic minority in Northern Ireland (Ulster) brings British troops from mainland.

1971: East Pakistan becomes Bangladesh.

1973: Britain, Denmark and Irish Republic join EC. Israel defeats Arab states in Yom Kippur war.

1979: Israel and Egypt sign peace treaty. Iran becomes Islamic republic.

1982: Argentina occupies Falkland Islands. Driven out by British troops.

1985–1991: **Mikhail Gorbachev** becomes leader of USSR.

1988: **Gorbachev** begins reforms in USSR – restructuring (*perestroika*) and openness (*glasnost*).

1989: Communist governments in East Germany, Poland, Romania, Bulgaria and Czechoslovakia overthrown by popular uprisings. Dismantling of Berlin Wall.

1990: Unification of Germany. Iraq invades Kuwait.

1991: The Gulf War – UN forces liberate Kuwait. Civil war begins in Yugoslavia. Apartheid laws in South Africa begin to be dismantled. Boris Yeltsin first democratically elected president of Russia.

1992: South African whites vote to negotiate end of white minority rule. Czechoslovakia moves towards separate Czech and Slovak states.

COUNTRIES
—OF THE—
WORLD

F acts about countries and people change all the
time. Over the centuries wars, revolutions and
independence movements have shaped our world.
Countries have changed their names, merged
with neighbours, gained or lost
territory. And as countries change,
so the culture and lifestyles of the
world's peoples have also changed. In
order for us to understand the world we live in, we need
detailed knowledge, including key facts and figures,
about its regions, countries, geography and lifestyles.
Countries of the World gives you all this information
at your fingertips.

The world today has many inequalities – in food,
healthcare, resources and income – and the North-
South divide between the richer and poorer nations
now overshadows the old East-West
confrontation of the Cold War.

Two comprehensive sections give a survey of
the world's different economic and political
systems and pinpoint key areas of
20th-century conflict. In a rapidly changing
world, *Countries of the World* is packed with
essential facts and figures about the countries
and peoples of today's world.

Brian Williams

THE WORLD

Continents and Countries

The Earth has existed for about 4600 million years, but modern humans, *Homo sapiens sapiens*, have been around for only 40,000 years. Civilizations did not begin to develop until 11,000 years ago, yet in that brief time people have spread to almost every habitable region, founding cultures and nations. Of the seven continents (Africa, Antarctica, Asia, Europe, North America, South America and Oceania) only Antarctica was not settled permanently. Asia is easily the biggest continent. It contains the most populous nation (China) and most of the biggest country by area (Russia). There are now more than 170 generally recognized independent countries in the world. Some are small islands such as Malta, Nauru or Singapore, others are giant countries such as Australia, Canada, China, the USA, and the largest of all, Russia.

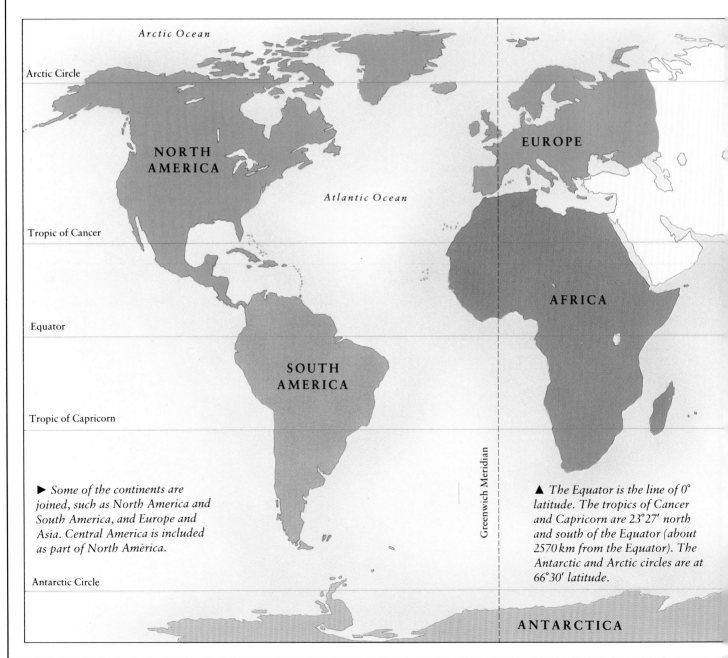

Arctic Ocean

Arctic Circle

NORTH AMERICA

EUROPE

Atlantic Ocean

Tropic of Cancer

AFRICA

Equator

SOUTH AMERICA

Tropic of Capricorn

Greenwich Meridian

▶ Some of the continents are joined, such as North America and South America, and Europe and Asia. Central America is included as part of North America.

▲ The Equator is the line of 0° latitude. The tropics of Cancer and Capricorn are 23°27′ north and south of the Equator (about 2570 km from the Equator). The Antarctic and Arctic circles are at 66°30′ latitude.

Antarctic Circle

ANTARCTICA

410

CONTINENTS	AREA (SQ KM)	% OF WORLD'S LAND AREA	POPULATION (MILLIONS)	NUMBER OF COUNTRIES	LARGEST COUNTRY
NORTH AMERICA	24,240,000	16.2	424	23	Canada
SOUTH AMERICA	17,817,000	11.9	298	12	Brazil
EUROPE	10,534,000	6.6	788[3]	45[4]	Russia[1]
ASIA	44,390,000	30.1	3173	44	China
AFRICA	30,313,000	20.2	657	52	Sudan
OCEANIA	9,510,000	5.7	26	11	Australia
ANTARCTICA	14,000,000	9.3	none[2]	0	–

[1] Part in Europe, part in Asia
[2] Population consists mainly of scientists
[3] Population includes Russia
[4] Number of countries includes 6 CIS states, 3 Baltic states (formerly within the Soviet Union).

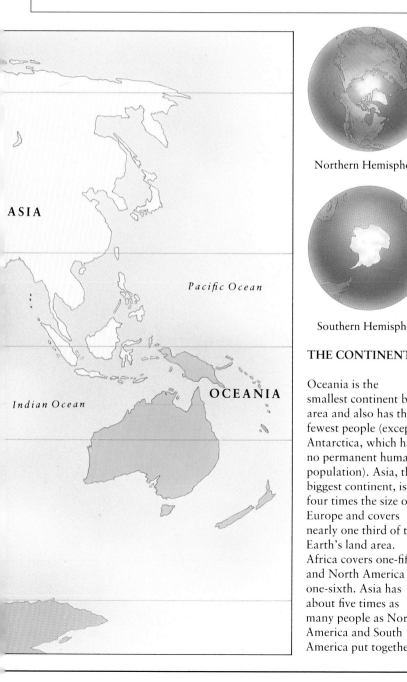

ASIA

Pacific Ocean

Indian Ocean

OCEANIA

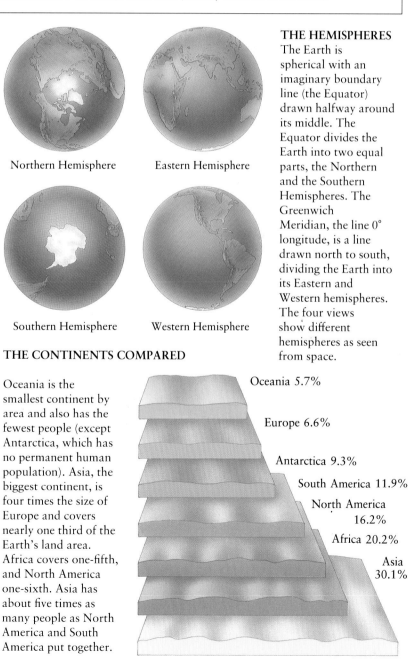

Northern Hemisphere

Eastern Hemisphere

Southern Hemisphere

Western Hemisphere

THE HEMISPHERES

The Earth is spherical with an imaginary boundary line (the Equator) drawn halfway around its middle. The Equator divides the Earth into two equal parts, the Northern and the Southern Hemispheres. The Greenwich Meridian, the line 0° longitude, is a line drawn north to south, dividing the Earth into its Eastern and Western hemispheres. The four views show different hemispheres as seen from space.

THE CONTINENTS COMPARED

Oceania is the smallest continent by area and also has the fewest people (except Antarctica, which has no permanent human population). Asia, the biggest continent, is four times the size of Europe and covers nearly one third of the Earth's land area. Africa covers one-fifth, and North America one-sixth. Asia has about five times as many people as North America and South America put together.

Oceania 5.7%

Europe 6.6%

Antarctica 9.3%

South America 11.9%

North America 16.2%

Africa 20.2%

Asia 30.1%

North America

North America is the world's third biggest continent, after Asia and Africa. It has a wide range of climates and landscapes, from the cold and snows of Alaska, northern Canada and Greenland to the warmth of Central America and the Caribbean islands. The continent has two very large nations, the United States and Canada. The United States is the world's only superpower. The countries of Central America and the Caribbean are smaller than the USA and Canada and many are comparatively poor.

▲ This lake is in the Canadian Rockies in Alberta, Canada. The Rocky Mountain chain is the major mountain system of North America. It stretches from New Mexico in the south to Alaska and the Yukon Territory of Canada.

NORTH AMERICAN DATAFILE

Number of Countries: 23
Coastline: 148,330 km long
Highest mountain: Mt McKinley in Alaska, USA, 6194 m
Lowest point: Death Valley, California, USA, 86 m below sea level
Hottest place: Amos, California, USA, with a top temperature of 54.4°C in 1885
Coldest place: Floeberg Bay, Canada, with a temperature of −58°C in 1852
Longest rivers: Mississippi (3779 km), Missouri (3726 km), Rio Grande (3034 km), Arkansas (2348 km)
Largest lake: Lake Superior, between the US and Canada; at 82,103 sq km the largest freshwater lake on Earth
Other large lakes: Huron, Michigan, Erie, Ontario, Winnipeg, Great Bear, Great Slave
Largest city: Mexico City (20 m people)
Major cities (by population): New York, Los Angeles, Chicago, Philadelphia, Miami, Toronto, Detroit

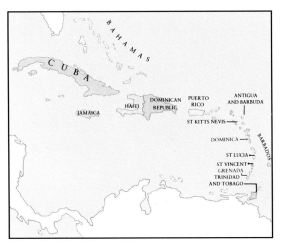

◄ The Caribbean islands form part of North America. There are three main island groups: the Bahamas, the Greater Antilles (Cuba, Jamaica, Haiti/Dominican Republic and Puerto Rico), and the Lesser Antilles.

▶ Chicago is the third largest city in the USA, as well as the birthplace of the skyscraper.

North America

ARCTIC OCEAN

BERING SEA

Queen Elizabeth
Islands

GREENLAND

Devon
Island

*BAFFIN
BAY*

Victoria
Island

DAVIS STRAIT

YUKON RIVER BASIN

Mt McKinley
6194 m
ALASKA RANGE

Baffin Island

*ATLANTIC
OCEAN*

GULF
OF
ALASKA

Mt Logan
5951 m

Great Bear
Lake

Cape Farewell

LABRADOR SEA

Alexander
Archipelago

Great
Slave Lake

*HUDSON
BAY*

Queen
Charlotte
Islands

L Athabasca

Reindeer
Lake

Labrador

Edmonton

Saskatchewan

Nelson

GULF OF
ST LAWRENCE

Calgary

L Winnipeg

Vancouver

L Manitoba

St Lawrence

Cape
Breton
Island

Seattle

L Superior

Quebec

Columbia

Missouri

Montreal

L Huron

Ottawa

Niagara Falls

Boston

San Francisco

GREAT PLAINS

L Michigan

Toronto

L Ontario

L Erie

New York
Philadelphia

Des Moines

Detroit

Washington
DC

Great Salt
Lake

GREAT
BASIN

Denver

Platte

Chicago

Springfield

CHESAPEAKE
BAY

Death Valley

Lincoln

Arkansas

St Louis

Nashville

Los Angeles

Mt Elbert
4399 m

MOJAVE
DESERT

Mt Elbert
4399 m

Phoenix

Little Rock

Mt Mitchell
2037 m

Mississippi

Tennessee

APPALACHIAN MTS

EDWARDS
PLATEAU

Dallas

Rio Grande

Houston

New Orleans

SIERRA MADRE OCCIDENTAL

CHIHUAHUA DESERT

Miami

GULF OF
MEXICO

Nassau

Cape San
Lucas

Havana

Paricutin
2808 m

Mexico City

San Juan

Port-au-Prince

Santo Domingo

Orizaba
5700 m

Kingston

CARIBBEAN

Belmopan

Guatemala City

SEA

San Salvador

Tegucigalpa

Managua

San José

Panama City

Panama Canal

*PACIFIC
OCEAN*

ROCKY MOUNTAINS

Mackenzie

COAST RANGE

Fraser

CASCADE RANGE

Sacramento

Snake

SIERRA NEVADA

GULF OF CALIFORNIA

▶ North America is
divided by the Rocky
Mountains, which
extend north to south.
The north of the
continent has many
lakes and rivers. The
Great Lakes include
Superior, the biggest
lake in North America.
The most important
river system is the
Mississippi-Missouri.

| 0 | 200 | 400 | 600 | 800 | 1000 | kilometres |

| 0 | 200 | 400 | 600 | miles |

COUNTRY	AREA (sq km)	POPULATION	CAPITAL	LANGUAGE
Antigua & Barbuda	433	64,000	St John's	English
Bahamas	13,933	251,000	Nassau	English
Barbados	430	260,000	Bridgetown	English
Belize	22,964	180,400	Belmopan	English, Spanish
Canada	9,970,610	26,527,000	Ottawa	English, French
Costa Rica	50,695	3,032,000	San José	Spanish
Cuba	114,516	10,582,000	Havana	Spanish
Dominica	751	85,000	Roseau	English
Dominican Republic	48,730	7,253,000	Santo Domingo	Spanish
El Salvador	21,392	5,221,000	San Salvador	Spanish, Nahuati
Grenada	344	84,000	St George's	English
Guatemala	108,880	9,340,000	Guatemala City	Spanish, Indian languages
Haiti	27,747	6,409,000	Port-au-Prince	French, Creole
Honduras	112,079	5,261,000	Tegucigalpa	Spanish
Jamaica	10,960	2,513,000	Kingston	English, Creole
Mexico	1,972,545	88,335,000	Mexico City	Spanish
Nicaragua	129,990	3,606,000	Managua	Spanish, English
Panama	75,643	2,423,000	Panama City	Spanish
St Kitts-Nevis	269	44,000	Basseterre	English
St Lucia	617	151,000	Castries	English
St Vincent & Grenadines	389	115,000	Kingstown	English
Trinidad & Tobago	5128	1,233,000	Port of Spain	English
USA	9,372,571	251,394,000	Washington DC	English

THE UNITED STATES OF AMERICA

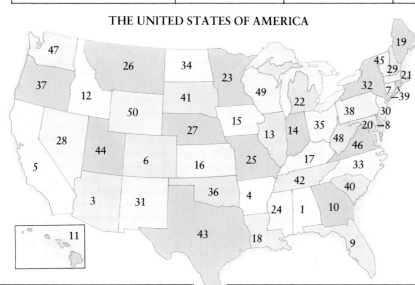

US STATES AND THEIR CAPITALS

1 **Alabama** Montgomery	11 **Hawaii** Honolulu	21 **Massachusetts** Boston
2 **Alaska** Juneau	12 **Idaho** Boise	22 **Michigan** Lansing
3 **Arizona** Phoenix	13 **Illinois** Springfield	23 **Minnesota** St Paul
4 **Arkansas** Little Rock	14 **Indiana** Indianapolis	24 **Mississippi** Jackson
5 **California** Sacramento	15 **Iowa** Des Moines	25 **Missouri** Jefferson City
6 **Colorado** Denver	16 **Kansas** Topeka	26 **Montana** Helena
7 **Connecticut** Hartford	17 **Kentucky** Frankfort	27 **Nebraska** Lincoln
8 **Delaware** Dover	18 **Louisiana** Baton Rouge	28 **Nevada** Carson City
9 **Florida** Tallahassee	19 **Maine** Augusta	29 **New Hampshire** Concord
10 **Georgia** Atlanta	20 **Maryland** Annapolis	30 **New Jersey** Trenton

MAJOR PRODUCTS	CURRENCY
Tourism	EC Dollar
Tourism, rum, banking	C Dollar
Rum, molasses, tourism	Dollar
Sugar, timber	Dollar
Minerals, timber, cereals, factory goods	Dollar
Coffee	Dollar
Sugar, molasses, bananas, fish	Peso
Bananas, fruit, tourism	EC Dollar
Sugar, minerals	Peso
Coffee, cotton	Colon
Cocoa, nutmeg, bananas	EC Dollar
Coffee, minerals	Quetzal
Coffee, sugar	Gourde
Bananas, coffee, timber	Lempira
Bauxite, bananas, sugar, tourism	Dollar
Oil, minerals, textiles, steel	Peso
Coffee, cotton, meat	New Cordoba
Canal traffic, banking, bananas, rice, sugar	Balboa
Sugar, tourism	EC Dollar
Bananas, cocoa, textiles	EC Dollar
Bananas, arrowroot, tourism	EC Dollar
Oil, sugar, cocoa, coffee	Dollar
Foods, minerals, industrial goods	Dollar

THE ORIGINAL 13 US COLONIES

1 Massachusetts
2 New Hampshire
3 Rhode Island
4 Connecticut
5 New York
6 Pennsylvania
7 New Jersey
8 Delaware
9 Maryland
10 Virginia
11 N Carolina
12 S Carolina
13 Georgia

The United States grew from 13 colonies founded by British settlers in the 1600s. The first colony was Virginia, which was first permanently settled in 1607, followed by Massachusetts (1620), New Hampshire (1623) and New York (1624). Last of the 13 was Georgia (1733). The British colonies were on the east coast. To the west and south were French and Spanish territories. The 13 colonies broke away from British rule in 1776 in an historic Declaration of Independence.

CANADA: PROVINCES AND TERRITORIES

PROVINCES
1 **Alberta**
  Edmonton
2 **British Columbia**
  Victoria
3 **Manitoba**
  Winnipeg

4 **New Brunswick**
  Fredericton
5 **Newfoundland**
  St John's
6 **Nova Scotia**
  Halifax
7 **Ontario**
  Toronto

8 **Prince Edward Island**
  Charlottetown
9 **Quebec**
  Quebec City
10 **Saskatchewan**
  Regina
TERRITORIES
11 **Northwest Territories**
  Yellowknife
12 **Yukon Territory**
  Whitehorse

31 **New Mexico**
  Santa Fé
32 **New York**
  Albany
33 **North Carolina**
  Raleigh
34 **North Dakota**
  Bismarck
35 **Ohio**
  Columbus
36 **Oklahoma**
  Oklahoma City
37 **Oregon**
  Salem
38 **Pennsylvania**
  Harrisburg
39 **Rhode Island**
  Providence
40 **South Carolina**
  Columbia

41 **South Dakota**
  Pierre
42 **Tennessee**
  Nashville
43 **Texas**
  Austin
44 **Utah**
  Salt Lake City
45 **Vermont**
  Montpelier
46 **Virginia**
  Richmond
47 **Washington**
  Olympia
48 **West Virginia**
  Charleston
49 **Wisconsin**
  Madison
50 **Wyoming**
  Cheyenne

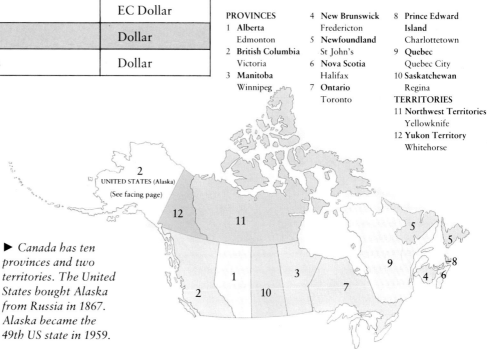

▶ *Canada has ten provinces and two territories. The United States bought Alaska from Russia in 1867. Alaska became the 49th US state in 1959.*

North America

North America is a continent of spectacle and superlatives, with some of the largest cities and most amazing natural wonders on Earth. Its peoples are as varied as its landscapes. The first Americans migrated from Asia thousands of years ago. Spreading across the great continent, they formed hunting and farming settlements and also built cities. Europeans first arrived in the 1500s, creating the United States of America in 1776. Canada became independent from the United Kingdom in 1867.

▲ *The longest river in the USA, the Mississippi River carries more than 40% of US inland freight.*

▼ *The city of St Louis was once called the 'Gateway to the West'. The Gateway Arch is on the city's riverfront.*

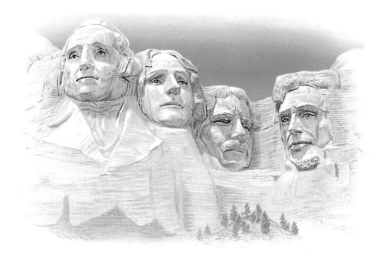

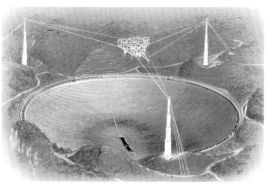

▲ *The faces of four US presidents are carved on a granite cliff at Mt Rushmore, South Dakota.*

◄ *A weekly market on the Caribbean island of Grenada. Formerly a British colony, it became independent in 1974.*

▲ *The world's biggest radio telescope dish, measuring almost 305 m across, is at Arecibo, Puerto Rico.*

◄ *The Grand Canyon in Arizona: it was cut by the Colorado River, and is the largest land gorge in the world.*

► *Old Faithful, in Yellowstone National Park, is a geyser that spouts a plume of hot water about 45 m high every 73 minutes.*

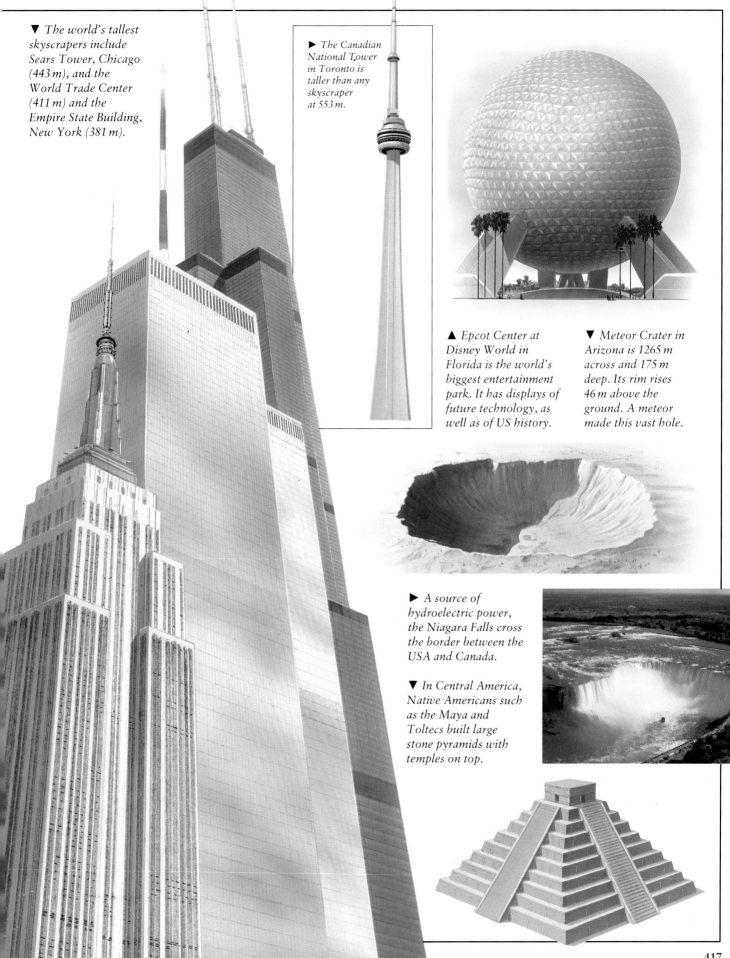

▼ The world's tallest skyscrapers include Sears Tower, Chicago (443 m), and the World Trade Center (411 m) and the Empire State Building, New York (381 m).

► The Canadian National Tower in Toronto is taller than any skyscraper at 553 m.

▲ Epcot Center at Disney World in Florida is the world's biggest entertainment park. It has displays of future technology, as well as of US history.

▼ Meteor Crater in Arizona is 1265 m across and 175 m deep. Its rim rises 46 m above the ground. A meteor made this vast hole.

► A source of hydroelectric power, the Niagara Falls cross the border between the USA and Canada.

▼ In Central America, Native Americans such as the Maya and Toltecs built large stone pyramids with temples on top.

South America

The fourth largest continent, South America is the largest part of Latin America (where most people speak Spanish or Portuguese). Much of the continent is thinly populated, including the Amazon rainforest region and the high Andes Mountains. The central plains include grasslands, known as *llanos* in the north and *pampas* in the south. About 75 percent of South Americans are city dwellers. South America is rich in natural resources, but many people in both the cities and the country live in poverty.

▲ *The beautiful opera house in Manaus, Brazil, was built with money from the region's wild rubber boom of 1890–1912.*

▼ *In Argentina's capital of Buenos Aires, the artistic quarter of La Boca is celebrated for its painted houses.*

THE AMAZON RAINFOREST
The Amazon rainforest is the world's greatest tropical forest and the home of thousands of species of birds, mammals, reptiles and insects. There are also more than 40,000 varieties of plants. However, much of the rainforest has now been cleared by farmers and new settlers.

◄ *In South American countries such as Brazil cattle raising is big business. Gauchos are the cowboys of the pampas, or plains. They are usually of mixed European and Indian blood.*

CARIBBEAN SEA

ATLANTIC OCEAN

• Caracas

Nevado
del Ruiz
5400 m △

L'Maracaibo

Orinoco

Angel Falls

Georgetown

GULF
OF PANAMA

Magdalena

LLANOS

GUYANA HIGHLANDS

Paramaribo

• Cayenne

PACIFIC OCEAN

• Bogotá

Branco

Maracá Island

Marajó Island

Negro

Japurá

Amazon

Manaus •

Cape
São Roque

Quito •

AMAZON RAINFOREST REGION

Tocantins

△ Chimborazo
6267 m

Paulo
Afonso
Falls

Marañón

Ucayali

Yavari

Purus

Madeira

Tapajós

Araguaia

São Francisco

Lima •

△ Huascarán
6768 m

MATO GROSSO

SERRA DOS PARECIS

BRAZILIAN
HIGHLANDS

▶ South America's
two main geographical
features are the Andes
Mountains stretching
down the western side
of the continent, and
the Amazon Basin
with its great river
systems. The
windswept far south
has few inhabitants.

A
N
D
E
S

L. Titicaca

PLATEAU

Brasília •

Ucayali

Coropuna △
6425 m

△ • La Paz

△ El Misti
5822 m

Sucre •

Brasília •

PACIFIC OCEAN

Lake
Poopó

GRAN
CHACO

Rio de Janeiro •

São Paulo •

Pilcomayo

Asunción •

Iguaçu Falls

Iguaçu

Cape Frio

△ Ojos del Salado
6880 m

Salado

Paraná

Uruguay

Patos
Lagoon

SOUTH AMERICAN
DATAFILE

Number of countries: 13
Greatest mountains: Andes,
over 7200 km long, longest
range on Earth
Highest point: Cerro
Aconcagua in Andes
(western Argentina), 6960 m
Driest spot: Atacama Desert
between southern Peru
and central Chile
Longest river: Amazon,
6448 km. Other important
rivers: Magdalena, Orinoco
Highest waterfall: Angel
Falls, Venezuela, 978 m
Biggest lake: Maracaibo, in
Venezuela, covering 16,300
sq km; Titicaca at 3812 m is
the highest lake in the world
**Biggest and most populous
country:** Brazil
Major cities (by population):
São Paulo, Buenos Aires,
Rio de Janeiro, Lima, Bogotá

ATACAMA DESERT

Cerro Aconcagua
6960 m

Santiago •

△ Tupungato
6800 m

Montevideo •

RIO DE LA PLATA

Buenos
Aires •

Cape San
Antonio

PAMPAS

Negro

Los Chonos
Archipelago

PATAGONIA

Cape Tres Puntas

kilometres 0 200 400 600 800 1000

miles 0 200 400 600

Falkland Islands

Reina Adelaida
Archipelago

Tierra del
Fuego

South Georgia

Strait of Magellan

Cape Horn

419

COUNTRY	AREA (sq km)	POPULATION	CAPITAL	LANGUAGE
Argentina	2,766,889	32,880,000	Buenos Aires	Spanish
Bolivia	1,098,581	7,400,000	La Paz	Spanish, Aymara, Quechua
Brazil	8,511,965	150,368,000	Brasília	Portuguese
Chile	756,945	13,173,000	Santiago	Spanish
Colombia	1,141,748	32,978,000	Bogotá	Spanish
Ecuador	269,178	10,782,000	Quito	Spanish
Guyana	215,083	756,000	Georgetown	English, Hindi, Urdu
Paraguay	406,752	4,277,000	Asunción	Spanish
Peru	1,285,216	22,332,000	Lima	Spanish, Aymara, Quechua
Surinam	163,265	411,000	Paramaribo	Dutch
Uruguay	176,215	3,033,000	Montevideo	Spanish
Venezuela	912,050	19,735,000	Caracas	Spanish

▲ *The Andes Mountains rise along the western side of South America. They are the world's longest mountain chain above sea level, with many peaks over 6000 m.*

◀ *A statue called Christ the Redeemer overlooks the bay at Rio de Janeiro, South America's finest natural harbour. Another of Rio's landmarks is Sugar Loaf Mountain.*

▲ *Reed boats on Lake Titicaca, the highest navigable lake in the world. The Atacama Desert (below) is the driest area in South America, stretching from southern Peru into northern Chile.*

MAJOR PRODUCTS AND INDUSTRIES	CURRENCY
Cereals, wool, vegetable oils, meat	Austral
Natural gas, metals (zinc, tin, gold)	Peso
Coffee, sugar, cattle, textiles	Cruzeiro
Copper, fruit, fish meal, paper	Peso
Coffee, bananas, minerals	Peso
Petroleum, shrimps, bananas	Sucre
Bauxite, sugar, rice	Dollar
Cotton, soya beans, meat, coffee, timber	Guarani
Coffee, sugar, minerals	Inti
Aluminium, shrimps, rice	Surinam Guilder
Textiles, meat, hides	New Peso
Petroleum, natural gas	Bolívar

◀ The cathedral in Brasília. The city was built to be capital of Brazil, replacing Rio de Janeiro.

▲ The Angel Falls: water plummets down a cliff on Mount Auyantepui in south-east Venezuela.

▶ The Incas of Peru built the mountain fortress-city of Machu Picchu, 'lost' until rediscovered in 1911.

▶ The Ambato market in Quito, the second largest city of Ecuador. Quito is famous for its weekly outdoor markets; held in different parts of the city, they attract large crowds. Most of the city's markets specialize in particular types of goods.

Europe

Europe is the second smallest of the continents, yet only Asia has more people. Europe is therefore the most crowded continent. It is the birthplace of Western civilization, and through trade, cultural contact and colonization has had an immense influence on the world. Its map has been redrawn many times in history. Changes in the 1990s include the growth of the European Community; the unification of Germany; and the break up of the Soviet Union, Czechoslovakia and Yugoslavia.

EUROPEAN DATAFILE

Number of countries: 45
Population: 788,000,000
Biggest cities: Moscow (Russia), London (UK), Paris (France), Essen (Germany)
Highest point: Mt Elbrus in the Caucasus range in Russia, 5633 m
Lowest point: shore of Caspian Sea, 28 m below sea level
Longest river: Volga, Russia, 3531 km. The Danube flows through Germany, Austria, Croatia, Slovakia, Hungary, Serbia, Bulgaria, Romania and Ukraine
Biggest lake: Caspian Sea 438,695 sq km
Largest country: Russia
Smallest independent country: Vatican City
Biggest island: Great Britain (England, Wales and Scotland), 218,041 sq km

▶ *Europe is the western part of the Eurasia land mass. It extends eastwards from the Atlantic Ocean to the Urals and contains about 20 percent of the world's population.*

BARENTS SEA

URAL MTS

Northern Dvina

Onega

Sukhona

Vyatka

Volga

Vetluga

Kuybyshev reservoir

● Moscow

Ural

Don

● Volgograd

Volga

Dnepr

CASPIAN SEA

SEA OF AZOV

Mt Elbrus 5633 m

BLACK SEA

CAUCASUS

● Tbilisi

Baku ●

Yerevan ●

Ankara ●

ICELAND

IRELAND

UNITED KINGDOM

DENMARK

NORWAY

SWEDEN

FINLAND

ESTONIA

LATVIA

LITHUANIA

RUSSIA

RUSSIA

BELARUS

UKRAINE

MOLDOVA

NETHERLANDS

POLAND

GERMANY

BELGIUM
LUXEMBOURG

FRANCE

PORTUGAL

SPAIN

ANDORRA

MONACO

CZECH REP

SLOVAK REP

AUSTRIA

LIECHTENSTEIN
SAN MARINO

SWITZERLAND

SLOVENIA

CROATIA

BOSNIA HERZ

YUGO

HUNGARY

ROMANIA

BULGARIA

MACE

ALBANIA

ITALY

VATICAN CITY

GREECE

TURKEY

GEORGIA

AZERBAIJAN

ARMENIA

AFRICA

MALTA

ASIA

▲ *Venice, with its canals and palaces, is one of Italy's most beautiful cities. It is built on islands in the Adriatic Sea.*

◄ *The Alps are the largest mountain system in Europe. In summer farmers move their cattle to higher pastures to graze. In winter the Alpine resorts are crowded with skiers.*

COUNTRY	AREA (sq km)	POPULATION	CAPITAL	LANGUAGE
Albania	28,748	3,278,000	Tirana	Albanian
Andorra	468	50,900	Andorra la Vella	Catalan, French, Spanish
Armenia	29,800	3,376,000	Yerevan	Armenian, Russian
Austria	83,856	7,623,000	Vienna	German
Azerbaijan	86,600	7,137,000	Baku	Azerbaijani, Russian
Belarus	207,600	10,260,000	Minsk	Byelrussian, Russian
Belgium	30,518	9,958,000	Brussels	Flemish, French
Bosnia-Herzegovina	51,129	4,479,000	Sarajevo	Šerbo-Croatian
Bulgaria	110,994	8,997,000	Sofia	Bulgarian, Turkish
Croatia	56,538	4,683,000	Zagreb	Croato-Serbian
Czech Republic	78,865	10,299,000	Prague	Czech
Denmark	40,093	5,139,000	Copenhagen	Danish
Estonia	45,100	1,573,000	Tallinn	Estonian
Finland	338,145	4,978,000	Helsinki	Finnish
France	543,965	56,647,000	Paris	French
Georgia	69,694	16,538,000	Tbilisi	Georgian, Russian
Germany	357,050	78,000,000	Berlin	German
Greece	131,944	10,141,000	Athens	Greek
Hungary	93,030	10,563,000	Budapest	Hungarian
Iceland	102,819	256,000	Reykjavik	Icelandic
Ireland	70,285	3,509,000	Dublin	Irish, English
Italy	301,277	57,512,000	Rome	Italian
Latvia	64,500	2,681,000	Riga	Latvian, Russian
Liechtenstein	160	28,700	Vaduz	German
Lithuania	65,200	3,690,000	Vilnius	Lithuanian
Luxembourg	2856	379,000	Luxembourg	Letzeburgish, French
Malta	316	353,000	Valletta	Maltese, English
Moldova	33,700	4,341,000	Chişinău	Moldovian, Russian
Monaco	1.9	29,300	Monaco	French, Monegasque
Netherlands	41,863	14,934,000	Amsterdam	Dutch
Norway	323,878	4,246,000	Oslo	Norwegian (two forms)
Poland	312,677	38,064,000	Warsaw	Polish
Portugal	92,389	10,388,000	Lisbon	Portuguese

MAJOR PRODUCTS AND INDUSTRIES	CURRENCY
Minerals, food products	Lek
Tourism, consumer goods	Spanish Peseta
Chemicals, agriculture, machinery	Rouble
Machinery, consumer goods, tourism	Schilling
Oil, iron, steel, textiles	Rouble
Livestock, timber	Rouble
Metals, textiles, chemicals, ceramics	Franc
Agriculture, chemicals, machinery	Dinar
Foods, wine, tobacco	Lev
Agriculture, machinery, clothing, textiles	Dinar
Machinery, vehicles, consumer goods	Koruna
Dairy foods, beer, chemicals	Krone
Petroleum, fertilizer, timber, machinery	Kroon
Wood products, engineering, fish	Markka
Foods, wine, engineering, consumer goods	Franc
Mining, agriculture	Rouble
Engineering, chemicals, textiles, vehicles	Deutsch Mark
Foods, clothing, petroleum products	Drachma
Machinery, foods, consumer goods	Forint
Fish	Krona
Manufactured goods, foods	Irish Pound
Foods, wine, textiles, engineering, vehicles	Lira
Machinery, electrical equipment, processed foods	Lat
Tourism, banking, precision engineering	Swiss Franc
Chemicals, metal goods, electrical equipment	Litas
Iron and steel	Luxembourg Fr
Ship repair, tourism	Maltese Lira
Agriculture, foods, chemicals	Rouble
Property, banking, tourism	Franc
Foods, flowers, manufacturing, natural gas	Guilder
Natural gas, petroleum, timber, fish	Krone
Machinery, chemicals, foods, textiles	Zloty
Foods, fish, cork, textiles, manufacturing	Escudo

THE EUROPEAN COMMUNITY

Twelve countries belong to the European Community (EC), and other European countries are seeking membership. Appointed by countries of the EC, the Commission meets in Brussels, Belgium. Here its members plan policy for the Community, now developing from a free trade area into a more close-knit political organization.

◄ *The EC Commission is the body that initiates Community proposals. Its headquarters are in Brussels, Belgium.*

CHANGES IN EASTERN EUROPE

The old Soviet Union of 15 republics broke up in 1990–1991. First to leave were the Baltic states of Estonia, Latvia and Lithuania. The Slav states are Russia, Ukraine and Belarus (Byelorussia). The Transcaucasian republics are Armenia, Georgia and Azerbaijan. Moldova is by language and history part of Romania. The central Asian republics were in the pre-1917 Russian empire.

▲ *The Soviet Union broke into 15 separate republics. By far the biggest is Russia, most of which is in Asia.*

▼ *The Hermitage Museum, once the Winter Palace, is in St Petersburg (formerly Leningrad).*

COUNTRY	AREA (sq km)	POPULATION	CAPITAL	LANGUAGE
Romania	237,500	23,265,000	Bucharest	Romanian, Hungarian
Russia	17,075,400	147,386,000	Moscow	Russian
San Marino	61	23,000	San Marino	Italian
Slovak Republic	49,035	5,269,000	Bratislava	Slovak
Slovenia	20,251	1,943,000	Ljubljana	Slovenian
Spain	504,783	38,959,000	Madrid	Spanish, Catalan
Sweden	449,964	8,529,000	Stockholm	Swedish
Switzerland	41,293	6,756,000	Bern	German, French, Italian, Romansch
Ukraine	603,700	51,800,000	Kiev	Ukrainian, Russian
United Kingdom	244,110	57,384,000	London	English
Vatican City	44 hectares	750	Vatican City	Italian, Latin
*Yugoslavia (former)	95,493	8,590,000	Belgrade	Serbo-Croatian

*By 1992 the federal republic of Yugoslavia had ceased to exist. At the time of printing the civil war in Bosnia continues. Macedonia has now been recognized as an independent country.

▶ Amsterdam is the capital city of the Netherlands; it is built on islands, separated by its famous canals.

◀ The Lloyd's Building was designed by Richard Rogers and finished in 1986. It lies in the City of London, the financial heart of the UK and an important world trading centre.

▲ The Eiffel Tower in Paris was built in 1889 to mark one hundred years since the French Revolution.

◀ Running through the Alps, the St Gotthard tunnel in Switzerland is the world's longest road tunnel (16.32 km).

MAJOR PRODUCTS AND INDUSTRIES	CURRENCY
Minerals, manufacturing, timber	Lev
Manufacturing, tourism	Rouble
Maize, pigs, steel, factory goods	Italian Lira
Agriculture, food products, wood products	Koruna
(Not available)	Dinar
Foods, wine, manufacturing, banking	Peseta
Uranium, iron, timber, pulp, engineering	Krona
Manufacturing, engineering, banking	Franc
Heavy industry, agriculture	Grivna
Manufacturing, petroleum, banking, tourism	Pound
None	Lira
Agriculture, clothing, textiles	Dinar

▲ The world's tallest statue, 'Motherland' (82 m) is in Volgograd (Stalingrad), Russia.

▲ The city of Krakow, once capital of Poland, has many historic buildings in its centre.

▼ Stonehenge, a 4000-year-old English stone monument, is believed to have been a temple.

◄ These vineyards are in Tuscany, a region of Italy noted for its beauty. Italy is the EC's leading wine producer, followed by France and Spain.

▲ The spire of Ulm Cathedral in southern Germany is the highest spire in the world at almost 161 m.

▼ On the Acropolis in Athens stands the Parthenon, the most famous temple built by the ancient Greeks.

Asia

About 60 percent of the Earth's population lives in Asia. The largest of all the continents, Asia has the world's highest mountains as well as great rivers, deserts, plains, polar wastes, forests and tropical jungles. The world's great religions began in Asia. So too did the first great civilizations. Since World War II (1939–1945), Asia has seen: an economic boom in the Gulf States and Japan; war in Korea, Vietnam and the Middle East; and poverty made worse by natural disasters such as flooding in Bangladesh.

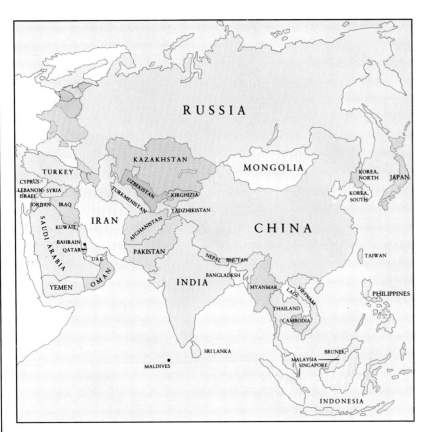

ASIAN DATAFILE

Number of countries: 44
Highest point: Mt Everest (8848 m). Next highest points: K2 (8610 m), Mt Kanchenjunga (8598 m). All in Himalayas
Longest river: Chang Jiang (Yangtze), 6300 km
Other major rivers: Yenisey (5540 km), Huang He (5464 km), Ob-Irtysh (5409 km), Lena (4400 km), Mekong (4350 km)
Lowest point: Dead Sea shore, 399 m below sea level
Largest deserts: Gobi, Kara Kum, Rub al Khali, Takli

Makan
Largest lake: Caspian Sea, 1225 km long, 371,800 sq km
Biggest country (excluding Russia, which is partly in Europe): China
Most populous country: China
Biggest city: Tokyo-Yokohama (Japan). Other major cities (by population): Seoul (South Korea), Osaka-Kobe-Kyoto (Japan), Bombay and Calcutta (India), Manila (Philippines), Jakarta (Indonesia); all over 9.5 million people

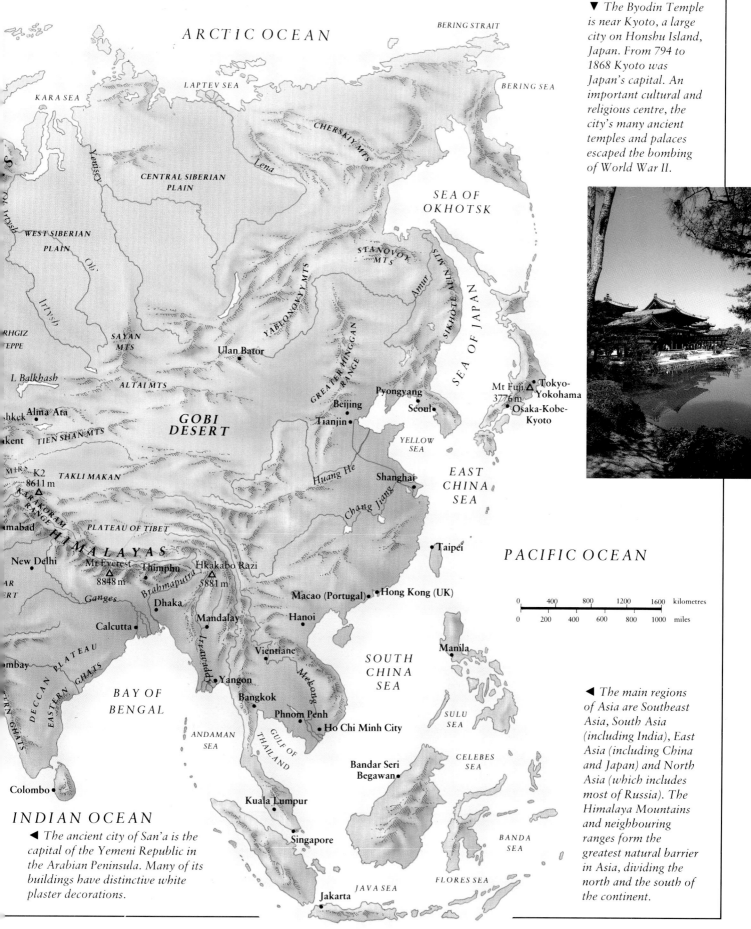

▼ *The Byodin Temple is near Kyoto, a large city on Honshu Island, Japan. From 794 to 1868 Kyoto was Japan's capital. An important cultural and religious centre, the city's many ancient temples and palaces escaped the bombing of World War II.*

ARCTIC OCEAN

BERING STRAIT

BERING SEA

LAPTEV SEA

KARA SEA

CENTRAL SIBERIAN PLAIN

Yenisey

Lena

CHERSKIY MTS

SEA OF OKHOTSK

WEST SIBERIAN PLAIN

Ob'

Irtysh

STANOVOY MTS

Amur

SIKHOTE ALIN MTS

SEA OF JAPAN

RHGIZ TEPPE

L Balkhash

SAYAN MTS

YABLONOVYY MTS

GREATER HINGGAN RANGE

Ulan Bator

hkck Alma Ata

ALTAI MTS

TIEN SHAN MTS

GOBI DESERT

Pyongyang

Beijing

Seoul

Mt Fuji 3776 m △ ● Tokyo-Yokohama

ent

Tianjin

● Osaka-Kobe-Kyoto

K2 8611 m △

TAKLI MAKAN

YELLOW SEA

MIRS

KARAKORAM RANGE

PLATEAU OF TIBET

Huang He

Shanghai

EAST CHINA SEA

abad

New Delhi

HIMALAYAS

Mt Everest 8848 m △

Thimphu

Hkakabo Razi 5881 m △

Brahmaputra

Chang Jiang

PACIFIC OCEAN

AR

ert

Ganges

Dhaka

Taipei

DECCAN PLATEAU

Calcutta

Mandalay

Irrawaddy

Hanoi

Macao (Portugal) ● Hong Kong (UK)

| 0 | 400 | 800 | 1200 | 1600 | kilometres |
| 0 | 200 | 400 | 600 | 800 | 1000 | miles |

EASTERN GHATS

ombay

Vientiane

Mekong

SOUTH CHINA SEA

Manila

BAY OF BENGAL

Yangon

Bangkok

Phnom Penh

● Ho Chi Minh City

SULU SEA

ERN GHATS

ANDAMAN SEA

GULF OF THAILAND

Colombo ●

CELEBES SEA

Bandar Seri Begawan ●

Kuala Lumpur

INDIAN OCEAN

◄ *The ancient city of San'a is the capital of the Yemeni Republic in the Arabian Peninsula. Many of its buildings have distinctive white plaster decorations.*

Singapore

BANDA SEA

JAVA SEA

FLORES SEA

Jakarta

◄ *The main regions of Asia are Southeast Asia, South Asia (including India), East Asia (including China and Japan) and North Asia (which includes most of Russia). The Himalaya Mountains and neighbouring ranges form the greatest natural barrier in Asia, dividing the north and the south of the continent.*

COUNTRY	AREA (sq km)	POPULATION	CAPITAL	LANGUAGE
Afghanistan	652,225	15,592,000	Kabul	Pushto, Dari
Bahrain	692	503,000	Manama	Arabic
Bangladesh	143,998	113,005,000	Dhaka	Bengali
Bhutan	47,000	1,442,000	Thimphu	Dzongkha
Brunei	5765	258,000	Bandar Seri Begawan	Malay
Cambodia	181,916	8,592,000	Phnom Penh	Khmer, French
China	9,572,900	1,133,683,000	Beijing	Mandarin Chinese
Cyprus[1]	9251	739,000	Nicosia	Greek, Turkish
India	3,166,414	853,373,000	New Delhi	Hindi, English and others
Indonesia	1,904,000	180,783,000	Jakarta	Bahasa Indonesia
Iran	1,648,196	56,923,000	Tehran	Farsi, Azerbaijani
Iraq	435,052	17,754,000	Baghdad	Arabic, Kirdish
Israel[2]	20,700	4,666,000	Jerusalem	Hebrew, Arabic
Japan	377,708	123,700,000	Tokyo	Japanese
Jordan	97,740	3,169,000	Amman	Arabic
Kazakhstan	2,717,300	16,793,000	Alma Ata	Turkic
Kirghizia	198,500	4,291,000	Bishkek	Turkic
Korea, North	122,370	22,937,000	Pyongyang	Korean
Korea, South	98,484	42,791,000	Seoul	Korean
Kuwait	17,818	2,143,000	Kuwait City	Arabic
Laos	236,800	4,024,000	Vientiane	Lao
Lebanon	10,230	2,965,000	Beirut	Arabic
Malaysia	329,749	17,886,000	Kuala Lumpur	Bahasa Malaysia
Maldives	298	214,000	Male	Divehi
Mongolia	1,565,000	2,150,000	Ulan Bator	Mongolian
Myanmar	676,552	41,675,000	Yangon	Burmese
Nepal	147,181	18,910,000	Kathmandu	Nepali
Oman	212,457	1,468,000	Muscat	Arabic
Pakistan	796,095	122,666,000	Islamabad	Urdu
Philippines	300,000	61,483,000	Manila	Filipino, English
Qatar	11,427	444,000	Doha	Arabic
Saudi Arabia	2,149,690	14,131,000	Riyadh	Arabic
Singapore	581	2,702,000	Singapore City	Chinese, English, Malay, Tamil

MAJOR PRODUCTS AND INDUSTRIES	CURRENCY
Cereals, dried fruit, wool, cotton	Afghani
Petroleum, natural gas	Dinar
Rice, jute, tea	Taka
Foods, timber	Ngultrum
Natural gas, petroleum	Brunei Dollar
Rice	Riel
Rice, minerals, fish, manufactured goods	Yuan
Foods, wine, tourism	Pound
Tea, cotton, sugar, jute, coal, manufactured goods	Rupee
Petroleum, natural gas	Rupiah
Petroleum, textiles, carpets	Rial
Petroleum, dates	Dinar
Fruit, vegetables, tourism	Sheqel
Vehicles, machinery, chemicals, textiles, electronics	Yen
Potash	Dinar
Cereals, cotton, petroleum	Rouble
Cotton	Som
Minerals, foods, textiles	Won
Vehicles, textiles, ships, steel, fish	Won
Petroleum, chemicals, fertilizer	Dinar
Farm products, timber, coffee, tin	Kip
Jewellery, clothes, pharmaceuticals	Lebanese Pound
Manufactured goods, palm oil, petroleum, rubber, tin	Malaysian Dollar
Fish, clothing	Rupee
Coal, metals, farm products	Tugrik
Teak, rice	Kyat Main
Foods, manufactured goods	Rupee
Petroleum	Rial
Cotton, textiles, foods, chemicals	Rupee
Electronics, clothing, farm products, wood	Peso
Petroleum, chemicals	Riyal
Petroleum	Riyal
Communications equipment, clothing, petroleum	Singapore Dollar

THE INDIAN SUBCONTINENT

Civilization in the Indian subcontinent began in the Indus Valley, about 5500 years ago. In the 300–500s and the 1500s–1700s Hindu and Islamic (Mogul) rulers created powerful empires. Between the 1700s and 1947 most of this territory was part of British-controlled India. In 1947 India (mostly Hindu) and Pakistan (Islamic) went their separate ways as independent republics. Bangladesh, formerly East Pakistan, broke away to gain its independence in 1971.

▲ *Devout Indian Hindus come to bathe in the sacred river Ganges at Varanasi (Benares).*

▼ *The Taj Mahal in India was built (1630–1650) by the Mogul emperor Shah Jahan as a tomb for his wife.*

431

COUNTRY	AREA (sq km)	POPULATION	CAPITAL	LANGUAGE
Sri Lanka	65,610	17,103,000	Colombo	Sinhalese, Tamil
Syria	185,180	12,116,000	Damascus	Arabic
Tadzhikistan	143,100	5,358,000	Dushanbe	Tadzhik
Taiwan	36,000	20,262,000	Taipei	Chinese
Thailand	514,000	56,147,000	Bangkok	Thai
Turkey	777,452[3]	56,941,000	Ankara	Turkish
Turkmenistan	488,100	3,622,000	Ashkhabad	Turkic
United Arab Emirates	83,600	1,881,000	Abu Dhabi	Arabic
Uzbekistan	447,400	20,708,000	Tashkent	Uzbek
Vietnam	329,556	66,111,000	Hanoi	Vietnamese
Yemen	531,869	11,546,000	San'a	Arabic

▼ *The Hindu temple of Angkor Wat, Cambodia (built in 1113–1150) is the world's largest religious structure.*

▼ *The port of Singapore is the key to the small city-state's economic prosperity.*

▲ *The Forbidden City was the central part of the Chinese emperor's palace in Beijing.*

MAJOR PRODUCTS AND INDUSTRIES	CURRENCY
Tea, rubber, gemstones	Rupee
Petroleum, chemicals, textiles	Pound
Cotton	Rouble
Electronics, clothes, plastic goods	Taiwan Dollar
Textiles, rice, rubber, tapioca, teak	Baht
Textiles, foods, metals	Lira
Cotton	Rouble
Petroleum	Dirham
Cotton	Rouble
Coal, farm produce, livestock, fish	Dong
Coffee, hides, foods, cigarettes	Dinar, Riyal

[1] Divided since 1974. Turkish Republic of Northern Cyprus not recognized by UN.
[2] Excludes territory occupied in 1967 war.
[3] 23,764 sq km in Europe.

▲ *Oil has made some Middle Eastern states very rich, despite their lack of other resources. This refinery is in Saudi Arabia, the largest oil producer in the region.*

▼ *This train is on the Trans-Siberian Railway, which runs from Moscow in Europe to Vladivostock in Asia. It is the world's longest railway.*

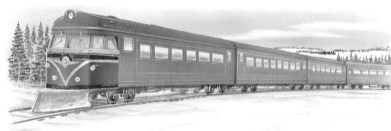

◄ *The Great Wall of China, at 2400 km, is the longest structure ever built. First built as a defensive wall c.210 BC, it was also used as a transport route.*

◄ *A bullet-shaped Japanese high-speed electric train. Japan's highly efficient rail network includes the world's longest rail tunnel, the Seikan Tunnel (54 km long); the first test run took place in 1988.*

► *Jerusalem is a city sacred to Christians, Jews and Muslims. Since 1967 the whole city has been occupied by Israel, whose capital it is.*

433

Africa

Africa covers about one-fifth of the Earth's land area, making it the second largest continent after Asia. It has more countries than any other continent, most of them independent only since the 1950s. Africa divides geographically north and south of the huge Sahara Desert. The people of the north are mostly Arabs and Berbers. In the south live mainly black Africans. In all, Africa is home to some 800 different-language groups, including people of European and Asian origin.

▲ *Kilimanjaro in Tanzania is an extinct volcano. One of its two peaks, Kibo, is the highest mountain in Africa and is always snow-capped. Lower slopes are covered with dense cloud forest, a type of wet forest found only at high altitudes.*

*The number of countries in Africa is now 53. In summer 1993, Ethiopia recognized the independence of Eritrea.

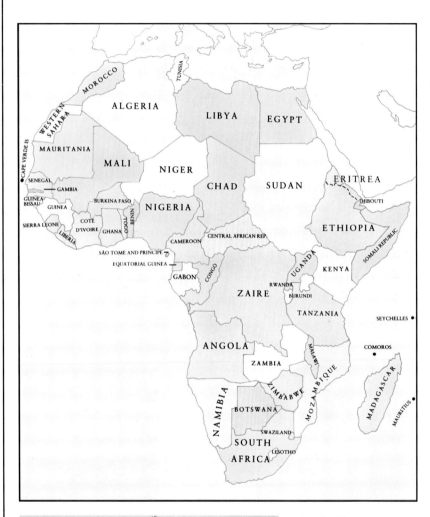

◀ *The Place Djema Al Fna lies in the centre of Marrakesh, the third largest city in Morocco, North Africa. Marrakesh was founded in 1062 and is one of Morocco's four traditional capital cities. A popular place for tourists to visit, this large square is always crowded with shoppers, traders and street entertainers.*

AFRICAN DATAFILE

Number of countries: 52*
Highest point: Kilimanjaro (Tanzania) 5895 m
Lowest point: Lake Assal (Djibouti) 155 m below sea level
Largest lake: Victoria, 360 km long; 69,500 sq km
Biggest deserts: Sahara, Kalahari, Namib
Hottest regions: Sahara and parts of Somalia (above 45°C)
Longest river: Nile (6670 km, the longest in the world)
Other important rivers: Zaïre (4700 km); Niger (4184 km); Zambezi (3540 km)
Greatest waterfalls: Victoria (highest, 355 m); Boyoma (most water, 730 m wide)
Largest country: Sudan
Most populous country: Nigeria
Most industrialized country: South Africa
Biggest city: Cairo (Egypt) 9.8 m. people
Other major cities (by population): Lagos (Nigeria), Kinshasa (Zaïre), Alexandria (Egypt), Casablanca (Morocco)
Biggest island: Madagascar (587,041 sq km)
Oldest civilizations: Egypt (*c*.3100 BC), Kush (*c*.2000 BC)

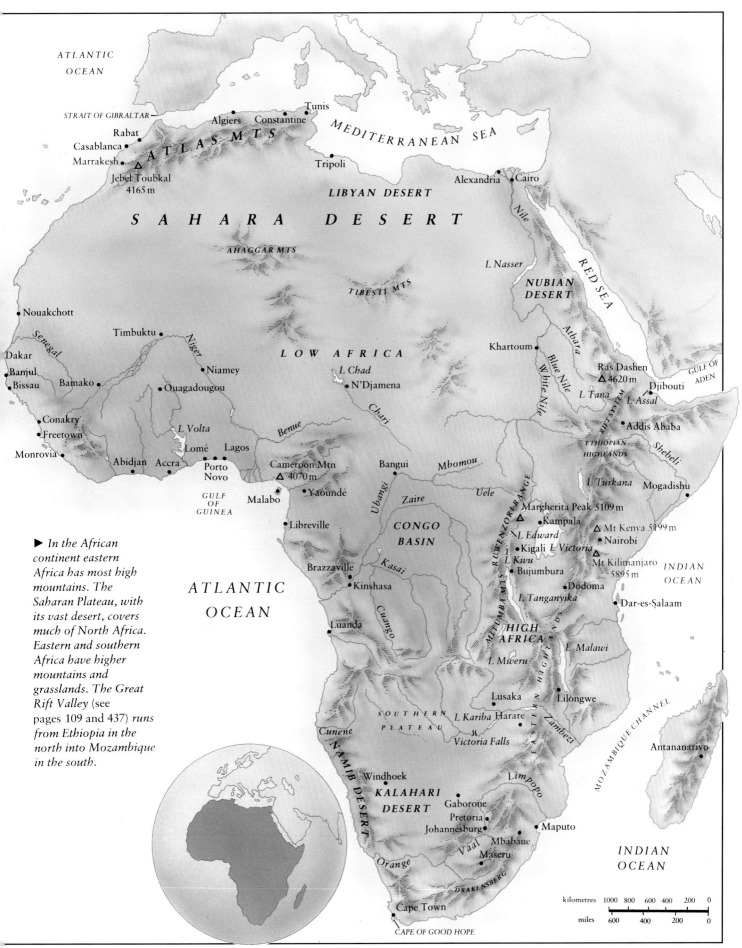

ATLANTIC
OCEAN

STRAIT OF GIBRALTAR

Rabat
Casablanca
Marrakesh
△ Jebel Toubkal
4165 m

Algiers   Constantine
Tunis

A T L A S   M T S

Tripoli

MEDITERRANEAN SEA

Alexandria   Cairo

LIBYAN DESERT

S A H A R A   D E S E R T

AHAGGAR MTS

L Nasser

NUBIAN
DESERT

RED SEA

TIBESTI MTS

Nouakchott

Timbuktu

L O W   A F R I C A

Khartoum

Ras Dashen
△ 4620 m

GULF OF
ADEN

Dakar
Banjul
Bissau

Senegal

Niger

Niamey

L Chad

N'Djamena

Djibouti

L Tana   L Assal

Bamako
Ouagadougou

Benue

Chari

White Nile   Blue Nile   Atbara

Addis Ababa

Conakry
Freetown
Monrovia

L Volta
Lomé   Lagos
Abidjan   Accra   Porto
Novo

Cameroon Mtn
△ 4070 m

Malabo

*ETHIOPIAN
HIGHLANDS*

Shebeli

GULF
OF
GUINEA

Yaoundé

Bangui

Mbomou

Uele

L Turkana   Mogadishu

Libreville

Ubangi   Zaire

Margherita Peak 5109 m
△
L Edward   Kampala
△ Mt Kenya 5199 m
Kigali   L Victoria   Nairobi
L Kivu   △ Mt Kilimanjaro
Bujumbura   5895 m

CONGO
BASIN

Brazzaville
Kinshasa

Kasai

INDIAN
OCEAN

Dodoma

L Tanganyika   Dar-es-Salaam

ATLANTIC
OCEAN

Cuango

Luanda

RUWENZORI RANGE

MITUMBA MTS

HIGH
AFRICA

EASTERN HIGHLANDS

L Mweru   L Malawi

► *In the African
continent eastern
Africa has most high
mountains. The
Saharan Plateau, with
its vast desert, covers
much of North Africa.
Eastern and southern
Africa have higher
mountains and
grasslands. The Great
Rift Valley (see
pages 109 and 437) runs
from Ethiopia in the
north into Mozambique
in the south.*

Lusaka   Lilongwe

SOUTHERN
PLATEAU   L Kariba   Harare

Zambezi

Cunene

Victoria Falls

MOZAMBIQUE CHANNEL

Antananarivo

Windhoek

NAMIB DESERT

KALAHARI
DESERT

Limpopo

Gaborone
Pretoria
Johannesburg

Maputo

INDIAN
OCEAN

Orange

Vaal   Mbabane
Maseru

DRAKENSBERG

Cape Town

CAPE OF GOOD HOPE

kilometres   1000 800 600 400 200 0

miles   600   400   200   0

COUNTRY	AREA (sq km)	POPULATION	CAPITAL	LANGUAGE
Algeria	2,381,714	25,337,000	Algiers	Arabic, French
Angola	1,246,700	10,002,000	Luanda	Portuguese
Benin	112,600	4,741,000	Porto-Novo	French
Botswana	581,730	1,295,000	Gaborone	Tswana, English
Burkina Faso	274,200	9,012,000	Ouagadougou	French
Burundi	27,834	5,439,000	Bujumbura	Kirundi, French
Cameroon	475,442	11,742,000	Yaoundé	French, English
Cape Verde Islands	4033	339,000	Praia	Portuguese
Central African Republic	622,984	2,875,000	Bangui	French
Chad	1,284,000	5,678,000	N'Djamena	Arabic, French
Comoros	1862	463,000	Moroni	Arabic, French
Congo	342,000	2,236,000	Brazzaville	French
Côte d'Ivoire	320,763	12,657,000	Abidjan	French
Djibouti	22,000	528,000	Djibouti	Arabic, French
Egypt	997,739	53,170,000	Cairo	Arabic, French
Equatorial Guinea	28,051	3,511,000	Malabo	Spanish
Ethiopia	1,221,900	50,341,000	Addis Ababa	Amharic
Gabon	267,667	1,171,000	Libreville	French
Gambia	10,689	860,000	Banjul	English
Ghana	238,533	15,020,000	Accra	English
Guinea	245,857	6,876,000	Conakry	French
Guinea-Bissau	36,125	973,000	Bissau	Portuguese
Kenya	582,646	24,872,000	Nairobi	Swahili, English
Lesotho	30,355	1,760,000	Maseru	Sesotho, English
Liberia	111,370	2,595,000	Monrovia	English
Libya	1,759,540	4,206,000	Tripoli	Arabic
Madagascar	587,041	11,980,000	Antananarivo	Malagasy, French
Malawi	118,484	8,831,000	Lilongwe	Chichewa, English
Mali	1,240,192	8,152,000	Bamako	French
Mauritania	1,030,700	2,000,000	Nouakchott	Arabic, French
Mauritius	2040	1,080,000	Port Louis	English
Morocco	458,730	25,113,000	Rabat	Arabic
Mozambique	799,380	15,696,000	Maputo	Portuguese

MAJOR PRODUCTS AND INDUSTRIES	CURRENCY
Petroleum, processed foods	Dinar
Petroleum, vegetable and animal products	Kwanza
Petroleum, palm products	CFA Franc
Minerals, livestock products	Pula
Gold, manganese, millet, peanuts	CFA Franc
Coffee, tea, cotton	Burundi Franc
Petroleum, coffee, cocoa, aluminium	CFA Franc
Bananas, coffee, fish	Escudo
Coffee, diamonds, wood, cotton	CFA Franc
Cotton, uranium	CFA Franc
Vanilla, copra, perfume	Franc
Petroleum, wood, diamonds	CFA Franc
Coffee, cocoa, diamonds	CFA Franc
Livestock (camels), food	Djibouti Franc
Petroleum, cotton, textiles	Pound
Cocoa, timber	CFA Franc
Coffee, hides, livestock, pulses	Birr
Petroleum, timber, manganese	CFA Franc
Peanut products, fish, tourism	Dalasi
Cocoa, gold, timber	Cedi
Bauxite, diamonds, gold	Guinean Franc
Cashews, peanuts	Peso
Coffee, tea, petroleum products, tourism	Kenya shilling
Wool, foods, manufactured goods	Loti
Iron ore, rubber, timber	Dollar
Petroleum	Dinar
Coffee, vanilla, cloves	Franc
Tobacco, tea, sugar	Kwacha
Cotton, livestock, nuts	CFA Franc
Fish, iron ore	Ouguiya
Textiles, sugar, diamonds, fish	Rupee
Foods, phosphates, fertilizer	Dirham
Shrimps, cashews, cotton, sugar	Metical

COLONIAL PARTITIONING OF AFRICA

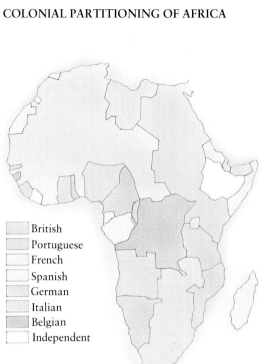

- British
- Portuguese
- French
- Spanish
- German
- Italian
- Belgian
- Independent

By the end of the 1800s, most of Africa was shared out between the European powers. The map of Africa was drawn by empire-builders and colonial frontier lines have shaped the boundaries of the independent nations of modern Africa. As a result national boundaries cut across the homelands of the more than 800 different ethnic groups of African people.

THE GREAT RIFT VALLEY
The Rift Valley is a series of cracks in the Earth's surface, running 6500 km from East Africa to Asia. In the steep-sided rift valleys lie rich farmland and Africa's great lakes.

COUNTRY	AREA (sq km)	POPULATION	CAPITAL	LANGUAGE
Namibia	823,144	1,302,000	Windhoek	Afrikaans, English
Niger	1,267,000	7,779,000	Niamey	French, Hausa
Nigeria	923,768	119,812,000	Lagos or Abuja	English
Rwanda	26,338	7,232,000	Kigali	Kinyarwanda, French
São Tomé & Príncipe	1001	121,000	São Tomé	Portuguese
Senegal	196,772	7,317,000	Dakar	French
Seychelles	453	68,700	Victoria	Creole, English, French
Sierra Leone	71,740	4,151,000	Freetown	English
Somalia	637,657	7,555,000	Mogadishu	Somali, Arabic
South Africa	1,240,167	37,419,000	Pretoria	Afrikaans, English
Sudan	2,508,813	28,311,000	Khartoum	Arabic
Swaziland	17,364	770,000	Mbabane	Swazi, English
Tanzania	945,087	24,403,000	Dodoma	Swahili, English
Togo	56,785	3,764,000	Lomé	French
Tunisia	154,530	8,182,000	Tunis	Arabic
Uganda	236,036	16,928,000	Kampala	Swahili, English
Zaïre	2,345,409	34,138,000	Kinshasa	French
Zambia	752,614	8,456,000	Lusaka	English
Zimbabwe	390,759	9,369,000	Harare	English

▶ The Sahara Desert has both the world's highest temperatures and the biggest sand dunes; some dunes are over 400 m high.

▼ The Pyramids at Giza in Egypt built c.2500s BC. Of the Seven Wonders of the Ancient World, only the Pyramids survive.

▶ The legislative capital of South Africa, Cape Town is a bustling trading and shipping centre on the southwest coast of Africa. The famous Table Mountain towers over the city and its harbour.

MAJOR PRODUCTS AND INDUSTRIES	CURRENCY
Diamonds, cattle, hides	Rand
Uranium, other minerals, livestock, vegetables	CFA Franc
Petroleum, palm products	Naira
Coffee, tea	Rwanda Franc
Cocoa, copra	Dobre
Peanut oil, shellfish, phosphates	CFA Franc
Petroleum, fish, tourism	S Rupee
Titanium dioxide, diamonds, bauxite, coffee	Leone
Livestock, bananas, hides, fish	Somali Shilling
Gold, minerals, foods, factory goods	Rand
Cotton, gum arabic, sesame, sheep	Sudanese Pound
Sugar, timber, coal, diamonds	Lilangeni
Coffee, cotton	Tanzanian Shilling
Fertilizer, coffee, tea, cocoa	CFA Franc
Clothing, petroleum, phosphates	Dinar
Coffee	Uganda Shilling
Copper, coffee, diamonds, petroleum	Zaïre
Copper, zinc, cobalt	Kwacha
Tobacco, gold	Zimbabwe Dollar

▲ The Zaire River, formerly known as the Congo, in west-central Africa is 4700 km long. Although it is an important transportation route, rapids prevent boats from navigating parts of the upper river.

▼ Muslims in Nigeria celebrate the end of Ramadan, the holy month of fasting. About half of Nigeria's population are Muslim, with some 40% Christian. Other Nigerians practise traditional religions.

◄ The river Nile, the longest river in the world, has always been the lifeblood of Egypt. Its waters made farming possible in an area of desert.

▼ The Great Mosque at Djenne in Mali, West Africa is a modern example (1907) of traditional building; it is built of sun-dried mud bricks.

▼ The Cullinan is the largest diamond ever mined; it is 3106 carats and was found in South Africa in 1905.

Oceania

Oceania is actually mostly water – the Pacific Ocean. By far the biggest landmass in Oceania is Australia, sometimes considered a continent in its own right. Much of Australia is empty desert. Next in size are Papua New Guinea and New Zealand. Scattered across the wide Pacific Ocean are about 30,000 islands. These islands form three main groups: Melanesia, Micronesia and Polynesia. The people of Oceania are mostly descendants of migrants who originally came from Asia or Europe.

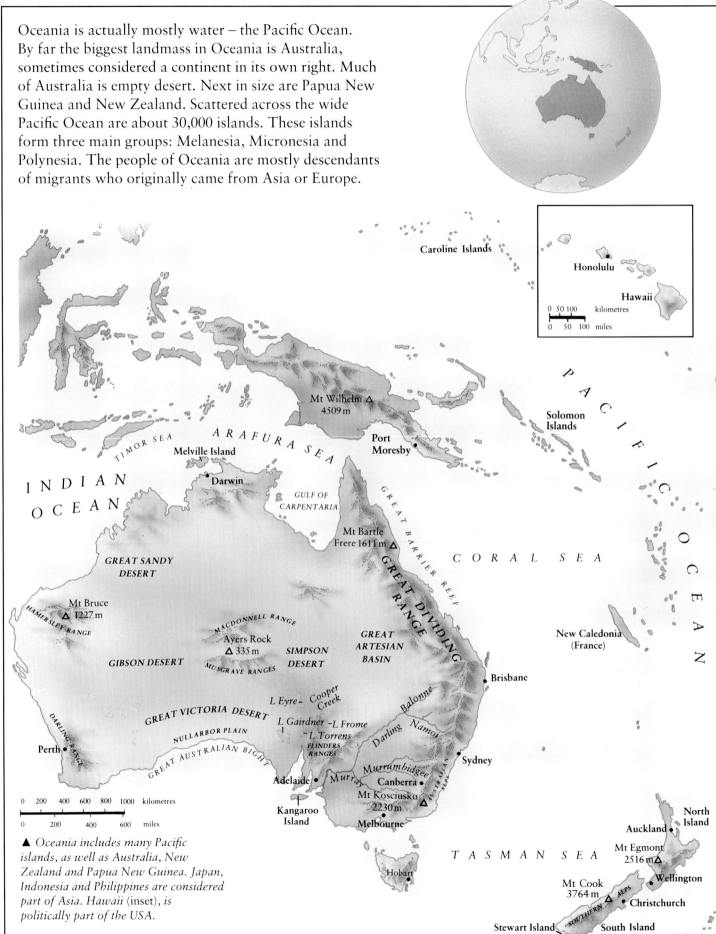

Caroline Islands

Honolulu

Hawaii

0 50 100   kilometres
0   50 100   miles

Mt Wilhelm △
4509 m

Solomon
Islands

Port
Moresby

TIMOR SEA   A R A F U R A   S E A

Melville Island

Darwin

I N D I A N
O C E A N

GULF OF
CARPENTARIA

P A C I F I C   O C E A N

C O R A L   S E A

Mt Bartle
Frere 1611 m △

GREAT BARRIER REEF

GREAT SANDY
DESERT

Mt Bruce
△ 1227 m

HAMERSLEY RANGE

MACDONNELL RANGE

Ayers Rock
△ 335 m

SIMPSON
DESERT

GREAT ARTESIAN
BASIN

GREAT DIVIDING RANGE

New Caledonia
(France)

GIBSON DESERT

MUSGRAVE RANGES

L Eyre Cooper
Creek

Brisbane

Balonne

GREAT VICTORIA DESERT

L Gairdner   L Frome

L Torrens

Darling

Namoi

NULLARBOR PLAIN

FLINDERS
RANGES

Perth

DARLING RANGE

GREAT AUSTRALIAN BIGHT

Murrumbidgee

Sydney

Murray

AUSTRALIAN ALPS

0   200   400   600   800 1000   kilometres

0   200   400   600   miles

Adelaide

Canberra

Mt Kosciusko
2230 m △

North
Island

Kangaroo
Island

Melbourne

Auckland

Mt Egmont
2516 m △

T A S M A N   S E A

▲ *Oceania includes many Pacific islands, as well as Australia, New Zealand and Papua New Guinea. Japan, Indonesia and Philippines are considered part of Asia. Hawaii (inset), is politically part of the USA.*

Hobart

Mt Cook
3764 m △

SOUTHERN ALPS

Wellington

Christchurch

Stewart Island

South Island

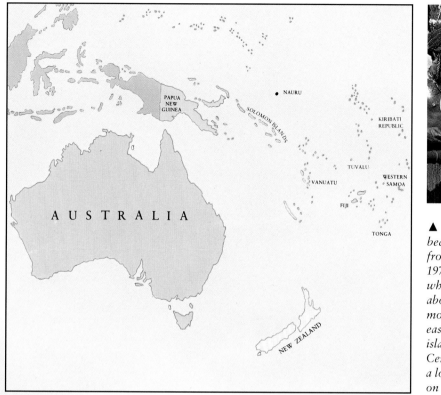

▲ *Papua New Guinea became independent from Australia in 1977. A country whose people speak about 700 languages, most of it occupies the eastern part of the island of New Guinea. Ceremonial dances are a longtime tradition on the islands.*

▼ *Australia's second largest city, Melbourne is a busy port and financial centre on the southeastern coast. Due to substantial post-war industrial growth, the city's population now includes people of Greek, Italian, Chinese and British origin.*

OCEANIC DATAFILE

Number of countries: 11
Biggest desert: Australian Desert (includes several deserts totalling 1.5 million sq km)
Highest mountain: Mt Wilhelm, Papua New Guinea, 4509 m
Longest river: Murray (Australia), 2575 km and its tributary, the Darling, 2740 km
Longest reef: Great Barrier Reef, Australia, over 2000 km long (longest in the world)
Largest country: Australia
Largest city (by population): Sydney (Australia). Other major cities: Melbourne, Adelaide, Perth, Brisbane, Hobart (all in Australia); Wellington, Auckland (both in New Zealand)

◄ *The British established six colonies in Australia from 1788–1859. When Australia became independent (1901) the colonies became states.*

► *The North Island of New Zealand has active volcanoes, spouting geysers and a region of bubbling hot thermal springs.*

COUNTRY	AREA (sq km)	POPULATION	CAPITAL	LANGUAGES
Australia	7,682,000	17,073,000	Canberra	English
Fiji	18,274	740,000	Suva	English, Fijian, Hindi
Kiribati	728	71,000	Bairiki	English, I-Kiribati
Nauru	21	9300	Domaneab	Nauruan, English
New Zealand	268,676	3,390,000	Wellington	English
Papua New Guinea	461,691	3,671,000	Port Moresby	English, local languages
Solomon Islands	28,370	319,000	Honiara	English, Pidgin
Tonga	699	96,300	Nuku'alofa	Tongan, English
Tuvalu	24	9100	Fongafale	Tuvaluan, English
Vanuatu	12,190	147,000	Vila	Bislama, English, French
Western Samoa	2831	165,000	Apia	Samoan, English

◀ A view of Sydney Harbour, Australia. The famous 1970s opera house (centre) confronts a steel arch bridge built in 1932.

▼ Ayers Rock in central Australia is an enormous solitary rock, 335 m high and 10 km around its base. It is a sacred place for the Aborigines.

THE GREAT BARRIER REEF
The world's longest reef, 2027 km long, is off the coast of Queensland, Australia. It is the biggest structure ever made by living creatures, and contains 350 different corals. The Great Barrier Reef is actually a chain of more than 2500 reefs and islands.

◀ Much of Australia is too dry for crop-raising, but is suitable for sheep-rearing. The world's longest fence is in Queensland, north-eastern Australia. Its 5500 km of wire was put up to protect sheep from attacks by dingos (wild dogs).

MAJOR PRODUCTS AND INDUSTRIES	CURRENCY
Minerals, machinery, foods, wool	Australian Dollar
Sugar, copra, fish, timber	Fiji Dollar
Copra, fish	Australian Dollar
Phosphates, financial services	Australian Dollar
Dairy foods, lamb, wool, fish	N Zealand Dollar
Copper, coffee, timber	Kina
Copra, cocoa, coconuts	Solomon Is. Dollar
Vanilla, vegetables, fish, coconuts	Pa'anga
Copra	Tuvalu Dollar
Copra, meat, cocoa, timber	Vatu
Coconut products, taro, timber	Tala

THE PACIFIC ISLANDS

It is estimated that there are between 20,000–30,000 islands in the Pacific Ocean. Easter Island is a remote speck of land 3800 km west of Chile in South America, from where the people who made its strange stone figures *(below)* probably came. Its current population is about 2000.

▲ *A fruit farm on Vitu Levu, or 'Great Fiji', the largest of 844 islands that make up the South Pacific state of Fiji. Only about 100 Fijian islands are inhabited.*

▼ *Fjordland is a region of spectacular scenery along the southwest coast of South Island, New Zealand. The fjords are long inlets cut into the land.*

Antarctica

Antarctica is larger than either Europe or Australia. It is a landmass, but it lies buried beneath a massive ice cap, which is on average 2000 m thick. Ice and snow cover 98 percent of Antarctica. Only a few mountains and rocky areas show above the ice cap. A small number of plants, insects and animals live on the mainland, but Antarctica has no permanent human population, although scientists work at research bases. The geographic South Pole is near the centre of Antarctica, on a high windy plateau.

ANTARCTIC DATAFILE

Number of countries: None, but several countries claim sectors of the continent
Area: About 14,000,000 sq km
Coastline: Measures almost 32,000 km
Highest point: Vinson Massif (5140 m)
Greatest mountain range: Transantarctic Mountains
Ice: The ice sheet has a volume of about 30 m sq km; deepest part is about 4800 m
Biggest glaciers: Amundsen, Beardmore, Lambert (world's longest), Scott
Largest ice shelf: Ross (up to 700 m thick)
Snowfall: About 60 cm a year at the coast, only 5 cm a year on the plateau
Lowest temperature: −89.2°C at Vostok Research Base, 1983

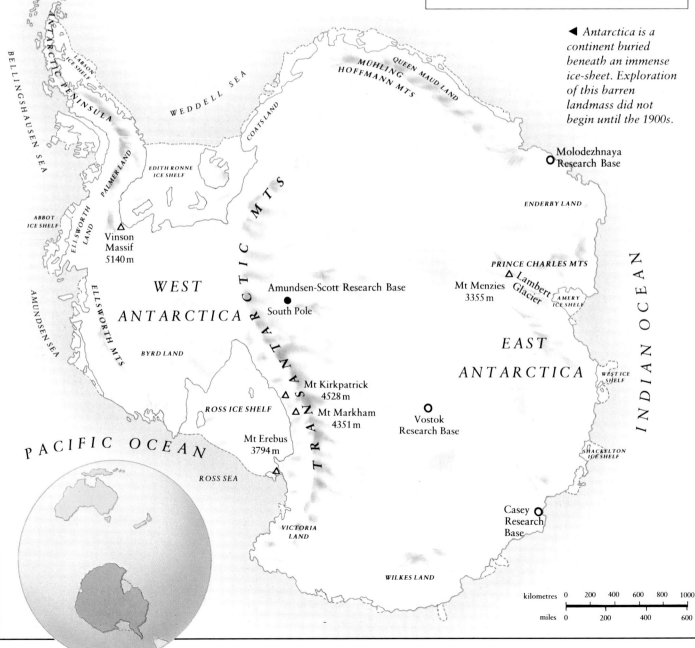

◀ *Antarctica is a continent buried beneath an immense ice-sheet. Exploration of this barren landmass did not begin until the 1900s.*

ATLANTIC OCEAN

ANTARCTIC PENINSULA

BELLINGHAUSEN SEA

LARSEN ICE SHELF

WEDDELL SEA

COATS LAND

MÜHLING HOFFMANN MTS

QUEEN MAUD LAND

Molodezhnaya Research Base

ENDERBY LAND

PALMER LAND

EDITH RONNE ICE SHELF

ABBOT ICE SHELF

ELLSWORTH LAND

Vinson Massif 5140 m

PRINCE CHARLES MTS

Lambert Glacier

Mt Menzies 3355 m

AMERY ICE SHELF

WEST ANTARCTICA

Amundsen-Scott Research Base

South Pole

AMUNDSEN SEA

ELLSWORTH MTS

BYRD LAND

TRANSANTARCTIC MTS

EAST ANTARCTICA

WEST ICE SHELF

INDIAN OCEAN

Mt Kirkpatrick 4528 m

Mt Markham 4351 m

Vostok Research Base

ROSS ICE SHELF

PACIFIC OCEAN

Mt Erebus 3794 m

ROSS SEA

SHACKELTON ICE SHELF

VICTORIA LAND

Casey Research Base

WILKES LAND

kilometres	0	200	400	600	800	1000

miles	0	200	400	600

▲ *An iceberg dwarfs a fishing boat. The biggest Antarctic iceberg ever seen was bigger than Belgium, covering 31,000 sq km.*

▶ *A colony of King penguins in the Antarctic. These flightless birds are the continent's largest non-human inhabitants.*

▲ *Mt Erebus on Ross Island is Antarctica's largest active volcano. From time to time it spews up volcanic rock. Its peak is 3794 m high.*

▼ *This member of the British Antarctic Survey is one of many scientists trying to protect Antarctica and the wildlife on its coasts from exploitation.*

EXPLORING ANTARCTICA

European sailors first sighted Antarctica in the early 1800s. In 1911 Roald Amundsen of Norway led the first explorers to the South Pole, beating a British expedition led by Robert F. Scott by five weeks. Scott and his men all died on the return journey. In 1929, the American Navy officer Richard Byrd flew over the South Pole for the first time. In 1957–1958 a British Commonwealth expedition, led by the British geologist Vivian Fuchs, made the first overland crossing of the continent.

▲ *Amundsen's party reached the South Pole in December 1911. Using skis and sled dogs, all the men returned safely.*

Countries

In the past, the boundaries of a people's territory were set either by natural barriers such as rivers or mountains, or by the power of its ruler. The idea of the nation-state, of people united by common laws, languages and customs, only developed gradually. But nationalism is a powerful but dangerous idea: it fired the American War of Independence and created new European countries in the 1800s. States are still being made and un-made. As people shift allegiances, the world map is once again redrawn.

THE ROMAN WORLD

The Roman Empire at its peak covered much of Europe, North Africa and the Mediterranean. Rome was the heart of an empire which included a number of tribes and kingdoms, first by conquest and then by the imposition of Roman law. There were no countries within the Roman Empire, only peoples.

▼ *Countries break records in many ways. Some are very big with many millions of inhabitants: at over 17 million sq km, Russia is easily the world's biggest country by area, while China has by far the most people. Other countries get into the record books because they are tiny: Monaco, a principality on the coast of southern France, has an area of only 1.9 sq km; it also has the shortest coastline of any country.*

TEN LARGEST COUNTRIES

1 Russia	17,075,400 sq km
2 Canada	9,970,610 sq km
3 China	9,572,900 sq km
4 USA	9,372,571 sq km
5 Brazil	8,511,965 sq km
6 Australia	7,682,000 sq km
7 India	3,166,414 sq km
8 Argentina	2,766,889 sq km
9 Sudan	2,508,813 sq km
10 Algeria	2,381,714 sq km

TEN SMALLEST COUNTRIES

1 Vatican City State	0.44 sq km
2 Monaco	1.9 sq km
3 Nauru	21 sq km
4 Tuvalu	24 sq km
5 San Marino	61 sq km
6 Liechtenstein	160 sq km
7 St Kitts-Nevis	269 sq km
8 Maldives	298 sq km
9 Malta	316 sq km
10 Grenada	344 sq km

THE AMERICAS

1 BELIZE
2 HONDURAS
3 NICARAGUA
4 GUATEMALA
5 EL SALVADOR
6 COSTA RICA
7 PANAMA
8 HAITI
9 DOMINICAN REPUBLIC
10 PUERTO RICO
11 GUYANA
12 SURINAME
13 FRENCH GUIANA
14 PARAGUAY
15 URUGUAY
16 ECUADOR

► *This map shows the world today. Political borders and country names can change dramatically, as happened when the Soviet Union broke up in the early 1990s.*

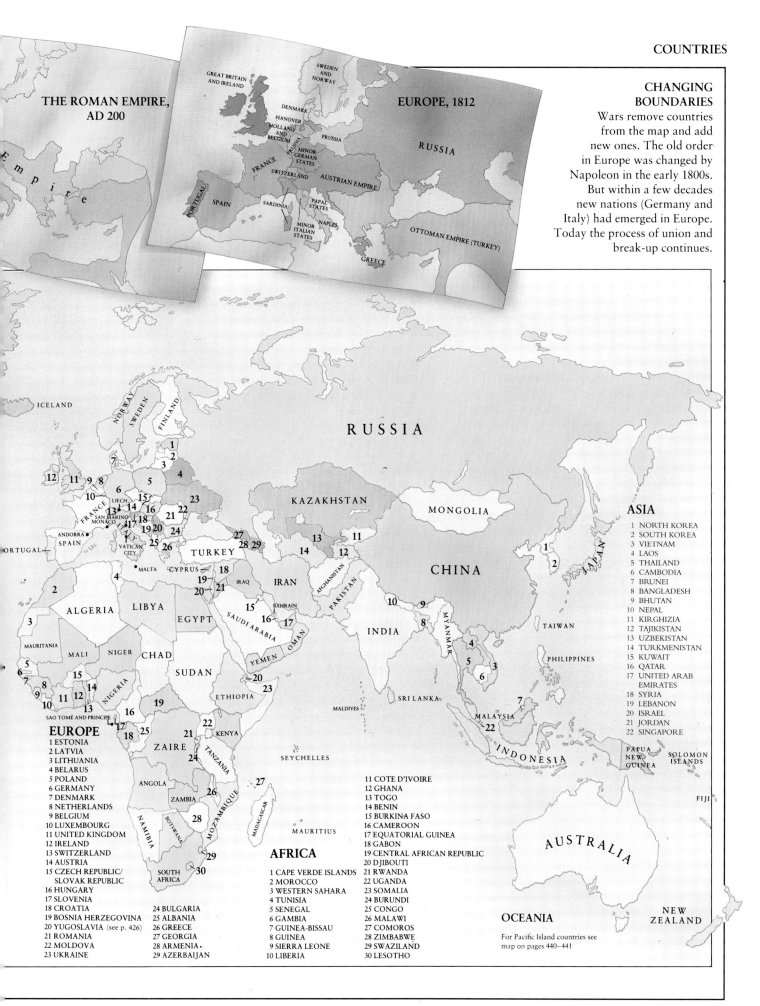

CULTURES

Population

Culture embraces many aspects of human life: art, religion, customs, language, technology. Cultures are amazingly diverse, even though in the 20th century 'world culture' (that is, western industrial culture) has touched almost every human group from the Amazon to the Arctic. Every year there are about 90 million extra people to share that culture. The human population grew slowly until the 1800s, since when the rate of increase has quickened dramatically. However, population growth is not the same worldwide. In the more prosperous countries birth rates roughly match the numbers of deaths, so that populations stay stable or grow only slowly. In developing countries, birth rates far outstrip death rates and consequently many of these countries have populations growing at two to three percent a year.

POPULATION DISTRIBUTION

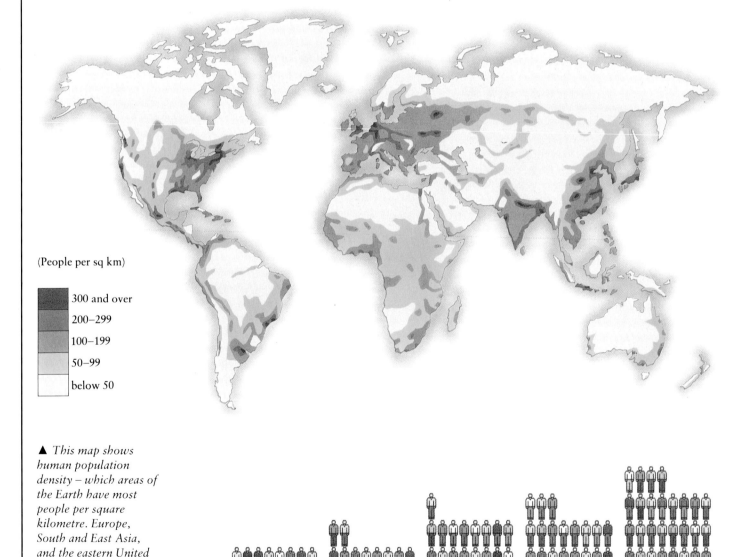

(People per sq km)

- 300 and over
- 200–299
- 100–199
- 50–99
- below 50

▲ *This map shows human population density – which areas of the Earth have most people per square kilometre. Europe, South and East Asia, and the eastern United States are the most densely populated regions in the world.*

AD 1	AD 1000	1500	1600	1750
200 million	255 million	420 million	470 million	700 million

ANNUAL RATES OF INCREASE

World	1.7%
Africa	3.0%
South America	1.9%
Asia	1.8%
Oceania	1.4%
North America	1.2%
Europe	0.2%

The world's population is rising fastest in the so-called developing world, particularly in Africa. In Kenya the population doubles every 18 to 23 years. But in some Western countries (Sweden, for example) the population is actually falling.

POPULATION DISTRIBUTION (*Right*)
Of the seven continents, Asia has by far the most people. Nearly six out of ten people live in Asia. Between them China and India have nearly 40 percent of all the world's people.

POPULATION EXPLOSION (*Below*)
The growth of human population was slow until the 1700s. It doubled from the mid-1600s to 1850, and has more than quadrupled since then. In 1950 the Earth's population was about 2.5 billion. In the year 2000 it will be over six billion.

 = 25 million people

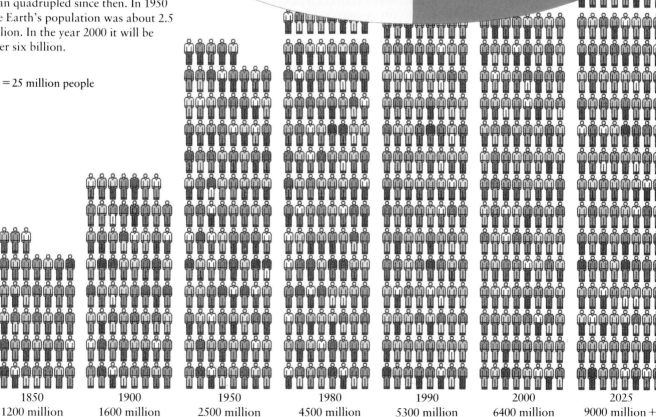

▲ *The Earth's five billion people occupy only about 15 percent of the planet's land area. Vast areas of the Earth are either too hot and dry, or too cold to support permanent human populations.*

Oceania
26 million

North and
Central America
420 million

Asia
3100 million

South America
290 million

Europe (inc Russia)
646 million

Africa
795 million

1850	1900	1950	1980	1990	2000	2025
1200 million	1600 million	2500 million	4500 million	5300 million	6400 million	9000 million +

Cities

In 1800 no more than one in every 20 people lived in a city. Most people lived in villages. City growth accelerated in the 1800s and today 8 in 20 people are city-dwellers. By the 2000s there will be more people living in towns and cities than in the countryside. People moving into towns in large numbers cause problems of inadequate housing, transport, food supply, public health and employment. In the developing countries in particular, there are insufficient resources to cope with these problems.

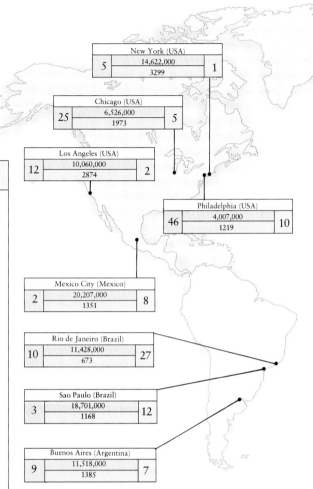

	New York (USA)	
5	14,622,000	1
	3299	

	Chicago (USA)	
25	6,526,000	5
	1973	

	Los Angeles (USA)	
12	10,060,000	2
	2874	

	Philadelphia (USA)	
46	4,007,000	10
	1219	

	Mexico City (Mexico)	
2	20,207,000	8
	1351	

	Rio de Janeiro (Brazil)	
10	11,428,000	27
	673	

	Sao Paulo (Brazil)	
3	18,701,000	12
	1168	

	Buenos Aires (Argentina)	
9	11,518,000	7
	1385	

FACTS ABOUT CITIES

- The world's oldest capital city is Damascus in Syria. It has been inhabited for about 4500 years.
- In 1800 less than three percent of the world's population lived in towns and cities. By the year 2000 it is expected that 50 percent of the world's population will live in cities or large towns.
- Cities grew rapidly in Europe and North America in the 1800s, during the Industrial Revolution. For example, Chicago in the USA grew from a town of 4000 people in 1840 to a booming city of more than one million inhabitants in 1890.
- Fires and earthquakes have devastated even the greatest cities. London's Great Fire of 1666 burned for six days. In 1906 an earthquake shook San Francisco in the USA. Fires broke out and more than 28,000 buildings were destroyed and about 3000 people died.
- Tokyo-Yokohama in Japan and Mexico City in Mexico rank as the two biggest urban areas in the world. Both have populations of more than 20 million people.
- India has two of the world's fastest-growing cities. By the year 2000 Calcutta and Bombay will probably rank fourth and fifth in the world, each topping 16 million people.

- Where are a city's limits? This is not always easy to say. Some city limits are fixed so they do not overlap neighbouring towns. Others include such towns, creating much larger metropolitan areas.
- Africa's biggest cities include Cairo (Egypt) 9.8 million people; Lagos (Nigeria), Alexandria (Egypt), Kinshasa (Zaïre), and Casablanca (Morocco) all have populations of over 2 million people.
- The biggest city in Australia is Sydney (about 3 million people).
- São Paulo, Brazil, is South America's largest city. Its metropolitan population is over 18.5 million.

▶ *Fast city growth often causes acute housing shortages. The self-built shacks in the* favelas *(slums) provide shelter for poor people on the hillsides around Rio de Janeiro in Brazil.*

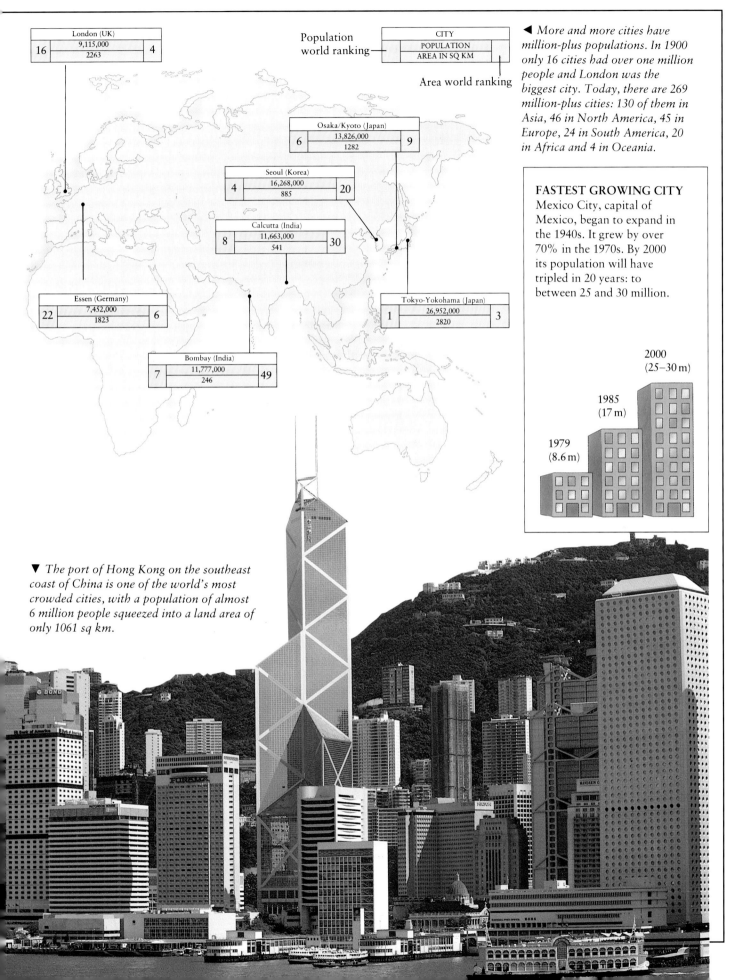

London (UK)		
16	9,115,000	4
	2263	

Population world ranking	CITY	Area world ranking
	POPULATION	
	AREA IN SQ KM	

Osaka/Kyoto (Japan)		
6	13,826,000	9
	1282	

Seoul (Korea)		
4	16,268,000	20
	885	

Calcutta (India)		
8	11,663,000	30
	541	

Essen (Germany)		
22	7,452,000	6
	1823	

Tokyo-Yokohama (Japan)		
1	26,952,000	3
	2820	

Bombay (India)		
7	11,777,000	49
	246	

◀ *More and more cities have million-plus populations. In 1900 only 16 cities had over one million people and London was the biggest city. Today, there are 269 million-plus cities: 130 of them in Asia, 46 in North America, 45 in Europe, 24 in South America, 20 in Africa and 4 in Oceania.*

FASTEST GROWING CITY
Mexico City, capital of Mexico, began to expand in the 1940s. It grew by over 70% in the 1970s. By 2000 its population will have tripled in 20 years: to between 25 and 30 million.

2000
(25–30 m)

1985
(17 m)

1979
(8.6 m)

▼ *The port of Hong Kong on the southeast coast of China is one of the world's most crowded cities, with a population of almost 6 million people squeezed into a land area of only 1061 sq km.*

Peoples

We all belong to the same species, *Homo sapiens sapiens*. Over many thousands of years people living in different parts of the Earth developed different characteristics. Groups of people that share the same characteristics belong to the same race. Their physical features are the result of heredity, the passing on of resemblances from parents to children through genetic inheritance. So members of a racial group are 'related' biologically in the same way as members of a family group are related.

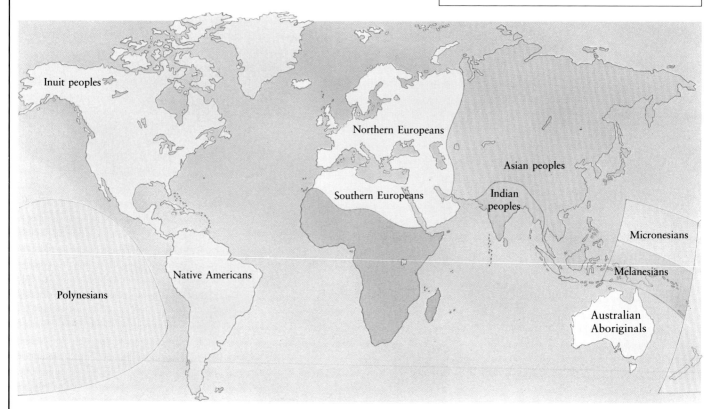

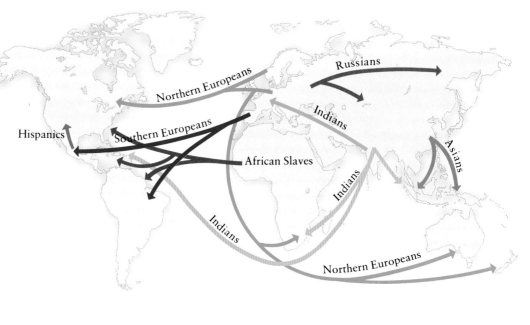

▲ This map shows the areas of the world where the main geographical races lived before the 1500s. They developed in comparative isolation, separated from one another by oceans, mountains and deserts.

► From the 1500s on, overseas exploration and mass migration altered the population map. For example, about half as many people of European descent now live outside Europe as in Europe. Arrows show major migrations.

HUMAN VARIATION
The United States' racial blend is the result of thousands of years of migration, colonization and slavery. On streets in cities such as New York you can see a varied population of predominantly English-speaking Americans whose ancestors came from Europe, Asia, South and Central America, Africa and the Pacific and Caribbean islands.

WORLDWIDE AGE DISTRIBUTION
In the developing world (countries in Africa and Asia), an average of about 37 percent of the total population is made up of children under 15 years old. However, in some African countries, the proportion of children is even higher – about 45 percent of the total population. This figure is based on the calculation that the average woman in Africa has more than 6 children.

DEVELOPING COUNTRY
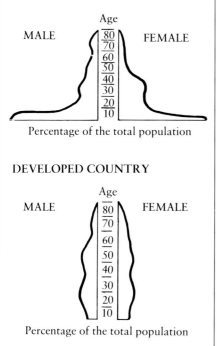

DEVELOPED COUNTRY

LIFE EXPECTANCY (1989)

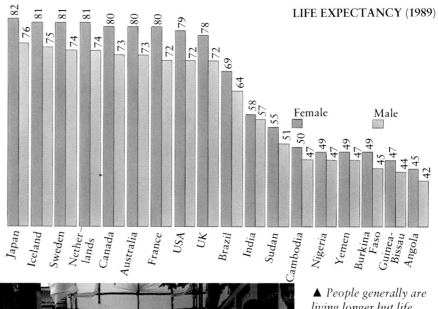

Female   Male

Japan 82/76, Iceland 81/76, Sweden 81/75, Netherlands 81/74, Canada 80/74, Australia 80/73, France 80/73, USA 79/72, UK 78/72, Brazil 69/64, India 58/57, Sudan 55/51, Cambodia 50/47, Nigeria 49/47, Yemen 49/47, Burkina Faso 49/45, Guinea-Bissau 47/44, Angola 45/42

▲ People generally are living longer but life expectancy varies greatly. Women everywhere live longer than men. The deaths of infants and of mothers in childbirth partly explain the difference between the developed and developing countries.

◄ In the developing world health workers in clinics (here administering vaccinations in Bangladesh) can cut child mortality rates, combat malnutrition, and check disease.

Languages

The world's people speak between 4000 and 5000 languages and dialects (local variations of a language). About 845 of these languages are spoken in India. The language spoken by most people in the world is Mandarin Chinese. English is the most widely spoken language. All languages change so long as people speak them. New words are added, others fall out of use. In a few hundred years, a language can become totally different. A language no longer spoken is called dead.

MAJOR LANGUAGE GROUPS

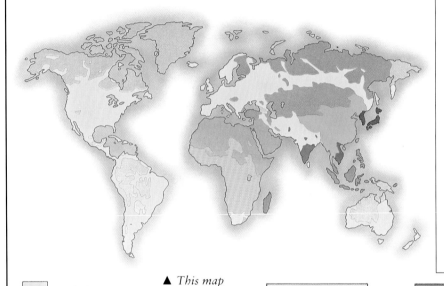

Indo-European
Sino-Tibetan
Black African
Malayo-Polynesian
Afro-Asian
Dravidian
Japanese & Korean
Uralic & Altaic
Mon-Khmer
Other Languages

▲ *This map shows the chief language groups and where they are most widely spoken. Almost half the world's peoples speak Indo-European languages. This group originated among peoples living in the area from northern India to Europe.*

FACTS ABOUT LANGUAGE

- Korean appears to be unrelated to any other language.
- Papua New Guinea has a remarkably large number of languages – over 700.
- Every language has the vowel sound 'a', as pronounced in the English word 'father'.
- Many words change languages. For example, English has borrowed planet (Greek), video (Latin), algebra (Arabic), chocolate (Native American), thug (Hindi) and knife (Norse) among others.

▼ *Most Canadians speak English but in Quebec, where 95% of the people have French ancestors, French is usually spoken.*

LANGUAGE FAMILIES

All languages within a family have developed from an original parent language. Indo-European has eight groups or branches, shown in the 'family tree' (*right*). English belongs to the Germanic branch, which also includes German, Dutch and the Scandinavian languages. Other language branches, such as Albanian, have no offshoots.

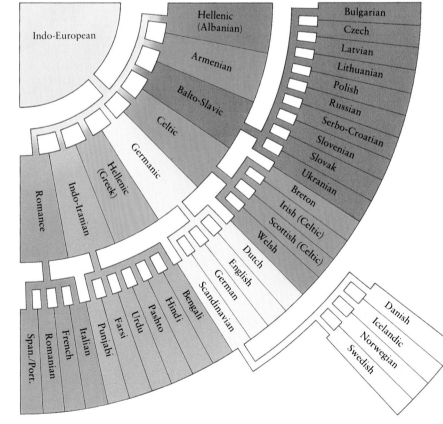

Indo-European

Hellenic (Albanian)
Armenian
Balto-Slavic
Celtic
Germanic
Hellenic (Greek)
Indo-Iranian
Romance

Bulgarian
Czech
Latvian
Lithuanian
Polish
Russian
Serbo-Croatian
Slovenian
Slovak
Ukranian
Breton
Irish (Celtic)
Scottish (Celtic)
Welsh
Dutch
English
German
Scandinavian

Bengali
Hindi
Pashto
Urdu
Punjabi
Farsi
Italian
French
Romanian
Span./Port.

Danish
Icelandic
Norwegian
Swedish

ALPHABETS

An alphabet is a collection of letters or signs that stand for sounds in speech. Alphabets were developed from ancient picture-writing systems. The oldest letter is 'O', unchanged in shape since it was used by the Phoenicians over 3000 years ago.

▲ *Egyptian hieroglyphs or picture-signs are about 5000 years old. The earliest signs represented objects.*

Russian

АБВГДЕЖЗИЙКЛМНОПРСТУФХЦЧ ШЩЪЫЬЭЮЯ

Greek

ΑΒΓΔΕΖΗΘΙΚΛΜΝΞΟΠΡΣΤΥΦΧ ΨΩ

Arabic

ابتثجحخدذرزسشصضطظغغفقكلمنهوي لا

Bengali

আমাদের পোস্টমাস্টার কলিকাতার ছেলে । জলের মাছকে ডাঙ্গায় তজলিলে যেরষ অবস্থা হয় এই গণ্ড ধগরামের মধ্যে আসিয়া পোস্টমাস্টারেরও সেই দশা

ARTIFICIAL LANGUAGES

Sign language is communication without speech. Finger-signing is a language used by deaf people.

'C' in both American and British sign language

'D' in British sign language

● There have been many attempts to invent artificial languages, such as Volapuk (1879) and Esperanto (1887). The inventors hoped a new language would help to break down old national rivalries.

● Esperanto has been the most successful artificial language, with some 10 million speakers. It has a 28-letter alphabet and its vocabulary contains many words common to the Indo-European group of languages. It was devised by a Pole, L.L. Zamenhof.

● Blind people can read and type using Braille, an alphabet of raised dots on paper invented by a young blind Frenchman, Louis Braille, in the 1820s. Blind people read Braille by running their fingertips over the dots. They can write Braille on a machine known as a Braillewriter.

OTHER IMPORTANT LANGUAGES

Afrikaans: From 17th-century Dutch; spoken by many in South Africa.
Gaelic: Spoken in Ireland and Scotland.
Greek: Many English words derive from ancient Greek.
Hebrew/Yiddish: Hebrew is the language of the Bible and modern Israel.

Latin: Originally language of the ancient Romans.
Sanskrit: Language of ancient India, from *c*.1500 BC.
Pidgin: Mixture of English and local words in the Pacific islands and New Guinea.
Creole: French, Spanish and Portuguese mixed with local words in the Americas.

THE WORLD'S MAJOR LANGUAGES

Mandarin, or standardized northern Chinese, is spoken by more people than any other language. English is the language spoken in most countries (Australia, Canada, the Caribbean, Ireland, New Zealand, the UK and the USA). English is also widely used in parts of Africa and Asia. Hindi is the most widely spoken language of India. Spanish and Portuguese are spoken in Latin America, as well as in Spain and Portugal.

Millions of persons

Chinese 845 m — 900
— 800
— 700
English 485 m — 600
— 500
— 400
Russian 291 m
Spanish 331 m
Hindi 338 m — 300
Malay-Indonesian 117 m
French 118 m
Japanese 124 m
German 138 m
Portuguese 171 m
Bengali 181 m
Arabic 192 m — 200
— 100
— 0

Religions

People in all times and cultures have tried to find the meaning of life. From this desire grew religious belief. Early religions were based on the worship of natural forces (the Sun, wind and fire) and animals. Some religions have many gods; for example, modern Hinduism. Other faiths teach belief in one supreme god. Religion gives believers a moral code and the concept of a spiritual world beyond the earthly one. An atheist is a person who holds no religious belief; an agnostic is someone who is undecided.

EARLY RELIGIONS

Early tribal religions, found worldwide, often involve beliefs in magic, witchcraft, and powerful spirits who may be good or evil and who dwell in animals, plants, rocks and water.

Polynesian head-dress worn in religious ceremonies

MAJOR RELIGIONS

Christian Cross

Crescent Moon

Hindu god Siva

Statue of the Buddha

Taoist symbol of *yin* and *yang*

CHRISTIANITY
Christianity is based on the life and teachings of Jesus Christ, born c.4 BC in Palestine and crucified by the Romans in c.AD 30. Christians believe that Jesus was the Son of God. Most Christians belong to one of three major groups: the Protestant, Roman Catholic or Eastern Orthodox Churches.

ISLAM
Founded in Arabia by the Prophet Muhammad in AD 622, the Islamic faith is derived largely from Judaism and Christianity. Islam's most sacred book is the Koran and its symbols are the crescent and the star. Followers of Islam are called Muslims, who submit to the will of God (Allah).

HINDUISM
Hinduism is an ancient Indian religion with no known founder. It is the major religion in India and has had an important effect on Indian culture. Hindus worship many gods, most Hindus believing that all gods are aspects of Brahman, one universal spirit. They also believe in reincarnation of the soul after death.

BUDDHISM
Buddhism is based on the teachings of an Indian, Siddhartha Gautama, in the 5th century BC. The name Buddha means 'Enlightened One'. Buddhists do not believe in any god. Instead, they believe that people can attain enlightenment (nirvana) through meditation and the right actions.

CHINESE
Taoism or Daoism is based on the teachings of Lao-tze who lived in China in the 6th century BC. Believers yield to Tao, the 'way' to restore harmony. The other Chinese ideology, Confucianism (from Confucius, also 500s BC), is a code of family and social behaviour rather than a mystical faith.

THE CITY OF MECCA
Islam has a number of holy cities, but none more sacred to Muslims than Mecca in Saudi Arabia, Muhammad's birthplace and the city from which he began his escape to Medina in AD 622. At least a million Muslims travel as pilgrims to Mecca every year; all Muslims are required to make a pilgrimage to Mecca once in their lifetime, if able to do so. The city's most sacred site is the Kaaba, a shrine that stands in the courtyard of the Great Mosque.

▲ *The Kaaba contains the Black Stone, by tradition given to Abraham by the angel Gabriel.*

OTHER RELIGIONS
Baha'i (Persian): founded in the 1800s in what is now Iraq. The founder was a Persian, Bahaullah.
Jainism (Indian): a sect of Hinduism, that teaches non-violence to all creatures.
Shinto (Japanese): Japan's oldest surviving religion. Shintoists worship their many gods (*kani*) at shrines or temples.

A Shinto pagoda (temple) in Japan

Membership of principal religions mid-1990

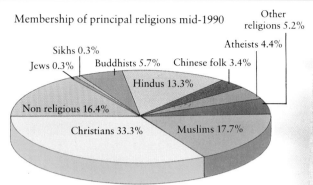

- Other religions 5.2%
- Sikhs 0.3%
- Jews 0.3%
- Buddhists 5.7%
- Hindus 13.3%
- Atheists 4.4%
- Chinese folk 3.4%
- Muslims 17.7%
- Christians 33.3%
- Non religious 16.4%

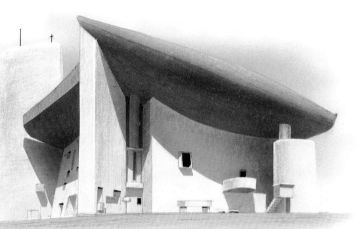

Star of David

Symbol of Sikhism

▲ *The pilgrimage chapel of Notre Dame du Haut is at Ronchamps in eastern France. The chapel is celebrated for its highly original style of church architecture; it was designed by France's most famous 20th-century architect, Le Corbusier, in the early 1950s.*

▼ *The Golden Temple in the sacred city of Amritsar in India is the holiest place of Sikh devotion. The city was built in the 1500s by the fourth Sikh guru (teacher), Ram Das. The temple stands on an island in a pool of fresh water, known as the 'tank of immortality'.*

JUDAISM

The ancient religion of the Jews, founded by Moses and Abraham, was the first religion to teach that there is one God. The main laws of Judaism come from the Torah, the first five books of the Hebrew Bible (the Christian Old Testament). Jews worship in synagogues and in their homes; many Jews follow strict dietary laws.

SIKHISM

A religion of India, the Sikhs' faith was first taught by Guru (teacher) Nanak (1469–1539). Nine gurus followed Nanak, but only God is considered the true guru. Sikhs have five 'k' symbols: kesh (uncut hair), kangha (comb), kara (bracelet), kaccha (breeches) and kirpan (dagger).

RELIGIONS GLOSSARY

Bible: the holy book of both Christians and Jews.
Caste: religious and social division in Hinduism.
Church: place of Christian worship, or organized Christian group.
Fast: giving up food and drink as a part of religious observance.
Hajj: the Islamic pilgrimage to Mecca.
Monks and nuns: men and women, usually living in communities, who take religious vows.

Mosque: the place where Muslims worship.
Pope: head of the Roman Catholic Church.
Orthodox Church: the Eastern Christian Church that split from the Western Church in the 4th century; national Church of Russia, Greece and Romania.
Protestant: a member of one of the Christian Churches that split from the Roman Catholic Church after the Reformation in the 1500s.

Rabbi: a Jewish religious leader or teacher.
Saint: a holy person worthy of worship.
Vedas: oldest and most sacred books of Hinduism.
Zoroastrianism: ancient religion of Iran founded by Zoroaster in the 6th *c.*BC.

▶ *The Church of the Holy Family is in Barcelona in Spain. The architect, Antonio Gaudi, died in 1926 while construction was still in progress.*

Customs and Celebrations

In all human societies, people mark the passage of time and the seasons by observing customs – such as having a feast to celebrate a good harvest. Our lives are marked by celebrations and festivals. We celebrate personal or family events, such as a birthday or a wedding. We observe national or religious holidays. Some of these customs are ancient. Their original meaning is forgotten as new beliefs and practices become more important. The variety of these celebrations adds colour and significance to our lives.

NON-RELIGIOUS FESTIVALS

Festivals usually take place once a year and last for at least a day. These include New Year, national holidays, independence days and bank holidays. Some festivals are connected to the history of a country, while others derive from seasonal feasts. Many festivals have moved far from their religious origins. For example, Hallowe'en came from an early pagan festival, associated with the onset of winter and death. In the Middle Ages this became the Christian festival of All Saints' Day on 1 November. The mass said on this day was *Allhallowmas* and the evening before became known as *Allhalloe'en*. In modern times, All Saints' Day (*Allhallowmas*) is still a religious feast day but in countries such as the USA and the UK Hallowe'en is a time when children dress up and play 'trick or treat'.

▲ *Once a Christian festival, Hallowe'en on 31st October is now when children carve Jack-o'-lanterns (hollowed-out pumpkins) and attend Hallowe'en parties.*

▼ *The eggs that are exchanged and eaten in many countries at Easter traditionally represent the renewal of life.*

▼ *The procession before the Palio horse races in Siena, Italy, has been held annually for hundreds of years.*

▲ *At carnival time in Rio de Janeiro, people in bright costumes fill the streets. Carnival or Mardi Gras marks the start of Lent.*

▼ *Every major religion has festivals or days of celebration. Some involve acts of pilgrimage by believers to holy places.*

MAJOR RELIGIOUS FESTIVALS

CHRISTIANITY

Christmas: celebrates the birth of Christ. Customs such as Christmas trees and Father Christmas come from old midwinter festivals.
Easter: celebrates Christ's death and resurrection. More important than Christmas in the Orthodox Churches.

ANIMAL	YEAR (The Chinese New Year starts in January or February)				
Rat	1936	1948	1960	1972	1984
Ox	1937	1949	1961	1973	1985
Tiger	1938	1950	1962	1974	1986
Hare (Rabbit)	1939	1951	1963	1975	1987
Dragon	1940	1952	1964	1976	1988
Snake	1941	1953	1965	1977	1989
Horse	1942	1954	1966	1978	1990
Sheep (Goat)	1943	1955	1967	1979	1991
Monkey	1944	1956	1968	1980	1992
Rooster	1945	1957	1969	1981	1993
Dog	1946	1958	1970	1982	1994
Pig	1947	1959	1971	1983	1995

SOME FESTIVALS AND SPECIAL DAYS

January:	New Year's Day
	Martin Luther King Day (USA)
February:	St Valentine's Day
March:	St David's Day (Wales)
	St Patrick's Day (Irl/USA)
	Mothering Sunday
April:	April Fool's Day
	St George's Day (England)
May:	May Day
June:	Father's Day (USA/Can/UK)
July:	Independence Day (USA)
	Bastille Day (France)
September:	Labor Day (USA)
October:	Oktoberfest (Germany),
	Hallowe'en
November:	Armistice/Veterans' Day
	Thanksgiving Day (USA)
	St Andrew's Day (Scotland)
December:	Boxing Day (UK/Canada)
	New Year's Eve
	(Hogmanay in Scotland)

▲ *The Chinese calendar is based on the lunar year. It begins at 2637 BC (traditionally, the year of its invention by the first emperor). The years run in cycles of 60, and involve the names of 12 animals.*

▶ *On every 4th July, Independence Day in the USA, Americans enjoy parades, picnics, pageants and fireworks.*

BUDDHISM

Wesak or Vesakha-puja: (Sri Lanka and Thailand) celebrates the birth, enlightenment and death of Buddha.
Flower festival: (Japan) celebrates Buddha's birth.
Rites of passage: (Japan) a child's coming of age.

JUDAISM

Rosh Hashanah: Jewish New Year.
Passover: commemorates the Exodus from Egypt.
Hanukkah and Purim: God's deliverance of the Jews in 165 BC.
Yom Kippur: a day of regret for faults.

HINDUISM

Navarati: in honour of goddess Shakti.
Dusserah: honouring Prince Rama.
Holi: an exuberant spring festival.
Diwali: festival of lights. There are many regional festivals.

ISLAM

The Great Festival: a time of sacrifice and giving to the poor after pilgrimage to the city of Mecca (which all Muslims try to make).
The Lesser Festival: Breaking of the Fast – marking the end of the fasting month of Ramadan.

Arts and Crafts

The visual arts, painting and sculpture, are ancient arts: there are carvings and cave paintings over 15,000 years old. Pottery and architecture developed when people first became settled farmers, about 10,000 years ago. The performing arts include music, dance, theatre and cinema. The first three all have their origins in our prehistoric past; cinema (and radio and television) are 19th and 20th-century inventions. Literature began with spoken story-telling; writing was only invented some 5000 years ago.

VISUAL ARTS

The visual arts include painting, sculpture, ceramics and textiles. Traditional arts (carpets or masks, for example) may change little in style over the centuries. Painters and sculptors have constantly sought fresh ways to express their vision of the world.

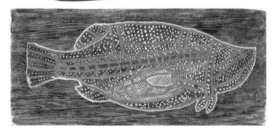

◀ *Venetians have been known for their beautiful glass-making since the 1200s.*

▲ *This selection of crafts from around the world includes a rug made by the Navajo people of New Mexico and Arizona (above); a neck ornament in gold and silver (right) from Kashmir in Asia and a bark painting (left) made by an Aboriginal artist in Australia.*

▲ *An American porcelain plate. Fine porcelain is also made in Europe and Asia.*

◀ *A ceremonial mask made by the BaLuba of Central Africa.*

THE PERFORMING ARTS

Dance was originally part of tribal ritual. It developed into drama – literature acted out with words and often accompanied by music. Western drama began in ancient Greece some 2500 years ago. Eastern drama includes the Kabuki and Noh theatre of Japan. The earliest written music is Indian, 3000 years old. Ballet and opera developed in Europe during the 1400s and 1500s.

◀ *Kabuki actors in Japan, where these colourful melodramas have been performed since the 1600s.*

▶ *A musician plays an important instrument in Indian music, the sitar or Indian lute.*

FACTS ABOUT THE ARTS

- English writers did not use English before the 1300s. Geoffrey Chaucer's *Canterbury Tales* (*c.*1387) was a landmark in the use of everyday language.
- About 800,000 people heard an open-air concert by the New York Philharmonic Orchestra in Central Park, New York, in 1986. This is thought to be the largest ever audience for a classical concert.
- Before graphite pencils became available in the 1600s, artists sketched with a metal silverpoint on prepared paper.
- The oldest piano in the world is one made by the Italian Bartolommeo Cristofori in 1720; it is now in New York's Metropolitan Museum.
- The largest library in the world is the United States Library of Congress with 97.5 million items.
- Walt Disney (1906–1966), the American cartoon-film maker, won a record total of 32 Oscar awards for his work.
- Wood-carving is probably the best known form of African sculpture. But artists in the Benin kingdom in West Africa (1500–1700) produced superb metalwork.
- The first purpose-built cinema was opened at the Atlanta Show in Georgia, USA, in 1895.
- The most successful pop group to date are the Beatles (John Lennon, Paul McCartney, Ringo Starr and George Harrison) with sales of over 1000 million tapes and discs as a group, and millions more as solo performers.

▶ *Watched by an audience of about 200,000 in Berlin, Germany, Pink Floyd's performance of 'The Wall' in 1990 was the biggest ever rock concert, involving 600 performers.*

LITERATURE

The first writings were practical records and business documents. Creative writing came later, in the form of songs and stories recording epic deeds, great kings and ancient folk-memories. Poetry (easier to recite and remember) came before prose. All major languages of East and West have literatures, each with their own major dramatists, novelists and poets. Critics generally agree that the English dramatist William Shakespeare (1564–1616) is the world's greatest playwright. As well as plays such as *Romeo and Juliet*, *Hamlet*, *Macbeth* and *A Midsummer's Night Dream*, he is also known for his poetry, such as the *Sonnets* (1609).

ARTS FESTIVALS

In the past, artists such as musicians and painters were often supported by wealthy patrons. Today, few artists can expect such backing. Arts festivals provide venues for artists to come together to exhibit and perform. Some festivals specialize: the Newport Jazz Festival in Rhode Island, USA, for example, or the Salzburg Music Festival in Austria which celebrates the music of Mozart. Others, such as Scotland's Edinburgh Festival, are showplaces for artists and performers from the theatre, musical arts, visual arts, comedy and literature.

▶ *The annual Edinburgh Festival Fringe – which includes music, art, drama and comedy – is the world's biggest arts festival.*

All Arts:	Edinburgh (Scotland)
	Avignon (France)
	Osaka (Japan)
Film:	Cannes (France)
	Berlin (Germany)
	Venice (Italy)
Music:	Salzburg [Mozart] (Austria)
	Bayreuth [Wagner] (Germany)
	Aldeburgh [classical] (England)
	Tanglewood [classical] (USA)
	Newport R.I. [jazz] (USA)
	Aix-en-Provence [classical] (France)
Television:	Montreux (Switzerland)
Theatre:	Stratford [Shakespeare] (Ont., Canada)

RESOURCES

Farming

The Earth is rich in resources such as farmland, minerals and energy. Yet the world population is growing so fast and consuming these resources so quickly that we must learn to conserve them. Farmers produce most of our food and many of the materials in the products we use. Important food crops grown worldwide include cereals (wheat, maize and rice), root crops (potatoes and cassava), pulses (beans and peas), fruits and vegetables, oil crops such as soya beans, sugar from cane and beet, nuts, and crops such as tea and coffee. Livestock includes cattle, chickens, pigs, sheep and goats. Fertile farmland and food resources are unevenly spread around the world. Europe, North America and Australasia produce more than enough food to feed their people. But in poorer countries farmers may lack resources and often cannot feed their own families.

LEADING PRODUCERS	Wheat	Rice	Potatoes	Sugar	Soya	Wine
1st	CIS	China	CIS	Brazil	USA	Italy
2nd	China	India	Poland	India	Brazil	France
3rd	USA	Indonesia	China	CIS	China	Spain

WORLD CROP OUTPUT

Asia 43%

Europe and CIS 27%

Africa 7%

USA and Canada 11%

Australia and Oceania 2%

South and Central America 10%

▲ The top three producers of six important agricultural products: wheat, rice, potatoes, sugar, soya beans and wine. (CIS = Commonwealth of Independent States, formerly the USSR).

▶ Terraced rice fields allow the maximum use of hillside farmland.

► *People are eating more poultry, but less beef and pork. The USA, CIS, China, Brazil and France have 60% of the world's chickens. Europe leads in the production of dairy foods (butter, milk and cheese). India has most cattle but India's Hindus do not eat beef.*

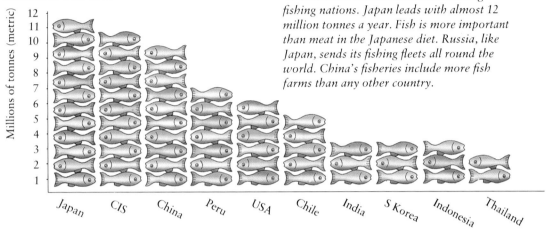

LEADING PRODUCERS	Beef	Pigs	Sheep	Poultry	Goats
1st	USA	China	Australia	USA	India
2nd	CIS	CIS	CIS	CIS	China
3rd	Brazil	USA	China	Brazil	Pakistan

FISHERIES TOP TEN

Millions of tonnes (metric)

12
11
10
9
8
7
6
5
4
3
2
1

Japan   CIS   China   Peru   USA   Chile   India   S Korea   Indonesia   Thailand

◄ *This chart shows the world's leading fishing nations. Japan leads with almost 12 million tonnes a year. Fish is more important than meat in the Japanese diet. Russia, like Japan, sends its fishing fleets all round the world. China's fisheries include more fish farms than any other country.*

FOOD AID
Many people in poorer countries eat less than 2000 calories a day. The daily requirement for a healthy diet is 3000 for a man and 2200 for a woman. Food aid from wealthier countries helps some of the world's hungry to survive.

HOW MANY PEOPLE WORK ON THE LAND?

Percentage of population employed in farming (1990)

Developed countries 8.4%

Developing countries 59.6%

◄ *In the poorer countries, roughly half the population works on the land. Many are subsistence farmers, growing only enough food to support their own families. In the richer countries (North America, Europe and Australia), farms are usually larger and are run as businesses. They need very few workers, since machines do most of the work.*

◄ *Portuguese fishermen sorting their catch. Over-fishing has reduced fish stocks in many seas. Fish must be conserved, not hunted to extinction. One solution is more fish farming.*

▼ *Combines harvesting wheat in North America. World wheat production is around 600 million tonnes a year. China grows the most wheat, but North America is the biggest exporter.*

Materials and Minerals

Timber is a precious material which can be renewed. Metals and minerals cannot be replaced once they have been mined: they include iron ore, copper, tin, gold, building stone and phosphates. Mining methods include deep-pit, open-cast or strip (surface) mining, dredging and quarrying. Two key materials are petroleum and bauxite. Petroleum is burned as a fuel; its by-products include many chemicals and plastics. From bauxite ore comes aluminium, a metal used to make many different goods.

FACTS ABOUT MINING

- The leading mining state for petroleum and gas in the USA is Texas.
- South Africa mines the world's most gold.
- The deepest coal shaft (2042 m) is in the Donbas coalfield in the Ukraine.
- Australia produces the most diamonds and bauxite of any country in the world.
- Canada mines the most uranium and zinc.

▶ *Most exported tropical hardwoods go to Japan; most of the rest go to China and Europe. Countries such as Brazil, the Philippines and Malaysia provide 70 percent of tropical hardwood exports. By 2000 the Philippines may have no usable forests left.*

▶ *In the developing world many people burn wood for fuel. Over 90 percent of India's timber-cut is burned for cooking.*

▼ *Rainforests are being felled at an alarming rate. The Amazon forest is the world's biggest natural plant resource.*

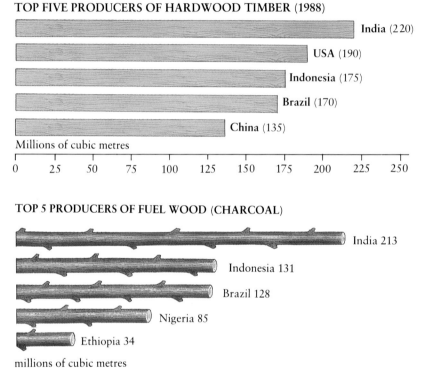

TOP FIVE PRODUCERS OF HARDWOOD TIMBER (1988)

India (220)
USA (190)
Indonesia (175)
Brazil (170)
China (135)

Millions of cubic metres

0 25 50 75 100 125 150 175 200 225 250

TOP 5 PRODUCERS OF FUEL WOOD (CHARCOAL)

India 213
Indonesia 131
Brazil 128
Nigeria 85
Ethiopia 34

millions of cubic metres

0 25 50 75 100 125 150 175 200 225 250

▼ *Open-cast mines are the cheapest way to get minerals. Bingham Canyon Copper Mine in Utah, USA, is the world's largest man-made quarry.*

DEPLETION OF THE BRAZILIAN RAINFOREST

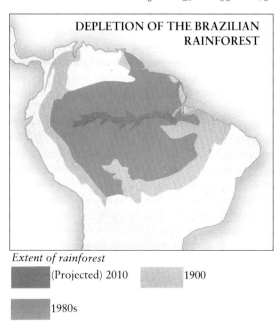

Extent of rainforest

(Projected) 2010 1900
1980s

UNDERSEA MINERALS

Mineral resources on land are being used up at an alarming rate. For new sources future generations may turn to the oceans. The valuable minerals found on land can also be extracted from the sea (although this is costly). About 20 percent of the world's oil comes from undersea wells. Huge reserves of minerals also lie deep on the sea bed in the form of manganese nodules.

An offshore oil platform

MAJOR OIL PRODUCERS

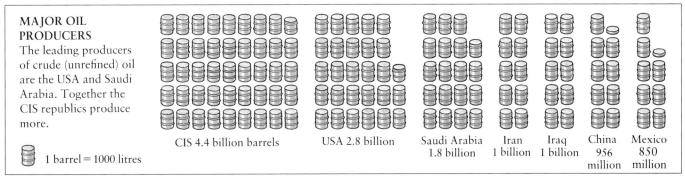

The leading producers of crude (unrefined) oil are the USA and Saudi Arabia. Together the CIS republics produce more.

🛢 1 barrel = 1000 litres

CIS 4.4 billion barrels

USA 2.8 billion

Saudi Arabia 1.8 billion

Iran 1 billion

Iraq 1 billion

China 956 million

Mexico 850 million

▶ *There are about 3000 different kinds of minerals. About a hundred minerals are quite common and those such as aluminium and iron are used in enormous amounts. Other minerals (such as titanium) are relatively scarce. The chart lists important minerals, their uses and the world's leading producers.*

COAL PRODUCTION

The USA and Australia are the world's leading exporters of coal. Canada, Poland, South Africa, Russia and Ukraine are also big exporters. China digs and burns more coal than any other nation. Coal production worldwide has risen since the 1970s, but the price of coal is being increased by environmental costs, such as clean-air scrubbers in coal-burning power stations. Also, as surface deposits are used up, mines are being dug more deeply, even though deep-pit mining costs more than open-cast or strip mining.

LEADING COAL PRODUCERS (million tonnes)

China 956   USA 862   CIS (mostly Russia and Ukraine) 785   Germany 500   Poland 284

METALS	USES	LEADING PRODUCERS
Aluminium	power cables, cooking foil, tennis racquets, food packaging, cans	USA, CIS, Canada, Australia, Brazil
Chromium	plating on metals, as an alloy to make stainless steel, as leather tanning	South Africa, Zimbabwe
Copper	electrical wiring, machinery, in alloys (bronze, brass), insecticides, paint	Chile, USA, Canada, CIS, Zambia, Zaire
Gold	currency, jewellery, gold leaf (alloyed with copper or silver), electronics	South Africa, CIS, Canada, USA, China, Australia
Iron	cast iron (moulded), wrought iron. Most iron used in steel-making	CIS, Brazil, Australia, China, Canada, S Africa, Sweden
Lead	lead acid batteries, petrol additive (declining use), paints, machine bearings	USA, CIS, Australia, Canada, Peru, China, Mexico, N Korea
Manganese	compounds of manganese in dry batteries, paints; vital alloy in steel-making	CIS, S Africa, Brazil, India, China, Australia
Nickel	electroplating (stainless), dry batteries, as an alloy in steel-making	CIS, Canada, Australia, New Caledonia
Platinum	chemical containers, jewellery, surgical instruments, electronics	CIS, South Africa, Canada, Japan, Australia
Silver	in coinage, jewellery, dentistry, photo film, batteries, electronics	Mexico, Peru, CIS, USA, Canada, Poland, Australia
Tin	on steel cans, in solder (with lead) in bronze, toothpaste, roofing	Malaysia, Peru, CIS, Indonesia, Brazil, China, Australia
Titanium	titanium dioxide in paint, paint, paper, tools, as an alloy in aircraft	CIS, Japan, USA, UK, China
Zinc	in alloys (brass, with copper), batteries, paints, electroplating, cosmetics	Canada, CIS, Australia, Peru, China, Mexico, Chile

Energy

The world relies heavily for energy on 'fossil fuels', such as coal, natural gas and petroleum. These fuels were formed millions of years ago. Existing reserves may be exhausted between 100 and 300 years. Untapped reserves would be very expensive to extract. We therefore need to use alternative energy sources (solar, wave and wind power) in order to conserve fossil fuel reserves. Nuclear power once promised cheap limitless energy, but its future now looks uncertain because of costs and concerns about its safety.

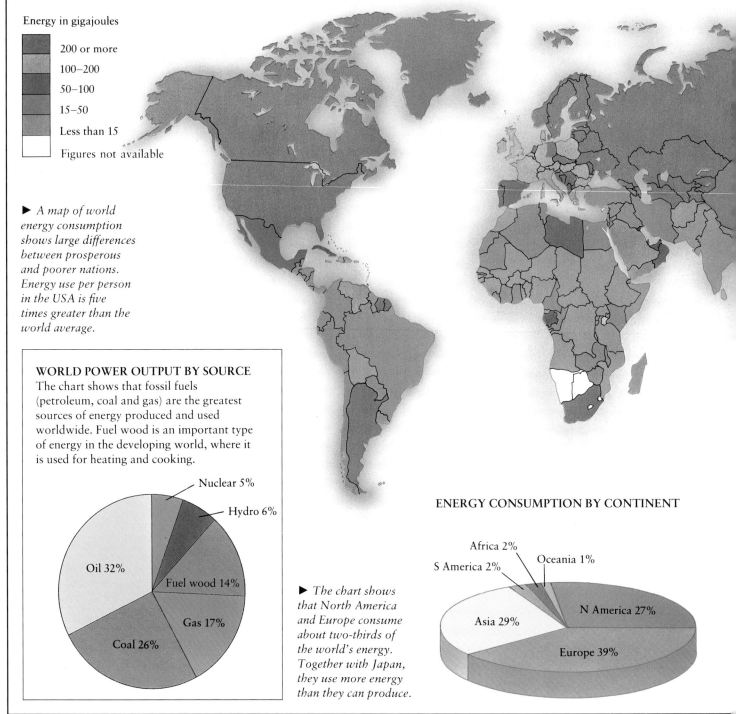

FACTS ABOUT ENERGY

● Energy is measured in units called joules (J) named after the British scientist James Prescott Joule (1818–1889).
● The watt (W) is a unit of power – the rate of producing or using energy, and is commonly used for measuring electric power. The watt is named after steam pioneer James Watt (1736–1819).

WORLD ENERGY CONSUMPTION

Energy in gigajoules

- 200 or more
- 100–200
- 50–100
- 15–50
- Less than 15
- Figures not available

▶ *A map of world energy consumption shows large differences between prosperous and poorer nations. Energy use per person in the USA is five times greater than the world average.*

WORLD POWER OUTPUT BY SOURCE

The chart shows that fossil fuels (petroleum, coal and gas) are the greatest sources of energy produced and used worldwide. Fuel wood is an important type of energy in the developing world, where it is used for heating and cooking.

Nuclear 5%
Hydro 6%
Oil 32%
Fuel wood 14%
Gas 17%
Coal 26%

ENERGY CONSUMPTION BY CONTINENT

Africa 2%
S America 2%
Oceania 1%
Asia 29%
N America 27%
Europe 39%

▶ *The chart shows that North America and Europe consume about two-thirds of the world's energy. Together with Japan, they use more energy than they can produce.*

NUCLEAR ENERGY

In a commercial nuclear reactor, the energy produced by the fission (splitting) of uranium atoms heats water to make steam to drive electricity generators. The first reactor was built at the University of Chicago in 1942. In recent years, rising costs and safety fears have made nuclear energy less attractive, although nuclear fusion (the joining together of atomic nuclei) may be an option for the next century.

TOP 6 NUCLEAR POWER PRODUCERS (amount per year in kilowatt-hours (kw/h))

Country		Amount
USA	☢☢☢☢☢☢☢☢☢☢☢☢☢	527 billion
France	☢☢☢☢☢☢	260 billion
CIS	☢☢☢☢☢	204 billion
Japan	☢☢☢☢	164 billion
Germany	☢☢☢	137 billion
Canada	☢☢	78 billion

☢ = 40 billion kw/h

◄ *Nuclear plants produce radioactivity and deadly waste. An accident, such as that at Chernobyl in Russia (1986) has disastrous consequences.*

◄ *The 12,600,000-kilowatt Itaipu Dam power plant on the Paraná River in Brazil is the world's most powerful hydroelectric dam. A hydroelectric dam can provide water as well as electricity.*

HYDROELECTRIC POWER

Most hydroelectric schemes involve the construction of huge dams to store water in artificial lakes. The water is released under great pressure to drive turbines which generate electricity. Some countries, Brazil for example, generate as much as 80 percent of their energy from water-power.

1 megawatt (MW) = 1 million watts

DAM	COUNTRY	OUTPUT
Guri Dam	Venezuela	10,300 MW
Grand Coulee	USA	7460 MW*
Itaipu	Brazil/Paraguay	7400 MW**
Sayano-Shushensk	Russia	6400 MW
Krasnoyarsk	Russia	6000 MW

* upgrading to 12,600 MW **upgrading to 10,800 MW

ALTERNATIVE POWER

On a wind farm a windmill called a wind turbine produces power as its blades turn in the wind. Our search for 'greener' energy sources (such as wind, tide and solar power) is spurred by the knowledge that oil and coal will not last for ever. Wind-power is practical in some areas: one generator can light 2000 homes.

◄ *Turbines on a wind farm on Long Island, USA. Most wind turbines have two propeller-shaped blades.*

Trade and Industry

The nations of the world live by trading goods such as cars and cotton, and by supplying services such as insurance and holidays. Goods and services are products of industry. The manufacturing industry is important to most industrial economies and depends on supplies of raw materials, such as oil and coal. Some countries have a lot of raw materials, while others have almost none. Countries such as Japan and Singapore can still prosper from trade despite having few natural resources of their own.

MAJOR INDUSTRIAL AREAS

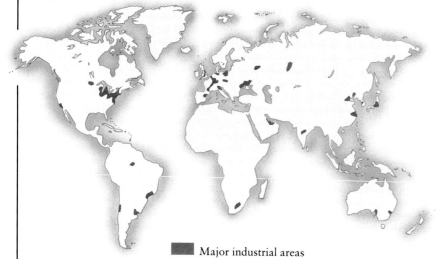

■ Major industrial areas

MAJOR INDUSTRIAL AREAS
North America: The United States is the most powerful industrial nation. Its main manufacturing regions are in the north-east, midwest, and on the west coast. Manufacturing employs a total of 17% of US workers.
South America: Brazil is the continent's major manufacturer followed by Argentina and Chile.
Europe: Europe, particularly in the west, has a powerful industrial economy. The EC dominates trade and industry; Germany is Europe's industrial leader.
Asia: Japan is the most successful trading nation. It is the world's biggest producer of vehicles, ships and TV sets. Singapore, South Korea and Taiwan all have thriving manufacturing export industries. China still relies mainly on state-run factories.
Russia: The industrial giant of the former USSR. It has high technology in some areas (space technology), but needs to modernize its financial structure and its industries.
Pacific: Australia, Indonesia and Philippines are the main industrial countries.
Africa: Some African states have very little industry. The North African countries have oil-based economies. Egypt and Nigeria are industrial, but South Africa is by far the richest manufacturing country.

MAJOR SECTORS IN TRADE AND INDUSTRY

Advertising: Goods have been advertised since pre-Roman times when people first hung signs outside their shops. The largest neon sign in the world today is an advertisement for cigarettes in Hong Kong.
Aerospace: The world's biggest plane-maker is Boeing of the USA.
Banks: The bank with the most branches is the State Bank of India (over 12,400 branches).
Cars: The General Motors Corporation of Detroit, USA, is the biggest industrial company of the world. Apart from vehicles, General Motors is involved in defence equipment, computer services and aircraft, and has more than 750,000 employees.
Clothing: The biggest US clothing manufacturer is Levi Strauss, best known for its jeans.
Games and toys: This industry is dominated by Asian factories making toys for Western markets.

Petrochemicals: Oil-rich nations such as Saudi Arabia are diversifying into petrochemicals.
Medicinal drugs: The world's largest pharmaceutical company is Johnson & Johnson of the USA.
Removals: The Shore Porters' Society of Aberdeen, Scotland, has been carrying and storing people's goods since before 1498.
Retail: The largest retail company in the world is Sears, Roebuck and Co, of Chicago, USA. The company was founded in 1886 and is noted for its mail order catalogue business as well as its stores.
Shipbuilding: Japan builds roughly 40% of the world's new ships.
Steel: The biggest producer is Japan's Nippon Steel Corporation.
Telecommunications: Japan makes the most TV sets, producing nearly 18 million a year.
Tourism: Americans earn more than any other country from tourism and spend most on it too.

▲ *About $110 billion is spent on advertising in the USA each year. These giant neon advertisements are in New York's Times Square.*

MAJOR EXPORTING COUNTRIES

☐ Major exporters of
primary (raw) materials

☐ Major exporters of
manufactured goods

▲ *This map illustrates
how raw materials and
manufactured goods
move between
developed and
developing nations. In
general, developing
countries supply raw
materials, not finished
goods. Japan, the
world's most
successful trader, relies
heavily on imported
raw materials.*

▶ *In poor and rich
nations alike, roads
carry most goods.
Farms and factories
use trucks to transport
their products.*

▼ *Cargo ships carry
bulky freight. Ships
using the Panama
Canal can take a short
route between the
Pacific and the
Atlantic oceans.*

FACTS ABOUT TRADE
AND INDUSTRY

● The world's largest
employer is Indian Railways
with 1.6 million people.
● Although agriculture is
often called the oldest
industry, the earliest
evidence of farming is in
about 9000 BC, thousands
of years after people began
to produce stone tools.
● With an output of over 8
million cars a year, Japan
makes more cars than any
other country.
● The developing world has
only about 14% of the
world's industry. Many poor
countries produce only one
main export item: for
example, 62 different
countries compete to sell
coffee abroad.
● The Faversham Oyster
Company in England claims
to have existed from 'time
immemorial'. In English law
this means before 1189,
making the firm the world's
oldest company.

Money and Debt

The world is growing richer. There are 20 times more goods and services today than there were in 1900. The few rich countries dominate the world economy. Poor countries borrow to finance development and are often unable to pay increasing debts. National wealth is compared by looking at gross national product (GNP) per head of population. For example, Switzerland (over US$35,000 worth of output per person per year) is much richer than Ethiopia (about $120 per person per year).

POPULAR CURRENCIES

Many countries use the same name for their money. The USA, Australia, Fiji, Jamaica, Singapore and Zimbabwe have dollars. France, Belgium and several African countries use francs. Dinars are used in Algeria, Iraq, Jordan and Tunisia. Ireland, Lebanon and Syria, as well as the UK, have pounds. Other currencies, such as Poland's zloty or Japan's yen, are unique.

AVERAGE WEALTH PER PERSON PER COUNTRY (PER CAPITA GNP)

WHAT IS GNP?

Gross national product (GNP) is what a country earns in a year minus its outgoings (imports, foreign debts). Divide by population to find the per capita (per head) figure. The map (right) shows how wealth is spread. Europe, North America, Japan and Australia have the highest per person GNPs in the world.

US$, 1988

20,000 and over	1500–2999
10,000–19,999	500–1499
5000–9999	Under 500
3000–4999	Figures not available

THE EARLIEST MONEY

- The first trade was done without money, by barter (exhange). Coins were first used in ancient Greece, India and China, where people used metal shaped like tools as money as early as 1100 BC.
- The Chinese invented paper money in the AD 800s. The Chinese use of paper money instead of coins amazed the Italian traveller Marco Polo in the 1200s. Europeans did not use paper money until the 1600s when the first bank notes were issued.

THE RICH GET RICHER

Taking the world as a whole, average income per person has doubled since 1950. But while an American is three times richer today than in 1950, an Ethiopian is no better off.

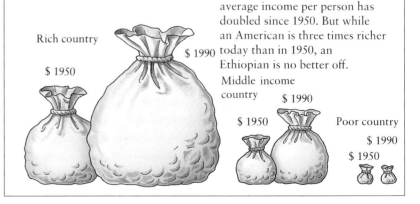

Rich country
$ 1950
$ 1990
Middle income country
$ 1950
$ 1990
Poor country
$ 1990
$ 1950

AID AND DEBT

Many poorer nations are deep in debt owing far more than they originally borrowed. As oil prices rose in the 1970s, developing nations borrowed to meet higher oil bills, and to finance development projects such as dams. When interest rates rose and world trade slumped, these countries faced crippling debt burdens. Aid can be measured in total cash given, or as a percentage of national income. The United States, Japan, France and Germany give the most aid; Norway comes top in terms of percentage of GNP (1.17%).

▼ *On the trading floor of the Paris Bourse in France vast amounts of money change hands every hour on the world's money and stock markets.*

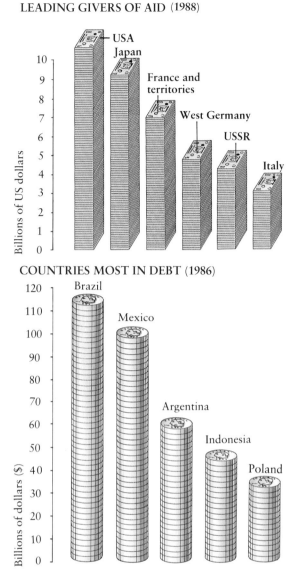

LEADING GIVERS OF AID (1988)

USA
Japan
France and territories
West Germany
USSR
Italy

Billions of US dollars

COUNTRIES MOST IN DEBT (1986)

Brazil
Mexico
Argentina
Indonesia
Poland

Billions of dollars ($)

Education and Health

A rich nation should have educated and healthy citizens. A poor nation also aspires to such ideals, but faces daunting problems. Poor countries have too few doctors and hospitals, too few teachers and schools. Every year nearly 5 million children in the developing world die from diarrhoea, caused in most cases by drinking unclean water. Education is particularly important – without it, hopes of a better life cannot be fulfilled. More than a quarter of the world's people cannot read and write.

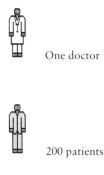

One doctor

200 patients

▼ *The illustration below compares the number of patients to doctors in selected countries. Burkina Faso, a poor country in West Africa, is typical of many African states: it has only one doctor for every 30,000 people. Compare the ratio of doctors to patients in the USA or Germany.*

PEOPLE PER DOCTOR (SELECTED COUNTRIES)

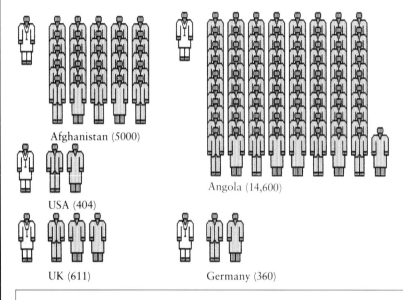

Afghanistan (5000)

USA (404)

UK (611)

Angola (14,600)

Germany (360)

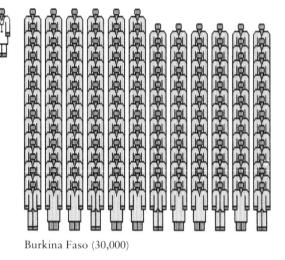

Burkina Faso (30,000)

HOSPITAL BEDS

A hospital cannot function without trained doctors and nurses, medicines and clean water, laundry and power. In parts of the developing world a sick person has little hope of a hospital bed. In Afghanistan there are five beds for every 10,000 people. In Norway 152 beds serve the same number of people.

▼ *A ward in a British eye hospital. Even if they have to go onto a waiting list, people in richer countries eventually get a hospital bed.*

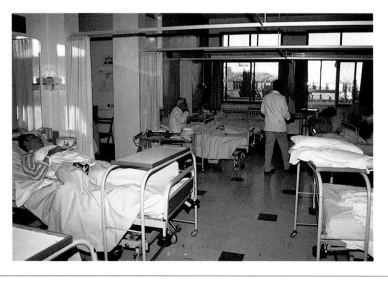

HEALTH AND WELFARE

Rich countries can afford to fund health and welfare programmes for their citizens – providing pensions for the elderly and payments to mothers of young children, for example. The table below contrasts what Australia and Ethiopia can afford as benefits to their people.

BENEFIT	Australia	Ethiopia
Work injury	✓	✓
Old age pension	✓	✗
Sickness/maternity benefit	✓	✗
Unemployment benefit	✓	✗
Family allowance	✓	✗

THE WORLD HEALTH ORGANIZATION

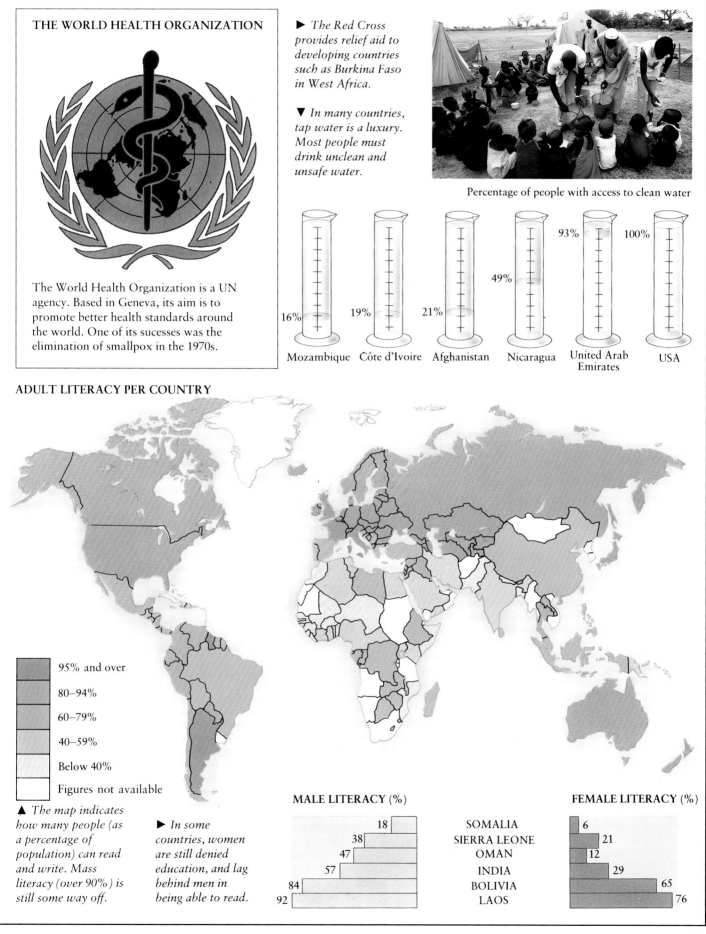

The World Health Organization is a UN agency. Based in Geneva, its aim is to promote better health standards around the world. One of its sucesses was the elimination of smallpox in the 1970s.

▶ *The Red Cross provides relief aid to developing countries such as Burkina Faso in West Africa.*

▼ *In many countries, tap water is a luxury. Most people must drink unclean and unsafe water.*

Percentage of people with access to clean water

Mozambique 16%   Côte d'Ivoire 19%   Afghanistan 21%   Nicaragua 49%   United Arab Emirates 93%   USA 100%

ADULT LITERACY PER COUNTRY

95% and over
80–94%
60–79%
40–59%
Below 40%
Figures not available

▲ *The map indicates how many people (as a percentage of population) can read and write. Mass literacy (over 90%) is still some way off.*

▶ *In some countries, women are still denied education, and lag behind men in being able to read.*

MALE LITERACY (%)

18
38
47
57
84
92

SOMALIA
SIERRA LEONE
OMAN
INDIA
BOLIVIA
LAOS

FEMALE LITERACY (%)

6
21
12
29
65
76

473

POLITICS

Government

Governments exist because society needs a structure to make laws, defend its citizens, set taxes and spend money for the common good. Early governments were authoritarian, imposed by powerful rulers. The ancient Greeks were the first civilization to experiment with democracy, or rule by the people, and today democracy still survives in various forms. The most common form of government worldwide is the republic, with an elected law-making parliament and president. Central to the idea of democracy is the concept of choice: political ideas are put forward by parties and chosen or rejected by voters in elections. Most true democracies have two or more political parties. However, one-party states are plentiful and, despite losing its grip in Europe, Communism still has a stronghold in the world's most populous country, China.

TYPES OF GOVERNMENT

- Monarchy
- Federal constitutional monarchy
- Republic
- Communist/Socialist state
- Federal republic

Communism: A system based on the 19th-century political theories of Karl Marx. Marx advocated class war and a society in which all property is publicly owned. Communist states are usually one-party and dictatorial.

Dictatorship: Rule by one person, a group or a committee whose word is law. The term *dictator* originated in ancient Rome when the Roman Senate could appoint individuals as 'dictators' in times of national emergency.

Federalism: A union of two or more self-governing states which agree to accept a single government's rule in certain matters. Countries which have federal systems include the USA, Australia, Canada and Switzerland.

Monarchy: Rule by a king, queen, emperor or empress. Usually a monarch would have supreme power, but a constitutional monarch's power is usually limited to mainly ceremonial duties by their country's constitution.

Oligarchy: Government by a small ruling group. A republic, for example, would be an oligarchy if only a few people were entitled to vote. Oligarchies in ancient times included most Greek city-states, where only certain citizens could vote.

Republic: A state where power is held by elected representatives acting on behalf of the people who elected them. An elected president rather than a monarch is head of state and/or head of the government.

GOVERNMENT SYSTEMS

Two important democratic government systems are represented in the diagram by those of the United States of America (a federal republic) and the United Kingdom (a parliamentary monarchy).

The British system, which has no written constitution, has evolved over centuries with parliament gradually asserting its power. The US system is based on a written constitution, approved in 1788.

THE CROWN

Monarch is head of state; the government acts on behalf of the crown. The monarch has no power, but is kept informed of government actions.

UNITED STATES OF AMERICA

PRESIDENT

Head of State with executive powers, also head of the armed forces. Elected for a four-year term. Has power to appoint officials and veto laws passed by Congress.

PRIME MINISTER

Head of government, usually chosen from the ruling party. Appoints government ministers, including senior Cabinet ministers. No fixed term of office.

LEGISLATURE

Congress has two Houses, the Senate and the House of Representatives. All members are elected for fixed terms. They can pass laws and overturn the president's vetoes.

PARLIAMENT

Two Houses, the elected Commons (650 members) and the non-elected Lords (hereditary and life peers, some bishops and judges). A general election must be held every five years.

JUDICIARY

The US Supreme Court is the highest court in the USA. The president appoints judges, subject to Senate consent, to decide whether laws are constitutional.

JUDICIARY

Judges in the House of Lords are the highest court in the UK. The judiciary is independent of government. No British court can overrule a decision of Parliament.

LOCAL GOVERNMENT

National governments run national affairs: taxation, finance, defence and foreign policy. Many countries also have state or provincial governments which have considerable powers. At local level, regional and city government is carried out by assemblies of elected members and by appointed full-time officials. The responsibilities of local government vary from country to country but often include such services as education, town planning, refuse collection, parks and recreation areas, police, fire services and roads. To pay for these services, local governments usually collect taxes, paid by tax payers in addition to national taxes.

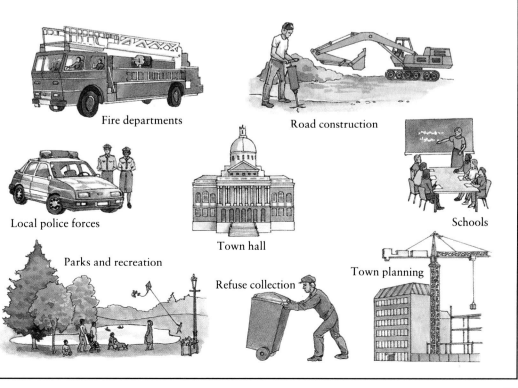

Fire departments

Road construction

Local police forces

Town hall

Schools

Parks and recreation

Refuse collection

Town planning

Government Facts and Records

The United Nations has more than 170 member-countries. Each has its own system of government, often modelled on one of the major world systems (such as the US or French presidential republics), but with their own distinctive characteristics. Monarchies survive in countries renowned for democratic liberalism, such as Sweden, as well as in more traditionally minded states such as Saudi Arabia. Today, as throughout history, dictators rise and fall, usually setting their own records of mis-government.

GOVERNMENT AND LAW-MAKING

National governments make laws that apply throughout a nation. Countries (like Canada) are unions or federations, with power shared between the central government and regional governments which make their own laws.
Laws are proposed by the president, by government ministers, or by members of the law-making assembly. A law begins as a bill, which is discussed by the assembly, often altered, and then voted on before becoming law as an act.
The democratic idea of **one person, one vote** is a modern concept, dating from the 1800s.

▲ *Under the United Nations charter, the Security Council has responsibility for keeping world peace.*

▼ *The Capitol in Washington DC, is the seat of the United States Congress.*

VOTING

Before the 1800s few people had the right to vote, even in parliamentary systems. Blacks in the USA had to struggle to win the vote and until the 1900s women took little part in government. Suffragette campaigns *(left)* won women the right to vote (1893 New Zealand, 1902 Australia, 1920 USA, 1928 UK). Voting in some countries is not compulsory. In others (Australia, for example) everyone registered to vote in elections must do so.

▶ *The Vatican City State in Rome, headquarters of government of the Roman Catholic Church, is the world's smallest self-governing state. It covers just 44 hectares.*

MONARCHY

Unlike other heads of state, monarchs usually inherit a throne from a member of their family such as their mother or father. In the past, monarchs often claimed that they were God's representatives; in Europe this belief was known as the 'divine right of kings'. The Japanese venerated their emperors as divine beings until 1946. After Japan's defeat in World War II, Emperor Hirohito renounced this ancient doctrine. Hirohito reigned as a constitutional monarch until his death in 1989, when his son Akihito succeeded him *(right)*.

Conflict

People fought wars long before history first recorded the victors' triumphs. Territorial rivalry and the pursuit of power are common factors in most conflicts. The 20th century has seen two world wars and many smaller wars. The 'Cold War' between the USSR and the USA ended in the early 1990s. The costly high-technology arms race between East and West has also stopped, but global peace remains an elusive goal. Terrorism and civil war still bring fear and devastation to the troublespots of the world.

▲ The Middle East has been a key area of 20th-century conflict. Saudi Arabians were in the allied force that fought Iraq in the 1991 Gulf War.

AREAS IN CONFLICT AROUND THE WORLD

Yugoslavia
N Ireland
Armenia
Azerbaijan
Afghanistan
W Sahara
Israel
Kashmir
Haiti
The Gulf
Liberia
Somalia
Chad
Rwanda
E Timor
Angola
Mozambique

SOME TROUBLESPOTS AROUND THE WORLD

Afghanistan: Soviet troops pulled out in 1989, but civil war continues between the government and guerrillas.
Angola: Civil war since 1970s between government and UNITA rebels.
Armenia: Newly independent ex-Soviet republic, fighting neighbour Azerbaijan over the disputed territory of Nagorno Karabakh.
Chad: Civil war, with Libya and France backing rival sides.
East Timor: Former Portuguese colony, ruled by Indonesia against the wishes of the local people.
Gulf: Iraq invaded Kuwait 1990, defeated by Allied forces in 1991.
Israel: At odds with its Arab neighbours since the foundation of a Jewish state in 1948.

Kashmir: Territory disputed between India and Pakistan.
Liberia: Civil war started in 1990 after rebels overthrew President Samuel Doe.
Mozambique: Civil war devastating the country and making five million people homeless.
Northern Ireland: A disputed part of UK; current terrorism began in the late 1960s.
Somalia: Civil war following the collapse of the government of Siyad Barrah in 1991.
Western Sahara: Claimed by Morocco, a claim disputed by nationalist Polisario Front.
Yugoslavia: A former federal republic torn apart by civil war. Croatia, Slovenia, Bosnia-Herzegovina and Macedonia are now independent.

▲ United Nations' soldiers in the former state of Yugoslavia in 1992. The UN lacks the military power to end conflicts but it can act as a peace-keeper between opposing sides in a conflict.

◄ *The end of the Cold War saw the end of the Soviet Union's influence: here, in 1989, crowds in Prague's main square cheer Czechoslovak democracy leaders.*

▼ *Aircraft of the major powers: the Russian MiG-29 is an advanced fighter plane. The US Air Force flies B-52 bombers, as well as the ultra-modern Stealth.*

THE COST OF A WORLD WAR

World War II (1939–1945) cost at least 55 million lives, more than all the previous wars in history put together. At least 40 million of those who died were civilians: the majority of them lived in Russia, Poland and China.

Stealth fighter

MiG-29

B-52

ARMED FORCES DATAFILE

The USA has the world's most powerful armed forces, but relies on technology rather than mass manpower. The forces of the old Soviet Union, numerically the world's largest, are at present controlled by the republics of the Commonwealth of Independent States (CIS). The graph *below* compares the world's five biggest armies.

LARGEST FIVE ARMIES

CIS

China

USA

N Korea

Vietnam

= 250,000 personnel

► *The US Star Wars defence system uses computers, lasers, satellites and missiles. It was originally designed to shoot down Soviet rockets. With the end of the Cold War, Russia and the US may co-operate to create a defensive shield in space.*

▼ *The largest ships in the US Navy, the world's biggest navy, are nuclear-powered aircraft carriers and three veteran battleships. Typhoon submarines (Russia) are the biggest in service.*

USS *Missouri*

USS *Nimitz*

Typhoon class submarine

Flags

Not all flags are national flags as are those shown here. Rulers (presidents or queens, for example) may have their own flags. So too do organizations, such as the United Nations and army regiments. Some national flags have very long histories. Denmark, for instance, has had the same flag for more than 700 years. The old Soviet Union's red flag of socialism, with its communist red star, hammer and sickle, has now given way to the flags of the independent republics. *For Flag Index see page 484.*

For Flag Index see page 484.

CANADIAN PROVINCES AND TERRITORIES

ALBERTA

NOVA SCOTIA

BRITISH COLUMBIA

ONTARIO

MANITOBA

PRINCE EDWARD I.

NEW BRUNSWICK

QUEBEC

NEWFOUNDLAND

SASKATCHEWAN

NW TERRITORIES

YUKON

NORTH AMERICA

9 COSTA RICA

18 DOMINICA

26 SURINAME

1 CANADA

10 PANAMA

19 ST. LUCIA

27 BRAZIL

2 UNITED STATES

11 BAHAMAS

20 BARBADOS

28 COLOMBIA

3 MEXICO

12 CUBA

21 GRENADA

29 ECUADOR

4 GUATEMALA

13 JAMAICA

22 ST. VINCENT & GRENADINES

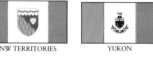
30 PERU

5 BELIZE

14 HAITI

23 TRINIDAD & TOBAGO

31 BOLIVIA

6 EL SALVADOR

15 DOMINICAN REPUBLIC

SOUTH AMERICA

32 PARAGUAY

7 HONDURAS

16 ANTIGUA & BARBUDA

24 VENEZUELA

33 URUGUAY

36 ICELAND

37 NORWAY

8 NICARAGUA

17 ST. KITTS-NEVIS

25 GUYANA

34 CHILE

38 SWEDEN

EUROPE

35 ARGENTINA

39 FINLAND

40 DENMARK

41 IRELAND

42 UNITED KINGDOM

43 NETHERLANDS

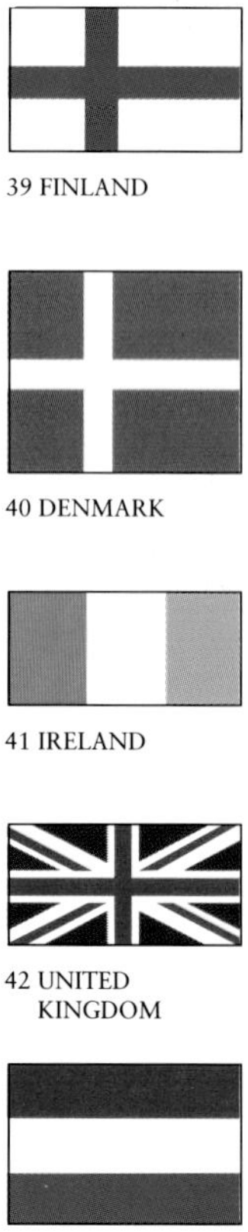

480

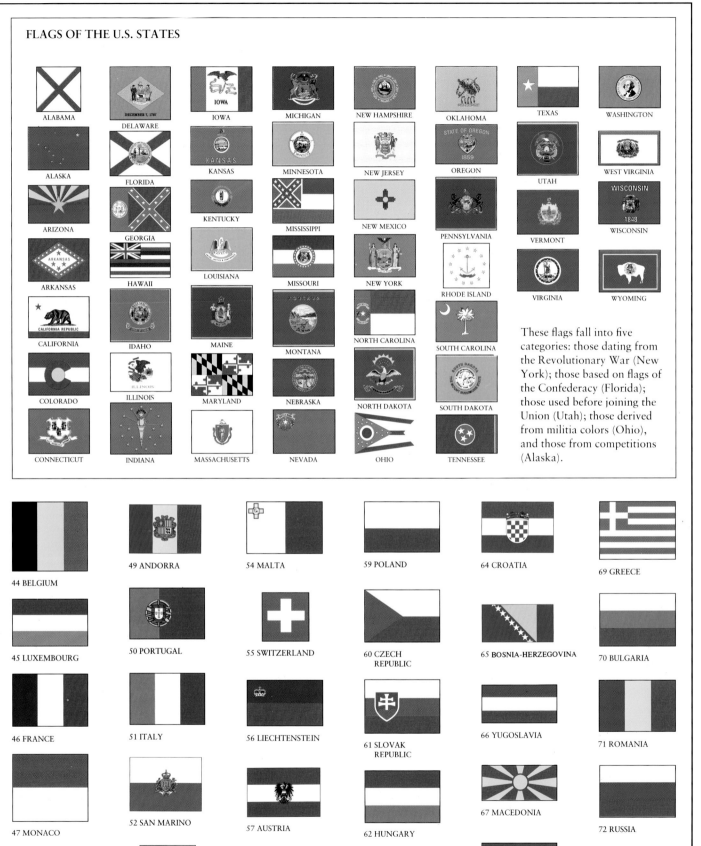

FLAGS OF THE U.S. STATES

ALABAMA

DELAWARE

IOWA

MICHIGAN

NEW HAMPSHIRE

OKLAHOMA

TEXAS

WASHINGTON

ALASKA

FLORIDA

KANSAS

MINNESOTA

NEW JERSEY

OREGON

UTAH

WEST VIRGINIA

ARIZONA

GEORGIA

KENTUCKY

MISSISSIPPI

NEW MEXICO

PENNSYLVANIA

VERMONT

WISCONSIN

ARKANSAS

HAWAII

LOUISIANA

MISSOURI

NEW YORK

RHODE ISLAND

VIRGINIA

WYOMING

CALIFORNIA

IDAHO

MAINE

MONTANA

NORTH CAROLINA

SOUTH CAROLINA

COLORADO

ILLINOIS

MARYLAND

NEBRASKA

NORTH DAKOTA

SOUTH DAKOTA

CONNECTICUT

INDIANA

MASSACHUSETTS

NEVADA

OHIO

TENNESSEE

These flags fall into five categories: those dating from the Revolutionary War (New York); those based on flags of the Confederacy (Florida); those used before joining the Union (Utah); those derived from militia colors (Ohio), and those from competitions (Alaska).

44 BELGIUM

49 ANDORRA

54 MALTA

59 POLAND

64 CROATIA

69 GREECE

45 LUXEMBOURG

50 PORTUGAL

55 SWITZERLAND

60 CZECH REPUBLIC

65 **BOSNIA-HERZEGOVINA**

70 BULGARIA

46 FRANCE

51 ITALY

56 LIECHTENSTEIN

61 SLOVAK REPUBLIC

66 YUGOSLAVIA

71 ROMANIA

47 MONACO

52 SAN MARINO

57 AUSTRIA

62 HUNGARY

67 MACEDONIA

72 RUSSIA

48 SPAIN

53 VATICAN CITY

58 GERMANY

63 SLOVENIA

68 ALBANIA

73 ESTONIA

FLAGS

74 LATVIA

84 UZBEKISTAN

94 YEMEN

105 NEPAL

115 CHINA

AFRICA

126 MOROCCO

75 LITHUANIA

85 TAJIKISTAN

95 OMAN

106 BHUTAN

116 MONGOLIA

127 ALGERIA

76 BELARUS

86 KIRGHIZIA

96 UNITED ARAB EMIRATES

107 BANGLADESH

117 KOREA, NORTH

128 TUNISIA

77 UKRAINE

87 TURKEY

97 QATAR

108 SRI LANKA

118 KOREA, SOUTH

129 MAURITANIA

78 MOLDOVA

88 CYPRUS

98 BAHRAIN

109 MALDIVES

119 JAPAN

130 SENEGAL

79 GEORGIA

89 SYRIA

99 KUWAIT

110 MYANMAR

120 TAIWAN

131 GAMBIA

80 ARMENIA

90 LEBANON

100 IRAQ

111 THAILAND

121 PHILIPPINES

132 GUINEA-BISSAU

81 AZERBAIJAN

101 IRAN

122 BRUNEI

ASIA

91 ISRAEL

102 AFGHANISTAN

112 CAMBODIA

123 MALAYSIA

133 GUINEA

82 KAZAKHSTAN

92 JORDAN

103 PAKISTAN

113 LAOS

124 SINGAPORE

83 TURKMENISTAN

93 SAUDI ARABIA

104 INDIA

114 VIETNAM

125 INDONESIA

134 SIERRA LEONE

135 LIBERIA

145 LIBYA

155 RWANDA

165 MALAWI

175 SEYCHELLES

182 NAURU

136 CÔTE D'IVOIRE

146 EGYPT

156 DEMOCRATIC REPUBLIC OF CONGO

166 MOZAMBIQUE

176 COMOROS

183 TUVALU

137 MALI

147 SUDAN

157 CENTRAL AFRICAN REPUBLIC

167 ZIMBABWE

177 MAURITIUS

184 KIRIBATI

138 BURKINA FASO

148 ETHIOPIA

158 CAMEROON

168 BOTSWANA

OCEANIA

185 VANUATU

139 GHANA

149 DJIBOUTI

159 EQUATORIAL GUINEA

169 NAMIBIA

178 PAPUA NEW GUINEA

186 FIJI

140 TOGO

150 SOMALIA

160 GABON

170 SOUTH AFRICA

179 AUSTRALIA

187 TONGA

141 BENIN

151 KENYA

161 SÃO TOMÉ & PRÍNCIPE

171 LESOTHO

180 NEW ZEALAND

188 WESTERN SAMOA

142 NIGERIA

152 UGANDA

162 CONGO

172 SWAZILAND

181 SOLOMON ISLANDS

Flags produced by Lovell Johns Ltd, Oxford and authenticated by the Flag Research Center Winchester, Mass. 018901 U.S.A.

143 NIGER

153 TANZANIA

163 ANGOLA

173 MADAGASCAR

AUSTRALIAN STATES

NEW SOUTH WALES

TASMANIA

NORTHERN TERRITORY

VICTORIA

144 CHAD

154 BURUNDI

162 ZAMBIA

174 CAPE VERDE IS

QUEENSLAND

WESTERN AUSTRALIA

SOUTH AUSTRALIA

Each state or territory of Australia has its own flag.

National flags recognized by the United Nations.

Index to Flags

GLOSSARY

Words in **bold** indicate an entry elsewhere in the **Glossary** or **Gazetteer**

Aborigines: The original inhabitants of **Australia**.

ASEAN: Association of Southeast Asian Nations, founded 1967. Members are Brunei, **Indonesia**, Malaysia, **Philippines**, **Singapore** and **Thailand**.

Autocracy: Government by one person, an absolute ruler or **dictator**.

Balance of Trade: Difference between a country's exports and imports.

Benelux: Economic union formed in 1948 by Belgium, Netherlands and Luxembourg.

Berlin Wall: Barricade in Berlin, **Germany**, built in 1961 by the East German communist government to prevent its citizens fleeing to the West. The Wall was opened up in November 1989, after the collapse of communism in East Germany.

Boom: Period of increased business activity; the opposite of a **slump**.

Bundestag: **Germany's** parliament.

CACM: Central American Common Market, founded 1960.

Capital: Money or property owned by a person or organization.

Caricom: Caribbean Community and Common Market founded 1973. Members include most Caribbean island states, but not Cuba.

Cash crop: Crop grown for sale, often for **export**, rather than for the farmer's own use.

Civil rights: Freedoms that people ought to enjoy, such as freedom of speech or worship, or the right not to be imprisoned without cause.

Civil war: War fought between different groups living in the same country.

Cold War: Mutual suspicion between communist and non-communist countries following World War II. It was at its height in the 1950s when the **USA** and USSR built up huge forces, including nuclear bombs and missiles; ended by the 1990s.

Colony: Territory fully or partly governed by a mother country.

Comecon: Council for Mutual Economic Assistance that coordinated economic activity amongst communist countries.

Command economy: Economic system in which agriculture, trade and industry are directed from central government – as under communism.

Commodity: Anything that is produced for sale.

Common market: Group of countries who have formed an economic alliance, to encourage **free trade** between them.

Commons, House of: Law-making body of British parliament, to which Members of Parliament (MPs) are democratically elected.

Commonwealth: Loose association of former British-ruled states, dating from 1949 but with its origins in the earlier British Empire. Heads of government meet every two years. The British monarch is the symbolic head of the Commonwealth. Its most recent member is Namibia.

Commonwealth of Independent States (CIS): Formed in 1991 as an attempt to preserve a loosely unified association of independent ex-**Soviet** republics.

Congress: **US** law-making assembly or parliament, consisting of the House of Representatives and the Senate.

Cortes: **Spain's** parliament.

Currency: A country's money; examples are the German mark, British pound, French franc and US dollar.

Customs duty: Tax paid on **imports** or **exports**.

Dail: **Ireland's** parliament.

Debt: Money owed by a person, a business or a country.

Dependent territory: One governed by another, for example a **colony**.

Detente: Easing of political tension or disagreement between countries.

Developing nation: A poor country that is building up its industries and modernizing its agriculture.

Dictator: Ruler with total authority over a country; a position often obtained by overthrowing the lawful authorities.

European Community (EC): Free trade and customs union originally set up by the ECSC Treaty of 1952. Its original members were Belgium, **France**, West Germany, Italy, Luxembourg and the Netherlands. By 1992 the EC was 12-strong (including the **UK**, Denmark, **Ireland**, Greece, **Spain** and Portugal) and was moving to become a closer union.

ECOWAS: Economic Community of West African States, founded 1975, with its headquarters in Nigeria.

EFTA: European Free Trade Association, formed 1960 (Austria, Iceland, Norway, Sweden, Finland and **Switzerland**). Entered into free trade agreements with **EC** in 1973.

Excise duty: Tax on goods produced or sold within the country of origin.

Exports: Goods a country sells to other countries.

FAO: Food and Agriculture Organization of the **United Nations**.

Federation: Group of states with some self-government but with some matters (such as defence) governed by a central authority.

Fertilizers: Substances added to soil to boost crop yields, can be artificial chemicals or natural (such as manure).

Fossil fuels: Hydrocarbon fuels such as petroleum, gas and coal. This resource will eventually run out.

Free trade area: An area covered by an agreement between certain countries to remove tariffs and other barriers to international trade.

G7 States: Informal group of seven leading Western nations: **Canada, France, Germany, Japan**, Italy, **United Kingdom** and the **United States**.

GATT: General Agreement on Tariffs and Trade, a **treaty** (1948) signed by about 100 countries, to promote trade between those countries.

Gross domestic product: Means of measuring a country's economic strength; the sum of all output (money spent, goods sold, income earned) in one year.

Gross national product: GNP is gross domestic product plus all income a country receives from abroad.

Guerilla: Irregular (i.e. non-army) soldier, usually fighting in a rebellion or **civil war**.

Gulf Cooperation Council: Set up in 1981 by Arab states in the Persian Gulf.

Gulf War: Fought in 1991 between **Iraq** and **UN**-backed international coalition of forces (including US, Canadian, British, French, Arab), following Iraq's invasion of **Kuwait** in 1990. Iraq withdrew from Kuwait and suffered considerable losses.

IMF: International Monetary Fund, a **United Nations** agency.

Imports: Goods a country buys from other countries.

Interest: Price paid for use of someone else's money.

International Court of Justice: A **United Nations** court of 15 elected judges, that meets at The Hague, Netherlands.

Kurds: A Middle Eastern people with no national territory of their own. Kurds live in **Turkey** and **Iraq**, and the plight of Iraqi Kurds during and after the **Gulf War** of 1991 brought their problems to worldwide notice.

Labour: Means work, but is used also to describe people who work for wages in factories, farms, offices, etc.

LAIA: Latin American Integration Association (also known as ALADI), a **free trade** community set up in 1980 by countries of South America.

League of Arab States: Known as The Arab League, founded in 1945 by Arab countries to foster cultural and economic ties among Arab states. It also represents member states in some international negotiations.

Market economy: System in which individuals and businesses control investment and production.

Mint: Government-run factory for making banknotes and coins.

Monarch: Hereditary ruler, such as a king, queen or emperor.

Nationalism: Belief in the idea that a national identity should be preserved.

NATO: North Atlantic Treaty Organization, a military alliance founded (1949) by Western nations to defend Europe and the North Atlantic Ocean from military aggression by the **Soviet Union**.

OAS: Organization of 35 American States, founded in 1948, with headquarters in **Washington DC, USA**. Cuba was excluded from OAS activities in 1962.

OAU: Organization of African Unity, founded (1963) to promote African unity and cooperation; by 1991 it had a membership of 50 countries. The headquarters are in Addis Ababa, Ethiopia.

OECD: Organization for Economic Cooperation and Development, founded (1961) to promote social and economic welfare in member countries. Headquarters in Paris, **France**. Members include most Western European states, **Japan, Australia, Canada** and the **USA**.

OPEC: Organization of Petroleum Exporting Countries, founded (1960) by oil-producing states to coordinate oil production and prices.

Patron saint: Christian saint believed by faithful to have special care for certain things: for example, St Christopher is the patron saint of travellers, St Patrick the patron saint of **Ireland**.

President: Elected (usually) head of state or government in a republic.

Private enterprise see **Market economy**

Product: Anything that is made.

Racism: Dislike, unfair treatment and persecution of one people by another on account of their race.

Referendum: National vote on a particular issue.

Refugee: Someone forced to flee their home by war or natural disaster.

Sanctions: Withholding goods or services as a punishment or as a means of persuasion. In recent years **UN** sanctions have been enforced against **Iraq** and **South Africa**, banning trade in certain goods with those countries.

Sect: In religion, a group of people within one faith but with their own separate beliefs and practices.

Security Council: 15-strong **UN** body concerned with maintaining peace and security between countries. The five permanent members are **China, France, Russia, UK** and the **USA**; the other ten members are elected for two-year terms.

Slump: Decline in trade and industry, causing business closures and unemployment.

Solar energy: Power derived from sunlight, for example, through heating panels in house roofs.

South Pacific: Forum founded in 1971 to further cooperation between Pacific nations, including **Australia**, New Zealand, Papua New Guinea and other island states.

Soviet Union: The former Union of Soviet Socialist Republics (USSR); the former republics of the USSR are now independent countries of the **CIS**.

Star Wars: Popular name for US Strategic Defense Initiative, a defensive anti-missile system. Work on developing the hugely costly system began in the 1980s but was slowed when relations between **USA** and **Soviet Union** improved.

START: Strategic Arms Reduction Treaty, signed in 1990 by **USA** and USSR and agreeing to cut their missile forces.

Subsistence farmers: Farmers who grow only enough food to feed their own families but have no surplus to sell.

Superpower: Countries such as the **USA** and the former **Soviet Union** that have the power to dominate world politics.

Third World, The: Term used to describe developing countries of Africa, Asia and Latin America; originally, those countries which did not support either the West or the **Soviet Union** during the **Cold War**.

Tidal power: Harnessing the ocean tides in a barrage or a dam to drive generators to make electricity.

Treaty: Written agreement between two or more nations.

United Nations (UN): An international organization, formed (1945) to promote world peace. By 1991 it had 166 member nations; its headquarters are in **New York, USA**.

UN Secretary-General: Chief administrative officer of the **United Nations**.

UNESCO: The United Nations Educational, Scientific and Cultural Organization is an agency of the **UN** set up to promote the exchange of information, ideas and culture. Its headquarters are in Paris.

UNICEF: The United Nations Children's Fund was set up by the **UN** to assist governments meet the long-term needs of child welfare. Its headquarters are in New York.

Wall Street: Located in Manhattan, New York, USA, a street that includes the New York Stock Exchange and many other financial institutions. Its name is often used in general reference to American money markets.

Warsaw Pact: Former military alliance (1955) of European communist countries, under the leadership of the **Soviet Union**. It was dissolved in 1991.

WHO: World Health Organization, a **UN** agency concerned with fighting disease and improving health standards.

GAZETTEER

Afghanistan: Republic in southwest Asia; has experienced long civil war between government and Islamic fundamentalist guerrillas, and invasion by Soviet troops (1979–1989).

Amazon: The most important river in South America. Second longest river in the world (6448 km).

Angel Falls, Venezuela: Highest waterfall in the world (978 m).

Arabia: Peninsula in southwest Asia; the Arabian Desert is the third biggest in the world.

Australia: Continent and largest island country in the Pacific Ocean; at first a British colony, in 1901 it became an independent federation of states.

Australian Desert: Several deserts combining to form the world's second largest desert region.

Balkans: Mountainous peninsula in southeast Europe.

Baltic States: Former Soviet republics of Estonia, Latvia and Lithuania.

Bangladesh: Country of the Indian subcontinent. It formed part of **India** from 1857 until 1947 when it became known as East **Pakistan**; it became an independent republic in 1971.

Borneo: A large island in Asia that includes Brunei and parts of Malaysia and **Indonesia**; the third biggest island in the world.

Bosnia-Herzegovina: Former Yugoslav republic, now an independent state.

Brazil: The largest country in South America and the world's fifth largest nation; Portuguese colony until 1826.

Brussels: Headquarters of the E.C.

Burma *see* **Myanmar**

Calcutta: Largest city in **India**.

California: US state with the most people (about 30 million).

Cambodia (Kampuchea 1976–1989): Country in southeast Asia recovering from a civil war (1970–1975), in which millions of its people died.

Canada: World's second-largest nation after **Russia**; covers entire northern part of North America excepting Alaska but with less than three people per sq km.

Cape Town: Important port and legislative capital of **South Africa**.

Caspian Sea: The world's largest lake (371,800 sq km); situated in Asia.

Channel Islands: Islands geographically close to France but part of the UK.

Chicago: Third largest city in the **USA**, situated on Lake Michigan, Illinois.

China: World's third biggest country by area and the largest by population; ruled by communists since 1949.

Croatia: Former Yugoslav republic, now independent.

Cyprus: Large island in the Mediterranean Sea, with population of mainly Greek and Turkish origin; a republic since 1960, the northern part of the island has been occupied by **Turkey** since 1974.

Czechoslovakia: Country in eastern Europe which threw off communist rule in 1989. In 1992 discussions began to split the country into two independent countries.

Danube: River in Europe (rises in **Germany**, flows east into Black Sea for 2850 km).

Elbrus: Mountain in Caucasus Mountains, Europe's highest peak (5633 m).

Eritrea: Part of Ethiopia in northeast Africa, which gained independence in 1993.

Everest: World's highest mountain (8848 km); situated in the **Himalayas** on the border of Tibet and Nepal.

France: Large country in western Europe; one of Europe's wealthiest and most powerful nations.

Ganges: River in northern **India**, sacred to Hindus.

Germany: Europe's most successful industrial nation, reunited in 1990 after being divided into two countries (East and West Germany) since the end of World War II in 1945.

Gibraltar: Rocky headland on the southern tip of **Spain**; a British **colony** since 1713.

Gobi: Desert in Mongolia and **China**; the fourth biggest desert in the world.

Grand Canyon, Arizona, USA: The world's longest inland gorge (about 350 km), formed by the Colorado River.

Greenland: Self-governing part of Denmark and the world's largest island (excluding **Australia**).

Himalayas: The great mountain range in Asia that stretches for over 1600 m and includes the world's highest peaks. *See* **Everest**.

Hong Kong: British **colony** on southeast coast of **China**, due to be returned to China in 1997.

Iberian Peninsula: The name for the southwest peninsula of Europe comprising **Spain** and **Portugal**.

India: The world and Asia's second largest country by population, and the world's largest democracy.

Indonesia: Large island group in southeast Asia; main islands include **Java**, Sumatra, South Borneo and West New Guinea (Irian Jaya).

Iran: Islamic republic in the Middle East. Iran was led by the Ayatollah Khomeini after the fall of the Shah in 1979; fought war with neighbouring **Iraq** (1980–1988).

Iraq: Islamic republic in the Middle East; a kingdom (under British administration) until 1958. Under President Saddam Hussein, Iraq was at war with **Iran** (1980–1988). After its invasion of **Kuwait** (1990), Iraq then fought an international coalition force in the **Gulf War** of 1991.

Ireland: The Republic of Ireland occupies four-fifths of an island situated west of Great Britain; an independent state since 1921.

Israel: Jewish state in what was formerly British-ruled Palestine. Israel was founded in 1948, since when it has fought four wars with its hostile Arab neighbours. It is the most highly industrialized country in the Middle East, especially for textiles.

Japan: Country in eastern Asia; it is the leading economic power in the region and the world's most successful trading nation.

Java: Most populated island of **Indonesia**, with 60 percent of the country's people.

Kilimanjaro, Tanzania: Highest mountain in Africa (5895 m).

Korea, North and South: Country of eastern Asia. Separate republics were declared in 1948.

Kuwait: Oil rich emirate in the Middle East; invaded by **Iraq** in 1990 and freed by an international coalition after the brief Gulf War of 1991.

Lapland: The most northerly region of **Scandinavia**; inhabited by Lapps.

Lake Superior: Largest lake in North America (82,103 sq km).

Lake Victoria: Largest lake in Africa (69,500 sq km).

Lebanon: Country in the Middle East; a prosperous trading centre for the region before civil war made it one of the world's most troubled countries.

Norway: Monarchy occupying northern and western part of **Scandinavia**.

Ottawa: Capital of **Canada**.

Pakistan: Country in southern Asia; part of **India** until 1947, when it became an independent Islamic state. In 1971 East Pakistan became **Bangladesh**.

Paraguay: Landlocked country in central South America; gained independence from **Spain** in 1811.

Paris: Capital of **France**.

Patagonia: Cool dry plateau at tip of South America; region is part of both southern Argentina and Chile.

Philippines: Republic in southeast Asia, consisting of more than 7000 islands.

Poland: Country in eastern Europe; under influence of USSR since the end of World War II, Poland abandoned communism in the late 1980s.

Portugal: Country in southwest Europe; a republic, Portugal occupies the western part of the Iberian Peninsula.

Pyrenees: Range of mountains separating **France** and **Spain**.

Quebec: French-speaking province of **Canada**.

Rhine: Important river in western Europe (1320 km), flowing from **Switzerland** through **Germany** and reaching the North Sea through the Netherlands.

Romania: Country in southeast Europe; after World War II Romania became a communist state, until the fall (1989) of the communist dictator Ceaucescu.

Rome: Capital of Italy.

Rotterdam: The Netherlands and Europe's biggest port.

Ruhr: Industrial region of western **Germany** and the greatest single manufacturing centre in Europe.

Russia: Largest of the republics making up the old Soviet Union, an independent country since 1991.

Sahara: Biggest desert in the world, covering much of northern Africa.

St Petersburg: Formerly Leningrad (1924–1991), second city and former capital of **Russia**.

San Marino: World's smallest independent republic; it claims to be Europe's oldest independent state (from 4th century AD).

Sardinia: Large island in the Mediterranean Sea, part of Italy.

Saudi Arabia: Oil-rich, conservatively ruled kingdom in southwest Asia, occupying most of Arabian Peninsula.

Scandinavia: Name used for four closely-linked countries of northern Europe: Denmark, Finland, **Norway,** Sweden. Iceland is often included as part of Scandinavia.

Serbia: Dominant (by population) republic of former Yugoslavia.

Sicily: Large island in the Mediterranean Sea, part of Italy.

Singapore: Prosperous small republic off the southern tip of Malay Peninsula in southeast Asia; consists of island of Singapore and over 50 smaller islands.

Slovenia: Former Yugoslav republic, now independent (1991).

Somalia (Somali Republic): Country in northeast Africa, torn by **civil war** since 1988.

South Africa: Republic in southern Africa. Until reforms began in late 1980s, the majority black population had few rights, and were ruled by a white minority government which enforced a system of apartheid (separation of the races).

Spain: Country in southwest Europe occupying most of the Iberian Peninsula. Spain became a monarchy in 1975; it was a republic (1931–1939) and a dictatorship under Franco (1939–1975).

Sri Lanka: Island off coast of **India** in southern Asia (formerly Ceylon); independent since 1972.

Stockholm: Capital of **Sweden**.

Sudan: Largest country in Africa; independent since 1956, it has suffered from prolonged **civil war**.

Sweden: Monarchy that occupies northeastern part of **Scandinavia**.

Switzerland: Prosperous small country in central Europe; divided into French, German and Italian-speaking areas, it was neutral in both World Wars.

Sydney: Largest city and most important port in **Australia**.

Syria: Country in Middle East; an Arab republic since 1941.

Taiwan (Nationalist China): Island republic, formerly Formosa, off the coast of **China**.

Thailand: Country in southest Asia (known as Siam until 1939).

Tokyo: Capital of **Japan** and the world's biggest city.

Toronto: Largest city in **Canada**.

Turkey: Republic in southwest Asia with a small region in southeast Europe.

Ukraine: Independent country on the borders of Europe and Asia; until 1990 a republic of the USSR.

United Kingdom: Kingdom of Great Britain (England, Scotland and Wales) and N Ireland (since 1922).

United States of America: Country occupying most of southern part of N America; the world's fourth largest country, it comprises 50 States and the Federal District of Columbia. Since World War II it has been the world's leading economic and military power.

Uruguay: Country in South America; a former Spanish **colony** that won its independence in 1825.

Vatican City: Independent papal State in **Rome**; seat of government of Roman Catholic Church.

Venezuela: Country in northern South America; one-time Spanish **colony** became fully independent in 1830.

Vienna: Capital of Austria.

Vietnam: Republic in southeast Asia, the setting for bitter fighting from 1946 (against French colonial rule) and from 1959 between South and North Vietnam. The **USA** became involved in the Vietnam War, which ended in 1975 with victory for the communist North, followed by reunification between the North and South.

Volga: Longest river in Europe (3531 km).

Washington DC: Capital of the **United States**; DC stands for District of Columbia.

Wellington: Capital of New Zealand.

West Indies: Group of islands off coast of N and S America that enclose the Caribbean Sea; they include Jamaica, Barbados, Cuba and Puerto Rico.

Yemen: Islamic republic in southern **Arabia**, formed by unification of Yemen Arab Republic and People's Democratic Republic of Yemen (1990).

Zaïre: Republic in central Africa, the second largest country in Africa. Before independence it was known as the Belgian Congo (1908–1960).

Zaïre River (formerly the Congo): Second longest river in Africa (4700 km).

Zimbabwe: Republic in southeast Africa; formerly the British **colony** of Rhodesia, it has been independent since 1980.

INDEX

The publishers would like to thank the following artists for contributing to this book:

Jonathan Adams; Kevin Addison; Marion Appleton; Andy Archer; Mike Atkinson (Garden Studio); Owain Bell (Aartverk Illustration); Richard Bonson; Peter Bull; Vanessa Card; Lynn Chadwick (Garden Studio); Kuo Kang Chen; Richard Coombes; Joanne Cowne; Richard Draper; Dean Entwistle; Michael Fisher (Garden Studio); Eugene Fleury; Chris Forsey; Mark Franklin; Terry Gabbey (Eva Morris AFA); Lee Gibbons (Wild Life Art Agency); Jeremy Gower; Peter Gregory; Ray Grinaway; Terry Hadler (Bernard Thornton Artists); Allan Hardcastle; Alan Harris; John Haysom; André Hrydziusko (Simon Girling and Associates); Simon Huson; Ian Jackson; Peter Jarvis; Ron Jobson (Kathy Jakeman Illustration); Kevin Jones Associates; Roger Kent (Garden Studio); Peter Kestervan (Garden Studio); Deborah Kindred (Simon Girling and Associates); Mike Lacey (Simon Girling and Associates); Adrian Lascom (Garden Studio); Jason Lewis; Shaun Lings; Jenny Lloyd (The Classroom); Bernhard Long (Temple Rogers); Chris Lyon; Louis Mackay (Linda Rogers Associates); Mainline Design (Guy Smith); Alan Male (Linden Artists); Maltings Partnership; Janos Marffy (Kathy Jakeman Illustration); Josephine Martin (Garden Studio); Dave McAllister (Simon Girling and Associates); Doreen McGuinness (Garden Studio); David More (Linden Artists); Tony Morris (Linda Rogers Associates); Oxford Illustrators Limited; Trevor Parkin (Linda Rogers Associates); Bruce Pearson (Wild Life Art Agency); Malcolm Porter; Sebastian Quigley; Elizabeth Rice (Wild Life Art Agency); Paul Richardson; John Ridyard; Eric Robson (Garden Studio); Michael Roffe; David Russell; Martin Salisbury (Linda Rogers Associates); John Scorey; Rodney Shackell; Nick Shewring (Garden Studio); Rob Shone; Mark Stacey; Paul Stangroom; Roger Stewart; Lucy Su; Graham Sumner (Simon Girling and Associates); Stephen Sweet (Simon Girling and Associates); Myke Taylor (Garden Studio); Kevin Toy (Garden Studio); Guy Troughton; Phil Weare (Linden Artists); Steve Weston; Keith Woodcock; and thanks to Mullard Radio Astronomy Observatory.

The publishers wish to thank the following for supplying photographs for this book:

Page 8 Science Photo Library; 11 Science Photo Library; 21 JPL/NASA; 23 Science Photo Library; 26 Science Photo Library; 27 ZEFA; 29 NASA; 31 NASA; 35 JPL/NASA; 37 JPL/NASA; 39 NASA; 40 NASA; 43 Science Photo Library; 44 Science Photo Library (top) ESA (bottom); 47 NASA (top) Anglo-Australian Observatory (centre right and bottom); 49 Anglo-Australian Observatory; 51 Science Photo Library; 54 Anglo-Australian Observatory; 58 Anglo-Australian Observatory; 59 Science Photo Library; 61 Royal Astronomical Society; 71 NASA; 75 Science Photo Library; 79 NASA; 95 NASA; 102 ZEFA; 108 ZEFA; 109 ARDEA; 111 AGE Fotostock; 112 ZEFA; 116 ZEFA; 122 Science Photo Library; 126 Frank Spooner Pictures; 131 NASA; 132 Science Photo Library; 135 Frank Spooner Pictures; 137 ZEFA; 141 Dundee University; 147 ZEFA; 149 Frank Spooner Pictures; 153 ZEFA; 155 Spectrum; 161 ZEFA; 179 ZEFA; 182 A-Z Botanical Collection; 187 Science Photo Library; 193 Heather Angel; 196 Tony Stone Pictures; 197 NHPA Spike Walker; 201 NHPA George Bernard; 205 ZEFA; 206 NHPA Tony Bannister; 211 Frank Lane Picture Agency; 216 Heather Angel; 220 ZEFA; 222 ZEFA; 225 Bruce Coleman (top) ZEFA (centre); 233 Allsport; 239 Robert Harding; 240 ZEFA; 243 TRIP Helene Rogers; 261 Allsport; 264 Science Photo Library; 273 Goodyear; 281 ZEFA; 283 Science Photo Library; 289 Science Photo Library; 290 Midnight Design Ltd; 295 Science Photo Library; 300 Sir Norman Foster & Partners; 303 QA Photo Library; 306 Quadrant Picture Library; 311 Boeing; 316 Science Photo Library; 336 SCALA; 338 AKG; 343 Permission of Town of Bayeux; 345 ZEFA; 347 British Museum; 348 British Library (top) Bridgeman Art Library (bottom); 351 AKG; 354 British Museum; 355 British Museum; 358 AKG; 359 British Museum; 362 Science Museum; 363 Bridgeman Art Library; 368 AKG; 372 Peter Newark Pictures (left) Library of Congress (right); 373 Peter Newark Pictures; 377 Bridgeman Art Library; 383 AKG; 385 Mary Evans Picture Library (left) Bettmann Archive (right); 388 Bridgeman Art Library; 389 National Army Museum; 391 AKG; 392 Bettmann Archive; 394 Imperial War Museum; 395 Wiener Library/Beate Klarsfeld Foundation (top) Associated Press (centre) Imperial War Museum(bottom); 397 Popperfoto; 399 Popperfoto (centre) Chatto and Windus (bottom); 400 Hulton-Deutsch Collection; 401 Popperfoto; 402 Frank Spooner Pictures; 412 ZEFA; 416 Spectrum (top) ZEFA (bottom); 417 ZEFA; 418 ZEFA (top and centre) The Hutchison Library (bottom); 421 TRIP Richard Powers (right) ZEFA (left); 423 ZEFA; 425 ZEFA; 426 Spectrum; 427 ZEFA (centre) Spectrum (bottom); 428 ZEFA; 429 Robert Harding; 431 ZEFA; 432 ZEFA; 434 ZEFA (top) Christine Osborne Pictures (bottom); 438 Robert Harding; 439 ZEFA; 441 ZEFA (top) Spectrum (centre); 442 ZEFA; 433 ZEFA; 445 ZEFA (right) British Antarctic Survey/ P Gurling (left); 450 ZEFA; 451 Robert Harding; 453 Frank Spooner Pictures (top) Panos Pictures (bottom); 454 ZEFA; 458 South American Pictures (top) Frank Spooner Pictures (bottom); 459 The Huthison Library; 460 Robert Harding; 461 Rex Features (top) Edinburgh Festival Fringe (bottom); 462 ZEFA; 463 Spectrum; 465 Robert Harding; 467 ZEFA (top) Robert Harding (bottom); 468 Spectrum; 471 Frank Spooner Pictures; 472 Rex Features; 473 British Red Cross; 476 Rex Features; 477 Mary Evans Picture Library (top) Frank Spooner Pictures (bottom); 478 Frank Spooner Pictures (top) Rex Features (bottom); 479 Frank Spooner Pictures.

(AKG = Archiv Fur Kunst Und Geschichte)

504